CLAN MACDOUGALL

Clan Line
Illustrated Fleet History

Clan Line

Illustrated Fleet History

John Clarkson, Roy Fenton and Archie Munro

Ships in Focus Publications

Published in the UK in 2007 by
Ships in Focus Publications,
18, Franklands, Longton, Preston PR4 5PD.

Printed by Amadeus Press, Cleckheaton.

ISBN 978-1-901703-47-4

Front end paper: *Clan Macdougall* (3) at Swansea on 1st June 1970. *[John Wiltshire/Nigel Jones collection]*
Back end paper: *Clan Roberston* (4) off the Alfred Entrance to Birkenhead Docks on 20th October 1974. *[Paul Boot]*
Frontispiece: *Clan Macilwraith* (2) was photographed from a boat as she passed Seaforth Dock, Liverpool inward bound on 29th May 1978. Note the solitary container on deck. *[Paul Boot]*
Title page: *Clan Campbell* (5) sails from the Tyne. *[Malcolm Donnelly]*

CONTENTS

A painting by Gordon Ellis of the *Clan Matheson* (4) at sea. *[British Mercantile Marine Memorial Collection]*

INTRODUCTION

Clan Line has been the subject of at least six previous works, so why publish another? Ships in Focus has long cherished the idea of celebrating some of the finest British cargo ships ever built with a book which includes the best set of photographs we can find and combining this with a detailed and accurate fleet list compiled largely from primary sources. Research for the latter has thrown up findings which suggest that some revision is needed to existing histories of the company, and has revealed some interesting links with other ship owners. More on this under 'Notes on the fleet list' and in the text. We have also been delighted to incorporate the writings of co-author Archie Munro who has uncovered a wealth of information on Charles Cayzer's early struggles to find sufficient cargoes and competent captains for his growing fleet, plus his detailed study of the design and war service of the big refrigerator ships launched from the mid 1930s. To add a personal perspective a few anecdotes have been included from individuals who knew the ships.

After much head scratching, we decided to limit coverage to steam and motor ships which were recognisably of Clan Line, rather than extending coverage to the entire fleets of companies which were acquired by Clan Line or by the Cayzer-inspired British and Commonwealth group. Clan liners are easier to identify than define, as not all were formally owned by Clan Line, whilst not all they owned had Clan names. Carrying a Clan name, ownership by The Clan Line Steamers Ltd. or regular use on Clan Line services are the criteria for inclusion. This admits ships nominally owned by Houston and Scottish Shire Lines following their acquisition in 1918 and which appeared frequently on Clan Line berths, and several later ships of King Line. It excludes the two sailing ships whose speculative purchase gave Charles Cayzer an early taste for ship owning, and the collection of tankers owned by Scottish Tanker Ltd. and Hector Whaling Ltd. In the final years, accountancy practices made ownership even more confusing, with the four *Clan Ranald* class reefers owned by Union-Castle, bareboat chartered to Houston, but with Clan names and running on Clan Line services. Clan Line's board treat these, the Houston, Scottish Shire and certain King Line ships as part of the fleet, and so have we. The limits set have allowed us to concentrate on a recognisable fleet of cargo ships, and have kept the work within reasonable bounds of size and cost. Nevertheless, there are over 300 ships detailed here and the majority are illustrated.

The ships covered here comprise the major part of the fleet managed by Cayzer, Irvine and Co. Ltd., and a substantial part of the tonnage controlled by the British and Commonwealth Group. Other fleets which came under the control or management of these two organisations have received considerable coverage in works still in print, notably in Peter Newall's 'Union-Castle Line', in Bill Harvey's 'Safmarine' and in features in our 'Ships in Focus Record' which dealt with Springbok Shipping Co. Ltd. (Ron Mapplebeck in 'Record' 4) and the managed fleet of Bowaters ('Record' 5 and 6).

As its title stresses, this is a fleet history and the focus is on the ships. This is reflected not only in the illustrated fleet list but also in the texts chronicling Clan Line's history, where we have concentrated on what the ships were doing (especially for the early years), why they were acquired, and how the trades they ran in developed. Anyone wishing to know more about the founder and the Cayzer dynasty is directed to *A Victorian Shipowner*. Neither have we attempted a business history. The material for such a history exists abundantly in the archives lodged with the National Maritime Museum, and would make an excellent basis for a doctoral thesis.

It is ironic that Scotland's finest fleet of cargo ships was founded by a Cornishman who was actually resident in Liverpool and was on only his second visit north of the border. Two factors influenced Charles Cayzer to start a company in Glasgow: the help of local financiers and the Clyde's excellent reputation for building iron steamers. However, Liverpool and Birkenhead provided much of the business for Clan Line, and the finest set of images of its ships have been provided by the Mersey photographers, who stretch in an unbroken line which includes John MacRoberts, M. Cooper, Basil Feilden, John Clarkson and Paul Boot, all of whose work is represented here.

We have broken with tradition by not presenting the fleet list in a purely chronological order. Instead, driven by the urge to accentuate the illustrative content, we have grouped similar ships together, although within each group they appear in order of build or acquisition. A further advantage of this method is that captions or headings can describe the design of a group of ships and discuss its fortunes. Those longing for a chronological list will find one on pages 329 to 333, whilst the index is the natural resort of anyone wishing to locate an individual ship.

Roy Fenton, June 2007

SOURCES AND ACKNOWLEDGEMENTS

For the history and some details of the ships, the Board Minutes of The Clan Line Steamers Ltd. and other material lodged with the National Maritime Museum at Greenwich have proved invaluable, and we thank the museum for preserving these, and its Caird Library staff for ferreting out most of the relevant pieces.

The fleet list has benefited from input by Malcolm Cooper (especially early histories and Second World War losses), Bill Harvey (launch dates), Duncan Haws and Bill Schell (especially fates, but also checking details), but the responsibility for any errors rests with Roy Fenton. For ships which left British and Commonwealth registers before 1955, the prime source for dimensions, dates, builders and owners has been the registration documents, classes BT108 and BT110 in the National Archives, Kew. For later vessels, *Lloyd's Register* and *Lloyd's Confidential Index* have been the major sources, whilst for all ships, Lloyd's Register *Wreck Returns*, the Board of Trade *Casualty Returns*, the Lloyd's of London war loss books for both world wars and Admiralty *Service Lists* have been consulted.

The following books have been consulted:
A Victorian Shipowner by Augustus Muir and Mair Davies; Cayzer, Irvine and Co. Ltd., London, 1978. This privately published biography of founder Charles Cayzer is an essential source, but tends towards hagiography and includes some received wisdom which is not born out by research.
Gathering of the Clans by Norman Middlemiss; Shield Publications Ltd., Newcastle-upon-Tyne, 1988. Provides a workmanlike fleet list but the typography in the history section could have been more reader friendly.

Merchant Fleets No. 33: Clan, Houston, Turnbull Martin and Scottish Tankers by Duncan Haws; TCL Publications, Pembroke, 1997. The drawings are useful for identification and assignment of vessels to groups, but the details of ships and their careers are not always reliable.
The Clan Line in the Great War by Archibald Hurd; Cassell and Co. Ltd. for The Clan Line Steamers Ltd., London, 1924. Heroics and dastardly enemies mean this is a far from objective account, but has much detail not available elsewhere.
In Danger's Hour by Gordon Holman; Hodder and Stoughton Ltd., 1948. This account of Clan Line ships in the Second World War reflects the mood of the conflict, but was written too soon after events to offer a full perspective.

House magazines *The Clansman* and *The British and Commonwealth Review* kindly loaned by Kevin O'Donoghue have been trawled for anecdotes and details.

Photographs have come from a number of sources, particularly the collections of the three authors and Ships in Focus. Credits are given below each photograph to the photographer (where known) and to the supplier of the print, but a special mention is needed for certain collectors who have made a significant contribution: Ian Farquhar, Nigel Farrell, Ambrose Greenway, Fred Hawks, Peter Newall, Kevin O'Donoghue, Bill Schell, George Scott and David Whiteside. Institutions to be thanked are Glasgow University Archives, The Ballast Trust, the National Maritime Museum and the Imperial War Museum. Paul Boot compiled the colour section with the help of Malcolm Donnelly, Mike Green, Eddie Jackson, Nigel Jones, Roy Kittle and Dave Salisbury. Thanks also to Captain A.W. Kinghorn and to Ian Farquhar, Bill Schell and Heather Fenton for help with proof reading and to Marion Clarkson for accountancy services

FLAGS AND FUNNELS
Illustrated by J.L. Loughran

The British and Commonwealth pennant.

Scottish Shire Line Ltd. (Turnbull, Martin and Co. Ltd).

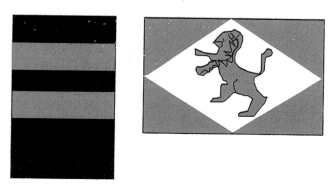

The Clan Line Steamers Ltd. (Cayzer, Irvine and Co. Ltd.).

British and South American Steam Navigation Co. Ltd. (R.P. Houston and Co.)

NOTES ON THE FLEET LIST

The fleet list is based wherever possible on data in the registration documents of British ships in Class BT108 and BT110 housed in the National Archives at Kew. Using these primary sources allows dates of registrations, sales and renamings to be quoted with great precision, and ownership changes to be plotted in much more detail than in contemporary publications such as *Lloyd's Register* or the *Mercantile Navy List*. Indeed, these sources have allowed many revisions to be made to Clan Line fleet lists previously compiled and published. However, the registration documents might at times be considered to give too much information. In common with all others, Clan Line ships were owned on a 64th share basis, and especially in the 1880s such shares were often traded individually. Tracking all these changes would make the fleet list extremely lengthy – for some of the early steamers there were 70 or so sales within a dozen years – and the convention has been adopted of quoting the initial shareholding in the vessel, and then only major changes. The practice in this period of transferring ships back and forth between The Clan Line Steamers Ltd. and various groups of shareholders, sometimes including and sometimes excluding Charles Cayzer, also leads to a certain repetitiveness in the entries. It was felt that these changes reflect the real ownership of the vessels, and also exemplify Cayzer's continuing struggle to finance a large and growing fleet, and hence they have been quoted in full. Contemporary editions of *Lloyd's Register* sidestep these issues by simply quoting the name of the managing company, Cayzer, Irvine and Co., as owners throughout, which does reflect the real unity of the fleet if not its actual legal ownership. A further peculiarity of registration documents is that they insist on an individual being quoted as ship's manager, whereas *Lloyd's Register* gives the much more familiar title of a company. The fleet list entries compromise by quoting company titles where known but recording changes as occurring on the dates when named individuals from these companies were appointed managers.

In all major respects, the fleet list follows the usual Ships in Focus format, shamelessly derived from that excellently developed by the World Ship Society. The first line of each entry gives the ship's name with the notation (1) to (5), to indicate that she is the first, second, third, fourth or fifth of that name in the fleet. The dates following are those of entering and leaving the fleet, or when management began and finished. Unless otherwise stated on this line, vessels are steam or motor ships with steel hulls.

On the second line is given the ship's official number (O.N.) in the British Register; then her tonnages at acquisition, gross (g) and net (n), followed by dimensions: registered length x breadth x depth in feet or, for vessels owned from 1955 onwards, the dimensions are length overall x breadth x draught in feet and in metres for vessels owned from 1974 onwards. For any substantial rebuild, new dimensions are given on a subsequent line.

On the following line is a description of the engine(s) fitted and the name of their builder. Steam reciprocating engines may be two-cylinder compound (C. 2-cyl.), three-cylinder triple-expansion (T. 3-cyl.) or quadruple-expansion four cylinder (Q. 4-cyl.). For oil engines are given the type (e.g. Sulzer, Burmeister & Wain), the number of cylinders, whether two stroke (2SC) or four stroke (4SC) cycle, single acting (SA) or double acting (DA). Next comes horsepower: nominal (NHP), brake (BHP), indicated (IHP) or shaft (SHP), and the ship's speed, all taken from registration documents. Figures for nominal horsepower should be taken with caution, as they are calculated from engine dimensions rather than measured, and are liable to change over time independently of any modifications to the machinery. Any changes of engine or major modifications are listed, with dates, on the next line.

Subsequent lines give the details of builder and the ship's full career. Where dates of completion are known only to the nearest month, they are not quoted if they fall within the same month as the registration date. The port indicated after the title of an owning company is the port in which the owners are domiciled. For ships sold to operators using flags of convenience, efforts have been made to indicate the actual owners and the managers (not always the same body). For these vessels, the flag is that of the state in which the ship owning company is domiciled unless otherwise stated. Dates of entering or leaving British government requisition in the First and Second World Wars are quoted, but not usually the type of service, as the details in the official Service Lists are either meaninglessly vague - e.g. simply 'liner service' – or include tedious detail about individual voyages.

Details of certain casualties which did not result in loss or scrapping of the ship have been incorporated. Very many more could have been included, as the board minutes report virtually every one, and small collisions in harbours or rivers, cargo fires and minor groundings are mentioned in almost every monthly meeting. Listing all would make tedious reading and double the length of the fleet list, so we have confined ourselves to the more major or dramatic incidents.

Clan Maclaren (2) docks at Liverpool on a stormy 29th December 1974. *[Paul Boot]*

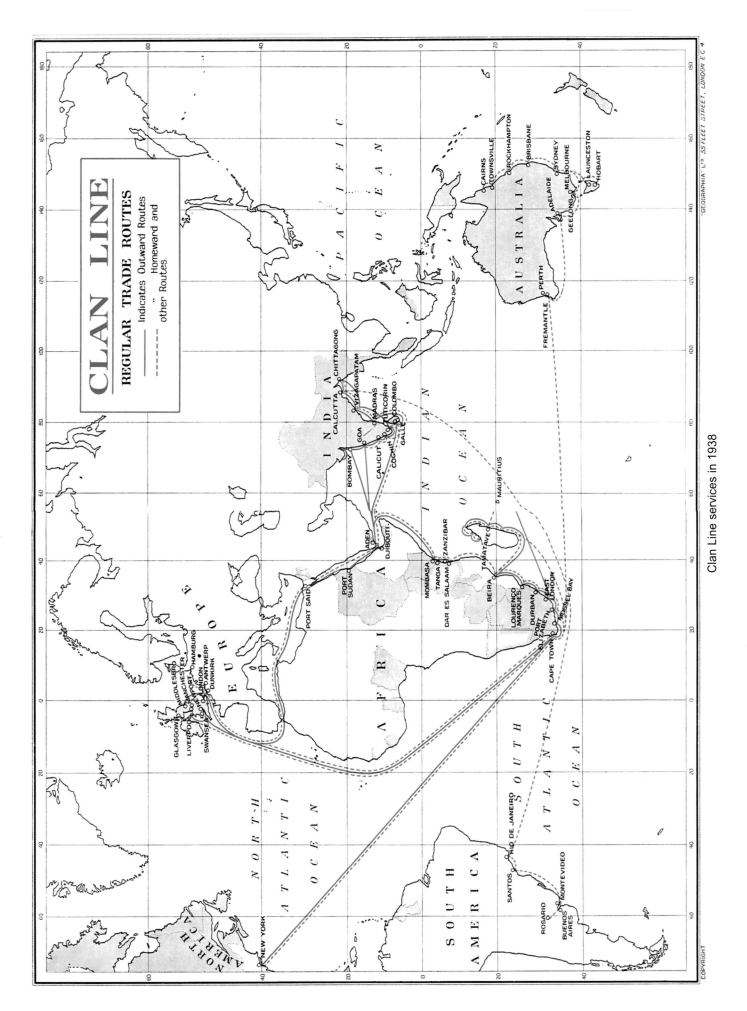

Clan Line services in 1938

EARLY YEARS, EARLY STRUGGLES: 1878-1890

At least three histories of Clan Line have been published, in addition to the comprehensive biography of the founder which appeared in 1978, 'A Victorian Shipowner'. Inevitably some items were repeated in these publications, as indeed some of the pertinent facts from that last-named volume must be here, but strangely for a company whose very existence depended on shipping and trade routes, very little has been told of the extreme difficulties of operating early steam ships with untried crews on liner routes already served by established companies.

Cayzer founds the line

The opening of the Suez Canal in 1869 created the opportunity to develop steamship routes to India and the Far East, and was soon capitalized upon. By using the shorter Mediterranean, Suez and Red Sea route the steam ship passage to India was at a stroke halved to 30 days, while the sailing ship confined to the long route around the Cape of Good Hope was unable to improve on 90 days. Of even greater significance was the ability of the steam ship to offer calls at secondary or intermediate ports along the way, and with a credibly reliable schedule the steamer could make three round trips per annum to India while the deep water sailing ship, limited by the vagaries and patterns of ocean winds and currents to a single voyage in any one year, became hopelessly uncompetitive to ports on the Indian continent.

Six years after the Canal opened, at least seven British companies were using the waterway to provide steamship services to India: three from London and east coast ports and the remainder from the west coast. The latter may sound sufficient but Hendersons sailed only to Rangoon (then part of India) and Harrisons only to Calcutta, leaving the Glasgow-owned Anchor and City Lines to serve Bombay and with the latter covering both Calcutta and Bombay with a fleet of just seven steam ships, it occurred to one Charles Cayzer that there could be an opening for an improved service from Liverpool to Bombay.

There was no shipping or seafaring background to the London-based Cayzer family, but this did not stop their only son Charles, at the age of 15, being engaged as a master's clerk on a sailing ship for a lengthy voyage to Japan. Following this he spent 12 years in Bombay, most of it looking after the stores and cargoes of a company (with Glasgow origins) which acted as agents for the well-established British India company. In 1873 Charles went home by steamer via Suez, and during his leave visited Liverpool and Glasgow, weighing up the prospects of establishing a regular steamer service to Bombay, and on returning to India promptly resigned his post and moved home permanently in October 1874. He took with him extensive experience of the shipping business in Bombay and a good knowledge gleaned on recent passages of what was required of a steam ship and crew; most especially their master.

After brief periods in Cardiff and London, Charles Cayzer moved to Liverpool in 1876 and found there that trade with India had doubled in the past ten years, confirming his earlier belief that a regular, direct service to Bombay would be well supported by shippers as an alternative to the expense and inconvenience of moving goods through London, although he personally did not have the means to finance such an undertaking. He did, however, gain control of the elderly wooden barque *Jalawar* (635/1850), which he had loaded with cotton goods and sent off to Bombay in November 1876, taking almost six months for the passage to India where both ship and cargo were promptly sold at a handsome profit. A further venture with the US built *North Star* (818/?), a full-rigged ship of doubtful vintage, bought in Hartlepool in May 1877, was less successful, possibly because a cargo for India could not be found, but he fixed her for an 18-month voyage out to the Plate and home with guano from Chile.

Late in 1877 Cayzer visited Glasgow where he had discussions with Alexander Stephen, the Linthouse shipbuilder, concerning the construction of two ships for a Bombay service while he was endeavouring to form a limited liability company. Negotiations began in earnest in January 1878 when Stephen offered to build them at one-third of their cost during construction with the remainder paid by bills of exchange within three years. Another financial supporter was John Muir of James Finlay and Co., prominent Glasgow merchants who even then could claim over a century of trading with India; this connection later proved to be of the greatest benefit to Finlay, to Cayzer and to Clan Line.

Towards the end of February 1878 agreement was reached to build the ships, with deliveries scheduled for November and December that year. Cayzer then set about raising the necessary finance and, having decided against a limited company, formed a partnership in Liverpool early in March with Captain Alexander Irvine, a former British India shipmaster with invaluable experience of the Indian trades, bringing into being Cayzer, Irvine and Company.

Sir Charles W. Cayzer had many other interests in addition to his shipping business. In 1892 he became Member of Parliament for Barrow-in-Furness, a position he held until 1906. He was knighted in 1897 in recognition of his shipping work and in 1904 created a baronet. To him a ship was not merely 'a tin box for carrying goods' and it was thought that depression caused by losing so many ships in the First World War contributed to his death in September 1916.

Whilst the two ships were under construction, and as a condition of John Muir's financial support, it was agreed that Finlay, Muir and Co. would act as inward and outward freight agents in Bombay, while James Finlay and Co. in Glasgow would give preference to Cayzer's ships when shipping goods to and from Bombay. This agreement was later amended to allow James Finlay alone to charter the Clan ships for country (i.e. Indian coastwise) cargoes and homeward employment for all ports east of Suez, but this was later modified. Meanwhile, although two ships were fine to get started, Cayzer was well aware that a minimum of six were necessary to sustain a fortnightly schedule of sailings to and from Bombay, so two further orders were given to Stephen and two to McMillan of Dumbarton; all four to be delivered in February and March 1879 when the intended schedule would become fully operational.

The first two ships were delivered a month early while the first ordered from McMillans was launched at Dumbarton on Christmas Eve to give a fleet of three before the end of 1878. The class as a whole was of modest dimensions. Accommodation was provided for 12 first class passengers while deck and engineering officers were British with Lascar crews carried from the outset.

With the ships being built in Scotland, as Alexander Stephen had agreed to become a partner in the venture, and having made many friends among the merchants and others in Glasgow, Charles Cayzer decided to name them after Scottish clans and to register them in Glasgow. For a number of years the naming system caused confusion with the sailing ships of Thomas Dunlop who had used a similar nomenclature since 1874. It is widely believed that the funnel colours - black with two red bands - were adopted because Cayzer wanted to use those of British India ships but with red in place of white.

The early voyages
When the first ship, Clan Alpine (1), was completed in October 1878 a large party was taken on a cruise around the upper Firth of Clyde to demonstrate and help publicise the beginning of the new service to India. For outward cargoes it was clear from the outset that shippers in Scotland would support the

service as much as those in Liverpool and so all Clan services from the west coast developed so that Liverpool was usually the last port outward and first inward, with Glasgow the turnround port and the base where repairs and surveys could be arranged while the ships were free of cargo. The Clan Alpine left Glasgow with a thousand tons of iron railway chairs and completed loading in the Sandon Dock in Liverpool, from where she departed for Bombay in the late evening of 26th October under the command of Captain George H. Cawley of Bristol, who had served as a sub-lieutenant in the Royal Naval Reserve 23 years earlier.

The maiden voyage of the second ship, Clan Fraser (1), began a month later and the others followed at intervals between March and May 1879, from which point onwards it might be assumed the new company was up and running with a regular service to and from Bombay, established within the space of eight months. However, difficulties soon arose in operating these early steam ships, some simply due to the failure of materials, others to the dependence on inexperienced personnel, while major problems arose in finding cargoes both in Bombay and in unfamiliar ports with shippers and agents as yet unknown to the new company.

On her first voyage the Clan Alpine averaged 10.5 knots to Malta, where bunkers were replenished. She reached Bombay in the advertised time of 30 days but it was here that delays began. Almost three weeks were spent in Bombay, in part probably seeking a homeward cargo which did not materialise. The ship then accepted a coastal cargo to Calcutta and another from there to Colombo before loading rice in Rangoon where the homeward voyage began at the end of February. On entering the Suez Canal two weeks later, the Clan Alpine took the ground and was only refloated after 24 hours by discharging 150 tons of cargo to lighten the ship. This lost cargo was not re-shipped and the Clan Alpine reached Liverpool on 6th April after a voyage lasting five and a half months and then had to wait four weeks to fit in with the next scheduled sailing for Bombay. Whilst in Liverpool, Captain Cawley was sent to Dumbarton to take over the Clan Stuart (1), then about to begin trials, and was replaced by Captain Edward Harley from Poole.

This painting of Clan Alpine (1) is one of the few images of the first Clans fully rigged. Following their sale in 1897 both Clan Alpine and her sister Clan Lamont almost immediately reverted to Clan Line registered ownership for two years, a precaution to provide security to Clan against a loan given to new owner John T. Lunn of Newcastle-upon-Tyne. It was intended to include Clan Gordon in the transaction, but she was wrecked before she could be handed over. [Newall Dunn collection]

The first voyage of the Clan Fraser under Captain William Cowie of Aberdeen echoed that of the Clan Alpine and lasted five months, returning to London on 1st May also with rice from Rangoon. Her second voyage was with ironwork from Middlesbrough to Karachi and she returned from Bombay with cotton to Genoa and Marseilles and in October 1879 brought a cargo from Tripoli to London, probably esparto grass. This ship was also out of step with the Bombay schedule and so made a six-week voyage under Captain McCann with coal from Cardiff to Brindisi on the heel of Italy and returned to Liverpool on 21st December with cotton from Alexandria.

In January 1880, Captain Richard Green of Liverpool, aged 33, was given command of Clan Fraser which sailed on the 18th and put into Malta with extensive heavy weather damage due to tarpaulins

An unidentified early Clan Line steamer in the Suez Canal. *[Newall Dunn collection]*

being torn away by seas allowing water into a hold, with cargo shifted and boats and cabin damaged. Her passage to Bombay occupied 35 days and after seven days discharging she was despatched to Calcutta and loaded for both Marseilles and London, berthing in the Millwall Dock on 14th May 1880.

A major blow was dealt Charles Cayzer while the first two ships were seeking homeward cargoes in Calcutta and Rangoon. His partner, Alexander Irvine, died suddenly from a heart attack on 27th January 1879 and, although Cayzer soon acquired another associate, out of loyalty to Irvine's family he never altered the name of the managing company which continued until Clan Line's demise in 1982.

The second voyage of the *Clan Alpine* was even longer than the first and required her to return to the Mersey for machinery adjustments. She eventually sailed on 6th May 1879 for Bombay, where Captain Harley exchanged commands with Captain Rule of the *Clan Lamont* (1) when that new ship arrived ten days later, and after transfer William Rule made a further six voyages on the *Clan Alpine* and continued as master in the company until his retirement in 1902. From Bombay the *Clan Alpine* proceeded to the Far East, loading homeward at Nagasaki, Hong Kong and Singapore to reach London on 11th November after a voyage of six months.

The next and third voyage of the *Clan Alpine* was from London to Bombay, returning from Pondicherry and Cocanada on the Madras coast to Marseilles, and then light ship to Cardiff for a short voyage with coal to Odessa and home with grain to Le Havre and thence to London to prepare for an outward ballast voyage to Bombay.

Clan Ranald (1) left the Clyde on 23rd February and Liverpool on 5th March for Bombay, under Captain John Hoole from Sheffield. The outward voyage was free of incident, Bombay being reached in the customary 30 days where the ship languished for six weeks until despatched to

Rangoon to load rice for London. Somewhere between Malta and the UK, this ship was reported as having jettisoned one thousand tons of cargo, almost half the total, without any stated reason, and on 25th June put into Falmouth where eight passengers landed. The voyage then resumed and the *Clan Ranald* berthed in Victoria Dock, London two days later. After completing discharge, Captain Hoole coasted the ship to Liverpool to begin loading for her second voyage and was there relieved by Captain James Joass, a Banffshire man who remained for the next three voyages. It later transpired that John Hoole had no steam certificate. This was the age of the early steam ships with many officers and crews brought up in sail, then willingly or otherwise transferred to the unfamiliar surroundings and quite different pace of life in steam. Certificates of competence only became mandatory in 1894.

While some ships proved reliable and free of incident or accident, others hardly completed a voyage without problems and *Clan Ranald* was certainly one of the latter. On her second voyage she discharged in Bombay at the end of August 1879 and again waited six weeks without obtaining a cargo until despatched with pilgrims to Jeddah. These were the first pilgrims carried by Clan, but thereafter for a number of years sailings were made each autumn. From Jeddah the *Clan Ranald* crossed the Red Sea to the remote anchorage of Rawaya, 70 miles north of Port Sudan, requiring the most dangerous approach through 20 miles of unmarked shoals and reefs. More pilgrims were embarked here from the village and fort of Muhammad Qol and conveyed to Jeddah and, on completion of these trips, the *Clan Ranald* was ordered first to Galle then Calcutta to load homewards. When approaching the entrance to the Hooghly at the Sandheads in the early hours of 18th November, the *Clan Ranald* collided with the anchored British India steamer *Chinsura* (2,033/1877), but sustained only minor damage and berthed safely in Calcutta later that day. From this port the first cargo from India to the UK was loaded and after a passage of five weeks the *Clan Ranald* berthed in London's East India Dock basin in the evening of 22nd January 1880.

The third ship built for the company by Alexander Stephen was launched as *Clan Gordon* (1) early in February 1879 and completed a month later when she was put under the command of Captain William Bigley, aged 32, born in Limerick and with an extra master's certificate in sail. The outward passage to Bombay began from Liverpool on 22nd March and was free of incident; 12 days after arrival the ship was despatched for Rangoon, later changed to Akyab where rice was loaded for Malta for orders. On 3rd June the *Clan Gordon* entered Trincomalee short of coals, where she grounded on the York Shoal inside the harbour but was refloated undamaged next day and proceeded round to Galle, where coals were obtained and departure made on the 10th. A bad passage was experienced across the Indian Ocean in the south west monsoon and damage suffered when approaching Ras Hafun on the Somali coast. Cabin doors were smashed, the saloon flooded, a boat stove in and the forward bulkhead of the amidships deckhouse started. She put into Malta for coaling and damage repairs before continuing to Antwerp for discharge.

The next voyage was from Middlesbrough and Sunderland, probably with ironwork, and also called at Gibraltar, Tangier, Algiers and Tunis en route to Bombay. After discharge the *Clan Gordon* loaded on the Madras coast, beginning at Gopalpore in Orissa and clearing from Galle on 20th December 1879 for Marseilles. Heavy weather was experienced in the Mediterranean, necessitating a call at Malta with shifted cargo and a portion jettisoned; three boats were lost when the decks were swept by seas fore and aft. In Malta 8,000 bags of damaged cargo were landed, the remainder restowed and the same 8,000 bags re-loaded. The *Clan Gordon* then part discharged in Marseilles with the balance in Elba before loading at three ports in Libya for Liverpool, arriving there on 1st March after a voyage of five and a half months. Captain Bigley then left the company's service on relief by William Cowie.

The second ship from Dumbarton, *Clan Stuart* (1), sailed from Liverpool on her maiden voyage on 27th April under Captain Cawley, who had transferred on arriving home with the *Clan Alpine*. The outward passage to Bombay was followed by rice from Rangoon to Falmouth for orders, and on arrival there on 21st August the ship was first ordered to Antwerp but changed to Liverpool and reached there two days later.

An irregular service

These were the earliest months of a company that quickly grew to become one of the major cargo carriers in the British merchant fleet, although its Bombay service was then struggling to establish some kind of regularity in departures from Liverpool. Since inception ten months earlier in October 1878, the frequency had varied from nine to 66 days and had latterly settled at two-monthly intervals; the most recent sailing being that of the *Clan Ranald* on 23rd July while the next would be *Clan Gordon* about 23rd September. Alternative employment had now to be found for *Clan Stuart* between these dates.

On 10th September 1879 the *Clan Stuart*, still under Captain Cawley, left Liverpool for South Carolina, taking 15 days on passage to Port Royal and Beaufort on the river of that name. This was an area captured by Union forces 17 years earlier: general cargo was likely carried outward and cotton most certainly homewards. The ship made Queenstown in 16 days and was ordered to Liverpool to discharge, arriving on 2nd November when Captain Cawley left both the ship and company's employ when replaced by Captain Harley from the *Clan Lamont*.

There had earlier been some dissension between Charles Cayzer and John Muir, ostensibly about mortgage payments, but it may also have been due to the lack of cargoes from Bombay and beyond, which from the outset were to be the responsibility of James Finlay and Co., while Finlay, Muir as agents were to benefit from commission on these cargoes. By October 1879 Charles Cayzer was threatening to turn his ships back at Port Said and trade to Mediterranean ports or even send them to North America. His frustration can be understood as by that date only one cargo had materialised from Bombay in the space of 12 months, and one good reason for trading to the Mediterranean or the United States would be to shorten the voyages and thus have more ships available for loading on the berth in Liverpool. It is claimed that Alexander Stephen dissuaded Cayzer from such action and from once again trying to form a limited liability company. Despite this, the voyage accounts show clearly that Cayzer's ships were indeed trading not only with Mediterranean ports but also with those on the other side of the Atlantic.

A second voyage to America began when the *Clan Stuart* left Liverpool on 13th November bound for New Orleans, where a further cotton cargo was loaded in two weeks, completing at Port Eads at the mouth of the Mississippi on Christmas Eve. This cargo was destined for Antwerp, but on

A painting of *Clan Lamont* (1), which almost failed to enter the fleet, as a cash-strapped Cayzer attempted to interest Lloyd Austriaco in purchasing her. The sale fell through when Alexander Stephen declined to guarantee that she could achieve 10.5 knots, although she exceeded this figure on subsequent trials. In September 1881 *Clan Lamont* took the first Clan Line sailing to South Africa. *[Newall Dunn collection]*

17th January 1880 the ship put into Falmouth, apparently for coals, left again next day and reached Flushing on the 20th with a draft of 20.5 feet. Navigation in the Scheldt was then restricted due to slush ice, but the vessel was allowed to continue up the river on condition that the consignees of cargo agreed to lighten the ship by means of 'iron river steamers'. Two days later the *Clan Stuart* was reported arriving in Antwerp Roads in tow of six tugs and 'with the hull tight and lightening continuing'. No further reports were made but whatever happened in the Scheldt between Flushing and Antwerp delayed the ship in that port for the ensuing seven months and must surely have been some form of litigation concerning the ship or cargo or both. The *Clan Stuart* ultimately sailed for Glasgow under Captain Beer and arrived there on 23rd August 1880 to begin loading for Bombay. Captain Harley was not further employed by the company.

A new homeward service

Last of the new ships to be delivered, *Clan Lamont* (1) left Liverpool on her first voyage on 20th May under Captain Rule, newly promoted from chief officer of the *Clan Fraser*, and who exchanged commands with Captain Harley of the *Clan Alpine* while these ships were discharging in Bombay. Homeward she loaded the first Cayzer, Irvine cargo from India at the Madras coast ports of Cocanada and Pondicherry - quite insignificant places then - while attention was focussed on securing cargoes from Bombay. However, the Madras coast had nine minor anchorage ports offering small consignments of ores, cotton piece-goods, tobacco, hemp and palmyra fibre, and by calling at one or more of these ports a ship could obtain a full cargo. The regular liner companies using Colombo, Madras and Calcutta as their main route could not afford to spend time calling at minor ports with all the difficulties of working cargo from surf boats at open anchorages, but Clan Line was to nurture and serve these small ports to good effect throughout its existence.

That homeward cargo from the Madras coast by the *Clan Lamont* in July 1879 was consigned to Marseilles, while another followed in *Clan Gordon* during December. During 1880 there were four similar cargoes from the Madras coast ports to Marseilles, one in 1882 and another four in 1884. In time loading at these small ports was combined with cargoes from the major ports, including Chittagong which opened in 1901. Clan ships continued to serve the small Madras coast ports until containerisation in the 1970s; their main interests served by Gordon, Woodroffe and Co. in Madras.

From Marseilles the *Clan Lamont* carried esparto grass from Tripoli to Liverpool, and it was while anchored in the river there awaiting the tide for docking that the Whitehaven brig *Excel* (100/1859) dragged across her bows causing some damage to the rigging of both ships, but not enough to delay her next departure for Bombay on 6th November under Captain Levack who assumed command in lieu of Edward Harley then transferred to the *Clan Stuart*. That voyage was similar to the previous one, Liverpool to Bombay, and homeward from Cocanada to Marseilles and Elba, then Tripoli to Liverpool arriving on 28th March 1880.

By this date the six ships of the fleet had completed 13 voyages but, while nine sailings were provided for shippers on the berths in Glasgow and Liverpool, there was no improvement in regularity, and this could only be achieved by employing more ships, which must have been a taxing thought

for the partners. Worse still was the situation in Bombay where the same nine ships had also been available on the homeward berth but only one had secured a cargo and that for Genoa and Marseilles. If Charles Cayzer complained of this it had the desired effect in that *Clan Lamont* loaded a first cargo for the UK and destined for Liverpool in May 1880, but this improvement was short lived and another four months passed before homeward cargoes became readily available from Bombay.

On her third voyage to Bombay, *Clan Ranald* sailed from Morpeth Dock in Birkenhead on 15th February 1880, on the same tide as Thomas Dunlop's barque *Clan Campbell* (729/1875) which served to emphasise how confusion might arise from the naming system used by both companies. The outward voyage extended to 36 days and after discharge the *Clan Ranald* was despatched to load on the Madras coast but, when passing around the south of Ceylon, lost her propeller and was towed into Galle by Harrison's *Inventor* (2,291/1878). The *Clan Ranald* was there ballasted by the head to expose the tailshaft which was found undamaged. A new propeller was sent down from Bombay and fitted by the ship's engineers, allowing the voyage to be continued after a delay of 27 days. The ship loaded at Pondicherry for discharge at Marseilles, before continuing to Sunderland to once again load for Bombay.

On this next voyage the *Clan Ranald* arrived in Malta two hours behind the *Clan Alpine*, then on her fifth voyage and in ballast from London. Both ships reached Port Said together, transited the Canal with the *Clan Ranald* two ships behind her consort and arrived in Bombay virtually together on 24th August. After six days anchored in the stream, the *Clan Alpine* entered Princes Dock, probably to discharge ballast or load coastal cargo, but in the process struck the quay and forced the pea of the anchor through the port bow and filled the collision compartment. On completion of repairs the *Clan Alpine* sailed for Calcutta and there loaded the first Clan cargo of jute for Dundee, arriving on 16th November and thereafter proceeding northabout to Glasgow, an awkward passage for a light ship, but which was to be repeated many times in the years ahead. Captain Rule continued as master of that ship for another four voyages until April 1882. Voyage six of the *Clan Alpine* was from Liverpool to Bombay and Karachi, returning from both ports to Marseilles then Falmouth for orders, when sent to Cardiff for a coal cargo, conveniently to Bombay and returned to Dunkirk, probably with cotton, on 30th July 1881.

Meanwhile, discharge of the *Clan Ranald* in Bombay at the end of September 1880 occupied a mere six days, after which the ship was ordered to Batavia and there diverted to load a mixed cargo in the open roadstead of Semarang on the north coast of Java. The ship left there on 7th October for Port Said, where discharge began on the 22nd and ten days later a serious fire broke out which necessitated scuttling the ship to extinguish it by allowing settlement on the bottom in 24 feet of water, still secured to her moorings. A survey soon revealed the upper deck planking burnt yet iron decks intact, hull undamaged with poop, bridge and forecastle above water but main deck submerged by eight feet and a slight list to port. Three weeks later the ship was refloated and the remaining cargo declared worthless. Repairs lasted four weeks and the *Clan Ranald* sailed on 27th December for the Clyde to berth in Glasgow on 11th January 1881. Four months' repair work was then undertaken to return the ship to service. Captain Joass then left the ship and returned to his former employers but was re-engaged by Cayzer, Irvine as master of the *Clan Gordon* in 1884 but sadly died during the course of that voyage, aged 64.

The third voyage of *Clan Gordon* was incident free out from Liverpool via Glasgow on 20th March 1880 to Bombay, returning from Madras, Pondicherry and Galle to Marseilles and then in ballast to Liverpool arriving at the end of July 1880. The fourth voyage of this ship under Captain Levack was a remarkably lengthy one which began at Liverpool on 31st July 1880, the ship making a good passage of 30 days to Bombay where 18 days were spent discharging and awaiting orders. The ship then embarked pilgrims for Jeddah and when leaving that port on 3rd October found herself aground on the Ulysses Shoal and making water at the rate of half an inch per hour. Unsuccessful attempts were made to refloat her but this was accomplished three days later, and after temporary repairs and coaling at Aden she returned to Bombay on the 22nd. The ship was docked three days later when the damage was found to be trifling and on completion the *Clan Gordon* made a second trip to Jeddah and was then despatched to Calcutta to embark more pilgrims. Whilst on passage there the propeller became suspect and with a speed of only six knots she took 23 days to reach the Sandheads. On arriving in Calcutta the vessel was tipped to expose the propeller which was found to be cracked in two places. A replacement was fitted in 17 days and the ship sailed on 8th January 1881 with pilgrims for Jeddah, then returned a further group to Bombay before continuing to Calcutta to load for Genoa and Marseilles. The *Clan Gordon* then reached the Clyde on 18th May and berthed in Glasgow on 1st June, having been absent from the scheduled Liverpool to Bombay service for 11 months.

Voyage five of *Clan Fraser* was from London to Karachi in June 1880 and thence via Galle to Java, where sugar was carried to Marseilles and thereafter ore from Bona and esparto grass from Arzew and Oran, both cargoes to Glasgow. On that homeward leg the *Clan Fraser* went ashore at Finisterre, probably due to fog, but managed to get off without assistance, making only a very little water in the ballast tank and reached Glasgow safely on 1st November. The next voyage was free of incident from Liverpool to Bombay and Karachi, returning on 12th March 1881 to London's West India Dock where Cayzer, Irvine and Co. had now established an office.

On her fourth voyage *Clan Stuart* left Liverpool on 6th September 1880 and, after spending two weeks in Bombay, made an intermediate trip with pilgrims to Jeddah before loading homewards from Bombay to Liverpool arriving on 28th January 1881. A further voyage under Captain Pratt, direct to Bombay and back to Liverpool in the space of 91 days, takes this ship up to 21st May 1881.

Captain Levack continued on *Clan Lamont* for a further Bombay voyage in April 1880, which as shown above was the first which returned direct to Liverpool in the short space of 13 weeks and must have given some hope that homeward cargoes could really be obtained from that port. At the end of this voyage Captain Levack left both the ship and the company's service, on replacement by Samuel Harrison Palmer, then aged 37, who had served as master in other steamers but lately as chief officer for two voyages on *Clan*

Ranald. Palmer remained as master of the *Clan Lamont* for four voyages until February 1882 when appointed the company's marine superintendent in South Africa. He returned to sea as a Clan Line master in 1886 and subsequently formed the partnership agency of Palmer, Womersley, which acted as Cayzer, Irvine's agents at Port Elizabeth where he remained until retirement in 1903.

The first two voyages under Palmer took the *Clan Lamont* out to Bombay and Karachi, returning from the former port to London on the first voyage and to Marseilles on the second, and from there in ballast to Penarth. His third voyage on the *Clan Lamont* was therefore with coal, sailing on 17th April 1881 for Singapore, from which port the ship returned via Penang to London's West India Dock on 13th August that year, and by which date three more ships had joined the fleet with others on order.

Increasing the fleet

It seems clear that Charles Cayzer's earliest intention was for the six original steamers to provide a fortnightly outward and homeward service between Liverpool and Bombay, which would have been possible had a turnround of 12 days been achieved at each of these ports. This in itself depended on efficient cargo handling and on shippers having cargoes on hand to meet the advertised sailing dates. There was no provision for delays in the schedules and these soon proved impossible to maintain.

The 32 voyages described above show how difficult it was to achieve the planned schedule. Even allowing half a day for coaling at Malta and a whole day for passage of the Suez Canal, Bombay should have been reached in 29 days at the scheduled 9.5 knots, but this was achieved on only three outward voyages out of 21: the average being almost 33 days and longest 37 days. Port time in Bombay was from four to seven weeks on six occasions when both discharging and loading or awaiting cargo or being ordered to load elsewhere. The average discharge time appeared to be 13 days, equivalent to working a mere 150 tons per day. At the UK end port time was even worse through having to make calls at two or three ports with two ships being there six or seven weeks, although the average was 25 days.

In-service conditions therefore showed that eight or ideally nine ships were required to maintain the fortnightly schedule to and from Bombay without allowance for diversions, such as those to load homewards from the Madras coast or beyond. By far the greatest delays and disruptions to schedules were those caused by accidents involving collision, grounding, machinery breakdown or loss of propeller which all continued to occur, although on a decreasing scale as engineering skills and navigational aids gradually improved and steam ships grew in size, power, speed and cargo handling facilities. Within 20 years Clan Line was taking delivery of ships with twice the capacity of the original six.

Despite the best endeavours of Charles Cayzer to attain a regular fortnightly schedule between Liverpool and Bombay, the irregular pattern of sailings was still evident during the first 30 months of operating with six new steamers. In that period 26 sailings were made to Bombay with a frequency which varied from two to 16 weeks, still averaging eight weeks apart, and was plainly insufficient to retain the interest of shippers. The fleet had to be increased to meet the needs of those who were supporting it. In October 1880, therefore, Stephen was asked to build two or four more steamers of slightly greater length and capacity to the original six, while negotiations began to form an association of Scottish banks and wealthy merchants to own the new ships, although Cayzer would manage them. Trade was then improving, and a small Cayzer, Irvine office was opened in Glasgow which dispensed with the need for Turnbull, Martin who had originally acted as agents at that port.

At the beginning of 1881 it became clear that the new ships from Stephen would not complete until well into 1882 and so, rather than risk losing the Bombay trade which had been acquired to date, it was decided to purchase secondhand ships of which the first available were three of George Smith's earliest City Line steamers, of almost the same dimensions and tonnage as the Stephen's ships yet to be built, and with ten years' proven service on the Bombay and Calcutta routes. The first of these, *City of Oxford*, was taken over in Glasgow towards the end of February 1881, was renamed *Clan Macduff*, and sailed from Liverpool for Bombay under Captain Thomas on 12th March and made a further smart voyage under that master which completed at Liverpool on 23rd September when Captain William Webster assumed command.

The *Clan Macduff* left Liverpool for Bombay on her third and fateful voyage on 18th October with 19 passengers and 43 locally engaged crew, and next day ran into a strong gale when large quantities of water were shipped; some of the boats were stove in and washed from their skids and with the bilges choked and unpumpable the ship began to settle. By the 20th the boiler fires were extinguished, the ship lost all power and the situation rapidly became hopeless with the ship barely afloat in a position about halfway between Fastnet and the Scillies. The master, passengers and part of the crew left the ship in the remaining three boats, leaving the remainder aboard to fend for themselves, which included the chief officer, second engineer, boatswain, two stewards, carpenter and ten seamen/firemen. The gale increased that night but next afternoon by sheer luck the small City of Cork packet steamer *Upupa* (948/1871) came across the *Clan Macduff* in a position about 40 miles south of Roche's Point (at the entrance to Queenstown harbour). With great risk and difficulty, the *Upupa* succeeded in taking off all the survivors, with the exception of a little girl who was accidentally lost overboard in transit. The *Upupa* remained with the wreck until 21.00 by which time the decks were almost awash and the *Clan Macduff* must have sunk soon afterwards as no further sightings were reported. On arrival at Plymouth two days later the *Upupa* reported losing some cattle in the severe weather but landed safely the 16 survivors. Of the three boats which got clear of the ship, one with four seamen and seven passengers was picked up on the morning of the 21st by the Liverpool steamer *Palestine* (2,128/1858) about eight miles south of Ballycotton, another with only three men aboard came ashore on the Irish coast seven miles east of Roche's Point in the evening of the 22nd, but the third boat was never recovered. Captain Webster and 31 others perished.

At the end of September 1881 the partnership of the Clan Line Association Steamers officially came into being and took ownership of the two other ex-City Line steamers, the *City of Cambridge* and *City of Mecca*, handed over in Glasgow during April 1881 to become *Clan Maclean* (1) and *Clan Macleod* (1) respectively. The first named began

her first voyage from Liverpool to Bombay on 23rd April and was followed by the *Clan Macleod* 14 days later.

Two further steamers were purchased in 1881. The *Muriel*, building on the Tyne, became *Clan Murray* (1) and loaded in Glasgow and Liverpool, departing on 29th October for Bombay under Captain Watson. The last acquisition that year was a three-island steamer completed as *Clan Monroe* (1). Also loading at Glasgow and Liverpool, this ship sailed from the Mersey for Bombay on 6th January 1882. As a result of these acquisitions, the combined fleet reached ten steamers and was set to more than double again by the end of that year.

The purchase of the three City Line steamers in the spring of 1881 had the desired effect on the frequency of the Bombay service, allowing it to become fortnightly from Liverpool. Homeward sailings from Bombay were also vastly improved; in 1879 only one sailing was made to continental ports (Genoa and Marseilles), in 1880 one to London and two for Liverpool, while in 1881 there were 20 sailings from Bombay to European ports: i.e. ten to Liverpool, two to

City of Oxford of 1870 bought in 1881, renamed *Clan Macduff* and lost on her third voyage. *[J. and M. Clarkson collection]*

An artist's impression of the rescue of the crew of the *Clan Macduff* by the *Upupa*. *[Newall Dunn collection]*

London, five to Marseilles, two for Genoa/Marseilles and one to Dunkirk. With good profits being reported on the Bombay voyages, Charles Cayzer and the Association partners felt it was time to look at the prospect of expanding into another trade quite separate from India.

A service to the Cape Colony

Some years prior to the formation of Cayzer, Irvine, Charles Cayzer had given consideration to starting a service to the Cape Colony. The principal traders were the rival Union and Castle Lines which from 1876 shared the lucrative mail contract and, although unlikely to welcome a newcomer on the Cape coast, could hardly prevent Clan ships loading for that destination in Glasgow and Liverpool while the mail companies confined themselves to London and south coast ports.

The distance from Liverpool to Bombay or Cape Town was much the same, coaling was available in the Cape Verde islands from where the Cape could be reached in 18 days, subject to the strength of the adverse Benguela Current and South East Trades in the South Atlantic. In Cape Town itself, the Alfred Basin with berths for five overseas ships and a sheltering breakwater was completed in 1870 while similar works and improvements were in progress at Durban and East London. Only at Mossel Bay and Algoa Bay (for Port Elizabeth) was it necessary to discharge overside into lighters at open roadsteads, with all the inherent difficulties that entailed in the Cape swell.

Throughout the formation of the Clan Line Association Steamers, one of the partners strongly supported Cayzer's desire to establish a service to the Cape and conveniently arranged to spend three months there making contacts once the service actually began. The first sailing to the Cape was made by *Clan Lamont* (1) under Captain Palmer, leaving Glasgow on 1st September 1881 and Liverpool on the 8th. Eleven days later a call was made at St Vincent in the Cape Verde islands for coaling, and Cape Town was reached on 7th October after a passage of 29 days at an average speed of 9.5 knots. Five days were spent in Cape Town whence the *Clan Lamont* continued to Algoa Bay then Durban and thereafter proceeded to Calcutta and loaded for London, where she berthed in the South West India Dock on 6th February 1882. Subsequent sailings to the Cape that year were made by *Clan Gordon* (1), *Clan Fraser* (1) and *Clan Macleod* (1) at roughly four-week intervals; the first named then loading home from Calcutta and the remaining two from Bombay.

An agreement was reached with the mail companies that Clan ships would not load homewards from the Cape, other than in exceptional circumstances and even then with no more than three loading in any one year. However, this arrangement suited Cayzer very well as it provided the opportunity to use the Cape ships for increased homeward sailings from India or elsewhere as occasion demanded. At the beginning of 1882 the Cape sailings were increased to a three-weekly frequency, calls were begun at East London and two or more in each year at Mauritius where sugar was loaded for Bombay. Two of the last sailings to the Cape in 1883 returned from that same coast with cargoes for London and in 1884 three for London, one for Glasgow and another for Savona in Italy. Occasionally, if no other cargoes were available, a ship from the Cape route would be sent to Java, where two sugar cargoes were carried to Marseilles in 1882.

At the end of 1881 after just three years in business, Cayzer, Irvine was therefore managing a fleet of ten Clan ships trading on two entirely separate routes to two continents, but this was by no means the end of Charles Cayzer's expansion plans. From his earlier experiences in Bombay, he knew that the jewel in the Indian crown was Calcutta, which exported all of India's valuable tea cargoes in addition to jute, hides and skins, linseed and numerous other commodities.

The start of the Calcutta service

Early in 1882 it became known that the Queen Line, which served Colombo, Madras and Calcutta from Glasgow and Liverpool, was withdrawing from that route. The City Line also served Calcutta from Glasgow but did not call at Colombo or Madras. Charles Cayzer felt it imperative that Clan ships should immediately replace those of the Queen Line before others such as the Anchor Line grasped the opportunity. John Muir agreed with Cayzer even although initially ships would have to be taken off the Bombay or Cape route until some of those on order were delivered. A further purchase was made in February from Sunderland shipbuilders who had launched a steamer in January for unidentified owners. This ship of similar tonnage to the original six Clans was completed as *Clan Mackay* (1) and sailed for the Cape on 19th March. The first of the four ships from Stephens, *Clan Cameron* (1), sailed initially for the Cape on 7th April but returned to the Mersey with machinery defects only to sail again six days later.

A further ten new ships were delivered in 1882 and five more in 1883. The first completion in 1882 was *Clan Macdonald* (1) which also made her first voyage to the Cape, leaving the Mersey on 1st May. After discharging at Durban, the *Clan Macdonald* proceeded via Galle to Bombay and was there ordered to Karachi where troops were embarked for Suez, a further contingent was then carried from Aden to Madras from where the ship loaded in Calcutta for London to return home after a voyage of almost eight months.

The *Clan Buchanan* (1) launched in Dumbarton in February 1882 was the first of a class of six with almost 50 per cent greater capacity than the *Clan Alpine* class of four years earlier. She left Liverpool on 20th May to begin the new service to Colombo, Madras and Calcutta and, unlike the Bombay route which had a most irregular service for the first two years, the Calcutta service was fortnightly from the outset, both outward and homeward. It would become one of the most important of the company's routes. Unfortunately the first voyage of the *Clan Buchanan,* although preceded on the homeward service by three ships routed to Calcutta from the Cape, was marred by her losing two blades of her propeller six hours after landing the Hooghly pilot at the Sandheads on 13th April. Undeterred by this loss, Captain Russell sailed the ship back to the Sandheads within four days, embarked a pilot and engaged a tug to tow her into the Saugor anchorage, where a second tug was secured for towage to Garden Reach at Calcutta. Some cargo had to be discharged to allow tipping to expose the propeller, new blades were fitted, the cargo re-loaded and the ship sailed 18 days later for London. On her next outward voyage, the *Clan Buchanan* went ashore, presumably in fog, some seven miles south of Cape Spartel, at the southern entrance to the Straits of Gibraltar. Divers, pumps and six tugs were sent from the Rock, the ship was found to be on a sandy bottom and, after jettisoning 100 tons of ironwork and bricks, refloating was achieved next day with

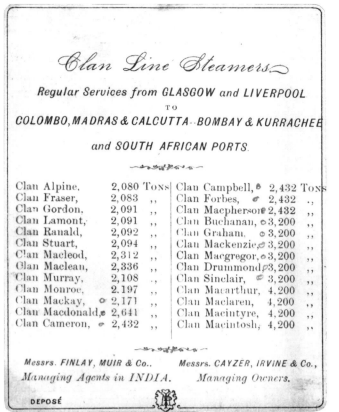

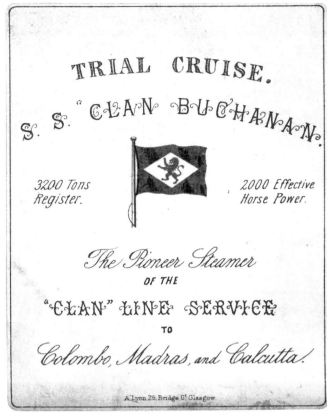

Clan Line Steamers

Regular Services from GLASGOW and LIVERPOOL
TO
COLOMBO, MADRAS & CALCUTTA--BOMBAY & KURRACHEE
and SOUTH AFRICAN PORTS.

Clan Alpine,	2,080 Tons	Clan Campbell,	2,432 Tons
Clan Fraser,	2,083 ,,	Clan Forbes,	2,432 .,
Clan Gordon,	2,091 ,,	Clan Macpherson	2,432 ,,
Clan Lamont,	2,091 ,,	Clan Buchanan,	3,200 ,,
Clan Ranald,	2,092 ,,	Clan Graham,	3,200 ,,
Clan Stuart,	2,094 ,,	Clan Mackenzie,	3,200 ,,
Clan Macleod,	2,312 ,,	Clan Macgregor,	3,200 ,,
Clan Maclean,	2,336 ,,	Clan Drummond	3,200 ,,
Clan Murray,	2,108 .,	Clan Sinclair,	3,200 ,,
Clan Monroe,	2,197 ,,	Clan Macarthur,	4,200 ,,
Clan Mackay,	2,171 ,,	Clan Maclaren,	4,200 ,,
Clan Macdonald,	2,641 ,,	Clan Macintyre,	4,200 ,,
Clan Cameron,	2,432 ,,	Clan Macintosh,	4,200 ,,

Messrs. FINLAY, MUIR & Co..   Messrs. CAYZER, IRVINE & Co.,
Managing Agents in INDIA.   Managing Owners.

DEPOSÉ

TRIAL CRUISE.
S. S. "CLAN BUCHANAN."

3200 Tons
Register.

2000 Effective
Horse Power.

The Pioneer Steamer
OF THE
"CLAN" LINE SERVICE
TO
Colombo, Madras, and Calcutta!

A. Lyon 25. Bridge St Glasgow.

MENU

Soups.
Clear Turtle.   A la reine.

Fish.
Salmon and Dutch Sauce.   Fillets of Soles and Lobster Sauce.

Entrees.
Veal Sweet-breads, à la financière.   Pigeons à la Marengo.
Rissoles de foie gras.

Grosses Pieces.
Roast Turkey aux truffes du Perigord.   Wiltshire Ham.
Hind Quarter of Lamb and Mint Sauce.
Roast Sirloin of Beef.   Spring Chickens.   Ox Tongues.

Prawn Curry and Bombay Duck.

Legumes.
Asparagus & White Sauce.   Cauliflower.   Green Peas.   New Potatoes.

Entremets.
Florence Pudding.   Cream à la Charlotte-russe.
Dantzic Jelly.   Meringues à la suisse.   Apricot Tart.
Peach Soufflé.   Pâtisserie française.

Glaces.
Strawberry Cream.   Pine-Apple Water.

Dessert.

Tea and Coffee.

Glasgow, 13th MAY, 1882.
Geo. R. MacKenzie, Purveyor, Glasgow, and PAISLEY.

TOAST LIST.

1	THE QUEEN,	THE CHAIRMAN.
2	The Prince and Princess of Wales,	THE CHAIRMAN.
3	The Army, Navy & Reserve Forces,	THE CHAIRMAN.

Replies,—COL. LAMBTON, Highland L.I. and MAJOR GLEN, 8th L.R.V.

4 THE "CLAN" LINE & the S.S. "CLAN BUCHANAN"   R. McMILLAN, Esq

5 The Builders & Engineers of the
    S.S. "CLAN BUCHANAN,"   JOHN MUIR, Esq.
    Replies—R. McMILLAN, Esq. and DAVID ROWAN, Esq.

6 Merchant Shippers and Manufacturers, ...C. W. CAYZER, Esq.
    Replies—D. S. CARGILL, Esq.; and THOMAS REID, Esq.

7 Prosperity to the Shipping Trade, ..   SIR JAMES WATSON.
    Reply, ... W. McEWEN, Esq.

8 The Guests, ..   JAMES ARTHUR, Esq.
    Reply,—PROVOST CAMPBELL, of Greenock.

9 The Clergy, ...   SIR WILLIAM COLLINS.
    Reply,—Rev. J. MARSHALL LANG, D.D.

10 The Press, ... SIR PETER COATS.
    Reply, ..   ————————

11 The Ladies, ..   DAVID GRAY, Esq.
    Reply,—T. G. ARTHUR, Esq.

12 The Chairman, ..   LORD DEAN OF GUILD.
    Reply,—THOMAS COATS, Esq.

A card issued to invited guests on the 1882 trial trip of *Clan Buchanan* (1), the first of a class of six new ships. Even more importantly, it marked the first sailing on the new Calcutta service. After disembarking the guests *Clan Buchanan* left the Clyde on 13th May and arrived on the Mersey the next day, sailing for Calcutta on 20th May. Note that one of the toasts given by Charles Cayzer was to 'merchant shippers and manufacturers', some of whom would number amongst the guests. Throughout Clan Line's history, shippers' parties were a regular event aboard the best of the company's ships in all manner of ports at home and abroad.

Inspection of the list of the company's ships on the back page of the card (top left) shows that at some stage the names of two of the four planned 4,200-ton steamers were changed, the names *Clan Maclaren* and *Clan Macintyre* being replaced by *Clan Macpherson* and *Clan Matheson*. [Archie Munro collection]

Clan Buchanan (1) in company with a fine array of deep-sea sailing vessels. Forty passengers were accommodated in her long poop. *[Ships in Focus]*

assistance from HMS *Osprey*. The ship was found to be watertight and, after making good repairs to her upperworks at Gibraltar, continued her voyage.

Two ships of the *Clan Buchanan* class, *Clan Graham* (1) and *Clan Sinclair* (1), were delivered from Napier, Shanks and Bell in June and November respectively. The second of the same class from McMillans was *Clan Drummond* which grounded near Dumbarton in a gale three weeks after launching while being towed to Glasgow for fitting boilers and machinery. The first voyage of this ship to and from Calcutta was free of incident, but on the next one while proceeding up the Mersey channel the *Clan Drummond* collided with the very large four-masted steamer *British Prince* (3,871/1882) between the Formby and Crosby Light Vessels. The *British Prince* was about to anchor and was struck amidships, had plates and frames broken, the bridge carried away and both bows and stern damaged. *Clan Drummond* suffered only minor damage which was repaired whilst loading outwards in Birkenhead.

Unfortunately, the bad luck of the relatively new *Clan Drummond* then carried forward into her third voyage which like the previous two was to Calcutta. While proceeding down the Gulf of Suez the *Clan Drummond* ran ashore six miles north of Ras Gharib, presumably on the four fathom shoal less than half a mile offshore. Soundings showed 26 feet of water aft, 24 feet forward and the ship touching the ground amidships on 20 feet. About 50 tons of coal was thrown overboard in an attempt to lighten the ship while an officer was sent to Suez on the Hartlepool steamer *Fannie* (1,684/1882) to request the immediate assistance of a tug and lighters to offload 250 tons of cargo. Before any of this could happen, the ship refloated without assistance next evening and, being undamaged, proceeded on her voyage and therefore minus the officer left at Suez. On arrival at Colombo 15 days later the master reported the ship 'quite tight, the cargo in good order and none jettisoned'.

Nine days later when proceeding up the Hooghly towards Calcutta, the *Clan Drummond* took the ground abreast

off Nurpore but came off almost immediately and, as her head payed off, collided with the French steamer *Cochin* (2,085/1881) outbound for Hull, which promptly sank in mid channel. The *Clan Drummond* had a large hole in both bows forward of the collision bulkhead and also had underwater plates damaged. Some water got into the fore hold but was kept in check by the pumps, although the cargo there was believed undamaged. Repairs and docking at Calcutta were estimated to take a month but actually delayed the ship seven weeks beyond her scheduled sailing date. With no chance of the sunken *Cochin* being lifted, the wreck was blown up to clear the channel. A subsequent court of enquiry held at Calcutta 'delivered judgement holding *Clan Drummond* blameless'.

The remaining two ships of the class were *Clan Mackenzie* (1) and *Clan Macgregor* (1), built at Leith. On her maiden voyage which began from Liverpool on 15th July, the *Clan Mackenzie* was delayed in Calcutta for 55 days, having to dock for leakages aft caused by several loose rivets in way of the aft bulkhead at the inner end of the stern tube. The damage was understood to have been caused by propeller vibration. On her third voyage to Calcutta in June 1883 the *Clan Mackenzie* suffered considerable damage when crossing the Indian Ocean at the height of the south west monsoon. By the morning of the 25th of that month the ship was 100 miles north east of Socotra and experiencing winds of force six with a short, choppy sea which then increased to hurricane force 12 and lasted for 14 hours. Large quantities of water were shipped, deck fittings carried away and some cases of acid washed overboard. At times the seas swept clean over the ship, carried away stanchions and the starboard quarter boat, stove in lifeboats and damaged rails and bulwarks. The vessel laboured badly, rolling in the trough of the sea as much as 45 degrees at times, but safely arrived at Colombo on 1st July.

At the launch of *Clan Macgregor* at Leith on 31st July, the ground underneath gave way and the vessel remained stationary but was successfully floated a few days later. This ship completed at the beginning of October and set out for

Table 1: Number and average frequency of Clan Line sailings from Liverpool, 1879-1888

Year	To Bombay		To Cape Colony		To Calcutta	
	Number	Frequency	Number	Frequency	Number	Frequency
1879	7	Infrequent	0	-	0	-
1880	10	Infrequent	0	-	0	-
1881	18	3 weeks	4	4 weeks	0	-
1882	12	4 weeks	15	3 weeks	11	2 weeks
1883	17	3 weeks	16	24 days	21	2 weeks
1884	34	10 days	12	4 weeks	24	2 weeks
1885	34	10 days	12	4 weeks	25	2 weeks
1886	28	2 weeks	10	5 weeks	20	2 weeks
1887	23	2 weeks	14	4 weeks	26	2 weeks
1888	21	2 weeks	18	3 weeks	29	2 weeks

Table 2: Number and average frequency of Clan Line homeward sailings, 1879-1888

Year	From Bombay		From Calcutta		From Madras coast	
	Number	Frequency	Number	Frequency	Number	Frequency
1879	1	-	1	-	2	-
1880	3	Infrequent	2	Infrequent	4	-
1881	20	3 weeks	2	Infrequent	0	-
1882	18	3 weeks	14	2 weeks	1	-
1883	17	3 weeks	21	2 weeks	0	-
1884	34	2 weeks	28	2 weeks	4	-
1885	43	10 days	27	2 weeks	3	-
1886	38	10 days	24	2 weeks	8	Irregular
1887	22	2 weeks	29	2 weeks	18	Irregular
1888	21	2 weeks	27	2 weeks	21	Irregular

Glasgow to begin loading, but when rounding Cape Wrath in a strong gale on the 5th, the skylight was smashed, a boat stove in, part of the bulwarks carried away while the main boom burst its lashings and broke adrift complete with crutch and starboard shrouds of the main rigging. Her maiden voyage began on 23rd October and due to engine breakdown she had to be towed into Colombo on 29th November by the brig *Audacious.* She was soon repaired and proceeded next day for Madras.

Of the remaining three ships from Stephen, the *Clan Campbell* (1) sailed from Liverpool for the Cape on 15th July. This class was built with scantlings considerably in excess of requirements and with extra watertight bulkheads to allow their names to be placed on the Admiralty list as suitable for transports. They were fitted with very airy, spacious and elegant passenger accommodation and launched with their machinery already installed. The *Clan Campbell* discharged in both Cape Town and East London, returned to Cape Town and then proceeded for Mauritius but stranded on the shore of that island 25 miles short of her destination at Port Louis harbour. The *Clan Campbell* had struck the coral reef which surrounds most of the island, and was almost a mile from the shore which made assistance difficult, in a position close to the Baie du Cap and three miles east of the south western extremity of the island. The first attempts to refloat her were unsuccessful, and another with tug assistance two days later also failed. Fortunately the weather remained fine and after being ashore for a week the vessel was fumigated to obtain pratique before lightening of cargo could begin; this was on

31st October but seven days later it was reported the ship had broken in two and the after part sunk. The sale of ship and cargo realised 32,000 rupees.

The third ship from Stephen, *Clan Forbes* (1), sailed from Liverpool for Calcutta on 10th September. The outward passage was incident-free, the ship loaded a full cargo of jute for Dundee and left Calcutta on 5th November. In the early evening of the 25th the *Clan Forbes* was making her way into Suez Bay when she collided with the port side midships section of the P&O steamer *Malwa* (2,957/1873) which had just exited the Canal. The main compartment of that liner filled with water and the ship had to be run ashore in the roads in 24 feet of water to prevent sinking, just as it was found the fore and aft compartments were also flooded. The leaks were stopped up within four days when the liner was towed into dry dock for repairs. On the *Clan Forbes* damage was restricted to smashed stem plates but required cargo to be discharged from the fore hold to gain access for repairs which were completed in four weeks when the voyage to Dundee was resumed on 28th December.

The last completion of 1882 was *Clan Ogilvie* from Stephens which sailed for Bombay on 8th December, and when manoeuvring in Princes Dock to leave that port on 24th January 1883, struck the Sunderland steamer *Inflexible* (2,300/1882) which had just arrived from Liverpool with a cargo of general goods and ironwork. The *Inflexible* sank at her berth in a few minutes with her after compartment full of water, but was subsequently refloated and continued her voyage. The *Clan Ogilvie* was able to resume her voyage three weeks later and reached Liverpool safely on 5th March.

Such were the hazards and difficulties encountered while increasing the fleet with 12 new units in 1882, but they were not the only ships then in trouble. On her seventh voyage the *Clan Ranald* (1) left Durban on 8th March under Captain Alexanderson bound for Calcutta to load homewards, and 11 days later when 180 miles north of the Seychelles lost her propeller and became helpless. The master had the vessel tipped and rigged the gear to fit a spare propeller but found the shaft damaged. Sails were then set and a course laid off for Bombay in lieu of Calcutta which was deemed impracticable in the circumstances. She was later seen and closed by the P&O *Khiva* (1,506/1873) which supplied her with provisions in latitude 16 degrees north. The *Clan Ranald* reached the approaches to Bombay on 28th May and was towed in by the steamer *Harvest* (1,338/1881), having sailed 1,740 miles in 70 days at an average speed of just over one knot. After fitting a new shaft in Bombay, the *Clan Ranald* was loaded and sailed for Marseilles three weeks later.

On 19th March the *Clan Gordon* (1) when proceeding up the Mersey from Glasgow was in collision with the sailing ship *Lake Leman* (1,035/1867), inward bound from Java. The *Clan Gordon* sustained considerable damage while the *Lake Leman* had her bowsprit and jib boom carried away. On 16th October *Clan Stuart* (1) homeward bound from Karachi went ashore on the Arabian coast 30 miles east of Perim. The *Clan Lamont* (1), following four days behind, was instructed at Aden to help but, prior to her arrival at the casualty site, a Finnish steamer had assisted the *Clan Stuart* to refloat undamaged and proceed on her voyage to Liverpool.

The first steel ships

The foregoing range of incidents involving Clan ships during their first four years of service was undoubtedly common to all the early steamships in that period of rapid development and expansion, for although Clan lost one ship by stranding and another by stress of weather, other well established companies had similar misfortunes. Such events were indeed symptomatic of the times and, quite undeterred by them, Charles Cayzer and his partners continued to add ships; the first delivered in 1883 being the *Procida* building by Stephens for the German owner Robert M. Sloman and bought whilst fitting out. Renamed *Clan Grant* (1) she left Glasgow on 12th March direct for Bombay. The ex-City liner *Clan Macleod* (1) which arrived in Glasgow that same month was transferred in part payment and assumed the name *Procida*.

Four more ships of an entirely new class and to a much enhanced specification were also delivered in 1883 for service on the Calcutta trade. As far back as December 1881 when John Muir was visiting Calcutta, he cabled Glasgow 'recommending the new Class to be fully equal to the new City steamers in speed and size'. At 381 feet in length and just under 4,000 tons gross they were indeed almost equal to the latest City liners and by far the largest ships in the Clan fleet and not subsequently surpassed until the Turret ships came out 14 years later. The greatest change was in the use of steel rather than iron for the hulls, framing and beams, with a consequent saving in weight. Their deadweight carrying capacity of 4,875 tons was two thirds greater than that of the early *Clan Alpine* class, and with increased boiler pressure and triple expansion engines they were capable of over 12 knots. Accommodation was provided for 40 first class passengers with saloons extending over the width of the ship and not only lit by electric light, but ventilated by large skylights and square ports.

Two of the new ships were ordered from Scotts and two from Napier, Shanks and Bell at Yoker. The first from Greenock was launched as *Clan Macarthur* (1) in March 1883 and completed three months later to sail from Liverpool on 12th June under the now familiar figure of Captain William Rule. The second from Scotts was the *Clan Macintosh* (1) which left Liverpool on 27th August with Captain Baines in command. The Yoker ships were *Clan Macpherson* (1) which sailed on 12th October and *Clan Matheson* (1), which completed and sailed on 22nd December. These four ships were all bound for Colombo, Madras and Calcutta.

With the delivery of *Clan Matheson* in December 1883, all three of the company's services had reached maturity with a regular and reliable frequency; every ten days in both directions between Glasgow, Liverpool and Bombay, and fortnightly both ways between Glasgow and Liverpool, to Colombo, Madras and Calcutta. The outward only service to Cape Colony was roughly monthly also from Liverpool and Glasgow, plus four homeward sailings from the Cape to Mediterranean ports. These three outward services continued to be the mainstay of the company's business with varying degrees of frequency according to shippers' demands, but there were further additions, prior to the turn of the century, including the increasing use of Madras coast ports for homeward sailings.

Expansion in India

The next eight years from 1883 were a period of consolidation for the fleet which had grown to 25 ships in just five years (see Table 3). The latter half of that decade was marred by the loss on 8th January 1888 of *Clan Ogilvie* which stranded on a small island on the Sardinian side of the Strait of Bonifacio while on a voyage from Bombay to Marseilles with a cargo of wheat. It may have been due to morning fog or mist as the ship entered the Strait and mistook one island for another where the course is normally altered 50 degrees to port for a clear passage through to the westward. Instead the vessel struck the rocky north east tip of Razzoli Island which tore the bottom out of her fore part which was soon underwater while the

A fine model of the *Clan Macarthur* (1) of 1883. *[Science Museum, London/Newall Dunn collection]*

Table 3: Size of Clan Line fleet and number of voyages at each year end, 1879-1888

Year	Fleet	Voyages	Average/ship
1879	6	10	1.7
1880	6	13	2.2
1881	9	22	4.7
1882	21	30	1.4
1883	25	53	2.1
1884	25	74	2.9
1885	25	78	3.1
1886	25	69	2.8
1887	25	67	2.7
1888	24	70	2.9

amidships and aft sections were stuck fast. As it appeared the vessel would sink, the crew and passengers were taken ashore in the ship's boats. Two days later when exposed to a strong north east breeze the ship developed a list to starboard and was submerged from the bridge forwards and that forenoon became partially dismasted and lost her funnel overboard. Next day the ship was broken in two places and impossible to approach and by next evening the local agents declared the ship and cargo as a total loss. Three days later a diver reported the fore part on its side on sand in six fathoms of water; the after part fixed firm on rocks and partly submerged. With all cargo underwater a prompt sale was recommended.

Reference has been made to the importance of a shipping service for the small anchorage ports on the Coromandel and Madras coasts of the Bay of Bengal, but mainly Cocanada, Pondicherry, Vizagapatam and Bimlipatam. Similar thought was later given to the corresponding small ports of the Malabar coast on the western side of India, extending from Tuticorin in the south to Mangalore 300 miles further north. Of these only Cochin provided a safe harbour, the remainder being quite open anchorages and inaccessible during the period of the south west monsoon. A vast range of cargoes, principally coconut oil and coir yarn with many others in small consignments, were available on this coast and were occasionally sufficient to fill an entire ship. From 1888 Tuticorin was sometimes used as an additional discharge port prior to the Calcutta ships reaching Colombo, while Mormugao was similarly used by the Bombay ships after leaving that port. The first homeward loading on the Malabar coast was by *Clan Alpine* (1) in March 1887 but the next cargo was not until *Clan Fraser* from the Cape coast loaded in Madras, Cochin and Colombo in September 1892. The following year *Clan Cameron* (1), also from the Cape, loaded in July at Galle, Tuticorin, Madras and Colombo. In 1894 Clan ships served the Malabar coast homeward in April, May, July, and November, and in 1895 during the months of February, April and December.

The Malabar Coast Chartering Coalition had come into being in 1886 to serve coffee growers in the hinterland, and ten years later invited the Clan Line to provide for shippers on the Malabar coast, resulting in 11 homeward calls that year from either Cochin, Tuticorin, Calicut or Tellicherry. In 1897 no less than 17 homeward calls were made at two or more Malabar coast ports and by November the Chartering Coalition had passed a resolution to give preference 'to the Clan Line as they have taken up the trade in earnest and done their best to meet its requirements'. The company was thereafter firmly entrenched in the trade of the Malabar coast and well served by the agency of Pierce, Leslie and Co. with its principal office at Cochin, while branches were maintained at four adjacent ports. In later years the outward Bombay

An early photograph of *Clan Matheson* (1) still with yards on the foremast. These were removed at the time the engines were tripled. *[Roy Fenton collection]*

service was extended to include Malabar coast ports and where homeward loading often began and this continued until containerisation dispensed with the need of all but Cochin and Mangalore.

Nor was the Malabar coast service the end of expansion in India. During the last years of the century a railway was built from Assam to a new jetty at the small, undeveloped port of Chittagong in the north east corner of the Bay of Bengal. Clan ships had carried much of that railway material into Calcutta and Charles Cayzer, aware that high freight-rate tea would soon be offering at Chittagong, wanted to provide shippers with regular sailings from the outset. *Clan Ogilvie* spent an exploratory week in the port in March 1887 before loading at Cochin. The next calls were by *Clan Murray* (1) and *Clan Sinclair* (1) in 1894, but regular sailings began only in August 1901 when *Clan Menzies* (1) lifted 12,000 chests of tea (a mere 650 tons) to be followed by nine other Clans at roughly fortnightly intervals before the end of that year, mostly of the smaller class but also the *Clan Macintosh* (1) of 4,000 deadweight in early November and the 5,000 deadweight Turret *Clan Monroe* (1) a month later. Clan was to have a monopoly of the tea trade until the outbreak of the Second World War, and continued to serve Chittagong until 1982. An early disadvantage of the port was the need for frequent dredging over the bar at the entrance to the Karnaphuli river, situated nine miles downstream from the railway jetty, but this was gradually overcome.

During the period from March 1888 through to September 1890, each of the six original ships was taken out of service in turn to have their compound machinery tripled by the addition of an extra cylinder and fitting of higher

pressure boilers, giving a 30% increase in power, although increasing speed by only two to three knots. This extra power did not come cheap: tripling the 1882-built *Clan Forbes* (1) in 1892 cost £8,600, about one third of the price of a new ship. Quadrupling the *Clan Monroe* (1) and *Clan Murray* (1) in 1892 and 1893 cost a total of £17,075.

Sir Charles Cayzer (left) with Hugh Gibb and John Joss in 1887 or 1888. At the time Hugh Gibb was manager of the Glagow office situated at 109 Hope Street. John Joss, a former sailing ship master, was the London manager with offices in Leadenhall Buildings, Bishopgate Street. *[The Clansman, Spring 1956]*

The staff of the Glasgow office in the early 1890s. Those seated are (left to right) Mr. Gyffin (superintendent steward), Thomas Barr (first secretary of The Clan Line Steamers Ltd. and manager from 1910 until his retirement in 1928), Captain Watson (marine superintendent), Hugh Gibb (manager), W. Bryden (assistant manager) and Henry Evans Jones (cashier). *[The Clansman, Spring 1956]*

THE FIRST CLANS

Early in 1878 the impecunious Charles Cayzer persuaded the respected shipbuilder Alexander Stephen to build him two ships at an advantageous price, a price obtained because Stephen's Linthouse yard was seriously short of work. Stephen had also to provide much of the finance, and agreed to the proposal only because he believed Cayzer was backed by the prosperous but ruthless Glasgow merchant John Muir. Realising that six ships would be needed for his planned fortnightly service from Glasgow and Liverpool to Bombay, Cayzer ordered two further steamers from Linthouse and two more from McMillan of Dumbarton, who also had to assist with finance.

CLAN ALPINE (1) 1878-1899 Iron
O.N. 78650 2,080g 1,349n
305.6 x 34.8 x 24.2 feet.
C.2-cyl. by Alexander Stephen and Sons, Linthouse, Glasgow; 250 NHP.
1889: T.3-cyl. by James Howden and Company, Glasgow; 200 NHP.
16.9.1878: Launched by Alexander Stephen and Sons, Linthouse, Glasgow (Yard No. 226).
14.10.1878: Registered in the ownership of Charles W. Cayzer, Liverpool (30/64) and Alexander Stephen, Glasgow (34/64) (Cayzer, Irvine and Co., Glasgow, managers) as CLAN ALPINE.
15.10.1878: Ran trials and delivered.
1889: Engine tripled.
12.1890: Transferred to John Muir, Alexander Moore, James Mackenzie (Cayzer, Irvine and Co., managers), Glasgow.
25.12.1896: Transferred to The Clan Line Steamers Ltd. (Cayzer, Irvine and Co., managers), Glasgow.
9.7.1897: Sold to Dene Steam Shipping Co. Ltd. (John T. Lunn and Co., managers), Newcastle-upon-Tyne.
2.9.1897: Re-acquired by The Clan Line Steamers Ltd. (Cayzer, Irvine and Co., managers), Glasgow.
26.8.1899: Sold to Dene Steam Shipping Co. Ltd. (John T. Lunn and Co., managers), Newcastle-upon-Tyne.
29.9.1899: Renamed ELMDENE.
22.10.1903: Register closed on sale to Saporta e Naar (P. Tassi, manager), Livorno, Italy and renamed IDA.
1908: Sold to the Bank of Athens (M. Vassilakis, Piraeus, manager), Greece and renamed SIMOPOULOS.
1909: Sold to J.J. King and Sons Ltd., Liverpool and broken up at Troon during the second quarter.

CLAN FRASER (1) 1878-1898 Iron
O.N. 80420 2,083g 1,350n
305.6 x 34.9 x 24.3 feet.
C.2-cyl. by Alexander Stephen and Sons, Linthouse, Glasgow; 250 NHP.
1889: T.3-cyl. by David Rowan and Son, Glasgow; 250 NHP.

7.11.1878: Launched by Alexander Stephen and Sons, Linthouse, Glasgow (Yard No. 227).
12.11.1878: Registered in the ownership of Charles William Cayzer, Liverpool (30/64) and Alexander Stephen, Glasgow (34/64) (Cayzer, Irvine and Co., Glasgow, managers) as CLAN FRASER.
15.11.1878: Completed.
2.1889: Engine tripled.
7.1890: Transferred to John Muir, Alexander Moore, James Mackenzie (Cayzer, Irvine and Co., managers), Glasgow.
5.3.1894: Transferred to The Clan Line Steamers Ltd. (Cayzer, Irvine and Co., managers), Glasgow.
30.8.1897: Sold to Dene Steam Shipping Co. Ltd. (John T. Lunn and Co., managers), Newcastle-upon-Tyne.
2.9.1897: Reacquired by The Clan Line Steamers Ltd. (Cayzer, Irvine and Co., managers), Glasgow.
21.8.1899: Sold to Dene Steam Shipping Co. Ltd. (John T. Lunn and Co., managers), Newcastle-upon-Tyne.
29.9.1899: Renamed OAKDENE.
1.2.1900: Sold to Walter S. Bailey, Hull.
6.2.1900: Register closed on sale to A. Tagliavia e Fratelli, Palermo, Italy, and renamed GIACOMO T.
1902: Renamed PRIMAVERA.
28.10.1902: Wrecked on the Burlings, Portugal whilst on a voyage from Palermo to Antwerp and Rotterdam with general cargo.

CLAN RANALD (1) 1879-1899 Iron
O.N. 80439 2,092g 1,357n
305.0 x 34.8 x 24.4 feet.
C.2-cyl. by David Rowan, Glasgow; 280 NHP.
1890: T.3-cyl. by Alexander Stephen and Sons, Linthouse, Glasgow; 280 NHP.
24.12.1878: Launched by Archibald McMillan and Son, Dumbarton (Yard No. 215).
21.2.1879: Registered in the ownership of Charles W. Cayzer, Liverpool (32/64) and Charles W. Cayzer and Robert McMillan, Dumbarton (32/64 jointly) (Cayzer, Irvine and Co., Glasgow, managers) as CLAN RANALD.
1890: Engine tripled.
7.1890: Transferred to The Clan Line Steamers Ltd. (Cayzer, Irvine and Co., managers), Glasgow.
27.2.1891: Transferred to John Muir, Alexander Moore, James Mackenzie (Cayzer, Irvine and Co., managers), Glasgow.
25.11.1896: Transferred to The Clan Line Steamers Ltd. (Cayzer, Irvine and Co., managers), Glasgow.
31.12.1897: Transferred to Sir Charles W. Cayzer, James Mackenzie and David Rennie (Cayzer, Irvine and Co., managers), Glasgow.
23.3.1899: Transferred to The Clan Line

Steamers Ltd. (Cayzer, Irvine and Co., managers), Glasgow.
20.11.1899: Sold to the Ranald Steamship Co. Ltd. (Thomas P. Purdie, manager), Glasgow for £10,500.
7.8.1900: Renamed RANALD.
4.6.1901: Foundered off Atlantic City, New Jersey, USA whilst on a voyage from Trinidad to New York with a cargo including asphalt and sugar.
9.8.1901: Register closed.

CLAN GORDON (1) 1879-1897 Iron
O.N. 80441 2,091g 1,355n
305.6 x 34.8 x 24.2 feet.
C.2-cyl. by Alexander Stephen and Sons, Linthouse, Glasgow; 250 NHP.
1888: T.3-cyl. by James Howden and Co., Glasgow; 200 NHP.
11.2.1879: Launched by Alexander Stephen and Sons, Linthouse, Glasgow (Yard No. 232).
14.3.1879: Registered in the ownership of Charles W. Cayzer, Liverpool (24/64) and Alexander Stephen, Glasgow (40/64) (Cayzer, Irvine and Co., Glasgow, managers) as CLAN GORDON.
1888: Engine tripled.
7.1890: Transferred to John Muir, Alexander Moore, James Mackenzie (Cayzer, Irvine and Co., managers), Glasgow.
25.11.1896: Transferred to The Clan Line Steamers Ltd. (Cayzer, Irvine and Co., managers), Glasgow.
16.10.1897: Wrecked in the River Umlalazi, Zululand, south of Durban, whilst on a voyage from the Clyde to Port Natal, Delagoa Bay and Beira with general cargo.
30.12.1897: Register closed

CLAN STUART (1) 1879-1890 Iron
O.N. 80447 2,094g 1,355n
305.4 x 34.8 x 24.4 feet.
C.2-cyl. by David Rowan, Glasgow; 250 HP.
1889: T.3-cyl. by Alexander Stephen and Sons, Linthouse, Glasgow; 280 HP.
21.2.1879: Launched by Archibald McMillan and Son, Dumbarton (Yard No. 216).
18.4.1879: Registered in the ownership of Charles W. Cayzer, Liverpool (32/64) and Charles W. Cayzer and Robert McMillan, Dumbarton (32/64 jointly) (Cayzer, Irvine and Co., Glasgow, managers) as CLAN STUART.
19.4.1879: Completed.
1889: Engine tripled.
7.1890: Transferred to John Muir, Alexander Moore, James Mackenzie (Cayzer, Irvine and Co., managers), Glasgow.
1897: Transferred to The Clan Line Steamers Ltd. (Cayzer, Irvine and Co., managers), Glasgow.
1898: Transferred to Sir Charles W. Cayzer, James Mackenzie and David Rennie

A superb view of *Clan Stuart* (1) after her engines had been tripled and her yards removed in 1889. Note the long deckhouse aft for the 32 passengers carried. *[Glasgow University Archives DC 101/0159]*

(Cayzer, Irvine and Co., managers), Glasgow.
16.10.1899: Registered at Bombay and sold to Hajee Goolam Mohamed Ajam, Bombay, India.
1900: Renamed RANDER REUNION.
1905: Sold to Essajee Tajbhoy, Bombay.
1906: Sold to Shah Steam Navigation Company of India Ltd., Bombay and renamed SHAH JADA.
11.1906: Broken up at Bombay.

CLAN LAMONT (1) 1879-1890 Iron
O.N. 80458 2,091g 1,334n
305.6 x 34.8 x 24.2 feet.
C.2-cyl. by Alexander Stephen and Sons, Linthouse, Glasgow; 250 NHP.
1889: T.3-cyl. by James Howden and Co., Glasgow; 250 NHP.
23.4.1879: Launched by Alexander Stephen and Sons, Linthouse, Glasgow (Yard No. 233).
12.5.1879: Ran trials, delivered and registered in the ownership of Charles W. Cayzer, Liverpool (32/64) and Alexander Stephen, Linthouse, Glasgow (32/64) (Cayzer, Irvine and Co., Glasgow, managers) as CLAN LAMONT.
8.1889: Engine tripled.
8.1890: Transferred to John Muir, Alexander Moore and James Mackenzie (Cayzer, Irvine and Co., managers), Glasgow.
30.5.1891: Wrecked off Vindiloas Point, Batticaloa on the east coast of Ceylon whilst on a voyage from Madras to London with general cargo.
13.6.1891: Register closed.

PURCHASES BY CLAN LINE ASSOCIATION STEAMERS
Although the first Clan Line ships were trading satisfactorily, Cayzer had too many problems in satisfying the demands of those from whom he had borrowed money to raise more capital to buy further ships. However, John Muir was so impressed with Cayzer's ability as a ship manager that in 1880 he approached other local investors with a proposal to form Clan Line Association Steamers. With such luminaries on board as Thomas Coats, thread manufacturer of Paisley, it was possible to persuade banks in Scotland and in London to give lines of credit. With almost three quarters of a million pounds available, expansion of the fleet could begin, and orders were placed for no fewer than 14 ships with a number of Scottish and English yards.

In the spring of 1881 the Association bought for £75,750 from the Glasgow-based City Line of George Smith and Sons three iron steamers which had substantial passenger capacities. One was lost within months – the company's first major casualty - one sold after just two years, and the third wrecked after lengthy service with Clan Line. A fourth steamer, Muriel, was bought soon after completion on the Tyne for £35,750.

As an unlimited partnership the Association was not eligible to own ships in its own right so all were initially registered in Cayzer's name. However, at various times in the 1890s Muir with a variety of partners took formal ownership of a number of Clan vessels.

CLAN MACDUFF 1881 Iron
O.N. 63796 2,328g 1,497n
326.1 x 36.1 x 27.7 feet.
C.2-cyl. by Barclay, Curle and Co., Whiteinch, Glasgow; 200 NHP.
18.10.1870: Launched by Barclay, Curle and Co., Whiteinch, Glasgow (Yard No. 206).
6.12.1870: Registered in the ownership of Robert Smith (28/64), George Smith (28/64), George Smith junior (4/64) and James Brown (4/64), trading as George Smith and Sons, Glasgow as CITY OF OXFORD.
9.3.1881: Registered in the ownership of Charles W. Cayzer (Cayzer, Irvine and Co., managers), Glasgow as CLAN MACDUFF.
21.10.1881: Foundered in heavy weather 40 miles south of Roche's Point, County Cork whilst on a voyage from Liverpool to Bombay with general cargo and 19 passengers. Thirty one lives were lost, 16 survivors being rescued by the steamer UPUPA (948/1871), 11 picked up from a boat by the steamer PALESTINE (2,128/1858), and three reached shore in another boat.
22.11.1881: Register closed.

CLAN MACLEAN (1) 1881-1903 Iron
O.N. 63807 2,336g 1,496n
326.5 x 36.1 x 27.7 feet.
C.2-cyl. by Barclay, Curle and Co., Whiteinch, Glasgow; 200 NHP.
1892: T.3-cyl. by Bow, McLachlan and Co., Paisley; 300 NHP, 1,000 IHP, 10.5 knots.
10.12.1870: Launched by Barclay, Curle and Co., Whiteinch, Glasgow (Yard No. 207).
2.2.1871: Registered in the ownership of

Robert Smith (28/64), George Smith (28/64), George Smith junior (4/64) and James Brown (4/64) trading as George Smith and Sons, Glasgow as CITY OF CAMBRIDGE.
14.4.1881: Registered in the ownership of Charles W. Cayzer (Cayzer, Irvine and Co., managers), Glasgow as CLAN MACLEAN.
1.7.1890: Transferred to The Clan Line Steamers Ltd. (Cayzer, Irvine and Co., managers), Glasgow.
27.2.1891: Transferred to John Muir, Alexander Moore and James Mackenzie, (Cayzer, Irvine and Co., managers), Glasgow.
9.1892: Engine tripled at a cost of £6,800.
25.11.1896: Transferred to The Clan Line Steamers Ltd. (Cayzer, Irvine and Co., managers), Glasgow.
31.12.1897: Transferred to Sir Charles W. Cayzer, James McKenzie and David Rennie (Cayzer, Irvine and Co., managers), Glasgow.
23.3.1899: Transferred to The Clan Line Steamers Ltd. (Cayzer, Irvine and Co., managers), Glasgow.
13.8.1903: Wrecked six miles north of Cape St. Vincent whilst on a voyage from Glasgow and Liverpool to Bombay with general cargo.
13.10.1903: Register closed.

CLAN MACLEOD (1) 1881-1883 Iron
O.N. 63821 2,300g 1,490n
325.7 x 36.2 x 27.4 feet.
C.2-cyl. by James Howden and Co., Glasgow; 240 NHP.
22.3.1871: Launched by Charles Connell and Co., Glasgow (Yard No. 75).
18.5.1871: Registered in the ownership of Robert Smith (28/64), George Smith (28/64), George Smith junior (4/64) and James Brown (4/64), trading as George Smith and Sons, Glasgow as CITY OF MECCA.
29.4.1881: Registered in the ownership of Charles W Cayzer (Cayzer, Irvine and Co., managers), Glasgow as CLAN MACLEOD.
14.2.1883: Register closed on sale to Robert M. Sloman & Company, Hamburg.
21.2.1883: Registered in the ownership of the Australia Sloman Linie A.G., Hamburg as PROCIDA.
28.12.1888: Transferred to Robert M Sloman & Company, Hamburg.
20.12.1900: Sold via G.H. Hammond, London to The Admiralty for use as a coal hulk at Simonstown and renamed NUBIAN.
1904: Renamed C.370.
15.7.1912: Left Simonstown in tow.
24.4.1913: Arrived at Morecambe to be broken up by T.W. Ward Ltd., Sheffield.

CLAN MURRAY (1) 1881-1897 Iron
O.N. 82745 2,108g 1,373n
290.0 x 36.2 x 23.3 feet.

The long-lived *Clan Maclean* (1) after the removal of her yards in 1893. *[Ian J. Farquhar collection]*

C.2-cyl. by the North Eastern Marine Engineering Co. Ltd., Sunderland; 250 NHP.
1893: Q.4-cyl. by Westray, Copeland and Company, Barrow-in-Furness; 259 NHP.
15.6.1881: Launched by the Tyne Iron Shipbuilding Co. Ltd. Willington Quay-on-Tyne (Yard No. 33). She had been ordered by W. B. Ritchie and Co., Dundee.
20.8.1881: Registered in the ownership of Robert S. Briggs, Sunderland as MURIEL.
9.1881: Acquired by Charles W. Cayzer (Cayzer, Irvine and Co., managers), Glasgow for £35,000.
19.10.1881: Renamed CLAN MURRAY.
8.1890: Transferred to John Muir, Alexander Moore, James Mackenzie (Cayzer, Irvine and Co., managers), Glasgow.
25.11.1896: Transferred to The Clan Line Steamers Ltd. (Cayzer, Irvine and Co., managers), Glasgow.
1893: Engine quadrupled.
7.4.1897: Sold to John T. Lunn, Newcastle-upon-Tyne.
12.8.1897: Renamed OLIVEDENE.
6.11.1897: Transferred to the Dene Steam Shipping Co. Ltd. (John T. Lunn and Company, managers), Newcastle-upon-Tyne.
3.8.1899: Sold to Lim Ching Tsong, Rangoon, Burma.
12.8.1899: Renamed SEANG LEONG.
25.7.1902: Left Singapore on a voyage to Amoy with general cargo and disappeared.
23.1.1903: Register closed.

WEAR DELIVERIES
The first new ships financed by the Association were a pair from Sunderland, costing £35,000 each. Some ten years later, when it was decided to quadruple the engines of Clan Monroe *and* Clan Murray, *the bill came to a total of £17,075. In Lunn's*

ownership the engines of Cedardene, *the former* Clan Monroe, *are described as 'tripled', the owners closing off one cylinder, although Westcott and Laurance opened it up again as a quadruple.*

CLAN MONROE (1) 1881-1897 Iron
O.N. 85879 2,197g 1,437n
285.5 x 37.2 x 24.4 feet.
C.2-cyl. by R. and W. Hawthorn, Newcastle-upon-Tyne; 300 NHP.
1892: Q.4-cyl. by Westray, Copeland and Co. Ltd., Barrow-in-Furness; 250 NHP, 1,000 IHP, 9 knots.
3.11.1881: Launched by Bartram, Haswell and Co., South Dock, Sunderland (Yard No. 116).
17.12.1881: Registered in the ownership of Charles W. Cayzer (Cayzer, Irvine and Co., managers), Glasgow as CLAN MONROE.
1.1882: Completed.
7.1890: Transferred to John Muir, Alexander Moore and James Mackenzie (Cayzer, Irvine and Co., managers), Glasgow.
1892: Engines quadrupled.
25.11.1896: Transferred to The Clan Line Steamers Ltd. (Cayzer, Irvine and Co., managers), Glasgow.
19.5.1897: Sold to John T. Lunn, Newcastle-upon-Tyne
11.6.1897: Renamed CEDARDENE.
6.11.1897: Transferred to the Dene Steam Shipping Co. Ltd. (John T. Lunn and Co., managers), Newcastle-upon-Tyne.
7.6.1899: Sold to Westcott and Laurance Line, London.
23.1.1902: Transferred to Cedardene Steamship Co. Ltd. (Westcott and Laurance, managers), London.
24.2.1903: Stranded north of Arzila, Morocco whilst on a voyage from the Clyde to Alexandria with a cargo of coal and became a total loss.
7.4.1903: Register closed.

Cedardene, the former *Clan Monroe* (1), at Bristol. *[Nigel Farrell collection]*

CLAN MACKAY (1) 1882-1891 Iron

O.N. 85906 2,171g 1,423n
285.8 x 37.2 x 24.4 feet.
C.2-cyl. by R. and W. Hawthorn,
Newcastle-upon-Tyne; 300 NHP.
19.1.1882: Launched by Bartram, Haswell
and Co., South Dock, Sunderland (Yard
No. 117).
7.3.1882: Registered in the ownership of
Charles W. Cayzer (Cayzer, Irvine and
Co., managers), Glasgow as CLAN
MACKAY.
7.1890: John Muir, Alexander Moore and
James Mackenzie (Cayzer, Irvine and Co.,
managers), Glasgow.
9.3.1891: Struck Belikata Wawa Rock in
the south west entrance to Galle, Ceylon
whilst leaving Galle during a voyage from

Madras to London with general cargo.
Although salvage attempts were made and
some cargo removed, she was declared a
constructive total loss.
26.5.1891: Register closed.

FIRST FROM SCOTTS

*The famous Greenock yard delivered its first
ship to Clan in early 1882, following it with
two larger cargo-passenger ships in 1883.
Clan Macdonald (1) was unusual in having
a single derrick serving her number 3 hold.*

CLAN MACDONALD (1) 1882-1897 Iron

O.N. 85914 2,642g 1,716n
335.5 x 39.4 x 26.9 feet.
C.2-cyl. by Scott and Co., Greenock; 400 NHP.

21.2.1882: Launched by Scott and
Company, Greenock (Yard No. 207).
1.4.1882: Registered in the ownership of
Charles W. Cayzer (Cayzer, Irvine and
Co., managers), Glasgow as CLAN
MACDONALD.
7-8.1890: Transferred to John Muir,
Alexander Moore and James Mackenzie
(Cayzer, Irvine and Co., managers),
Glasgow.
25.11.1896: Transferred to The Clan Line
Steamers Ltd. (Cayzer, Irvine and Co.,
managers), Glasgow.
29.1.1897: Sold to John T. Lunn,
Newcastle-upon-Tyne for £10,250.
27.3.1897: Renamed BRIARDENE.
27.12.1897: Transferred to the Dene
Steam Shipping Co. Ltd. (John T. Lunn
and Co., managers) (14/64) and John T.
Lunn (46/64), Newcastle-upon-Tyne.
25.10.1898: Sold to the Briardene
Steamship Co. Ltd. (Anglo-American
Agency Co. Ltd., managers), Halifax,
Nova Scotia.
25.1.1900: Sold to Martin Dickie, Truro,
Nova Scotia (32/64) and Alfred Dickie,
Stewiacke, Nova Scotia (32/64).
14.7.1902: Alfred Dickie, Stewiacke
became sole owner.
5.7.1904: Transferred to the Colchester
Steamship Co. Ltd. (Alfred Dickie,
manager), Truro, Nova Scotia.
30.6.1916: Sold to the Overseas Shipping
Co. Ltd., Halifax, Nova Scotia.

The hull form of *Clan Macdonald* (1) was unusual, with a long bridge deck at the fore end of which was a single derrick, and with two well decks aft. Prominent are the pole compass on her bridge and the 'lighthouses' carrying navigation lights on either side forward and connected by a walkway. Like a number of early Clan Line ships she has a grey hull. *[Glasgow University Archives DC101/0147]*

1.12.1916: Captured and sunk by bombs by the German submarine UC 19 12.5 miles south east by south of Bishop's Rock in position 49.45 north by 06.11 west whilst on a voyage from New York to London with general cargo.
8.3.1917: Register closed.

FOUR FROM LINTHOUSE
Of four steamers ordered from Stephen in 1880, the Clan Campbell *had the unfortunate distinction of being lost on her maiden voyage. She was diverted to Cape Town, and was wrecked carrying cargo from there to Mauritius. Attempts to refloat her were so long delayed by local authorities who insisted on applying outdated quarantine regulations that she began to break up in heavy seas. Despite her loss, the name was to be repeated, unlike that of* Clan Macduff.

CLAN CAMERON (1) 1882-1900 Iron
O.N. 85913 2,433g 1,585n
324.5 x 38.1 x 23.8 feet.
C.2-cyl. by Alexander Stephen and Sons, Linthouse, Glasgow; 300 NHP.
1892: T.3-cyl. by the Naval Construction and Armaments Co. Ltd., Barrow-in-Furness; 350 NHP, 1,700 IHP, 11.5 knots.
22.2.1882: Launched by Alexander Stephen and Sons, Linthouse, Glasgow (Yard No. 261).
1.4.1882: Completed.
12.4.1882: Registered in the ownership of Charles W. Cayzer (Cayzer, Irvine and Co., managers), Glasgow as CLAN CAMERON.
7-8.1890: Transferred to John Muir, Alexander Moore, James Mackenzie (Cayzer, Irvine and Co., managers), Glasgow.

1892: Engine tripled at a cost of £8,400.
30.9.1897: Transferred to Sir Charles W. Cayzer, James Mackenzie and David Rennie (Cayzer, Irvine and Co., managers), Glasgow.
23.3.1899: Transferred to The Clan Line Steamers Ltd. (Cayzer, Irvine and Co., managers), Glasgow.
12.1.1900: Sold to Trinidad Shipping and Trading Co. Ltd. (George Christall, manager), Glasgow for £14,850.
16.2.1900: Renamed MARAVAL.
4.1910: Broken up on the Clyde.
15.6.1910: Register closed on sale for demolition.

CLAN CAMPBELL (1) 1882 Iron
O.N. 86663 2,434g 1,586n
324.5 x 38.1 x 23.8 feet.
C.2-cyl. by Alexander Stephen and Sons, Linthouse, Glasgow; 300 NHP.
5.6.1882: Launched by Alexander Stephen and Sons, Linthouse, Glasgow (Yard No. 262).
7.7.1882: Registered in the ownership of Charles W. Cayzer (Cayzer, Irvine and Co., managers), Glasgow as CLAN CAMPBELL.
22.9.1882: Wrecked at Baie du Cap, south coast of Mauritius, en route from Cape Town to Mauritius with general cargo during her maiden voyage.
11.12.1882: Register closed.

CLAN FORBES (1) 1882-1902 Iron
O.N. 86680 2,441g 1,591n
324.5 x 38.1 x 23.8 feet.
C.2-cyl. by Alexander Stephen and Sons, Linthouse, Glasgow; 300 NHP.

1892: T.3-cyl. by Westray, Coupland and Co., Barrow-in-Furness; 350 NHP, 1,600 IHP, 11 knots.
15.8.1882: Launched by Alexander Stephen and Sons, Linthouse, Glasgow (Yard No. 263).
1.9.1882: Registered in the ownership of Charles W. Cayzer (Cayzer, Irvine and Co., managers), Glasgow as CLAN FORBES.
7.1890: Transferred to John Muir, Alexander Moore and James Mackenzie (Cayzer, Irvine and Co., managers), Glasgow.
1892: Engine tripled at a cost of £8,600.
30.9.1897: Transferred to Charles W. Cayzer, James MacKenzie and David Rennie (Cayzer, Irvine and Co., managers), Glasgow.
23.3.1899: Transferred to The Clan Line Steamers Ltd. (Cayzer, Irvine and Co., managers), Glasgow.
13.11.1902: Sold to Furness, Withy and Co. Ltd., West Hartlepool.
22.11.1902: Renamed LONDON CITY.
13.4.1910: Sold to Denaby and Cadeby Main Collieries Ltd., London.
19.2.1920: Transferred to the Denaby Shipping and Commercial Co. Ltd., London.
27.3.1922: Register closed on sale to ship breakers in Hamburg, who demolished her during the third quarter.

CLAN OGILVIE 1882-1888 Iron
O.N. 86718 2,425g 1,584n
324.5 x 38.1 x 23.8 feet.
C.2-cyl. by Alexander Stephen and Sons, Linthouse, Glasgow; 300 NHP.

Although she has lost her yards, *Clan Forbes* (1) carries a sail on her forestay. *[J. and M. Clarkson collection]*

24.11.1882: Launched by Alexander Stephen and Sons, Linthouse, Glasgow (Yard No. 264)
1.12.1882: Registered in the ownership Charles W. Cayzer (Cayzer, Irvine and Co., managers), Glasgow as CLAN OGILVIE.
1.1883: Completed.
8.1.1888: Wrecked off Maddelena in the Straits of Bonifacio, Corsica whilst on a voyage from Bombay via Naples to Marseilles and London with a cargo of wheat.
9.3.1888: Register closed.

SIX PASSENGER CARGO SHIPS

The largest order of the period was for six steamers with accommodation in their poops for first class passengers. McMillan built three at Dumbarton, with two others built at Yoker and one at Leith. Two were lost in Clan service, but the four survivors found buyers in India who used them in the pilgrim trade. These sales were expedited by Clan Line's well-established agents in Bombay, Finlay, Muir and Co., and by Clan offering mortgages to the buyers.

CLAN BUCHANAN (1) 1882-1905 Iron

O.N. 85927 2,933g 1,913n
330.3 x 40.1 x 26.3 feet.
C.2-cyl. by David Rowan and Son, Glasgow; 223 NHP, 2,000 IHP, 11.5 knots.
1899: T.3-cyl. by Vickers, Son and Maxim Ltd., Barrow-in-Furness; 360 NHP.
22.2.1882: Launched by Archibald McMillan and Son, Dumbarton (Yard No. 237).
10.5.1882: Registered in the ownership of Charles W. Cayzer (Cayzer, Irvine and Co., managers), Glasgow as CLAN BUCHANAN.
13.5.1882: Completed.
10.1890: Transferred to William A. Coats, John Muir and Charles W. Cayzer (Cayzer, Irvine and Co., managers), Glasgow.
23.8.1897: Transferred to The Clan Line Steamers Ltd. (Cayzer, Irvine and Co., managers), Glasgow.
8.10.1897: Transferred to Sir Charles W. Cayzer, James MacKenzie and David Rennie (Cayzer, Irvine and Co., managers), Glasgow.
1899: Engines tripled at a cost of £9,900.
24.3.1899: Transferred to The Clan Line Steamers Ltd. (Cayzer, Irvine and Co., managers), Glasgow.
28.8.1900: Transferred to Sir Charles W. Cayzer, James MacKenzie and David Rennie (Cayzer, Irvine and Co., managers), Glasgow.
18.12.1900: Transferred to The Clan Line Steamers Ltd. (Cayzer, Irvine and Co., managers), Glasgow.
9.2.1905: Sold to Essajee Tajbhoy, Bombay, India for £9,750.
17.11.1905: Renamed SHAH ALLUM.
5.9.1906: Sold to the Shah Steam Navigation Co. of India Ltd., Bombay.

1.10.1907: Resold to Essajee Tajbhoy, Bombay.
18.10.1907: Sold to Hajee Ahmad Hassum, Bombay.
15.10.1908: Resold to the Shah Steam Navigation Co. of India Ltd., Bombay.
10.6.1909: Wrecked on Piram Island, near Gogho, Gulf of Cambay, western India whilst on a voyage from Rangoon to Bhownuggar with a cargo of rice.
2.9.1909: Register closed.

CLAN GRAHAM (1) 1882-1905 Iron

O.N. 85943 2,926g 1,911n
330.5 x 40.2 x 26.4 feet.
C.2-cyl. by David Rowan and Son, Glasgow; 400 NHP.
1894: T.3-cyl. by the Naval Construction and Armaments Co. Ltd., Barrow-in-Furness; 310 NHP, 2,000 IHP, 12 knots.
21.3.1882: Launched by Napier, Shanks and Bell, Yoker (Yard No. 14).
22.6.1882: Registered in the ownership of Charles W. Cayzer (Cayzer, Irvine and Co., managers), Glasgow as CLAN GRAHAM.
10.1890: Transferred to William A. Coats, John Muir and Charles W. Cayzer (Cayzer, Irvine and Co., managers), Glasgow.
4.6.1891: Transferred to John Muir, Alexander Moore and James Mackenzie (Cayzer, Irvine and Co., managers), Glasgow.
2.1894: Engine tripled at a cost of £11,000.
30.9.1897: Transferred to Charles W. Cayzer, James MacKenzie and David Rennie (Cayzer, Irvine and Co., managers), Glasgow.
1.6.1899: Transferred to The Clan Line Steamers Ltd. (Cayzer, Irvine and Co., managers), Glasgow.
28.8.1900: Transferred to Sir Charles W. Cayzer, James MacKenzie and David Rennie (Cayzer, Irvine and Co., managers), Glasgow.
18.12.1900: Transferred to The Clan Line Steamers Ltd. (Cayzer, Irvine and Co., managers), Glasgow.
30.8.1905: Sold to the Bombay and Persia Steam Navigation Co. Ltd., Bombay, India for £13,750.
5.1.1906: Renamed MAJIDI.
28.6.1912: Register closed on sale to T. Astarita, Mela, Italy, and renamed MARIA VITTORIA.
1913: Renamed MARIA DELLE VITTORIE.
1915: Laid up at Naples for disposal and sold 1915 to the British Admiralty for use as a block ship, probably in the Eastern Mediterranean

CLAN MACKENZIE (1) 1882-1905 Iron

O.N. 85944 2,954g 1,930n
329.6 x 40.0 x 26.3 feet.
C.2-cyl. by David Rowan and Son, Glasgow; 400 NHP.

1898: T.3-cyl. by Vickers, Son and Maxim Ltd., Barrow-in-Furness; 362 NHP.
20.4.1882: Launched by Ramage and Ferguson, Leith (Yard No. 35).
24.6.1882: Registered in the ownership of Charles W. Cayzer (Cayzer, Irvine and Co., managers), Glasgow as CLAN MACKENZIE.
10.1890: Transferred to John Muir, Alexander Moore, James Mackenzie (Cayzer, Irvine and Co., managers), Glasgow.
23.8.1897: Transferred to The Clan Line Steamers Ltd. (Cayzer, Irvine and Co., managers), Glasgow.
8.8.1897: Transferred to Sir Charles W. Cayzer, James Mackenzie and David Rennie (Cayzer, Irvine and Co., managers), Glasgow.
8.1898: Engine tripled at a cost of £9,900.
1.6.1899: Transferred to The Clan Line Steamers Ltd. (Cayzer, Irvine and Co., managers), Glasgow.
28.8.1900: Transferred to Sir Charles W. Cayzer, James Mackenzie and David Rennie (Cayzer, Irvine and Co., managers), Glasgow.
15.12.1900: Transferred to The Clan Line Steamers Ltd. (Cayzer, Irvine and Co., managers), Glasgow.
22.2.1905: Sold to Essajee Tajbhoy, Bombay, India for £9,750.
2.10.1905: Renamed SHAH AMEER.
5.9.1906: Sold to Shah Steam Navigation Co. of India Ltd., Bombay.
1.10.1907: Resold to Essajee Tajbhoy, Bombay, India.
18.10.1907: Resold to Hajee Ahmad Hassum, Bombay.
15.10.1908: Resold to Shah Steam Navigation Co. of India Ltd., Bombay.
4.1.1909: Owners became the Bombay and Hujaz Steam Navigation Co. of India Ltd., Bombay.
3.7.1912: Register closed on sale for demolition in Bombay.

CLAN DRUMMOND 1882-1898 Iron

O.N. 86669 2,922g 1,904n
330.3 x 40.1 x 26.3 feet.
C.2-cyl. by David Rowan and Son, Glasgow; 400 NHP.
1893: T.3-cyl. by the Naval Construction and Armaments Co. Ltd., Barrow-in-Furness; 226 NHP, 2,100 IHP, 11.5 knots.
5.1882: Launched by Archibald McMillan and Son, Dumbarton (Yard No. 238).
14.8.1882: Registered in the ownership of Charles W. Cayzer (Cayzer, Irvine and Co., managers), Glasgow as CLAN DRUMMOND.
10.1890: Transferred to John Muir, William A. Coats, Thomas G. Arthur and Charles W. Cayzer (Cayzer, Irvine and Co., managers), Glasgow.
14.8.1891: Transferred to John Muir, Alexander Moore and James Mackenzie (Cayzer, Irvine and Co., managers), Glasgow.

A fine view of the *Clan Drummond* with a grey hull. Noteworthy are the mast arrangements, with gaffs which are not apparent on the photograph of *Clan Buchanan* and the high-mounted mainmast derricks. *Clan Drummond* was the first Clan to transit the Manchester Ship Canal, and her tall masts had to be modified to clear the canal's bridges. Her foundering in January 1898 was attributed to her number two hatch being stove in by heavy seas, and ensured *Clan Drummond's* name was never repeated. *[Glasgow University Archives DC/101/0143]*

1893: Engine tripled at a cost of £11,000.
30.9.1897: Transferred to the Clan Line Steamers Ltd. (Cayzer, Irvine and Co., managers), Glasgow.
30.9.1897: Transferred to Charles W. Cayzer, James MacKenzie and David Rennie (Cayzer, Irvine and Co., managers), Glasgow.
28.1.1898: Foundered in heavy weather off the northern coast of Spain in approximate position 45.30 north by 08.40 west whilst on a voyage from Glasgow and Liverpool to Algoa Bay with general cargo. 37 members of the crew were lost, 27 being picked up by the steamer HOLBEIN (2,050/1882).
28.12.1898: Register closed.

CLAN MACGREGOR (1) 1882-1899 Iron
O.N. 86692 2,956g 1,927n
329.6 x 40.3 x 26.4 feet.
C.2-cyl. by David Rowan and Son, Glasgow; 400 NHP.
1898: T. 3-cyl. by Vickers, Son and Maxim Ltd., Barrow-in-Furness; 223 NHP, 2,000 IHP, 11.5 knots.
2.8.1882: Launched by Ramage and Ferguson, Leith (Yard No. 36).
28.9.1882: Registered in the ownership of Charles W. Cayzer (Cayzer, Irvine and Co., managers), Glasgow as CLAN MACGREGOR.
30.9.1882: Completed.
10.1890: Transferred to William A. Coats, John Muir, Thomas G. Arthur and Charles

W. Cayzer (Cayzer, Irvine and Co., managers), Glasgow.
23.8.1897: Transferred to The Clan Line Steamers Ltd. (Cayzer, Irvine and Co., managers), Glasgow.
8.10.1897: Transferred to Charles W. Cayzer, James MacKenzie and David Rennie (Cayzer, Irvine and Co., managers), Glasgow.
1898: Engine tripled at a cost of £9,900.
1.6.1899: Transferred to The Clan Line Steamers Ltd. (Cayzer, Irvine and Co., managers), Glasgow.
4.8.1899: Sank after colliding with the Danish steamer CATHAY (4,111/1898) off Cape St. Vincent, Portugal whilst on a voyage from Madras to London with general cargo. The crew was saved.
2.11.1899: Register closed.

CLAN SINCLAIR (1) 1882-1905 Iron
O.N. 86705 2,933g 1,912n
330.5 x 40.3 x 26.4 feet.
C.2-cyl. by Davd Rowan and Son, Glasgow; 225 NHP, 2,000 IHP, 12 knots.
1897: T.3-cyl. by the Naval Armaments and Construction Co. Ltd., Barrow-in-Furness; 362 NHP.
15.8.1882: Launched by Napier, Shanks and Bell, Yoker (Yard No. 15).
8.11.1882: Registered in the ownership of Charles W. Cayzer (Cayzer, Irvine and Co., managers), Glasgow.
13.11.1882: Completed.
10.1890: Transferred to William A. Coats, John Muir, Thomas G. Arthur and Charles

W. Cayzer (Cayzer, Irvine and Co., managers), Glasgow.
14.4.1896: Transferred to The Clan Line Steamers Ltd. (Cayzer, Irvine and Co., managers), Glasgow.
25.11.1896: Transferred to Sir John Muir, Alexander Moore and James Mackenzie (Cayzer, Irvine and Co., managers), Glasgow.
2.1897: Engine tripled at a cost of £9,000.
30.9.1897: Transferred to Sir Charles W. Cayzer, James Mackenzie and David Rennie (Cayzer, Irvine and Co., managers), Glasgow.
1.6.1899: Transferred to The Clan Line Steamers Ltd. (Cayzer, Irvine and Co., managers), Glasgow.
28.8.1900: Transferred to Sir Charles W. Cayzer, James Mackenzie and David Rennie (Cayzer, Irvine and Co., managers), Glasgow.
18.12.1900: Transferred to The Clan Line Steamers Ltd. (Cayzer, Irvine and Co. managers), Glasgow.
27.7.1905: Sold to the Bombay and Persia Steam Navigation Co. Ltd., Bombay, India.
24.11.1905: Renamed RAHMANI.
9.1.1917: Sold to Framjee, Sons and Co., Bombay.
20.7.1917: Lost in collision in the Mediterranean in position 35.02 north by 19.07 east during a voyage from Bombay to Genoa and London.
25.8.1917: Register closed.

Clan Sinclair (1). [Ian J. Farquhar collection]

GERMAN ORDER

This ship had been ordered by Sloman of Hamburg, who then decided she was too large, or too expensive. She was sold to Clan, who paid for her in part by selling the smaller and much older Clan Macleod *(1) to the German company. After her sale in 1900, the former* Clan Grant *had a long and interesting career in the Far East.*

CLAN GRANT (1) 1883-1900 Iron

O.N. 86745 3,545g 2,306n
350.5 x 41.1 x 26.6 feet.
C.2-cyl. by Alexander Stephen and Sons, Linthouse, Glasgow; 400 NHP.
24.1.1883: Launched by Alexander Stephen and Sons, Linthouse, Glasgow (Yard No. 272) for Robert M. Sloman, Hamburg, Germany as PROCIDA but sold before completion.
24.2.1883: Registered in the ownership of Charles W. Cayzer (Cayzer, Irvine and Co., managers), Glasgow as CLAN GRANT.
8.10.1890: Transferred to William A. Coats, John Muir, Thomas G. Arthur and Charles W. Cayzer (Cayzer, Irvine and Co., managers), Glasgow.
23.8.1897: Transferred to the Clan Line

Steamers Ltd. (Cayzer, Irvine and Co., managers), Glasgow.
8.10.1897: Transferred to Charles W. Cayzer, James Mackenzie and David Rennie (Cayzer, Irvine and Co., managers), Glasgow.
25.3.1899: Transferred to The Clan Line Steamers Ltd. (Cayzer, Irvine and Co., managers), Glasgow.
7.8.1900: Register closed on sale to Pacific Whaling and Fishery, Joint Stock Company of Count H.H. Keyserling and Company, Vladivostok, Russia and renamed MICHAIL.
10.2.1904: Captured by Japanese warships in the Korea Strait whilst on a voyage to Vladivostok with a cargo of iron.
1905: Sold to the Japanese Government, Department of Agriculture and Commerce, Tokyo and renamed MIHAIRU MARU.
1914: Sold to Ishikari Sekitan K.K., Yokohama, Japan, and name rendered MIHARU MARU.
1923: Sold to Hokkaido Tanko K.K., Tokyo, Japan.
1927: Sold to Sugaya K.K., Kobe, Japan.
1928: Sold to Kikutaro Aoyagi, Japan and broken up

CLANS FOR PASSENGERS

These four ships were the first with steel hulls, and had the largest passenger capacity of any built for Clan, with 40 in first class and an unspecified number in third class. The owners were particularly keen to build ships to compete with the City Line who were serving Calcutta, and were prepared to spend the large sum of £80,000 on each.

Two of this class had particularly close associations with Charles Cayzer. He chose Clan Matheson *for his cruise to the Baltic in 1895, whilst* Clan Macpherson *represented Clan Line at the Diamond Jubilee Naval Review in June 1897, and Cayzer was knighted on board.*

All four ships ended their lives in the Far East, three with Diederichsen, Jebsen & Co., a German company based in Tsingtao who used the Totti *and probably others to run the blockade of Vladivostok during the Russo-Japanese War. The* Totti *reverted to her original name* Clan Macintosh *when sold on to Burmese owners, the name obviously reflecting the high regard in which Clan liners were held in the East.*

CLAN MACARTHUR (1) 1883-1905

O.N. 87657 3,984g 2,635n
381.2 x 43.3 x 27.9 feet.
C.2-cyl. by Scott and Company, Greenock; 332 NHP, 2,500 IHP, 12.5 knots.
1893: T. 3-cyl. by the Naval Construction and Armaments Co. Ltd., Barrow-in-Furness.
12.3.1883: Launched by Scott and Co., Greenock (Yard No. 223).
30.5.1883: Registered in the ownership of Charles W. Cayzer (Cayzer, Irvine and Co., managers), Glasgow.
6.6.1883: Ran trials.
9.6.1883: Completed.
8.10.1890: Transferred to William A. Coats, John Muir, Thomas G. Arthur and Charles W. Cayzer (Cayzer, Irvine and Co., managers), Glasgow.
1893: Engine tripled.
23.8.1897: Transferred to The Clan Line Steamers Ltd. (Cayzer, Irvine and Co., managers), Glasgow.
8.10.1897: Transferred to Sir Charles W. Cayzer, James Mackenzie and David Rennie (Cayzer, Irvine and Co., managers), Glasgow.
29.11.1899: Transferred to The Clan Line Steamers Ltd. (Cayzer, Irvine and Co., managers), Glasgow.
28.8.1900: Transferred to Sir Charles W. Cayzer, James Mackenzie and David Rennie (Cayzer, Irvine and Co., managers), Glasgow.
9.9.1901: Transferred to The Clan Line Steamers Ltd. (Cayzer, Irvine and Co., managers), Glasgow.
9.2.1905: Sold to Essajee Tajbhoy, Bombay, India for £11,000.
16.8.1905: Renamed SHAH JEHAN.
5.9.1906: Sold to Shah Steam Navigation Co. of India Ltd., Bombay.

Clan Macarthur (1) on the Clyde, still carrying her foremast yards. *[Glasgow University Archives DC101/1792]*

1.10.1907: Resold to Essajee Tajbhoy, Bombay.
12.11.1907: Sold to Hajee Amed Hassum, Bombay.
15.10.1908: Resold to Shah Steam Navigation Co. of India Ltd., Bombay.
4.1.1909: Owners became the Bombay and Hujaz Steam Navigation Co. of India Ltd., Bombay.
21.8.1912: Register closed on sale for demolition at Bombay.

CLAN MACINTOSH (1) 1883-1905
O.N. 87690 3,985g 2,636n
381.2 x 43.3 x 27.9 feet.
C.2-cyl. by Scott and Co., Greenock; 475 NHP, 2,500 IHP, 12.5 knots.
1892: T.3-cyl. by the Naval Construction and Armaments Co. Ltd., Barrow. 600 NHP.
6.6.1883: Launched by Scott and Co., Greenock (Yard No. 224).
6.8.1883: Ran trials and delivered.
8.8.1883: Registered in the ownership of Charles W. Cayzer (Cayzer, Irvine and Co., managers), Glasgow as CLAN MACINTOSH.
8.10.1890: Transferred to Willam A. Coats, John Muir, Thomas G. Arthur and Charles W. Cayzer (Cayzer, Irvine and Co., managers), Glasgow.
1892: Engine tripled.
23.8.1897: Transferred to The Clan Line Steamers Ltd. (Cayzer, Irvine and Co., managers), Glasgow.
8.10.1897: Transferred to Sir Charles W. Cayzer, James Mackenzie and David Rennie (Cayzer, Irvine and Co., managers), Glasgow.
29.11.1899: Transferred to The Clan Line Steamers Ltd. (Cayzer, Irvine and Co., managers), Glasgow.
28.8.1900: Transferred to Sir Charles W. Cayzer, James Mackenzie and David

Rennie (Cayzer, Irvine and Co., managers), Glasgow.
9.9.1901: Transferred to The Clan Line Steamers Ltd. (Cayzer, Irvine and Co., managers), Glasgow.
18.2.1905: Registered in the ownership of M. Jebsen, Hamburg, Germany as TOTTI.
2.3.1905: British register closed.
7.8.1905: Transferred to Gustav Diederichsen junior, Hamburg, Germany.
7.6.1906: Transferred to M. Jebsen, Hamburg, Germany.
23.7.1907: Registered in the ownership of the Madras Steam Navigation Co. Ltd., Rangoon, Burma as CLAN MACINTOSH.
7.10.1914: Register closed on sale for demolition.

CLAN MACPHERSON (1) 1883-1905
O.N. 87709 3,971g 2,587n
380.7 x 43.2 x 28.3 feet.
C.2-cyl. by David Rowan and Son, Glasgow; 600 NHP.
1892: T.3-cyl. by D. and W. Henderson and Co., Glasgow; 470 NHP, 3,070 IHP, 13.25 knots.
25.5.1883: Launched by Napier, Shanks and Bell, Yoker, Glasgow (Yard No. 20).
29.9.1883: Ran trials and delivered.
4.10.1883: Registered in the ownership of Charles W. Cayzer (Cayzer, Irvine and Co., managers), Glasgow as CLAN MACPHERSON.
8.10.1890: Transferred to John Muir, Willam A. Coats, Thomas G. Arthur and Charles W. Cayzer (Cayzer, Irvine and Co., managers), Glasgow.
9.1892: Engine tripled.
23.8.1897: Transferred to The Clan Line Steamers Ltd. (Cayzer, Irvine and Co., managers), Glasgow.
8.10.1897: Transferred to Sir Charles W. Cayzer, James McKenzie and David

Rennie (Cayzer, Irvine and Co., managers), Glasgow.
13.10.1899: Transferred to The Clan Line Steamers Ltd. (Cayzer, Irvine and Co., managers), Glasgow.
28.8.1900: Transferred to Sir Charles W. Cayzer, James McKenzie and David Rennie (Cayzer, Irvine and Co., managers), Glasgow.
9.9.1901: Transferred to The Clan Line Steamers Ltd. (Cayzer, Irvine and Co., managers), Glasgow.
7.2.1905: Registered in the ownership of M. Jebsen, Hamburg, Germany as HANNA
14.2.1905: British register closed.
7.8.1905: Transferred to Gustav Diederichsen junior, Hamburg.
1906: Transferred to M. Jebsen, Hamburg.
13.10.1906: Sold to Kishimoto Kanetaro, Kobe, Japan, and renamed SHINKOKU MARU.
1909: Transferred to Kishimoto Kisen K.K., Hamadera, Japan.
1914: Broken up at Osaka during the third quarter.

CLAN MATHESON (1) 1883-1905
O.N. 87725 3,917g 2,581n
380.7 x 43.2 x 28.3 feet.
C.2-cyl. by David Rowan and Son, Glasgow; 600 NHP.
1892: T. 3.cyl. by D. and W. Henderson and Co., Glasgow; 600 NHP, 3,000 IHP, 12.5 knots.
20.8.1883: Launched by Napier, Shanks and Bell, Yoker, Glasgow (Yard No. 21).
1.12.1883: Ran trials and delivered.
17.12.1883: Registered in the ownership of Charles W. Cayzer, (Cayzer, Irvine and Co., managers), Glasgow as CLAN MATHESON.
8.10.1890: Transferred to John Muir, Willam A. Coats, Thomas G. Arthur, and

Charles W. Cayzer (Cayzer, Irvine and Co., managers), Glasgow.
6.1892: Engines tripled.
23.8.1897: Transferred to the Clan Line Association (Cayzer, Irvine and Co., managers), Glasgow.
8.10.1897: Transferred to Sir Charles W. Cayzer, James McKenzie and David Rennie (Cayzer, Irvine and Co., managers), Glasgow.
13.10.1899: Transferred to The Clan Line Steamers Ltd. (Cayzer, Irvine and Co., managers), Glasgow.

28.8.1900: Transferred to Sir Charles W. Cayzer, James McKenzie and David Rennie (Cayzer, Irvine and Co., managers), Glasgow.
9.9.1901: Transferred to The Clan Line Steamers Ltd. (Cayzer, Irvine and Co., managers), Glasgow.
17.2.1905: British register closed.
18.2.1905: Registered in the ownership of M. Jebsen, Hamburg Germany as MARIECHEN.
7.8.1905: Transferred to Gustav Diederichsen junior, Hamburg, Germany,

1906: Transferred to M. Jebsen, Hamburg.
24.1.1906: Stranded at Chicagof Island, Alaska whilst on a voyage from San Francisco and Seattle to Vladivostok. Subsequently refloated.
28.7.1906: Sold, beached in Smith Cove, Seattle, stripped of machinery and woodwork.
1916: Hull broken up in situ during the summer.

Her accommodation having been extended in a recent refit, *Clan Matheson* (1) was chosen by Charles Cayzer in June 1895 to take guests on a cruise from Tilbury to Kiel to attend the celebrations for the opening of the Nord-Ostsee Canal. Cayzer had determined on the jaunt on learning that his arch-rival on South African routes, Sir Donald Currie, was taking his guests on his *Tantallon Castle*. The cruise was judged a social success, but several of the guests who were Members of Parliament had to hurry home to defend their seats, as the government had fallen whilst they were away enjoying themselves. Note the grey hull, and the long bridge deck with passenger accommodation. *[Glasgow University Archives DC101/0154]*

Engineers and deck officers on board the *Clan Matheson* (1). Dougald Fletcher is second from the right in the front row. *[Colin Fletcher]*

LIMITED LIABILITY, UNLIMITED CONFIDENCE: 1890-1914

The years from 1890 to the outbreak of the First World War were marked by continued growth of services, increased sailings in line with growing demand, and improvements to both the size and performance of the fleet. Mistakes were made, but overall the story is of confident, organic growth that established Clan Line as one of the world's foremost cargo carriers.

The limited company

Despite the closeness of their business interests, Charles Cayzer and John Muir were not always on good terms. During the late 1880s increasing testiness on the part of Muir, probably in the face of growing confidence and arrogance on the part of Cayzer, seems to have decided the latter to put the business on a different footing and establish a limited liability company. He had been strongly advised against this course in 1879 when he was an ambitious but impecunious beginner in shipping, but his success, reputation and growing personal wealth made matters very different in 1890. His main difficulty was not selling shares but persuading some of his business associates that transferring ownership of the steamers to the new company would not harm their interests. The issued capital of The Clan Line Steamers Ltd. was £375,000 in shares and debentures, representing half of the authorised capital. In return for his interests in the steamers which were transferred, Charles Cayzer received shares and debentures worth £231,600, making him the majority shareholder, a position which he and his successors were to enjoy throughout Clan Line's existence as a ship owning company.

The Clan Line Steamers Ltd. was formed in July 1890 with Charles Cayzer as chairman, his 21-year-old son at his side, while two of the appointed directors had served as representatives of James Finlay and Company in the Clan Line Association partnership. It is impossible in any story involving India and the Clan Line to ignore the close association between these two companies both with registered offices in Glasgow. James Finlay and Company became a private limited company in 1909, by which date it had offices representing the Clan Line in Bombay, Karachi, Colombo, Calcutta and Chittagong. By far the largest of these offices was at Calcutta which after the Second World War employed no less than 470 people, of whom 30 were Europeans.

The board minutes record that the company acquired a majority of the shares in 13 of the 24 steamers managed by Cayzer, Irvine and Co. in July 1890 for a total of £301,048. In fact, only two were immediately registered in the new company's name, and 11 others were registered in the names of trustees for the debenture holders who accounted for half of the company's issued capital. The remaining 11 steamers were registered in the names of the surviving Association partners (see Table 4). Consolidation of ownership was achieved only gradually, with *Clan Drummond* and *Clan Graham* (1) bought from the Clan Line Association partners in 1891, and further batches following in 1896, 1897 and 1899. This resolved the somewhat clumsy situation in which the important Calcutta services could in theory employ only steamers belonging to The Clan Line Association Calcutta Steamers, as the Association was now termed. However, as the fleet list entries testify, ownership was fluid and, to provide

the necessary security for debenture holders, ships were from time to time re-registered in the names of trustees. New vessels were registered initially in Charles Cayzer's name, in recognition of his guaranteeing payments to their builders, and consolidation of ownership of all ships in the name of The Clan Line Steamers Ltd. was not completed until 1916. Nevertheless, all the Clan ships continued to be treated as if they were one fleet, all managed by Cayzer, Irvine and Co., and all dealt with equally in the board minutes of the new company.

Table 4. Registered ownership of ships on the formation of The Clan Line Steamers Ltd.

The Clan Line Steamers Ltd.	Trustees for debenture holders:	Clan Line Association partners:
	John Muir,	John Muir,
	Alexander Moore,	William Coats,
	James Mackenzie	Thomas Arthur,
		Charles Cayzer
Clan Maclean	*Clan Alpine*	*Clan Buchanan*
Clan Ranald	*Clan Cameron*	*Clan Drummond*
	Clan Forbes	*Clan Graham*
	Clan Fraser	*Clan Grant*
	Clan Gordon	*Clan Macarthur*
	Clan Lamont	*Clan Macgregor*
	Clan Macdonald	*Clan Macintosh*
	Clan Mackay	*Clan Mackenzie**
	Clan Maclean	*Clan Macpherson*
	Clan Monroe	*Clan Matheson*
	Clan Murray	*Clan Sinclair*

* *Clan Mackenzie* was transferred to the trustees in October 1890.

One of the first actions taken by the new board was to decide that, as ten ships were on charter during the first six months of 1890, the fleet had to be expanded and no fewer than 23 shipbuilders were asked to tender for six ships. Stephen's tender at £32,600 each and Doxford's at £31,000 were accepted. Alongside this expansion was a continuing programme of tripling older ships, intended to improve performance and hence service. The 1890s were also marked by the disposal of the last four of the original six Clans and by the loss of six more ships, but in the same period 31 new ships joined the fleet from yards at Sunderland, Glasgow and Barrow-in-Furness, so that by 1900 the fleet had increased to 44. To cope with the repairs needed by this growing fleet, a workshop was set up during 1891 in Glasgow, the port at which homeward sailings usually terminated.

More sailings, more trades

The last decade of the nineteenth century saw a remarkable increase in the number of sailings to the Cape, mainly the result of an expansion in trade to South Africa and later the outbreak of the Boer War in October 1899. This route operated on a two-week frequency until 1894, thereafter 32 sailings were made in 1895, 49 in 1896 and 60 in 1897. Sailings peaked the following year when 62 Clan ships sailed for South African ports, alternate sailings being for Cape Town and East London, then for Algoa Bay and Natal. In accordance with agreements with previously established lines, no Clan steamer was employed on homeward cargoes from the Cape that year; all made a light ship passage to India and loaded either in Calcutta, or on the Madras or Malabar coasts. In return, Cayzer insisted that the mail companies did not load outward at Liverpool or Glasgow. Payments of £10,000 a year were made to Clan by the mail companies for not carrying passengers to South Africa. The important Calcutta service continued on the firm two-week outward and homeward frequency, supplemented on the homeward berth by a further 20 or more ships brought up from the Cape. On the Bombay berth an average of 14 outward sailings were made annually, but only ten or fewer homeward from that port. A feature of the Indian trade was that P&O paid Clan £3,000 per year for not carrying passengers to India.

In 1893 two of Clan's rivals on the Cape services, Donald Currie's Castle Line and Bucknall Brothers, began a service from United States ports to South Africa under the title American and African Steamship Line. The combative Cayzer could not take this lying down, and in conjunction with the Union Line instituted sailings in May 1893 between New York and South African ports. As no Clan ships could be spared, the chartered steamer *Arroyo* (3,564/ 1890) was used initially, Cayzer admitting to his board that it could not expect to make a profit, but the line's interests had to be protected. Indeed, it soon became obvious that no-one could make a profit on this route in a competitive situation, and an amicable agreement was soon reached to share the trade. This service grew to be important enough to warrant Clan Line having two ships specially constructed, although the advent of competition in 1903 and 1904

Clan Macnab (1) completed at Linthouse, Glasgow in 1891. *[Newall Dunn collection]*

Clan Ross (1) completed at Barrow in 1894. *[Ian J. Farquhar collection]*

Few pictures have been found of the two ships built for the USA to South Africa service - two of the *Clan Macmillan* (1) and none of the *Clan Macgregor* (2). This view of the *Clan Macmillan* shows her on the slipway in McMillan's yard where she was almost destroyed in a serious fire. Note the forward bridge which is just discernable on the other view of her on page 74. *[The Ballast Trust]*

The *Clan Menzies* (1) completed in 1896 at Barrow-in-Furness. Note the small hatch which can be clearly seen between bridge and engine room. *[Ambrose Greenway collection]*

meant that Clan made a loss that year. The competitor, who also made himself felt in the United Kingdom to South Africa trade, was to figure prominently in the further story of Clan Line, Robert P. Houston.

In 1893 Cayzer had the idea that his original, smaller ships of the *Clan Alpine*-type might be profitably employed on services to the Persian Gulf ports. Wool was shipped homeward, and dates were important exports from Iran and Iraq during the last three months of the year, small in tonnage but profitable if delivered in time for Christmas. An added attraction for ships returning from India to load in the Gulf ports was the seasonal carriage of Muslim pilgrims to Jeddah. As a way of entering this trade without having to fight the existing lines, the four steamers of the Persian Gulf Steamship Company were bought in 1895, part of the price of £63,750 being paid in Clan Line shares and debentures. Although Clan names were allocated to three of these, only the newest, the *Shat el Arab*, received its intended name, *Clan Macrae* (1). The other three were quickly sold at a profit of £2,800 and, as originally intended, the smaller and older Clan ships were used on the service. The Gulf trade proved harder to enter, and much less profitable, than Cayzer had supposed. For instance, at Bussorah (now Basra) date cargoes had to be ferried out to the steamers by lighter, the cost of which quickly ate up any anticipated profit.

The opening of the Manchester Ship Canal in January 1894 saw a modest extension of Clan Line routes. The Canal expedited the export of cotton goods made in Lancashire to India, and Cayzer was anxious that his rivals in the Bombay and Calcutta trades did not steal a march on him by using Manchester first. By promising to run regular services from Manchester to India and Ceylon for at least five years, he was able to extract special terms and concessions from the Manchester Ship Canal Company, who were anxious to have as many lines as possible serving Manchester.

Of growing importance to Clan was the East African trade, including that to Beira, a port in the Portuguese colony of Mozambique which was of most significance because it served the Rhodesias with their copper and tobacco exports. In 1897 in anticipation of the growth in trade which a railway between Salisbury and Beira would bring, Cayzer acquired shares in the Beira Boating Company which handled lighterage in the port.

The Turret years

In 1892 Doxford introduced their Turret design to a cautious shipping industry, the first example built having to be classed with Bureau Veritas in view of Lloyd's Register's conservatism. Cayzer was a belated but latterly enthusiastic convert to her design. In June 1896 Clan Line agreed with Doxford and the owners to bareboat charter at a rate of £2,275 for one year the *Imperialist* which was then building for Angier Brothers. She was delivered and registered in Clan ownership early in July. It has been suggested that this was simply to evaluate the idea, but there was no time to do so before Clan Line placed an order for two Turrets in August. Comparison of the Turrets with a conventional design proposed by Stephens had established that the former would save £519 on port and Suez Canal charges during a voyage to Calcutta, a total of about £2,000 per year. There was also a saving on initial cost. Indeed, Turret mania seems to have gripped the board. In August the *Bullionist,* also building for Angier Brothers, was taken on charter for £2,318 per year, whilst in September the Turret order was increased to four ships at a cost of £49,000 each. The charters of *Imperialist* and *Bullionist* were renewed for a further year in 1897 for £3,000, partly because of the need for additional sailings to the Cape (now running at between four and five a month) and partly because older ships continued to be taken out of service for their engines to be tripled. *Imperialist* was actually purchased for £30,000 in April 1898 during the second year of her charter and renamed *Clan Shaw* (1), nominally a replacement for the recently lost *Clan Lindsay* (1). This was a hasty move as it was quickly decided that she was not uniform with the other Turrets being built, and in July she was sold to Doxford for £32,000. The almost instant profit was probably achieved because the builder

This double-page spread illustrates each of the six batches of Turrets built for Clan Line.

The first Turret ordered by the company, as opposed to being chartered as a completed ship, was *Clan Macdonald* (2), ordered in August 1896 (top). Of the initial group of seven, two were built at Barrow-in-Furness by a yard which had recently become Vickers, Son and Maxim Ltd. The yard was granted a licence in October 1897, and Doxfords received a payment of 7/6d per registered ton from Clan Line. *[Ian J. Farquhar]*

The second batch of Turrets, led by *Clan Colquhoun* (1) of 1899, saw length increase from 400 to 440 feet, requiring more powerful engines. Not only were these three the longest Turrets built for Clan, they were not surpassed in length in the fleet until the refrigerator ships of 1912. *Clan Colquhoun* has its topmasts telescoped in order to transit the Manchester Ship Canal (middle). *[Kevin O'Donoghue collection]*

Hard on the heels of the lengthy batch 2 Turrets came the first of seven to the much reduced length of 355 feet. *Clan Gordon* (2) (bottom) was one of two from this group which had the misfortune to capsize. *[Ambrose Greenway collection]*

The fourth batch of Turrets, begun in 1902 after an 18-month break in deliveries, saw length increase slightly to 360 feet. They again numbered seven, the last being *Clan Macneil* (2) (top). There were variations in the hull form of this group, with this vessel and *Clan Forbes* (2) having a poop. *[Newall Dunn collection]*

A further modest increase in length to 385 feet characterised the three Turrets of batch 5. Note the awnings rigged at bow and stern of *Clan Maclean* (2) (middle). *[Simon Oliver collection]*

The final three Turrets for Clan reverted to the 400-foot length of the first batch. All had full height poops. This is *Clan Sinclair* (2), the last Turret to remain in the fleet. *[Ships in Focus]*

received an order valued at £44,500 for a larger replacement. On *Bullionist's* bareboat charter ending in September 1898, she was immediately re-chartered for a voyage to Bombay, despite her non-uniformity: Cayzer's decisions were not always consistent.

Alongside fewer but more conventional ships from Linthouse, Port Glasgow, Dumbarton and West Hartlepool, a steady stream of two- and three-deck Turrets emerged from Sunderland for Clan, plus two license-built at Barrow-in-Furness, an order almost certainly gained by the yard because Charles Cayzer was the town's Member of Parliament. Partly in replacement of its oldest ships, several of which passed initially to Doxfords in part payment, Clan took a total of 32 Turrets and, although not all were in service together, this comprised the largest number with any one owner.

Clan Line made another, less welcome, contribution to the Turret saga when *Clan Ranald* (2) capsized off the Australian coast in January 1909. She sailed from Adelaide on 31st January with 6,500 tons of grain and flour, and 50 tons of bunker coal stowed on the starboard Turret deck and 20 tons to port, plus 50 tons more on the weather deck. The slight starboard list with which she had sailed increased that afternoon so that her harbour deck was under water. She headed for shore and anchored, laying head-on to a moderate sea, but that evening capsized and sank with the loss of 40 lives. A Board of Trade enquiry cast doubts on the stability of the Turret design, and Doxfords issued detailed instructions for loading Turrets, stressing for instance the importance of filling double bottom tanks if bunker coal was stowed on the harbour deck. The second capsize of a Clan Turret involved the *Clan Gordon* (2) in 1919. After sailing from New York on 28th July 1919 with a cargo of case oil the master put the helm over both ways to check stability, and found she did not heel. Two days later he decided to pump out water from certain ballast tanks to put the ship down by the stern to improve power and in the mistaken belief that it would improve bad weather behaviour. Later that day she took a five-degree list, but when her helm was put over to port the list increased and she capsized, although slowly enough for all but four of her crew to get on to her bottom to await rescue. Her loss was blamed on her master emptying the ballast tanks. After lengthy legal action, Clan had to meet a claim of £97,000 from the owners of her cargo. The findings after the loss of *Clan Ranald* may have turned owners against the Turret design, as only two more were built after 1909, although changes in the basis of port and canal charges which made the design less favourable were probably a bigger factor. Nevertheless, the type remained in service with Clan until 1933, and Turrets were a feature of the fleet for 37 years.

By 1902 the freight market which had been particularly buoyant during the Boer War began to show signs of depression, and for two Turrets ordered that year the price fell back from the £49,500 quoted in August 1901 to £47,000. Early in 1904 a particularly bold initiative was to order six Turrets, but a further depression in freight rates was noted, and three of the orders were quickly cancelled. It was now thought prudent for the chairman to advance money to The Clan Line Steamers Ltd. from his personal fortune, he being careful to obtain interest at 1% above the Bank of England base rate on this loan. A sure sign of the depression was that no ships were taken on charter, all sailings in Clan's various trades being taken by its own ships. By 1907 the situation was bad enough to cause real concern over the company's liabilities for ships on order, and it was resolved to order no more until liabilities were reduced. A symptom of poor loadings was that eight of the company's ships were fixed outside Clan's regular trades. No new ships were ordered until 1910, by when developments in trade required a new type of ship.

Not all losses of Turret ships were due to stability problems. The *Clan Monroe* (2) was wrecked on the South African coast in 1905. *[Newall Dunn collection]*

Although Clan Line ships became frequent visitors to Australia, they were much less common in New Zealand ports. On 5th January 1910 *Clan Macneil* (2) became the first ship of the Line to enter Westport (right). The Union Steamship Company of New Zealand were attempting to control coal supplies on the west coast, and Clan Line did not endear themselves to this company by taking coal from a rival mine. *[Ian J. Farquhar collection]*

Failures and successes

With the freight market quiet following the Boer War, there were few developments concerning Clan Line routes. In 1902 the Caledonia Landing, Shipping and Salvage Co. Ltd. was formed to undertake lighterage work at South African ports, where Clan Line were particularly concerned that lengthy detentions were losing them money. Local tugs were bought, *Scotia* at Algoa Bay, *Caledonia* at Port Elizabeth and *Portia* at Cape Town, and lighters shipped out from the UK. It was not to be a fortunate venture. *Scotia* was lost in a gale in 1902 and *Caledonia* in 1905. In 1908 it was decided to wind up the company, which had failed to prosper when faced with competition in Algoa Bay from the Port Elizabeth Harbour Board.

Cayzer was nothing if not pugnacious, and in 1905 he made an attempt to enter the trade to Karachi by loading rails and locomotives for the port. Karachi had long been the preserve of the City and Hall Lines, now both under the control of another man of Cayzer's calibre although somewhat younger, John Ellerman. Perfectly reasonably, Ellerman objected to Clan running to Karachi, as in agreements concerning the trade to other Indian ports between Clan, City and Hall it was explicitly stated that the signatories should not interfere in the others' spheres of influence. Nevertheless, it raised Cayzer's hackles when in retaliation Ellerman's ships started loading for Madras in Liverpool and Glasgow. Strongly advised to desist from the Karachi trade by associates and friends, Cayzer did back off, partly because he was persuaded that Ellerman was not getting that much profit out of the Karachi trade.

Cayzer's associates probably recognised that more was to be lost than gained from such bickering with partners in shipping conferences, where Clan's best interests were served by cooperation. Three years after this spat, Clan, Ellerman, and T. and J. Harrison were working together 'to protect the interests of West Coast lines in the South African trade' by initiating a six-weekly service from the West Coast of the United Kingdom via the Suez Canal to Red Sea and East African ports. These included Port Sudan, Massawa, Aden, Mombasa, Kilindini and Zanzibar. It is not clear who the aggressor was in this case, but the service was to prove an enduring one for Clan Line.

Cayzer senior's judgement was fallible, and perhaps more so as he grew older, as with his opposition to Clan's entry into the trade from Australia to the United Kingdom. Clan had been invited in by an important wool shipper, the McArthur Shipping and Agency Co. Ltd., so although the established lines were unhappy, they could do little about it. Clan sailings from Australia began in 1906 with *Clan Matheson* (2) loading in Port Pirie and other ports, and steadily built up, with calls at New Zealand beginning in 1908. Initially, there was little profit in the few yearly sailings with wool and some wheat, as steamers had to be sent out in ballast from South Africa, but their importance was in bringing to the company's attention other Australian trades, notably fruit. Against Charles Cayzer senior's judgement, his sons felt this trade had potential, and were prepared to invest heavily, to the extent of ordering ships with refrigerating machinery. The satisfaction with Clan's services expressed by McArthur saw agents in Tasmania and New Zealand begin to use the line, which gained contracts for meat, dairy products, and apples. It is probable that Cayzer senior's antipathy to Australian business may have been responsible for the company not taking up a promising opportunity. In November 1911 Cayzer's friend Lord Furness offered him first refusal of rights in the Australian homeward trade held by Houlder Brothers, which he had recently taken over and which was to concentrate on the South American trades. Not displaying his characteristic dynamism, Cayzer professed to be awaiting further details of the rights, but when these were not forthcoming the matter was allowed to lapse. The sons were proved correct in their predictions about the Australian trade and, reinforced by a timely acquisition later in the decade, it was to become a mainstay of Clan's business. It was probably no coincidence that the name *Clan Macarthur* (2) was given to a big refrigerated ship in 1912.

Perhaps more so than other cargo lines, Clan were perfectly willing to enter the preserve of tramp owners, especially if so doing put their ship into a favourable position to fill a berth on a regular trade. Over the years their ships lifted many bulk cargoes, including sugar from Java, rice from Burma, guano from the Seychelles, phosphates from Pacific Islands, coal from the Tyne or Natal, timber for Vladivostok, grain from the United States to Rotterdam, coal from South

The short-lived sister of the *Clan Macarthur* was the *Clan Mactavish* (1), seen above. Delivered in 1913 she was lost to the German auxilliary cruiser *Moewe* in 1916. *[Nautical Photo Agency/Archie Munro collection]*

Wales or Hull to the River Plate, china clay from Fowey to Bombay. Such willingness to get their ships' holds dirty was a factor in Clan's prospering through good times and bad.

Deliveries recommence

The years immediately before the First World War saw freight rates improve and with them a spate of new orders. The most important was for a class of nine large, flush-decked ships from six different builders, including Doxford and Stephen who were familiar to Clan, and also from yards on the Tyne and Tees which were not. Significantly, it was decided to install refrigeration machinery and the necessary hold insulation in three ships of this group, a first for Clan and a decision prompted by the younger Cayzers' optimistic views on the prospects for the Australian trade. But this machinery did not come cheap. Figures for the extra cost of refrigeration do not appear in board minutes, but some idea can be had from the increase in price between the ships of the *Clan Macphee* group,

which started at £64,000 for a non-reefer, and the £92,250 each tendered by Armstrong, Whitworth for the admittedly bigger reefers *Clan Macarthur* (2) and *Clan Mactavish* (1). Doxford and Palmer's had tendered even higher for these ships, £104,000 and £97,000, respectively.

In March 1912 there was debate amongst board members about the wisdom of continuing to order steamers, with Charles Cayzer senior being excited by favourable reports of the pioneering ocean-going motor vessel *Selandia* (4,964/ 1912) which had just paid a visit to London. Caution prevailed, however, and it was decided to await further development of the diesel engine. In fact, Clan were to be relatively late and indecisive users of the oil engine, and only became committed to it in the 1950s. There was a need to replace the *Clan Macinnes* (1) and *Clan Maciver* (1) which were due to be returned to Furness, Withy at the conclusion of their bareboat charters at the end of 1913, and because of the urgency two basically-similar three-island ships of around 390 feet were

Clan Macquarrie (1) was the last of the nine-ship *Clan Macphee* class to be delivered. *[Ian J. Farquhar collection]*

taken over whilst building, one by Laing and the other by Ropner, to become *Clan Macbeth* (1) and *Clan Macbride* (1). Possibly prompted by the loss of the almost-new *Clan Mackenzie* (2) in February 1913, was the purchase of J. and C. Harrison's *Harflete*, which was completed on the Tyne as *Clan Mackellar* (1). Three ships ordered in October 1913 from Napier and Miller, Swan, Hunter and Doxford introduced the cruiser stern to the fleet. *Clan Campbell* (3), *Clan Ross* (2) and *Clan Ogilvy* (2) were not delivered until after the outbreak of war in August 1914, but fortunately were sufficiently far advanced that diversion of shipbuilding resources from merchant to warship construction did not significantly delay them. However, all three and their crews were to suffer grievously during wartime, with one sunk in 1916, another badly damaged by torpedo in 1918 and then sunk in 1942, and the third torpedoed in 1941.

The last five years of peace saw trade recover, and with it Clan Line's profits, so that a dividend of 33% was paid in 1912. Reserves had grown too, and £250,000 was taken out of the reserve fund to provide each shareholder with an additional share for every two they held. Needless to say, the main beneficiary was Sir Charles Cayzer, who held 80% of the equity. The company's success did not

Clan Mackellar (1), the former *Harflete* of J. and C. Harrison. *[Roy Fenton collection]*

Clan Macbride (1). *[Kevin O'Donoghue collection]*

go unnoticed, and an offer to buy it was made by Owen Phillips, the *infant terrible* of contemporary shipping who was in the process of turning round the fortunes of the ailing but venerable Royal Mail Steam Packet Company. Surprisingly, as the company had been his life's work, Charles Cayzer was minded to accept the offer, but his sons strongly counselled against it, all but Charles junior who had left the business in 1910. The sons' argument carried

the day, probably because they persuaded their father that Phillips' offer was far too low, given their company's value and earning potential.

On the outbreak of the First World War the Clan Line fleet had grown to 62 ships. Although this was not to be its peak figure, a changing world and a new chairman would mean an end to the days of confident expansion in trade and with it a growing fleet.

The Turret *Clan Lindsay* (2) about to enter Tilbury. *[Newall Dunn collection]*

CLIPPER BOWS FROM STEPHENS

Three of the orders that followed the setting up of The Clan Line Steamers Ltd. in 1890 went to the Linthouse yard, which rather surprisingly for this date produced a clipper-bowed design. They were, however, the first Clan Line ships built with triple-expansion engines.

In 1902 and 1903 all three ships were sold to Furness, Withy for their service from London to Newfoundland, Nova Scotia and New Brunswick, for which passenger accommodation was added. The transaction was perhaps linked to the close friendship between Charles Cayzer and Christopher Furness.

CLAN MACKINNON (1) 1891-1902

O.N. 98627 2,268g 1,473n
305.0 x 39.0 x 23.4 feet.
T.3-cyl. by Alexander Stephen and Sons, Linthouse, Glasgow; 300 NHP.
21.4.1891: Launched by Alexander Stephen and Sons, Linthouse, Glasgow (Yard No. 332).
15.5.1891: Registered in the ownership of Charles W. Cayzer (Cayzer, Irvine and Co., managers), Glasgow as CLAN MACKINNON.
20.5.1891: Ran trials and completed.
3.7.1896: Transferred to The Clan Line Steamers Ltd. (Cayzer, Irvine and Co., managers), Glasgow.
25.11.1896: Transferred to Sir John Muir, Alexander Moore and James Mackenzie (Cayzer, Irvine and Co., managers), Glasgow.
30.9.1897: Transferred to Sir Charles W.

Evangeline, the former *Clan Mackinnon* (1), loading coal. *[Nigel Farrell collection]*

Cayzer, James McKenzie and David Rennie (Cayzer, Irvine and Co., managers), Glasgow.
18.12.1900: Transferred to The Clan Line Steamers Ltd. (Cayzer, Irvine and Co., managers), Glasgow.
15.7.1902: Sold to Furness, Withy and Co. Ltd., West Hartlepool.
18.7.1902: Renamed EVANGELINE.
22.7.1909: Register closed on sale to Anglo Hellenic Steamship Co. Ltd. (A.A. Embiricos, manager), Piraeus, Greece and renamed PELAGOS
11.8.1912: Grounded on Cold Knap, off Barry whilst on a voyage from Barry to Livorno with a cargo of coal. Subsequently refloated.
11.1912: Sold to T.W. Ward Ltd., Sheffield and broken up at Morecambe.

CLAN MACNAB (1) 1891-1903

O.N. 98645 2,268g 1,472n
305.0 x 39.0 x 23.4 feet.
T.3-cyl. by Alexander Stephen and Sons, Linthouse, Glasgow; 300 NHP.
9.6.1891: Launched by Alexander Stephen and Sons, Linthouse, Glasgow (Yard No. 333).
19.6.1891: Registered in the ownership of Charles W. Cayzer (Cayzer, Irvine and Co., managers), Glasgow as CLAN MACNAB.
7.1891: Completed.
10.9.1897: Transferred to Sir Charles W. Cayzer, James Mackenzie and David Rennie (Cayzer, Irvine and Co., managers), Glasgow.
10.8.1899: Transferred to The Clan Line Steamers Ltd. (Cayzer, Irvine and Co., managers), Glasgow.
28.8.1900: Transferred to Sir Charles W. Cayzer, James Mackenzie and David Rennie (Cayzer, Irvine and Co., managers), Glasgow.
18.12.1900: Transferred to The Clan Line Steamers Ltd. (Cayzer, Irvine and Co., managers), Glasgow.
21.1.1903: Sold to Furness, Withy and Co. Ltd., West Hartlepool.
23.1.1903: Renamed ST. JOHN CITY.
28.7.1909: Register closed on sale to the Anglo Hellenic Steamship Co. Ltd. (A.A. Embiricos, manager), Piraeus, Greece and renamed PONTOS.
1913: Sold to Tassos N. Caruso, Piraeus, Greece.
1915: Taken over by the Admiralty, and scuttled as a block ship at Scapa Flow.
1922: Raised and broken up.

Clan Macnab (1) displays the elegance of her clipper-bowed design. *[Glasgow University Archives DC101/0149]*

CLAN MACALISTER (1) 1891-1902

O.N. 98662 2,270g 1,173n
305.0 x 39.0 x 23.3 feet.
T.3-cyl. by Alexander Stephen and Sons, Linthouse, Glasgow; 300 NHP.
5.8.1891: Launched by Alexander Stephen and Sons, Linthouse, Glasgow (Yard No. 334).
18.8.1891: Registered in the ownership of Charles W. Cayzer (Cayzer, Irvine and Co., managers), Glasgow as CLAN MACALISTER.
3.7.1896: Transferred to Sir John Muir, Alexander Moore and James Mackenzie (Cayzer, Irvine and Co., managers), Glasgow.
30.9.1897: Transferred to Sir Charles W. Cayzer, James Mackenzie and David Rennie (Cayzer, Irvine and Co., managers), Glasgow.
16.8.1899: Transferred to The Clan Line Steamers Ltd. (Cayzer, Irvine and Co., managers), Glasgow.
28.8.1900: Transferred to Sir Charles W. Cayzer, James Mackenzie and David Rennie (Cayzer, Irvine and Co., managers), Glasgow.
18.12.1900: Transferred to The Clan Line Steamers Ltd. (Cayzer, Irvine and Co., managers), Glasgow.
26.7.1902: Sold to Furness, Withy and Co. Ltd., West Hartlepool.
29.7.1902: Renamed LOYALIST.
27.9.1904: Wrecked at Freshwater Cove, Trepassey Bay, Newfoundland whilst on a voyage from Halifax, Nova Scotia to London with general cargo.
14.10.1904: Register closed.

DOXFORD DELIVERIES

Doxford built three of the clipper-bowed ships ordered by Cayzer in 1890, undercutting Stephen's price (£31,000 compared with £32,600) and beating him thoroughly on delivery times, the first being delivered in just six and a half months compared with nine months from the Linthouse yard.

After barely a decade of service, all three were purchased for £31,500 by Ellermans for the Westcott and Laurance services to the Mediterranean, another example of a whole class being sold and employed together.

CLAN MACNEIL (1) 1891-1902

O.N. 98611 2,487g 1,595n
312.0 x 39.0 x 23.5 feet.
T.3-cyl. by William Doxford and Sons Ltd., Sunderland; 300 NHP, 1,400 IHP, 10 knots.
14.2.1891: Launched by William Doxford and Sons Ltd., Sunderland (Yard No. 203).
26.3.1891: Registered in the ownership of Charles W. Cayzer (Cayzer, Irvine and Co., managers), Glasgow as CLAN MACNEIL.
3.1891: Completed.

The clipper-bowed *Clan Macneil* (1) with a paddle tug alongside. Note the narrowness of the deckhouses on the Clan Liner's bridge deck. *[Glasgow University Archives DC101/0151]*

Clan Macneil (1) lying alongside the North Jetty at Port Elizabeth in 1895, the first ocean-going ship to do so. Port Elizabeth, formerly Algoa Bay, was the main port of supply for the army during the Boer War and at times there could be as many as one hundred sailing vessels anhored off. As a result some Clan Line steamers suffered delays of up to three months. *[The Clansman, Spring 1956]*

7.7.1891: Transferred to John Muir, Alxaman Moore and James Mackenzie (Cayzer, Irvine and Co., managers), Glasgow.
30.9.1897: Transferred to Sir Charles W. Cayzer, James Mackenzie and David Rennie (Cayzer, Irvine and Co., managers), Glasgow.
13.10.1899: Transferred to The Clan Line Steamers Ltd. (Cayzer, Irvine and Co., managers), Glasgow.

26.8.1902: Sold to Ellerman Lines Ltd., London (Fred Swift, Liverpool, manager).
15.9.1902: Renamed BELGRAVIAN.
6.11.1914: Manager became Graham Swift, Liverpool.
27.5.1922: Sold to Kenneth Saunders, London.
3.7.1929: Arrived at La Spezia.
29.7.1929: Register closed following sale for demolition at La Spezia.

CLAN MACLEOD (2) 1891-1902

O.N. 98620 2,517g 1,614n
312.0 x 39.0 x 23.5 feet.
T.3-cyl. by William Doxford and Sons
Ltd., Sunderland; 300 NHP; 1,400 IHP, 10
knots.
25.3.1891: Launched by William Doxford
and Sons Ltd., Sunderland (Yard No. 204).
1.5.1891: Registered in the ownership of
Charles W. Cayzer (Cayzer, Irvine and
Co., managers), Glasgow as CLAN
MACLEOD.
3.7.1896: Transferred to Sir John Muir,
Alxander Moore and James Mackenzie
(Cayzer, Irvine and Co., managers),
Glasgow.
30.9.1897: Transferred to Sir Charles W.
Cayzer, James Mackenzie and David
Rennie (Cayzer, Irvine and Co.,
managers), Glasgow.
13.10.1899: Transferred to The Clan Line
Steamers Ltd. (Cayzer, Irvine and Co.,
managers), Glasgow.
17.9.1902: Sold to Ellerman Lines Ltd.,
London (Fred Swift, Liverpool, manager).
22.9.1902: Renamed BOSNIAN.
6.11.1914: Manager became Graham
Swift, Liverpool.
2.5.1922: Sold to Olivier and Co. Ltd.
(Ernest Olivier, manager), London.
20.9.1922: Register closed on sale to
Michael Basiliades, Chios, Greece and
renamed PSARA.
1924: Sold for demolition.

CLAN MACINTYRE (1) 1891-1902

O.N. 98936 2,517g 1,615n
312.0 x 39.0 x 23.5 feet.
T.3-cyl. by William Doxford and Sons
Ltd., Sunderland; 300 NHP, 1,400 IHP,
10 knots.
28.4.1891: Launched by William Doxford
and Sons Ltd., Sunderland (Yard No. 205).
3.6.1891: Registered in the ownership of
Charles W. Cayzer (Cayzer, Irvine and
Co., managers), Glasgow as CLAN
MACINTYRE.
3.7.1896: Transferred to Sir John Muir,
Alexander Moore and James Mackenzie
(Cayzer, Irvine and Co., managers),
Glasgow.
30.9.1897: Transferred to Sir Charles W.
Cayzer, James Mackenzie and David
Rennie (Cayzer, Irvine and Co.,
managers), Glasgow.
24.3.1899: Transferred to The Clan Line
Steamers Ltd. (Cayzer, Irvine and Co.,
managers), Glasgow.
12.4.1902: Sold to Ellerman Lines Ltd.,
London (Fred Swift, Liverpool, manager).
21.5.1902: Renamed BULGARIAN.
20.1.1917: Torpedoed and sunk by the
German submarine U 84 south west of
Ireland whilst on a voyage from
Cartagena to Garston with a cargo of iron
ore, with the loss of her master and 13
crew, the remaining 9 being taken
prisoner.
4.4.1917: Register closed.

The Greek *Psara,* formerly *Clan Macleod* (2), approaching Bristol towards the end
of a long career. Alterations since Clan Line days include a more substantial
bridge and modified bow which has lost its bowsprit. *[Nigel Farrell collection]*

Bulgarian, the former *Clan Macintyre* (1) bought by Ellerman Lines in 1902.
[Newall Dunn collection]

POLITICAL ORDERS

*Charles Cayzer became the Conservative
Member of Parliament for the Barrow-in-
Furness constituency in July 1892. In his
election speeches he promised to bring work
to the town's shipyard. He kept his word,
with work on tripling the compound engines
of his fleet, and with an order for three ships.
These were identical in dimensions to the
preceding three from Doxford, although they
had conventional bows and there is evidence
that they were more powerful and hence
faster. They were cheaper, too, at £28,500
each.*

*This was another class that stayed
together almost throughout their careers,
with sale for £15,500 each to the Adelaide
Steamship Co Ltd. (now better known for
being the international tug operator
Adsteam) being followed by further service
in China or Indochina.*

CLAN ROSS (1) 1894-1913

O.N. 104539 2,602g 1,664n
312.0 x 40.2 x 24.7 feet.
T.3-cyl. by the Naval Construction and
Armaments Co. Ltd., Barrow-in-Furness;
300 NHP, 2,300 IHP, 12.25 knots.
7.6.1894: Launched by the Naval
Construction and Armaments Co. Ltd.,
Barrow-in-Furness (Yard No. 227).
6.7.1894: Registered in the ownership of
Charles W. Cayzer (Cayzer, Irvine and
Co., managers), Glasgow as CLAN ROSS.
10.9.1897: Transferred to Sir Charles W.
Cayzer, James Mackenzie and David
Rennie (Cayzer, Irvine and Co., managers),
Glasgow.
9.9.1901: Transferred to The Clan Line
Steamers Ltd. (Cayzer, Irvine and Co.,
managers), Glasgow.
1.7.1907: Managers became Cayzer, Irvine
and Co. Ltd.
17.2.1909: Transferred to Sir Charles W.
Cayzer, James Mackenzie and David
Rennie (Cayzer, Irvine and Co. Ltd.,
managers), Glasgow.
31.12.1909: Transferred to The Clan Line
Steamers Ltd. (Cayzer, Irvine and Co.,
managers), Glasgow.
8.5.1913: Sold to the Adelaide Steamship
Co. Ltd., Adelaide, South Australia.
18.7.1913: Renamed CANTARA.
28.4.1924: Sold to John McLeod Bolton,
Sydney, New South Wales.
17.10.1924: Register closed on sale to
South China Steamship Co. Ltd., Shanghai,
China and renamed HWAH CHENG.

1929: Sold to Yee Cheong and Company, Saigon, Indochina.
1930: Sold for demolition and broken up during the first quarter.

CLAN CAMPBELL (2) 1894-1913
O.N. 104576 2,600g 1,662n
312.0 x 40.2 x 24.7 feet.
T.3-cyl. by the Naval Construction and Armaments Co. Ltd., Barrow-in-Furness; 300 NHP, 2,300 IHP.
3.9.1894: Launched by the Naval Construction and Armaments Co. Ltd., Barrow-in-Furness (Yard No. 228).
10.1894: Completed.
11.11.1894: Registered in the ownership of Charles W. Cayzer (Cayzer, Irvine and Co., managers), Glasgow as CLAN CAMPBELL.
10.9.1897: Transferred to Sir Charles W. Cayzer, James Mackenzie and David Rennie (Cayzer, Irvine and Co., managers), Glasgow.
9.9.1901: Transferred to The Clan Line Steamers Ltd. (Cayzer, Irvine and Co., managers), Glasgow.
1.7.1907: Managers became Cayzer, Irvine and Co. Ltd.
17.2.1909: Transferred to Sir Charles W. Cayzer, James Mackenzie and David Rennie (Cayzer, Irvine and Co. Ltd., managers), Glasgow.
31.2.1909: Transferred to The Clan Line Steamers Ltd. (Cayzer, Irvine and Co., managers), Glasgow.
8.5.1913: Sold to the Adelaide Steamship Co. Ltd., Adelaide, South Australia.
28.6.1913: Renamed CAMIRA.
19.1.1925: Register closed on sale to W. McBain, Shanghai, China and renamed YUNG NING.
1927: Sold to Compagnie Extrême Orientale, Haiphong, Indochina.
1928: Sold to Louis Dubest (Alex. Gerondal, manager), Haiphong and renamed COMMANDANT HENRI RIVIERE.
1936: Sold to Shiu Tsing Hong (Far East Shipping Co. Ltd., managers), Canton, China.
Lost during the Sino-Japanese War or the Second World War.

CLAN MACKAY (2) 1894-1913
O.N. 104593 2,600g 1,665n
312.0 x 40.2 x 24.7 feet.
T.3-cyl. by the Naval Construction and Armaments Co. Ltd., Barrow-in-Furness; 300 NHP, 2,300 IHP, 12.25 knots.
31.10.1894: Launched by the Naval Construction and Armaments Co. Ltd., Barrow-in-Furness (Yard No. 229).
6.12.1894: Registered in the ownership of Charles W. Cayzer (Cayzer, Irvine and Co., managers), Glasgow as CLAN MACKAY.
10.9.1897: Transferred to Sir Charles W. Cayzer, James Mackenzie and David

The first Clan Line ship from Barrow, *Clan Ross* (1). *[Nigel Farrell collection]*

The second *Clan Campbell*, Barrow-built. Note the single derrick, with no post, ahead of number three hold. *[Ships in Focus]*

Clan Mackay (2). *[Kevin O'Donoghue collection]*

In May 1913, all three Barrow-built ships were sold to the Adelaide Steamship Co. Ltd. Pictured above are, from top to bottom, *Cantara* the former *Clan Ross* (1), *Camira* formerly *Clan Campbell* (2), and *Ceduna* the former *Clan Mackay* (2). Since being built they had been fitted with kingposts between holds two and three, those on *Camira* being noticeably taller. There are other minor differences apparent between these supposed sisters, including the presence or absence of cabs on the bridge wings, the height of the topmasts, and the ventilators near the foremast. After just over a decade of service in South Australia, all three were sold to work in China. *[All: Ian J. Farquhar]*

Rennie (Cayzer, Irvine and Co., managers), Glasgow.
9.9.1901: Transferred to The Clan Line Steamers Ltd. (Cayzer, Irvine and Co., managers), Glasgow.
1.7.1907: Managers became Cayzer, Irvine and Co. Ltd.
17.2.1909: Transferred to Sir Charles W. Cayzer, James Mackenzie and David Rennie (Cayzer, Irvine and Co. Ltd., managers), Glasgow.
31.12.1909: Transferred to The Clan Line Steamers Ltd. (Cayzer, Irvine and Co., managers), Glasgow.
8.5.1913: Sold to the Adelaide Steamship Co. Ltd., Adelaide, South Australia
30.7.1913: Renamed CEDUNA.
28.4.1924: Sold to John McLeod Bolton, Sydney, New South Wales.
28.7.1924: Register closed on sale to Woo Kuei Fen (Tung, Tuck and Co., managers), Shanghai, China and renamed TUNG TUCK.
1937: Sold to Lee Yuen Steamship Co. Ltd., Shanghai, China and renamed CHANG TEH.
1937: Sold to J.D. Tsounias (China Hellenic Lines Ltd., managers), Piraeus, Greece and renamed PANANIS.
12.1941: Seized by Imperial Japanese Forces and owners became the Japanese Government, Tokyo.
1943: Placed in service as SHINYO MARU.
7.9.1944: Torpedoed and sunk by the US submarine PADDLE off Liloy, Mindanao in position 08.11 north by 122.40 east.

PERSIAN GULF PURCHASES
When Cayzer wanted to enter the Persian Gulf trade he acquired the ships owned or operated by the Persian Gulf Steamship Co. Ltd. for £63,750. He was more interested in the steamship company's share of the trade, however, and three of the Persian Gulf ships were quickly sold, in one case within days of acquisition, to London brokers. Only the most modern ship was retained and renamed Clan Macrae, *but even she was kept for barely four years.*

GORJI 1895 Iron
O.N. 87156 1,768g 1,110n
255.5 x 35.1 x 24.5 feet.
C.2-cyl. by Wigham, Richardson and Co., Newcastle-upon-Tyne; 180 NHP.
7.1883: Launched by Wigham, Richardson and Co., Newcastle-upon-Tyne (Yard No. 157).
7.9.1883: Registered in the ownership of James Darby, London, trading as the Persian Gulf Steamship Co., as GORJI.
29.7.1886: Transferred to Benjamin Jenkins, Kenward W. Elmslie and Herbert Jones, London.

18.4.1891: Transferred to Kenward W. Elmslie and Herbert Jones, London.
31.7.1891: Sold to the Persian Gulf Steamship Co. Ltd., London.
21.3.1895: Acquired by The Clan Line Steamers Ltd. (Cayzer, Irvine and Co., managers), Glasgow.
4.4.1895: Sold to Joseph R.K. Johnson, London.
17.4.1895: Renamed MOSHTARI.
8.12.1896: Sold to the Bombay and Persia Steam Navigation Co. Ltd., Bombay, India.
8.2.1914: Register closed on sale to Abe Shokai, Dairen, Manchuria and renamed FUKUJU MARU under the Japanese flag.
1917: Sold to Murao Kisen Goshi Kaisha, Amagasaki, Japan.
3.3.1930: Wrecked near Shiriyasaki whilst on a voyage from Ofunato to Muroran with a cargo of ore.

AMARA 1895
O.N. 98197 2,454g 1,566n
289.5 x 40.3 x 22.8 feet.
T.3-cyl. by the North Eastern Marine Engineering Co. Ltd., Sunderland; 220 NHP, 1,320 IHP, 10.5 knots.
15.11.1890: Launched by John Blumer and Co., Sunderland (Yard No. 108).
5.1.1891: Registered in the ownership of the Persian Gulf Steam Ship Co. Ltd., London as AMARA.
31.1.1895: Acquired by The Clan Line Steamers Ltd. (Cayzer, Irvine and Co., managers), Glasgow. It was intended to rename her CLAN MENZIES but this was not carried out.
16.7.1895: Sold to William Keswick, London.
17.7.1896: Sold to the Indo-China Steam Navigation Co. Ltd., London.
14.2.1911: Register closed on sale to N. Aso, Nishinomaya, Japan and renamed TAGA MARU.
1917: Sold to Fukugawa Ringyo K.K, Osaka, Japan.
1920: Owners became Fukugawa Kisen K.K., Tokyo, Japan.
1922: Sold to Tajima Nobukazu, Kobe, Japan.
12.3.1925: Wrecked in Heki Ki Channel, near Icheyezaki, Wakayama whilst on a voyage from Shibaura to Osaka in ballast.

TIGRIS 1895
O.N. 98167 2,412g 1,536n
290.0 x 40.1 x 24.4 feet.
T.3-cyl. by the North Eastern Marine Engineering Co. Ltd., Sunderland; 220 NHP, 1,750 IHP, 10 knots.
30.8.1890: Launched by John Blumer and Co., Sunderland (Yard No. 107).
3.10.1890: Registered in the ownership of the Persian Gulf Steamship Co. Ltd., London as TIGRIS.

14.5.1895: Acquired by The Clan Line Steamers Ltd. (Cayzer, Irvine and Co., managers), Glasgow. It was intended to rename her CLAN CHISHOLM but this was not carried out.
29.5.1895: Sold to William Keswick, London.
17.7.1896: Sold to Indo-China Steam Navigation Co. Ltd., London
2.3.1896: Renamed HIN SANG.
14.2.1911: Register closed on sale to C. Yamaki, Uraga, Japan and renamed KAIHEI MARU.
21.7.1911: Wrecked in the Soya Strait, Japan.

CLAN MACRAE (1) 1895-1899
O.N. 99099 2,604g 1,664n
305.0 x 41.2 x 18.9 feet.
T.3-cyl. by the North Eastern Marine Engineering Co. Ltd., Sunderland; 220 NHP, 1,200 IHP, 10 knots.
13.5.1892: Launched by John Blumer and Co., Sunderland (Yard No. 122).
17.6.1892: Registered in the ownership of the Persian Gulf Steamship Co. Ltd., London as SHAT-EL-ARAB.
14.5.1895: Acquired by The Clan Line Steamers Ltd. (Cayzer, Irvine and Co., managers), Glasgow.
30.9.1895: Renamed CLAN MACRAE.
31.12.1897: Transferred to Sir Charles W. Cayzer, James Mackenzie and David Rennie (Cayzer, Irvine and Co., managers), Glasgow.
24.3.1897: Transferred to The Clan Line Steamers Ltd. (Cayzer, Irvine and Co., managers), Glasgow.
16.5.1899: Sold to the Chadwick Steamship Co. Ltd. (Robert B. Avery, manager), Newcastle-upon-Tyne for £18,750.
5.6.1899: Renamed CARMELITE.
8.2.1915: Stranded near Ile d'Yeu, whilst on a voyage from Blyth to La Pallice with a cargo of coal. Later refloated but declared a constructive total loss.
22.11.1915: Register closed. Later repaired.
22.3.1916: Registered in the ownership of Thorolf G. Berg, Cardiff.
28.3.1916: Sold to the Page Shipping Co. Ltd. (Hopkins, Jones and Co. Ltd., managers), Cardiff.
22.11.1916: Manager became Maurice Ramet, London.
20.3.1917: Manager became Albert H. Page, London.
20.6.1917: Managers became John I. Jacobs and Co., London
2.3.1918: Torpedoed and sunk by the German submarine U 105 ten miles south west by west of the Calf of Man whilst on a voyage from Bilbao to Cardiff with a cargo of iron ore.
16.3.1918: Register closed.

CONVENTIONAL SHIPS OF 1896

The year in which Clan Line largely standardised on Turret types, 1896, also saw a number of conventional ships delivered. The first four from Barrow and Linthouse were of similar dimensions, whilst Clan Menzies *(1),* Clan Ogilvy *(1) and the slightly larger* Clan Sutherland *(1) had a short hatch between bridge and funnel.   The Barrow-built ships cost £34,500,* Clan Ogilvy *£32,125 and* Clan Sutherland *£35,750.*

CLAN MENZIES (1) 1896-1925
O.N. 105979 2,669g 1,704n
312.3 x 40.2 x 23.6 feet.
T.3-cyl. by the Naval Construction and Armaments Co. Ltd., Barrow-in-Furness; 300 NHP, 2,300 IHP, 12.25 knots.
1.2.1896: Launched by the Naval Construction and Armaments Co. Ltd., Barrow-in-Furness (Yard No. 245).
2.3.1896: Registered in the ownership of Charles W. Cayzer (Cayzer, Irvine and Co., managers), Glasgow as CLAN MENZIES.
10.9.1897: Transferred to Sir Charles W. Cayzer, James Mackenzie and David Rennie (Cayzer, Irvine and Co., managers), Glasgow.
9.9.1901: Transferred to The Clan Line Steamers Ltd. (Cayzer, Irvine and Co., managers), Glasgow.
1.7.1907: Managers became Cayzer, Irvine and Co. Ltd.
24.2.1909: Transferred to Sir Charles W. Cayzer, James Mackenzie and David Rennie (Cayzer, Irvine and Co. Ltd., managers), Glasgow.
31.12.1909: Transferred to The Clan Line Steamers Ltd. (Cayzer, Irvine and Co. Ltd., managers), Glasgow.

Clan Menzies (1). Note the bunker hatch between bridge and funnel. *[George Scott collection]*

8.5.1917: Requisitioned by the British government until 5.4.1919.
17.11.1925: Register closed on sale to Attilio Ardito, Genoa, Italy and renamed NOSTRA SIGNORA DI CORONATA.
7.1928: Lying at Savona awaiting demolition, which began in the fourth quarter.

CLAN OGILVY (1) 1896-1913
O.N. 106030 2,647g 1,690n
312.5 x 40.2 x 23.5 feet.
T.3-cyl. by Alexander Stephen and Sons, Linthouse, Glasgow; 320 NHP.
25.8.1896: Launched by Alexander Stephen and Sons, Linthouse, Glasgow (Yard No. 367).
9.9.1896: Registered in the ownership of The Clan Line Steamers Ltd. (Cayzer, Irvine and Co., managers), Glasgow as CLAN OGILVY.
25.11.1906: Sold to Sir John Muir, Alexander Moore and James Mackenzie

(Cayzer, Irvine and Co., managers), Glasgow.
30.9.1897: Sold to Charles W. Cayzer, James Mackenzie and David Rennie (Cayzer, Irvine and Co., managers), Glasgow.
9.9.1901: Transferred to The Clan Line Steamers Ltd. (Cayzer, Irvine and Co., managers), Glasgow.
1.7.1907: Managers became Cayzer, Irvine and Co. Ltd.
17.2.1909: Transferred to Charles W. Cayzer, James Mackenzie and David Rennie (Cayzer, Irvine and Co. Ltd., managers), Glasgow.
1.12.1909: Transferred to The Clan Line Steamers Ltd. (Cayzer, Irvine and Co. Ltd., managers), Glasgow.
25.8.1913: Register closed on sale to Iwaki Ukichi, Dairen, Manchuria for £15,500 and renamed TAIYO MARU under the Japanese flag.
1918: Sold to Hamaguchi Kisen K.K., Osaka, Japan.

The Manchurian-owned, Japanese-flagged *Taiyo Maru,* formerly the *Clan Ogilvy* (1). *[Ian J. Farquhar collection]*

A splendid shot of *Clan Chisholm* (1), almost certainly running trials in the Firth of Clyde on 25th July 1896. Unprotected even by a canvas dodger, those on the bridge were enjoying a stimulating ride. *[Glasgow University Archives DC101/0142]*

1924: Owners became Hamaguchi Kisen Gosen Kaisha, Osaka.
1925: Sold to Taiyo Kisen Goshi Kaisha, Dairen.
1926: Sold to Uyeda Mitsujiro, Dairen.
1927: Sold to Uyeda Kisen Goshi Kaisha, Dairen.
1929: Sold to Dalgosrybtrest, Vladivostok, USSR, converted into a floating crab cannery, and renamed PERVYI KRABOLOV.
During the 1940s used as an oil storage hulk by the Soviet Navy.
1960: Deleted from 'Lloyd's Register' due to lack of up to date information.

CLAN CHISHOLM (1) 1896-1924
O.N. 106017 2,647g 1,690n
312.5 x 40.2 x 23.5 feet.
T.3-cyl. by Alexander Stephen and Sons, Linthouse, Glasgow; 320 NHP.
30.6.1896: Launched by Alexander Stephen and Sons, Linthouse, Glasgow (Yard No. 366).
15.7.1896: Registered in the ownership of The Clan Line Steamers Ltd. (Cayzer, Irvine and Co., managers), Glasgow as CLAN CHISHOLM.
25.7.1896: Ran trials and delivered.
25.11.1896: Transferred to Sir John Muir,

Alexander Moore and James Mackenzie (Charles W. Cayzer, manager), Glasgow.
30.9.1897: Transferred to Sir Charles W. Cayzer, James Mackenzie and David Rennie (Charles W. Cayzer, manager), Glasgow.
9.9.1901: Transferred to The Clan Line Steamers Ltd. (Cayzer, Irvine and Co., managers), Glasgow.
1.7.1907: Managers became Cayzer, Irvine and Co. Ltd.
17.2.1909: Transferred to Sir Charles W. Cayzer, James Mackenzie and David Rennie (Cayzer, Irvine and Co. Ltd., managers), Glasgow

CLAN LINDSAY (1) 1896-1898
O.N. 105997 2,668g 1,705n
312.3 x 40.2 x 23.6 feet.
T.3-cyl. by the Naval Construction and Armaments Co. Ltd., Barrow-in-Furness; 300 NHP, 2,300 IHP, 12.25 knots.
2.4.1896: Launched by the Naval Construction and Armaments Co. Ltd., Barrow-in-Furness (Yard No. 246).
1.5.1896: Registered in the ownership of Charles W. Cayzer (Cayzer, Irvine and Co., managers), Glasgow as CLAN LINDSAY.
10.9.1897: Transferred to Charles W. Cayzer, John MacKenzie and David Rennie (Cayzer, Irvine and Co., managers), Glasgow.
21.3.1898: Wrecked at Mazeppa Bay, north of the Great Kei River, East London, Cape Colony whilst on a voyage from Glasgow and Liverpool to South Africa with general cargo.
7.5.1898: Register closed.

A deep-laden *Clan Chisholm* (1) approaches Avonmouth. *Clan Chisholm* had a remarkably lucky war. She was attacked on several occasions by U-boats, and on each drove off her assailants with gunfire. Indeed, she almost sank *U 49*, which attacked her off Cape Finisterre in November 1916 having hidden alongside a schooner. During this attack a second submarine appeared on the scene, but went to the aid of *U 49* when *Clan Chisholm's* appeared to score a direct hit, allowing the Clan liner to escape. On 8th July 1917 she fired at another submarine which immediately submerged, the *Clan Chisholm's* cargo consisting of an interesting and rather inflammable combination of wheat, shells and cordite which she was carrying from Portland, Maine and New York to Hull. *[J. and M. Clarkson collection]*

Clan Sutherland (1) in New Zealand waters.   The Wellington-based firm of George H. Scales was owned by the sheep farmers of New Zealand and each year they chartered three ships to lift their shareholders' wool at freight rates below Conference rates. The Conference condoned this as it was only a small part of their trade and the farmers had significant clout with the government of the day. They had started with sailing ships in 1897 and switched to steamers for the 1909 season, going to Clan Line for tonnage to charter. *Clan Macaulay* (1) and *Clan Sutherland* (1) took the first two cargoes and Clan Line continued to do so until 1913. The war intervened and it was not until April 1929 that Thomas Barr of the Clan Line went to New Zealand to meet Scales about a new contract. Nothing came of the approach and the company continued to charter on the open market until the 1960s. So ended the Clan Line involvement in the New Zealand trade.   *[Archie Munro collection]*

31.12.1909: Transferred to The Clan Line Steamers Ltd. (Cayzer, Irvine and Co. Ltd., managers), Glasgow.
3.3.1916: In French Government service until 2.5.1916.
13.11.1916: Attacked by the German submarine U 49 and one other off Cape Finisterre but returned fire and both broke off the attack. She was on a voyage from Birkenhead to South Africa with general cargo.
22.5.1917: Requisitioned by the British government until 18.3.1919.
31.7.1924: Register closed on sale to Nippon Kaiun K.K., Yokohama, Japan for £13,000 and renamed FUKKO MARU.
7.2.1926: Stranded at Katsuura, near Tokyo, whilst on a voyage from Muroran to Yokohama with a cargo of coal. Subsequently became a total loss.

CLAN SUTHERLAND (1) 1896-1921
O.N. 106037 2,820g 1,810n
326.0 x 40.2 x 23.5 feet.
T.3-cyl. by the Naval Construction and Armaments Co. Ltd., Barrow-in-Furness; 198 NHP, 2,300 IHP, 12 knots.
26.9.1896: Launched by the Naval Construction and Armaments Co. Ltd., Barrow-in-Furness (Yard No. 252).
22.10.1896: Registered in the ownership of The Clan Line Steamers Ltd. (Cayzer, Irvine and Co., managers), Glasgow as

CLAN SUTHERLAND.
25.11.1896: Transferred to Sir John Muir, Alexander Moore and James Mackenzie (Cayzer, Irvine and Co., managers), Glasgow.
30.9.1897: Transferred to Sir Charles W. Cayzer, James Mackenzie and David Rennie (Cayzer, Irvine and Co., managers), Glasgow.
9.9.1901: Transferred to The Clan Line Steamers Ltd. (Cayzer, Irvine and Co., managers), Glasgow.
1.7.1907: Managers became Cayzer, Irvine and Co. Ltd.
17.2.1909: Transferred to Sir Charles W. Cayzer, James Mackenzie and David Rennie (Cayzer, Irvine and Co. Ltd., managers), Glasgow
31.12.1909: Transferred to The Clan Line Steamers Ltd. (Cayzer, Irvine and Co. Ltd., managers), Glasgow.
17.4.1917: Damaged by torpedo from the German submarine UC 66 18 miles south east of Start Point and beached at Dartmouth whilst on a voyage from Cochin to London. Eight lives were lost. Subsequently refloated and repaired at Falmouth.
19.11.1917: Requisitioned by the British government until 20.3.1919.
29.11.1921: Register closed on sale to Sato Shokai Goshi Kaisha (T. Sato and Co., managers), Otaru, Japan, and renamed

SHINSHU MARU.
1924: Sold to Azuma Kisen Goshi Kaisha, Dairen, Manchuria.
1933: Broken up in Japan during the fourth quarter.

TURRET EVALUATION
Ostensibly to evaluate the Turret design, Clan bareboat chartered two from Doxford with an option to purchase. The Imperialist *and* Bullionist *were building for Angier Brothers and, despite Doxford retaining control, they appear in registration documents as wholly owned by The Clan Line Steamers Ltd. Cayzer had probably already made his mind up about the design, as within six weeks of fixing these charters he placed orders with Doxford for two Turrets at £49,000 each, and followed it up with two more in October. Clan were eventually to have the largest fleet of Turrets: the one third reduction of Suez Canal dues being an important attraction on Clan's Indian routes. Imperialist was acquired at the end of the two-year charter - signified by her being renamed* Clan Shaw *- as a replacement for the wrecked* Clan Lindsay *(1). However, Cayzer then had a change of heart, and considering her 'non uniform' sold her to Ritsons of Sunderland, who also took the* Bullionist *at the conclusion of her charter.*

Imperialist on trials. [Glasgow University Archives DC101/0301]

IMPERIALIST/CLAN SHAW (1) 1896-1898

O.N. 106016 3,442g 2,177n
340.2 x 45.6 x 24.6 feet.
T.3-cyl. by William Doxford and Sons
Ltd., Sunderland; 350 NHP, 1,600 NHP,
10 knots.
25.4.1896: Launched by William Doxford
and Sons Ltd., Sunderland (Yard No. 242)
for Angier Brothers, London as
IMPERIALIST.
8.7.1896: Registered in the ownership of
The Clan Line Steamers Ltd. (Cayzer,
Irvine and Co., managers), Glasgow as
IMPERIALIST.
2.7.1898: Renamed CLAN SHAW.
14.10.1898: Sold to the Nautilus Steam
Shipping Co. Ltd. (Frank W. Ritson,
manager), Sunderland for £32,000 and
renamed VINE BRANCH.
6.4.1917: Torpedoed and sunk by the
German submarine U 55 south west of
Ireland whilst on a voyage from Valparaiso
to Liverpool with a cargo of nitrate and
frozen meat. There were no survivors
from her crew of 44.
4.7.1917: Posted missing.
19.7.1917: Register closed.

BULLIONIST 1896-1898

O.N. 106021 3,435g 2,196n
340.3 x 45.6 x 24.6 feet.
T.3-cyl. by William Doxford and Sons
Ltd., Sunderland; 350 NHP, 1,600 IHP, 10
knots.
27.6.1896: Launched by William Doxford

and Sons Ltd., Sunderland (Yard No. 243)
for Angier Brothers, London as
BULLIONIST.
12.8.1896: Registered in the ownership of
The Clan Line Steamers Ltd. (Cayzer,
Irvine and Co., managers), Glasgow as
BULLIONIST.
15.9.1898: Renamed ORANGE
BRANCH.
19.9.1898: Sold to the Nautilus Steam
Shipping Co. Ltd. (Frank W. Ritson,
manager), Sunderland.
12.11.1919: Sold to the 'K' Steamship Co.
Ltd. (Kaye, Son and Co. Ltd., managers),
London.
18.11.1919: Renamed KEMMEL.

23.2.1920: Wrecked at St. Vincent, Cape
Verde Islands whilst on a voyage from
Rosario to Constantinople with a cargo of
meat and flour.
1.9.1921: Register closed.

TURRETS BATCH ONE

*The first Turret order by Clan was for ships
substantially larger than* Imperialist *and*
Bullionist *for £49,500 each. Presumably
because of Cayzer's position as Member of
Parliament for Barrow, two of this batch
were constructed under licence by Vickers,
Sons and Maxim Ltd. for £51,500. Only six
of the 182 Turrets came from builders other
than Doxford.*

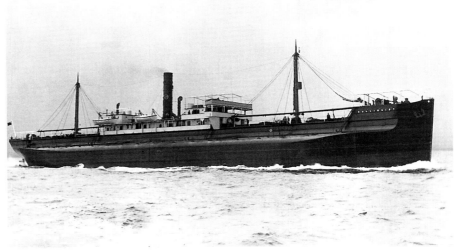

Bullionist. [Nigel Farrell collection]

The increased length of the first Turrets ordered by Clan is apparent in this view of *Clan Macdonald* (2). *[J. and M. Clarkson collection]*

CLAN MACDONALD (2) 1897-1922
O.N. 106067 4,839g 3,113n
400.6 x 50.2 x 27.7 feet.
T.3-cyl. by William Doxford and Sons
Ltd., Sunderland; 437 NHP, 2,800 IHP, 12
knots.
3.3.1897: Launched by William Doxford
and Sons Ltd., Sunderland (Yard No. 250).
14.4.1897: Registered in the ownership of
The Clan Line Steamers Ltd. (Cayzer,
Irvine and Co., managers), Glasgow as

CLAN MACDONALD.
10.9.1897: Transferred to Sir Charles W.
Cayzer, James Mackenzie and David
Rennie (Cayzer, Irvine and Co.,
managers), Glasgow.
1.7.1907: Managers became Cayzer, Irvine
and Co. Ltd.
31.12.1909: Transferred to The Clan Line
Steamers Ltd. (Cayzer, Irvine and Co. Ltd.,
managers), Glasgow.
20.11.1916: Requisitioned by the British

government until 14.7.1919.
8.6.1922: Register closed on sale to
Hokuyo Kisen Goshi Kaisha, Dairen,
Manchuria, and renamed HOKUYO
MARU under the Japanese flag.
1928: Broken up in Japan during the
second quarter.

CLAN MURRAY (2) 1897-1917
O.N. 106077 4,830g 3,107n
400.0 x 50.2 x 27.8 feet.

Clan Murray (2) dressed overall in the Mersey as part of the shipping display to mark the Diamond Jubilee day holiday in 1897.
   The 64 casualties when *Clan Murray* was sunk in May 1917 made her one of the most disastrous of Clan Line's losses during the First World War. A measure of the stress to which officers were subjected at the height of the U-boat war was that her master, Captain Woodhall, had not left the bridge for two days and nights prior to her torpedoing. Tragically, he went below to recover the code books and was trapped when his ship sank. The only survivors appear to have been the third officer, who was blown off the bridge by the force of the explosion, and the third engineer, both of whom were rescued by *UC 55* and spent the rest of the war in a prison camp. *[Kevin O'Donoghue collection]*

T.3-cyl. by William Doxford and Sons Ltd., Sunderland; 437 NHP, 2,800 IHP, 12 knots.
17.4.1897: Launched by William Doxford and Sons Ltd., Sunderland (Yard No. 251).
5.1897: Completed.
1.6.1897: Registered in the ownership of The Clan Line Steamers Ltd. (Cayzer, Irvine and Co., managers), Glasgow as CLAN MURRAY.
10.9.1897: Transferred to Charles W. Cayzer, James Mackenzie and David Rennie (Cayzer, Irvine and Co., managers), Glasgow.
1.7.1907: Managers became Cayzer, Irvine and Co. Ltd.
31.12.1909: Transferred to The Clan Line Steamers Ltd. (Cayzer, Irvine and Co. Ltd., managers), Glasgow.
23.10.1915: Requisitioned by the British government.
29.5.1917: Torpedoed and sunk by the German submarine UC 55 40 miles west by south of Fastnet in position 50.57 north by 10.12 west whilst on a voyage from Port Pirie to Belfast with a cargo of wheat. 64 lives were lost including her master and members of the crew of the CLAN CUMMING (1). Two were taken prisoner.
19.6.1917: Register closed.

CLAN MONROE (2) 1897-1905
O.N. 106097 4,853g 3,121n
400.1 x 50.2 x 27.8 feet.
T.3-cyl. by William Doxford and Sons Ltd., Sunderland; 437 NHP, 2,800 IHP, 12 knots.
3.6.1897: Launched by William Doxford and Sons Ltd., Sunderland (Yard No. 254).
12.7.1897: Registered in the ownership of The Clan Line Steamers Ltd. (Cayzer, Irvine and Co., managers), Glasgow as CLAN MONROE.
7.1897: Completed.
16.9.1897: Transferred to Sir Charles W. Cayzer, James McKenzie and David Rennie (Cayzer, Irvine and Co., managers), Glasgow.
1.7.1905: Wrecked at Slangkop Point, Cape Peninsula, South Africa whilst on a voyage from Glasgow and Liverpool to South African ports with general cargo.
3.10.1905: Register closed.

CLAN ROBERTSON (1) 1897-1922
O.N. 108684 4,826g 3,104n
400.2 x 50.2 x 27.7 feet.
T.3-cyl. by William Doxford and Sons Ltd., Sunderland; 437 NHP, 2,800 IHP, 12 knots.
17.7.1897: Launched by William Doxford and Sons Ltd., Sunderland (Yard No. 255).
30.8.1897: Registered in the ownership of The Clan Line Steamers Ltd. (Cayzer, Irvine and Co., managers), Glasgow as CLAN ROBERTSON.
9.1897: Completed.
10.9.1897: Transferred to Sir Charles W. Cayzer, James Mackenzie and David

Clan Murray (2) lying in Mossel Bay, South Africa, in March 1908. In *Clan Murray* and her sisters an unusual feature was derrick posts alongside both masts. It has been suggested these were provided because conventional derricks, rigged on the masts, would not have the necessary outreach over the harbour deck. *[Kevin O'Donoghue collection]*

The end of *Clan Monroe* (2), breaking up on the Cape Peninsula. *[Kevin O'Donoghue collection]*

There were some detail differences between the individual ships in the first group of Turret ships, including the crow's nest on the foremast of *Clan Robertson* (1). *[J. and M. Clarkson collection]*

Rennie (Cayzer, Irvine and Co., managers), Glasgow.

1.7.1907: Managers became Cayzer, Irvine and Co. Ltd.

31.12.1909: Transferred to The Clan Line Steamers Ltd. (Cayzer, Irvine and Co. Ltd., managers), Glasgow.

9.5.1917: Requisitioned by the British government until 11.1.1919.

18.8.1922: Register closed on sale to Kyosei Kisen K.K., Kobe, Japan and renamed KYOSEI MARU.

6.1.1924: Abandoned south of the Aleutian Islands in position 49.36 north by 179.02 east whilst on a voyage from Victoria and Vancouver, British Columbia to Yokohama with a cargo of lumber and wheat.

CLAN MACFARLANE (1) 1898-1915

O.N. 108742 4,823g 3,107n
400.5 x 50.2 x 27.6 feet.
T.3-cyl. by William Doxford and Sons Ltd., Sunderland; 437 NHP, 2,800 IHP, 12 knots.

6.5.1898: Launched by William Doxford and Sons Ltd., Sunderland (Yard No. 261).

23.6.1898: Registered in the ownership of The Clan Line Steamers Ltd. (Cayzer, Irvine and Co., managers), Glasgow as CLAN MACFARLANE.

7.1898: Completed.

24.6.1898: Transferred to Sir Charles W. Cayzer, James McKenzie and David Rennie (Cayzer, Irvine and Co., managers), Glasgow.

1.7.1907: Managers became Cayzer, Irvine and Co. Ltd.

27.12.1909: Transferred to The Clan Line Steamers Ltd. (Cayzer, Irvine and Co. Ltd., managers), Glasgow.

29.8.1914: Requisitioned as an Indian Expeditionary Force Transport until 7.12.1914.

30.12.1915: Torpedoed and sunk by the German submarine U 38 66 miles south east by south from Cape Martello, Crete, in position 34.50 north by 25.55 east on a voyage from Glasgow and Liverpool to Bombay with general cargo. 52 lives were lost, 24 survivors being picked up from their boats after seven and a half days and landed at Valetta by the steamer CROWN OF ARRAGON (4,500/1905).

7.2.1916: Register closed.

CLAN FERGUSON (1) 1898-1917

O.N. 108779 4,808g 3,107n
400.6 x 50.2 x 27.5 feet.
T.3-cyl. by Vickers, Sons and Maxim Ltd., Barrow-in-Furness; 282 NHP, 2,800 IHP, 11.5 knots.

4.10.1898: Launched by Vickers, Sons and Maxim Ltd., Barrow-in-Furness (Yard No. 267).

12.12.1898: Registered in the ownership of The Clan Line Steamers Ltd. (Cayzer, Irvine and Co., managers), Glasgow as CLAN FERGUSON.

16.12.1898: Transferred to Sir Charles W. Cayzer, James McKenzie and David Rennie (Cayzer, Irvine and Co., managers), Glasgow.

Clan Macfarlane (1). *[Nigel Farrell collection]*

Comparison of the views above shows that the Barrow-built *Clan Ferguson* (1) at some point lost the white line along the upper edge of the hull carried by most Clan Line Turrets.

    Clan Ferguson was sunk around midnight on 6th September 1917 in an area of the Mediterranean which was becoming increasingly dangerous, partly due to the belated introduction of a convoy system having made British waters less of a happy hunting ground for U-boats. Loss of life might well have been heavier than ten, *Clan Ferguson* sinking in seven minutes, but all the port boats got away. Captain Laird remained on board whilst she sank, but after swimming for half an hour in the dark reached a raft, which also rescued two other officers and five members of the crew. One of the boats took them from the raft, and all the 63 survivors were picked up in the morning by a patrol vessel and landed at Gibraltar. *[Upper: Ships in Focus; lower: J. and M. Clarkson collection]*

1.7.1907: Managers became Cayzer, Irvine and Co. Ltd.
31.12.1909: Transferred to The Clan Line Steamers Ltd. (Cayzer, Irvine and Co. Ltd., managers), Glasgow.
9.8.1917: Requisitioned by the British government.
6.9.1917: Torpedoed and sunk by the German submarine UB 49 15 miles north west of Cape Spartel in position 35.50 north by 06.10 west with the loss of 10 of her crew. She was on a voyage from Glasgow to Alexandria and Bombay via Gibraltar with coal and general cargo. Ten lives were lost.
28.9.1917: Register closed.

CLAN CUMMING (1) 1899-1925
O.N. 108797 4,808g 3,108n
400.6 x 50.2 x 27.5 feet.
T.3-cyl. by Vickers, Sons and Maxim Ltd., Barrow-in-Furness; 282 NHP, 2,800 IHP, 11.5 knots.
26.1.1899: Launched by Vickers, Sons and Maxim Ltd., Barrow-in-Furness (Yard No. 268).
24.2.1899: Registered in the ownership of The Clan Line Steamers Ltd. (Cayzer, Irvine and Co., managers), Glasgow as CLAN CUMMING.
25.2.1899: Transferred to Sir Charles W. Cayzer, James Mackenzie and David Rennie (Cayzer, Irvine and Co., managers), Glasgow.
1.7.1907: Managers became Cayzer, Irvine and Co. Ltd.
31.12.1909: Transferred to The Clan Line Steamers Ltd. (Cayzer, Irvine and Co. Ltd., managers), Glasgow.
17.1.1917: Requisitioned by the British government until 12.3.1919.
5.11.1917: Seriously damaged by a torpedo from the German submarine UB 55 20 miles south west of the Lizard whilst on a voyage from Baltimore to Brest with a cargo of copper, steel and timber. Thirteen lives were lost, and the escorting armed trawler HMS ISABELLA FOWLIE took off the survivors. Subsequently towed to Falmouth and beached. Later refloated by the Western Marine Salvage Company, taken to Liverpool for repair, and returned to service.

Above: *Clan Cumming* (1). *[J. and M. Clarkson collection]*
Middle: *Clan Cumming* (1) in Eastham Locks, Manchester Ship Canal. The masts of Clan's Turrets were telescopic and could be readily lowered to pass under the Ship Canal's bridges. *[Kevin O'Donoghue collection]*
Bottom left: *Clan Cumming* (1) beached following a torpedo attack in November 1917.
Bottom right: The 30-foot by 25-foot wooden patch fitted at Falmouth over the hole made by a torpedo in the hull of *Clan Cumming* (1). The patch allowed her to be taken in easy stages to Liverpool for repair. *[Bottom left and right: The Clan Line in the Great War, Archibald Hurd]*

Clan Colquhoun (1). *[J. and M. Clarkson collection]*

7.4.1925: Register closed on sale to Società Anonima Cantiere Olivo, Genoa, Italy, and renamed ETTORE.
1926: Sold to Tito Campanella Società Anonima., Genoa, Italy, and renamed ELISA CAMPANELLA.
5.2.1932: Arrived at Savona to be broken up.

TURRETS BATCH TWO
Clan's Turrets represented a considerable size increase over anything they had previously owned, and at 440 feet this batch of three were the largest of the type owned. The three cost a total of £184,000.

CLAN COLQUHOUN (1) 1899-1925
O.N. 111187 5,856g 3,760n
440.0 x 51.6 x 28.9 feet.
T.3-cyl. by William Doxford and Sons Ltd., Sunderland; 477 NHP, 3,080 IHP, 11.5 knots.
11.3.1899: Launched by William Doxford and Sons Ltd., Sunderland (Yard No. 269).
4.1899: Completed.
2.5.1899: Registered in the ownership of The Clan Line Steamers Ltd. (Cayzer, Irvine and Co., managers), Glasgow as CLAN COLQUHOUN.
26.5.1899: Transferred to Sir Charles W. Cayzer, James Mackenzie and David Rennie (Cayzer, Irvine and Co. Ltd., managers), Glasgow.
1.7.1907: Managers became Cayzer, Irvine and Co. Ltd.
15.5.1913: Transferred to The Clan Line Steamers Ltd. (Cayzer, Irvine and Co. Ltd., managers), Glasgow.
25.11.1916: Attacked with gunfire by the German submarine U 38 off Algeria whilst on a voyage from Liverpool to India, but fought off the attack.

13.4.1917: Requisitioned by the British government until 8.7.1919.
5.2.1925: Register closed on sale to Villain and Fassio, Genoa, Italy and renamed NASCO.
1927: Sold to Società Anonima Parodi and Corrado, Genoa and renamed CENGIO.
1929: Sold to Corrado Società Anonima di Navigazione, Genoa.
16.6.1929: Arrived at Genoa to be broken up.

CLAN FARQUHAR (1) 1899-1917
O.N. 111209 5,858g 3,757n
439.0 x 51.6 x 28.9 feet.

T.3-cyl. by William Doxford and Sons Ltd., Sunderland; 477 NHP, 3,080 IHP, 11.5 knots.
24.6.1899: Launched by William Doxford and Sons Ltd., Sunderland (Yard No. 271).
3.8.1899: Registered in the ownership of The Clan Line Steamers Ltd. (Cayzer, Irvine and Co., managers), Glasgow as CLAN FARQUHAR.
8.8.1899: Transferred to Sir Charles W. Cayzer, James McKenzie and David Rennie (Cayzer, Irvine and Co., managers), Glasgow.
10.1899: Completed.
1.7.1907: Managers became Cayzer, Irvine and Co. Ltd.

Clan Farquhar (1) at Hull in 1907. When torpedoed in February 1917 she sank so rapidly that only two boats could be launched, and there was heavy loss of life including the master and chief engineer. The second engineer was taken prisoner and spent some time as a prisoner-of-war in Austria until exchanged. *[Kevin O'Donoghue collection]*

15.5.1913: Transferred to The Clan Line Steamers Ltd. (Cayzer, Irvine and Co., managers), Glasgow.

26.2.1917: Torpedoed and sunk by the German submarine UB 43 80 miles north of Benghazi in position 33.30 north by 20.50 east whilst on a voyage from Calcutta to London with a cargo of cotton, jute and tea with the loss of 49 lives. The survivors were picked up from their boats by HMS VERBENA and landed at Malta.

22.3.1917: Register closed.

CLAN URQUHART (1) 1899-1929

O.N. 111219 5,855g 3,757n
440.0 x 51.6 x 28.9 feet.
T.3-cyl. by William Doxford and Sons Ltd., Sunderland; 477 NHP, 3,080 IHP, 11.5 knots.

22.8.1899: Launched by William Doxford and Sons Ltd., Sunderland (Yard No. 272).

23.9.1899: Registered in the ownership of The Clan Line Steamers Ltd. (Cayzer, Irvine and Co., managers), Glasgow as CLAN URQUHART.

10.10.1899: Transferred to Sir Charles W. Cayzer, James Mackenzie and David Rennie (Cayzer, Irvine and Co., managers), Glasgow.

1.7.1907: Managers became Cayzer, Irvine and Co. Ltd.

15.5.1913: Transferred to The Clan Line Steamers Ltd. (Cayzer, Irvine and Co. Ltd., managers), Glasgow.

30.6.1917: Requisitioned by the British government until 26.7.1919.

21.2.1929: Sold to Emil R. Retzlaff, Stettin, Germany for £12,000 and renamed GENERALDIREKTOR SONNENSCHEIN.

4.1931: Sold to W. Kuntsmann, Stettin, Germany.

1.1933: Sold to Stettiner Oderwerke A.G., Stettin and broken up during the third quarter of 1933.

TURRETS BATCH THREE

The Turrets were rumoured to have stability problems, and two of this batch capsized, Clan Gordon (2) and Clan Ranald (2). Investigations by Doxford after the latter capsized in 1909 led to revised instructions for stowing cargo, which specified that the lower deck had to be loaded first, irrespective of where on the voyage this cargo was destined. Understandably, this reduced the appeal of Turrets for liner companies like Clan.

CLAN ALPINE (2) 1899-1917

O.N. 111232 3,587g 2,285n
355.0 x 45.6 x 24.7 feet.
T.3-cyl. by William Doxford and Sons Ltd., Sunderland; 342 NHP, 2,080 IHP, 11 knots.

22.9.1899: Launched by William Doxford and Sons Ltd., Sunderland (Yard No. 273).

10.1899: Completed.

Clan Urquhart (1) in the Manchester Ship Canal. *[Kevin O'Donoghue collection]*

Clan Alpine (2) berthed (above) and at anchor (below). The photograph above emphasises the ungainly hull form of the Turrets. Note also, particularly in the photograph below, how the white band on the hull is parallel to the waterline, rather than following the contour of the forecastle as in the *Clan Urquhart* (1) in the top photograph. *[Above: Kevin O'Donoghue collection; below: Newall Dunn collection]*

7.11.1899: Registered in the ownership of The Clan Line Steamers Ltd. (Cayzer, Irvine and Co., managers), Glasgow as CLAN ALPINE.

22.11.1899: Transferred to Sir Charles W. Cayzer, James McKenzie and David Rennie (Cayzer, Irvine and Co., managers), Glasgow.

The batch three Turret *Clan Fraser* (2) anchored in Table Bay with a fleet of sailing ships. *[Martin Leendertz Collection/Ship Society of South Africa]*

1.7.1907: Managers became Cayzer, Irvine and Co. Ltd.
15.5.1913: Transferred to The Clan Line Steamers Ltd. (Cayzer, Irvine and Co. Ltd., managers), Glasgow.
29.10.1915: Requisitioned by the British government.
9.6.1917: Torpedoed and sunk by the German submarine U 60 40 miles north by east half east of Muckle Flugga whilst on a voyage from the Tyne to Archangel. Eight lives were lost.
22.6.1917: Register closed.

CLAN FRASER (2) 1900-1919
O.N. 111259 3,589g 2,285n
355.0 x 45.6 x 24.7 feet.
T.3-cyl. by William Doxford and Sons Ltd., Sunderland; 342 NHP, 2,080 IHP, 11 knots.
30.3.1900: Launched by William Doxford and Sons Ltd., Sunderland (Yard No. 276).
19.5.1900: Registered in the ownership of The Clan Line Steamers Ltd. (Cayzer, Irvine and Co., managers), Glasgow as CLAN FRASER.
9.6.1900: Transferred to Sir Charles W. Cayzer, James McKenzie and David Rennie (Cayzer, Irvine and Co., managers), Glasgow.
1.7.1907: Managers became Cayzer, Irvine and Co. Ltd.
15.5.1913: Transferred to The Clan Line Steamers Ltd. (Cayzer, Irvine and Co. Ltd., managers), Glasgow.
25.5.1917: Requisitioned by the British government until 3.5.1919.
26.11.1919: Register closed on sale to A.S. and A.G. Coutsodontis, Syra, Greece for £142,500 and renamed AGHIA PARASKEVI.
20.2.1920: Capsized and foundered off Cape St. Thomas, Brazil whilst on a voyage from Buenos Aires to Malta with a cargo of flour and coal. 32 lives were lost.

CLAN GORDON (2) 1900-1919
O.N. 111269 3,589g 2,286n
355.0 x 45.6 x 24.7 feet.
T.3-cyl. by William Doxford and Sons Ltd., Sunderland; 342 NHP, 2,080 IHP, 11 knots.

Photographed in a North American port, probably Boston, *Clan Gordon* (2) helped confirm the propensity of Turrets to capsize with her loss in July 1919. Already exhibiting a five degree list, this increased dramatically to 70 degrees when the helm was put over. She then turned turtle, but slowly enough for the crew to be able to get on to her upturned bottom and wait to be rescued. *[J. and M. Clarkson collection]*

12.5.1900: Launched by William Doxford and Sons Ltd., Sunderland (Yard No. 277).
13.6.1900: Registered in the ownership of The Clan Line Steamers Ltd. (Cayzer, Irvine and Co., managers), Glasgow as CLAN GORDON.
26.6.1900: Delivered.
28.8.1900: Transferred to Sir Charles W. Cayzer, James McKenzie and David Rennie (Cayzer, Irvine and Co., managers), Glasgow.
1.7.1907: Managers became Cayzer, Irvine and Co. Ltd.
15.5.1913: Transferred to The Clan Line Steamers Ltd. (Cayzer, Irvine and Co. Ltd., managers), Glasgow.
8.12.1917: Requisitioned by the British government until 5.7.1919.
30.7.1919: Capsized and sank 140 miles south east of Cape Hatteras, North Carolina whilst on a voyage from New York to Darien with a cargo of case oil and wax. Four of her crew were lost.
12.9.1919: Register closed.

CLAN LAMONT (2) 1900-1928
O.N. 111280 3,594g 2,286n
355.0 x 45.6 x 24.7 feet.
T.3-cyl. by William Doxford and Sons Ltd., Sunderland; 342 NHP, 2,080 IHP, 11 knots.
16.6.1900: Launched by William Doxford and Sons Ltd., Sunderland (Yard No. 278).
24.7.1900: Registered in the ownership of The Clan Line Steamers Ltd. (Cayzer, Irvine and Co., managers), Glasgow as CLAN LAMONT.
28.8.1900: Transferred to Sir Charles W. Cayzer, James Mackenzie and David Rennie (Cayzer, Irvine and Co., managers), Glasgow.
1.7.1907: Managers became Cayzer, Irvine and Co. Ltd.
15.5.1913: Transferred to The Clan Line Steamers Ltd. (Cayzer, Irvine and Co. Ltd., managers), Glasgow.
21.9.1917: Requisition by the British government until 14.8.1919.
3.9.1928: Towed into Port Elizabeth by the steamer PAPIPAKI (7,166/1914) following engine failure whilst on a voyage from

Clan Lamont (2), showing how far the davits had to overhang the harbour deck in the Turret design. *[Ships in Focus]*

Madagascar, Natal and East London to Algoa Bay. One member of the crew was lost. Following temporary repairs she returned to the United Kingdom.
12.1928: Sold to P. and W. Maclellan for £6,450.
5.12.1928: Register closed.
1.1929: Delivered to Bo'ness for breaking up.

CLAN RANALD (2) 1900-1909
O.N. 111290 3,596 2,285n
355.0 x 45.6 x 24.7 feet.
T.3-cyl. by William Doxford and Sons Ltd., Sunderland; 342 NHP, 2,080 IHP, 11 knots.
31.7.1900: Launched by William Doxford and Sons Ltd., Sunderland (Yard No. 279).
6.9.1900: Registered in the ownership of The Clan Line Steamers Ltd. (Cayzer, Irvine and Co., managers), Glasgow as CLAN RANALD.
20.9.1900: Transferred to Sir Charles W. Cayzer, James McKenzie and David Rennie (Cayzer, Irvine and Co., managers), Glasgow.
1.7.1907: Managers became Cayzer, Irvine and Co. Ltd.
31.1.1909: Capsized and sank off Edithburgh, Spencer Gulf, South Australia whilst on a voyage from Adelaide to Durban, East London and Cape Town with a cargo of flour and wheat. Forty lives were lost. Some seventy tons of bunker coal was stowed on the Turret deck.
22.2.1910: Register closed.

Clan Ranald (2). The lower deck was sometimes referred to as the harbour deck. As this photograph shows, at certain states of loading it was indeed at the same level as a quay. *[Nigel Farrell collection]*

Clan Stuart (2) wrecked in Simon's Bay. Over 90 years later, the tops of her cylinders are still visible. *[J. and M. Clarkson collection]*

CLAN STUART (2) 1900-1914 Turret
O.N. 113911 3,594g 2,285n
355.0 x 45.6 x 24.7 feet.
T.3-cyl. by William Doxford and Sons Ltd., Sunderland; 342 NHP, 2,080 IHP, 11 knots.
8.9.1900: Launched by William Doxford and Sons Ltd., Sunderland (Yard No. 280).
9.10.1900: Registered in the ownership of The Clan Line Steamers Ltd. (Cayzer, Irvine and Co., managers), Glasgow as CLAN STUART.
18.12.1900: Sold to Charles W. Cayzer, James Mackenzie and David Rennie (Cayzer, Irvine and Co., managers), Glasgow.
1.7.1907: Managers became Cayzer, Irvine and Co. Ltd.
15.5.1913: Transferred to The Clan Line Steamers Ltd. (Cayzer, Irvine and Co. Ltd., managers), Glasgow.
3.8.1914: Requisitioned by the British government.
21.11.1914: Wrecked in Simon's Bay, False Bay, Cape Colony, South Africa whilst on a voyage from Glasgow to Simonstown with a cargo of coal.
24.9.1915: Register closed.

CLAN CAMERON (2) 1900-1917
O.N. 113919 3,595g 2,285n
355.0 x 45.6 x 24.7 feet.
T.3-cyl. by William Doxford and Sons Ltd., Sunderland; 342 NHP, 2,080 IHP, 11 knots.
11.10.1900: Launched by William Doxford and Sons Ltd., Sunderland (Yard No. 281) as CLAN MACRAE.
12.11.1900: Registered in the ownership of The Clan Line Steamers Ltd. (Cayzer, Irvine and Co., managers), Glasgow as CLAN CAMERON.
18.12.1900: Transferred to Sir Charles W. Cayzer, James McKenzie and David Rennie (Cayzer, Irvine and Co., managers), Glasgow.
1.7.1907: Managers became Cayzer, Irvine and Co. Ltd.
15.5.1913: Transferred to The Clan Line Steamers Ltd. (Cayzer, Irvine and Co. Ltd., managers), Glasgow.
11.7.1917: Requisitioned by the British government.
22.12.1917: Torpedoed and sunk by the German submarine UB 58 23 miles south west by south half south from Portland Bill whilst on a voyage from Chittagong to London and Dundee with a cargo of tea and jute. She was steaming slowly having previously been damaged by a collision with the escorting destroyer HMS ACASTA. The whole of the crew were rescued by the tug VULCAN.
8.1.1918: Register closed.

TURRETS BATCH FOUR
The prices of this batch of Turrets reflected the depression in shipping which followed the Boer War. The first three,

Right: *Clan Stuart* (2) at Cape Town. *[Martin Leendertz collection/Ship Society of South Africa]*
Below: A mysterious photo showing a stranding of *Clan Stuart* (2) prior to her loss in 1914. The puzzle is why her funnel colours have been painted out. *[Kevin O'Donoghue collection]*

ordered in April 1901, cost £53,000; by the time Clan Lindsay *and* Clan Chattan *were ordered in August 1901, the price had fallen to £49,000, whilst* Clan Forbes *and* Clan Macneil *cost £47,000 when ordered in October 1902. This was the most unfortunate group of Turrets, with only two of the seven surviving the First World War.*

CLAN GRANT (2) 1902-1914
O.N. 115683 3,948g 2,505n
360.4 x 48.1 x 24.5 feet.
T.3-cyl. by William Doxford and Sons Ltd., Sunderland; 394 NHP, 2,080 IHP, 11 knots.
12.4.1902: Launched by William Doxford and Sons Ltd., Sunderland (Yard No. 296).
21.5.1902: Registered in the ownership of the Clan Line Steamers Ltd. (Cayzer, Irvine and Co., managers), Glasgow as CLAN GRANT.
27.10.1902: Transferred to Sir Charles W. Cayzer, James McKenzie and David Rennie (Cayzer, Irvine and Co., managers), Glasgow.
1.7.1907: Managers became Cayzer, Irvine and Co. Ltd.

Two photographs of *Clan Grant* (2) on charter to George H. Scales. She was to become the second Clan Line victim of SMS *Emden*. *[Ian J. Farquhar collection]*

15.5.1913: Transferred to the Clan Line Steamers Ltd. (Cayzer, Irvine and Co. Ltd., managers), Glasgow.
16.10.1914: Captured and sunk with gunfire by the German cruiser EMDEN 150 miles south west of Minicoy, Maldive Islands whilst on a voyage from Liverpool to Colombo, Madras and Calcutta with general cargo. Her crew landed at Cochin.
27.10.1914: Register closed.

CLAN SHAW (2) 1902-1917
O.N. 115691 3,943g 2,503n
360.0 x 48.1 x 24.5 feet.
T.3-cyl. by William Doxford and Sons Ltd., Sunderland; 394 NHP, 2,080 IHP, 11 knots.
10.5.1902: Launched by William Doxford and Sons Ltd., Sunderland (Yard No. 297).
20.6.1902: Registered in the ownership of The Clan Line Steamers Ltd. (Cayzer, Irvine and Co., managers), Glasgow as CLAN SHAW.
27.10.1902: Transferred to Charles W. Cayzer, James Mackenzie and David Rennie (Cayzer, Irvine and Co., managers), Glasgow.
1.7.1907: Managers became Cayzer, Irvine and Co. Ltd.
13.5.1913: Transferred to The Clan Line Steamers Ltd. (Cayzer, Irvine and Co. Ltd., managers), Glasgow.
23.1.1917: Mined eight miles north east of St. Andrews and although beached at the entrance to the River Tay became a total loss. She was on a voyage from Calcutta to Dundee with a cargo of jute. Two lives were lost. The mine was laid the previous day by the German submarine UC 29.
6.2.1917: Register closed.

The second Turret named *Clan Shaw*. *[J. and M. Clarkson collection]*

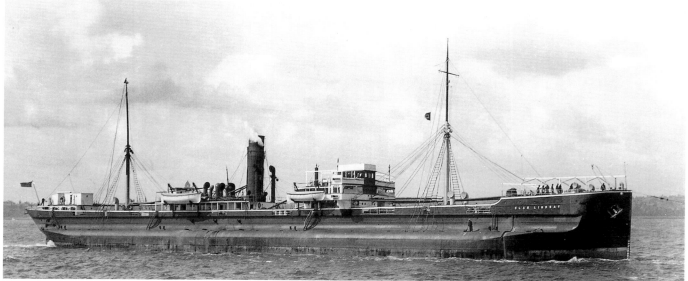

Middle: *Clan Leslie* photographed on the River Clyde by W. Robertson. *[Kevin O'Donoghue collection]*
Bottom: A particularly fine study of the Turret *Clan Lindsay* (2). A crew member has ventured on to the harbour deck which, unlike in former ships, no longer has the protection of rails. It was proposed that this deck could be used for cargo, especially timber. Note too how the ratlines from the masts are secured to the outboard edge of this deck. *[J. and M. Clarkson collection]*

CLAN LESLIE 1902-1916

O.N. 115697 3,937g 2,499n
359.8 x 48.1 x 24.5 feet.
T.3-cyl. by William Doxford and Sons Ltd., Sunderland; 394 NHP, 2,080 IHP, 11 knots.
20.6 1902: Launched by William Doxford and Sons Ltd., Sunderland (Yard No. 298).
24.7.1902: Registered in the ownership of The Clan Line Steamers Ltd. (Cayzer, Irvine and Co., managers), Glasgow as CLAN LESLIE.
9.5.1903: Transferred to Sir Charles W. Cayzer, James McKenzie and David Rennie (Cayzer, Irvine and Co., managers), Glasgow.
1.7.1907: Managers became Cayzer, Irvine and Co. Ltd.
15.5.1913: Transferred to The Clan Line Steamers Ltd. (Cayzer, Irvine and Co. Ltd., managers), Glasgow.
22.8.1915: Rescued the crew of the steamer PALMGROVE (3,100/1896) which had been torpedoed by the German submarine U 38, 58 miles west of the Isles of Scilly, and was herself attacked by the submarine, which was driven off by gunfire and the arrival of a naval vessel.
4.11.1916: Torpedoed and sunk by the German submarine UB 43 200 miles east by half south from Malta in position 35.56 north by 18.37 east with the loss of three of the crew. She was on a voyage from Bombay to London with general cargo including tea and jute.
21.11.1916: Register closed.

CLAN LINDSAY (2) 1902-1931

O.N. 115704 3,935g 2,499n
360.2 x 48.1 x 24.5 feet.
T.3-cyl. by William Doxford and Sons Ltd., Sunderland; 394 NHP, 2,080 IHP, 11 knots.
25.7.1902: Launched by William Doxford and Sons Ltd., Sunderland (Yard No. 299).
28.8.1902: Registered in the ownership of The Clan Line Steamers Ltd. (Cayzer, Irvine and Co., managers), Glasgow as CLAN LINDSAY.
9.1902: Completed.
9.5.1903: Transferred to Sir Charles W. Cayzer, James Mackenzie and David Rennie (Cayzer, Irvine and Co., managers), Glasgow.
1.7.1907: Managers became Cayzer, Irvine and Co. Ltd.
15.5.1913: Transferred to The Clan Line Steamers Ltd. (Cayzer, Irvine and Co. Ltd., managers), Glasgow.
3.5.1916: Attacked with gunfire by the German submarine U 20 whilst in the Bay of Biscay but returned fire from her 4.7 inch gun and the submarine broke off the attack.
4.5.1917: Requisitioned by the British government until 9.4.1919.
21.1.1931: Arrived at Inverkeithing to be broken up by T.W. Ward Ltd., Sheffield.
23.3.1931: Breaking up began.
20.10.1931: Register closed.

CLAN CHATTAN (1) 1902-1930

O.N. 115711 3,938g 2,500n
359.8 x 48.1 x 24.5 feet.
T.3-cyl. by William Doxford and Sons Ltd., Sunderland; 394 NHP, 2,080 IHP, 11 knots.
3.9.1902: Launched by William Doxford and Sons Ltd., Sunderland (Yard No. 300).
25.9.1902: Registered in the ownership of The Clan Line Steamers Ltd. (Cayzer, Irvine and Co., managers), Glasgow as CLAN CHATTAN.
10.1902: Completed.
9.5.1903: Transferred to Sir Charles W. Cayzer, James Mackenzie and David Rennie (Cayzer, Irvine and Co., managers), Glasgow.
1.7.1907: Managers became Cayzer, Irvine and Co. Ltd.
15.5.1913: Transferred to The Clan Line Steamers Ltd. (Cayzer, Irvine and Co. Ltd., managers), Glasgow.
31.7.1917: Requisitioned by the British government until 14.5.1919.
1930: Sold to P. and W. MacLellan Ltd. for £4,075 to be broken up at Bo'ness.
23.12.1930: Arrived.
11.2.1931: Register closed.

CLAN FORBES (2) 1903-1918

O.N. 115762 3,946g 2,516n
360.3 x 48.1 x 24.5 feet.
T.3-cyl. William Doxford and Sons Ltd., Sunderland; 394 NHP, 2,080 IHP, 11 knots.
25.4.1903: Launched by William Doxford and Sons Ltd., Sunderland (Yard No. 306).

Top: *Clan Chattan* (1) at Cape Town. *[Ian J. Farquhar collection]*
Bottom: Discharging Australian wool at Calais, *Clan Chattan* (1) shows one of the disadvantages of the Turret hull and what passed for a poop in these early Turrets. *[Kevin O'Donoghue collection]*

Clan Forbes (2) on trials. She has a white forecastle, seen in few other photographs of Clan's Turrets.

Two members of her Lascar crew were lost and several injured when *Clan Forbes* was torpedoed in the Mediterranean during June 1918, but the death toll could have been much worse. The ship, travelling at ten knots when hit, sank within six minutes. Her boats were launched, but in the heavy sea that was running one was washed on to the harbour deck and off again, capsizing in the process and trapping the 16 men previously on board. All but one managed to get out, and he had a remarkable escape when the boat was smashed by one of the escorting armed trawlers coming to the ship's aid. Another boat with 27 men on board also capsized, but fortunately there were rafts in the vicinity, washed off the *Clan Forbes'* deck, and the escorting trawlers rescued the survivors from these and landed them at Alexandria. *[J. and M. Clarkson collection]*

19.5.1903: Registered in the ownership of The Clan Line Steamers Ltd. (Cayzer, Irvine and Co., managers), Glasgow as CLAN FORBES.
6.1903: Completed.
1.7.1907: Managers became Cayzer, Irvine and Co. Ltd.
17.2.1909: Transferred to Sir Charles W. Cayzer, James McKenzie and David Rennie (Cayzer, Irvine and Co. Ltd., managers), Glasgow.
15.5.1913: Transferred to The Clan Line Steamers Ltd. (Cayzer, Irvine and Co. Ltd., managers), Glasgow.
6.1.1917: Requisitioned by the British government.
9.6.1918: Torpedoed and sunk by the German submarine UB 105 115 miles west north west of Alexandria in position 31.55 north by 27.50 east. Two lives were lost, the others being landed at Alexandria. She was on a voyage from Newport, Monmouthshire to Port Said with a cargo of coal.
11.7.1918: Register closed.

CLAN MACNEIL (2) 1903-1918
O.N. 115770 3,939g 2,504n
360.1 x 48.1 x 24.5 feet.
T.3-cyl. by William Doxford and Sons Ltd., Sunderland; 394 NHP, 2,080 IHP, 11 knots.
13.5.1903: Launched by William Doxford and Sons Ltd., Sunderland (Yard No. 307).
17.6.1903: Registered in the ownership of The Clan Line Steamers Ltd. (Cayzer,

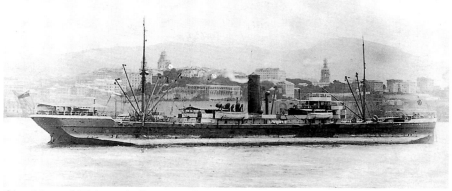

Clan Macneil (2) in an Italian port. *[Kevin O'Donoghue collection]*

Irvine and Co., managers), Glasgow as CLAN MACNEIL.
7.1903: Completed.
5.5.1904: Transferred to Charles W. Cayzer, James Mackenzie and David Rennie (Cayzer, Irvine and Co., managers), Glasgow.
1.7.1907: Managers became Cayzer, Irvine and Co. Ltd.
15.5.1913: Transferred to The Clan Line Steamers Ltd. (Cayzer, Irvine and Co. Ltd., managers), Glasgow.
4.2.1916: Requisitioned by the British government.
6.8.1918: Torpedoed and sunk by the German submarine UC 34 ten miles north of Alexandria whilst on a voyage from Karachi to Marseilles in convoy with a cargo of grain and onions. No lives were lost.
1.10.1918: Register closed.

TURRET BATCH FIVE
In January 1901 Clan placed its largest order yet with Doxfords, for six Turrets slightly larger than the previous batch at £53,500 each. However, a depression in the freight market saw three cancelled within months.

CLAN MACDOUGALL (1) 1904-1918
O.N. 119184 4,710g 2,976n
385.2 x 50.1 x 26.3 feet.
T.3-cyl. by William Doxford and Sons Ltd., Sunderland; 504 NHP, 2,800 IHP, 11.5 knots.
12.10.1904: Launched by William Doxford and Sons Ltd., Sunderland (Yard No. 325).
18.11.1904: Registered in the ownership of The Clan Line Steamers Ltd. (Cayzer,

Irvine and Co., managers), Glasgow as
CLAN MACDOUGALL.
12.1904: Completed.
1.7.1907: Managers became Cayzer, Irvine
and Co. Ltd.
21.12.1904: Transferred to Sir Charles W.
Cayzer, James McKenzie and David
Rennie (Cayzer, Irvine and Co. Ltd.,
managers), Glasgow.
15.5.1913: Transferred to The Clan Line
Steamers Ltd. (Cayzer, Irvine and Co. Ltd.,
managers), Glasgow.
23.2.1917: Requisitioned by the British
government until 10.3.1918.
15.3.1918: Torpedoed and sunk by the
German submarine UB 49 60 miles south east
by east half east from Cape Carbonara,
Sardinia whilst on a voyage from Naples to
Bizerta in ballast. Her master and 32 crew
were lost after taking to the boats. The
surviving 42 landed in Sardinia.
13.4.1918: Register closed.

CLAN MACNAB (2) 1905-1918
O.N. 119199 4,675g 2,952n
385.1 x 50.0 x 26.3 feet.
T.3-cyl. by William Doxford and Sons Ltd.,
Sunderland; 504 NHP, 2,800 IHP, 11.5 knots.
22.11.1904: Launched by William Doxford
and Sons Ltd., Sunderland (Yard No. 327).
6.1.1905: Registered in the ownership of The
Clan Line Steamers Ltd. (Cayzer, Irvine and
Co., managers), Glasgow as CLAN
MACNAB.
31.10.1907: Transferred to Charles W.
Cayzer, James Mackenzie and David Rennie
(Cayzer, Irvine and Co., managers), Glasgow.
15.5.1913: Transferred to The Clan Line
Steamers Ltd. (Cayzer, Irvine and Co.,
managers), Glasgow.
1.7.1907: Managers became Cayzer, Irvine
and Co. Ltd.
30.1.1917: Requisitioned by the British
government until 1.8.1918.
4.8.1918: Torpedoed and sunk by the German
submarine U 113 14 miles north north west
from the Pendeen Lighthouse whilst on a
ballast voyage from Plymouth to Glasgow in
convoy. 22 lives were lost, the survivors
being rescued by the Belgian steamer
KASBEK (2,716/1888).
16.8.1918: Register closed.

CLAN MACLEAN (2) 1905-1919
O.N. 121211 4,676g 2,952n
385.2 x 50.1 x 26.3 feet.
T.3-cyl. by William Doxford and Sons Ltd.,
Sunderland; 504 NHP, 2,800 IHP, 11.5 knots.
23.1.1905: Launched by William Doxford
and Sons Ltd., Sunderland (Yard No. 329).
2.1905: Completed.
2.3.1905: Registered in the ownership of The
Clan Line Steamers Ltd. (Cayzer, Irvine and
Co., managers), Glasgow as CLAN
MACLEAN.
5.10.1905: Transferred to Charles W. Cayzer,
James Mackenzie and David Rennie (Cayzer,
Irvine and Co., managers), Glasgow.

Clan Macdougall (1) was the first of the group of three batch five Turrets. All had a proper poop. *[Kevin O'Donoghue collection]*

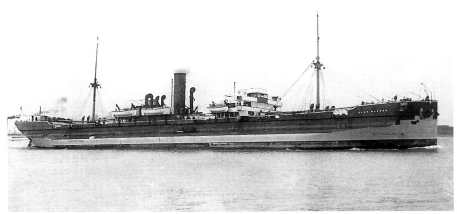
Clan Macnab (2). It appears that one of her freeing ports has been removed, probably to facilitate cargo handling. *[Roy Fenton collection]*

Clan Maclean (2) at Manchester. *[C. Downs/Kevin O'Donoghue collection]*

On a voyage from Calcutta to Naples on 26th May 1917 *Clan Graham* (2) had an encounter with a German submarine which she claimed was disguised as a patrol vessel, even carrying a dummy funnel from which smoke was coming. In her next meeting with a U-boat in March 1918 she was so seriously damaged that the British government, in the person of the Shipping Controller, took her over, having paid out war risk insurance. Clan Line bought her back, only to lose her again following a collision at the mouth of the River Scheldt in 1920. *[J. and M. Clarkson collection]*

1.7.1907: Managers became Cayzer, Irvine and Co. Ltd.
15.5.1913: Transferred to The Clan Line Steamers Ltd. (Cayzer, Irvine and Co. Ltd., managers), Glasgow.
29.3.1917: Requisitioned by the British government until 16.4.1919.
23.11.1919: Wrecked near Mafamede Island whilst on a voyage from Liverpool via Delagoa Bay to Kilindini with a cargo of coal. No lives were lost.
2.2.1920: Register closed.

TURRET FINALE
Turrets were successful partly because they exploited loopholes in regulations for calculating dues for harbours and, particularly, transiting the Suez Canal. Not surprisingly, these loopholes were closed, and with the Turrets propensity to capsize occasionally, their popularity waned, although they were delivered until 1911. These three were Clan's last batch, two giving very respectable 27 years' of service.

CLAN GRAHAM (2) 1907-1918/ 1919-1920
O.N. 124211 5,213g 3,289n
400.2 x 52.1 x 27.5 feet.
T.3-cyl. by William Doxford and Sons Ltd., Sunderland; 504 NHP, 2,800 IHP, 11 knots.
1919: T.3-cyl. made by Mackie and Baxter Ltd., Glasgow in 1917; 557 NHP.
24.7.1907: Launched by William Doxford and Sons Ltd., Sunderland (Yard No. 331).

20.8.1907: Registered in the ownership of The Clan Line Steamers Ltd. (Cayzer, Irvine and Co. Ltd., managers), Glasgow as CLAN GRAHAM.
10.1907: Completed.
17.2.1909: Transferred to Sir Charles W. Cayzer, James Mackenzie and David Rennie (Cayzer, Irvine and Co. Ltd., managers), Glasgow.
23.3.1915: Transferred to The Clan Line Steamers Ltd. (Cayzer, Irvine and Co. Ltd., managers), Glasgow.
14.11.1915: Requisitioned by the British Government until 17.7.1918.
4.3.1918: Torpedoed by the German submarine UC 74 in Kasos Strait, 15 miles south south east of Cape Sidero, Crete whilst on a voyage from Avonmouth to Port Said in ballast, but although abandoned was reboarded and towed into Suda Bay and then Mudros. Three lives were lost.
2.10.1918: Registered in the ownership of the Shipping Controller (Sir Ernest W. Glover, manager), London.
6.8.1919: Re-acquired by The Clan Line Steamers Ltd. (Cayzer, Irvine and Co. Ltd., managers), Glasgow for £60,000. Towed by the Dutch tug WITTE ZEE to Rotterdam for repair by the Rotterdam Dry Dock Co. Ltd. and fitting with a new engine.
10.3.1920: Work completed.
11.11.1920: Collided in fog with the steamer CHOLMLEY (1,368/1880) in the Wielingen and beached on Rommelan

Bank near Vlissingen whilst on a voyage from Chittagong and London to Antwerp with general cargo.
13.11.1920: Heavily damaged when her cargo caught fire from oxy-acetylene cutting equipment being used in an effort to repair a hole in her hull.
25.11.1920: Refloated, taken to Antwerp and later declared a constructive total loss.
21.12.1922: Register closed on sale to ship breakers for £3,000.
1923: Broken up by Produits Métallurgiques S.A. at Antwerp during the first quarter. The almost-new engines and boiler were taken out, brought to Glasgow and used in CLAN MACILWRAITH (1).

CLAN SINCLAIR (2) 1907-1933
O.N. 124222 5,215g 3,291n
400.1 x 52.1 x 27.5 feet.
T.3-cyl. by William Doxford and Sons Ltd., Sunderland; 504 NHP, 2,800 IHP, 11 knots.
28.8.1907: Launched by William Doxford and Sons Ltd., Sunderland (Yard No. 333).
18.9.1907: Registered in the ownership of The Clan Line Steamers Ltd. (Cayzer, Irvine and Co. Ltd, managers), Glasgow as CLAN SINCLAIR.
10.1907: Completed.
15.9.1908: Transferred to Sir Charles W. Cayzer, James Mackenzie and David Rennie (Cayzer, Irvine and Co. Ltd., managers), Glasgow.
23.3.1915: Transferred to The Clan Line Steamers Ltd. (Cayzer, Irvine and Co. Ltd., managers), Glasgow.

18.4.1917: Attacked by gunfire from the German submarine U 43 in the North Atlantic whilst on a voyage from South Africa to Liverpool but when she returned fire the submarine broke off the engagement.
10.5.1917: Requisitioned by the British government until 27.3.1919.
10.1933: Sold to Hughes Bolckow and Co. Ltd., Blyth for demolition.

21.11.1933: Arrived at Blyth.
10.12.1933: Register closed.

CLAN BUCHANAN (2) 1907-1933
O.N. 124232 5,212g 3,288n
400.1 x 52.1 x 27.4 feet.
T.3-cyl. by William Doxford and Sons Ltd., Sunderland; 504 NHP, 2,800, 11 knots.
24.9.1907: Launched by William Doxford

and Sons Ltd., Sunderland (Yard No. 335).
17.10.1907: Registered in the ownership of The Clan Line Steamers Ltd. (Cayzer, Irvine and Co. Ltd, managers), Glasgow as CLAN BUCHANAN.
11.1907: Completed.
15.9.1908: Transferred to Sir Charles W. Cayzer, James Mackenzie and David Rennie (Cayzer, Irvine and Co. Ltd., managers), Glasgow.

Clan Sinclair (2). Although identical in length to the first batch of Turrets, the final vessels delivered to Clan had a lower profile, making them appear bigger. *[Ships in Focus]*

The last Turret built for Clan, and almost the last one to remain in the fleet, *Clan Buchanan* (2) is seen on the Mersey. Note how the white hull line is carried across the forecastle and poop on this ship, differently from the treatment on other Turrets. *[J. and M. Clarkson]*

A fine shot of a well-laden *Clan Macaulay* (1). Her war record was rather singular: between September 1915 and July 1917 she made no fewer than 116 voyages across the English Channel with 115,000 tons of supplies for the British Expeditionary Force. *[Glasgow University Archives DC/101/0145]*

23.3.1915: Transferred to The Clan Line Steamers Ltd. (Cayzer, Irvine and Co. Ltd., managers), Glasgow.
24.5.1917: Requisitioned by the British government until 14.9.1919.
29.10.1933: Arrived at Blyth to be broken up by Hughes Bolckow and Co. Ltd.
6.4.1934: Register closed.

CLAN MACAULAY AND SISTERS

Whilst the large fleet of turrets was being built up, more conventional hulls were being ordered, including two three-deck ships from Clan's original supplier, Stephen of Linthouse These cost £36,750, whilst the third of the class, from Blackwood and Gordon, was cheaper at £34,500. All three members of the class came through the First World War unscathed, although both Clan Macfadyen *and* Clan Maclaren *were attacked by submarines.*

CLAN MACAULAY (1) 1899-1929
O.N. 108800 2,834g 1,775n
326.0 x 40.2 x 23.7 feet.
T.3-cyl. by Alexander Stephen and Sons, Linthouse, Glasgow; 313 NHP.
27.2.1899: Launched by Alexander Stephen and Sons, Linthouse, Glasgow (Yard No. 381).
24.3.1899: Registered in the ownership of The Clan Line Steamers Ltd. (Cayzer, Irvine and Co., managers), Glasgow as CLAN MACAULAY.
24.3.1899: Transferred to Sir Charles W. Cayzer, James Mackenzie and David Rennie (Cayzer, Irvine and Co., managers), Glasgow.
1.4.1899: Ran trials and delivered.

9.9.1901: Transferred to The Clan Line Steamers Ltd. (Cayzer, Irvine and Co., managers), Glasgow.
1.7.1907: Managers became Cayzer, Irvine and Co. Ltd.
17.2.1909: Transferred to Sir Charles W. Cayzer, James Mackenzie and David Rennie (Cayzer, Irvine and Co. Ltd., managers), Glasgow.
31.12.1909: Transferred to The Clan Line Steamers Ltd. (Cayzer, Irvine and Co. Ltd., managers), Glasgow.
25.9.1915: In French Government service until 9.11.1915.
10.11.1915: In British and Italian government service until 8.2.1918.

17.6.1929: Register closed following sale to breakers for £6,750.
26.6.1929: Arrived at Charlestown, Fife to be broken up by the Alloa Shipbreaking Co. Ltd.
3.7.1929: Work began.

CLAN MACLAREN (1) 1899-1924
O.N. 111188 2,832g 1,775n
326.0 x 40.2 x 23.6 feet.
T.3-cyl. by Alexander Stephen and Sons, Linthouse, Glasgow; 313 NHP.
24.4.1899: Launched by Alexander Stephen and Sons, Linthouse, Glasgow (Yard No. 382).

Clan Maclaren (1). *[Ian J. Farquhar collection]*

19.5.1899: Registered in the ownership of The Clan Line Steamers Ltd. (Cayzer, Irvine and Co., managers), Glasgow as CLAN MACLAREN.
26.5.1899: Transferred to Sir Charles W. Cayzer, James Mackenzie and David Rennie (Cayzer, Irvine and Co., managers), Glasgow.
9.9.1901: Transferred to The Clan Line Steamers Ltd. (Cayzer, Irvine and Co., managers), Glasgow.
1.7.1907: Managers became Cayzer, Irvine and Co. Ltd.
17.2.1909: Transferred to Sir Charles W. Cayzer, James Mackenzie and David Rennie (Cayzer, Irvine and Co. Ltd., managers), Glasgow.
31.12.1909: Transferred to The Clan Line Steamers Ltd. (Cayzer, Irvine and Co. Ltd., managers), Glasgow.
11.8.1917: Requisitioned by the British government until 23.5.1919.
20.6.1918: Attacked by the German submarine U 100 in North Atlantic but avoided the torpedo by turning towards the submarine and attempting to ram.
14.3.1924: Register closed on sale to Kuribayashi Shosen K.K., Tokyo, Japan for £17,000 and renamed MURORAN MARU No. 6.
1933: Demolished in Japan during the second quarter.

CLAN MACFADYEN (1) 1899-1921
O.N. 111220 2,816g 1,755n
326.2 x 40.2 x 23.5 feet.
T.3-cyl. by Blackwood and Gordon, Port Glasgow; 317 NHP, 1,700 IHP, 12 knots.
9.8.1899: Launched by Blackwood and Gordon, Port Glasgow (Yard No. 241).
9.1899: Registered in the ownership of The Clan Line Steamers Ltd. (Cayzer, Irvine and Co., managers), Glasgow as CLAN MACFADYEN.
10.10.1899: Transferred to Sir Charles W. Cayzer, James Mackenzie and David Rennie (Cayzer, Irvine and Co., managers), Glasgow.
9.9.1901: Transferred to The Clan Line Steamers Ltd. (Cayzer, Irvine and Co., managers), Glasgow.
9.5.1903: Transferred to Sir Charles W. Cayzer, James Mackenzie and David Rennie (Cayzer, Irvine and Co., managers), Glasgow.
1.7.1907: Managers became Cayzer, Irvine and Co. Ltd.
31.12.1909: Transferred to The Clan Line Steamers Ltd. (Cayzer, Irvine and Co. Ltd., managers), Glasgow.
2.5.1916: Hit by gunfire from the German submarine U 20 in the Bay of Biscay 180 miles north west of Ushant but returned fire and escaped. She was on a voyage from Mauritius to London.
9.9.1916: Requisitioned by the British government until 27.2.1919.
3.9.1921: Register closed on sale to Yamamoto Shoji K.K., Amagasaki, Japan and renamed SHUNKA MARU.

Clan Macfadyen (1) had an odd adventure in 1921, when two of the three blades of her propellor broke off in the Atlantic whilst she was steaming from Chittagong to New York. It is said she steamed 600 miles to the nearest harbour in Bermuda on the one remaining blade, but this must have put great strain on her machinery. *[Ships in Focus]*

Precursor of the *Clan Mackinnon* class, *Clan Maclachlan* (1) was photographed off Penarth. Detail differences include a leaner funnel and no plating below the bridge wings. She was also slightly narrower. *[Kevin O'Donoghue collection]*

19.7.1932: Wrecked in position 37.03 north by 125.58 east whilst on a voyage from Tsingtao to Chemulpo, Korea with a cargo of salt.

CLAN MACKINNON CLASS AND A PRECURSOR
At 395 feet, these basically similar ships were the largest conventional ships for almost 20 years, although many of the Turrets were larger. Although the type has been referred to as the Clan Mackinnon *class,* Clan Maclachlan, *delivered from Linthouse three years earlier, was the first of the group.*

CLAN MACLACHLAN (1) 1900-1917
O.N. 111252 4,729g 3,008n
395.3 x 48.0 x 27.1 feet.
T.3-cyl. by Alexander Stephen and Sons, Linthouse, Glasgow; 398 NHP.
20.2.1900: Launched by Alexander Stephen and Sons, Linthouse, Glasgow (Yard No. 385).
5.4.1900: Registered in the ownership of The Clan Line Steamers Ltd. (Cayzer, Irvine and Co., managers), Glasgow as CLAN MACLACHLAN.
4.1900: Completed.
28.8.1900: Transferred to Sir Charles W. Cayzer, James Mackenzie and David Rennie (Cayzer, Irvine and Co., managers), Glasgow.
1.7.1907: Managers became Cayzer, Irvine and Co. Ltd.
15.5.1913: Transferred to The Clan Line Steamers Ltd. (Cayzer, Irvine and Co. Ltd., managers), Glasgow.
13.7.1915: Requisitioned as an Indian Expeditionary Force transport until 1.10.1915.
22.5.1917: Requisitioned by the British government.
19.7.1917: Sank following a collision with the Italian steamer EUROPA (7,870/1907) when both vessels were steaming without lights 60 miles south west of Cape Spartel. Six lives were lost. She was on a voyage from Cardiff to Gibraltar with general cargo and coal.
7.8.1917: Register closed.

THE SECOND MATE GOES BOATING

In 1911 C.A. Cahill joined Clan Macfadyen *(1) as second mate under Captain William Isaac Mason for a voyage to South and East Africa and then India. This is a lightly-edited extract from his account of his experiences which appeared in 'The Clansman' for Summer 1956.*

After discharge at East London we received orders to proceed to Ananalava and Majunga in Madagascar to load mangrove bark. Both ports were in a primitive stage of development. The bark in bags was carried down to the beaches by natives and stacked. In the south west monsoon dhows from the Malabar coast acted as lighters and were brought in empty towards the shore at high water and anchored at a pre-arranged depth. When the tide fell the natives carried the bags out to the dhows which, when loaded, awaited the next high water to come off to the ship. After loading at these ports we were still short of capacity and our adventures thereafter became curiouser and curiouser. A cable was received from head office telling us to proceed to position 17.05 south and 38.30 east where we would find 900 tons of bark stacked on the beach. Looking up our small scale chart of the East African coast, we saw the spot indicated was near the mouth of the Moebazi River.

On our way from Majunga Captain Isaac Mason thought it prudent to call at Quelimane in an effort to collect more information about the Moebazi River which appeared on our small chart to bristle with bars and reefs. We anchored off the town of Quelimane for 24 hours and contacted the harbour master, a Portuguese gentleman who informed us that the Moebazi River was easily navigable. He also added that we were neaped in Quelimane for three days.

We at last proceeded towards our position and on the way the master discussed the situation with me saying that he had little faith in the harbour master and that he would send me in a lifeboat to survey the place and seek out a passage between the bars. Accordingly, on Sunday 13th August 1911 we anchored four miles off the coast and prepared the boat with the necessary tackle; ten buoys being made of dunnage weighted with firebars and moorings of wire. The boat was watered and the master personally instructed the steward to see that the boat was properly provisioned for 48 hours. I had picked ten Lascar seamen to accompany me and after a hasty lunch we set off. All went well for the first mile when we encountered the first broken water where the boat commenced to behave in an alarming manner not assisted by the ten crude, eight-feet high, home-made buoys sticking up above the gunwales with a mass of moorings, all under the feet of inexpert oarsmen.

The shore approaches were guarded by an inner and outer bar, the seaward end of which overlapped, and as we approached the bars the sea was breaking and eight to ten feet of broken water threw the boat in all directions. I managed to take soundings as far as the bar and found that there was 15 to 12 feet all the way, this at high water. As the *Clan Macfadyen* was drawing 19 feet, I realised that our journey hadn't been necessary. The closer we approached the bars, the more violent became the motion of the boat and the confusion became more confounded when the home-made buoys joined in the dance and nearly knocked half the crew out. I gave orders to dump the lot, backed out to sea and baled the boat out properly. On the second attempt we shipped a lot of water, but made a better approach, crossed the bar and got into smooth water at the mouth of the river. I anchored the boat and thought that some refreshment would help us. The crew thought so too, and they were well provided with chappatis and curry. I opened my parcel - marmalade sandwiches, a piece of hard cheese and a ship's biscuit. The bottle, which I thought would be of whisky and water, I found to contain cold tea whereupon I cursed the steward heartily.

We all had a smoke and I pitched bits of biscuit into the water to see when the tide would turn - it flowed at about one and a half knots and didn't turn at all, due perhaps to the backwater formation. It was now getting dusk and I was anxious to make the ship before darkness fell. Hauling up the anchor, we paddled easily towards the bar in order to conserve our strength for the tussle in the broken water. At 11 pm the crew were tiring and a quarter of an hour later the boat shipped some very heavy water and was being washed towards the shore out of control. At about midnight we grounded and the boat turned over but we were able to salvage much of the boat's gear including a white-painted canvas package containing matches. It was not long before the Lascars had a fire going using driftwood and the boat's bottom boards. After drying out I made up my mind to reach Moebazi about one and a half miles away to gain assistance. Influenced by the cosiness of the fire and the weird shrieks and howls coming from the surrounding countryside, none of the crew would accompany me.

After crossing a black, stinking, muddy creek I eventually came upon a village surrounded by a number of poles with boxes on top and monkeys secured to them. As soon as I was scented or seen the most unearthly chattering and scrambling up and down the poles took place. The sleepy village awoke and I was interviewed by one I took to be the headman who led me to a hut and set a pot of stew on the fire. The meat was too small for sheep or goat and there were no rabbits, but it tasted good and I was too cold and hungry to worry about the niceties. It was whilst I was eating that the blanket wrapped around my host dropped a little and I saw that my host was in fact my hostess.

I awoke at daybreak and explained in mime what had happened and, after some food, accompanied by a score of natives I returned to the scene of our grounding. The Lascars were all asleep round the fire and the boat bottom up and damaged. The villagers soon had the boat righted and launched, patching up the damage with palm leaves and sticky black gum. The boat's crew and I waited all day for these patches to harden and when night came I resolved to make a start at sun up. My hostess detailed half a dozen men to help us, and these natives perched on the gunwale of the lifeboat between my rowers and paddled for dear life at the critical time crossing the bar, then dived overboard and swam ashore.

Captain Mason met me at the gangway and was very pleased to see me back, having been in ignorance of what had become of the boat. I told him my story and one of his remarks was 'Anyway, you had plenty of provisions.' I told him what I had been issued with and he sent for the steward and reprimanded him severely.

Returning to Quelimane we were instructed to rendezvous with the *Clan Alpine* (2) and discharge our 2,000 tons of bark into her holds. In turn we proceeded to Chittagong to load jute and tea for London.

In the fullness of time we arrived in Glasgow and I presented myself at 109 Hope Street. My losses, amounting to nine pounds and sixteen shillings for my uniform, were made good, and when Sir August Cayzer heard the yarn he ordered that I should have an extra fiver.

CLAN MACKINNON (2) 1903-1927

O.N. 115746 4,788g 3,049n
395.4 x 50.9 x 27.1 feet.
T.3-cyl. by Denny and Company,
Dumbarton; 252 NHP.
30.12.1902: Launched by William Denny
and Brothers, Dumbarton (Yard No. 675).
28.2.1903: Registered in the ownership of
The Clan Line Steamers Ltd. (Cayzer,
Irvine and Co., managers), Glasgow as
CLAN MACKINNON.
28.2.1903: Delivered at a cost of £64,000.
9.5.1903: Transferred to Sir Charles W.
Cayzer, James Mackenzie and David
Rennie (Cayzer, Irvine and Co.,
managers), Glasgow.
1.7.1907: Managers became Cayzer, Irvine
and Co. Ltd.
15.5.1913: Transferred to The Clan Line
Steamers Ltd. (Cayzer, Irvine and Co. Ltd.,
managers), Glasgow.
3.10.1917: Requisitioned by the British
government until 3.5.1919.
3.11.1927: Register closed on sale to
Aktiebolag Oceanfart (Lars Krogius,
manager), Helsingfors, Finland for
£16,000 and renamed HERAKLES.
1935: Sold to Stephens, Sutton Ltd.,
Newcastle-upon-Tyne for £11,000 to trade
in under the 'Scrap and Build Scheme'
1936: Sold to P. and W. MacLellan Ltd.
27.4.1936: Arrived at Bo'ness for
demolition.

Sold in 1927, *Clan Mackinnon* (2) went to the Finnish flag to become the *Herakles*.
But the UK had not seen the last of her. The British Shipping (Assistance) Act of
1935 encouraged owners to scrap old tonnage and build new with the promise of
a loan against every ship broken up. But the act did not specify whether the
scrapped ships had to be long term units of the owner's fleet, or even British.
Hence a number of foreign ships were bought especially to be scrapped and
traded in against a loan. *Herakles* was bought for £11,000 by Stephens, Sutton of
Newcastle-upon-Tyne who - on her sale to breakers at Bo'ness - qualified for a
loan against their new steamer *Ripley* (4,997/1936).
[J. and M. Clarkson collection]

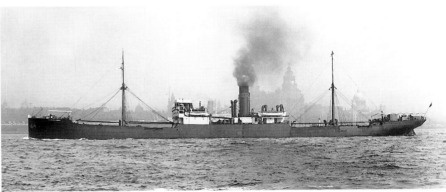

Clan Mackinnon (2) with a black hull,
as opposed to grey in the top picture, in
the Mersey off Birkenhead (middle) and
on passage in the Manchester Ship
Canal (bottom). *[Middle: B. and A.
Feilden/J. and M. Clarkson, bottom:
Nigel Farrell collection]*

CLAN MACKINNON AND ELISE
Captain R. Hinton Browne

I was third officer of the *Clan Mackinnon* and we loaded under charter a mixed cargo in Savannah, Georgia, sailing from there on 30th November 1910. We loaded a few poplar logs on deck, weighing up to two tons each, which, as we were destined for Antwerp, was in order; had our destination been a British port it would not have been as deck cargoes are not allowed in Britain in the winter. From the time we left Savannah we had bad weather; on 8th December the logs on deck broke adrift and, with a dangerous wamp, bashed into the forward bulkhead of the saloon house. The captain turned the ship round and we ran all night before the storm for safety. On the following day we got ready and I, being young and sprightly, put on rubber beach shoes the better to hop about on top, or out of the way of, a rolling log. The logs were to be dumped overboard; all the Europeans, except those on duty, were on the job and we hove the logs forward to the bulwark opening at number one hatch. Getting the logs into position was comparatively easy on account of the rolling of the ship, though one had to be quick to avoid being crushed; when a log was in position and the ship rolled appropriately, the log was tipped into the briny. The captain, with a seacunny, held the bridge, allowing all the rest of the Europeans to 'enjoy' the sport of log dumping. We had no lunch but the steward came round with coffee. Whenever a log was dumped the ship was swung to prevent any damage to the propeller. We were warm and quite cheerful and at five o'clock the last log disappeared; we cleared up the decks and sat down to lunch and supper combined - being hungry I had a jolly good tuck-in.

During the forenoon of Tuesday, 13th December 1910 we came across the ketch *Elise* of Mandal in a sinking condition.

The weather was still bad and the little ketch was in sore straits; her main boom was swinging from side to side with every roll, her canvas was in ribbons, and the whole was a dreadful sight. Captain Rayner East was a good sailor, knowing what was required, and did it. It was not possible to go alongside, so we were manoeuvred in such a way as to bring the ketch right ahead, watching the waves coming up from astern, the engines were put astern and so prevented our crashing down on the little vessel; it worked fairly well, but on one occasion we did come down on her and landed alongside. We had had communication by rope before this. As soon as we were alongside the captain of the ketch made a spring for it, but this was neither quick enough nor high enough, and he was crushed between the two vessels. The mate, who had been standing naked on the deck, dived overboard. Diving under the great big curlers that came along with a regular frequency, he swam under our ship and came on board himself by a rope that was hanging down; a wonderful swimmer, a wonderful sight. The others put a rope round their body and we pulled them on board without much ado. The score now was three saved, one dead, and one to get. The one that remained was a small boy aged fifteen, the cook; he was frightened, and I can assure you that the sea was not a pleasant sight when you thought of going into and through it, so, poor lad, he hesitated. We yelled at him, but to no avail; one strong, almighty pull got him overboard and he was dragged through the raging sea, and the boy was the best of them all as regards saving. Poor little devil, the few seconds he was in the water he will never forget. We got going towards our destination, and the *Elise* to her destination, which was the bottom of the deep blue sea. The *Elise* was from Labrador bound to Gibraltar with about seventy tons of salt cod. The rock scorpions there apparently like it.

This account appeared in 'The British and Commonwealth Review' for June 1961.

Clan Macalister (2) dressed overall. In December 1915 she became the first Clan Line ship to be sunk by a submarine, torpedoed in the Mediterranean after being chased and shelled for about two hours. *[Kevin O'Donoghue collection]*

CLAN MACALISTER (2) 1903-1915

O.N. 115756 4,835g 3,065n
395.0 x 51.1 x 27.0 feet.
T.3-cyl. by Dunsmuir and Jackson,
Glasgow; 440 NHP, 2,200 IHP.
18.3.1903: Launched by Archibald
McMillan and Son Ltd., Dumbarton (Yard
No. 389).
25.4.1903: Registered in the ownership of
The Clan Line Steamers Ltd. (Cayzer,
Irvine and Co., managers), Glasgow as
CLAN MACALISTER.
9.5.1903: Transferred to Sir Charles W.
Cayzer, James McKenzie and David
Rennie (Cayzer, Irvine and Co.,
managers), Glasgow.
1.7.1907: Managers became Cayzer, Irvine
and Co. Ltd.
15.5.1913: Transferred to The Clan Line
Steamers Ltd. (Cayzer, Irvine and Co. Ltd.,
managers), Glasgow.
6.11.1915: Captured and sunk with a
torpedo by the German submarine U 35
120 miles south by east of Cape Martello,
Crete in position 33.10 north by 25.50 east
whilst on a voyage from Liverpool to
Calcutta, with general cargo. Her entire
crew took to the boats and were either
picked up by other craft or landed on
Crete.
18.11.1915: Register closed.

Clan Macalister (2) at Manchester. *[Ships in Focus]*

CLAN MACINTYRE (2) 1903-1928

O.N. 115775 4,807g 3,053n
395.5 x 51.1 x 27.4 feet.
T.3-cyl. by Richardsons, Westgarth and
Co. Ltd., Hartlepool; 448 NHP, 2,300 IHP,
10.75 knots.
1.4.1903: Launched by Furness, Withy and
Co. Ltd., Hartlepool (Yard No. 266).
1.7.1903: Registered in the ownership of
The Clan Line Steamers Ltd. (Cayzer,
Irvine and Co., managers), Glasgow as
CLAN MACINTYRE.
8.7.1903: Delivered at a cost of £65,600.
26.10.1903: Transferred to Sir Charles W.
Cayzer, James Mackenzie and David
Rennie (Cayzer, Irvine and Co.,
managers), Glasgow.
1.7.1907: Managers became Cayzer, Irvine
and Co. Ltd.
15.5.1913: Transferred to The Clan Line
Steamers Ltd. (Cayzer, Irvine and Co. Ltd.,
managers), Glasgow.
2.7.1917: Requisitioned by the British
government until 1.3.1919.
4.6.1928: Register closed on sale to
Società Anonima di Navigazione Marco U.
Martinolich, Lussinpiccolo, Italy for
£16,200 and renamed NORMA.
3.7.1932: Arrived Genoa to be broken up.

Seen arriving at Avonmouth, *Clan Macintyre* (2) was an example of the larger, three-island ships built alongside the Turrets.
She was the last vessel to contact Lund's *Waratah* (9,339/1908) before she disappeared on 27th July 1909. *[J. and M.
Clarkson collection]*

The fate of *Clan Macleod* (3) demonstrated both the inhumanity and humanity of the earlier, and generally more chivalrous, phase of the submarine war. Homeward bound from India in the Mediterranean in December 1915, she was ordered to stop by *U 33*. *Clan Macleod* ignored the warning shots which landed ahead of her, turning away and making smoke by putting oil into the boiler fires. However, when *U 33* started shooting at her, the Clan Liner signalled that she was surrendering. The U-boat commander ignored this, continuing to shell *Clan Macleod* until she was abandoned, causing twelve deaths and several injuries. The wounded master of *Clan Macleod* was taken on board the submarine and had his injuries dressed, but only after he had been harangued by the commander for not stopping sooner and hence avoiding casualties. He and the 51 survivors were put into the two remaining boats and given a course to steer for Malta. Both were picked up within days. *[Newall Dunn collection]*

Clan Macmillan (1) at Cape Town. In September 1914 she took part in the campaign to capture German South West Africa. She carried some 1,300 mules, the stalls for some of which can be seen on her deck. *[J. and M. Clarkson collection]*

CLAN MACLEOD (3) 1903-1915

O.N. 115783 4,796g 3,043n
395.5 x 51.1 x 27.1 feet.
T.3-cyl. by Richardsons, Westgarth and Co. Ltd., Hartlepool; 448 NHP, 2,300 IHP, 10.75 knots.
10.6.1903: Launched by Furness, Withy, and Co. Ltd., West Hartlepool (Yard No. 267).
3.9.1903: Registered in the ownership of The Clan Line Steamers Ltd. (Cayzer, Irvine and Co., managers), Glasgow.
8.9.1903: Ran trials and delivered at a cost of £64,000.
11.3.1904: Transferred to Sir Charles W. Cayzer, (Cayzer, Irvine and Co., managers), Glasgow.
21.12.1904: Transferred to the Clan Line Steamers Ltd. (Cayzer, Irvine and Co., managers), Glasgow.
1.5.1905: Transferred to Sir Charles W. Cayzer, James McKenzie and David Rennie (Cayzer, Irvine and Co., managers), Glasgow.
1.7.1907: Managers became Cayzer, Irvine and Co. Ltd.
15.5.1913: Transferred to the Clan Line Steamers Ltd. (Cayzer, Irvine and Co. Ltd., managers), Glasgow.
1.12.1915: Captured and sunk with gunfire by the German submarine U 33 100 miles east south east of Malta whilst on a voyage from Chittagong to London with general cargo. Twelve of her crew were lost.
10.12.1915: Register closed.

USA TO SOUTH AFRICA SHIPS

This pair were the first flush-decked ships delivered to Clan Line. With all-European crews, rather than Lascars, they were intended for a service from New York to South Africa, on which service Clan Macgregor *was quickly lost.*

CLAN MACMILLAN (1) 1901-1917

O.N. 113992 4,525g 2,805n
396.5 x 48.2 x 27.0 feet.
T.3-cyl. by the Greenock Foundry Co., Greenock; 399 NHP, 1,950 IHP.
16.10.1901: Launched by Archibald McMillan and Son Ltd., Dumbarton (Yard No. 380).
30.11.1901: Ran trials.
3.12.1901: Completed.
6.12.1901: Registered in the ownership of The Clan Line Steamers Ltd. (Cayzer, Irvine and Co., managers), Glasgow as CLAN MACMILLAN.
16.6.1902: Transferred to Sir Charles W. Cayzer, James McKenzie and David Rennie (Cayzer, Irvine and Co., managers), Glasgow.
1.7.1907: Managers became Cayzer, Irvine and Co. Ltd.
15.5.1913: Transferred to The Clan Line Steamers Ltd. (Cayzer, Irvine and Co. Ltd., managers), Glasgow.
22.3.1917: Requisitioned by the British government.

23.3.1917: Torpedoed and sunk by the German submarine UB 39 ten miles west of Beachy Head in position 50.41 north by 00.01 west. The crew took to the boats and were picked up by an armed trawler the next day. She had sailed from Chittagong to London with a cargo of coir matting, and was proceeding to Glasgow when lost.
5.4.1917: Register closed.

CLAN MACGREGOR (2) 1902

O.N. 114013 4,511g 2,796n
395.7 x 48.2 x 27.0 feet.
T.3-cyl. by the Greenock Foundry Co., Greenock; 399 NHP, 1,950 IHP.
14.12.1901: Launched by Archibald McMillan and Son Ltd., Dumbarton (Yard No. 381).
7.2.1902: Registered in the ownership of the Clan Line Steamers Ltd. (Cayzer, Irvine and Co., managers), Glasgow as CLAN MACGREGOR.
1.6.1902: Wrecked on Atlas Reef, Martha's Point, near Cape Agulhas, Cape Colony whilst on a voyage from Port Natal to New York in ballast.
2.12.1902: Register closed.

FURNESS-BUILT

The order placed in October 1904 for three steamers from the West Hartlepool yard of Furness, Withy may well have been a result of Cayzer's close friendship with Christopher Furness. They were by a few feet the longest conventional hulls yet built for Clan and cost £63,500 each.

CLAN MACPHERSON (2) 1905-1918

O.N. 121274 4,779g 3,041n
400.0 x 51.0 x 27.2 feet.
T.3-cyl. by Richardsons, Westgarth and Co. Ltd., Hartlepool; 448 NHP, 2,300 IHP, 10.75 knots.

1.9.1905: Launched by Furness, Withy and Co. Ltd., West Hartlepool (Yard No. 287).
23.11.1905: Registered in the ownership of The Clan Line Steamers Ltd. (Cayzer, Irvine and Co., managers), Glasgow as CLAN MACPHERSON.
1.7.1907: Managers became Cayzer, Irvine and Co. Ltd.
31.10.1907: Transferred to Sir Charles W. Cayzer, James Mackenzie and David Rennie (Cayzer, Irvine and Co. Ltd., managers), Glasgow.
23.3.1915: Transferred to The Clan Line Steamers Ltd. (Cayzer, Irvine and Co. Ltd., managers), Glasgow.
13.3.1915: Requisitioned by the British government.
23.7.1917: Beached to prevent her sinking in Belfast Lough following a collision in fog near Corsewall Point with the steamer SCINDIA (5,127/1900) whilst on a voyage in convoy from New Orleans to Manchester with a cargo of grain. Refloated and repaired at Glasgow.
4.3.1918: Torpedoed and sunk by the German submarine UC 27 24 miles north of Cape Serrat, North Africa whilst on a voyage from Malta and Bizerta to Colon with government stores. A total of 20 lives were lost, 18 of them when the foremast collapsed and smashed one of the boats. The survivors were landed at Bizerta.
13.4.1918: Register closed.

CLAN MACINTOSH (2) 1906-1932

O.N. 121290 4,774g 3,043n
400.0 x 51.0 x 27.2 feet.
T.3-cyl. by Richardsons, Westgarth and Co. Ltd., Hartlepool; 448 NHP, 2,300 IHP, 10.75 knots.
13.10.1905: Launched by Furness, Withy and Co. Ltd., West Hartlepool (Yard No. 288).
23.1.1906: Ran trials, delivered and registered in the ownership of The Clan

Clan Macintosh (2) at Cape Town.   *[F. W. Hawks]*

Clan Macintosh (2) in the Mersey. [J. and M. Clarkson collection]

Line Steamers Ltd. (Cayzer, Irvine and Co., managers), Glasgow as CLAN MACINTOSH.
10.8.1906: Transferred to Sir Charles W. Cayzer, James Mackenzie and David Rennie (Cayzer, Irvine and Co., managers), Glasgow.
1.7.1907: Managers became Cayzer, Irvine and Co. Ltd.
23.3.1915: Transferred to The Clan Line Steamers Ltd. (Cayzer, Irvine and Co. Ltd., managers), Glasgow.
5.7.1915: Attacked by gunfire from the German submarine UC 71 in the Bristol Channel whilst on a voyage from Montreal to Portishead, but escaped thanks to bad visibility.
9.10.1915: Requisitioned by the British government until 3.3.1919.
4.2.1932: Arrived in the Clyde for demolition by Smith and Houston Ltd., Port Glasgow.
30.5.1933: Register closed.

CLAN MATHESON (2) 1906-1914
O.N. 121305 4,775g 3,053n
400.0 x 51.0 x 27.2 feet.
T.3-cyl. by Richardsons, Westgarth and Co. Ltd., Hartlepool; 448 NHP, 2,300 IHP, 10.75 knots.
27.11.1905: Launched by Furness, Withy and Co. Ltd., West Hartlepool (Yard No. 289).
28.2.1906: Registered in the ownership of The Clan Line Steamers Ltd. (Cayzer, Irvine and Co., managers), Glasgow as CLAN MATHESON.
10.4.1906: Delivered.
10.8.1906: Transferred to Sir Charles W. Cayzer, James Mackenzie and David Rennie (Cayzer, Irvine and Co., managers), Glasgow
1.7.1907: Managers became Cayzer, Irvine and Co. Ltd.
14.9.1914: Captured by the German light cruiser EMDEN and sunk with explosives

60 miles south west by south from the Pilot's Light at the mouth of the Hooghly whilst on a voyage from Glasgow and Liverpool to Calcutta River with general cargo. The crew of 70 were transferred to the Norwegian steamer DOVRE (1,181/ 1906) and landed at Rangoon.
2.10.1914: Register closed.

FURNESS CLIPPER-BOWED SHIPS
These two elegant steamers were built to serve the port of Newport News, which belonged to the Chesapeake and Ohio Railroad, and were owned by a British company set up jointly by the railroad and Furness, Withy. Soon after completion the ships were chartered to Clan Line for seven years, but both had problems. On 30th January 1913, Clan Macinnes was run into by the Danish steamer Jens Bang (1,543/ 1907) near Cape St. Vincent, the owners of the latter admitting liability. Furness refused

to extend their charters in 1913, and when the ships were handed back disputed the condition of the boiler, propellers and ventilators of Clan Maciver, and after arbitration received an award of £1,155.

CLAN MACINNES (1) 1907-1914
O.N. 124329 3,709g 2,418n
368.4 x 49.0 x 25.9 feet.
T.3-cyl. by Richardsons, Westgarth and Co. Ltd., Hartlepool; 380 NHP, 1,800 IHP, 9.75 knots.
28.12.1906: Launched by Furness, Withy and Co. Ltd., West Hartlepool (Yard No. 299).
27.2.1907: Registered in the ownership of Chesapeake and Ohio Steamship Co. Ltd. (Furness, Withy and Co. Ltd., managers), London as ROANOKE.
13.3.1907: Ran trials and completed.
16.11.1907: Transferred to Furness, Withy and Co. Ltd., West Hartlepool and London.

Clan Matheson (2) was Clan's first casualty of the First World War, captured by SMS Emden in September 1914. She was the sixth ship captured during a highly successful cruise by the raider, which ended when Emden was sunk by HMAS Sydney in November 1914. [J. and M. Clarkson collection]

23.11.1907: Acquired by The Clan Line Steamers Ltd. (Cayzer, Irvine and Co. Ltd., managers), Glasgow and renamed CLAN MACINNES.
2.5.1908: Transferred to Sir Charles W. Cayzer, Glasgow and Christopher Furness, West Hartlepool (Cayzer, Irvine and Co. Ltd., managers), Glasgow.
26.1.1911: Transferred to The Clan Line Steamers Ltd. (Cayzer, Irvine and Co. Ltd., managers), Glasgow.
13.2.1914: Renamed ROANOKE.
17.2.1914: Sold to Furness, Withy and Co. Ltd., West Hartlepool.
11.2.1917: Damaged by a submarine torpedo four miles south east of Girdleness whilst on a voyage from Dundee to New York with general cargo. Towed into Dundee for repair.
12.8.1917: Captured and sunk with bombs by the German submarine UB 48 100 miles west north west from the Butt of Lewis in position 58.39 north by 09.08 west whilst on a voyage from Leith to Philadelphia with general cargo.
28.9.1917: Register closed.

CLAN MACIVER (1) 1907-1913
O.N. 124334 3,705g 2,411n
368.4 x 49.0 x 29.4 feet.
T.3-cyl. by Richardsons, Westgarth and Co. Ltd., Hartlepool; 380 NHP, 1,800 IHP, 9.75 knots.
28.2.1907: Launched by Furness, Withy and Co. Ltd., Hartlepool (Yard No. 300).
25.4.1907: Registered in the ownership of Chesapeake and Ohio Steamship Co. Ltd. (Furness, Withy and Co. Ltd., managers), London as RAPIDAN.
5.1907: Completed.
16.10.1907: Transferred to Furness, Withy and Co. Ltd., London and West Hartlepool.
5.12.1907: Acquired by The Clan Line Steamers Ltd. (Cayzer, Irvine and Co. Ltd., managers), Glasgow and renamed CLAN MACIVER.
2.5.1908: Transferred to Sir Charles W. Cayzer, James Mackenzie and David Rennie (Cayzer, Irvine and Co. Ltd., managers), Glasgow.
26.1.1911: Transferred to The Clan Line Steamers Ltd. (Cayzer, Irvine and Co. Ltd., managers), Glasgow.
18.12.1913: Sold to Furness Withy and Co. Ltd., West Hartlepool.
19.12.1913: Renamed RAPIDAN.
24.10.1923: Sold to the Charles G. Dunn Shipping Co. Ltd., Liverpool.
14.11.1923: Renamed DOVENBY HALL.
1927: Sold to Panaghis M. Hadoulis and Partners, Andros, Greece and renamed PANAGHIS M. HADOULIS.
7.9.1929: Register closed.
1933: Sold to Olivier and Company, Algiers and renamed MIREILLE under the Panama flag.
9.8.1934: Arrived at La Spezia for breaking up.

Above: *Clan Macinnes* (1). *[Ian J. Farquhar]*
Below: After return to Furness as *Roanoke* at Fowey in June 1915. *[Kevin O'Donoghue collection]*

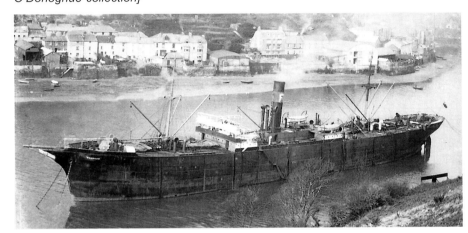

Clan Maciver (1) as the *Rapidan* (above) and and late in her life as the *Panaghis M. Hadoulis* (below). *[Above: World Ship Society Limited, below: Ian J. Farquhar collection]*

Clan Macphee was one of Clan Line's oldest ships when torpedoed on 16th August 1940, sinking in eight minutes with heavy loss of life. The survivors were soon picked up by the Hungarian steamer *Kelet*, but she was herself torpedoed on the 19th August. The crews from both vessels spent five days in boats and rafts until picked up by a Norwegian ship which landed them at Galway. *[J. and M. Clarkson collection]*

430-FOOT FLUSH-DECKERS

Due to a depression in shipping, there was a lull in deliveries between the last batch of Turret completions in 1907 and 1911 when the first of nine 430-foot flush-decked steamers arrived. Clan Macrae, Clan Davidson *and* Clan Macewen *were the first Clan Line ships to have refrigeration machinery, to suit the needs of the Australian trade. The final pair,* Clan Maccorquodale *and* Clan Macquarrie, *ordered in June 1912, had detail differences, with the deckhouse alongside the funnel extending the width of the ship for its full length.*

CLAN MACPHEE 1911-1940

O.N. 129578 5,177g 3,225n
430.0 x 53.5 x 26.4 feet.
T.3-cyl. by Richardsons, Westgarth and Co. Ltd., Hartlepool, 657 NHP, 3,600 IHP, 12 knots.
23.4.1911: Launched by Irvine's Ship Building and Dry Docks Co. Ltd., West Hartlepool (Yard No. 499).
13.6.1911: Registered in the ownership of The Clan Line Steamers Ltd. (Cayzer, Irvine and Co. Ltd., managers), Glasgow as CLAN MACPHEE having been completed at a cost of £66,000.
25.7.1911: Transferred to Sir Charles W. Cayzer (Cayzer, Irvine and Co. Ltd., managers), Glasgow.
10.9.1914: Requisitioned as an Indian Expeditionary Force Transport until 23.12.1914.
23.3.1915: Transferred to The Clan Line Steamers Ltd. (Cayzer, Irvine and Co. Ltd.,

managers), Glasgow.
2.9.1916: Requisitioned as an East African Transport until 22.3.1918.
22.2.1940: Requisitioned by the British government.
16.8.1940: Torpedoed and sunk by the German submarine U 30 400 miles south of Iceland and 350 miles west of North Uist in position 57.30 north by 17.14 west whilst on a voyage from Glasgow and Liverpool to East Africa and Bombay with general cargo. 67 lives were lost, the remaining 25 being picked up by the Hungarian steamer KELET (4,295/1913).
2.4.1941: Register closed.

CLAN MACKENZIE (2) 1911-1912

O.N. 129584. 5,018g 3,134n
430.0 x 53.6 x 26.6 feet.
T.3-cyl. by William Doxford and Sons Ltd., Sunderland; 670 NHP, 3,600 IHP, 12 knots.
8.6.1911: Launched by William Doxford and Sons Ltd., Sunderland (Yard No. 421).
13.7.1911: Registered in the ownership of The Clan Line Steamers Ltd. (Cayzer, Irvine and Co. Ltd., managers), Glasgow as CLAN MACKENZIE having been completed at a cost of £64,250.
30.12.1912: Wrecked in fog at Torre Nueva near Cadiz whilst on a voyage from

The unfortunate *Clan Mackenzie* (2). She stranded in fog on Conil Shoals near Cape Trafalgar on 30th December 1912, although fortunately her crew was rescued and taken to Gibraltar. Three thousand tons of her general cargo was salved before she broke in two on 27th February, the rest being sold for £2,500, the remnants of the almost-new ship fetching just £2,000. *[Kevin O'Donoghue collection]*

Clan Macgillivray (1) came largely unscathed through two world wars, and gave the company an unprecedented 37 years' service. The upper photograph shows her about to sail from Pinkenba Wharf, Brisbane, Australia for Gallipoli with a full complement of infantry men who are hanging off the funnel, stays and cross trees. One wonders how many of these Australians came home alive or even uninjured: they were landed under fire at Mudros, and such were the casualties in the Dardanelles campaign that *Clan Macgillivray* then became a hospital ship. She is seen in the lower photograph on a peaceful Mersey between the wars: note the length of the spreader on her foremast. *[Top; Australian War Memorial, H02222, bottom: J. and M. Clarkson collection]*

the River Clyde and Newport to Colombo and Calcutta with general cargo.
9.4.1913: Register closed.

CLAN MACGILLIVRAY (1) 1911-1948
O.N. 129596 5,023g 3,107n
430.6 x 53.6 x 26.6 feet.
T.3-cyl. by the Wallsend Slipway and Engineering Co. Ltd., Newcastle-upon-Tyne; 496 NHP.

12.6.1911: Launched by Sir W.G. Armstrong, Whitworth and Co. Ltd., Newcastle-upon-Tyne (Yard No. 834).
29.8.1911: Registered in the ownership of The Clan Line Steamers Ltd. (Cayzer, Irvine and Co. Ltd., managers), Glasgow as CLAN MACGILLIVRAY.
9.1911: Delivered at a cost of £66,000.
15.8.1914: Requisitioned by the British government until 17.5.1919.

1.7.1940: Requisitioned by the British government until 12.3.1946.
10.1948: Sold to Eastern Asia Navigation Co. Ltd. (Wheelock, Marden and Co. Ltd., managers), Hong Kong.
12.1948: Renamed MACLOCK.
16.1.1949: Arrived at Bruges for demolition by van Heyghen Frères.
12.1.1949: Register closed.
3.2.1949: Demolition commenced.

CLAN MACNAUGHTON (1) 1911-1915

O.N. 129592 4,985g 3,103n
429.8 x 53.7 x 34.6 feet.
T.3-cyl by Alexander Stephen and Sons Ltd., Linthouse, Glasgow; 666 NHP, 4,000 IHP.
28.6.1911: Launched by Alexander Stephen and Sons Ltd., Linthouse, Glasgow (Yard No. 443).
8.8.1911: Registered in the ownership of The Clan Line Steamers Ltd. (Cayzer, Irvine and Co. Ltd., managers), Glasgow as CLAN MACNAUGHTON having been completed at a cost of £66,750.
10.5.1913: Transferred to Sir Charles W. Cayzer (Cayzer, Irvine and Co. Ltd., managers), Glasgow.
19.11.1914: Hired by the Admiralty for service as an armed merchant cruiser and served with the Tenth Cruiser Squadron under the pennant number M.81.
3.2.1915: Last reported on patrol west of the Hebrides. Lost with her 20 officers and 261 men.
27.2.1915: Register closed.

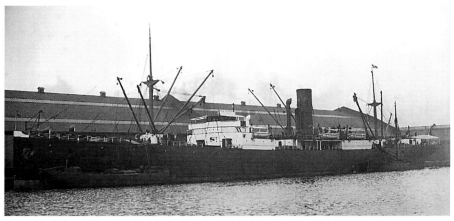

The short-lived *Clan Macnaughton* (1) which disappeared whilst serving as an armed merchant cruiser in February 1915. Whether the cause of her loss was striking a mine or foundering in an Atlantic gale has never been determined. *[Nigel Farrell collection]*

CLAN MACRAE (2)/BANFFSHIRE 1912-1943

O.N. 133005 5,058g 3,166n
430.0 x 53.5 x 30.0 feet.
T.3-cyl. by William Doxford and Sons Ltd., Sunderland; 670 NHP, 3,600, 12 knots.
1931: Fitted with low pressure exhaust turbine.
21.11.1911: Launched by William Doxford and Sons Ltd., Sunderland (Yard No. 429).
2.1.1912: Registered in the ownership of The Clan Line Steamers Ltd. (Cayzer, Irvine and Co. Ltd., managers), Glasgow as CLAN MACRAE.
13.1.1912: Ran trials and delivered.
25.7.1913: Transferred to Sir Charles W. Cayzer (Cayzer, Irvine and Co. Ltd., managers), Glasgow.
23.3.1915: Transferred to The Clan Line Steamers Ltd. (Cayzer, Irvine and Co. Ltd., managers), Glasgow.
23.3.1915: Requisitioned by the British government as an Expeditionary Force transport until 20.4.1916.
24.8.1917: Requisitioned by the British government until 9.5.1919.
23.6.1920: Transferred to the Scottish Shire Line Ltd. (Turnbull, Martin and Co. Ltd., managers), Glasgow.
28.6.1920: Renamed BANFFSHIRE.
15.5.1936: Transferred to the British and South American Steam Navigation Co. Ltd. (Houston Line (London) Ltd., managers), London.
11.5.1940: Requisitioned by the British government.
29.9.1943: Torpedoed and sunk by the German submarine U 532 380 miles south west of Mangalore in a position 09.26 north by 71.20 east whilst on a voyage from Colombo to Aden and the United Kingdom with a cargo of tea, rubber, plumbago, coconut oil and copra. One life was lost from the complement of 101.
27.1.1944: Register closed.

Above: *Clan Macrae* (2). She cost £64,000 without her refrigeration equipment. *[Ian J. Farquhar collection]*
Below: *Banffshire. [Ships in Focus]*

CLAN DAVIDSON (1) 1912-1917

O.N. 133017 5,058g 3,167n
430.0 x 53.5 x 26.6 feet.
T.3-cyl. by William Doxford and Sons Ltd., Sunderland; 670 NHP, 3,600 IHP, 12 knots.
19.12.1911: Launched by William Doxford and Sons Ltd., Sunderland (Yard No. 431).
29.2.1912: Registered in the ownership of The Clan Line Steamers Ltd. (Cayzer, Irvine and Co. Ltd., managers), Glasgow as CLAN DAVIDSON.
13.3.1912: Ran trials and delivered. The contract price without refrigeration machinery was £64,000.
15.5.1913: Transferred to Sir Charles W. Cayzer, James Mackenzie and David Rennie (Cayzer, Irvine and Co. Ltd., managers), Glasgow.

23.3.1915: Sold to The Clan Line Steamers Ltd. (Cayzer, Irvine and Co. Ltd., managers), Glasgow.
24.6.1917: Torpedo and sunk by the German submarine UC 17 130 miles south west by a quarter west from the Scilly Isles in position 48.16 north by 08.36 whilst on a voyage from Sydney, New South Wales to London with a general cargo including maize and butter. 14 lives were lost, the remainder of the crew being picked up by the steamer CROWN OF ARRAGON (4,500/1905) which was herself torpedoed later that day. Both sets of survivors were rescued by HMS LYRA and landed at Plymouth.
10.7.1917: Register closed.

CLAN MACEWEN/BUTESHIRE
1912-1948

O.N. 133053 5,140g 3,190n
430.5 x 53.6 x 26.6 feet.
T.3-cyl. by Palmer's Shipbuilding and Iron
Co. Ltd., Newcastle-upon-Tyne; 666 NHP,
3,600 IHP, 12 knots.
1931: Low-pressure exhaust steam turbine
fitted.
16.3.1912: Launched by Palmer's
Shipbuilding and Iron Co. Ltd., Newcastle-
upon-Tyne (Yard No. 817).
5.1912: Completed. The contract price
without refrigeration machinery was £64,250.
15.6.1912: Registered in the ownership of
The Clan Line Steamers Ltd. (Cayzer, Irvine
and Co. Ltd., managers), Glasgow as CLAN
MACEWEN.
10.5.1913: Transferred to Sir Charles W.
Cayzer (Cayzer, Irvine and Co. Ltd.,
managers), Glasgow.
23.3.1915: Transferred to The Clan Line
Steamers Ltd. (Cayzer, Irvine and Co. Ltd.,
managers), Glasgow.
12.5.1915: Requisitioned by the British
government until 20.2.1919.
17.11.1920: Transferred to the Scottish Shire
Line (Turnbull, Martin and Co. Ltd.,
managers), Glasgow.
23.11.1920: Renamed BUTESHIRE.
16.4.1936: Transferred to the British and
South American Steam Navigation Co. Ltd.
(Houston Line (London) Ltd., managers),
London.
4.4.1940: Requisitioned by the British
government until 21.6.1946.
17.2.1948: Sold to the British Iron and Steel
Corporation and allocated to T.W. Ward Ltd.,
Sheffield.
25.2.1948: Arrived at Preston for breaking up.
25.6.1948: Register closed.

Above: Although *Clan Macewen* seems to have led a blameless existence, managing to survive two world wars, her name was not perpetuated. *[Archie Munro collection]*
Below: As *Buteshire* she served both Scottish Shire and Houston Lines. *[Middle: F. W. Hawks, bottom: J. and M. Clarkson collection]*

The only photograph found of the short-lived *Clan Maccorquodale,* showing the larger deckhouse amidships compared with her near sisters. The letter 'L' seen on her hull in this photograph identifies her as a transport during the First World War, probably in Australian waters. *[Australian War Memorial, PO1122.003]*

CLAN MACCORQUODALE 1913-1917
O.N. 133153 5,121g 3,180n
430.2 x 53.4 x 26.7 feet.
T.3-cyl. by Dunsmuir and Jackson Ltd.,
Govan; 680 NHP, 3,600 IHP, 12.5 knots.
4.9.1913: Launched by Charles Connell and
Co. Ltd., Glasgow (Yard No. 354).
16.10.1913: Registered in the ownership of
The Clan Line Steamers Ltd. (Cayzer, Irvine
and Co. Ltd, managers), Glasgow as CLAN
MACCORQUODALE.
11.1913: Delivered at a cost of £82,000.
3.9.1914: Requisitioned by the British
government.
17.11.1917: Torpedoed and sunk by the
German submarine UB 51 165 miles north
west by north of Alexandria in a position 33.26

north by 27.52 east whilst on a voyage from
Chittagong and Madras to London with
general cargo. The entire crew took to the
boats and were picked up by HMS LOBELIA.
31.12.1917: Register closed.

CLAN MACQUARRIE (1) 1913-1942
O.N. 133157 5,060g 3,152n
429.2 x 53.7 x 26.6 feet.
20.5.1915: 6,430g 4,083n.
T.3-cyl. by Alexander Stephen and Sons Ltd,
Linthouse, Glasgow; 670 NHP, 4,500 IHP.
16.9.1913: Launched by Alexander Stephen
and Sons Ltd, Linthouse, Glasgow (Yard No.
456).
25.10.1913: Registered in the ownership of
The Clan Line Steamers Ltd. (Cayzer, Irvine

and Co. Ltd., managers), Glasgow as
CLAN MACQUARRIE.
11.1913: Delivered at a cost of £82,500.
15.8.1914: Requisitioned by the British
government until 14.9.1914.
19.7.1917: Requisitioned by the British
government until 5.4.1919.
25.5.1940: Requisitioned by the British
government.
13.6.1942: Sunk by torpedo and gunfire
from the Italian submarine LEONARDO
DA VINCI 600 miles west from Freetown
in position 05.30 north by 23.30 west
whilst on a voyage from Bombay and
Durban to New York in ballast. There was
one casualty.
12.1.1943: Register closed.

Clan Macquarrie (1) and her exact sister *Clan Maccorquodale* had the amidships deckhouse extended to be flush with the hull plating. *Clan Macquarrie* was to be the last ship built for Clan Line by Stephen. *[J. and M. Clarkson collection]*

Clan Macarthur (2) (above) and her sister were the largest Clan liners yet built. As *Berwickshire* (below) she was the fleet's final loss in the Second World War. *[Both: J. and M. Clarkson collection]*

BIG REEFERS

The first steamers to exceed in length the three big Turrets of 1899, these refrigerator ships were given a third additional boiler to act as a standby and also provide steam for auxiliaries including the refrigeration plant, generators and winches. The contract price was £92,500 each.

CLAN MACARTHUR (2)/ BERWICKSHIRE 1912-1944

O.N. 133085 5,815g 3,614n
450.1 x 57.1 x 30.4 feet.
9.7.1915: 7,382g 4,679n.
T.3-cyl. by the Wallsend Slipway and Engineering Co. Ltd., Wallsend-on-Tyne; 840 NHP, 4,500 IHP, 12 knots.

1931: Fitted with Bauer-Wach exhaust steam turbine by Deutsche Schiff und Maschinenbau A.G. 'Weser', Bremen, Germany; 1,600 BHP.
26.9.1912: Launched by Armstrong, Whitworth and Co. Ltd., Newcastle-upon-Tyne (Yard No. 846).
10.12.1912: Ran trials, delivered and registered in the ownership of The Clan Line Steamers Ltd. (Cayzer, Irvine and Co. Ltd., managers), Glasgow as CLAN MACARTHUR.
10.5.1913: Transferred to Sir Charles W. Cayzer, James Mackenzie and David Rennie (Cayzer, Irvine and Co. Ltd., managers), Glasgow.
23.3.1915: Transferred to The Clan Line Steamers Ltd. (Cayzer, Irvine and Co. Ltd.,

managers), Glasgow.
19.5.1917: Requisitioned by the British government until 3.4.1919.
25.6.1920: Transferred to the Scottish Shire Line Ltd. (Turnbull, Martin and Co. Ltd., managers), Glasgow.
28.6.1920: Renamed BERWICKSHIRE.
9.3.1940: Requisitioned by the British government.
20.8.1944: Torpedoed and sunk by the German submarine U 861 500 miles east south east of Durban in position 30.58 south by 38.50 east whilst on a voyage from Liverpool via Durban to Tamatave and Mauritius with general cargo. Eight lives were lost from the complement of 102.
18.11.1944: Register closed.

Clan Mactavish (1), *seen above* in an Australian port, was sunk after a short and one-sided gun battle with SMS *Moewe* which drew within 300 yards by identifying herself as the *Trader* of T. and J. Harrison. *[Archie Munro collection]*

CLAN MACTAVISH (1) 1913-1916
O.N. 133100 5,816g 3,626n
450.1 x 57.1 x 26.8 feet.
19.5.1915: 7,385g. 4,693n.
T.3-cyl. by the Wallsend Slipway and Engineering Co. Ltd., Newcastle-upon-Tyne; 840 NHP, 4,500 IHP, 12 knots.
9.12.1912: Launched by Sir W.G. Armstrong, Whitworth and Co. Ltd., Newcastle-upon-Tyne (Yard No. 847).
19.2.1913: Registered in the ownership of The Clan Line Steamers Ltd. (Cayzer,

Irvine and Co. Ltd., managers), Glasgow as CLAN MACTAVISH.
27.2.1913: Ran trials and delivered.
10.5.1913: Transferred to Sir Charles W. Cayzer, James Mackenzie and David Rennie (Cayzer, Irvine and Co. Ltd., managers), Glasgow.
26.3.1915: Transferred to The Clan Line Steamers Ltd. (Cayzer, Irvine and Co. Ltd., managers), Glasgow.
16.1.1916: Sunk during a running fight with the German auxiliary cruiser MOEWE 120 miles south by west from Funchal in position

30.52 north by 17.20 west whilst on a voyage from Wellington to London with general cargo including frozen meat. 18 lives were lost, and the master and one other were taken prisoner on the MOEWE. The survivors were divided between two captured British steamers, the WESTBURN (3,300/1893) which landed them at Teneriffe on 22nd February 1916, and the Elder, Dempster passenger steamer APPAM (7,781/1913) which landed four of them at Norfolk, Virginia on 1st February 1916.
21.3.1916: Register closed.

Clan Macbride (1) in South African waters. *[Ships in Focus]*

PURCHASES

The need to replace the clipper-bowed ships on charter from Furness, Withy meant Clan had to shop urgently for ships. In 1912 two quite similar three-island vessels were bought on the stocks at Stockton-on-Tees and Sunderland, Clan Macbride *and* Clan Macbeth. *A repeat of the former was also bought from Ropners for a massive £150,000, becoming* Clan Macbrayne *on her delivery in 1916. The somewhat bigger shelter-decker* Harflete *which became* Clan Mackellar *had a flush-decked hull and was described as '...almost a duplicate of* Clan Mackenzie, *but slower.'*

CLAN MACBRIDE (1) 1912-1937

O.N. 133087 4,886g 3,009n
390.0 x 50.5 x 31.6 feet.
T.3-cyl. by Blair and Co. Ltd., Stockton; 393 NHP, 2,000 IHP, 10.5 knots.
9.1912: Launched by Ropner and Sons Ltd., Stockton (Yard No. 474).
She had been ordered by H. W. Dillon, London.
17.12.1912: Registered in the ownership of The Clan Line Steamers Ltd. (Cayzer, Irvine and Co. Ltd., managers), Glasgow as CLAN MACBRIDE.
19.12.1912: Ran trials and delivered at a cost of £64,000.
10.5.1913: Transferred to Sir Charles W. Cayzer, James Mackenzie and David Rennie (Cayzer, Irvine and Co. Ltd., managers), Glasgow.
23.3.1915: Transferred to The Clan Line Steamers Ltd. (Cayzer, Irvine and Co. Ltd., managers), Glasgow.
5.1.1916: Requisitioned by the British government until 30.3.1919.
26.1.1937: Sold to McCowen and Gross Ltd., London.
4.2.1937: Renamed HEATHCOT.
1938: Sold for £17,000 to be broken up under the 'Scrap and Build' scheme.
12.4.38: Arrived at Osaka to be demolished.
10.5.1938: Register closed.

CLAN MACBRIDE'S PRECIOUS CARGOES

In 1965, Captain H.S. Pengelley recalled a voyage he made as chief officer of the 1912-built *Clan Macbride* in December 1931. Outward bound for Bombay, eight racehorses were loaded in horse boxes stowed on the after deck alongside number five hatch. The *Clan Macbride* had a good run down into the Mediterranean, but ran into a north westerly gale on Christmas Eve. By Christmas morning the seas were breaking over the after deck, and Chief Officer Pengelley found it had partly washed away the boarding from the box holding the smallest and most frightened of the horses. He asked permission of the master, Captain Last, to move those to port on to the hatch, clear of the swirling water. The master considered it very risky, but agreed to let the mate have his way. It was a cold, tough job, as work had to stop every time a sea broke aboard whilst the rather inadequate wash ports let it run away. Although the chief officer missed his Christmas dinner, he was pleased to have relieved the suffering of the animals, which were eventually landed at Bombay in good condition.

The return cargo loaded in Bombay was even more valuable than the race horses and, as it turned out, almost as vulnerable: gold bullion. The bullion arrived on board a lorry on the morning *Clan Macbride* was due to sail, but there were no papers, and the driver simply left the boxes sitting on the quay. About three hours later, a bank official arrived and the bars of gold and sovereigns in the boxes were tallied, signed for, and placed in the safest place on the ship, the chief steward's store. The mate and steward checked the seals on bullion boxes night and morning. At Port Said a clerk came on board and said to the master, 'I believe you have a lot of bullion on board'. 'Who the devil told you that?' was the astonished reply. 'Why,' said the clerk, it's in all Reuter's telegrams.' Captain Last then decided to have an armed guard on the bullion until the ship sailed for Tilbury. On arrival, the bullion was unloaded and taken away in a very different manner to that which it had came on board at Bombay.

This story appeared in 'The British and Commonwealth Review'
for December 1965.

Clan Macbride (1) in the Mersey off the entrance to Birkenhead docks. Note the topgallant mast and heavy derrick for number 2 hatch. *[J. and M. Clarkson collection]*

Although to the same basic design as *Clan Macbride* (1), the Laing-built *Clan Macbeth* (1) had a number of detail differences, including the treatment of the bridge front and the plating of the deckhouses alongside the funnel. *[F. W. Hawks]*

CLAN MACBETH (1) 1913-1937
O.N. 133120 4,650g 2,881n
385.0 x 51.7 x 27.4 feet.
T.3-cyl. by Richardsons, Westgarth and Co. Ltd., West Hartlepool; 394 NHP.
9.2.1913: Launched by Sir James Laing and Sons Ltd., Sunderland (Yard No. 640). She had been ordered by W. Lowden and Co., Liverpool.
12.5.1913: Registered in the ownership of Sir Charles W. Cayzer, James Mackenzie and David Rennie (Cayzer, Irvine and Co. Ltd., managers), Glasgow as CLAN MACBETH.
14.5.1913: Ran trials and delivered at a cost of £65,500.
1915: Transferred to The Clan Line Steamers Ltd. (Cayzer, Irvine and Co. Ltd., managers), Glasgow.
27.4.1917: Requisitioned by the British government until 2.4.1919.
22.12.1936: Sold to the Nailsea Steamship Co. Ltd. (E.R. Management Co. Ltd., managers), Cardiff for £16,250 and renamed NAILSEA VALE.
1938: Sold for £11,000 W.H. Arnott, Young (Shipbreaking) Ltd., Dalmuir to be broken up under the 'Scrap and Build' scheme.
2.1.1938: Arrived in the Clyde.

CLAN MACBRAYNE (1) 1916-1947
O.N. 137811 4,818g 2,978n
390.0 x 50.5 x 28.0 feet.
T.3-cyl. by Blair and Co. Ltd., Stockton-on-Tees; 402 NHP, 3,000 IHP, 10.5 knots.
3.2.1916: Launched by Ropner and Sons Ltd., Stockton-on-Tees (Yard No. 504).
1.4.1916: Registered in the ownership of The Clan Line Steamers Ltd. (Cayzer,

Irvine and Co. Ltd., managers), Glasgow as CLAN MACBRAYNE.
4.5.1917: Requisitioned by the British government until 11.6.1919.
5.9.1939: Requisitioned by the British government until 11.5.1946.
23.3.1944: Transferred to the British and South American Steam Navigation Co. Ltd. (Houston Line (London) Ltd., managers), London.
25.3.1947: Register closed on sale to C. Galanos Steam Ship Company of Panama S.A., Panama and renamed SAN GEORGIO.
1950: Sold to the British Iron and Steel Corporation and allocated to T.W. Ward Ltd., Sheffield.

24.10.1950: Arrived at Barrow-in-Furness to be broken up.

CLAN MACKELLAR (1) 1913-1937
O.N. 133105 4,925g 3,062n
410.2 x 52.0 x 27.9 feet.
T.3-cyl. by Earle's Shipbuilding and Engineering Co. Ltd., Hull; 602 NHP, 3,000 NHP, 11.5 knots.
7.12.1912: Launched by the Northumberland Shipbuilding Co. Ltd., Howdon-on-Tyne (Yard No. 202) for J. and C. Harrison Ltd., London as HARFLETE.
8.3.1913: Registered in the ownership of The Clan Line Steamers Ltd. (Cayzer, Irvine and Co. Ltd., managers), Glasgow

Clan Macbrayne (1). *[Ships in Focus]*

Although not ordered by Clan, *Clan Mackellar* (1) was not dissimilar to contemporary ships built for them, and may well have been modified to suit the company's ideas during the period of three months between her launch and completion.

In 1937 London tramp ship owners McCowen and Gross Ltd. bought *Clan Mackellar* (1) and *Clan Macbride* (1) to trade in to secure a loan of £117,200 to build their *Derrymore* (4,799/1938) at Burntisland. The *Clan Mackellar* was bought jointly with Springwell Shipping Co. Ltd. who used part of the credit from her sale for scrap to obtain a loan for their *Springtide* (1,579/1937). *[J. and M. Clarkson collection]*

as CLAN MACKELLAR having been bought for £86,750.
16.3.1913: Ran trials and delivered.
10.5.1913: Transferred to Sir Charles W. Cayzer, James Mackenzie and David Rennie (Cayzer, Irvine and Co. Ltd., managers), Glasgow.
23.3.1915: Transferred to The Clan Line Steamers Ltd. (Cayzer, Irvine and Co. Ltd., managers), Glasgow.
16.11.1916: Requisitioned by the British government until 26.6.1919.
25.1.1937: Sold jointly to McCowen and Gross Ltd., London and Springwell Shipping Co Ltd., London for £20,000 and renamed MOORCOT.
3.2.1938: Arrived at Osaka to be broken up under the 'Scrap and Build' scheme. She had been sold to Japanese breakers for £19,250.
11.3.1938: Register closed.

CRUISER STERNS
Indecision over hull forms continued, and this group reverted to a three-island design. Their cruiser sterns gave them a more modern appearance, and they represent a distinct stage in the evolution of the designs that culminated in the classic 1930s refrigerator ships.

CLAN CAMPBELL (3) 1914-1916
O.N. 136320 5,897g 3,680n
430.3 x 54.3 x 29.4 feet.

T.3-cyl. by Dunsmuir and Jackson Ltd., Glasgow; 413 NHP.
6.8.1914: Launched by Napier and Miller Ltd., Old Kilpatrick, Glasgow (Yard No. 196).
16.9.1914: Registered in the ownership of The Clan Line Steamers Ltd. (Cayzer, Irvine and Co. Ltd., managers), Glasgow as CLAN CAMPBELL.
18.9.1914: Ran trials and delivered at a cost of £83,500.

11.2.1915: Requisitioned by the British government as an East African Expeditionary Force transport until 31.1.1916.
3.4.1916: Sunk by torpedoes and gunfire from the German submarine U 39 29 miles south east of Cape Bon, Tunisia whilst on a voyage from Tuticorin to London with general cargo including cotton. There were no casualties, the crew being landed at Kalibia.
18.4.1916: Register closed.

Clan Campbell (3) at Cape Town during her tragically short career. She did not sink immediately on being torpedoed in April 1916, allowing her crew to take to the boats, and it required 14 shells from *U 39* to complete her destruction. *[Newall Dunn collection]*

CLAN ROSS (2) 1914-1938

O.N. 136330 5,971g 3,757n
430.0 x 54.3 x 29.4 feet.
T.3-cyl. by Swan, Hunter and Wigham
Richardsons Ltd., Wallsend-on-Tyne; 565
NHP, 3,400 IHP, 13 knots.
4.9.1914: Launched by Swan, Hunter and
Wigham Richardsons Ltd., Wallsend-on-
Tyne (Yard No. 959).
19.10.1914: Registered in the ownership
of The Clan Line Steamers Ltd. (Cayzer,
Irvine and Co. Ltd., managers), Glasgow
as CLAN ROSS.
24.10.1914: Delivered at a cost of
£84,000.
22.8.1917: Requisitioned by the British
government until 5.7.1919.
5.5.1918: Torpedoed and later shelled by
the German submarine UB 48 28 miles
east of Cape Camaret, Gulf of Lyons
whilst on a ballast voyage from Genoa to
Buenos Aires in convoy with the loss of
nine lives. Partly abandoned, but with HM
Trawler ACHERNAR standing by, she was

Clan Ross (2) experienced determined
enemy action at least three times
during her career. On the first
occasion, in May 1918, a torpedo blew
a hole 55 feet by 27 feet in her port
side amidships, partly flooding two of
her holds. Some of the crew were
transferred to an escorting trawler,
HMS *Achernar*, the rest of the convoy
and its escort steaming away as fast as
possible. Despite *Clan Ross* taking a
severe list, those remaining on board
worked for six hours to reduce the
inflow of water. That night with an
increasing list and deteriorating
weather, her remaining complement
were taken off by the trawler which
stood by the *Clan Ross*. It was as well
they did, as the U-boat returned and
fired 32 shells at the *Clan Ross* and
two at the trawler, whose master
decided that discretion was the better
part of valour, and steamed away.
Returning in the morning, the trawler
could not find the ship and assumed
she had been sunk, but proceeding to
Toulon was surprised to see *Clan Ross*
anchoring in the roads, having been
towed in by a French naval tug.   On
the third occasion she was attacked, in
April 1942, *Clan Ross* had no time to
avoid the torpedo from a Japanese
submarine. Although *I-6* surfaced to
inspect the wreckage, it neither helped
nor harmed the survivors. Those in
one boat were picked up by a
Norwegian steamer, whilst those in the
other were rescued by a native craft
after a six-day voyage.
        The bottom photograph clearly
shows her cruiser stern. *[Top: J. and
M. Clarkson, middle: Kevin
O'Donoghue collection, bottom: Ships
in Focus]*

towed into Toulon by the French tug
MILON.
2.5.1938: Transferred to the British and
South American Steam Navigation Co.
Ltd. (Houston Line (London Ltd.,
managers), London.
10.9.1939: Requisitioned by the British
government.
24.6.1940: Attacked by German aircraft in
St. George's Channel in position 46.17
north by 14.35 west whilst on a voyage

from India to Liverpool but reached
Milford Haven.
2.4.1942: Torpedoed and sunk by the
Japanese submarine I-6 in position 15.58
north by 68.24 east whilst on a voyage
from Liverpool to Durban, Bombay and
Cochin with general cargo including
explosives. Of the complement of 86, 11
were lost.
25.6.1942: Register closed.

CLAN OGILVY (2) 1914-1941

O.N. 137782 5,909g 3,716n
430.0 x 54.2 x 29.4 feet.
T.3-cyl. by William Doxford and Sons Ltd., Sunderland; 564 NHP, 3,000 IHP, 11.75 knots.
20.10.1914: Launched by William Doxford and Sons Ltd., Sunderland (Yard No. 470).
12.1914: Delivered at a cost of £83,000.
18.12.1914: Registered in the ownership of The Clan Line Steamers Ltd. (Cayzer,

Irvine and Co. Ltd., managers), Glasgow as CLAN OGILVY.
16.11.1915: Requisitioned by the British government until 3.5.1919.
8.7.1938: Transferred to the British and South American Steam Navigation Co. Ltd. (Houston Line (London) Ltd., managers), London.
23.8.1940: Requisitioned by the British government.
30.6.1940: Damaged by gunfire from a German E-boat off St. Catherines Point.

20.3.1941: Torpedoed and sunk by the German submarine U 105 550 miles north west of Dakar in position 20.04 north by 24.45 west whilst on a voyage from Chittagong to the United Kingdom with general cargo including tea, pig iron and groundnuts in convoy SL 68 from Freetown. A total of 61 lives were lost.
5.9.1941: Register closed.

In the top and middle photographs, *Clan Ogilvy* (2) is seen on the Mersey, the latter being taken by John McRoberts on 29th June 1938. In the bottom photograph she is working cargo at Naples.

The ship met her end during March 1941 in a desperate battle over convoy SL 68 in which six ships were lost to just two submarines, *U 105* and *U 106*. *Clan Ogilvy's* stern was blown off, and ammunition exploded, resulting in her sinking in minutes with a heavy loss of life. The survivors got away in three boats, and next morning came across a boat and a raft from the *Benwyvis* (5,920/1929) which had also been sunk in the attack. The Ben Line men were distributed amongst the boats, which set sail for the Cape Verde Islands. Accounts of what happened next are incomplete, but the first officer's boat sailed past the islands and its exhausted crew made a landfall on Portugese territory in mainland Africa on 5th April. The captain's boat sailed for ten days before it was obvious that they had missed the islands and, running short of water, the course was altered to take them into shipping lanes. On 1st April the boat met the Spanish steamer *Cabo Vilano* (4,282/ 1920) which broadcast radio messages requesting other ships to look out for the *Clan Ogilvy's* boats. The crew of a third boat are reported to have been picked up by the British motor ship *King Edgar* (4,536/1927). *[Top and middle: J. and M. Clarkson collection; bottom: National Maritime Museum P28566]*

SURVIVING WAR, SURVIVING PEACE: 1914-1934

Business almost as usual

From the Clan Line's board minutes during the First World War it is not always apparent that a very bloody conflict was underway. There is the occasional announcement of regret at a war loss and accompanying casualties, and reports of protests at government requisition of ships, but otherwise the minutes concern themselves mainly with reports of trade continuing and record voyage profits being made.

The outbreak of the war saw a decision made in mid-August 1914 to keep ships in port or have them make for a safe port, but sailings began again when the government stepped in to provide war risk insurance. However, congestion in British ports, shortage of labour as dock workers went to enlist, and government fixtures of ships combined to cause disruption of services. Clan Line ships were quickly involved in the conflict, with *Clan Matheson* (2) and then *Clan Grant* (2) falling victim to the German light cruiser *Emden*, although in neither case were there casualties amongst the crews. *Clan Macnaughton* (1) was taken up for commissioning as an armed merchant cruiser, for which role she was converted on the Thames; her career was to be tragically short, with her huge naval complement she disappeared in February 1915. A further loss was the wreck in November 1914 of *Clan Stuart* (2) whilst delivering a cargo of coal to the naval base at Simonstown. Although prospects of refloating seemed good, and experts from Glasgow went out to supervise salvage, a heavy swell damaged the ship in April 1915 just as she was on the point of being refloated, and salvage attempts were abandoned. As the coal was to Admiralty account, an attempt was made to get their lordships to stand part of the loss, but not surprisingly was rejected. There were to be further unsuccessful attempts to get the government to pay for damage done whilst ships were under some form of naval control, for instance when the *Clan Macpherson* (2) collided in fog with Anchor Line's *Scindia* (5,106/1900) in July 1917, the fact that she was manoeuvring in convoy was felt to be the basis for a claim on the government's war risk insurance.

Congestion was worst on Merseyside, with ships for Liverpool waiting up to five weeks for a discharge berth by mid-1915, with London and Glasgow less affected. It quickly became necessary to charter steamers to maintain sailings, and a number of captured German ships were so employed including *Pagenturm* (5,000/1909), *Warturm* (4,965/1908) and *Diyatalawa* ex-*Rappenfels* (5,883/1912), plus some British ships such as *Zayani* (3,505/1899). Where possible these steamers were put on outward sailings from the United Kingdom. It was admitted that there was little profit from these charters, but it was explained to the board that they meant the chartered steamers ran the risks from submarines and mines in home waters, allowing Clan steamers to stay as far as possible outside danger zones, and to profit from lucrative fixtures from various governments. For instance, *Clan Macbeth* (1) was fixed from Manila to New York and earned a profit of £15,500 in 110 days. In 1916 *Clan Cumming* (1) made £28,000 in profit in 88 days by carrying rice from Burma, and *Clan Macquarrie* (1) £40,000 on a similar voyage. But not all the promised profits materialised. In June 1915 *Clan Graham* (2) was fixed to carry flour from New York to Marseilles where, after guaranteed discharge, she was expected to earn £11,000 in just 65 days. Unfortunately, before she could take up this charter she was requisitioned by the Indian government, which action resulted in a protest to the government about the 'considerable hardship' caused by such 'indiscriminate chartering'. From time to time Charles Cayzer senior used what remained of his political clout (he had lost his seat in Parliament in 1906) to lobby the government. In December 1915 he met First Lord of the Admiralty, A.J. Balfour, to complain that the largely untaxed profits being earned by neutral ship owners were enabling them to oust British ships, and enter trades against the British interest. Apart from reversing the policy which had brought merchant shipbuilding virtually to a standstill in favour of naval construction, there seems little that Balfour could do about this, although he promised to consider the question. A legitimate grumble of the ship owner was that a ship could be requisitioned on the point of loading a cargo, which disrupted schedules on liner berths and increased congestion in ports. On this issue the government did show some sympathy, and

Taken at Brisbane on 30th October 1915 this shows the *Clan Macmillan* (1) (lost in 1917), the *Clan Mactavish* (1) (sunk 78 days later on her homeward voyage to London) and the *Clan Macarthur* (2), later the *Berwickshire* (sunk in 1942). This is a most interesting picture as the two latter ships were refrigerated sister ships and this may have been the only occasion when they were in port together. Both were heading home, having first gone out to the Cape on the Durban express service. *[Archie Munro collection]*

allowed owners to substitute another suitable steamer for one about to be requisitioned. But it continued to be an issue, and in 1918 August Cayzer had an interview with the Shipping Controller about 'excessive requisitioning'. Obtaining no satisfaction he wondered if legal action could be taken. So much for a ship owner's patriotism.

Despite the Cayzers' grumbling, their company was doing very well financially. Government war insurance was covering the lost steamers at their inflated wartime values. For instance, the 12-year-old *Clan Macalister* (2) had a book value of £34,000 but £77,760 was paid in war risk insurance when she was torpedoed in November 1915. Voyage profits of £434,000 in 1914 increased to £852,000 in 1915 and jumped to no less than £2,333,000 in 1916, although they then declined somewhat from this peak. Costs were up too, but overall profits were excellent, dividends of 25% were paid in 1915 and 1916, much of them going to the Cayzers themselves as major shareholders, and a generous amount was salted away in reserves for future acquisitions.

The cost of war
It is difficult to read what the Clan Line board, sitting safely in Glasgow, were recording in their minutes about record freight rates and profits, without thinking of their crews who faced unprecedented dangers at sea. The *Clan Mactavish* (1), for instance, was attacked by the German auxiliary cruiser *Moewe* in January 1916, which got close by identifying herself as a Harrison Line ship which she had recently sunk. Captain Oliver believed that the attacker was a German merchant ship, no better armed than *Clan Mactavish* herself, and when *Moewe* fired a shell across her bows he responded with the order for full ahead and a shot from her own modest gun. But the *Moewe's* much heavier armament quickly made itself felt, and there were heavy casualties on *Clan Mactavish* which was forced to surrender. News of her sinking reached home after Elder, Dempster's *Appam* (7,781/1913) carrying some of *Clan Mactavish's* crew put into Newport News on 1st February under the German flag, having been captured by *Moewe* prior to the fight with the Clan liner. The British propaganda machine made much of Captain Oliver's gallant fight in the *Clan Mactavish* against the piratical Hun (in this case, Captain Graf Nikolaus zu Dohna-Schlodien, who had actually behaved chivalrously towards the survivors). With later examples of the company's vessels engaging surfaced U-boats with gunfire, there was much jingoistic comment about 'the fighting Clans'. This was of little consolation to the relatives of the dead or of those like Captain Oliver who spent two years in a German prisoner-of-war camp. Cayzers' generosity to their crews went little further than writing to congratulate them on surviving yet another voyage. The award of two months' pay to members of the crew of *Clan Macfadyen* (1) when she fought off *U 20* in the Western Approaches during May 1916 was unusual enough to be mentioned in the board minutes, which record that it was only paid to those who participated in defending the ship. Table 5 is a chronological list of vessels totally lost during the First World War. It includes an indication of the numbers of deaths: a total of 329 not including the 281 naval personnel lost on the armed merchant cruiser *Clan Macnaughton* (1). To the casualty figures must be added the unrecorded number of those physically or mentally wounded, who spent days in open boats, or years in captivity. It is notable that the Mediterranean was the most dangerous place for a

Table 5: Vessels totally lost during the First World War through all causes.

Name	Date	Cause	Lost*
Clan Matheson (3)	14.9.1914	Gunfire from *Emden* in Indian Ocean	0
Clan Grant (2)	16.10.1914	Gunfire from *Emden* in Indian Ocean	0
Clan Stuart (2)	21.11.1914	Wrecked South Africa	0
Clan Macnaughton (1)	3.2.1915	Lost whilst serving as AMC in North Atlantic	281
Clan Macalister (2)	6.11.1915	Torpedoed by *U 35* in Mediterranean	0
Clan Macleod (3)	1.12.1915	Gunfire from *U 33* in Mediterranean	12
Clan Macfarlane (1)	30.12.1915	Torpedoed by *U 38* in Mediterranean	52
Clan Mactavish (1)	22.2.1916	Gunfire and bombs from *Moewe* in North Atlantic	18
Clan Campbell (3)	3.4.1916	Torpedoed by *U 39* in Mediterranean	0
Clan Leslie	4.11.1916	Torpedoed by *UB 43* in Mediterranean	3
Clan Shaw (2)	23.1.1917	Mined in North Atlantic	2
Clan Farquhar (1)	26.2.1917	Torpedoed by *UB 43* in Mediterranean	49
Clan Macmillan (1)	23.3.1917	Torpedoed by *UB 39* in English Channel	0
Clan Murray (2)	29.5.1917	Torpedoed by *UC 55* in North Atlantic	64
Clan Alpine (2)	9.6.1917	Torpedoed by *U 60* in North Atlantic	8
Clan Davidson (1)	24.6.1917	Torpedoed by *UC 17* in North Atlantic	14
Clan Maclachlan (1)	19.7.1917	Collision with *Europa* in Mediterranean	6
Clan Ferguson (1)	6.9.1917	Torpedoed by *UB 49* in Mediterranean	10
Clan Maccorquodale	17.11.1917	Torpedoed by *UB 51* in Mediterranean	0
Clan Cameron (2)	22.12.1917	Torpedoed by *UB 58* in English Channel	0
Clan Macpherson (2)	4.3.1918	Torpedoed by *UC 27* in Mediterranean	20
Clan Macdougall (1)	15.3.1918	Torpedoed by *UB 49* in Mediterranean	33
Clan Mackay (3)	11.5.1918	Convoy collision with *Eurypylus* in North Atlantic	0
Clan Matheson (3)	23.5.1918	Convoy collision with *Western Front* in North Atlantic	0
Clan Forbes (2)	9.6.1918	Torpedoed by *UB 105* in Mediterranean	2
Hyperia	28.7.1918.	Torpedoed by *UB 51* in Mediterranean	
Clan Macnab (3)	4.8.1918	Torpedoed by *U 113* in English Channel	22
Clan Macneil (2)	6.8.1918	Torpedoed by *UC 34* in Mediterranean	0
Clan Macvey	8.8.1918	Torpedoed by *UB 57* in English Channel	7

* Figures for lives lost are, unfortunately, approximate. They vary from source to source and are subject to variation if, for example, an injured man later died of his wounds, or was killed during the loss of a ship which had rescued him or taken him prisoner.

In dazzle paint and war rig, this is clearly one of the ships built by Ayrshire Dockyard at Irvine, and is believed to be *Clan Morrison*. She is light ship and very clean, and the photograph was probably taken around the day she was handed over, 20th March 1918. The wartime censor has removed all background detail.

Clan Line steamer during the war: 14 of the 24 losses through enemy action occurred in this sea. Avoiding the Mediterranean would have meant longer voyages, but would undoubtedly have saved ships and lives.

The negative aspect of the high freights earned during wartime was that the price of new or replacement steamers was also inflated. To compound the problem were extreme delays in deliveries from shipyards, partly through priority being given to naval work. In January 1915 Clan placed orders with three shipbuilders with promised delivery dates between November 1915 and January 1916. The best performing of the three yards was that of the Northumberland Shipbuilding Co. Ltd. which delivered the *Clan Mackay* (3) in December 1916, having promised November 1915, and then only after the original price of £78,500 had been increased by £12,500. Craig, Taylor and Co. Ltd. delivered the *Clan Malcolm* (1) 14 months late in March 1917, again at an extra cost of £19,500. Sir James Laing and Sons only completed *Clan Matheson* (3) in September 1917, having promised January 1916, and then only after the original price of £71,250 had been increased by £12,750 and the ship classified, somewhat obviously, as 'war work'. Even ships which were bought whilst under construction were not immune from severe delays, and in February 1915 Napier and Miller promised a ship for August 1915, but she did not materialise as *Clan Ranald* (3) until February 1917. Russell and Company did somewhat better with *Clan Stuart* (3), delivered in October 1916 but at the high price of £178,000. As a consequence of the delays in delivery, ship prices were rising: in December 1915 Ayrshire Dockyard quoted a price of £124,700 but by June 1916 the price for a similar ship had risen to £159,000. Clan had little choice but to pay and progressively increased the size of this order so that eventually Ayrshire built six ships, although only two were completed in wartime, *Clan Morrison* in March 1918 and *Clan Monroe* (3) in June 1918. Clan were lucky that

these orders were allowed to proceed at all, as the government in the person of the Shipping Controller was now taking berths for a belated programme of building standard merchant ships. This pressure on the yards meant that in 1917 orders placed with Laing for a repeat of *Clan Matheson* (3) and Napier and Miller for a replacement of *Clan Campbell* (3) were cancelled by the builders, prompting Clan Line to raise the question of compensation from the government. In mid-1917 concern at losses to enemy action and requisitioning, and despair at getting new ships ordered, led to a decision to buy ships already built or building for other owners, at whatever the cost. These came from a variety of builders and are listed, with other ships bought under construction earlier, in table 6. In addition, five second-hand ships were bought, becoming *Clan Macmaster*, the sisters *Clan Kenneth* (1) and *Clan Kennedy* (1), *Clan Macbeolan* and *Clan Keith* (1). Needless to say, none came cheap, the highest price recorded being the £280,000 paid for the *Clan Alpine* (3), bought in January 1918 whilst building for Denholm at Greenock, war having inflated building costs three or fourfold. One can have a little sympathy with Clan Line that, going to such trouble and expense to acquire tonnage, their ships were requisitioned almost immediately on delivery. Tragically, the new ships were no less likely to be sunk than old ones: *Clan Macvey*, which cost £243,000, lasted precisely 16 days.

The gradual extension of government control of shipping had some interesting consequences, taking Clan ships on unusual routes and to ports which were quite out of their usual range. In February 1917, *Clan Macfadyen* (1) loaded 1,000 tons of cocoa in Nigeria, with her cargo being completed by John Holt and Co. For this, Clan received a lump sum of £14,000, to be paid even if the ship was lost. In June of 1917, *Clan Chisholm* (1) was reported to be loading for Hull on an Ellerman Wilson berth in New York, and *Clan Macintyre* (2) was loading in New Orleans for a T. and J. Harrison sailing to Liverpool.

Table 6: Vessels bought whilst building during the First World War

Builder	Name	Delivered
Russell and Co.	*Clan Stuart* (3)	10.1916
Napier and Miller Ltd.	*Clan Ranald* (3)	2.1917
Northumberland Shipbuilding Co Ltd.	*Clan Mackenzie* (3)	6.1917
	Clan Macvicar	3.1918
	Clan Macvey	7.1918
Bartram and Sons Ltd.	*Clan Macbean* (1)	3.1918
Greenock and Grangemouth Dockyard Co. Ltd.	*Clan Alpine* (3)	4.1918
	Clan Macwilliam	11.1918
William Doxford and Sons Ltd.	*Clan Macmillan* (2)	6.1918
Lloyd Royal Belge (Great Britain) Ltd.	*Halizones* (1)	7.1918
William Hamilton and Co. Ltd.	*Clan Mackinlay* (1)	11.1918
	Clan Matheson (3)	4.1919

The founder dies

Sir Charles Cayzer's attendance at board meetings was sporadic from September 1915, and at the meeting on 27th September 1916 it was announced that he was seriously ill. He died the next day, aged 73. He had been only 35 years of age when he founded Cayzer, Irvine and Co., and it is remarkable to consider his ascendance from humble shipping clerk to a ship owner with substantial personal wealth, and his transition from a humble Thameside home to extensive Scottish estates. His success was achieved through overwhelming ambition, a pugnacious attitude to opponents (and often to friends as well), attention to detail, and close control over money. However, the meticulousness which served him well in early days later exhibited itself as a tendency to micro-manage those around him, especially his family. Surviving letter books show a huge outpouring of memoranda from his desk, largely on trivial matters like the purchase of a typewriter or copying letters. The economy he habitually practised was laudable in an aspiring businessman, but in later life was close to parsimony in a millionaire advising his wife on buying the cheapest available blinds for one of large houses he had bought. Relationships with his sons were not always easy: the eldest, also Charles, showed some reluctance to enter the business wholeheartedly and left it in 1910 following many disputes with his father. It fell to the third son, August Cayzer (1876-1943), to become chairman in 1916, with fifth son Herbert (1881-1958) as vice-chairman and succeeding as chairman in 1943. The sixth son, Harold (1882-1948), was also a director in 1916 but was on active service. The second and fourth sons had both died relatively young.

The decision to move the headquarters and all board meetings from Glasgow to London was taken in May 1917, allowing a decent interval after Charles Cayzer's death. The move had been proposed in 1906, but the founder had opposed it on the grounds that Clan was a west coast line, with voyages that started and finished in Glasgow, where it had workshop facilities. Tellingly, given his closeness with money, the lower cost of operating from Scotland was also a factor. Board meetings had in fact alternated between London and Glasgow until Sir Charles became too ill to travel from Scotland.

Acquisitions and adventures

A change in business strategy followed the change in leadership. Growth had previously been achieved largely by aggressive entry into existing services or the pioneering of new routes. The few acquisitions, such as that of the Persian Gulf Steamship Company ships, had not been particularly successful, and other opportunities to acquire shipping lines or rights had not been pursued, for instance Houlder's Australian rights in 1911, and the chance to buy Glen Line in 1912. Now, however, three major acquisitions followed in quick succession, enabled by the huge wartime profits which had swelled the company's reserves.

The first move was to complete the acquisition of the Scottish Shire Line Ltd., taken over with effect from 31st December 1917, but in which the Cayzers had held an interest since 1910. A modest company now with just two ships, *Ayrshire* (1) and *Argyllshire* (1), it could trace its ancestry back to 1874, and its managers, Turnbull, Martin and Co., had once been Clan's agents in Glasgow. The company was attractive enough for Clan to offer £750,000 as it had rights in the Australasian trades. There was to be some interchange between the Scottish Shire and Clan ships in terms of routes served, but essentially the Scottish Shires stayed in the Australian trade where their refrigerated capacity was essential for homeward carriage of produce. Subsequently, the occasional transfers from Clan to Scottish Shire involved refrigerated ships.

Much larger was the British and South American Steam Navigation Co. Ltd., fully acquired in 1918 for £4,000,000, and in which Cayzers again had an existing interest. The company was formed in 1898, but its founder and manager, Robert P. Houston, had been a shipowner since the early 1880s. Houston was an aggressively ambitious self-made man like Charles Cayzer, and indeed had been a thorn in Clan's side in the 1900s when forcing his way into the South African trades from both the United Kingdom and North America. The appeal of his line to the Cayzers was the company's interests in the trade to South America, and certainly not the fleet which was badly run down and elderly, varying in

Ayrshire (1) of 1903, taken over by Clan at the end of 1917 along with the *Argyllshire* of 1911 and their owners, Scottish Shire Line Ltd. *[National Maritime Museum P.8984]*

Hortensius, one of the elderly Houston ships taken over in 1918. She was sold for breaking up in 1925. *[Ian J. Farquhar collection]*

age from 16 to 28 years. The first mention of the acquisition is in board minutes for September 1918, and at this point war losses had reduced the Houston fleet to 15 ships (listed from page 114 onwards). As with Scottish Shire, Houston's naming tradition - giving ships classical names beginning with the letter H - was continued, but there was more cross-over of the ships in terms of usage on the various Clan and Houston routes. What transfers there were between ownerships seem to have been largely for accountancy purposes, and were not necessarily straightforward: Clan's ships having accommodation for Lascar crews whilst Houston (like Scottish Shire) employed white crews.

The third acquisition was to have a long-term effect on the fleet. The Greenock Dockyard Co. Ltd. was bought by the management company Cayzer, Irvine and Co. Ltd. in 1919. At first the yard was allowed to function independently of its parent, which did not in fact need to order more ships, and was allowed to sink into the depression-era torpor which so

affected many British yards. It was not even entrusted with the work of converting sloops to cargo ships for Clan's Mexican business. However, it came into its own from 1928 when it delivered the *Clan Macdonald* (3), the first of four refrigerator ships, and went on to build the majority of Clan Line's ships, establishing a style which was second to none.

With one exception, Clan Line's attempts to expand their routes were not particularly bold. In 1919 a joint service with Ellerman and Andrew Weir was begun from Chittagong and other Indian ports and Red Sea ports to the Atlantic seaboard of the USA. *Clan Gordon* (2) and *Clan Murray* (3) took the first Clan sailings, but no more is heard of this 'American and Indian Line Branch Service'. Probably as a result of Houston's presence in South America, sailings were also begun from Calcutta to the River Plate in 1926, but again do not seem to have survived long. The one entirely novel service was that proposed in 1921, from west coast Mexican ports to Los Angeles and San Francisco. The story of this

Clan Skene was the only ship bought directly from the Shipping Controller and placed in Clan Line ownership. During a brief spell with Houston Line she had an unfortunate stranding off Nova Scotia, and after repair was taken back by Clan Line, as if their new subsidiary was not to be trusted with the ship. *[John McRoberts/J. and M. Clakson collection]*

singularly unsuccessful adventure is told from page 140 onwards.

Surviving the peace

The Armistice still left Clan short of ships, a situation made worse by the need to re-equip the Houston fleet. Government war loss insurance had covered the cost of Turret *Clan Graham* (2) which had been torpedoed in March 1918, but rather than pay in cash the Shipping Controller offered in replacement one of the war-built standard ships, *War Adder*, with Clan to make a cash adjustment. She became *Clan Skene* and was to be the only standard ship in the Clan fleet for some years, as the offer of one of the refrigerated G class to replace the lost *Clan Macvey* was turned down. However, war-built standard ships were felt good enough for Houston which was allocated four. This line also received

Hesione (2) of 1915, formerly the German *Itajahy*, bought in 1921 from the Shipping Controller for Houston services. *[National Maritime Museum P.10798.]*

three of the four ex-German ships bought from the Admiralty or the Shipping Controller in 1920 and 1921: they had been taken in prize or surrendered as reparations at the end of the war. The saga of the *Clan Graham* (2) was not over with the settlement of the insurance claim, as she was reacquired and towed to Rotterdam for extensive repairs.

Buying back the aged and obsolescent *Clan Graham* was symptomatic of the continuing desperation felt over replacing losses and rebuilding the fleet. This was made even more critical by a series of losses, with the Turret *Clan Gordon* (2) capsizing off North Carolina in June 1919, *Clan Maclean* (2) wrecked in East Africa in November 1919, and the recently repaired *Clan Graham* herself coming to grief in 1920. At one point towards the end of 1919, eight ships were on order from Ayrshire Dockyard, as well as orders with Lithgows. Anxiety about there not being sufficient steel available for building these ships was allayed by buying shares in the Steel Company of Scotland Ltd. But 1920 saw freight rates tumble

dramatically, and with them ship prices, leaving Clan very worried about their massive commitment to ships from Ayrshire Dockyard. In July the possibility was discussed of substituting tankers for two of the hulls yet to be laid down at the yard, although Clan did not intend to operate them but to sell them on. In March 1921 it was admitted that the order was not viable, and five ships, allocated yard numbers 492 to 496, were cancelled for a payment of £265,000. This expense coupled with other recent purchases and ships on order which were too advanced to cancel left Clan Line financially embarrassed, to the extent it needed to take large loans from a bank and from its recently acquired Houston subsidiary. The steel company shares were also quickly sold.

A symptom of the rapid deterioration in the market was that in mid-1922 came some of the first reports of ships being laid up, with the old Houston vessels *Hostilius*, *Hortensius* and *Hyacinthus* inactive at Liverpool, with *Clan Macvicar* at Colombo, and *Clan Macnaughton* (2) and *Clan*

Clan Mactavish (2), built by Ayrshire Dockyard, but seen here in Victoria Harbour, Greenock, adjacent to Scotts' fitting-out basin, on 30th May 1921 after having her turbines fitted. She went out on trials the following day. The tug under her bow is Clyde Shipping's *Flying Foam* (217/1917). *[Glasgow University Archives]*

1927

S.S. "CLAN *Macnaughton* VOY. X 12
(Capt. A.W. Simpson)

For *Natal Delagoa Bay & Beira*

CLOSING DATE AT GLASGOW 4th Aug SAILED 6th Aug 27
Do. do. LIVERPOOL 10th do. " 14th do -

GLASGOW COAL, 908
Less CONSUMED 167   741 D/W.   Mt.   W/M.
DISCHARGED AT LIVERPOOL, ——— " ——— " ——— "
                          741
SHIPPED AT LIVERPOOL, 694 " ——— " ——— "
TOTAL COAL, 1435 " 1614 " 1435 "
TOTAL CARGO, 6788 " 6525 " 8467 "
         8223   8139   9902

ESTIMATED EARNINGS (Gross)
Amouth & GLASGOW, 10.617.
      LIVERPOOL 11.947
      £ 22,564.

NOTES ON CARGO.
GLASGOW,   LIVERPOOL *Livestock*
                 4 Rabbits } for
                 1 Bull   } Natal

TOTAL COAL ON SHIP'S A/c. ———
PERMANENT BUNKERS, ———
            @...........................

GLASGOW TO
Natal   739 D/W. 938 Mt. 1009 W/M.
Delagoa Bay 370 " 381 " 448 "
Beira   1705 " 1348 " 2133 "
            2814   2667   3590 "

LIVERPOOL TO
Natal   2201 D/W. 2327 Mt. 2769 W/M.
Delagoa Bay 544 " 394 " 605 "
Beira   977 " 1011 " 1251 "
            3722   3732   4625 "
Avonmouth/Natal 238 . 119 . 238 .
   " /Delagoa Bay 1 . 1 . 1 .
   " /Beira 13 . 6 . 13 .
            252   126   252

TOTAL FOR
Natal   3178 D/W. 3384 Mt. 4016 W/M.
Delagoa Bay 915 " 776 " 1054 "
Beira   2695 " 2365 " 3397 "
            6788. " 6525. " 8467 ".

ON SAILING SHE WAS *fully down* AND HAD 837 T. SPACE.

The cargo book for the second *Clan Macnaughton* (below) for her voyage to Natal, Delagoa Bay and Beira in August 1927. The detail is impressive: note the four rabbits listed under 'livestock'. Despite being down to her marks, she still had space unfilled. *[Upper: Kevin O'Donoghue collection; lower: B. and A. Feilden/J. and M. Clarkson]*

1927

S.S. "CLAN *Mactaggart*" Voy. 12
Capt. Mee.

CLOSING DATE AT GLASGOW 16th Dec SAILED 28th Dec.
Do. do. LIVERPOOL 22nd " " 5th Jan
a.m.

GLASGOW COAL, 2208
Less CONSUMED 147 2061 D/W. Mt. W/M.

DISCHARGED AT LIVERPOOL, " ___ " ___ "
2061
SHIPPED AT LIVERPOOL, 201 " ___ " ___ "
TOTAL COAL, 2262 " 2545 " 2262 "
" Oil 420
TOTAL CARGO, 6824 " 5920 " 8067
9506 8465 10329

ESTIMATED EARNINGS (GROSS)
'mouth Newpat GLASGOW, 5,624.
LIVERPOOL, 10,573
£16,197.

NOTES ON CARGO.

GLASGOW, Amounts deducted from Freight
Gw. (4th) Gal. Iron Cash Refunds. 2667
(Apt) " " 588.
(—) Ewart " 40.
Buck Rodric " 5
L. Gal. Iron " " 2918.
TOTAL COAL ON SHIP'S A/C. E'ware " " 187.
Gran " " 1.
PERMANENT BUNKERS, Utensils H.
Glassware @ 3
Beer
£6413.

Cape Town, Mossel Bay
For Algoa Bay & East London

GLASGOW TO		D/W		Mt		W/M
Cape Town	430	D/W	474	Mt	533	W/M.
Mossel Bay	7	"	9	"	9	"
Algoa Bay	105	"	197	"	229	"
East London	245		253		275	"
	847		933		1046	
Liverpool						
Cape Town	2175	D/w	2325	Mt.	2843	W/M
Mossel Bay	49		45		56	
Algoa Bay	946	D/W.	955	Mt.	1203	W/M.
East London	752	"	531	"	846	"
	3922	"	3856	"	4948	"
Avonmouth						
Cape Town	694	D/W.	347	Mt	694	W/M.
Mossel Bay	111	"	55	"	111	"
Algoa Bay	6	"	3	"	6	"
East London	75	"	38	"	75	"
Natal	415	"	208	"	415	"
TOTAL FOR	1301		651		1301	
Cape Town	2623	D/W.	3349	Mt.	4608	W/M.
Mossel Bay	176		114		185	
Algoa Bay	1304	"	1249	"	1628	
East London	1306	"	1000	"	1434	"
Natal	415		208		415	
	6824		5920		8067	
Newport:						
Cape Town	324		203		338	
Mossel Bay	9		5		9	
Algoa Bay	187		94		187	
East London	234		178		238	
	754		480		772	

ON SAILING SHE WAS 1½ light AND HAD 3530 Tons SPACE.

4

A similar cargo book for the first *Clan Mactaggart* (below). Cargo loaded in Birkenhead (listed as 'Liverpool') and for Cape Town preponderates, and one wonders at the economics of calling at Newport. The 'Amounts to deduct' may relate to discounts given to loyal conference customers on certain cargoes. *Clan Mactaggart* is shown with a 50-ton derrick at number 2 hatch. *[Upper: Kevin O'Donoghue collection; lower: Ships in Focus]*

1920s acquisitions. Above: *Clan Macfadyen* (2) completed at Irvine in 1923, the last in a series of six ships built by the Ayrshire Dockyard. *[Archie Munro collection]* Below: A fine view of the *Clan Macilwraith* (1). She had been delivered by the Greenock Dockyard in 1924 and was the first Clan from there. *[Newall Dunn collection]*

Sinclair (2) also facing the possibility of lay up. However, these problems proved to be temporary, and Clan fell back on its practice of fixing ships for what were regarded as tramp voyages, with *Clan Mactaggart* (1) carrying US grain to Rotterdam in November 1922, coal being loaded in South Wales for the River Plate, and iron ore cargoes delivered to the Scheldt ports. Indeed, with the notable exception of its Mexican company, Clan and its subsidiaries were singularly successful in keeping their ships out of lay up throughout the depression which was to stretch through the interwar years.

The accounts of both Houston and Scottish Shire now began to record losses, £146,000 for the former in 1922 and £190,000 in 1923. Houston was having difficulties with its

routes from UK and North America to South America, the latter in particular facing severe competition. However, a contributing factor to their poor performance on paper was the very high prices at which ships had been transferred from Clan Line to these fleets. For instance, the company owning Houston ships, the British and South American Steam Navigation Co. Ltd., had been charged no less than £705,000 in total for the *Clan Skene,* the less-than-new *Clan Macbeolan* and *Clan Keith* (1).

Although the spread of Clan's routes mitigated the impact of the depression, as ships could be quickly switched from a poorly performing trade to a better one, its services were far from immune from problems. Clan's share of the

Further acquisitions in the 1920s were the *Clan Grant* (3) and *Clan Graham* (3) (above). *Clan Graham,* the former *Port Lincoln,* was bought from William Thomas as the *Cambrian Baroness* in 1929. *[Ships in Focus]*

Australian wool trade was affected by continental owners putting on faster ships. Hansa Line, eliminated from the trades by the First World War, returned and began a service from New York to South Africa supported strongly by a major shipper of case oil. The aggressively expansionist Blue Star Line were making inroads into both the South African and homeward Australian trades. In India import cargoes were hit by the boycott of British goods which was part of the agitation for independence. In South Africa negotiations over a renewal of the contract between the conference lines and the government's South African Shipping Board dragged on for years, the latter being anxious to help and protect local farmers and other industries by setting low rates for exports and high rates for imported goods. Even more worrying to the Clan Line board, judged by the amount of time devoted to its discussion, was an incursion into the South African trade by a non-conference service begun by R.J. Thomas and Co. Robert Thomas was the son of the highly successful Anglesey-born tramp ship owner William Thomas who, faced with straitened conditions in post-First World War years, tried to force his way into several liner trades. Thomas' monthly service from Antwerp and Newport received some support from shippers of galvanised iron products in South Wales and fertiliser manufacturers in Holland and Belgium, and loaded coal and timber to fill spare capacity. The response of Clan and its conference partners was ferocious, with a 'fighting steamer' put on to precede Thomas' ships and match his offer of 5% below the prevailing conference homeward rates. Thomas countered by extending his services to East Africa. The fight dragged on from April 1927 until December 1928, when it was agreed that the conference lines would carry some cargo on Thomas' behalf, and that Clan Line would buy two of his ships, *Cambrian Baroness* and *Cambrian Marchioness,* for £40,000.

Modernising the fleet

The lesson Clan learned from the difficulties of the 1920s was that it needed faster and better equipped ships. A start was made in 1928 to fit Bauer-Wach exhaust turbines to the more modern steamers, which were taken out of service one by one and sent to Hamburg or the Clyde for these modifications. Enthusiasm for the economy and extra speed expected led to some quite elderly steamers being included in this programme, including the 1912-built *Buteshire* sent to William Beardmore for conversion in 1930. More significant, however, was the 1928 delivery from Greenock Dockyard of Clan's first motor ship, the *Clan Macdonald* (3). This was not the first time Clan had made use of its 1919 acquisition of the Greenock yard, as *Clan Macilwraith* (1) of 1924 had been delivered in 1924, albeit to an existing design and with an engine salvaged from *Clan Graham* (2) and boilers left over from the Mexican conversions. *Clan Macdonald's* significance lay in her being planned carefully for Clan's needs with her refrigerated capacity, modestly increased speed, and facilities including heavy-lift derricks and strengthened decks. However, pride in the new ship was tempered by the prospect of a quick profit: Clan were prepared to consider an offer for *Clan Macdonald* from Hamburg-Amerika Line, but in the event decided that the German offer was too low.

The heavy-lift derricks on Clan Line ships had a long pedigree. Resulting from a mishap in delivering a heavy boiler on the Malabar coast of India in 1909, Clan Line fitted their new tonnage with cargo gear suitable for handling heavy items. Five of the eleven ships built between 1911 and 1913 were fitted with a 30-ton derrick on the foremast (40 tons in the last of class), while those completed by the Ayrshire Dockyard between 1918 and 1923 were similarly equipped, but with an additional 15-ton derrick on the mainmast to serve number 4 hatch. Four of this latter class later exchanged their 30-ton derricks for ones of 50 tons. The *Clan Macdonald* was also delivered with 50- and

15-ton derricks while the next two ships, *Clan Macdougall* (2) and *Clan Macpherson* (3), were each fitted with a derrick of 120 tons for handling the 101-ton Vulcan Foundry locomotives then being built for Indian Railways, and for other heavy lifts such as electric stators for South Africa and Australia weighing in at 80 to 105 tons. The beam of these ships was also increased by five feet to make it easier to carry such heavy loads. The *Clan Macalister* (3) of 1930 reverted to the 50-ton derrick.

As motor ships, *Clan Macdonald* and her near sister *Clan Macdougall* were a false dawn in the fleet. The succeeding two vessels of this class, *Clan Macpherson* and *Clan Macalister* (3), reverted to steam propulsion, it being reckoned that the addition of an exhaust turbine would provide the same speed as the diesels but at reduced first cost. And they were followed in the early 1930s by the purchase of three ageing steamers bought simply to enhance the line's refrigerated capacity. However, the 1928 class were significant as the precursors of a group of ships discussed fully in the next chapter, which were to give exceptional service to both Clan Line and to their country in time of war.

These two pictures of *the Clan Macdougall* (2), a motor ship (above) and *Clan Macalister* (3), a steamer (below), make it easy to compare the different layouts, especially regarding the position of number 3 hold. *[Both: Ian J. Farquhar collection]*

Clan Line brochure published about 1936. *[Newall Dunn collection]*

CLAN MACDOUGALL LIFTS LOCOS

Carrying heavy loads such as railway locomotives and rolling stock became part of Clan Line's stock-in-trade, and indeed a brochure was commissioned to promote this activity (see previous page). These photographs show a particularly intensive loading session, which took place at Birkenhead between 17th and 19th January 1929, just prior to the maiden voyage of *Clan Macdougall* (2). Her cargo consists of at least ten locomotives and their tenders, from two builders in Lancashire and destined for various railways in India.

In the upper photograph, four 106-ton 2-8-2 locomotives built by Vulcan Foundry at Newton-le-Willows await lifting. A Mersey Docks and Harbour Board floating crane is at work, probably arranging the locomotives so that they are within reach of *Clan Macdougall's* heavy derrick. Note the mixed-gauge track on which these 5 foot 6 inch gauge locomotives are standing, and that two have their cab roofs removed to facilitate lifting: beams were fitted above the firebox.

In the foreground of the lower photograph are three bogie tenders lettered NWR for the North Western Railway of India with beyond them a group of locomotives built by Beyer-Peacock of Gorton.

In the foreground of the photograph top left are two locomotives, numbered 912 and 913, from Beyer-Peacock, with the Vulcan Foundry 2-8-2s beyond. Tenders had already been stowed in lower holds.

The photograph above is interesting in showing two spreader beams. That to the right is lifting one of the Vulcan locos using *Clan Macdougall's* own gear, whilst that to the right is lettered for Beyer-Peacock and is in use by the MDHB crane. The photograph to the left has another view of a Vulcan 2-8-2 coming aboard. Below, three Vulcan locomotives are stowed on the foredeck, whilst a Beyer-Peacock type is having its cab roof put in place by fitters now the lifting is complete. Note the extensive lashings for each locomotive.

With loading on the foredeck complete, the locomotives are lashed down. In the upper photograph, Vulcan locomotive number 221 has been placed on rails which rest on wooden baulks. Wooden stops have been fitted to her buffer beam. The work is being overseen by a Clan Line officer and a bowler-hatted foreman, probably from Clan's in-house stevedoring outfit, Caledonia Stevedoring Co. Ltd.

The locomotives, looking particularly large on the dockside, seem dwarfed when seen on *Clan Macdougall's* deck in the lower photograph. Having a track gauge wider than Britain's standard gauge, and being well outside the loading gauge, they would have been brought from Lancashire by road to Birkenhead on a low-loading trailer.

The photographs were taken by Liverpool professional photographers, Stewart Bale, on behalf of the Caledonia Stevedoring Co. Ltd. They came to this publisher's attention thanks to Ian Pope of Lightmoor Press and Campbell McCutcheon who are thanked for allowing their reproduction here.

Clan Stuart (3) being assisted by a Cock tug into Birkenhead Docks. She was bought for £178,000 during February 1916 whilst building at Port Glasgow and although expected to be ready in August 1916 was not completed until October.
[B. and A. Feilden/J. and M. Clarkson]

WARTIME DELIVERIES

With priority given to naval building on the outbreak of the First World War, no new ships were delivered to Clan Line between the Clan Ogilvy *(2) in November 1914 and* Clan Macbrayne *(1) in April 1916. When merchant shipbuilding was allowed to recommence once the Government realised the seriousness of shipping losses, Clan took what ships it could, including some whose design it specified itself, others that were building or had been completed for other owners, and wartime standard ships. Many were bought at high prices born of frustration with trying to get ships ordered or completed once they were ordered.* Clan Matheson *(1), for instance, had been ordered at the beginning of 1915, but Clan could only get the builders to expedite her construction by getting her construction classed as 'war work' and paying an extra £6,000 to the builders and £6,250 to the engine builders. Similarly, sums of £5,000 to the builder and £3,500 to the engine builders were necessary to encourage Napier and Miller to complete* Clan Ranald *(3). Even then, the ships were late: the* Clan Mackay *(3) was expected in September but was not delivered until December. Craig, Taylor's* Clan Malcolm *(1) cost an extra £19,500, but the builder lost out on a further payment of £1,000 as it could not deliver the ship by November 1916.*

The photographic record is, sadly, incomplete, as not a few of the war built ships were lost, sometimes within months, including the Clan Mackay *and* Clan Matheson. *The ships are presented roughly in chronological order of registration in Clan's ownership, with sisters grouped together.*

CLAN STUART (3) 1916-1940
O.N. 137827 5,775g. 3,639n
423.5 x 56.0 x 28.7 feet.
T.3-cyl. by John G. Kincaid and Co. Ltd., Greenock; 538 NHP, 2,400 IHP, 11 knots.
1930: Fitted with a Bauer-Wach low-pressure exhaust steam turbine; increasing total output to 627 NHP.
29.7.1916: Launched by Russell and Co., Port Glasgow (Yard No. 689).
17.10.1916: Registered in the ownership of The Clan Line Steamers Ltd. (Cayzer, Irvine and Co. Ltd., managers), Glasgow as CLAN STUART
16.5.1917: Requisitioned by the British government until 8.5.1919.
11.3.1940: Sank following a collision in fog with the British steamship ORLOCK HEAD (1,563/1921) 18 miles south east of Start Point whilst on a voyage in convoy from the Tyne via Antwerp to Beira and East London. The crew took to the boats and were picked up later that day by the French fishing vessel NOTRE DAME DE MONTLIGNON.
13.5.1940: Register closed.

CLAN MACKAY (3) 1916-1918
O.N. 137829 6,580g 4,190n
420.2 x 53.4 x 36.3 feet.
T.3-cyl. by the North Eastern Marine Engineering Co. Ltd., Newcastle; 660 NHP, 4,000 IHP, 12.5 knots.
17.7.1916: Launched by the Northumberland Shipbuilding Co. Ltd., Newcastle (Yard No. 229).
22.12.1916: Registered in the ownership of The Clan Line Steamers Ltd. (Cayzer, Irvine and Co. Ltd., managers), Glasgow as CLAN MACKAY.
27.12.1916: Delivered.
8.1917: Requisitioned by the British government.
11.5.1918: Sank following a collision with the British steamship EURYPYLUS (5,691/1912) in convoy 520 miles south west of the Scilly Isles whilst on a voyage from Liverpool to Calcutta with general cargo. The crew were picked up by the cruiser USS BIRMINGHAM and landed at Gibraltar.
3.8.1919: Register closed.

Clan Stuart (3) at Manchester. *[Kevin O'Donoghue collection]*

CLAN MACKENZIE (3) 1917-1937

O.N. 137849 6,544g 4,142n
420.1 x 53.4 x 36.4 feet.
T.3-cyl. by the North Eastern Marine
Engineering Co. Ltd., Newcastle-upon-Tyne;
662 NHP, 4,000 IHP, 12.5 knots.
1918: T. 3-cyl. by D. and W. Henderson and
Co. Ltd., Glasgow; 610 NHP, 2,500 IHP, 10
knots.
1930: Fitted with a Bauer-Wach low-pressure
exhaust steam turbine; increasing total output
to 698 NHP.
1.1917: Launched by the Northumberland
Shipbuilding Co. Ltd., Willington-on-Tyne
(Yard No. 231).
18.6.1917: Registered in the ownership of
The Clan Line Steamers Ltd. (Cayzer, Irvine
and Co. Ltd., managers), Glasgow as CLAN
MACKENZIE.
23.6.1917: Requisitioned by the British
government until 19.2.1919.
5.3.1918: Hit by a torpedo fired by the
German submarine UB 30 off St. Catherine's
Point whilst on a voyage from Liverpool to
Plymouth. Six members of her crew were
killed, and the remaining 82 taken off by
HMS GARLAND. She was reboarded the
next day, towed into the Solent and beached
near Portsmouth where she was later repaired,
requiring a new set of engines.
5.4.1933: Fire reported in tobacco in number
2 hold whilst on a voyage from the Phillipines
to the Mediterranean and Continental ports.
Proceeded to Syracuse, Sicily where the fire
was extinguished on 10.4.1933. She was
repaired by Greenock Dockyard Co. Ltd.
23.10.1937: Collided with the British steamer
MANCHESTER REGIMENT (7,930/1922)
in Liverpool Bay whilst outward bound to
East London. Subsequently beached to
prevent her from sinking. The crew were
taken off by the Mersey Docks and Harbour
Board's salvage tender VIGILANT (344/
1903).
28.10.1937: Register closed.
18.11.1937: Refloated and anchored in the
Queen's Channel.
19.11.1937: Arrived in Gladstone Dock after
she had been sufficiently lightened.
29.3.1938: Arrived at Troon to be broken up
by the West of Scotland Shipbreaking Co.
Ltd.

Bought whilst under construction, *Clan Mackenzie* (3) was a virtual repeat of *Clan Mackay* of 1916. In 1926, the government was belated in claiming £18,500 as a contribution towards the new engine which had been fitted following her torpedoeing in March 1918, and paid for by the government's war risk managers. Clan countered that the new, less powerful engines had caused her to depreciate in value. The argument was settled by Clan paying back some of her hire fee.

Having survived torpedoes in 1918, and fire in 1933, she met her end due to what might be called friendly fire. Leaving Liverpool in October 1937 she was overtaking the *Manchester Regiment*, which was flying the flags 'JT' signifying that she was adjusting her compasses. Suddenly she changed course and hit *Clan Mackenzie* on the port side, so disabling her that she had to be beached, although contemporary newspaper photographs show that at high water she was practically covered with water. Salvage was expensive: £10,000 having been quoted, but the 20-year old *Clan Mackenzie* was fit only for scrap. Applying the rule of the road, a judge subsequently decided that the Manchester Liner was 80% to blame.

Clan Mackenzie is seen, first in dazzle paint when leaving Portsmouth Dockyard after being repaired in 1918, in peacetime colours in the Mersey, and in the ignominious position of resting on the bottom of the Mersey estuary in 1937. *[Top: Kevin O'Donoghue collection, middle: Ian J. Farquhar collection]*

CLAN RANALD (3) 1917-1944

O.N. 137833 5,503g 3,445n
409.1 x 54.0 x 28.9 feet.
T.3-cyl. by John G. Kincaid and Co. Ltd.,
Glasgow; 537 NHP, 2,100 IHP, 11 knots.
28.12.1916: Launched by Napier and
Miller Ltd., Old Kilpatrick, Glasgow (Yard
No. 199).
24.2.1917: Registered in the ownership of
The Clan Line Steamers Ltd. (Cayzer,
Irvine and Co. Ltd., managers), Glasgow
as CLAN RANALD.
27.2.1917: Delivered
13.11.1917: Requisitioned by the British
government until 11.8.1919.
4.7.1940: Requisitioned by the British
government until 27.5.1946
17.3.1944: Transferred to the British and
South American Steam Navigation Co.
Ltd., (Houston Line (London) Ltd.,
managers), London.
29.8.1947: Sold to Pace Brothers Ltd.
Valetta, Malta (Gordon O. Till, London,
manager).
24.2.1948: Renamed VALETTA CITY.
23.5.1951: Register closed on sale to
Società di Navigazione Vecchia Genova,
Genoa, Italy and renamed LA VALETTA.
1953: Sold to Ditta Pala e Franceschini,
Genoa.
25.3.1958: Arrived at La Spezia and laid
up.
5.1958: Breaking up began by Cantiere
Navale del Golfo.

The third *Clan Ranald* was bought from her builders in February 1915, with the promise of delivery in August. As soon as she had been launched, much later than expected, Clan asked Napier and Miller to lay down another steamer on the vacated berth for a price of £156,000, and even decided to name her *Clan Campbell*. But pressure on the yard to build standard ships for the government proved too intense, and her contract was cancelled at the builders' suggestion in April 1917.

    Clan Ranald's entry into service was most unfortunate: arriving on the Mersey to load in February 1917 she was in collision with the *Cufic* (8,249/1895) - which was later found to blame - requiring a trip to Manchester for dry docking. Despite this bad start, *Clan Ranald* managed over 30 years with the company, and when sold was still good for a further decade of trading. She was photographed in the Mersey on 16th September 1934 by John McRoberts (top), approaching Eastham Locks during the Second World War (middle), and as the *La Valetta* after her 1951 sale to Italian buyers. [*Top: J. and M. Clarkson collection, middle: National Maritime Museum P22124, and bottom: Ships in Focus collection*]

Clan Malcolm (1) is seen, first in Australia, and again after she ran ashore in fog just beneath the Lizard Coastguard Station shortly before 8.00pm on 26th September 1935. She was reported as filling fast, and a boat quickly went alongside to take off most of the crew who were landed at Cadgwith. Although the German salvage tug Seefalke anchored astern of her, salvage proved a vain hope: she was hard aground with her engine room and all forward holds flooded. In two days her position was being described as 'critical' and on 4th November she broke her back. The last two pictures, of her remains, show what the sea can do to a ship in a short time. Clan Malcolm's master was held to blame and had his certificate suspended for a year.

She was indeed an unfortunate ship, having contributed to the loss of the Burns and Laird passenger steamer Rowan in October 1921. Whilst outward bound from Greenock to Belfast in fog, Rowan had been hit by the inward bound US steamer West Camak (5,881/1920). Whilst orders were given to abandon ship, Rowan swung across the channel and was hit by Clan Malcolm which was following her. At the subsequent enquiry, Clan Malcolm was held two thirds to blame for proceeding too fast in fog, escaping complete responsibility only because the Rowan had not sounded her whistle as a vessel stopped in the water. As she was busy evacuating her passengers at the time, this judgement seems a little harsh on Rowan. [Top: Ian J. Farquhar collection, middle: Nigel Farrell collection, bottom and left: J. and M. Clarkson collection]

CLAN MALCOLM (1) 1917-1935

O.N. 137837 5,994g 3,724n
405.1 x 53.4 x 33.5 feet.
T.3-cyl. by Blair and Co. Ltd., Stockton-on-Tees; 560 NHP, 2,600 IHP, 11 knots.
9.11.1916: Launched by Craig, Taylor and Co. Ltd., Stockton-on-Tees (Yard No. 172).
31.3.1917: Registered in the ownership of The Clan Line Steamers Ltd. (Cayzer, Irvine and Co. Ltd., managers), Glasgow as CLAN MALCOLM.
5.4.1917: Delivered.
7.4.1917: Requisitioned by the British government until 6.3.1919.
8.10.1921: Whilst on a voyage from Glasgow to Liverpool collided in fog off Corsewall Point, Wigtownshire with the steamer ROWAN (1,103/1909) which sank with the loss of 20 lives.
26.9.1935: Wrecked on Tregwin Rocks, Green Lane Cove, The Lizard, Cornwall whilst on a voyage from Port Natal and Durban to Glasgow via London with a cargo of maize.
8.10.1935: Register closed.

CLAN MATHESON (3) 1917-1918

O.N. 137858 5,960g. 3,736n
405.0 x 53.5 x 33.5 feet.
T.3-cyl. by George Clark Ltd., Sunderland. 560 NHP, 2,900 IHP, 11° knots.
14.8.1916: Launched by Sir James Laing and Sons, Sunderland (Yard No. 657).
1.1917: Completed.
13.9.1917: Registered in the ownership of The Clan Line Steamers Ltd. (Cayzer, Irvine and Co. Ltd, managers), Glasgow as CLAN MATHESON.
15.9.1917: Requisitioned by the British government.
17.9.1917: Delivered.
23.5.1918: Sank following a collision with the United States steamer WESTERN FRONT (5,743/1917) in position 40.32 north by 49.10 west whilst on a voyage in convoy from New Orleans, Newport News and New York to Nantes with a cargo of barley, oats and steel. The entire crew were picked up by the WESTERN FRONT and landed in New York.
3.8.1918: Register closed.

The Clan Line board authorised a repeat of Clan Matheson *soon after she was launched in August 1916, but in March 1917 recognised that pressure on the yards to build standard ships was too intense, and the order was abandoned.*

SUTHERLAND SHIPS

Two ships completed or about to be delivered by Doxford to B.J. Sutherland were acquired at the cost of £250,000 each. A measure of the rapid fall in value of ships in the early 1920s is that Clan Macmaster *was insured for just £102,000 at the time of her loss in 1923.* Clan Macmillan *was equally short lived, her loss in the Bay of Bengal in 1924 being attributed to a gross error of judgement by her master.*

CLAN MACMASTER 1917-1923

O.N. 140696 6,563g 4,137n
420.0 x 54.0 x 34.4 feet.
T.3-cyl. by William Doxford and Sons Ltd., Sunderland; 568 NHP, 2,600 IHP, 11 knots.

Clan Macmaster had a short career and an ignominious end, which is undoubtedly why her name was not repeated. On 30th September 1923 while on a routine coasting voyage from the Clyde to the Mersey she encountered fog and fetched up on Thousla Rock on the Isle of Man, to have the dubious distinction of becoming the largest Manx shipwreck. The two ships bought from B.J. Sutherland were singularly unfortunate; the *Clan Macmillan* being just as short lived. *[J. and M. Clarkson collection,]*

Clan Macmaster aground on Thousla Rock, near Port Erin, Isle of Man. *[Left: Archie Munro collection, right: Nigel Farrell collection*

24.2.1917: Launched by William Doxford and Sons Ltd., Sunderland (Yard No. 481).
3.9.1917: Registered in the ownership of Munro Shipping Co. Ltd. (B.J. Sutherland and Co. Ltd., managers), Newcastle-upon-Tyne as SUTHERLAND.
29.12.1917: Acquired by The Clan Line Steamers Ltd. (Cayzer, Irvine and Co. Ltd., managers), London for £250,000.
9.1.1918: Renamed CLAN MACMASTER.
15.1.1918: Requisitioned by the British government until 30.5.1918.
30.9.1923: Wrecked on Thousla Rock, Calf of Man whilst on a voyage from Glasgow to Liverpool, from where she was due to sail to Colombo, Madras and Calcutta. There were no casualties. Efforts by the salvage steamer RANGER failed to refloat her, although some cargo was recovered.
17.10.1923: Register closed.

CLAN MACMILLAN (2) 1918-1924
O.N. 141883 6,608g 4,109n
420.0 x 54.0 x 34.4 feet.
T.3-cyl. by Richardsons, Westgarth and Co. Ltd., Hartlepool; 568 NHP, 2,800 IHP, 11 knots.
29.12.1917: Launched by William Doxford and Sons Ltd., Sunderland (Yard No. 517) for the Munro Shipping Co. Ltd. (B.J. Sutherland and Co. Ltd., managers), Newcastle-upon-Tyne as DUMFRIES.
21.6.1918: Registered in the ownership of The Clan Line Steamers Ltd. (Cayzer, Irvine and Co. Ltd., managers), London as CLAN MACMILLAN, having been acquired for £250,000.
4.7.1918: Requisitioned by the British government until 28.7.1919.
21.6.1924: Wrecked on a reef off Preparis Island in the Bay of Bengal north of the Andaman Islands whilst on a voyage from the United Kingdom to Calcutta and the

Pacific Islands with general cargo. There were no casualties, the crew being picked up by passing vessels including the tanker MINHLA (1,300/1909) and landed at Rangoon or Chittagong.
22.9.1924: Register closed.

SCOTTISH SHIRES TAKEN OVER
At a meeting of the Clan Line board in February 1918 it was minuted that as from 31st December 1917 Scottish Shire Line Ltd. of Turnbull, Martin and Co. had been taken over for £710,000. The company had but two ships, the Ayrshire and Argyllshire, but its attraction was its loading rights in Australia. It was undoubtedly a good investment, and the line was eventually to benefit from the transfer of several relatively new ships from the Clan Line fleet, and four new buildings.

Clan Macmillan (2) was very unusual for Clan in having only kingposts. *[Allan C. Green/State Library of Victoria, b.42926]*

AYRSHIRE (1) 1918-1926

O.N. 119066 9,188g 5,931n
460.0 58.8 x 31.8 feet.
Two T.3-cyl. by the North Eastern
Marine Engineering Co. Ltd.,
Wallsend-on-Tyne driving twin
screws; 893 NHP, 5,400 IHP total,
13 knots.
28.8.1903: Launched by R. and W.
Hawthorn, Leslie and Co. Ltd.,
Hebburn-on-Tyne (Yard No. 389).
10.11.1903: Registered in the
ownership of D'Arcy M. Dawes
and David C. Leck, London
(Turnbull, Martin and Co.,
managers), Glasgow as
AYRSHIRE.
23.6.1908: Transferred to the
Elderslie Steamship Co. Ltd.
(Turnbull, Martin and Co.,
managers), Glasgow.
10.8.1910: Transferred to the
Scottish Shire Line Ltd. (Turnbull,
Martin and Co. Ltd., managers),
Glasgow and later London.
28.11.1926: Abandoned on fire in
the Indian Ocean in position 07.50
north by 73.50 east whilst on a
voyage from Brisbane to the United
Kingdom and the Continent with
general cargo including tallow and
frozen meat. The crew were taken
off by the steamers AENEAS
(10,058/1910) and CITY OF
NAGPUR (10,138/1922). HMS
LUPIN stood by, and tried to take
her in tow, but then decided to sink
her as a danger to navigation.
29.11.1926: Sunk by HMS LUPIN
in position 09.12 north by 73.28
east.
17.12.1926: Register closed.

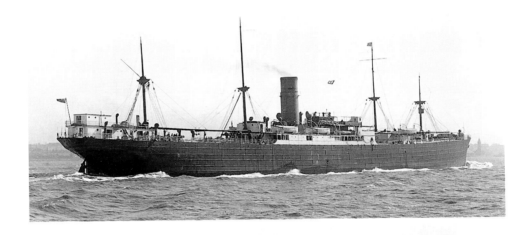

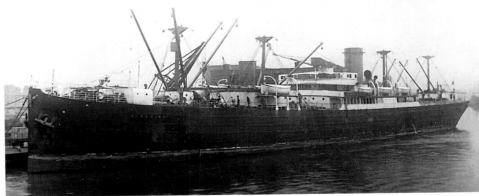

When delivered in 1903 *Ayrshire* was one of the largest and finest refrigerated ships serving New Zealand, and still looked impressive when Clan took over Scottish Shire Line in 1918. This book describes her as *Ayrshire* (1) as she was the first in the Clan fleet to use the name, but was in fact Turnbull, Martin's second *Ayrshire*.

The upper two photographs were taken on the Mersey: prominent are the flanges for removing the funnel top. The bottom picture shows her in Manchester with the funnel top and topmasts removed. *[All: J. and M. Clarkson collection]*

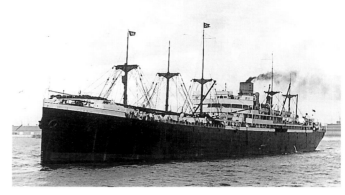

In 1904 Scottish Shire Line in conjunction with Federal Steam Navigation Co. Ltd. and Houlder Brothers began a joint service on behalf of the State of Victoria to take out emigrants and bring frozen meat back to the United Kingdom. In 1911 three massive ships were delivered for this service, Scottish Shire's contribution being the *Argyllshire*, originally having accommodation for 130 first class passengers (quickly reduced to 62) and several hundred emigrants in dormitories. Houlders withdrew from this service in April 1912 but the other partners continued six-weekly sailings, mainly from Liverpool but with discharge at Manchester which required the ships to have telescopic top masts and the facility for the removal of the upper part of the funnel top for passage along the Ship Canal (middle left). Not surprisingly, *Argyllshire* was requisitioned as a troop ship by the Australian government immediately on the outbreak of the First World War (top left).

The joint service was not resumed after the First World War, although all three ships continued to trade to

Australasia, *Argyllshire* now having a nominal capacity of 113 first class and 76 third class passengers, although this was not always full. As trading conditions became depressed, it was found increasingly difficult to employ her. During the coal shortage occasioned by the miner's strike in 1926 she was taken out of lay up on the Thames and sent to the USA to bring a cargo of coal back to Birkenhead, her holds requiring careful cleaning before being put on a Clan Line berth. Subsequent voyages included a round-the-world trip, before she went back into lay up in late 1928, this time in the Gareloch, and was then sold to Federal together with homeward loading rights for £145,000. The improvement in trade in the 1930s saw her bought back by Clan Line, for whom she spent her last years running to South and East Africa as *Clan Urquhart* (2)(bottom). Of her sisters, the Federal-owned *Wiltshire* (10,390/1912) was wrecked in May 1922 and their *Shropshire* (10,347/1911) was torpedoed under the name *Rotorua* in December 1940. *[Top: B. and A. Feilden/J. and M. Clarkson collection, middle: Ian J. Farquhar collection]*

ARGYLLSHIRE (1) / CLAN URQUHART (2) 1918-1929/1932-1936

O.N. 129581 10,236g 6,054n
526.2 x 61.4 x 33.3 feet.
Two Q.4-cyl. by John Brown and Co. Ltd.,
Clydebank driving twin screws; 644 NHP,
5,500 IHP, 14 knots.
27.2.1911: Launched by John Brown and
Co. Ltd., Clydebank (Yard No. 399).
6.1911: Completed.
1.7.1911: Registered in the ownership of
the Scottish Shire Line Ltd. (Turnbull,
Martin and Co. Ltd., managers), Glasgow
as ARGYLLSHIRE.
5.2.1917: Torpedoed about three miles off
Start Point, but succeeded in reaching
Falmouth. Later repaired.
7.10.1929: Sold to the Federal Steam
Navigation Co. Ltd., London.
15.11.1932: Acquired by The Clan Line
Steamers Ltd. (Cayzer, Irvine and Co. Ltd.,
managers), London for £12,000.
21.12.1932: Renamed CLAN
URQUHART.
1936: Sold to T.W. Ward Ltd., Sheffield
for £22,000.
30.10.1936: Arrived at Briton Ferry.
14.3.1937: During demolition damaged by
fire and scuttled in shallow water.
12.10.1937: Register closed.

RUSSELL PAIR

CLAN KENNETH (1) 1918-1934

O.N. 127551 4,897g 3,159n
400.0 x 52.0 x 27.4 feet.
T.3-cyl. by Rankin and Blackmore Ltd.,
Glasgow; 479 NHP, 2,300 IHP, 10.5 knots.
17.8.1909: Launched by Russell and
Company, Port Glasgow (Yard No. 588).
4.9.1909: Registered in the ownership of
the Steamship Ardgryfe Co. Ltd. (Lang
and Fulton Ltd., managers), Greenock as
ARDGRYFE.
30.9.1916: Requisitioned by the British
government until 15.12.1916.
17.3.1917: Requisitioned by the British
government until 7.4.1919.
16.1.1918: Acquired by The Clan Line
Steamers Ltd. (Cayzer, Irvine and Co. Ltd.,
managers), London for £150,000.
22.5.1918: Renamed CLAN KENNETH.
1934: Sold to Hughes Bolckow Ltd.
4.1.1934: Arrived at Blyth to be broken up.
19.1.1934: Register closed.

CLAN KENNEDY (1) 1918-1924

O.N. 123539 4,936g 3,160n
400.0 x 52.0 x 27.3 feet.
T.3-cyl. by Rankin and Blackmore Ltd.,
Greenock; 471 NHP, 2,300 IHP, 10.5
knots.
11.9.1907: Launched by Russell and
Company, Port Glasgow (Yard No. 570).
30.9.1907: Registered in the ownership of
the Burn Line Ltd. (R. Shankland and Co.
Ltd., managers), Greenock as
OTTERBURN.

The *Ardgryfe* at Boston, U.S.A. on 2nd April 1916. She later became the *Clan Kenneth* (1). *[Wm. A. Schell]*

Clan Kenneth (1) on the Mersey. *[B. and A. Feilden/J. and M. Clarkson]*

Ardgarroch. Although built for different owners, she was a near sister of *Clan Kenneth* and was bought by Clan Line from the same Greenock-based fleet of Lang and Fulton and became *Clan Kennedy* (1). *[Nigel Farrell collection]*

10.1907: Completed.
1.9.1911: Sold to the Steamship
Ardgarroch Co. Ltd. (Lang and Fulton
Ltd., managers), Greenock.
7.9.1911: Renamed ARDGARROCH.
2.12.1916: Requisitioned by the British
government until 23.8.1919.
18.2.1918: Acquired by The Clan Line
Steamers Ltd. (Cayzer, Irvine and Co. Ltd.,
managers), London for £135,000.

15.4.1918: Renamed CLAN KENNEDY.
16.1.1924: Stranded on Sizewell Bank, one
mile north from Thorpeness, Suffolk, whilst
on a voyage from New Caledonia to
Hamburg and London with a cargo of nickel
ore and copra. Subsequently salvaged.
28.3.1924: Register closed following sale to
John Cashmore Ltd. for demolition.
3.4.1924: Arrived at Newport, Monmouthshire in tow for breaking up.

HOUSTON SHIPS TAKEN OVER

A much more substantial acquisition than Scottish Shire was announced in September 1918, that of R.P. Houston and Co. and the British and South American Steam Navigation Co. Ltd. This was no great surprise, as the Cayzer family already had a substantial enough shareholding to have appointed directors to the Houston board. As the list below shows, the fleet was decidedly elderly, with nothing younger than 16 years and the oldest ship having been in service for 28 years. In fact, the company had not built a new ship since 1902 or bought anything since 1903. As with Scottish Shire, the attraction was its services, giving Clan routes from the UK and the USA to South America, a London to South Africa service, and other interests in South Africa, where Houston was soon to buy the coastal operator Thesens Steamship Co. Ltd.

Houston was treated as a poor relation. Its urgent need for fleet renewal was met by buying war-built tonnage and ships taken over from Germany. Indeed, it was decided to put some ships under Houston ownership not to improve the fleet but because the government had made it plain that ship owners had to buy war-built or German reparation tonnage to replace any ships that were sold foreign, as were Herminius *and* Hilarius.

Because of the depressed state of the South American trades in the 1920s, and particularly that from the Eastern seaboard of the USA which was hit by continuing heavy competition and the depression, Houston did not receive priority for new tonnage. For the rest of its existence it had to make do with vessels transferred from Clan plus a couple of Second World War standards. Even the transfers were somewhat arbitrary, as Clan and Houston ships were often used on the other company's berths, as sailing schedules and availability of vessels dictated. Although the fleets were not fully merged, there was from now on little but a difference in naming scheme (and initially in funnel colours) to outwardly distinguish Clan and Houston ships, and later Houston ships have been placed in the main fleet list.

HERMINIUS (1) 1918-1919

O.N. 109442 3,525g 2,276n
339.4 x 45.9 x 29.8 feet.
T.3-cyl. by Hutson and Son, Glasgow; 299 NHP, 1,600 IHP, 9 knots.
3.5.1898: Launched by Russell and Co., Port Glasgow (Yard No. 428).
17.6.1898: Registered in the ownership of the British and South American Steam Navigation Co. Ltd. (R.P. Houston and Co., managers), Liverpool as HERMINIUS.
18.7.1919: Register closed on sale to N.G. Livanos, Piraeus, Greece and renamed SPYRIDON.

18.6.1922: Wrecked in fog on Bidvido Rocks, off Vigo, Spain whilst on a voyage from Seriphos to Rotterdam with a cargo of minerals.

HORATIUS 1918-1919

O.N. 109462 3,552g 2,297n
339.2 x 45.9 x 29.8 feet.
T.3-cyl. by Hutson and Son, Glasgow; 298 NHP, 1,600 IHP, 9 knots.
27.6.1898: Launched by Russell and Company, Port Glasgow (Yard No. 430).
28.9.1898: Registered in the ownership of the British and South American Steam Navigation Co. Ltd. (R.P. Houston and Co., managers), Liverpool as HORATIUS.
7.4.1919: Sold to the London Transport Co. Ltd. (Brown, Jenkinson and Co., managers), London for £86,400.
6.5.1919: Renamed MONNETTE
12.4.1920: Managers became E.J. Heinz (London) Ltd.

22.11.1926: Register closed on sale to F. Marchese Pucci, Catania, Italy and renamed NICE.
1932: Sold to Belgian shipbreakers while laid up at Antwerp.
1932: Resold to O. Rosini, Genoa, Italy and renamed ALGA for delivery voyage.
1933: Broken up in Italy during the first quarter

HYANTHES 1918-1923

O.N. 110565 4,354g 2,793n
350.0 x 47.0 x 32.3 feet.
T.3-cyl. by John Dickinson and Sons Ltd., Sunderland; 432 NHP, 2,400 IHP, 12.5 knots.
9.2.1899: Launched by Bartram and Sons, Sunderland (Yard No. 173).
30.3.1899: Registered in the ownership of the British and South American Steam Navigation Co. Ltd. (R.P. Houston and Co., managers), Liverpool as HYANTHES.
4.1899: Completed.

Horatius. [J. and M. Clarkson collection]

Hyanthes was the sole surviving member of a class of four built for Houston at Sunderland. The others were *Hermes*, wrecked in Table Bay during May 1901, *Hyades* sunk by the German cruiser *Dresden* in August 1914, and *Hesperides* torpedoed off Fastnet in April 1917. *[George Scott collection]*

12.1916: Requisitioned by the Admiralty until 10.1918, operating as a submarine decoy or Q-ship under the names CRAVEN, LORIMER and OOMA.
18.6.1923: Arrived at Rotterdam to be broken up by Frank Rijsdijk & Co., Hendrik-Ido-Ambacht, but resold to Eisen-und-Metall G.m.b.H. and towed to Hamburg by the tug ZWARTE ZEE for breaking up.
22.6.1923: Register closed.

HONORIUS 1918-1925
O.N. 110594 3,476g 2,126n
350.0 x 47.0 x 25.0 feet.
T.3-cyl. by David Rowan and Co., Glasgow; 438 NHP, 1,900 IHP, 11 knots.
28.1.1899: Launched by Archibald McMillan and Son Ltd., Dumbarton (Yard No. 364).
7.1899: Completed.
12.8.1899: Registered in the ownership of the British and South American Steam Navigation Co. Ltd. (R.P. Houston and Co., managers), Liverpool as HONORIUS.
1925: Sold to T.W. Ward Ltd., Sheffield.
21.10.1925: Arrived at Preston to be broken up.
22.10.1925: Work began.
26.4.1926: Register closed.

HORTENSIUS 1918-1925
O.N. 110606 3,472g 2,125n
350.0 x 47.0 x 25.0 feet.
T.3-cyl. by David Rowan and Co., Glasgow; 438 NHP; 1,900 IHP, 11 knots.
28.3.1899: Launched by Archibald McMillan and Son Ltd., Dumbarton (Yard No. 365).
9.9.1899: Registered in the ownership of the British and South American Steam Navigation Co. Ltd. (R.P. Houston and Co., managers), Liverpool as HORTENSIUS.
1925: Sold to the Alloa Shipbreaking Co. Ltd., Alloa.
20.2.1926: Arrived at Charlestown, Fife.
3.3.1926: Breaking up began.
14.7.1928: Register closed.

HOSTILIUS 1918-1926
O.N. 113374 3,322g 2,089n
350.0 x 47.0 x 24.9 feet.
T.3-cyl. by David Rowan and Co., Glasgow; 600 NHP; 3,000 IHP, 13.5 knots.
15.5.1900: Launched by Archibald McMillan and Son Ltd., Dumbarton (Yard No. 372).
2.7.1900: Registered in the ownership of the British and South American Steam Navigation Co. Ltd. (R.P. Houston and Co., managers), Liverpool as HOSTILIUS.
4.7.1900: Ran trials.
19.1.1926: Sold to the Byron Steamship Co. Ltd. (Michael A. Embiricos, manager), London.

Honorius, seen here at the breakers, was the first of four sisters built at Dumbarton for Houston, all of which survived the First World War. *[Nigel Farrell collection]*

Hortensius. *[George Scott collection]*

Hostilius. *[Newall Dunn collection]*

21.1.1926: Renamed GENERAL NAPIER.
6.1928: Sold to Alloa Shipbreaking Co. Ltd., Alloa.
4.7.1928: Arrived at Rosyth.
25.7.1928: Work began.
4.12.1929: Register closed.

HELLENES (1) 1918-1925
O.N. 113410 3,332g 2,029n
350.2 x 47.0 x 25.0 feet.
T.3-cyl. by David Rowan and Co., Glasgow; 600 NHP, 3,000 IHP, 13.5 knots.
1900: Laid down by Archibald McMillan and Son Ltd., Dumbarton (Yard No. 373) as HORUS.

13.7.1900: Launched as HELLENES.
24.9.1900: Registered in the ownership of the British and South American Steam Navigation Co. Ltd. (R.P. Houston and Co., managers), Liverpool as HELLENES.
27.9.1900: Ran trials.
11.1925: Sold to T.W. Ward Ltd., Sheffield.
21.10.1925: Breaking up began at Grays, Essex.
6.4.1926: Register closed.

HILARIUS (1) 1918-1919
O.N. 104255 3,969g 2,538n
344.6 x 43.1 x 26.8 feet.
T.3-cyl. by Robert Stephenson and Co. Ltd., Hebburn-on-Tyne; 400 NHP, 2,200 IHP, 12 knots.
7.5.1894: Launched by Robert Stephenson and Co. Ltd., Hebburn-on-Tyne (Yard No. 30).
29.6.1894: Registered in the ownership of Prince Steam Shipping Insurance Association (James Knott, manager), Newcastle-upon-Tyne as AFGHAN PRINCE.
27.1.1895: Transferred to Prince Line Ltd. (James Knott, manager), Newcastle-upon-Tyne.
5.8.1899: Acquired by the British and South American Steam Navigation Co. Ltd. (R.P. Houston and Co., managers), Liverpool.
16.8.1899: Renamed HILARIUS.
14.11.1919: Register closed on sale to M.G. Livanos, Piraeus, Greece and renamed LIVANOS.
27.8.1923: Wrecked at Chapelet in the Straits of Bonifacio whilst on a voyage from Follonica to Hamburg with a cargo of iron ore.

HARMODIUS (1) 1918-1919
O.N. 101917 3,513g 2,213n
360.0 x 43.5 x 26.1 feet.
T.3-cyl. by Wigham, Richardson and Co., Newcastle-upon-Tyne; 500 NHP, 2,600 IHP, 12 knots.
23.6.1892: Launched by the Sunderland Shipbuilding Co. Ltd., Sunderland (Yard No. 173).
8.1892: Completed.
24.8.1892: Registered in the ownership of William Lund, London as WARRNAMBOOL.
28.11.1900: Acquired by the British and South American Steam Navigation Co. Ltd. (R.P. Houston and Co., managers), Liverpool.
28.11.1900: Renamed HARMODIUS.
15.2.1919: Sold to Kaye, Son and Co. Ltd., London.
7.3.1919: Transferred to the 'K' Steamship Co. Ltd. (Kaye, Son and Co. Ltd., managers), London.
28.4.1919: Renamed KUT.
1926: Sold to T.W. Ward Ltd., Sheffield.
16.11.1926: Arrived at Briton Ferry to be broken up.
22.12.1927: Register closed.

Hellenes. [George Scott collection]

Elegant but anachronistic: the *Afghan Prince* briefly joined the fleet as the *Hilarius* and brought the clipper bow back to the fleet after an absence of 16 years. [*Nigel Farrell collection*]

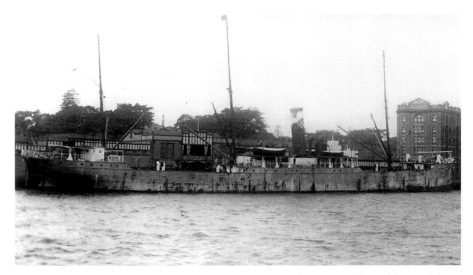

Following the Clan Line take over *Harmodius* (above) and her sister *Harmonides* were quickly sold to Kaye, Son and Co. Ltd. in a deal worth £160,000. [*Newall Dunn collection*]

HARMONIDES (1) 1918-1919

O.N. 98954 3,521g 2,221n
360.0 x 44.4 x 26.0 feet.
T.3-cyl. by Wigham, Richardson and Co.,
Newcastle-upon-Tyne; 500 NHP, 2,000
IHP, 12 knots.
26.5.1891: Launched by Wigham,
Richardson and Co., Newcastle-upon-Tyne
(Yard No. 262).
6.7.1891: Registered in the ownership of
William Lund, London as
WOOLLOOMOOLOO.
21.3.1901: Acquired by the British and
South American Steam Navigation Co.
Ltd. (R.P. Houston and Co., managers),
Liverpool.
22.3.1901: Renamed HARMONIDES.
7.3.1902: In collision off Anglesey with
the Belgian steamer WAESLAND (4,752/
1867) which sank.
20.1.1918: Damaged by a torpedo from
the German submarine UC 71 off St.
Catherine's Point in the English Channel
whilst on a voyage from London to
Newport. Reached Falmouth, and
continued to Newport.
15.2.1919: Sold to Kaye, Son and Co.
Ltd., London.
7.3.1919: Transferred to the 'K' Steamship
Co. Ltd. (Kaye, Son and Co. Ltd.,
managers), London.
12.6.1919: Renamed KHARTUM.
20.12.1926: Register closed on sale to A.
Ardito for demolition at Genoa.

HYDASPES 1918-1930

O.N. 108840 5,658g 3,630n
452.0 x 52.2 x 28.2 feet.
T. 3-cyl. by Palmers' Shipbuilding and
Iron Co. Ltd., Jarrow-on-Tyne; 750 NHP,
3,500 IHP, 12 knots.
26.4.1899: Launched by Palmers'
Shipbuilding and Iron Co. Ltd., Jarrow-on-
Tyne (Yard No. 740).
She had been ordered by Furness, Withy
and Co. Ltd., West Hartlepool.
6.1899: Completed.

Woolloomooloo, bought in 1901 and renamed *Harmonides.* [Nigel Farrell collection]

Hydaspes was the largest ship yet in the Houston fleet at the time of acquisition, and was followed by two sisters, *Hypatia* and *Hyacinthus,* which were presumably bought whilst completing for companies in the Furness, Withy group. *Hydaspes* was modified for carrying cattle in August 1926. [F. W. Hawks/Newall Dunn collection]

17.6.1899: Registered in the ownership of
Manchester Liners Ltd., Manchester as
MANCHESTER PORT.
2.8.1900: Acquired by Robert P. Houston,
London.
14.8.1900: Transferred to the British and
South American Steam Navigation Co.

Ltd. (R.P. Houston and Co., managers),
Liverpool.
18.8.1900: Renamed HYDASPES.
1.1930: Sold to Luigi Pittaluga, Genoa,
Italy for £14,000.
1.4.1930: Arrived at Genoa to be broken
up.
12.4.1930: Register closed.

Hypatia was lost whilst taking a Clan Line sailing from East Africa to the USA, the mainstay of this trade being the carriage of chrome ore westbound. [Ambrose Greenway collection]

HYPATIA 1918-1929

O.N. 115246 7,305g 4,778n
452.0 x 52.2 x 28.3 feet.
T.3-cyl. by Palmer's Shipbuilding and Iron
Co. Ltd., Jarrow-on-Tyne; 750 NHP, 3,500
IHP, 12 knots.
26.11.1901: Launched by Palmer's
Shipbuilding and Iron Co. Ltd., Jarrow-on-
Tyne (Yard No. 760).
27.1.1902: Registered in the ownership of
the British and South American Steam
Navigation Co. Ltd. (R.P. Houston and
Co., managers), Liverpool as HYPATIA.
29.10.1929: Wrecked on Whale Rock,
Robben Island, Cape of Good Hope whilst
on a voyage from Beira and Port Natal to
New York with general cargo, chrome ore
and copper.
13.12.1929: Register closed.

HYACINTHUS 1918-1930

O.N. 115279 7,356g 4,769n
452.0 x 52.2 x 28.3 feet.
T.3-cyl. by Palmer's Shipbuilding and Iron
Co. Ltd., Jarrow-on-Tyne; 750 NHP, 3,500
IHP, 12.25 knots.
12.3.1902: Launched by Palmer's
Shipbuilding and Iron Co. Ltd., Jarrow-on-
Tyne (Yard No. 761).
14.5.1902: Registered in the ownership of
the British and South American Steam
Navigation Co. Ltd. (R.P. Houston and
Co., managers), Liverpool as
HYACINTHUS.
25.12.1917: Damaged by torpedo from the
German submarine UC 71 in the English
Channel. The hole was covered by a tar-
paulin and she was towed into Stokes Bay,
repaired and returned to service.
1930: Sold to Dutch breakers for £8,250.
17.10.1930: Arrived at Rotterdam to be
broken up.
21.10.1930: Register closed.

HYPERIA 1918

O.N. 105342 3,908g 2,518n
358.0 x 45.2 x 27.0 feet.
T.3-cyl. by John Dickinson and Sons Ltd.,
Sunderland; 500 NHP, 2,500 IHP, 10 knots.
7.8.1895: Launched by Joseph L.
Thompson and Sons Ltd., Sunderland (Yard
No. 323).
26.9.1895: Registered in the ownership of
the Norfolk and North American Steamship
Co. Ltd. (Simpson, Spence and Young,
managers), Newcastle-upon-Tyne as
PINNERS POINT.
13.8.1903: Acquired by the British and
South American Steam Navigation Co. Ltd.
(R.P. Houston and Co., managers),
Liverpool.
17.8.1903: Renamed HYPERIA.
28.7.1918: Torpedoed and sunk by the
German submarine UB 51 84 miles north
west by north of Port Said whilst on a
voyage from Marseilles to Port Said with
military equipment. Seven lives were lost.
2.9.1918: Register closed.

HOMEREUS 1918-1919

O.N. 98094 3,279g 2,097n
340.0 x 42.7 x 26.2 feet.
T.3-cyl. by Thomas Richardson and Co.,
Hartlepool, 450 NHP, 12.5 knots.
18.2.1890: Launched by Raylton Dixon
and Co., Middlesbrough (Yard No. 304).
14.5.1890: Registered in the ownership of
William Ross and Co., London as STORM
KING.
20.11.1893: Sold to Frank Ross, Quebec,
Canada.
3.11.1899: Sold to Thomas Ronaldson,
London.
6.5.1902: Transferred to Thomas
Ronaldson and Co. Ltd., London.
12.10.1903: Acquired by the British and
South American Steam Navigation Co.
Ltd. (R.P. Houston and Co., managers),
Liverpool.

The remains of the *Hypatia* after her stranding on Robben Island, South Africa.
[John Marsh collection]

Hyacinthus off Birkenhead. *[J. and M. Clarkson collection]*

Ronaldson's *Storm King* was acquired in October 1903 and renamed *Homereus*
later the same month. *[Nigel Farrell collection]*

22.10.1903: Renamed HOMEREUS.
21.10.1919: Sold to Burns, Philp and Co.
Ltd., Sydney, New South Wales.
1.12.1919: Renamed MALAYAN
1924: Sold to B. B. Wiltshire, Sydney.

11.5.1925: Register closed on sale to
Ninomiya Junichi, Hiogo-ken, Japan and
renamed HAKUYO MARU
1930: Dismantled at Uraga, Japan during
the fourth quarter.

Clan Macbeolan as *Halesius,* in the Mersey on 20th September 1931 in Houston ownership. *[John McRoberts/J. and M. Clarkson collection]*

ONE-OFF ACQUISITIONS
Despairing of getting ships built, the Clan Line board decided early in 1918 that whatever the price it would have to buy ships to replace losses so that it could carry on its business when the war was over. Two of these three non-standard ships were later transferred to Houston ownership.

CLAN MACBEOLAN/HALESIUS (1) 1918-1936
O.N. 131427 4,652g 2,903n
385.0 x 51.5 x 27.4 feet.
T.3-cyl. by Blair and Co. Ltd., Stockton-on-Tees; 419 NHP, 1,900 IHP, 10 knots.
2.2.1912: Launched by Craig, Taylor and Co. Ltd., Stockton-on-Tees (Yard No. 149).
11.3.1912: Registered in the ownership of the Steamship Lord Lathom Co. Ltd. (John Herron and Co., managers), Liverpool as LORD CROMER.

14.3.1912: Ran trials and completed.
1.5.1917: Requisitioned by the British government until 23.4.1919.
25.9.1917: Managers became Frank E. Dixon and Frederick W. Lund, London.
7.2.1918: Acquired by The Clan Line Steamers Ltd. (Cayzer, Irvine and Co. Ltd, managers), London.
16.2.1918: Renamed CLAN MACBEOLAN.
23.3.1920: Transferred to the British and South American Steam Navigation Co. Ltd. (R.P. Houston and Co., managers), Liverpool for £225,000.
7.4.1920: Renamed HALESIUS.
6.1.1936: Register closed on sale to M. Sitinis and Company, Andros, Greece, and renamed AVRA.
25.9.1941: Sank following a collision in fog with the British steamer MARVIA (1,989/1914) off Duncansby Head whilst on

a voyage from London to Montreal in ballast.

CLAN MACBEAN (1) 1918-1946
O.N. 141876 5,052g 3,082n
400.0 x 52.4 x 28.0 feet.
T.3-cyl. by John Dickinson and Sons Ltd., Sunderland; 476 NHP, 2,290 IHP, 11.5 knots.
31.10.1917: Launched by Bartram and Sons Ltd., Sunderland (Yard No. 243). She had been laid down for G. Swainton and Co., Newcastle-upon-Tyne and was acquired for £220,000.
26.2.1918: Registered in the ownership of The Clan Line Steamers Ltd. (Cayzer, Irvine and Co. Ltd., managers), London as CLAN MACBEAN.
3.1918: Completed.
6.3.1918: Requisitioned by the British government until 19.2.1919.

Clan Macbean (1). *[Ships in Focus]*

119

17.9.1939: Missed when attacked by a torpedo and gunfire from a German submarine and attempted to ram the submarine by turning into the track of the torpedo.

18.10.1939: Attacked by torpedo and gunfire by a German submarine in approximate position 45 north by 15 west whilst on a voyage from India to Liverpool via Gibraltar. The submarine crash-dived as CLAN MACBEAN headed straight towards her. One member of the crew was lost.

9.5.1940: Requisitioned by the British government until 15.3.1946.

30.12.1946: Sold to Okeanis Shipping Co. Ltd. (Goulandris Brothers Ltd., managers), London for £62,500.

29.3.1947: Renamed ANGLOS.

18.10.1949: Register closed on sale to G.N. Louloudis, Paris, France (Goulandris Brothers (Hellas) Ltd., Piraeus, Greece, managers) and renamed KORTHION under the Greek flag.

1950: Sold to Ubaldo Gennari fu Torquato & C., Pesaro, Italy and renamed AUDAX.

1.1959: Sold to Primo Armatori Shipbreakers, Ancona for demolition.

21.1.1959: Delivered at Ancona.

12.3.1959: Resold to Matsukura Co. Ltd., Tokyo for demolition.

8.6.1959: Arrived at Yamata, Japan for demolition.

19.6.1959: Work commenced.

CLAN KEITH (1)/HILARIUS (2) 1918-1937

O.N. 136654 4,306g 2,685n
385.0 x 52.0 x 25.1 feet.
T.3-cyl. by John Dickinson and Sons Ltd., Sunderland; 401 NHP, 1,960 IHP, 11 knots.

Clan Macbean (1) as the Italian *Audax*. [J. and M. Clarkson collection]

12.1.1914: Launched by Bartram and Sons Ltd., Sunderland (Yard No. 231).

23.3.1914: Registered in the ownership of the Cambrian Steam Navigation Co. Ltd. (J. Mathias and Sons, managers), Cardiff as ETONIAN.

16.2.1916: Requisitioned by the British government until 26.4.1919.

13.3.1918: Acquired by The Clan Line Steamers Ltd. (Cayzer, Irvine and Co. Ltd., managers), London for £140,000.

18.3.1918: Renamed CLAN KEITH.

11.1.1921: Transferred to the British and South American Steam Navigation Co. Ltd. (R.P. Houston and Co., managers), Liverpool for £200,000.

17.2.1921: Renamed HILARIUS.

15.11.1923: Transferred to The Clan Line Steamers Ltd. (Cayzer, Irvine and Co. Ltd., managers), Glasgow.

23.11.1923: Renamed CLAN KEITH.

12.2.1937: Sold to the Minster Steamship Co. Ltd. (Thomas Eeles and Co., manager), London for £23,000.

19.2.1937: Renamed ORMINSTER.

25.2.1940: Requisitioned by the British government.

9.6.1940: Sold to The South American Saint Line Ltd. (Richard G.M. Street, manager), Newport, Monmouthshire.

25.8.1944: Torpedoed and sunk by the German submarine U 480 35 miles north west of Cap d'Antifer in position 50.07.48 north by 00.41.54 west whilst a straggler from convoy FTM74 on a voyage from Arromanches to Southampton in ballast. Six lives were lost, and the 57 survivors were rescued by escorts and landed at Portsmouth.

30.8.1944: Register closed.

Clan Keith (1) in the Mersey on 24th May 1924. *[M. Cooper/B. and A. Feilden/J. and M. Clarkson collection]*

THE NORTHUMBERLAND MACVS

The Clan Macvicar *was bought after launch for Cardiff owners, and the* Clan Macvey *was probably building for the same people.*

CLAN MACVICAR 1918-1936

O.N. 141878 5,815g 3,621n
400.1 x 53.0 x 32.9 feet.
T.3-cyl. by the North Eastern Marine
Engineering Co. Ltd., Wallsend-on-Tyne;
570 NHP, 3,400 IHP, 12 knots.
15.12.1917: Launched by the
Northumberland Shipbuilding Co. Ltd.,
Howdon-on-Tyne (Yard No. 244) for W.
and C.T. Jones Steamship Co. Ltd., Cardiff
as MAENWEN.
27.3.1918: Registered in the ownership of
The Clan Line Steamers Ltd. (Cayzer,
Irvine and Co. Ltd, managers), London as
CLAN MACVICAR, having been bought
for £243,000.
23.12.1936: Sold to Dover Hill Steamship
Co. Ltd. (Counties Ship Management Co.
Ltd., managers), London for £29,000.
28.12.1936: Renamed DOVER HILL.
22.3.1940: Requisitioned by the British
government.
4.4.1943: Hit by a bomb dropped by a Ju
88 aircraft at Michukov Anchorage, Kola
Inlet, in a position 68.53 north by 33.10
east having arrived from Loch Ewe in
convoy JW 53. The bomb failed to
explode and was removed from the coal
bunker.
26.11.1943: Returned to Loch Ewe in
convoy RA 54B.
4.2.1944: Register closed when taken over
by the Ministry of War Transport, London.
6.5.1944: Registered in the ownership of
the Ministry of War Transport, London (J.
and J. Denholm Ltd., Glasgow, managers).
8.6.1944: Planted as part of Gooseberry
No. 5 off Sword Beach, Normandy in a

Above: *Clan Macvicar.* [B. and A. Feilden/J. and M. Clarkson collection]
Below: After being sold and renamed *Dover Hill.* [Ships in Focus collection]

position 49.30.00 north by 00.20.00 west.
5.7.1944: Register closed.

CLAN MACVEY 1918

O.N. 141884 5,818g 3,623n
400.1 x 53.0 x 32.8 feet.
T.3-cyl. by the North Eastern Marine
Engineering Co. Ltd., Sunderland; 570
NHP, 3,400 IHP, 12 knots.
25.4.1918: Launched by the
Northumberland Shipbuilding Co. Ltd.,
Howdon-on-Tyne (Yard No. 245).
19.7.1918: Registered in the ownership of
The Clan Line Steamers Ltd. (Cayzer,
Irvine and Co. Ltd., managers), London as
CLAN MACVEY, having been bought for
£243,000
23.7.1918: Delivered.
8.8.1918: Damaged by a torpedo from the
German submarine UB 57 half a mile
south east of Anvil Point and sank five
miles north west of the Needles with the
loss of seven lives. She was on her
maiden voyage from Newcastle-upon-Tyne
to Port Said with a cargo of coal.
19.8.1918: Register closed.

Probably the only image to survive of
Clan Macvey, Clan's final First World
War loss, is this one of her last
moments. She was a sister of *Clan
Macvicar,* and it is assumed that her
original owners were also the W. and
C.T. Jones Steamship Co. Ltd. of
Cardiff.

Clan Morrison. [Ian J. Farquhar]

AYRSHIRE QUARTET

The nearest Clan could come to standardisation during the First World War was this group of flush-deckers built at Irvine, and ordered in stages. Only two saw service during this war, but they were deeply involved in the subsequent conflict, when two were mined on the East Coast. The two survivors were transferred to Houston Line.

CLAN MORRISON 1918-1940

O.N. 141877 5,931g 3,698n
409.6 x 53.5 x 33.5 feet.
T.3-cyl. by Dunsmuir and Jackson Ltd., Glasgow;413 NHP, 3,000 IHP, 12 knots.
1.11.1917: Launched by the Ayrshire Dockyard Co. Ltd., Irvine (Yard No. 457).
20.3.1918: Registered in the ownership of The Clan Line Steamers Ltd. (Cayzer, Irvine and Co. Ltd., managers), London as CLAN MORRISON.
16.3.1918: Requisitioned by the British government until 8.8.1919.
5.9.1939: Requisitioned by the British government.

24.2.1940: Mined and sunk off Cromer in position 53.07.21 north by 01.15.50 east whilst on a ballast voyage from Southampton to Blyth in convoy FN102. The crew took to the boats and were picked up by naval craft and landed at Grimsby. The minefield had been laid on the night of 9/10.2.1940 by the German destroyers BRUNO HEINEMANN (Z 8), WOLFGANG ZENKER (Z 9) and ERICH KOELLNER (Z 13).
14.3.1940: Register closed.

CLAN MONROE (3) 1918-1940

O.N. 141882 5,919 3,656n
409.6 x 53.4 x 33.5 feet.
T.3-cyl. by Dunsmuir and Jackson Ltd., Glasgow; 561 NHP, 3,000 IHP, 12 knots.
28.3.1918: Launched by the Ayrshire Dockyard Co. Ltd., Irvine (Yard No. 466).
1.6.1918: Delivered.
4.6.1918: Requisitioned by the British government until 5.3.1919.
13.6.1918: Registered in the ownership of The Clan Line Steamers Ltd. (Cayzer,

Irvine and Co. Ltd., managers), London as CLAN MONROE.
4.1925: In collision in the River Scheldt with the Dutch JONGE CATHARINA which sank. Dutch courts subsequently judged CLAN MONROE wholly to blame, although this decision was vigorously opposed by Clan Line.
7.9.1939: Requisitioned by the British government.
29.7.1940: Damaged by mine 25 miles east of Harwich in position 51.52 north by 01.48 east whilst on a voyage from Cochin to the Tees with manganese ore and bound northwards from London in convoy FN236. 13 lives were lost.
30.7.1940: After being taken in tow, anchored off South Shipwash with back broken.
31.7.1940: Beached at Hollesley in a position 52.02.22 north by 01.30.08 east to prevent sinking. Subsequently declared a constructive total loss.
13.12.1940: Register closed.

Clan Monroe (3). Note the spreaders either side of her crosstrees, and the heavy lift derrick on the foremast, features of this class of four from the Ayrshire Dockyard. The two-month delay in delivering this ship after her trials suggests problems, but there is no explanation in the Clan Line board's minutes. *[John McRoberts/J. and M. Clarkson]*

CLAN MURRAY (3) / HALIZONES (3)
1919-1952

O.N. 141894 5,926g 3,678n
409.5 x 53.5 x 33.5 feet.
T.3-cyl. by Dunsmuir and Jackson Ltd.,
Glasgow; 561 NHP, 3,000 IHP, 12 knots.
1932: Fitted with a Bauer-Wach low-
pressure exhaust steam turbine by
William Beardmore and Co. Ltd.,
Dalmuir; increasing total output to 622
NHP, 4,350 IHP.
22.10.1918: Launched by the Ayrshire
Dockyard Co. Ltd., Irvine (Yard No.
472).
17.1.1919: Registered in the ownership of
The Clan Line Steamers Ltd. (Cayzer,
Irvine and Co. Ltd., managers), London
as CLAN MURRAY.
18.1.1919: Requisitioned by the British
government until 6.8.1919.
12.7.1940: Requisitioned by the British
government until 9.3.1946.
4.2.1948: Transferred to the British and
South American Steam Navigation Co.
Ltd., (Houston Line (London) Ltd.,
managers), London.
14.3.1949: Renamed HALIZONES.
1952: Sold to the British Iron and Steel
Corporation and allocated to P. and W.
Maclellan Ltd.
17.6.1952: Arrived at Bo'ness to be
broken up.
24.9.1952: Register closed.

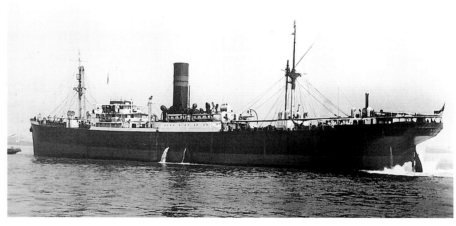

Clan Murray (3) served Clan and its associates for 33 years. She is seen at Sydney still in wartime rig, loading for home in December 1919 (top), towards the end of her long Clan career on 17th April 1947 (middle), and as Houston's *Halizones* (bottom). A list of ships being built which appears in Clan Line's board minutes for October 1917 suggests she was intended to have been named *Clan Morgan,* a name briefly given to *Clan Matheson* (4). *[Top: William Livermore/J. and M. Clarkson collection, middle: John McRoberts/J. and M. Clarkson, bottom: B. and A. Feilden/J. and M. Clarkson collection]*

CLAN MURDOCH (1) / HALESIUS (2) 1919-1952

O.N. 141911. 5,930g. 3,683n.
409.6 x 53.5 x 33.5 feet.
T.3-cyl. by Dunsmuir and Jackson Ltd., Glasgow; 561 NHP, 3,000 IHP, 12 knots.
1930: Fitted with a Bauer-Wach low-pressure exhaust steam turbine by Deutsche Schiff und Maschinenbau, Bremen, Germany; increasing total output to 674 NHP, 4,051 IHP.
15.4.1919: Launched by the Ayrshire Dockyard Co. Ltd., Irvine (Yard No. 473).
30.6.1919: Registered in the ownership of The Clan Line Steamers Ltd. (Cayzer, Irvine and Co. Ltd., managers), London as CLAN MURDOCH.
7.1919: Completed.
20.7.1940: Requisitioned by the British government until 29.6.1946.
4.2.1948: Transferred to the British and South American Steam Navigation Co. Ltd. (Houston Line (London) Ltd., managers), London.
14.5.1948: Renamed HALESIUS.
4.1.1952: Register closed on sale to Compañia Limitada Capo Bona Esperanza S.A., Panama and renamed JANKIKI.
30.5.1952: Grounded 25 miles from Cape Tenes, Algeria whilst on a voyage from Macoris, Dominican Republic to Colombo.
6.1952: Refloated, taken to Algiers and laid up.
28.11.1953: Capsized and sank after her cargo of phosphates had shifted in heavy weather about 10 miles north west of Ilha Berlenga, 50 miles north of Lisbon, whilst on a voyage from Casablanca to Vlaardingen, Holland.

LONG BRIDGE DECKS

Long-bridge-deck steamers were unusual in the Clan Line fleet. Two were acquired on the stocks at Greenock, having been ordered by Denholms, and a third had been launched by Lloyd Royal Belge's Whiteinch yard for their own account as Ypresville, *but taken over on completion by the Shipping Controller. She was bought by Clan and then transferred to Houston as* Halizones.

CLAN ALPINE (3) 1918-1943

O.N. 141879 6,465g 4,762n
410.2 x 53.5 x 28.4 feet.
T.3-cyl. by John G. Kincaid and Co. Ltd., Greenock; 538 NHP, 2,300 IHP, 11 knots.
1930: Fitted with a Bauer-Wach low-pressure exhaust turbine; increasing total output to 627 NHP.
28.1.1918: Launched by the Greenock and Grangemouth Dockyard Co. Ltd., Greenock (Yard No. 379).
She had been laid down for J. and J. Denholm Ltd., Glasgow.
3.1918: Completed.
22.4.1918: Registered in the ownership of The Clan Line Steamers Ltd. (Cayzer, Irvine and Co. Ltd., managers), London as CLAN ALPINE, having been acquired for £280,000.

Top: Clan Murdoch (1) in Australian waters. Middle: As *Halesius* after her change of name in 1948. There is evidence from board minutes that this ship was intended to be *Clan Morran*, a name not otherwise used. *[Top: Ian J. Farquhar collection, lower: Archie Munro collection]*
Below: The long bridge deck of *Clan Alpine* (3) was unusual in the fleet. *[John McRoberts/Roy Fenton collection]*

4.1918: Requisitioned by the British government until 23.5.1919.
10.4.1940: Requisitioned by the British government.
13.3.1943: Badly damaged by a torpedo from the German submarine U 107 190 miles west of Cape Finisterre in position 42.45 north by 13.31 west whilst on a voyage from Liverpool to Walvis Bay and Port Sudan as part of convoy OS 44. A total of 26 lives were lost, four boats getting away with 68 survivors. Later sunk by HMS SCARBOROUGH which picked up the survivors.
29.6.1943: Register closed.

CLAN QUHELE/
CLAN MACWILLIAM 1918-1927

O.N. 141892 7,234g 5,370n
423.3 x 55.9 x 28.8 feet.
T.3-cyl. by John G. Kincaid and Co. Ltd.,
Greenock; 267 NHP.
23.10.1918: Launched by the Greenock
and Grangemouth Dockyard Co. Ltd.,
Greenock (Yard No. 385) as CLAN
QUHELE.
She had been laid down for J. and J.
Denholm Ltd., Glasgow and was to have
been named LEAPARK.
28.11.1918: Registered in the ownership
of The Clan Line Steamers Ltd. (Cayzer,
Irvine and Co. Ltd., managers), London as
CLAN MACWILLIAM having been
acquired for £240,000.
28.11.1918: Requisitioned by the British
government until 12.6.1919.
24.12.1927: Caught fire whilst loading
copra and general cargo at Vavau, Friendly
Islands. Subsequently moved to the Upper
harbour, but sank and broke her back. Her
master and chief engineer were lost. She
was on a voyage from Pagoumene and
Nukualofa to European ports with a cargo
of copra.
25.2.1928: Register closed.

HALIZONES (1)/WILLCASINO/CLAN
MACWHIRTER 1918-1920/1922-1942

O.N. 142598 7,062g 5,351n
424.4 x 55.8 x 28.8 feet.
T.3-cyl. by John G. Kincaid and Co. Ltd.,
Greenock; 279 NHP, 2,800 IHP, 11.25
knots.
26.4.1918: Launched by Lloyd Royal
Belge (Great Britain) Ltd., Whiteinch,
Glasgow (Yard No. 3).
25.7.1918: Registered in the ownership of
the Shipping Controller, London (James
Gardiner and Co., Glasgow, managers) as
YPRESVILLE.
31.7.1918: Acquired by The Clan Line
Steamers Ltd. (Cayzer, Irvine and Co. Ltd.,
managers), London for £285,000.
7.1918: Requisitioned by the British
government until 22.12.1918.
13.11.1918: Transferred to the British and
South American Steam Navigation Co.
Ltd. (R.P. Houston and Co., managers),
Liverpool.
17.3.1919: Renamed HALIZONES.
19.1.1920: Sold to the Convoy Steamship
Co. Ltd. (Hector D. Kempt, manager),
Halifax, Nova Scotia.
22.1.1920: Renamed WILLCASINO.
9.7.1922: Reacquired by the mortgagees,
the British and South American Steam
Navigation Co. (R.P. Houston and
Co., managers), Liverpool.
26.3.1923: Renamed CLAN
MACWHIRTER.
18.7.1923: Transferred to The Clan Line
Steamers Ltd. (Cayzer, Irvine and Co. Ltd.,
managers), London.
9.3.1942: Requisitioned by the British
government.

A second purchase from J. and J. Denholm Ltd., *Clan Macwilliam* is seen (above) in dazzle paint and war rig, with a gun mounted aft, and in peacetime condition in Australia (below). Her bridge deck extended right to the bow, leaving only a short well aft. She was the first Clan Line ship equipped for oil burning. *[Above: National Maritime Museum, P.15738, below: Ian J. Farquhar collection]*

Houston sold *Halizones* within a year, but the buyers failed to keep up the mortgage repayments, and she returned to Houston under her new name *Willcasino*. In 1923 she was transferred to Clan as *Clan Macwhirter*, as seen above. The board minutes are coy about the reason for this transfer, citing 'certain advantages' in her being operated by Clan Line. These were undoubtedly the savings they enjoyed when using a Lascar crew. *[B. and A. Feilden/J. and M. Clarkson collection]*

26.8.1942: Torpedoed and sunk by the German submarine U 156 about 200 miles north of Madeira in position 35.45 north by 18.45 west as a straggler from convoy SL 119 whilst on a voyage from Bombay, Durban and Bathurst to Hull with a cargo of manganese ore, linseed, pig iron and general. Nine of the seventy nine crew and two of the nine gunners were lost. The survivors were rescued by the Portuguese sloop PEDRO NUNES and were landed at Funchal.
29.10.1942: Register closed.

HAMILTON-BUILT

CLAN MACKINLAY (1) 1918-1940
O.N. 141890 6,418g 3,964n
420.0 x 54.5 x 34.0 feet.
T.3-cyl. by David Rowan and Co. Ltd., Glasgow;
667 NHP, 3,500 IHP, 12˜ knots.
1930: Fitted with Bauer-Wach low-pressure
exhaust steam turbine by William Beardmore and
Co. Ltd., Dalmuir; increasing total output to 781
NHP, 4,850 IHP.
20.9.1918: Launched by William Hamilton and
Co. Ltd., Port Glasgow (Yard No. 308). She had
been laid down for W. and A. Graham, Glasgow.
31.10.1918: Registered in the ownership of The
Clan Line Steamers Ltd. (Cayzer, Irvine and Co.
Ltd., managers), London as CLAN
MACKINLAY.
11.1918: Completed.
2.11.1918: Requisitioned by the British
government until 25.4.1919.
4.6.1940: Requisitioned by the British
government.
6.11.1940: Bombed by German aircraft off Noss
Head, Wick and sank in position 58.32.05 north
by 02.53.00 west whilst on a voyage from
Bombay to Oban, Methil and London with
general cargo in convoy WN31. Five of her
crew of 82 were lost.
29.9.1940: Register closed.

CLAN MORGAN/CLAN MATHESON (4)/ HARMODIUS (3) 1919-1951
O.N. 141896 5,613g 3,453n
397.1 x 51.5 x 34.0 feet.
T.3-cyl. by David Rowan and Co. Ltd., Glasgow;
517 NHP, 3,000 IHP, 11.5 knots.
18.2.1919: Launched by William Hamilton and
Co. Ltd., Port Glasgow (Yard No. 311) as CLAN
MORGAN.
She had been ordered by Australian Steamships
Ltd., Melbourne, and acquired in September
1917 soon after the keel had been laid.
4.4.1919: Registered in the ownership of The
Clan Line Steamers Ltd. (Cayzer, Irvine and Co.
Ltd., managers), London as CLAN
MATHESON.
21.2.1940: Requisitioned by the British
government until 19.8.1946.
5.12.1943: Bombed and damaged by Japanese
aircraft at Calcutta.
4.2.1948: Transferred to the British and South
American Steam Navigation Co. Ltd. (Houston
Line (London) Ltd., managers), London.
1.7.1948: Renamed HARMODIUS.
23.5.1951: Sold to the Heron Steamship Co. Ltd.
(Tsavliris (Shipping) Ltd., managers), London.
28.5.1951: Renamed CLAIRE T.
19.12.1953: Transferred to the Romney
Steamship Co. Ltd. (Tsavliris (Shipping) Ltd.,
managers), London.
27.1.1955: Sold to the Ministry of Transport,
London.
15.2.1955: Renamed EMPIRE CLAIRE.
27.7.1955: Left Stranraer to be scuttled in the
Atlantic in position 12.00 west by 56.30 north
with obsolete ammunition including poison gas
canisters.
29.10.1955: Register closed.

Although ordered by another owner, the Clyde-built *Clan Mackinlay* (1) was dimensionally similar to *Clan Macmillan* from Doxford. She was bought by Clan in 1916 for a massive £200,000, with an anticipated delivery date in 1917, but was not actually completed until days before the end of the war. *[Ian J. Farquhar collection]*

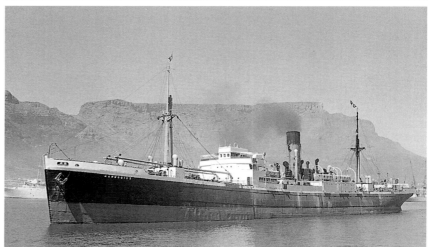

This ship was originally to be *Clan Morgan* but became *Clan Matheson* (4) (middle) probably because the third ship of the name had recently been lost in collision. The change was decided on by a board meeting on 15th January 1919, although no-one told the ship yard, which launched her as *Clan Morgan*.

Clan Matheson survived the Second World War, but was unfortunate enough to be set on fire during one of the few air raids experienced by India, when the Japanese bombed Calcutta on 5th December 1943. She became *Harmodius* (3) (bottom) in 1948. *[Both: Ships in Focus]*

WAR STANDARDS

The Connell-built War Adder *was offered to Clan Line in part payment of the government war loss insurance on the* Clan Graham, *Clan paying just £37,500 to make up the difference in values. The regular price for one of these B-type standard ships was £165,000.*

Early in 1919 three similar B-type ships building at Irvine were bought on the stocks. It was considered prudent to place these in the ownership of the British and South American Steam Navigation Co. Ltd. Three old ships from this fleet had been sold foreign, and the government had stipulated that any owner so doing should use the proceeds to buy a new ship. As Harmodius of 1892 and Harmonides of 1891 had realised £160,000 and Horatius of 1894 £86,400, and the new Ayrshire vessels were costing just £165,000, Clan were replacing old with new ships at minimal cost. The £230,000 paid in October 1919 for the Dennistoun, which became Haliartus, reflected the true market value of standard ships.

The names intended for the three Irvine-built standards are not known, although Mitchell and Sawyer list the following six names as being allocated to the yard for its contribution to the B-type programme: War Beaver, War Condor, War Falcon, War Grouse, War Wren *and* War Wryneck.

CLAN SKENE/HALOCRATES/CLAN SKENE 1918-1942

O.N. 141893 5,623g 3,993n
401.0 x 52.3 x 28.5 feet.

Clan Skene. [Ships in Focus]

T.3-cyl. by David Rowan and Co. Ltd., Glasgow; 517 NHP, 3,000 IHP, 11.5 knots.
12.1930: Fitted with a Bauer-Wach low-pressure exhaust steam turbine; increasing total output to 599 NHP.
3.2.1918: Launched by Charles Connell and Co. Ltd., Glasgow (Yard No. 389) for the Shipping Controller, London as WAR ADDER.
12.1918: Acquired by The Clan Line Steamers Ltd. (Cayzer, Irvine and Co. Ltd., managers), London.
1.1.1919: Requisitioned by the British government until 20.8.1919.
17.1.1919: Registered as CLAN SKENE.
29.7.1920: Transferred to the British and South American Steam Navigation Co. Ltd. (R.P. Houston and Co., managers), Liverpool for £280,000.

2.9.1920: Renamed HALOCRATES.
4.7.1923: Grounded in the Straits of Canso, Nova Scotia. Refloated and taken to New York for repair.
18.7.1923: Transferred to The Clan Line Steamers Ltd. (Cayzer, Irvine and Co. Ltd., managers), Glasgow.
1.8.1923: Renamed CLAN SKENE.
29.4.1940: Requisitioned by the British government.
10.5.1942: Torpedoed and sunk by the German submarine U 333 360 miles south east of Cape Hatteras in position 31.43 north by 70.43 west whilst on an independent voyage from Cape Town to New York with a cargo of chrome ore. Nine lives were lost, the survivors being taken on board USS MCKEAN and landed at San Juan, Puerto Rico.
10.7.1942: Register closed.

HALIARTUS 1919-1932

O.N. 142832 5,294g 3,255n
400.2 x 52.4 x 28.5 feet.
T.3-cyl. by John Readhead and Sons Ltd., South Shields; 513 NHP, 3,000 IHP, 11.5 knots.
31.3.1919: Launched by John Readhead and Sons Ltd., South Shields (Yard No. 10).
She had been laid down for the Shipping Controller, London as WAR MOORHEN.
16.5.1919: Registered in the ownership of the Fernley Shipping Co. Ltd. (Shankland, Russell and Co., managers), Glasgow as DENNISTOUN.
23.10.1919: Acquired by the British and South American Steam Navigation Co. Ltd. (R.P. Houston and Co., managers), Liverpool for £230,000.
29.10.1919: Renamed HALIARTUS.
1932: Managers became Houston Line (London) Ltd.
4.5.1932: Wrecked off Bull Point, 22 miles west of Mossel Bay, whilst on a voyage from the Tees, Antwerp and London to Cape Town, Simonstown and Beira with general cargo.
16.6.1932: Register closed.

In explanation of the low yard number allocated to *Haliartus*, formerly *War Moorhen*, it should be noted that Readheads, perhaps uniquely, used a separate series of numbers for its First World War standard ship completions. Her stranding in 1932 (bottom) led to her master being dismissed for making an error of judgement in proceeding in bad visibility without having taken good bearings. *[Middle: B. and A. Feilden/J. and M. Clarkson collection; bottom: Newall Dunn collection]*

HARMODIUS (2) 1919-1941

O.N. 140657 5,229g 3,179n
400.7 x 52.3 x 28.5 feet.
T.3-cyl. by Dunsmuir and Jackson Ltd.,
Glasgow; 517 NHP, 3,000 IHP, 11.5 knots.
28.6.1919: Launched by the Ayrshire
Dockyard Co. Ltd., Irvine (Yard No. 476)
as HERMIONE.
She had been laid down for the Shipping
Controller.
9.10.1919: Registered in the ownership of
the British and South American Steam
Navigation Co. Ltd. (R.P. Houston and
Co., managers), Liverpool as
HARMODIUS.
1932: Managers became Houston Line
(London) Ltd.
8.3.1941: Torpedoed and sunk by the
German submarine U 105 north of Cape
Verde in position 20.35 north by 20.40
west whilst on a voyage from Cochin and
Table Bay to Glasgow and London in
convoy SL 67 with general cargo. Eleven
lives were lost. The survivors were picked
up by HMS FAULKNOR and eventually
landed at Gibraltar.
14.7.1941: Register closed.

Harmodius (2) loading china clay at Fowey. *[Ambrose Greenway collection]*

HARMONIDES (2) 1920-1942

O.N. 143610 5,288g 3,147n
400.2 x 52.3 x 28.5 feet.
T.3-cyl. by John G. Kincaid and Co. Ltd.,
Greenock; 517 NHP, 2,700 IHP, 11 knots.
1930: Exhaust steam turbine fitted by
Willam Beardmore and Co. Ltd., Dalmuir;
increasing total output to 599 NHP, 3,740
IHP.
11.11.1919: Launched by the Ayrshire
Dockyard Co. Ltd., Irvine (Yard No. 484)
as HESIONE.
She had been laid down for the Shipping
Controller.
13.1.1920: Registered in the ownership of
the British and South American Steam
Navigation Co. Ltd. (R.P. Houston and
Co., managers), Liverpool as
HARMONIDES.
21.1.1920: Ran trials.
1932: Managers became Houston Line
(London) Ltd.

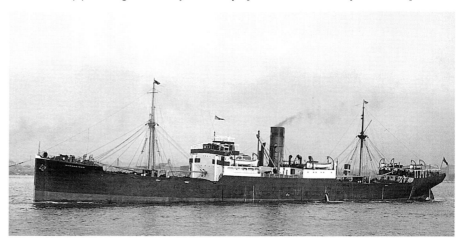

Harmonides (2) in the Mersey in Houston colours on 8th April 1934. *[John McRoberts/J. and M. Clarkson collection]*

25.8.1942: Torpedoed and sunk by the
Japanese submarine I-165 in the Indian
Ocean 300 miles from Galle in position
01.47 north by 77.27 east whilst on a
voyage from Calcutta, Trincomalee and
Lourenco Marques to the USA with
general cargo including pig iron, tea,
castor and linseed oils. 14 lives were lost.
The survivors were rescued by HMS
SHOREHAM and landed at Colombo.
24.3.1943: Register closed.

HALIZONES (2) 1920-1943

O.N. 143626 5,298g 3,137n
400.7 x 52.2 x 28.5 feet.
T.3-cyl. by Dunsmuir and Jackson Ltd.,
Glasgow; 517 NHP, 3,000 IHP, 11.5
knots.
6.2.1920: Launched by the Ayrshire
Dockyard Co. Ltd., Irvine (Yard No.
487).
She had been laid down for the
Shipping Controller.
27.3.1920: Registered in the ownership
of the British and South American
Steam Navigation Co. Ltd. (R.P.
Houston and Co., managers), Liverpool
as HALIZONES.
4.1920: Completed.
1932: Managers bacame Houston Line
(London) Ltd.
27.7.1943: Bombed by German aircraft
200 miles west north west of Cape St.
Vincent in position 38.04 north by
12.59 west whilst on a voyage from
Glasgow to Montevideo and Buenos
Aires with general cargo in convoy OS
52.
30.7.1943: Sank whilst under tow in
position 37.22 north by 13.03 west.
Her crew was rescued.
20.9.1943: Register closed.

Halizones (2) approaching the locks at Avonmouth. *[Nigel Farrell collection]*

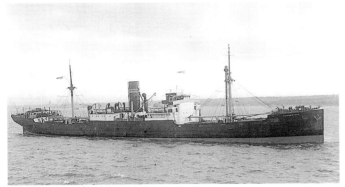

Ships sometimes changed funnel colours as they sailed for different companies in the group. The *Harmonides* (left) is in Clan Line colours and *Halizones* (right) is in Bullard, King funnel colours. *[Both: George Scott collection]*

GERMAN PRIZES

Clan bought from the government Huntscraft, *a ship which had been taken in prize in the opening weeks of the war. Despite what other authors have written, only days elapsed before she was renamed* Clan Mackay. *Three German ships taken as reparations from Germany at the end of the First World War were also bought for Houston. At various times during 1920, there were negotiations with the government to buy the German steamers* Atte *(5,169/1911) for £170,000 and the twin-screw* Kurland *(10,900/1920) for £160,000, but these fell through.*

When *Clan Mackay* (4) was bought as *Huntscraft* she was described as a duplicate of *Clan Macmillan* but with 'tween decks. *[B. and A. Feilden/J. and M. Clarkson collection]*

CLAN MACKAY (4) 1920-1934

O.N. 136793 5,166g 3,210n
420.0 x 54.1 x 26.3 feet.
T.3-cyl. by William Doxford and Sons Ltd., Sunderland; 577 NHP.
3.6.1913: Launched by William Doxford and Sons Ltd., Sunderland (Yard No. 455) for Hamburg-Amerikanische Packetfahrt A.G., Hamburg, Germany as SÜDMARK.
7.1913: Completed.
17.8.1914: Captured by HMS BLACK PRINCE in the Indian Ocean whilst on a voyage from Yokohama to Hamburg.
9.1914: Condemned by the Prize Court.
23.2.1915: Registered in the ownership of The Admiralty (Harris and Dixon Ltd., managers), London.
23.9.1915: Renamed HUNTSCRAFT.
5.1917: Managers became the Union-Castle Mail Steamship Co. Ltd., London.
6.7.1918: Torpedoed by a German submarine 10 miles south east of St. Catherine's Point but towed in to Netley and later repaired.
7.1.1920: Acquired by The Clan Line Steamers Ltd. (Cayzer, Irvine and Co. Ltd., managers), London for £285,000.
24.1.1920: Renamed CLAN MACKAY.
19.10.1934: Wrecked in mist on Carpenter's Rock, Sierra Leone whilst on a voyage from Cairns to Montreal.
23.11.1934: Register closed.

HESPERIA (1) 1921-1938

O.N. 144661 3,895g 2,380n
384.5 x 52.0 x 22.5 feet.
T.3-cyl. by Flensburger Schiffsbau

Gesellschaft, Flensburg, Germany; 531 NHP, 2,800 IHP, 12 knots.
12.1919: Completed by Flensburger Schiffsbau Gesellschaft, Flensburg, Germany (Yard No. 351) as PATRIA. She had been laid down for Hamburg-Amerikanische Packetfahrt Actien Gesellschaft, Hamburg, Germany, but had been surrendered to the Allied Shipping Commission.
15.7.1920: Delivered to Leith.

21.7.1920: Registered in the ownership of the Shipping Controller (Royal Mail Steam Packet Company, managers), London as PATRIA.
22.2.1921: Acquired by the British and South American Steam Navigation Co. Ltd. (R.P. Houston and Co., managers), Liverpool for £56,000.
28.6.1921: Renamed HESPERIA.
1932: Managers became Houston Line (London) Ltd.

Hesperia. [B. and A. Feilden/J. and M. Clarkson collection]

9.2.1938: Sold to Euxine Shipping Co. Ltd., London.
24.3.1938: Renamed CHRISTINE MARIE.
25.3.1947: Register closed on sale to S.A. Cargueros Panamenos (O.E. Bertin) (Wallem and Co., managers), Hong Kong and renamed COSTA RICA under the Panama flag.
1947: Sold to Rederi A/B Ledsund (Uno Adolfsson, manager), Mariehamn, Finland and renamed LEDSUND.
1952: Paul Kåhre became manager.
1956: Leonard Johnsson became manager.
1959: Sold to the Omega Shipping Co., Hong Kong for breaking up.
21.11.1959: Arrived at Hong Kong and later broken up by Hong Kong Chiap Hua Manufactory Co. (1947) Ltd.

Hesperia (1), seen at Cape Town in January 1957 as the Finnish *Ledsund*. [J. and M. Clarkson collection]

HESPERIDES (1) 1921-1937

O.N. 144694 3,929g 2,392n
384.2 x 52.9 x 22.4 feet.
T.3-cyl. by Flensburger Schiffsbau Gesellschaft, Flensburg, Germany; 531 NHP, 2,800 IHP, 12 knots.
10.1919: Completed by Flensburger Schiffsbau Gesellschaft, Flensburg, Germany (Yard No. 353) as PARTHIA.

Hesperides (1) at anchor in the Mersey.   [B. and A. Feilden/J. and M. Clarkson collection]

She had been laid down for Hamburg-Amerikanische Packetfahrt Actien Gesellschaft, Hamburg, Germany but was surrendered to the Allied Shipping Commission.
6.8.1920: Delivered to Leith.
18.8.1920: Registered in the ownership of the Shipping Controller (Royal Mail Steam Packet Company, managers), London as PARTHIA.
22.2.1921: Acquired by the British and South American Steam Navigation Co. Ltd. (R.P. Houston and Co., managers), Liverpool for £56,000.
13.5.1921: Renamed HESPERIDES.
1932: Managers became Houston Line (London) Ltd.
3.1937: Sold to Reunert & Co. m.b.H. (Fisser & van Doornum, managers), Emden, Germany for £38,000 and renamed BERTHA FISSER.
22.4.1937: British register closed.
29.12.1938: Transferred to Fisser & van Doornum Reederei GmbH. (Fisser and von Doornum, managers), Emden.

20.11.1939: Scuttled by her crew after interception by the armed merchant cruiser HMS CHITRAL south of Iceland whilst on a voyage from Pernambuco to Germany with a cargo of grain. She was masquerading as the Norwegian ATA.

HESIONE (1) 1921-1937

O.N. 143802 4,125g 2,516n
361.6 x 51.2 x 25.7 feet.
T.3-cyl. by Reihersteig Schiffswerfte und Maschinenfabrik, Hamburg, Germany; 300 NHP, 2,000 IHP, 10.5 knots.
27.3.1915: Launched by Reihersteig Schiffswerfte & Maschinenfabrik Abt. Hamburg, Germany (Yard No. 459) for Hamburg-Südamerikanische Dampschifffahrts Gesellschaft, Hamburg, Germany as ITAJAHY
11.1915: Completed.
22.3.1919: Surrendered to the Allied Shipping Commission.
5.4.1919: Registered in the ownership of the Shipping Controller (Elder, Dempster and Co. Ltd., managers), London as ITAJAHY.

Hesione (1) in the Mersey. She was bought for feeder services between UK and the Continent, but in 1931 was employed in the River Plate. By 1935 she was running on Clan Line voyages. [B. and A. Feilden/J. and M. Clarkson collection]

11.3.1921: Acquired by the British and South American Steam Navigation Co. Ltd. (R.P. Houston and Co., managers), Liverpool for £58,500.
28.4.1921: Renamed HESIONE.
1932: Managers became Houston Line (London) Ltd.
20.7.1937: Sold to the Stanhope Shipping Co. Ltd. (J.A. Billmeir and Co. Ltd., managers), London.
28.7.1937: Renamed STANWOOD.
5.12.1939: Cargo of coal caught fire in position 50.10.18 north by 02.05.06 west whilst on a voyage from Methil, Leith and London for Dakar and Buenos Aires.
7.12.1939: Put into Falmouth.
10.12.1939: Sank in 90 feet of water on the Mylor side of Trefusis Point whilst being flooded to extinguish the fire. Wreck subsequently dispersed.
29.8.1940: Register closed.

In 1947 a mast and one of the king-posts at the after end of the super-structure of the *Stanwood*, the former *Hesione*, were still standing in Falmouth Harbour. *[Newall Dunn collection]*

Top: The Dundee-built and owned *Perth* bought by Houstons in 1920 and renamed *Hellopes*. *[George Scott collection]*
Bottom: *Perth* as the South African coaster *Hellopes*. *[John Marsh collection]*

SOUTH AFRICAN COASTER

This coaster was bought for Houston's African coastal services to Mombasa, Mauritius and Madagascar. Following the purchase of Thesens, there seems to have been some difficulty employing the old ship, and in 1923 there was discussion about transferring her to the Mexican operations, but this did not happen. She was brought back to London in 1927 to await sale.

HELLOPES 1920-1927
O.N. 96411   1,703g 839n
280.0 x 36.6 x 16.9 feet.
T.3-cyl. by W.B. Thompson and Co. Ltd., Dundee; 450 NHP, 2,800 IHP, 16 knots.
1918: T.3-cyl. by the Caledon Shipbuilding Co. Ltd., Dundee; 206 NHP, 2,000 IHP, 13 knots.

21.5.1890: Launched by W.B. Thompson and Co. Ltd., Dundee (Yard No. 95).
17.7.1890: Registered in the ownership of James W. Kidd, Robert Guild, William Lowson and Alexander Hutton, Dundee as PERTH.
25.6.1914: Transferred to the Dundee, Perth and London Shipping Co. Ltd. (James W. Kidd, manager), Dundee.
22.2.1915: Renamed ARBROATH.
12.1917: Requisitioned by the Admiralty until 7.1919.
8.4.1920: Acquired by the British and South American Steam Navigation Co. Ltd. (R.P. Houston and Co., managers), Liverpool for £83,500.
7.5.1920: Renamed HELLOPES.
21.4.1927: Register closed on sale to Türkiye Seyr-I Sefain Ydaresi, Istanbul, Turkey for £11,000 and renamed KONYA.
7.1933: Transferred to Denizyollari Iletmesi U.M., Istanbul.
1.1938: Transferred to Denizbank - Denizyollari Iletmesi U.M., Istanbul.
7.1939: Transferred to T.C. Münakalât Vekâleti - Devlet Denizyollari Iletmesi U.M., Istanbul.

5.1944: Transferred to Denizyollari ve Limanlari, Istanbul.
3.1952: Transferred to Denizcilik Bankasi T.A.O., Istanbul.
12.1955: Laid up at Istanbul.
3.1959: Breaking up began by Hürdaçilik T.A.S. at Haliç near Istanbul.

CLAN MACINNES *CLASS*
At least two of this class were bought on the stocks at Port Glasgow during October 1919 for £218,000 each. The yard was previously known as Russell and Company, but became Lithgows Ltd. in 1918, belatedly recognising that the Lithgow family had been in control for many years.

CLAN MACINNES (2) 1920-1947
O.N. 141940   4,672g 2,826n
384.8 x 52.0 x 26.7 feet.
T.3-cyl. by Rankin and Blackmore Ltd., Greenock; 517 NHP, 3,000 IHP, 11.5 knots.
6.11.1919: Launched by Lithgows Ltd., Port Glasgow (Yard No. 727).
5.1.1920: Registered in the ownership of The Clan Line Steamers Ltd. (Cayzer,

Clan Macinnes had more than her share of lucky escapes during the Second World War. On 5th May 1941 she was in Liverpool when the town, and particularly the docks, experienced one of its heaviest air raids. Whilst many ships around her were hit or caught fire, *Clan Macinnes* was hit by just one bomb which failed to explode. Whilst in a convoy during December 1942 she was missed by a torpedo which went on to hit one of the escorts, and during 1942 was missed whilst at anchor by two torpedoes fired by a Japanese submarine.

And for an encore she survived a Japanese air attack on Trincomalee. Above we see her in the Mersey and right at anchor off Beira, East Africa in August 1932. *[Above: B. and A. Feilden/J. and M. Clarkson collection, right: Ships in Focus]*

Irvine and Co. Ltd., managers), London as CLAN MACINNES.
21.5.1940: Requisitioned by the British government until 27.3.1946.
1947: Sold to the Noemijulia Steamship Co. Ltd. (S. Catsell and Co. Ltd., managers), London and renamed SAN GEORGE.
1949: Transferred to the Kenfig Steamship Co. Ltd. (S. Catsell and Co. Ltd., managers), London.
1951: Sold to the Indian National Steamship Co. Ltd., Calcutta, India and renamed SIVA-SHAMBHU.
1955: Broken up at Calcutta during the third quarter.

CLAN MACINDOE (1) 1920-1943
O.N. 144233 4,635g 2,775n
384.8 x 52.0 x 26.6 feet.
T.3-cyl. by Rankin and Blackmore Ltd., Greenock; 518 NHP, 3,000 IHP, 11.5 knots.
1930: Fitted with a Bauer-Wach low-pressure exhaust steam turbine by Deutsche Schiff-und Maschinenbau A.G. Weser, Bremen, Germany; increasing total output to 613 NHP, 4,100 BHP.
11.11.1920: Launched by Lithgows Ltd., Port Glasgow (Yard No. 728).

14.12.1920: Registered in the ownership of The Clan Line Steamers Ltd. (Cayzer, Irvine and Co. Ltd., managers), London as CLAN MACINDOE.
24.2.1940: Requisitioned by the British government.
26.4.1943: Fire broke out in number 4 hold whilst at Alexandria discharging a

cargo of tinned aviation fuel and explosives.
27.4.1943: Beached outside the harbour.
6.5.1943: Fire still burning in the partly submerged vessel, explosions having blown open her starboard side and broken her back.
4.9.1943: Register closed.

Clan Macindoe (1) at Cape Town. *[Ships in Focus]*

CLAN MACIVER (2) 1921-1951

O.N. 144253 4,507g 2,729n
384.8 x 52.0 x 26.5 feet.
T.3-cyl. by Rankin and Blackmore
Ltd., Greenock; 517 NHP, 3,000
IHP, 11.5 knots.
6.5.1921: Launched by Lithgows
Ltd., Port Glasgow (Yard No. 737).
6.1921: Completed for The Clan
Line Steamers Ltd. (Cayzer, Irvine
and Co. Ltd., managers), London as
CLAN MACIVER.
20.3.1940: Requisitioned by the
British government until 2.3.1946.
1951: Sold to Compañia Maritima
Carrena S.A., Panama (Vlassopoulo
Brothers Ltd., London, managers)
and renamed CARRENA under the
Costa Rican flag.
1953: Sold to Gulf Steamships Ltd.,
Karachi, Pakistan and renamed
MUSTALI.
9.1960: Broken up by the Sind
Steel Corporation, Karachi.

CLAN MACILWRAITH (1) 1924-1950

O.N. 147931 4,958g 2,928n
387.4 x 52.2 x 27.6 feet.
T.3-cyl. made by McKie and Baxter
Ltd., Glasgow in 1917; 557 NHP.
1930: Fitted with a Bauer-Wach
low-pressure exhaust steam turbine
by Deutsche Schiff-und
Maschinenbau A.G. Weser, Bremen,
Germany; increasing total output to
653 NHP, 2,500 IHP, 12.5 knots.
14.8.1924: Launched by the
Greenock Dockyard Co. Ltd.,
Greenock (Yard No. 403).
17.11.1924: Delivered.
20.11.1924: Registered in the
ownership of The Clan Line
Steamers Ltd. (Cayzer, Irvine and
Co. Ltd., managers), London as
CLAN MACILWRAITH.
7.5.1942: Requisitioned by the
British government until 21.4.1946.
27.7.1950: Sold to F.A. Vinnen und
Co., Bremen, West Germany for
£45,000 and renamed
MAGDALENE VINNEN.
1.8.1950: British register closed.
12.12.1955: Sold to Companhia
Naviera Vaptistis S.A., Panama
(Lemos and Pateras Ltd., London,
managers) and renamed SAN
GEORGE under the Costa Rican
flag.
18.4.1958: Arrived at Antwerp to
be broken up by Scrappingco S.r.l.

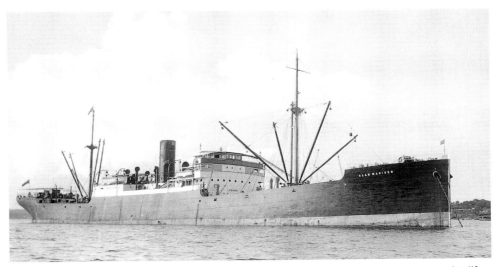

Clan Maciver (2) had one of the few adventures in what seems to have been a quiet life in 1924. On 2nd April 1924, the steamer *Frangestan* (9,683/1899) carrying 1,221 pilgrims from Bombay to Jeddah caught fire in the Red Sea. First on the scene was the *Clan Maciver*, and soon after her arrival the master of the *Frangestan* decided that his passengers should be transferred to the Clan liner. This was accomplished with *Clan Maciver's* four boats, each - it is said - being followed hopefully by sharks. The passengers were taken into Port Sudan, and *Clan Maciver* continued on her voyage to Suez. *Frangestan* - still burning and a danger to navigation - was dispatched by Royal Navy submarine *K 26*. [Ships in Focus]

Early in 1923 Greenock Dockyard offered to build a new vessel for Clan Line for just £63,700. The company decided to have a virtual repeat of the Lithgows-built ships, and to use the relatively new machinery taken from the *Clan Graham* (2) which was being broken up at Antwerp, and boilers from the sloops bought for the Mexican venture, reducing the building price accordingly. The result was *Clan Macilwraith* (1), notable as the first Clan Line ship built at Greenock Dockyard. In the upper view she is seen in the Mersey in peacetime and below at Cape Town in March 1946 with a grey hull and still with wartime gun tubs. [Middle: Ships in Focus, bottom: National Maritime Museum P15696]

TURBINES FROM AYRSHIRE

This pair from Ayrshire Dockyard were by a few feet the longest yet delivered to Clan. They were intended to be duplicates of Clan Macarthur *of 1912 with a raised forecastle and geared turbines, but dimensions differed slightly when they were delivered well over three years after the order was placed in January 1917. In fact, Clan were fortunate to get them at all, as the Shipping Controller wanted their berths for standard ships. It was originally intended to insulate the ships for refrigerated cargoes, but as an economy measure this was not carried out. Requisitioned for government service during the Second World War almost simultaneously, both were to become war losses late in 1942.*

Clan Mactaggart (1) as built (upper). Like all the ships built for Clan by Ayrshire Dockyard, she had her funnel extended in later life. Her turbine installation was photographed on 24th August 1920 (lower). *[Upper: Ian J. Farquhar collection, lower: Glasgow University Archives]*

CLAN MACTAGGART (1) 1920-1942

O.N. 144223 7,603g 4,776n
452.7 x 57.7 x 35.2 feet.
Two steam turbines by Scotts' Shipbuilding and Engineering Co. Ltd., Glasgow, double-reduction geared to twin screw shafts; 4,250 IHP, 13 knots.
17.6.1920: Launched by the Ayrshire Dockyard Co. Ltd., Irvine (Yard No. 474).
15.10.1920: Registered in the ownership of The Clan Line Steamers Ltd. (Cayzer, Irvine and Co. Ltd., managers), London as CLAN MACTAGGART.
10.11.1920: Ran trials in loaded condition.
6.1936: Transferred to the Scottish Shire Line (Turnbull, Martin and Co. Ltd., managers), London for £74,000.
10.2.1940: Requisitioned by the British government.
11.10.1940: Damaged in an air raid at Liverpool.
16.11.1942: Torpedoed and sunk by the German submarine U 92 100 miles west of Gibraltar and 60 miles west by south of Cadiz, in position 36.08 north by 07.23 west whilst on a ballast voyage from North Africa and Gibraltar to the Clyde and Liverpool. Two of

the crew of 100 and one of the 55 naval personnel on board were lost. There were also 19 gunners on board. The survivors were picked up by the Royal Navy corvette HMS COREOPSIS. CLAN MACTAGGART was returning home after taking part in KMS 1, the convoy for the assault on Oran.
17.5.1943: Register closed.

CLAN MACTAVISH (2) 1921-1942

O.N. 144252 7,619g 4,765n
452.6 x 57.7 x 29.6 feet.
Two steam turbines by Scotts' Shipbuilding and Engineering Co. Ltd., Greenock, double reduction geared to a single screw shaft; 4,250 BHP, 13 knots.
20.11.1920: Launched by the Ayrshire Dockyard Co. Ltd., Irvine (Yard No. 475).
31.5.1921: Ran trials and completed.
16.6.1921: Registered in the ownership of The Clan Line Steamers Ltd. (Cayzer, Irvine

and Co. Ltd, managers), London as CLAN MACTAVISH.
9.2.1940: Requisitioned by the British government.
8.10.1942: Torpedoed and sunk by the German submarine U 159 off Cape of Good Hope in position 34.53 south by 16.45 east whilst on an independent voyage from Beira and Durban to Trinidad, New York and the United Kingdom with a cargo of copper and general cargo. Of the 88 crew and passengers, 52 were lost and two of the five gunners. Amongst the 35 passengers lost were seven survivors from the Danish motor vessel BORINGIA (5,821/1930) sunk by the same submarine and whom the CLAN MACTAVISH was attempting to pick up at the time she was torpedoed. The survivors were picked up by the steamer MATHERAN (8,007/1942) and landed at Cape Town.
23.8.1943: Register closed.

CLAN MACNAB CLASS

The relationship with the Irvine shipbuilder continued with six slightly smaller ships, which represented the core of the fleet renewal programme in the early 1920s. The class was to have been even larger, and five more were ordered from Irvine, yard numbers 492 to 496. Doubts about the wisdom of these orders emerged in July 1920, when the possibility of substituting two tankers for two of the ships ordered from Irvine but not yet laid down was discussed, Clan Line being prepared to sell these on behalf of Ayrshire Dockyard. With the economic situation worsening, in March 1921 these five contracts were cancelled, at a cost of £265,000. The class suffered heavily during the Second World War, four of the six being lost.

In December 1919 a severe storm blew down the frames of *Clan Mactavish* (2) which was building at Irvine. Completion was further delayed by a joiners' strike and she was completed by apprentices. As with her sister ships her funnel was extended at some time in her career: compare the top and middle photographs. *[Top: B. and A. Feilden/J. and M. Clarkson collection, middle: Ships in Focus]*
Photographed sailing from Brisbane (below) with a full cargo on 27th May 1933, *Clan Macnab* (3) sank as a result of a collision with a Norwegian tanker in the confusion when her convoy homeward from Freetown was attacked by the German submarines *U 105* and *U 106*. The latter sank the *Clan Ogilvy* (2) three days later. *[J. and M. Clarkson collection]*

CLAN MACNAB (3) 1920-1941
O.N. 144229 6,114g 3,816n
410.6 x 53.3 x 33.4 feet.
T.3-cyl. by Dunsmuir and Jackson Ltd., Glasgow; 561 NHP, 3,000 IHP, 12 knots.
8.1929: Fitted with a Bauer-Wach low-pressure exhaust steam turbine by Deutsche Schiff-und Maschinenbau A.G., Hamburg, Germany; increasing total output to 692 NHP, 4,650 IHP.
12.8.1920: Launched by the Ayrshire Dockyard Co. Ltd., Irvine (Yard No. 485).
1.12.1920: Registered in the ownership of The Clan Line Steamers Ltd. (Cayzer, Irvine and Co. Ltd., managers), London as CLAN MACNAB.
2.4.1940: Requisitioned by the British government.
17.3.1941: Collided with the Norwegian motor tanker STRIX (6,219/1930) in convoy SL 68 whilst on a voyage from Bombay, Durban and Freetown to the Clyde.
18.3.1941: Sank east of the Cape Verde Islands in a position 17.13 north by 21.22 west.
18.6.1941: Register closed.

Two views of *Clan Macnair* (1). The lower view, taken post war, with a deep white top strake and extended funnel shows her in superb condition, despite her age. *[Above: B. and A. Feilden/J. and M. Clarkson collection, below: J. and M. Clarkson collection]*

CLAN MACNAIR (1) 1921-1952
O.N. 144259 6,078g 4,079n
410.7 x 53.3 x 33.5 feet.
T.3-cyl. by Dunsmuir and Jackson Ltd.,
Govan; 5,610 NHP, 3,000 IHP, 12
knots.
1930: Fitted with a Bauer-Wach low-
pressure exhaust steam turbine;
increasing total output to 639 NHP.

25.3.1921: Launched by the Ayrshire
Dockyard Co. Ltd., Irvine (Yard No.
486).
28.6.1921: Registered in the ownership
of The Clan Line Steamers Ltd.
(Cayzer, Irvine and Co. Ltd.,
managers), London as CLAN
MACNAIR.
10.1921: Completed after joinery work

had been carried out at Portsmouth due to a
strike at Irvine.
5.7.1940: Requisitioned by the British
government until 16.3.1946.
1952: Sold to the British Iron and Steel
Corporation and allocated to Hughes,
Bolckow Ltd., Blyth.
15.9.1952: Arrived at Blyth to be broken up.
18.10.1954: Register closed.

Clan Macnaughton (2) had singularly heavy derricks at both masts. *[Ian J. Farquhar collection]*

CLAN MACNAUGHTON (2)
1921-1942
O.N. 146259 6,111g 3,784n
410.5 x 53.3 x 33.4 feet.
T.3-cyl. by Dunsmuir and Jackson Ltd., Glasgow; 561 NHP, 3,000 IHP, 12 knots.
12.1930: Fitted with a Bauer-Wach low pressure exhaust steam turbine increasing total output to 639 NHP.
9.8.1921: Launched by the Ayrshire Dockyard Co. Ltd., Irvine (Yard No. 488).
14.10.1921: Registered in the ownership of The Clan Line Steamers Ltd. (Cayzer, Irvine and Co. Ltd., managers), London as CLAN MACNAUGHTON.
19.10.1921: Delivered at a cost of £330,000.
24.2.1940: Requisitioned by the British government.
1.8.1942: Torpedoed and sunk by the German submarine U 155 in position

11.54 north by 54.25 west lives whilst on an independent voyage from Alexandria and Freetown to Trinidad and New York with a cargo of cotton. Of the 86 on board, five of the crew and one gunner were lost. The survivors took to the boats, one boat landing on Trinidad, one on Tobago and one being picked up by the EMPIRE BEDE (6,959/1942).
12.4.1943: Register closed.

CLAN MACNEIL (3) 1922-1952
O.N. 146281 6,111g 3,788n
410.5 x 53.3 x 33.5 feet.
T.3-cyl. by Dunsmuir and Jackson Ltd., Glasgow; 561 NHP, 3,000 IHP, 12 knots.
10.1929: Fitted with a Bauer-Wach low-pressure exhaust steam turbine by Deutsche Schiff und Maschinenbau A.G., Hamburg, Germany; increasing total output to 691 NHP.

1.12.1921: Launched by the Ayrshire Dockyard Co. Ltd., Irvine (Yard No. 489).
3.2.1922: Registered in the ownership of The Clan Line Steamers Ltd. (Cayzer, Irvine and Co. Ltd., managers), London as CLAN MACNEIL.
14.2.1922: Ran trials and delivered at a cost of £330,000.
8.8.1937: In collision with the Belgian steamer PRINCESSE MARIE JOSE (2,477/1925) whilst on a voyage from London to Dunkirk. The Belgian ship had to be beached and five passengers were badly injured.
23.3.1940: Requisitioned by the British government until 11.3.1946.
1952: Sold to the British Iron and Steel Corporation and allocated to Smith and Houston Ltd., Port Glasgow.
1.5.1952: Arrived at Port Glasgow.
2.5.1952: Moved to breakers' yard.
24.9.1952: Register closed.

In contrast to her sister, *Clan Macneil* (3) had a heavy derrick only at her foremast. *[J. and M. Clarkson collection]*

CLAN MACFARLANE (2) 1922-1940
O.N. 146317 6,222g 3,850n
418.1 x 53.4 x 33.6 feet.
T.3-cyl. by Dunsmuir and Jackson Ltd.,
Glasgow; 630 NHP, 3,300 IHP, 12 knots.
1929: Fitted with Bauer-Wach low-
pressure exhaust steam turbine by
Deutsche Schiff und Maschinenbau A.G.,
Hamburg, Germany; increasing total
output to 743 NHP.

24.8.1922: Launched by the Ayrshire
Dockyard Co. Ltd., Irvine (Yard No. 491).
It was intended to use the name HERMIONE.
17.10.1922: Registered in the ownership
of The Clan Line Steamers Ltd. (Cayzer,
Irvine and Co. Ltd., managers), London as
CLAN MACFARLANE.
11.1922: Completed.
25.5.1940: Requisitioned by the British
government.

17.7.1940: Sank following a collision with
the British steamer GANGES (6,246/1930)
in the Indian Ocean 250 miles east of
Italian Somaliland in position 12.38 north
by 55.31 east. She was on a voyage from
Glasgow and Liverpool to Mombasa to
Cochin. From her complement of 88, 41
were lost.
24.10.1940: Register closed.

These two photographs of the *Clan Macfarlane* on the Mersey show her with her original and extended funnel. Note the
railway carriages on deck in the lower photo.   *[B. and A. Feilden/J. and M. Clarkson collection]*

CLAN MACFADYEN (2) 1923-1942
O.N. 146335 6,224g 3,864n
418.2 x 53.4 x 25.6/33.6 feet.
T.3-cyl. by Dunsmuir and Jackson Ltd.,
Glasgow; 630 NHP, 3,300 IHP, 12 knots.
8.1928: Fitted with Bauer-Wach low-
pressure exhaust steam turbine increasing
total output to 743 NHP.
15.2.1923: Launched by the Ayrshire
Dockyard Co. Ltd., Irvine (Yard No. 490).
It was intended to use the name
HERCULES.

8.5.1923: Registered in the ownership of
The Clan Line Steamers Ltd. (Cayzer,
Irvine and Co. Ltd., managers), London as
CLAN MACFADYEN.
12.5.1923: Delivered.
7.2.1940: Requisitioned by the British
government.
26.11.1942: Torpedoed and sunk by the
German submarine U 508 200 miles north
west of Georgetown, British Guiana in

position 08.57 north by 59. 48 west whilst
on an independent voyage from Mauritius
and Pernambuco to Trinidad and the
United Kingdom with a cargo of sugar. 75
of her 84 crew and seven of eight gunners
were lost. The survivors were rescued
from a raft by the British schooner
HARVARD (114/1891) and landed at Port
of Spain, Trinidad.
16.8.1943: Register closed.

Two superb photographs of *Clan Macfadyen* (2). The right hand view was taken by the photographer E. Fluck as she sailed down the Adelaide River. She has her gear down and is fairly light but with native crews ships probably sailed between ports with the derricks stowed. *[Ian J. Farquhar collection]*

Above we see John McRoberts' view of the *Clan Macfadyen (2)* sailing from Liverpool with the assistance of a Cock tug on 11th September 1937. She was the first Clan Line ship to be fitted with a Bauer-Wach exhaust turbine, installed in Germany in 1928, and which set the company back £10,000. The initial results were disappointing, giving increased speed but no improvement in fuel consumption due to a problem with the condenser. Nevertheless, Clan were enthusiastic enough to send almost all their modern steamers to German or Clydeside yards for similar modifications, and to specify exhaust turbines for all new steamers. *[John McRoberts/J. and M. Clarkson]*

MEXICAN MISADVENTURE

A most unlikely service for Clan Line was that along the south west coast of North America. The ships employed were equally unlikely: Flower-class sloops of various sub-types which were converted for mercantile use.

The original suggestion may have come from a Houston contact in Mexico, and was based on the professed willingness of the Mexican government to provide a subsidy for a service from its west coast ports to Los Angeles and San Francisco. Recognising the government's involvement, the owning company was named Compañia Naviera de los Estados de Mexico S.A. (the Mexican State Lines). The whole venture attracted misfortune, and everyone involved came out of it worse off – Clan themselves, the Admiralty, the Mexican government and the shipbuilders who carried out the conversions.

The first three sloops selected were HMS Mistletoe, Montbretia *and* Polyanthus, *bought from the Admiralty at a bargain price of £14,500 each for vessels which according to Clan's board minutes were 'lavishly equipped'. Cramptons (Shipbuilders) Ltd. of Portsmouth offered to convert them for £7,500 each, the specification including removal of one of the two boilers, conversion of the other to oil fuel, and installing passenger accommodation. Clan retained the boilers removed from these ships, some being subsequently fitted as replacements in Scottish Shire's* Ayrshire. *Delighted with such bargains, Clan then bought a further three,* HMS Ivy, Silene *and* Convolvulus, *noting that these were 'practically the last on offer'. Before they could all be delivered, however, the two which were at Queenstown,* HMS Silene *and* Convolvulus, *suffered 'malicious damage' – presumably during the civil war in Ireland – and were substituted by* HMS Dianthus *and* Pelargonium. *Cramptons quoted £84,000 for the three further conversions, having seriously underestimated the work required on the first three. Indeed, Cramptons later threatened to sue Clan on the basis that alterations in the specifications had increased the cost by £90,000, but this was dismissed by Clan as the actual changes were minor, although as a gesture of goodwill they offered £15,000. Unwisely, Cramptons turned this down, and the next heard of this claim is from the shipyard's liquidators who some years later received just £3,500 from Clan. The choice of an obscure yard in Portsmouth to carry out this work was undoubtedly due to Cayzer being the local member of Parliament.*

When converted the vessels sailed out to Mexico via the Azores, where their bunkers were replenished. Although Cramptons seem to have worked quite speedily, given that the conversions contributed to their bankruptcy, there were delays in getting all the ships out to Mexico and on to the service, which was due to begin

HMS *Polyanthus*, one of the first batch of three sloops purchased, which became the *Colima*. [Imperial War Museum SP.1656]

in November 1921. Oaxaca, *for instance, was not in operation until the summer of 1922. Partly because of the delay, ships owned by the Mexican government continued on the route, somewhat bizarrely as the same government had promised Clan a subsidy. In service, the ships proved unsuccessful, although the Clan Line board minutes are somewhat ambiguous about the reasons for this. On a number of occasions they are laid up for want of cargo, but on others blamed for being too small for the cargoes offered, the government-owned ships being larger. To remedy this situation, in 1923 a larger, Dutch-built ship was bought and renamed* Sinaloa *(2). She had accommodation for 30 first and 30 second class passengers, and usually managed to remain trading whilst the smaller ships were laid up. Early in 1923 it was decided to extend the service south to Panama, and there was even talk of* Clan Menzies *(2) taking a sailing on the berth from Panama to San Francisco, although this was quickly cancelled.*

The Clan Line board became frustrated with the operation, and particularly the difficulty of getting replies to queries from the local managers. In desperation, a director was sent out to Mexico during 1923, visiting the company's offices at Mazatlan and San Francisco, agents at Guadalajara and Los Angeles, and even government officials in Mexico City. He learnt that the four government-owned ships were bigger and better suited to the trade. However, crew and other problems meant they could not match the regularity of sailings of the Clan-owned company's ships. There was great confidence that it would only be a matter of time before their ships were sold by the government, who had lost a reported £120,000. In anticipation, the director went to Mexico City, where long hours were spent waiting for interviews with government officials. These proved singularly unproductive: the price quoted for

the government steamers was much too high, and it was not even possible to secure payment of the promised government subsidy, officials claiming that the Clan-owned company had not kept to their schedules. It was concluded, however, that despite these difficulties and a loss of about £32,000 in the first year, the Clan-owned service should continue, as it was expected that the US government would soon officially recognise the current Mexican regime, which would immediately increase trade.

This proved far too optimistic. Within months Mexico was experiencing a civil war, the rebels briefly seizing the Oaxaca *and helping themselves to the contents of the company's oil hulk. Five of the ships were now laid up at San Francisco. The rebellion was crushed, but despite the government offering pooling arrangements, trade continued at a low level, with only* Sinaloa *running regularly. Efforts now began to sell the other ships but, although several South American governments showed interest, they were not prepared to pay a reasonable price. In 1925* Colima *and* Nayarit *were chartered to Clarke Steamship Co. Ltd. of Quebec, and were sent round to the St. Lawrence, being re-registered in Montreal in Clan Line ownership. Even this produced problems, as the charterers were blamed when one of* Nayarit's *cylinders was found cracked, probably due to it not being properly drained of water during winter lay up. Eventually she was sold to Clarke when Clan refused to renew her charter. Despairing of a sale for* Colima, *it was decided to bring her home to Glasgow. Again disaster struck: she broke down in mid-Atlantic and the bill of £3,750 for towage and assistance almost matched the price received when she was eventually sold in 1929.*

By then even Sinaloa *was laid up, and the others began to be sold for sums as low as £3,000. In 1930 it was decided to bring* Sinaloa *to the 'other side' as the*

140

minutes described it, and she was sent up to Vancouver to load a full cargo of wines and spirits for the St.Pierre Islands. She then enjoyed a short career running mainly on Clan Line berths from East Africa to Birkenhead, but was rather small for this service and was sold in 1933. Clan Line applied to the British Foreign Office to help with their claim on the Mexican government for the still-unpaid subsidy. The final ignominy was the Foreign Office declining to pursue this claim as it was on behalf of a Mexican-registered company. In 1930 a debt of almost £160,000 on behalf of Compañia Naviera de los Estados de Mexico S.A. was written off by Clan Line.

The blame for the Mexican misadventure could be put on unreasonable assumptions of profitability, unsuitable ships, civil unrest, Mexican government intransigence and, probably most telling, a remote operation with local managers who did not understand the country and could hardly speak its language. The poor outcome was untypical of the enterprises of Clan Line, which succeeded in surviving the depression of the 1930s with none of their other ships laid up.

CHIHUAHUA 1921
O.N. 146258 1,471g 849n
254.4 x 35.1 x 17.3 feet.
T. 4-cyl. by Richardsons, Westgarth and Co. Ltd., Hartlepool; 236 NHP.
3.9.1917: Launched by Irvine's Shipbuilding and Drydock Co. Ltd., West Hartlepool (Yard No. 588).
12.1917: Completed for the Admiralty as the Aubrietia-type sloop HMS MONTBRETIA. Also served as ROCHFORT.
25.1.1921: Acquired by The Clan Line Steamers Ltd. (Cayzer, Irvine and Co. Ltd., managers), London and converted for commercial use by Cramptons (Shipbuilders) Ltd., Portsmouth.
20.9.1921: Registered as CHIHUAHUA.
1921: Transferred to Compañia Naviera de los Estados de Mexico S.A., Mazatlan, Mexico.
1932: Sold to the Pacific Deep Sea Fishing Corporation, Wilmington, California, USA, remaining registered at Mazatlan, Mexico.
1935: Dismantled during the second quarter.

COLIMA 1921-1922/1925-1929
O.N. 146269 1,393g 819n
255.9 x 35.0 x 15.4 feet.
T.4-cyl. by Lobnitz and Co. Ltd., Renfrew; 181 NHP, 1,000 IHP, 12 knots.
24.9.1917: Launched by Lobnitz and Co. Ltd., Renfrew (Yard No. 826).
11.1917: Completed for the Admiralty, London as HMS POLYANTHUS.
25.1.1921: Acquired by The Clan Line Steamers Ltd. (Cayzer, Irvine and Co.

Ltd., managers), London and converted for commercial use by Cramptons (Shipbuilders) Ltd., Portsmouth.
24.11.1921: Registered as COLIMA.
2.3.1922: Register closed on transfer to Compañia Naviera de los Estados de Mexico S.A., Mazatlan, Mexico.
26.8.1925: Registered at Montreal in the ownership of The Clan Line Steamers Ltd. (Cayzer, Irvine and Co. Ltd., managers), London.
12.1927: Whilst on a voyage from the St. Lawrence to Glasgow broke down in mid-Atlantic with boiler problems and adrift for seven days until taken in tow to Glasgow by the German tug SEEFALKE (570/1924), for which she was awarded £2,500. The US steamer WEST COHAS (5,624/1918) stood by and was awarded £1,250.
21.3.1928: Registered at Glasgow.
11.11.1929: Sold to British Trade Crusades Ltd. (Noel P. Billing, manager), London for £4,500.
3.5.1933: Register closed on sale to N.D. Antoniou, Piraeus, Greece, and renamed ACROPOLIS
6.4.1941: Sunk when CLAN FRASER (3) exploded during an air raid at Piraeus in position 37.57.00 north by 23.42.00 east.

CHIAPAS 1921
O.N. 146277 1,473g 841n
254.6 x 35.2 x 17.2 feet.
T. 4-cyl. by Dunsmuir and Jackson Ltd., Glasgow; 228 NHP.
17.11.1917: Launched by the Greenock and Grangemouth Dockyard Co. Ltd., Grangemouth (Yard No.382).
5.1918: Completed for the Admiralty as the Anchusa-type sloop HMS MISTLETOE.
25.1.1921: Acquired by The Clan Line Steamers Ltd. (Cayzer, Irvine and Co. Ltd., managers), London and converted for commercial use by Cramptons (Shipbuilders) Ltd., Portsmouth.

22.12.1921: Registered as CHIAPAS.
1921: Transferred to the Compañia Naviera de los Estados de Mexico S.A., Mazatlan, Mexico.
2.8.1930: Sold to J. Dale Gentry, Panama for £3,000 and renamed PLAYA ENSENADA.
1932: Sold to G.A. McLoney, Panama and renamed LA PLAYA.
1933: Sold to Martin S. Lewis, Panama and renamed CITY OF PANAMA.
1934: Transferred to Martin S. Lewis junior, Los Angeles, USA and renamed STAR OF HOLLYWOOD.
1938: Sold to S.G. Murphy, Los Angeles.
3.1939: Reported sold to Harry C. Wilson and Co. and in use as an offshore fishing barge at Los Angeles.

GUERRERO 1921-1922
O.N. 146288 1,415g 859n
254.9 x 35.1 x 17.3 feet.
T. 4-cyl. by Barclay, Curle and Co. Ltd., Stobcross, Glasgow; 170 NHP, 11 knots.
1.2.1917: Launched by Barclay, Curle and Co. Ltd., Stobcross, Glasgow (Yard No. 557).
12.1917: Completed for the Admiralty as the Anchusa-type sloop HMS DIANTHUS. Also served as DHOBY.
3.6.1921: Acquired by The Clan Line Steamers Ltd. (Cayzer, Irvine and Co. Ltd., managers), London and converted for commercial use by Cramptons (Shipbuilders) Ltd., Portsmouth.
24.3.1922: Registered as GUERRERO.
16.6.1922: Register closed on transfer to Compañia Naviera de los Estados de Mexico S.A., Mazatlan, Mexico.
1932: Sold to C.G. Krueger and Co., Los Angeles, USA, remaining registered at Mazatlan, Mexico.
1933: Sold to William J. Maggio, San Pedro, California, USA.
1938: Broken up at Los Angeles

The sloop *HMS Dianthus*, later the *Guerrero*. Some of the sloops bought for conversion were intended for use as decoy, or Q-ships, and the various yards building them were instructed to vary their appearance. *[National Maritime Museum N.3849]*

SINALOA (1) 1921-1922/NAYARIT 1925-1929

O.N. 146296 1,461g 892n
254.1 x 35.1 x 17.4 feet.
T.4-cyl. by Richardsons, Westgarth and Co. Ltd., Hartlepool; 192 NHP, 850 IHP, 12 knots.
31.10.1917: Launched by the Blyth Shipbuilding and Dry Dock Co. Ltd., Blyth (Yard No. 203).
4.1918: Completed for the Admiralty, London as the Anchusa-type sloop HMS IVY.
2.1920: Sold to Howard, Ipswich.
2.6.1921: Acquired by The Clan Line Steamers Ltd. (Cayzer, Irvine and Co. Ltd., managers), London and converted for commercial use by Cramptons (Shipbuilders) Ltd., Portsmouth.
2.6.1922: Registered as SINALOA.
22.8.1922: Register closed on transfer to Compañia Naviera de los Estados de Mexico S.A., Mazatlan, Mexico.
1923: Renamed NAYARIT.
26.8.1925: Registered at Montreal in the ownership of The Clan Line Steamers Ltd. (Cayzer, Irvine and Co. Ltd., managers), London.
3.4.1929: Sold to Desmond A. and Wilfrid G. Clarke, Quebec for £7,000.
30.4.1929: Transferred to the Clarke Steamship Co. Ltd., Quebec.
7.5.1929: Renamed NORTH VOYAGEUR.
5.10.1937: Register closed on sale to Hellenic Shipping and Commercial Co. Ltd., Athens, Greece, and renamed ESPEROS.
21.4.1941: Bombed and sunk off Missolonghi, Greece in position 38.19.54 north by 21.24.42 east whilst serving as a hospital ship.

OAXACA 1921-1922

O.N. 146305 1,468g 897n
254.7 x 35.1 x 17.3 feet.
T. 4-cyl. by John G. Kincaid and Co. Ltd., Greenock; 221 NHP, 1,350 IHP, 11 knots.
18.3.1918: Launched by William Hamilton and Co. Ltd., Port Glasgow (Yard No. 354).
5.1918: Completed for the Admiralty as the Anchusa-type sloop HMS PELARGONIUM.
25.1.1921: Acquired by The Clan Line Steamers Ltd. (Cayzer, Irvine and Co. Ltd., managers), London and converted for commercial use by Cramptons (Shipbuilders) Ltd., Portsmouth.
5.8.1922: Registered as OAXACA.
20.9.1922: Register closed on transfer to the Compañia Naviera de los Estados de Mexico S.A., Mazatlan, Mexico.
1927: Sold to the West Coast Transportation Co. Inc., Los Angeles, USA under the Panama flag.
1929: Sold to J.W. Hobbs (Hobbs Brothers Ltd., managers), Vancouver, British Columbia under the Panama flag.
18.4.1929: Registered in the ownership of Hobbs Brothers Ltd., Vancouver.

HM convoy sloop *Ivy* leaving Malta. Bought and refitted she was renamed *Sinaloa* in 1922 and *Nayarit* in 1923. *[Imperial War Museum SP.2060]*

28.1.1932: Register closed on sale to J. Dale Gentry, San Bernardino, California, USA.
1938: Sold to M.P. Nomikos (Petros M. Nomikos Ltd., managers), Piraeus, Greece and renamed SOFIA
1939: Sold to John Toyias Steam Ship Co., Piraeus.
25.4.1941: Bombed and sunk at Aghios Georgios, Greece.

SINALOA (2) 1923-1933

O.N. 145240 1,364g 627n
238.6 x 36.6 x 15.6 feet.
T.3-cyl. by N.V. Van de Kuy & van der Ree's Machinefabriek & Scheepswerf, Rotterdam, Holland; 127 NHP, 900 IHP, 10 knots.
26.3.1921: Launched by N.V. Scheepsbouwwerf 'de Merwede' v/h Van Vliet & Co., Neder-Hardinxveld, Holland (Yard No. 132) for the Anglo-Mexican Petroleum Co. Ltd., London.

14.6.1921: Registered in the ownership of the San Antonio Steamship Co. Ltd. (John S. Evernden, manager), London as SANTA GERTRUDIS.
6.11.1923: Acquired by The Clan Line Steamers Ltd. (Cayzer, Irvine and Co. Ltd., managers), London for £21,000.
18.1.1924: Register closed on transfer to Compañia Naviera de los Estados de Mexico S.A., Mazatlan, Mexico and renamed SINALOA.
4.2.1932: Registered in the ownership of The Clan Line Steamers Ltd. (Cayzer, Irvine and Co. Ltd., managers), Glasgow.
10.11.1933: Register closed on sale to Constantine M. Lemos, Syra, Greece, and renamed ARCHON for £4,800.
1939: Sold to B. Yiadikiaroglou, B. Kalogheras and Th. Vranas, Piraeus, Greece.
21.4.1941: Bombed and sunk off Chalkis, Euboea.

Note the cowl top to the plain black funnel of the Dutch-built *Sinaloa* (2). *[B. and A. Feilden/J. and M. Clarkson collection]*

Port Macquarie. [Ian J. Farquhar collection]

Port Lincoln. [Ian J. Farquhar collection]

THOMAS PURCHASES

In the late 1920s Robert Thomas tried to emulate his highly successful, Anglesey-born shipowning father, William Thomas, by trying to break in to trades to South America and South Africa. In both he was bitterly opposed by the respective conferences, and in the South African trades Clan Line and others put on 'fighting ships' to offer even lower rates than Thomas could give. As part of an eventual settlement, two of his ships were bought by Clan for £40,000 the pair and although 17 years old were described as 'most satisfactory'. Each ship gave Clan and its Houston subsidiary ten years of service.

CLAN GRANT (3) 1929-1939

O.N. 135132 7,235g 4,638n
426.0 x 54.1 x 37.3 feet.
Q.4-cyl. by the North Eastern Marine Engineering Co. Ltd., Newcastle-upon-Tyne; 786 NHP, 4,100 IHP, 12.25 knots.

30.5.1912: Launched by R. and W. Hawthorn, Leslie and Co. Ltd., Hebburn (Yard No. 456).
2.9.1912: Registered in the ownership of the Anglo-Australasian Steam Navigation Co. Ltd. (William Milburn and Co., managers), London as PORT MACQUARIE
5.9.1912: Ran trials.
12.9.1912: Delivered.
11.2.1914: Transferred to the Commonwealth and Dominion Line Ltd., London.
21.5.1927: Sold to William Thomas Shipping Co. Ltd. (R.J. Thomas and Co. Ltd., managers), Holyhead.
15.6.1927: Renamed CAMBRIAN MARCHIONESS.
29.12.1928: Sold to C.W. Kellock and Co. Ltd., London.
2.5.1929: Acquired by The Clan Line Steamers Ltd. (Cayzer, Irvine and Co. Ltd., managers), London.
18.5.1929: Renamed CLAN GRANT.

14.1.1935: Transferred to the British and South American Steam Navigation Co. Ltd. (Houston Line (London) Ltd., managers), London.
19.1.1939: Sold to the Stanhope Steamship Co. Ltd. (J.A. Billmeir and Co. Ltd., manager), London.
25.1.1939: Renamed STANGRANT.
14.4.1940: Requisitioned by the British government.
13.10.1940: Torpedoed and sunk by the German submarine U 37 220 miles west of the Butt of Lewis in position 58.27 north by 12.36 west whilst a straggler from convoy HX 77 and on a voyage from Hampton Roads to Belfast with a cargo of steel and scrap metal. Eight of the crew of 37 were lost, the survivors including the one gunner being rescued by a Sunderland flying boat.
15.11.1940: Register closed.

Clan Grant (3) and her sister had a distinctive profile in the Clan fleet. [B. and A. Feilden/J. and M. Clarkson collection]

CLAN GRAHAM (3) 1929-1938

O.N. 132733 7,134g 4,568n
426.0 x 54.1 x 37.3 feet.
Q.4-cyl. by the North Eastern Marine Engineering Co. Ltd., Newcastle-upon-Tyne; 777 NHP, 13 knots.
3.4.1912: Launched by R. and W. Hawthorn, Leslie and Co. Ltd., Hebburn (Yard No. 452).
22.6.1912: Ran trials.
24.6.1912: Registered in the ownership of William Milburn and Co., London as PORT LINCOLN.
3.7.1912: Delivered.
13.2.1914: Transferred to the Commonwealth and Dominion Line Ltd., London.

27.7.1927: Sold to William Thomas Shipping Co. Ltd. (R.J. Thomas and Co. Ltd., managers), Holyhead.
3.8.1927: Renamed CAMBRIAN BARONESS.
13.12.1928: Sold to C.W. Kellock and Co. Ltd., London.
9.5.1929: Acquired by The Clan Line Steamers Ltd. (Cayzer, Irvine and Co. Ltd., managers), London.
18.5.1929: Renamed CLAN GRAHAM.
4.1.1935: Transferred to British and South American Steam Navigation Co. Ltd. (Houston Line (London) Ltd., managers), London.

14.12.1938: Sold to Neill and Pandelis Ltd., London for £17,500.
24.12.1938: Renamed MARITIMA.
16.4.1940: Requisitioned by the British government.
2.11.1942: Torpedoed and sunk by the German submarine U 522 370 miles north east by east from St. Johns, Newfoundland in position 52.20 north by 45.40 west, whilst on a voyage in convoy SC 107 from New York and Sydney, Nova Scotia to Glasgow with general cargo including explosives. 29 of the 51 crew and three of the eight gunners were lost.
16.6.1943: Register closed.

Clan Graham (4). Comparison of the funnels of *Clan Grant* and *Clan Graham* with the photographs of *Port Macquarie* and *Port Lincoln* on the previous page shows they have been considerably shortened, probably before Clan bought them.
[Above: Archie Munro collection, below: Ships in Focus]

GREENOCK DOCKYARD QUARTET

The four ships built in the late 1920s at Greenock represented the first new Clan Line design since the Clan Macnab had been ordered almost a decade earlier. The increasing need for fast, refrigerated ships for both the South African and Australian trades was behind the order, although the possibility of government assistance under the Trade Facilities Act was also a factor. In the event, the government would only provide a loan of £400,000 if both the two new ships and two of the Clan Macnab class were provided as security, a condition which Clan found too onerous, and decided to proceed without the loan.

It is tempting to assume that different types of machinery were fitted in order to carry out comparative tests of diesel and steam engines, but there is nothing to support this in the board minutes. More likely cost was a deciding factor in fitting the later pair with steam engines: the contract price for Clan Macalister was £165,000 compared with £195,000 for Clan Macdonald and £205,000 for the larger Clan Macdougall. There was also enthusiasm for the benefits of the extra speed and reduced fuel consumption expected from the Bauer-Wach exhaust turbine which were specified for the steamers, and were in the process of being retro-fitted to many earlier ships.

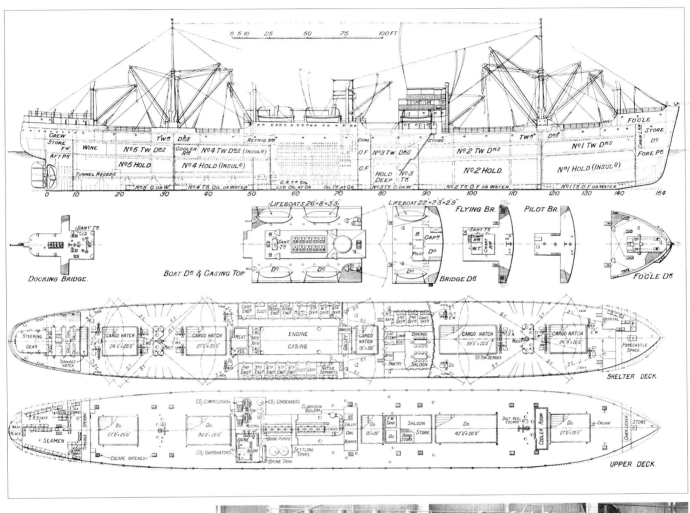

General arrangement drawing of *Clan Macdonald* (3) (above). Her two-stroke, double-acting, oil engine was built by J.G. Kincaid and Co. Ltd. of Greenock to a Burmeister & Wain design (right). *[Shipbuilding and Shipping Record]*

**CLAN MACDONALD (3) /
STIRLINGSHIRE (1) 1928-1940**
O.N. 160210 6,051g 3,591n
434.2 x 57.7 x 33.7 feet.
8-cyl. 4SCDA Burmeister & Wain-type
oil engine by John G. Kincaid and Co.
Ltd., Greenock; 4,830 BHP, 6,440 IHP,
13.5 knots.
21.2.1928: Launched by the Greenock
Dockyard Co. Ltd., Greenock (Yard No.
414).
20.6.1928: Registered in the ownership

of The Clan Line Steamers Ltd.
(Cayzer, Irvine and Co. Ltd.,
managers), London as CLAN
MACDONALD.
22.6.1928: Ran trials and delivered at a
cost of £195,000.
8.1.1930: Transferred to the Scottish
Shire Line (Turnbull, Martin and Co.
Ltd., managers), Glasgow.
18.1.1930: Renamed STIRLINGSHIRE.
20.6.1940: Requisitioned by the British
government.

2.12.1940: Torpedoed by the German
submarine U 94 350 miles north west of
Malin Head, Ireland and sunk in position
55.36 north by 16.22 west whilst in
convoy HX 90 on a voyage from
Townsville and Sydney, New South Wales
via Bermuda and Halifax, Nova Scotia to
Liverpool with general cargo including
sugar and lead. The crew of 73 and one
gunner were rescued by the steamer
EMPIRE PUMA (7,777/1920).
27.2.1941: Register closed.

Clan Macdonald (3) had the distinction of being Clan's first motor ship, but between the two parts of the superstructure retained a hatch which was originally intended as a coal bunker. During construction Clan received an offer for her from HAPAG, but turned it down as being too low. *[M. Cooper/J. and M. Clarkson]*

As *Stirlingshire* (1) she was the first ship sunk by *U 94* which went on to be one of the more successful U-boats sinking a total of 25 merchant ships and an armed trawler before her loss on 28th August 1942. Note the containers on deck in this photograph, which also shows that her funnel had been heightened. *[J. and M. Clarkson]*

For *Clan Macdougall* (2) the design was modified to have a hull beamier and longer than *Clan Macdonald* in order to take heavy lifts such as locomotives weighing up to 120 tons. This requirement also resulted in a more sensible configuration for a motor ship with a compact superstructure and number 3 hold ahead of the bridge. Her engine was a four-stroke, for comparison with that of *Clan Macdonald*. She was photographed on 29th January 1938 when outward bound on the Brisbane River. *[W. Elliot]*

CLAN MACDOUGALL (2) 1929-1941
O.N. 160234 6,843g 4,079n
454.0 x 62.3 x 28.9 feet.
8-cyl. 4SCDA Burmeister & Wain-type oil engine by John G. Kincaid and Co. Ltd., Greenock; 4,830 BHP, 6,440 IHP, 13-14 knots.
28.9.1928: Launched by the Greenock Dockyard Co. Ltd., Greenock (Yard No. 415).
28.12.1928: Ran trials.
7.1.1929: Registered in the ownership of The Clan Line Steamers Ltd. (Cayzer,

Irvine and Co. Ltd., managers), London as CLAN MACDOUGALL.
28.1.1935: In King's Dock, Swansea on sailing for Glasgow damaged in collision with the Danish steamer HJORTHOLM (1,471/1905) which sank, and was subsequently raised and broken up at Llanelli. CLAN MACDOUGALL was repaired and returned to service.
8.6.1940: Requisitioned by the British government.
31.5.1941: Torpedoed by the German submarine U 106 near St. Vincent, Cape

Verde Islands and sank in position 16.46 north by 25.25 west whilst on an independent voyage from Glasgow to East London with general cargo. From her complement of 81 crew and four gunners, two members of the crew were lost.
17.12.1941: Register closed.

CLAN MACPHERSON (3) 1929-1943
O.N. 160249 6,940g 4,191n
454.0 x 62.3 x 28.9 feet.
T.3-cyl. by Rankin and Blackmore Ltd., Glasgow with a low pressure Bauer-Wach

Clan Macpherson (3) in the Antipodes. In contrast to her two immediate predecessors, which completed their trials quite successfully despite their relatively novel diesel engines, *Clan Macpherson* (3) had considerable trouble with her much more conventional machinery. When the exhaust turbine was engaged the gearing was very noisy, due to the teeth not meshing and led to trials being abandoned. Careful running in solved the problem, and allowed her to take her maiden sailing on time, but when her engines were opened up on arrival at Colombo the low-pressure piston was found to be cracked. Until a new piston could be cast, she ran on the intermediate and high pressure cylinders, plus the exhaust turbine. Both mishaps led to strong words being said to engine builders Rankin and Blackmore Ltd. *[Ian J. Farquhar]*

exhaust steam turbine; 973 NHP, 5,800 IHP, 14 knots.

9.3.1929: Launched by the Greenock Dockyard Co. Ltd., Greenock (Yard No. 416).

12.5.1929: Ran trials.

14.5.1929: Registered in the ownership of The Clan Line Steamers Ltd. (Cayzer, Irvine and Co. Ltd., managers), London as CLAN MACPHERSON.

16.2.1940: Requisitioned by the British government.

1.5.1943: Torpedoed by the German submarine U 515 75 miles south west of Freetown in position 07.58 north by 14.14 west and sank in position 08.04 north by 14.12 west. She was on a voyage from Calcutta, Durban and Takoradi to Freetown and the United Kingdom with pig iron and general cargo in convoy TS 37. Of the complement of 132, four of the crew were lost, the survivors being taken on board the trawler HMS ARRAN.

4.9.1943: Register closed.

Clan Macpherson (3) is seen above in Birkenhead (top) and early in the Second World War (bottom), carrying a gun on her poop and with boats slung out. In May 1943 she was one of seven ships from convoy TS 37 to be sunk by *U 515* in two separate attacks. Hit on the starboard beam and abandoned within ten minutes, *Clan Macpherson* remained afloat and her crew later re-boarded her but could not stop the flooding and abandoned her again. She drifted 10 miles before sinking.
[Top: B. and A. Feilden/J. and M. Clarkson collection, bottom: National Maritime Museum P.15723]

CLAN MACALISTER (3) 1930-1940

O.N. 161909 6,795g 4,097n
453.8 x 62.3 x 28.9 feet.
T.3-cyl. by John G. Kincaid and Co. Ltd.,
Greenock with a Bauer-Wach low pressure
exhaust steam turbine; 719 NHP, 5,150
IHP, 13 knots.
29.1.1930: Launched by the Greenock
Dockyard Co. Ltd., Greenock (Yard No.
418).
4.1930: Completed.
7.5.1930: Registered in the ownership of
The Clan Line Steamers Ltd. (Cayzer,
Irvine and Co. Ltd., managers), London as
CLAN MACALISTER.
8.5.1930: Ran trials and delivered.
29.8.1939: Requisitioned by the British
government.
29.5.1940: Bombed, set on fire and
eventually sunk by German Ju 87 aircraft
whilst unloading landing craft near Bray
Dunes, Dunkirk in position 51.04.41 north
by 02.28 east during Operation Dynamo.
She was on a voyage from Southampton to
Dunkirk carrying landing craft and their
crews. Of the crew of 75 and 4 gunners,
18 members of the crew were lost.
13.12.1940: Register closed.

Dressed over-all, the newly launched
Clan Macalister enters the Garvel Dry
Dock at Greenock (top right) after her
launch. *(Glasgow University Archives
GD323/7/9/2/418/1]*
In the undated view of her in the
Mersey (right) the funnel appears to be
taller than in the view below. *[B. and A.
Feilden/J. and M. Clarkson]*

Above: Although credited with a modest 13 knots in her registration documents, *Clan Macalister* (3) managed an impressive
16.5 knots on trials, justifying the £10,000 extra cost of fitting a Bauer-Wach turbine.
    Clan Macalister had the unhappy distinction of being the largest ship to take part in the evacuation of Dunkirk. She
was anchored about one and a half miles off Dunkirk, acting as a mother ship to landing craft which were helping to ferry
troops out from the beaches to waiting ships. Her size singled her out for unwelcome attention from the Luftwaffe, and she
received three hits, sinking in such shallow water that she appeared to be still afloat and was attacked further. The destroyer
HMS *Malcolm* attempted unsuccessfully to extinguish the flames, and took off the troops and wounded members of the crew.
The remainder of the crew were taken off by the minesweeper HMS *Pangbourne*. *[B. and A. Feilden/J. and M. Clarkson
collection]*

HOUSTON PURCHASE

The British and South American Steam Navigation Co. Ltd. was something of a poor relation of Clan Line, probably because its routes to South America (and particularly that from New York) were never as profitable as some Clan services. After a flurry of acquisitions in 1919 and 1920, no ships were built for the company, and it made do with former Clan or other second hand ships, including this middle-aged vessel bought in 1930.

HERACLIDES 1930-1939

O.N. 139163 7,131g 4,379n
470.0 x 58.3 x 37.8 feet.
Q.4-cyl. by George Clark Ltd., Sunderland; 629 NHP, 3,000 IHP, 11 knots.
2.5.1916: Launched by Short Brothers Ltd., Sunderland (Yard No. 390).
2.11.1916: Registered in the ownership of Nitrate Producers' Steamship Co. Ltd. (Lawther, Latta and Co. Ltd., managers), London as ANGLO CHILEAN.
30.11.1916: Completed.
1.8.1930: Acquired by the British and South American Steam Navigation Co. Ltd. (R.P. Houston and Co., managers), London for £40,000.
12.8.1930: Renamed HERACLIDES.
1932: Managers became Houston Line (London) Ltd.
4.3.1939: Sold to Hermes Steamship Co. Ltd. (Vergottis Ltd.), London.
10.3.1939: Renamed HERMES.
25.6.1940: Detained at Algiers following the Franco-German Armistice, subsequently seized by the Vichy authorities, managed by Compagnie des Bateaux à Vapeur du Nord and renamed ST. FRANÇOIS.
9.12.1942: Seized by Germany at Marseilles and transferred to the Italian Government, Rome ('Adriatica' Società Anonima di Navigazione, Venice,

Upper: *Anglo Chilean* purchased in 1930 to become *Heraclides*. *[George Scott collection]*
Middle: *Heraclides*. *[Ships in Focus]*

managers) and renamed ALCAMO.
25.2.1943: Sunk by torpedoes and bombs from Bristol Beauforts of 39 Squadron, Royal Air Force, 73 miles north of Trapani in position 39.14 north by 12.30 east whilst on a voyage in convoy from Bizerta to Naples.
8.10.1947: British register closed.

WAR G-TYPE

Increasingly concerned about having sufficient refrigerated space for its South African and Australian services, in 1933 Clan took the opportunity of buying two big, war-built, G-type ships when White Star gave up its services to Australia. A third was bought from the New Zealand Shipping Co. Ltd. in 1934.

CLAN COLQUHOUN (2) 1933-1947

O.N. 142741 7,912g 4,888n
450.0 x 58.5 x 37.1 feet.
Two T.3-cyl. by Workman, Clark and Co. Ltd., Belfast driving twin screws; 1,476 NHP.
12.12.1918: Launched by Workman, Clark and Co. Ltd., Belfast (Yard No. 436).
11.12.1918: Registered in the ownership of the Shipping Controller (Federal Steam Navigation Co. Ltd., managers), London as WAR ARGUS

White Star's *Gallic* bought in 1933 to become *Clan Colquhoun* (2). *[J. and M. Clarkson collection]*

4.7.1919: Sold to the Oceanic Steam Navigation Co. Ltd. (White Star Line, managers), Liverpool.
9.8.1919: Renamed GALLIC.
14.9.1933: Acquired by The Clan Line Steamers Ltd. (Cayzer, Irvine and Co. Ltd., managers), London for £22,500.
30.10.1933: Renamed CLAN COLQUHOUN.
12.8.1940: Requisitioned by the British government until 18.4.1946.
3.2.1947: Register closed on sale to the Zarate Steamship Co. Ltd., Panama (John Livanos and Sons Ltd., London, managers) for £52,500 and renamed IOANNIS LIVANOS.
1949: Transferred to Dos Oceanos Compañia de Navigation S.A., Panama (John Livanos and Sons Ltd., London, managers) and renamed JENNY.
1951: Sold to Djakarta Lloyd N.V., Djakarta, Indonesia and renamed IMAM BONDJOL.
1952: Renamed DJATINEGRA.
22.10.1955: Delivered to Hong Kong Salvage and Towage Co. Ltd. at Djakarta for delivery to Japan for breaking up.
1.12.1955: Whilst under tow to Osaka beached at Lingayen, near Manila, Philippines after springing leaks.
21.2.1956: Refloated after patches had been fitted.
19.3.1956: Arrived at Hong Kong where it was decided that the vessel was not sufficiently seaworthy to complete the journey to Japan and she was subsequently resold to Peninsula Shipbreakers Ltd., Hong Kong.
6.1956: Demolition began.

Clan Colquhoun (2) was the first of five Gs built by Workman Clark, Belfast. Note the flange on her funnel to facilitate removing the top to negotiate the Manchester Ship Canal. *[B. and A. Feilden/J. and M. Clarkson collection]*

Clan Colquhoun shabby in her drab wartime grey. Clan Line must have been popular with funnel builders - compare the funnel on *Gallic* with the two later views - at some stage it has been shortened and later lengthened. *[National Maritime Museum P22119]*

Whilst in Livanos ownership between 1947 and 1951, the ship was fitted out as an emigrant carrier, as seen under the name *Jenny* at Montevideo on 4th April 1950. *[Wm. A. Schell]*

CLAN FARQUHAR (2) 1933-1948

O.N. 142695 8,005g 4,894n
450.4 x 58.4 x 37.2 feet.
Two T.3-cyl. by Harland and Wolff
Ltd., Glasgow driving twin screws;
944 NHP, 7,000 IHP, 14.25 knots.
19.9.1918: Launched by Harland and
Wolff Ltd., Belfast (Yard No. 540).
26.10.1918: Registered in the
ownership of the Shipping Controller,
London (Booth Steamship Co. Ltd.,
Liverpool, managers) as WAR
ICARUS
31.10.1918: Completed.
10.6.1919: Sold to the Atlantic
Transport Co. Ltd., London.
8.7.1919: Renamed MESABA.
21.10.1925: Renamed DELPHIC.
23.11.1925: The Oceanic Steam
Navigation Co. Ltd. (White Star Line,
managers), Liverpool became part
owners (32/64 shares).
2.10.1933: Acquired by The Clan
Line Steamers Ltd. (Cayzer, Irvine
and Co. Ltd., managers), London for
£15,000.
16.10.1933: Renamed CLAN
FARQUHAR.
16.5.1940: Requisitioned by the
British government until 26.7.1946.
1.7.1948: Sold to the British Iron and
Steel Corporation for £19,250 and
allocated to T.W. Ward Ltd., Sheffield.
8.7.1948: Delivered by the tugs
MASTERMAN and TRADESMAN
from the Mersey to Milford Haven for
breaking up.
1.11.1948: Register closed.

The G class frozen meat carriers were the most impressive of the First World War
standard ships, appearing even more striking once Greenock Dockyard had modified
them with taller funnels. *Clan Farquhar* (2) had been completed as *War Icarus*, the only
one of 29 ordered which was delivered before the Armistice. The second view shows
her as *Delphic* and the third with her taller funnel during the Second World War. *[Top:
B. and A. Feilden/J. and M. Clarkson collection, middle: J. and M. Clarkson collection,
bottom: National Maritime Museum P22120]*

CLAN ROBERTSON (2) 1934-1938
O.N. 132763 7,976g 4,934n
449.1 x 58.3 x 37.1 feet.
Two T.3-cyl. by Barclay, Curle and Co. Ltd., Whiteinch, Glasgow driving twin screws; 752 NHP, 7,000 BHP, 14 knots.
1919: Keel laid by Barclay, Curle and Co. Ltd., Whiteinch, Glasgow (Yard No. 574) for the Shipping Controller as WAR JUPITER.
29.10.1919: Launched for the New Zealand Shipping Co. Ltd., London.
22.1.1920: Registered as OTAKI.
2.1920: Completed.
31.5.1934: Acquired by The Clan Line Steamers Ltd. (Cayzer, Irvine and Co. Ltd., managers), London for £17,500.
8.11.1934: Renamed CLAN ROBERTSON.
8.12.1938: Sold to the Stanhope Steamship Co. Ltd. (J.A. Billmeir and Co. Ltd., managers), London for £72,500.
17.12.1938: Renamed STANFLEET.
5.7.1939: Sold to Zubi Shipping Co. Ltd. (Alejandro Zubizarreta, manager), London.
20.11.1939: Sold to Blue Star Line Ltd., London for £65,000.
5.12.1939: Renamed PACIFIC STAR.
24.4.1940: Requisitioned by the British government.
27.10.1942: Torpedoed by the German submarine U 509 north west of the Canary Islands in position 29.16 north by 20.57 west whilst in convoy SL 125 on a voyage from Rosario and Freetown to Liverpool with general cargo including 5,037 tons of frozen meat.
28.10.1942: Abandoned in position 29.21 north by 19.28 west. The crew of 86 and 11 gunners were all rescued.
7.1.1943: Register closed.

Like the majority of the G class, *Clan Robertson* (2) was laid down for the Shipping Controller but launched for commercial owners, in her case the New Zealand Shipping Co. Ltd. She was photographed on the Mersey (above) on 3rd August 1935 and below after her funnel had been extended (below). *[Above: J. and M. Clarkson, below: Archie Munro collection]*

Pacific Star as the former *Clan Robertson* became in 1939 was torpedoed off the Canaries in October 1942, fell out of her convoy and headed first for Gibraltar and then for Las Palmas when she continued to take in water. Sadly, the crew's efforts were in vain, and she was abandoned again and was last seen afloat on 30th October and is assumed to have sunk soon afterwards. She was one of six ships from convoy SL 125 sunk by *U 509* over two nights. *[Nigel Farrell collection]*

DESIGNED IN PEACE, PROVEN IN WAR: 1934-1946

Twin screws

Towards the end of 1934 Clan Line placed one of its most important orders at Greenock Dockyard. Convinced that fast, well-equipped reefers were the way forward, the design specified 10,000 gross tons, up to half a million cubic feet of refrigerated space with an average speed of 15 knots and 16 in good weather. To achieve this performance twin screws were necessary, but the machinery was the tried-and-tested triple-expansion engine with Bauer-Wach exhaust turbine. The price of £285,000 included testing of the hull form in the tank at Teddington.

The ship, to be named *Clan Macarthur* (3), was laid down in March 1935. In June a sister was ordered for Scottish Shire Line, to become the *Perthshire*. The third hull, *Clan Macaulay* (2), was not actually ordered until the *Clan Macarthur* was completed, but two further ships were then ordered to a modified design. To be named *Clan Cameron* (3) and *Clan Campbell* (3), they were non-refrigerated, open shelter-deck ships, and to suit the Calcutta trade were ten feet shorter in length and three feet less in beam giving a gross tonnage of around 7,200. The steam machinery was similar to the freezer trio with twin screws driven by triple-expansion engines with Bauer-Wach low pressure turbines, but having five rather than six single-ended Scotch boilers arranged to burn coal or oil, which suited the trades for which they were designed if not the engineers and Indian crews of the time. Designed for a loaded service speed of 15.5 knots, they were indeed capable of this when burning oil but not when using coal. The freezer trio and the new class, which was soon expanded to five, were equipped with 80- and 30-ton derricks in addition to the usual outfit of 3-, 5- and 15-ton derricks.

Clan Cameron was completed in January 1937 and was followed at three-monthly intervals by ten more until the *Clan Lamont* (3). At a glance the first eight appeared identical but minor differences appeared as the class progressed, as noted in the captions to the individual photographs. The Greenock Dockyard also completed two larger refrigerated ships each with six hatches, the motor ship *Clan Macdonald* (4) in December 1939 and the turbine-driven *Lanarkshire* in April 1940, which together with the 1936 trio made a total of 16 modern, 15-knot ships all with similar 80- and 30- ton heavy lifting gear which made them unique amongst the British merchant fleet. At the beginning of the 1930s there were hardly any cargo liners in the world capable of making 15 knots or more but, during the decade that followed to April 1940, eight British companies took delivery of 56 such ships of which nearly a third were for Clan Line.

Table 7 summarises Clan's services in mid-1936, just as the twin-screw ships were beginning to arrive. The 11 non-refrigerated ships were designed to operate on any of these services to South or East Africa, to India, Ceylon or Australia but most of all on the premier Durban Express route direct from Birkenhead. They quickly came to dominate this service, and of the 56 outward loadings of these ships up to December 1939, 71 per cent were on the Durban service and another 14 per cent on the Cape Town to Beira range of ports, while four sailings were to Australia via the Cape and only one to India. Of homeward sailings the South African route accounted for a mere eight loadings, sugar from Mauritius made up 40 per cent of the cargoes, those from India 30 per cent while six ships had to make the long and profitless ballast voyages to Australia to find homeward cargoes.

Clan Macaulay (2), the third of the *Clan Macarthur* class. The design incorporated the twin-screw, triple-expansion, raised forecastle and poop arrangement of the war-built G class refrigerator ships, but with a ten percent increase in carrying capacity. *[Ian J. Farquhar collection]*

Table 7: Clan Line services and approximate frequencies in 1936.	
Frequency	**Trade (from/to UK unless indicated)**
Two per month	Natal
Two per month	Calcutta
Two per month	Bombay
Three per month	Cape Town
Monthly	Red Sea and East Africa
Monthly	Malabar Coast and Chittagong
Two-monthly	US to South and East Africa
Seasonal	Australia
Yearly contracts	Mauritius (sugar)
Yearly contracts	Queensland (sugar)
Occasional	Calcutta to River Plate

Not only were the twin-screw ships considered somewhat special, so were their engineers. A new wage scale was introduced in February 1939, with pay to some extent based on the class of ship, which in turn was probably based on insured values. There were six classes, with the two existing motor ships *Clan Macdougall* (2) and *Stirlingshire* (1) regarded as a special case. The ships in each of the six classes are listed in table 8.

Table 8: Ships listed by class, February 1939			
Class 1	*Clan Macbean* (1)	**Class 3**	*Clan Macquarrie* (1)
	Clan Macbrayne (1)	**(cont)**	*Clan Murdoch* (1)
	Clan Macilwraith (1)		*Clan Murray* (3)
	Clan Macindoe (1)		*Clan Stuart* (3)
	Clan Macinnes (2)	**Class 4**	*Banffshire*
	Clan Maciver (2)		*Berwickshire*
Class 2	*Clan Alpine* (3)		*Buteshire*
	Clan Macwhirter		*Clan Macalister* (3)
	Clan Matheson (3)		*Clan Macpherson* (3)
	Clan Monroe (3)		*Clan Mactaggart* (1)
	Clan Morrison		*Clan Mactavish* (2)
	Clan Ogilvy (2)	**Class 5**	*Clan Buchanan* (3)
	Clan Ranald (3)		*Clan Campbell* (4)
	Clan Ross (2)		*Clan Cameron* (3)
	Clan Skene		*Clan Chattan* (2)
	Halizones (2)		*Clan Chisholm* (2)
	Harmonides (2)		*Clan Colquhoun* (2)
Class 3	*Clan Macfadyen* (2)		*Clan Cumming* (2)
	Clan Macfarlane (2)		*Clan Farquhar* (2)
	Clan Macgillivray (1)		*Clan Ferguson* (2)
	Clan Mackinlay (1)		*Clan Forbes* (3)
	Clan Macnab (3)		*Clan Fraser* (3)
	Clan Macnair (1)		*Clan Menzies* (2)
	Clan Macnaughton (2)	**Class 6**	*Clan Macarthur* (3)
	Clan Macneil (3)		*Clan Macaulay* (2)
	Clan Macphee		*Perthshire*

War, disruption and requisition

The first British cargo liner taken up for military service in the Second World War had been requisitioned even before war broke out. The *Clan Ferguson* (2), which had begun loading in Glasgow on the Durban service, was suddenly ordered to discharge, shifted berth and began loading a consignment of military stores and supplies for Turkey. This was a government scheme to pave the way for British military access in the event of Axis attacks through the Balkans. Requisitioned on 28th August 1939, the *Clan Ferguson* left the Clyde on 5th September

as the sole cargo liner in the GC convoy of ten passenger liners carrying reinforcements for the Middle and Far East. In the eastern Mediterranean the *Clan Ferguson* detached from the convoy to discharge at Izmir and Istanbul before completing at Alexandria, where she was released to load homewards on her owner's berth from Bombay and Cochin. A further Turkish consignment was carried on *Clan Menzies* (2), which loaded in Ellesmere Port and sailed on 18th September to discharge first at Malta, then Istanbul, at the Roumanian ports of Galati (80 miles up the Danube) and Constanza, and finally at Burgas in Bulgaria. From this Black Sea port the *Clan Menzies* proceeded to Alexandria and loaded a small cargo for Hull where she was released back to her owners.

Further requisitions quickly followed: *Clan Ross* (2) on the 3rd September, *Clan Macbrayne* (1) and *Clan Morrison* on the 4th, and *Clan Menzies* (2) on the 10th September for her voyage to Turkey. The Clan Line board felt quite unable to maintain schedules, and blamed this on the requisitioning, as well as on delays whilst waiting for convoys and Admiralty routeing of ships. With more cargo available than space to ship it, the government were compounding the problem by requisitioning space to bring in foodstuffs. To add to Clan's difficulties, many Lascar seamen were refusing to sail under war conditions, a problem only partly solved by increasing their pay by 100%. Of the British officers, 20 were officers in the Royal Naval Reserve and were called for war service. Clan Line's response to all these problems was to put a surcharge of between 25% and 50% on most freight rates.

The British government's Liner Requisition Scheme became effective for all ships discharging after 1st February 1940, and this sent cargo liners wherever they were best employed. Thus more and more Clan ships found themselves running on berths for other lines, both conference partners and rivals, including Anchor, Brocklebank, T. and J. Harrison, and Union-Castle Lines. It was usual practice for homeward-bound troop ships to load on whatever berths could offer cargo at Bombay, Mombasa, Durban or Cape Town. This saw Clan and their agents involved with a fascinating variety of ships outside their usual experience, including a number of substantial passenger liners such as Furness Withy's *Monarch of Bermuda* (22,424/1931), Cunard-White Star's *Britannic* (26,943/1930), Booth's *Anselm* (5,954/1935) and Royal Mail's *Highland Brigade* (14,134/1929). Oddities not to be repeated were the two Italian ships which Clan loaded homeward from Calcutta in March 1940, *Gabbiano* (6,584/1923) and *Iris* (5,175/1918), both owned by Achille Lauro.

Further rationalisation introduced by the government meant that all ships for one destination, irrespective of their ownership, would load on the same berth where possible in order to make it simpler for the railways to deliver cargo. For instance, Clan's Vittoria Dock berths in Birkenhead were used by all

CLANS IN GREY

Top: *Clan Macbrayne* (1) of 1916. *[National Maritime Museum P21921]*

Middle: *Clan Murray* (3) on war service. Note the guns on the poop. *[National Maritime Museum P22123]*

Bottom: *Lanarkshire.* *[Archie Munro collection]*

ships loading for South Africa. But despite the war, inter-company rivalry died hard. With London and Southampton more or less closed to shipping in 1940, Union-Castle and members of the Indian conference who traditionally loaded in East Coast ports wanted to use the open ports of Liverpool and Glasgow, but Clan objected and succeeded in restricting the tonnage other lines could load in these ports and demanded prior notice of these loadings. Another spat broke out with Brocklebank and British India which were loading for Trincomalee and Colombo at Leith and Rosyth, ports which Clan Line considered to be reserved to themselves. These rows must have taken some explaining to a government determined to expedite cargo movements, and the Ministry of Shipping (later the Ministry of War Transport) were adamant that peacetime conference arrangements were not to be applied.

Perhaps it was fortunate that Clan's vice-chairman, Herbert Cayzer, now Lord Rotherwick, was deeply involved on behalf of the Chamber of Shipping in negotiations with the Ministry of Shipping. Herbert took over the chairmanship of Clan Line in January 1943 when Sir August Cayzer offered his resignation on health grounds. Sir August had been Clan Line's chairman for 26 years, and his quiet restrained approach contrasts with his father's impatience. He died soon after relinquishing the chair.

Sir August Cayzer (1876-1943) and Sir Herbert Cayzer (1882-1968). *[Newall Dunn collection]*

The heavy derricks on the company's ships were maintained in a high state of readiness with the purchase and topping lifts rigged at all times. This did not escape the attention of the Ministry of Shipping who, in the autumn of 1940, found themselves seeking 15-knot cargo liners not only able to carry military stores and hardware around the Cape to the Middle East, but also able to ship the British Army's 28-ton tanks of that era and land them at destinations where no shoreside facilities existed. Requisition often meant ships had to carry military cargoes into or across active operational theatres such as the Middle East and especially the Mediterranean. The part the big twin-screw Clan Liners played in this theatre is so important that a full account is an essential part of the fleet's history.

Malta convoys

From the inception of Clan Line sailings from Glasgow and Birkenhead to Bombay in 1878, calls were made at Malta, probably for coaling, at least until the turn of the century and then occasionally homeward from India as late as the 1920s. In June 1940 the entry of Italy into the war invested Malta by closure of the Mediterranean for through traffic. This brought

the fast Clans into the front line and they returned to the island in profusion bringing vital stores and supplies to help in its maintenance and defence. The saga of the Malta convoys has been well recorded, but in reviewing the operations today it is extraordinary to find that Clan provided one quarter of the 99 merchant ships involved up to the end of the Pedestal convoy in August 1942. No other company provided even half that number. Indeed, more than a quarter of the most hazardous trips were made by *Clan Ferguson* (2) before she was sunk in Operation Pedestal.

Undoubtedly the speed and cargo handling gear of the fast twin-screw Clans made them eminently suitable for inclusion in the WS convoys which sailed around the Cape to the Middle East from the summer of 1940. Once in the Mediterranean theatre and discharged, usually at Alexandria where the Malta Shipping Committee was set up to co-ordinate civil and military supplies for the island, their further requisition to load for Malta followed as a matter of course and they frequently made repeat trips. Thus in the six months up until March 1941 eight convoys sailed for Malta (and others for Piraeus) involving 30 cargo liners of which 14 were Clan Line owned or managed. *Clan Ferguson* (2) and *Clan Macaulay* (2) each made three round trips, *Lanarkshire* two and *Perthshire* one while the *Clan Forbes* (3) and *Clan Fraser* (3) made a special trip in November from the Clyde direct to Malta as Operation Collar, the former disguised as the depot ship *Maidstone* with a dummy second funnel. Building on the success of this trip, Operation Excess in January 1941 comprised *Clan Cumming* (2), *Clan Macdonald* (4) and *Empire Song* which sailed direct from the Clyde also through the Mediterranean to land supplies for Greek forces at Piraeus. Another through convoy of five ships codenamed Tiger included *Clan Campbell* (4), *Clan Chattan* (2), *Clan Lamont* (3) and *Empire Song* and ran from the Clyde to Alexandria in May 1941 carrying tanks, guns and vehicles for the British Army in the desert.

Few of these operations were free of incident and from the very first Malta convoy at the end of June 1940 Italian naval and air units contested every passage while bombing was frequent in both Malta and Alexandria. The *Clan Macarthur* (3) reported in October 1940 that of 17 nights spent in Alexandria, only three were free from bombing raids, but in Valetta harbour at Malta there was little interference with the discharge of ships until the Luftwaffe arrived on Sicily in January 1941. The Italians bombed Malta 40 times in June, once in October and then attacks dwindled almost to nothing, but the Luftwaffe attacks throughout 1941 and much of 1942 were severe and exceeded in intensity even the London blitz. *Clan Macaulay* (2) was near-missed by two bombs while discharging in Malta in January 1941, and in April that year the *Perthshire* received a direct hit in the forehold while in Malta but was able to continue in service.

The winter months of 1940/1941 were also a period of severe congestion in the Middle East ports where ships were often discharged illogically by the military in seeking to reach whatever items then seemed the most urgent. Ships were also held up unnecessarily, some of the freezer ships being used as cold stores instead of maintaining the vital food and import programme to the United Kingdom. The worst case was that of the *Perthshire* being held in the Middle East for over six months during which time she made only a single trip to Malta. The *Clan Macaulay* (2) spent a similar time in the area and

Lanarkshire almost five months. When brought to the attention of the Prime Minister on 23rd March, these ships were quickly released and despatched to Australia to load refrigerated produce homewards.

In the spring of 1941 the Clans suffered severe losses. When leaving Piraeus after discharge in January 1941, *Clan Cumming* (2) was torpedoed by an Italian submarine but did not sink and put back for repair which lasted three months and ultimately sealed her fate. On 6th April the Germans bombed Piraeus where *Clan Fraser* (3) was discharging military supplies brought around the Cape from Glasgow. The ship was struck by two bombs which set her alight and she burned fiercely for four hours then blew up. *Clan Cumming* finally cleared the port on 14th April only to be mined and sunk in the approaches. Two weeks later *Clan Buchanan* (3) was sunk by the German raider *Pinguin* in the Indian Ocean en route to Chittagong. All the officers and crew were accommodated aboard the raider for ten days until that ship was sunk by the cruiser HMS *Cornwall*. When *Pinguin* was hit, the mines she was carrying exploded with heavy casualties. Only eight Europeans and five of the Indian crew out of the 121 who had been aboard the *Clan Buchanan* were picked up.

On the same day as the *Pinguin* was sunk, 9th May 1941, *Empire Song* in the Tiger convoy for Alexandria struck a mine when passing through the Sicilian Narrows. Fires broke out, the ship fell

Two ships involved in Malta convoys: *Clan Macdonald* (4) (upper) and *Clan Lamont* (3) (lower). Both carry Carley floats. The *Clan Lamont* has the extra accommodation added when she became a troop carrier, and on the reverse of this photograph one of her passengers has written 'Sailed from Greenock to the Mediterranean on this ship by way of the Azores – lucky to get there. July 1944'.
[Upper: Archie Monroe collection; lower: J. and M. Clarkson collection]

behind shaken by internal explosions and had to be abandoned and was later almost re-boarded before she blew up and sank. Miraculously only 19 personnel were lost out of 146 crew and service personnel aboard.

With the arrival of the Tiger convoy at Alexandria the involvement of Clan ships in Mediterranean convoys was much reduced. *Clan Macdonald* (4) and *Clan Ferguson* (2) formed part of the nine-ship Halberd convoy from the Clyde direct to Malta in September 1941. After discharge the 17.5-knot *Clan Macdonald* was sailed independently and unescorted to Gibraltar and successfully completed this passage, despite attacks by three torpedo-carrying aircraft which missed thanks to rapid and evasive alterations of course by the ship. One week later the *Clan Ferguson* set off at 16 knots on a similar attempt to reach Gibraltar but was attacked by two torpedo bombers seven hours after leaving Malta and was ordered back, only to languish there for three months until opportunity allowed a convoy to be sailed for Alexandria. The *Clan Ferguson* made one further round trip to Malta in January 1942 and then returned home via the Cape and New York to the Clyde.

Captain Arthur Young, a former harbour master of the Clyde Port Authority, served two years as indentured

apprentice on the *Clan Ferguson*, making all of her Malta trips except Pedestal, and vividly recalls much of that perilous time. He first joined the ship aged 16 in June 1940 and made two short trips evacuating personnel from western France, the first with members of the British Expeditionary Force from St. Nazaire and another with Czech and Polish refugees from Le Verdon. Thereafter the *Clan Ferguson* carried a reinforcement cargo around the Cape to Alexandria in company with *Reina del Pacifico* (17,702/1931). From this port the *Clan Ferguson* made three round trips to Malta up to April 1941 before returning home from Indian ports and the Cape, her voyage lasting 13 months.

The *Clan Ferguson* then sailed from Glasgow to Malta in the Halberd convoy of September 1941, experiencing several air attacks en route with guns manned round the clock. This visit to the island lasted in total 89 days with air raids from the Luftwaffe almost daily, sometimes three each day and on one occasion eleven. The coal bunkers were discharged to supplement a shortage on shore. When trying to reach Gibraltar unescorted and disguised under the French flag, the ship was attacked by torpedo bombers and ordered back: she finally sailed for Alexandria on Boxing Day 1941. During that passage the *Clan Ferguson* was dive-bombed but near

The ship centre left has been identified as *Clan Macaulay* (2): the derrick to the mast immediately abaft the superstructure distinguishes her from her sisters. The location is an eastern Mediterranean port, most likely Port Said, during the period September 1940 to March 1941. Note the extensive damage to the bows of the ship to the right. *[Newall Dunn collection]*

missed by a Junkers Ju-87 causing a few holes and damage to the lifeboats. This was followed by attacks from six torpedo bombers which all missed.

When in Alexandria the absence of air raids brought great relief to the crew. However, loading began immediately for a return trip and went on day and night. With grain, flour, sugar, beans, aviation spirit, bombs, shells and 150 troops the *Clan Ferguson* again sailed for Malta. Several air attacks developed during the passage but all ships arrived safely in the midst of an air raid to a great welcome. Discharge was partly carried out by service personnel, especially during air raids which were very heavy at this time with as many as ten or fifteen in a single day and some lasting as long as five hours. On one occasion a stick of bombs burst 20 feet from the bows causing several holes in the hull while a further stick of bombs riddled the port side of the ship.

The *Clan Ferguson* left Malta in the midst of an air raid on Friday 13th February, the same date as three loaded ships left Alexandria for the island, and had a particularly hair-raising passage to Port Said, with several torpedo and dive-bomber attacks which continued by day and at night with the use of flares. This convoy also passed the westbound one in which the *Clan Chattan* (2) was seen to be ablaze before being torpedoed by the destroyer HMS *Decoy* after which she blew up and sank. From Suez the *Clan Ferguson* carried troops and military vehicles to Bombay before returning home with a full cargo from New York to Glasgow. After a spell of leave Arthur Young was transferred to another ship. In remembrance of these times, he returned to Malta in 1992 to watch the Queen dedicate the Siege Bell Memorial to the 7,000 who lost their lives in the island's heroic defence.

Amongst the three ships from Alexandria in February 1942 were *Clan Campbell* (4) and *Clan Chattan* (2), neither of which reached the island. Both Clans had arrived in the Middle East by way of the Cape, following which *Clan Campbell*, with assistance from Ellerman's *City of Sydney* (6,986/1930), towed the burnt-out troopship *Georgic* (27,759/

1932) from Suez to Port Sudan before returning to Suez and loading for Malta. The convoy was heavily bombed, the *Clan Campbell* with her speed reduced had to be sent into Tobruk and then returned to Alexandria. The *Clan Chattan* received a direct hit and the cased petrol she was carrying burned so furiously that she had to be abandoned. The third ship in the convoy was also sunk.

The repaired *Clan Campbell* was able to join the next convoy of four ships which left Alexandria on 20th March but fared little better. The convoy became involved with the Italian fleet in the Second Battle of Sirte but escaped harm until approaching Malta when it was heavily attacked from the air. *Breconshire* (8,982/1939) made it to within eight miles of the harbour but *Clan Campbell*, with just 20 miles to go and lagging behind the convoy due to damage previously received, was hit by a bomb and quickly sank with the loss of Captain J.F. Vooght and nine others. The remaining two ships reached harbour but were bombed and sunk at their berths while discharging.

The final Clan sailing to Malta was the *Clan Ferguson* (2) in the Pedestal convoy of August 1942. Few of the officers and crew had taken part in the previous trips to the island and the Admiralty had instructed the owners to exchange the Indian ratings for their British counterparts who were engaged from the Glasgow Pool. From this point onwards the *Clan Ferguson* seems to have run out of the luck that had carried her through half of the war. She was one of nine cargo liners sunk in the 14-ship Pedestal convoy, torpedoed by a Heinkel He-111 near the Skerki Channel off Cape Bon in the evening of the 12th. The hit ignited the 2,000 tons of aviation spirit on board, which in turn set off 1,500 tons of ammunition. Blazing furiously, the ship came to a stop and soon had to be abandoned. Captain Arthur Cossar and 62 of her complement survived overnight on rafts until picked up next morning. Some were rescued by German seaplanes which took them to Sicily, others fell into the hands of the Vichy French and also became prisoners-of-war in Algeria until released following the Torch landings three months later.

Wartime deliveries of twin-screw ships

Clan Line minutes report that in May 1939 four twin-screw ships had been ordered from Greenock Dockyard, including one for Houston Line. It seems that after the outbreak of war the government took over the orders, or possibly cancelled them and issued fresh instructions. The next of the twin-screw ships to emerge from Greenock was the Ministry-owned *Empire Song* launched on 18th June 1940. She completed fitting out under Clan Line management in late October, when she was requisitioned to load a military cargo for Piraeus. The next hull from Greenock Dockyard, number 444, was reportedly to be *Clan Brodie*, but work was suspended on the outbreak of war and she was later taken over by the Admiralty to emerge as the aircraft transport HMS *Athene*. Further government intervention saw one order diverted to Denny of Dumbarton to expedite delivery as the Greenock yard was then heavily committed to five of the X and Y type standard tramps. There is some evidence that the Denny hull was to be named *Clan Buchanan*, but Admiralty requisition and dithering saw her become first the armed boarding vessel *Empire Might* (a name later reallocated to a Greenock Dockyard hull), then a seaplane carrier, and finally emerge as the aircraft transport HMS *Engadine*. These two ships were used simply to carry aircraft for most of the war and, given the immense value of these fast merchant ships to the war effort as the Malta convoys proved, the Admiralty's need for the hulls must be questioned, especially as they seemed to struggle to find a role for them. During her 64 months of Admiralty service, HMS *Engadine* spent six months fitting out, 11 under repair or refit, 15 in reserve, and seven months reconverting. Thus a mere 25 months was spent on passage to or under orders in the war zone in the Far East or Pacific. HMS *Athene* fared little better, spending 12 months fitting out, seven under repair, 18 in reserve, and eight whilst reconditioning, giving 31 months on passage or under orders. In comparison, *Clan Cameron* (3) completed 12 voyages and carried 26 cargoes over the same time period.

The fourth vessel of the May 1939 order may well have been cancelled, as the next two hulls were to Ministry orders for 488-foot hulls fitted out as refrigerated ships and with the heavy derrick at number 4 hatch reduced to one of 20 tons capacity. The first was delivered to Blue Star management as *Empire Might* in August 1942 and her sister as *Empire Wisdom* to Clan management three months later. Both ships continued as such until they exchanged managements, the former becoming *Clan Macrae* (3) and the latter *Royal Star*.

Further replacements were ordered from Greenock Dockyard in September 1941 when Clan Line was issued licences to build two more of the *Clan Forbes* design to a wartime specification with a shortened funnel and three boats on each side of the boat deck. The first ship was taken over by the Admiralty whilst on the stocks and launched as HMS *Bonaventure* in October 1942. Fitting out was by the adjacent Scotts' yard and when commissioned in January 1943 this ship served thereafter as a depot ship for midget submarines. The second ship was launched as *Clan Campbell* (4) and completed in May 1943. Two further ships of the class, each with slightly different bridge structures, were completed as *Clan Chattan* (3)

The aircraft transport HMS *Engadine*. [Imperial War Museum FL 22647/Newall Dunn collection]

Top: The recently-completed HMS *Bonaventure* at anchor in the Clyde. *[Glasgow University Archives GD323/7/9/2/452/1]*

Middle: HMS *Bonaventure* arriving at Portsmouth from the Far East in April 1947. *[Newall Dunn collection]*

Left: On the quarter deck of HMS *Bonaventure* are Captain W.R. Fell OBE, DSC, RN and Lieutenant Commander J.R.F. Brown DSC, RN. Captain Fell was the instigator of the human torpedo in 1942, and from 1943 to 1944 was responsible for the development of the midget submarines or 'X craft' and training their personnel. On 21st February 1945 he sailed on HMS *Bonaventure* to the Far East, and remained there as Captain Submarine Flotilla 14 until this flotilla was disbanded in Sydney at the end of hostilities.

Captain Fell's post-war career was equally distinguished, involving clearing the war damage from Malta harbour. On his retirement he was immediately re-employed by the Admiralty as a Grade 1 Salvage Officer. His other achievements included cutting up a sunken minelayer with 500 live mines still aboard, but perhaps his greatest was the epic clearance of Port Said in 1956. *[Imperial War Museum A26928]*

and *Clan Chisholm* (3) in June and October of 1944. The completion of the final unit of the series was delayed by priority being given to four heavy-lift ships. The last of these was launched in December 1945 as *Empire Canute* (and then was simply left at a lay-by berth under management by Cayzer, Irvine), and so the last twin-screw ship for Clan was not launched until May 1946 as *Clan Cumming* (3). She was delivered in August 1946 with a streamlined bridge structure and a slightly outward sloping stern. Two further refrigerated ships to the *Clan Macdonald* (4) design had been built under wartime licence, the first completing as the triple-expansion *Clan Urquhart* (3) (but with Babcock and Wilcox watertube boilers) in December 1943 and the second as the motor ship *Clan Macdougall* (3) in May 1944, both 'utility' sisters of *Lanarkshire* and *Clan Macdonald* (4), respectively.

Gains and losses

As the land war intensified from mid-1940, and one country after another was overrun by Germany, Clan was given the management of foreign tonnage now under the control of the Ministry of War Transport, mostly French but also Dutch and Danish. There were problems with some of their crews, leading to Clan relinquishing management in the case of the *Robert Mærsk*.

In 1943 Clan was requested to supply crews for a number of Liberty ships which were being supplied by the USA on bareboat charter to the Ministry of War Transport. Also in 1943 a decision was taken to apply to the government for three tramp-type steamers to replace losses. A trio of wartime standard ships was transferred to the company's management with an agreed price at which Clan Line would buy them following the end of hostilities. Their experience with heavy loads also saw the company manage two large and two small vessels with heavy-lift capacity. Management eventually extended to well over 30 ships, in marked contrast with the First World War when none were managed.

However, the major theme of the war was to be losses of ships and even more grievously of their crews as aircraft and mines added to the dangers from submarines familiar from the First World War. All 37 complete losses during the war are listed in table 9, with more detail given in the fleet lists. One loss was by fire in a military cargo, three by collision

Above: *Clan Chisholm* (2) seen at Stobcross Quay, Glasgow was Clan's first loss during the Second World War. *[Archie Munro collection]*

Right: *Clan Mactavish* (2) in Australian waters. The death toll of 89 when she was torpedoed in the South Atlantic in October 1942 was surpassed only by the 109 lost on *Clan Buchanan* (3). *[Ian J. Farquhar collection]*

(two in convoys), four ships were mined, seven sunk by aircraft, one by an auxiliary cruiser, and the rest torpedoed - one by an Italian submarine, two by Japanese, and the remaining 18 by German boats. Of the total of 674 deaths, the largest and most tragic loss was sustained when the complement of *Clan Buchanan* (3) – having been picked up by the raider *Pinguin* – were killed when the auxiliary cruiser was sunk by HMS *Cornwall*. However, the sinkings by torpedo of *Clan Mactacvish* (2) and of *Clan Macfadyen* (3) ran this close in terms of casualties. The most dangerous place to be on a Clan Liner in the Second World War was the North Atlantic, which accounted for 16 of 37 losses. Losses were spread wider geographically than in the First World War, with seven each in the Mediterranean and the Indian Ocean.

Table 9 (right) shows that casualties declined dramatically during the final two years of the war, and indeed the last three losses were in the Indian Ocean, remote from the convoys and air cover that had turned the tide of losses in the North Atlantic and Mediterranean. The last loss was that of *Berwickshire* in August 1944, yet it should not be supposed that the final years of the war were less valiant ones for Clan. For instance, *Clan Chattan* (3) served with the British Pacific Fleet for the last four months of the war, and right until the end of the European war the Clan-manned Liberty *Adolph S. Ochs* was sailing in North Russian convoys.

Although based on reputable sources, the figures for lives lost in table 9 are probably incomplete for reasons discussed below table 5. The numbers include not just crew members, but also gunners and other naval personnel, passengers, survivors from other ships and prisoners-of-war.

Completing the twin-screw class

At the end of the war one of the twin-screw ships was still building, the *Clan Cumming* (3), and remaining in service were just three of the pre-war units and three delivered during wartime. However, other hulls were available and Clan gradually bought these back. HMS *Engadine* and *Athene* were purchased and converted by the Greenock Dockyard emerging as *Clan Buchanan* (4) and *Clan Brodie* in October 1946 and February 1947. *Clan Macrae* (3) ex-*Empire Might* became operational for the company in July 1946 while the *Clan Lamont* (3), which served from February 1944 as an infantry landing ship and as a troop transport until September 1947, completed reconversion in February 1948. Finally *Bonaventure* returned from the Far East in April 1947, began conversion eight months later, and emerged as the 12-passenger *Clan Davidson* for the Calcutta service in October 1948. Thus the class of 11 were re-established three years after the end of hostilities.

A chronological list of all the twin-screw ships appears in table 10. A total of 28 were built, and although all were either owned or managed by the company at some time in their eventful careers, the maximum in service at any one time was 14 on the outbreak of war. Although Clan was still to have some fine ships in its fleet, it was never again to build such a large and iconic class.

Table 9: Vessels totally lost during the Second World War through all causes.

Name	Date	Cause	Lost
Clan Chisholm (2)	17.10.1939	Torpedoed by *U 48* in N. Atlantic	4
Clan Morrison	24.2.1940	Mined in North Sea	0
Clan Stuart (3)	11.3.1940	Convoy collision with *Orlock Head* in English Channel	0
Clan Macalister (3)	29.5.1940	Bombed off Dunkirk	18
Clan Macfarlane (2)	17.7.1940	Collision with *Ganges* in Indian Ocean	41
Clan Monroe (3)	29.7.1940	Mined in North Sea	13
Clan Menzies (2)	29.7.1940	Torpedoed by *U 99* in N. Atlantic	6
Clan Macphee	16.8.1940	Torpedoed by *U 30* in N. Atlantic	67
Clan Mackinlay (1)	6.11.1940	Bombed off Scotland	5
Stirlingshire	2.12.1940	Torpedoed by *U 94* in N. Atlantic	0
Harmodius	8.3.1941	Torpedoed by *U 124* in N. Atlantic	11
Clan Macnab (3)	17.3.1941	Convoy collision with *Strix* in N. Atlantic	0
Clan Ogilvy (2)	21.3.1941	Torpedoed by *U 105* in N. Atlantic	61
Clan Fraser (3)	6.4.1941	Bombed in Mediterranean	12
Clan Cumming (2)	14.4.1941	Mined in Mediterranean	0
Clan Buchanan (3)	28.4.1941	Sunk by *Pinguin* in Indian Ocean	106
Empire Song	9.5.1941	Mined in Mediterranean	17
Clan Macdougall (2)	31.5.1941	Torpedoed by *U 106* in the N. Atlantic	2
Clan Chattan (2)	14.2.1942	Bombed in Mediterranean	0
Clan Campbell (4)	23.3.1942	Bombed in Mediterranean	10
Clan Ross (2)	2.4.1942	Torpedoed by *I-6* in Indian Ocean	11
Clan Skene	10.5.1942	Torpedoed by *U 333* in N. Atlantic	9
Clan Macquarrie (1)	13.6.1942	Torpedoed by *Leonardo da Vinci* off West Africa	1
Clan Macnaughton (2)	1.8.1942	Torpedoed by *U 155* N. Atlantic	6
Clan Ferguson (2)	12.8.1942	Torpedoed by a Heinkel 111 aircraft in Mediterranean	18
Harmonides	25.8.1942	Torpedoed by *I-165* in Indian Ocean	14
Clan Macwhirter	26.8.1942	Torpedoed by *U 156* in N. Atlantic	9
Clan Mactavish (2)	8.10.1942	Torpedoed by *U 159* in S. Atlantic	89
Clan Mactaggart (1)	16.11.1942	Torpedoed by *U 92* in N. Atlantic	3
Clan Macfadyen (2)	27.11.1942	Torpedoed by *U 508* in N. Atlantic	82
Clan Alpine (3)	13.3.1943	Torpedoed by *U 107* in N. Atlantic	26
Clan Macindoe (1)	26.4.1943	Fire and explosion in Mediterranean	0
Clan Macpherson (3)	1.5.1943	Torpedoed by *U 515* in the N. Atlantic	4
Halizones	27.7.1943	Bombed off Spanish coast	0
Clan Macarthur (3)	11.8.1943	Torpedoed by *U 181* in Indian Ocean	20
Banffshire	29.9.1943	Torpedoed by *U 532* in Indian Ocean	1
Berwickshire	20.8.1944	Torpedoed by *U 861* in Indian Ocean	8

Preparing for peace

A successor class to the twin-screw ships had been ordered as early as 1944, but government work at Greenock Dockyard meant the first of the new class would not be ready until late in 1946. Shipyard

163

Table 10: Ships completed to the Clan Line twin-screw design, 1936 to 1948

All reciprocating-engined steamers except where shown, and all built by Greenock Dockyard Co. Ltd. except *Engadine/Clan Buchanan* built by Denny.

Built as	Yard no.	Delivered	Feet	Notes
Clan Macarthur (3)	423	1.1936	499	Reefer
Perthshire	424	6.1936	499	Reefer
Clan Macaulay (2)	425	11.1936	499	Reefer
Clan Cameron (3)	426	2.1937	485	
Clan Campbell (4)	427	4.1937	485	
Clan Chattan (2)	428	7.1937	488	
Clan Chisholm (2)	429	10.1937	488	
Clan Cumming (2)	430	1.1938	488	
Clan Buchanan (3)	431	2.1938	488	
Clan Ferguson (2)	432	5.1938	488	
Clan Menzies (2)	433	9.1938	488	
Clan Forbes (3)	434	12.1938	488	
Clan Fraser (3)	435	2.1939	488	
Clan Lamont (3)	438	5.1939	488	
Clan Macdonald (4)	436	12.1939	505	Six holds, motor reefer
Lanarkshire	437	4.194	505	Six holds, turbine reefer
Empire Song	443	8.194	488	
Athene (HMS)	444	10.1941	488	1946: *Clan Brodie*
Engadine (HMS)	Denny 1356	11.1941	488	1946: *Clan Buchanan* (4)
Empire Might	450	8.1942	488	Reefer. 1946: *Clan Macrae* (3)
Empire Wisdom	451	11.1942	488	Reefer. 1946: *Royal Star*
Bonaventure (HMS)	452	1.1943	488	1948: *Clan Davidson* (2)
Clan Campbell (5)	453	5.1943	488	
Clan Urquhart (3)	454	1.1944	500	Six holds, reefer
Clan Macdougall (3)	455	5.1944	505	Six holds, motor reefer
Clan Chattan (3)	456	6.1944	488	
Clan Chisholm (3)	457	10.1944	488	
Clan Cumming (3)	459	8.1946	487	

capacity was restricted and building prices too high for Clan to replace all its war losses with new buildings, and the shortfall was filled by wholesale acquisitions of war-built standard ships, a process which had started in 1943. In March 1946 it was decided to buy eight further UK-built freighters, and to take on bareboat charter for five years three others plus seven of the very similar Ocean type which had been built for British account in United States yards. The British government did not permit Clan to rename these ships, and they ran with Empire or Ocean names until the end of 1947 when Clan exercised its option to purchase them. Towards the end of 1946 Liberty ships became available for purchase, and Clan bid for three of those it was managing, although it was only successful in acquiring two. Two further Oceans were bought in the early 1950s. Therefore alongside the survivors of the fast, twin-screw steamers and their post-war successors, Clan was to operate 25 basic steam tramps, barely capable of 11 knots. This situation was not unprecedented, as Clan had long had such a mixed fleet to suit the varied requirements of its many services. It is interesting to speculate just what a fine fleet Clan would have had if the war had not intervened and it had continued to take the twin-screw ships from Greenock Dockyard. It was not until the 1960s that Clan could boast of a relatively homogenous fleet all built to its specification, but – as the next chapter will tell – this was to be a relatively brief period of stability.

Empire Lankester at Cape Town in September 1945 still with her armaments. She was chartered by Clan in 1946, bought in 1947 and renamed *Clan Mackellar* (2). *[J. and M. Clarkson collection]*

The Liberty *Sambrian* was purchased and renamed *Clan Macfarlane* (3) (right) in 1947. She ran for the company until 1961 when she was sold to London Greeks. *[Malcolm Cranfield collection]* *Ocean Verity* (middle) was chartered from September 1946 until the end of December 1947 when she was acquired and renamed *Clan Keith* (2). Only five of her crew survived when she was lost in 1961. *[Archie Munro collection]* Never owned but chartered to carry locomotives to Beira for Rhodesian Railways was the *Empire Byng* (below). Completed by the Greenock Dockyard in 1945, she was sold in 1951 to London buyers and renamed *Peter Dahl II*. In 1954 she was bought by the Ben Line of Edinburgh becoming the *Benwyvis*. Staying with them for only eight years she passed to Panamanian buyers in 1963. The beginning of her end came in 1970 when she grounded in Manila Bay in a typhoon. *[Glasgow University Archives GD323/7/9/2/457/3C]*

CLANS AT WAR

Lanarkshire fully loaded arriving on the Clyde from Australian ports via Panama on 16th May 1941. Note that the hull and funnel are both black, while her upper works are probably yellow ochre.

    The photographs on this page were taken, quite illegally, by a Mr Paterson from his home in Dunoon. He set his camera up on a tripod, pretended to read his newspaper, and used a cable release to fire the shutter when the ship's bow passed a tree on the opposite bank of the Clyde. *[Paterson/Archie Munro collection]*

Clan Macdonald (4), part loaded, in two tones of grey, and carrying landing craft (LCAs) during the three-month period when she was engaged in combined operations training based at Inverary. The photograph was taken either on 17th July 1941 when she arrived on the Clyde from Inverary or on 17th August 1941 when arriving from exercises at Scapa Flow. *[Paterson/Archie Munro collection]*

Clan Macarthur (3), all grey and fully loaded, arriving on the Clyde on 16th May 1943 from New Zealand via Panama and New York. She left Glasgow four weeks later on a voyage during which she was torpedoed and sunk near Mauritius. *[Paterson/Archie Munro collection]*

Clan Macaulay (2) sails from Glasgow and the Clyde direct to Bombay via Suez. Note that the life rafts remain although the gun tubs have been removed and her funnel repainted in Clan colours. She had arrived in Glasgow direct from the Cape for full discharge, three weeks after the end of the war with Japan. *[Paterson/Archie Munro collection]*

TWIN-SCREW FREEZER TRIO

The twin-screw steamers completed at Greenock in 1936 determined the look of Clan Line ships for well over two decades, although war losses and sales of hulls to the Admiralty reduced much of the impact of this standardisation. First of the group, the third Clan MacArthur, was Clan's biggest ship yet in terms of tonnage (Clan Urquhart (2) was longer) and the first twin-screw ship built for the company (again, several recent second hand additions had twin screws). Like all Clan advances, however, the influence of their immediate predecessors could be seen, in this case the Clan Macdonald class. A feature of these steamers was the ability to burn either coal or oil, which gave them considerable flexibility when bunkering in ports around the world. Note that all lengths quoted from this point are overall, unless shown (b.p. = between perpendiculars).

Above: *Clan Macarthur* (3) returning from her trials. *[Glasgow University Archives GD 319/18/2/2/7]*
Below: Berthed at Liverpool. *[B. and A. Feilden/J. and M. Clarkson]*

CLAN MACARTHUR (3) 1936-1943
O.N. 164066 10,528g 6,105n
498.5 x 66.2 x 31.8 feet.
Two T.3-cyl. by the North Eastern Marine Engineering Co. Ltd., Wallsend-on-Tyne, each with a low-pressure exhaust steam turbine, double-reduction geared to twin screws; 1,552 NHP, 15.75 knots.
14.10.1935: Launched by the Greenock

Dockyard Co. Ltd., Greenock (Yard No. 423).
15.1.1936: Registered in the ownership of The Clan Line Steamers Ltd. (Cayzer, Irvine and Co. Ltd., managers), London as CLAN MACARTHUR.
17.1.1936: Ran trials and delivered at a cost of £280,000.
4.2.1940: Requisitioned by the British government.

11.8.1943: Torpedoed and sunk by the German submarine U 181 350 miles east from Farafangana, Madagascar in position 23.00 south by 53.10 east whilst on an independent voyage from Glasgow via Table Bay and Durban to Mauritius with general cargo, mail and military stores. Of the 127 people onboard, 50 crew were lost; 1 of the 18 gunners; and 1 of 6 passengers.
4.9.1943: Register closed.

PERTHSHIRE (2) 1936-1964

O.N. 164087 10,496g 6,121n
498.5 x 66.2 x 40.2 feet.
Two T.3-cyl. by the North Eastern
Marine Engineering Co. Ltd.,
Wallsend-on-Tyne, each with a low-
pressure exhaust steam turbine,
double-reduction geared to twin
screws; 1,685 NHP, 17 knots.
26.3.1936: Launched by the Greenock
Dockyard Co. Ltd., Greenock (Yard
No. 424).
24.6.1936: Ran trials and delivered at
a cost of £265,000.
5.7.1936: Registered in the ownership
of the Scottish Shire Line Ltd.
(Turnbull, Martin and Co. Ltd.,
managers), London as PERTHSHIRE.
13.1.1960: The tug APPLEGARTH
(231/1951) which was assisting her to
enter Birkenhead Docks was sunk
with the loss of seven lives.
22.11.1960: Transferred to Houston
Line Ltd. (Cayzer, Irvine and Co.
Ltd., managers), London.
30.11.1962: Transferred to Huntley,
Cook and Co. Ltd., London.
11.7.1963: Serious fire in the engine
room whilst at Southampton. Bunker
oil was contaminated by water, which
put out a burner, resulting in a leak of
hot oil, which caught fire. It was
initially decided to sell her for scrap,
but a shortage of fruit ships meant she
was put back into service for two
voyages to South Africa.
29.7.1964: Sold to Margalante
Compania Naviera S.A., Panama
(Mavroleon Brothers Ltd., London)
for £102,500 and renamed BORIAS
under the Greek flag.
9.12.1965: Arrived at Shikama, Japan
to be broken up.
1.4.1965: Demolition began at Hirao
by Matsukara Kaiji K.K.

Top: Launch of the *Perthshire* on
26th March 1936. *[Archie Munro
collection]*
Upper middle: *Perthshire* in pre-war
condition off Gourock on Christmas
Day 1936. *[Archie Munro collection]*
Lower middle: *Perthshire* in wartime
grey. *[National Maritime Museum
P.23762]*
Bottom: *Perthshire* in Shire Line
colours berthing at the Bluff,
Durban. *[Archie Munro collection]*

CLAN MACAULAY (2) 1936-1963

O.N. 164100 10,492g 6,046n
498.6 x 66.2 x 40.2 feet.
Two T.3-cyl. by the North Eastern
Marine Engineering Co. Ltd., Wallsend-
on-Tyne, each with a low-pressure
exhaust steam turbine, double-reduction
geared to twin screws; 1,586 NHP, 17
knots.
7.8.1936: Launched by the Greenock
Dockyard Co. Ltd., Greenock (Yard No.
425).
2.11.1936: Registered in the ownership of
The Clan Line Steamers Ltd. (Cayzer,
Irvine and Co. Ltd., managers), London
as CLAN MACAULAY. She cost
£265,000
11.4.1940: Requisitioned by the British
government until 22.3.1946.
19.1.1941: Damaged by bombs at Malta.
3.10.1960: Transferred to Houston Line
Ltd. (Cayzer, Irvine and Co. Ltd.,
managers), London.
30.11.1962: Transferred to Huntley, Cook
and Co. Ltd., London.
18.11.1963: Arrived at Dalmuir.
6.12.1963: Handed over to W.H. Arnott,
Young and Co. Ltd. for £77,000.
20.12.1963: Breaking up began.

Top: On 7th August 1936 the newly-
launched *Clan Macaulay* (2) is assisted
into dock by Steel and Bennie's tugs
Strongbow (197/1927), *Campaigner*
(163/1911) and *Warrior* (249/1935) for
fitting out. *[Glasgow University
Archives GD323/7/9/2/425/1]*
Middle: A classic view of *Clan
Macaulay* in the Mersey being assisted
by Cock tugs of the Liverpool Screw
Towing Co. Ltd. *[B. and A. Feilden/J.
and M. Clarkson collection]*
Bottom: *Clan Macaulay* at Cape Town
in February 1958. *[J. and M. Clarkson
collection]*

TWIN-SCREW GENERAL CARGO STEAMERS

The ships of the non-refrigerated Clan Cameron *class were slightly smaller than their predecessors. A total of 19 hulls were eventually built to these dimensions.*

CLAN CAMERON (3) 1936-1959

O.N. 164108 7,243g 3,659n
484.6 x 63.0 x 29.9 feet.
Two T.3-cyl. by John G. Kincaid and Co. Ltd., Greenock, each with a Bauer-Wach low-pressure exhaust steam turbine, double-reduction geared to twin screws; 1,362 NHP, 17 knots.

15.10.1936: Launched by the Greenock Dockyard Co. Ltd., Greenock (Yard No. 426).

26.1.1937: Registered in the ownership of The Clan Line Steamers Ltd. (Cayzer, Irvine and Co. Ltd., managers), London as CLAN CAMERON.

30.1.1937: Delivered.

12.4.1939: In collision with the motor coaster SAPPHIRE (933/1935) in fog seven miles off the South Bishop Lighthouse whilst on a voyage from Mauritius to Liverpool with a cargo of sugar. The SAPPHIRE sank with the loss of two lives and was later found 60% to blame.

31.7.1940: Requisitioned by the British government until 12.3.1946.

5.2.1959: Sold to Dah Chong Hong for £90,500.

4.3.1959: Arrived at Hong Kong for demolition.

Following her launch on 15th October 1936 (top) *Clan Cameron* (3) was towed through the Garvel Basin towards the James Watt Dock by Clyde Shipping's tugs, led by *Flying Eagle* (260/1928) (above). *[Glasgow University Archives GD323/7/9/2/426/2 and 1]*

It is an indication of the action seen by these fine ships that *Clan Cameron* (3) was the only one of this group of eight to come through the war. These pre- and post-war views emphasise the difference in appearance made by the deep white strake on her hull. Note that there are no vents to the king posts ahead of the funnel. *[Above: B. and A. Feilden/J. and M. Clarkson collection, right: J. and M. Clarkson collection]*

CLAN CAMPBELL (4) 1937-1942

O.N. 164112 7,255g 3,662n.
463.7 (b.p.) x 63.0 x 29.9 feet.
Two T.3-cyl. by John G. Kincaid and Co. Ltd., Greenock, each with a Bauer-Wach low-pressure exhaust steam turbine, double-reduction geared to twin screws; 9,500 IHP, 17 knots.
14.1.1937: Launched by the Greenock

Dockyard Co. Ltd., Greenock (Yard No. 427).
25.3.1937: Registered in the ownership of The Clan Line Steamers Ltd. (Cayzer, Irvine and Co. Ltd., managers), London as CLAN CAMPBELL.
30.3.1937: Delivered.
1.4.1940: Requisitioned by the British government.
13.2.1942: Damaged by bombs 45 miles

north east of Tobruk in position 32.22 north by 24.22 east whilst on a voyage from Alexandria to Malta.
23.3.1942: Bombed and sunk eight miles and 245 degrees from Filfola Island, Malta whilst on a voyage from Alexandria to Malta with general cargo and government stores. Of the 57 crew, 7 were lost, and 3 of the 12 gunners.
27.4.1942: Register closed.

Clan Campbell (4) with derricks stowed and ready for sea at Beira (upper) and on a peaceful Mersey (lower). *[Upper: Ships in Focus, lower: B. and A. Feilden/J. and M. Clarkson]*

CLAN CHATTAN (2) 1937-1942

O.N. 165907 7,262g 3,666n
487.6 x 63.0 x 29.9 feet.
Two T.3-cyl. by John G. Kincaid and Co.
Ltd., Greenock, each with a Bauer-Wach
low-pressure exhaust steam turbine,
double-reduction geared to twin screws;
9,500 IHP, 17 knots.
12.4.1937: Launched by the Greenock
Dockyard Co. Ltd., Greenock (Yard No.
428).
26.6.1937: Delivered.
5.7.1937: Registered in the ownership of
The Clan Line Steamers Ltd. (Cayzer,
Irvine and Co. Ltd., managers), London as
CLAN CHATTAN.
20.4.1940: Requisitioned by the British
government.
14.2.1942: Bombed and sunk 190 miles
north of Benghazi in position 35.01 north
by 20.11 east whilst on a voyage from
Alexandria to Malta in convoy MW9B
with a cargo of military and naval stores.
The 128 crew and 230 troops on board
were rescued by a naval vessel.
10.7.1942: Register closed.

Top: Two views of the launch of *Clan
Chattan* (2), first as she goes down the
ways and then after Clyde Shipping's
tugs have taken charge of her. The
head tug is *Flying Eagle* (260/1928).
[Kevin O'Donoghue collection]

Middle: *Clan Chattan* (2)
photographed on 25th July 1937
sailed from the Clyde on her maiden
voyage to Durban. She would
complete loading at Newport,
Swansea and Liverpool. *[Archie Munro
collection]*

Bottom: A fine three quarter stern view
in the Mersey. *[B. and A. Feilden/J.
and M. Clarkson collection]*

CLAN CHISHOLM (2) 1937-1939

O.N. 165915 7,256g 3,671n
463.7 (b.p.) x 63.0 x 29.9 feet.
Two T.3-cyl. by John G. Kincaid and
Co. Ltd., Greenock, each with a
Bauer-Wach low-pressure exhaust
steam turbine, double-reduction
geared to twin screws; 1,362 NHP, 17
knots.
21.7.1937: Launched by the
Greenock Dockyard Co. Ltd.,
Greenock (Yard No. 429).
24.9.1937: Delivered.
8.10.1937: Registered in the
ownership of The Clan Line Steamers
Ltd. (Cayzer, Irvine and Co. Ltd.,
managers), London as CLAN
CHISHOLM.
17.10.1939: Torpedoed and sunk by
the German submarine U 48 north
north west of Cape Finisterre in
approximate position 45 north by 15
west whilst on a voyage from
Calcutta to Liverpool and Glasgow
and from Gibraltar in convoy HG3
with general cargo including tea, jute,
pig iron and cotton. Four lives were
lost. The survivors were picked up
from their boats by the Swedish
motor ship BARDALAND (2,595/
1936) and landed at Kirkwall. The
WARWICK CASTLE (17,383/1939)
and Norwegian steamer SKUDD
(1,247/1929) also took part in the
rescue.
18.11.1939: Register closed.

CLAN CUMMING (2) 1938-1941

O.N. 165924 7,264g 3,676n
487.6 x 63.0 x 29.9 feet.
Two T.3-cyl. by John G. Kincaid and
Co. Ltd., Greenock, each with a
Bauer-Wach low-pressure exhaust
steam turbine, double-reduction
geared to twin screws; 9,500 IHP, 17
knots.
18.10.1937: Launched by the
Greenock Dockyard Co. Ltd.,
Greenock (Yard No. 430).
21.12.1937: Completed.
3.1.1938: Registered in the
ownership of The Clan Line Steamers
Ltd. (Cayzer, Irvine and Co. Ltd.,
managers), London as CLAN
CUMMING.
24.4.1940: Requisitioned by the
British government.
10.10.1940: Damaged by bombs at
Liverpool.
7.4.1941: Damaged at Piraeus when
CLAN FRASER blew up.
15.4.1941: Mined and sunk in the
Gulf of Athens in position 37.49
north by 23.38.30 east whilst on a
voyage from Piraeus to Alexandria in
ballast. Of 110 crew and three
gunners, all were saved but 77 of the
crew became prisoners of war.
28.1.1942: Register closed.

The tragically short-lived *Clan Chisholm* (2), Clan's first loss during the Second World War, is seen moored to a buoy at Beira. She had taller stokehold vents and the sidelight boxes were moved down to the master's deck from the bridge. *[John G. Callis]*

Bystanders watch as the newly-launched *Clan Cumming* (2) is brought into dock by the tug *Flying Eagle* (260/1928). *[Glasgow University Archives GD323/7/9/2/430/1]*

Clan Cumming (2). Compared to their refrigerated predecessors, the Clan Cs had fewer boats. Beginning with the *Clan Cumming* a pair of derrick posts replaced the single kingpost at number 4 hatch and vents reappeared on the kingposts ahead of the funnel. *[B. and A. Feilden/J. and M. Clarkson]*

Clan Buchanan (3) seen arriving at Brisbane on 28th August 1938. Compared with the immediately preceding group of ships, the sides of the lower bridge deck, housing the navigating officers, were opened out as on the one above, which reduced the area of that space and relegated the cadets' accommodation to the port side forward of the engineers' space on the casing. In terms of lives lost, *Clan Buchanan* was to become Clan's worst war casualty. *[W. Elliot/J. and M. Clarkson]*

CLAN BUCHANAN (3) 1938-1941
O.N. 165929 7,266g 3,692n
487.6 x 63.0 x 29.9 feet.
Two T.3-cyl. by John G. Kincaid and Co. Ltd., Greenock, each with a Bauer-Wach low-pressure exhaust steam turbine, double-reduction geared to twin screws; 9,500 IHP, 17 knots.
21.12.1937: Launched by the Greenock Dockyard Co. Ltd., Greenock (Yard No. 431).
18.2.1938: Delivered.
22.2.1938: Registered in the ownership of The Clan Line Steamers Ltd. (Cayzer,

Irvine and Co. Ltd., managers), London as CLAN BUCHANAN.
5.4.1940: Requisitioned by the British government.
28.4.1941: Sunk by the German auxiliary cruiser PINGUIN (SCHIFF NO. 33) west of the Maldive Islands, Indian Ocean in a position 04.15 north by 63.00 east whilst on a voyage from the Clyde to Durban, Colombo and Chittagong with general cargo, military stores and mail. Of the crew of 119 and two gunners, a total of 106 were lost when PINGUIN was sunk by HMS CORNWALL on 9.5.1941.
9.1.1942: Register closed.

CLAN FERGUSON (2) 1938-1942
O.N. 165937 7,347g 3,563n
463.7 (b.p.) x 63.0 x 29.9 feet.
Two T.3-cyl. by John G. Kincaid and Co. Ltd., Greenock, each with a low-pressure exhaust steam turbine, double-reduction geared to twin screws; 9,500 IHP, 17 knots.
22.3.1938: Launched by the Greenock Dockyard Co. Ltd., Greenock (Yard No. 432).
26.5.1938: Registered in the ownership of The Clan Line Steamers Ltd. (Cayzer, Irvine and Co. Ltd., managers), London as CLAN FERGUSON.
24.5.1938: Delivered.

Clan Ferguson (2) photographed leaving Cape Town. For her and *Clan Menzies*, the bridge and engine casing structures were lengthened by a reduction of the break at number 3 hatch, three stokehold vents were fitted in lieu of two and most prominent of all the funnel was repositioned twelve feet forward which considerably enhanced their profile. *[Ships in Focus]*

28.8.1939: Requisitioned by the British government.
21.9.1940: Attacked by aircraft off Alexandria.
12.8.1942: Torpedoed and sunk 20 miles north of Zembra Island whilst on a voyage from the Clyde to Gibraltar and Malta as part of Operation Pedestal. Her cargo of military stores included aviation spirit and explosives. The torpedo was fired by a German Heinkel He-111 aircraft. Of her crew of 81, 11 were lost; of 20 gunners, one was lost; and of 13 passengers six were lost, the remainder becoming prisoners of war when picked up by German seaplanes and taken to Sicily or getting ashore in Vichy French territory.
5.6.1943: Register closed.

Servicemen watch as *Clan Ferguson* (2) enters Grand Harbour, Malta, on 19th January 1942. *[Imperial War Museum, GM341]*

CLAN MENZIES (2) 1938-1940
O.N. 165947 7,336g 3,555n
463.7 (b.p.) x 63.0 x 29.9 feet.
Two T.3-cyl. by John G. Kincaid and Co. Ltd., Greenock, each with a low-pressure exhaust steam turbine, double-reduction geared to twin screws; 1,370 NHP, 9,500 IHP, 17 knots.
15.6.1938: Launched by the Greenock Dockyard Co. Ltd., Greenock (Yard No. 433).
24.8.1938: Delivered.
25.8.1938: Registered in the ownership of The Clan Line Steamers Ltd. (Cayzer, Irvine and Co. Ltd., managers), London as CLAN MENZIES.
11.9.1939: Requisitioned by the British government.
29.7.1940: Torpedoed and sunk by the German submarine U 99 160 miles west south west of Tory Island off the west coast of Ireland in position 54.10 north by 12.00 west whilst on an independent voyage from

Sydney and Melbourne to Liverpool with general cargo including zinc, dried fruit and wheat. Six of the crew of 94 were lost.
10.8.1940: Register closed.

Clan Menzies (2) seen following trials on the Clyde in September 1938 (middle) and during her first visit to Liverpool to load on 1st October 1938 (bottom). *[Middle: Archie Munro collection; bottom: J. and M. Clarkson]*

EXTRA ACCOMMODATION

This group had higher mast tables and an accommodation deck for the engineers above the engine casing.

CLAN FORBES (3) 1938-1959

O.N. 165951 7,529g 3,689n
487.6 x 63.0 x 29.9 feet.
Two T.3-cyl. by John G. Kincaid and Co. Ltd., Greenock, each with a low-pressure exhaust steam turbine, double-reduction geared to twin screws; 1,370 NHP.
8.9.1938: Launched by the Greenock Dockyard Co. Ltd., Greenock (Yard No. 434).
10.11.1938: Registered in the ownership of The Clan Line Steamers Ltd. (Cayzer, Irvine and Co. Ltd., managers), London as CLAN FORBES.
11.11.1938: Delivered.
22.3.1940: Requisitioned by the British government.
16.8.1940: Damaged during an air raid at Tilbury.
6.8.1959: Arrived at Hong Kong for breaking up by Dah Chong Hong having been sold for £96,500.
23.10.1959: Work began.

The newly-launched *Clan Forbes* (3) is assisted into James Watt Dock by Clyde Shipping's tug *Flying Condor* (202/1914) on 8th September 1938 (upper). The middle view shows her leaving the Mersey with railway carriages in July 1939, and the bottom in post-war condition with extra white paint and additional navigational equipment atop the bridge. Note in the post-war view the wide spreaders beneath the cross trees which carried portable cargo lights. When at sea they were stowed against the masts.
[Upper: Glasgow University Archives GD323/7/9/2/434/3; middle : B. and A. Feilden/J. and M. Clarkson; lower: J. K. Byass/Roy Fenton collection]

Clan Forbes (3) on the Riverside Wharf, King George V Dock, Glasgow in her final post-war livery. Alongside is a tanker which is almost her contemporary, *Peter M* (972/1937), owned by Metcalf Motor Coasters Ltd. of London, and probably delivering bunker oil. *Clan Forbes* and the other steamers of this class were designed to burn either coal or oil, a feature which gave them maximum flexibility when bunkering at ports round the world. It is likely that, when this photograph was taken, she was burning only oil. *[Archie Munro collection]*

CLAN FRASER (3) 1939-1941
O.N. 165960 7,529g 3,524n
487.6 x 63.0 x 29.9 feet.
Two T.3-cyl. John G. Kincaid and Co. Ltd., Greenock, each with a low-pressure exhaust steam turbine, double-reduction geared to twin screws; 9,500 IHP, 17 knots.
20.12.1938: Launched by the Greenock Dockyard Co. Ltd., Greenock (Yard No. 435).
20.2.1939: Registered in the ownership of The Clan Line Steamers Ltd. (Cayzer, Irvine and Co. Ltd., managers), London as CLAN FRASER.
22.2.1939: Delivered.
12.4.1940: Requisitioned by the British government.
6.4.1941: Caught fire when bombed by enemy aircraft whilst discharging a cargo of military vehicles and stores at Piraeus. Of the crew of 106 plus six gunners, six of the crew were lost, along with six prisoners.
7.4.1941: Blew up, damaging other ships in the port, including the British steamer CITY OF ROUBAIX (7,108/1928) and the Greek steamer PETALLI (6,565/1917).
25.4.1941: Register closed.

Clan Fraser (3) in the Mersey (middle) and looking war-like when sailing from Cape Town early during the Second World War (lower). On her final voyage *Clan Fraser* brought military supplies around the Cape from Glasgow and was discharging at Piraeus in 6th April 1941. During an air raid the ship was struck by two bombs which set her alight. After burning fiercely for several hours she blew up, causing considerable damage to several other ships, including *Clan Cumming* (2). *[Middle: B. and A. Feilden/J. and M. Clarkson; lower: F. W. Hawks]*

CLAN LAMONT (3) 1939-1944/1948-1961

O.N. 165965 7,673g 3,501n
487.7 x 63.0 x 29.9 feet.
Two T.3-cyl. by John G. Kincaid and Co. Ltd., Greenock, each with a low-pressure exhaust steam turbine, double-reduction geared to twin screws; 1,370 NHP, 15 knots.
22.3.1939: Launched by the Greenock Dockyard Co. Ltd., Greenock (Yard No. 438).
24.5.1939: Delivered and registered in the ownership of The Clan Line Steamers Ltd.

(Cayzer, Irvine and Co. Ltd., managers), London as CLAN LAMONT.
2.5.1940: Requisitioned by the British government.
25.4.1944: Commissioned into the Royal Navy as an infantry landing ship.
1.5.1944: Renamed HMS LAMONT.
8.8.1945: Renamed HMS ARD PATRICK.
5.10.1945: Transferred from Royal Navy to management of Cayzer, Irvine and Co. Ltd. Subsequently fitted with extra accommodation for ferrying troops between United Kingdom, Germany and Poland and in the Mediterranean.

16.9.1947: Arrived at Greenock Dockyard Co. Ltd., Greenock for reconversion to a cargo vessel.
17.2.1948: Redelivered by The Clan Line Steamers Ltd. (Cayzer, Irvine and Co. Ltd., managers), London as CLAN LAMONT.
18.5.1961: Transferred to King Line Ltd., London (Cayzer, Irvine and Co. Ltd., London, managers).
24.8.1961: Arrived at Moji.
31.8.1961: Sold to Nichimen K.K., Mihara for demolition.
31.8.1961: Arrived at Mihaharo for breaking up.

Despite the urgent need for fast, modern cargo liners, the Admiralty persisted in taking them over and carrying out expensive and protracted conversions, only to produce specialised vessels whose use was limited. In January 1944, the *Clan Lamont* (3) was taken in hand for conversion (opposite page upper, in pre-war condition) to a landing ship infantry, with a capacity of 18 small landing craft and over 1,000 troops (opposite bottom and right, on the Clyde in April 1944), on the Clyde in April 1944. Her contribution to Operation Neptune was impressive, as HMS *Lamont* she landed over 8,000 troops on Normandy beaches and made five crossings, during which her master, Captain Angus Campbell, insisted on flying the Royal Standard of Scotland at a masthead as well as the more official white ensign.

But this was to remain her only moment of glory. On 3rd August 1944 she left Greenock for New York to take on troops for Pacific operations. But after passing through the Panama Canal she experienced engine troubles which meant she was left behind by the other members of the British squadron. Proud Clan Line personnel blamed her problems on a non-Clan engine room crew who did not understand her plumbing.

Late in the war, and after being sent home, she was renamed HMS *Ard Patrick* and used for training, as an accommodation ship and, after the war, as a short-distance troop transport. All these activities were no doubt worthy, but did they justify depriving the country of the services of a first class cargo carrier?

The middle photograph on this page shows her as a troop transport, with additional deck houses and carrying Clan Line funnel, in recognition of her being managed by Cayzer, Irvine and Co. Ltd. In the deck houses and in the lower and upper 'tween decks she had berths which would accom-modate 1,624 men.

When rebuilt (right), *Clan Lamont* was very similar in appearance to the *Clan Forbes* and *Clan Fraser*. She had one 80-ton and one 30-ton heavy-lift derrick. Originally fitted for coal or oil firing, she burned only oil after her refit, and her coal bunkers provided extra cargo space. *[Opposite bottom and top right: Imperial War Museum 25030C and 25028; middle right: Newall Dunn collection; top left and bottom right: J. and M. Clarkson collection]*

179

EMPIRE SONG 1940-1941
O.N. 166991 9,228g 4,950n
463.8 (b.p.) x 63.0 x 32.7 feet.
Two T.3-cyl. by John G. Kincaid and Co.
Ltd., Greenock each with a Bauer-Wach
low pressure exhaust steam turbine,
double-reduction geared to twin screws;
1,210 NHP, 9,500 IHP, 16 knots.
18.6.1940: Launched by the Greenock
Dockyard Co. Ltd., Greenock (Yard No.
443).
4.10.1940: Registered in the ownership of
the Ministry of Shipping, (Cayzer, Irvine
and Co. Ltd., managers), London as
EMPIRE SONG.
11.10.1940: Completed.
21.10.1940: Began military stores service.
9.5.1941: Exploded a mine, caught fire
and sank in the Mediterranean about 45
miles west of Pantelleria whilst on a
voyage from the Clyde and Gibraltar to
Malta in convoy Tiger with a cargo of
military stores including ammunition. Of
her complement of 113 crew and 33
service personnel, 10 members of the crew,
five military personnel and two gunlayers
were lost.
11.7.1941: Register closed.

CLAN CAMPBELL (5) 1943-1961
O.N. 168761 9,545g 5,090n
487.6 x 63.0 x 29.9 feet.
Two T.3-cyl. by John G. Kincaid and Co.
Ltd., Greenock, each with a Bauer-Wach
low-pressure exhaust steam turbine,
double-reduction geared to twin screws;
1,370 NHP, 17 knots.
23.2.1943: Launched by the Greenock
Dockyard Co. Ltd., Greenock (Yard No.
453).
3.5.1943: Registered in the ownership of
The Clan Line Steamers Ltd. (Cayzer,
Irvine and Co. Ltd., managers), London as
CLAN CAMPBELL.
9.5.1943: Completed.
28.2.1961: Transferred to King Line Ltd.
(Cayzer, Irvine and Co. Ltd., managers),
London.
27.9.1961: Arrived at Hong Kong.
30.9.1961: Sold for £123,500 to Shiu
Wing Hong and Co., Hong Kong for
demolition.
16.3.1962: Work commenced.

Clan Campbell (5) is seen first on the
Clyde in June 1943 on trials (upper
middle), with landing craft on deck and
fitted with a radar lantern (lower middle)
and in South African waters with a
peacetime cargo of railway rolling stock
(bottom). Her design and that of
subsequent war-built Clans was based
on that of *Clan Fraser* (3), with an extra
accommodation deck for engineers and
a stump mast aft rather than kingposts.
*[Upper middle: Glasgow University
Archives GD319/18/2/5/1, lower middle:
National Maritime Museum; P22116;
bottom: Ships in Focus]*

The short-lived *Empire Song*, built for British government account to Clan Line design, arriving on the Clyde on 27th March 1941 at the end of her maiden voyage, during which she brought sugar from Mauritius for discharge at Greenock. During her second voyage, taking tanks and other military vehicles to Alexandria as part of the Tiger Convoy, she was mined and sunk in the Sicilian Narrows. *[Scottish Maritime Museum]*

CLAN CHATTAN (3) 1944-1962

O.N. 169413 9,585g 5,090n
487.7 x 63.0 x 29.9 feet.
Two T.3-cyl. by John G. Kincaid and Co.
Ltd., Greenock, with a low-pressure exhaust
steam turbine, double-reduction geared to
twin screws; 1,370 NHP.
9.3.1943: Launched by the Greenock
Dockyard Co. Ltd., Greenock (Yard No. 456).

15.6.1944: Registered in the ownership of
The Clan Line Steamers Ltd. (Cayzer, Irvine
and Co. Ltd., managers), London as CLAN
CHATTAN.
22.6.1944: Delivered.
3.7.1945: Damaged in collision with the
transport USS BLOUNT (AK-163) whilst
leaving Manus Island in the Pacific. She

proceeded to Sydney for repairs. BLOUNT
was found 75% to blame.
29.1.1962: Transferred to King Line Ltd.
(Cayzer, Irvine and Co. Ltd., managers),
London.
14.5.1962: Arrived at Hong Kong to be
broken up by Sigma Shipping Co. Ltd.
26.5.1962: Work commenced.

The upper picture shows the *Clan Chattan* (3) in the Clyde, on trials, in June 1944. She is armed, fitted with Carley floats and her radar lantern can be seen on top of the bridge, a feature often painted out by the censor. In the lower photo we see her in the Mersey with the Liver Buildings in the background. In 1949 *Clan Chattan* was reported as suffering from fractures in her framing, a problem which Clan Line management admitted was not uncommon in ships from Greenock Dockyard. *[Top: Glasgow University Archives GD319/18/2/8/6; lower: B. and A. Feilden/J. and M. Clarkson]*

Clan Chisholm (3) is seen first on trials in October 1944 (top), and in peacetime still retaining her signal mast (middle). She is also seen off Birkenhead, with the usual deck cargo of railway coaches stowed aft (bottom) and at Cape Town (opposite top). [Top and middle: Archie Munro collection, bottom: B. and A. Feilden/J. and M. Clarkson, opposite top: F. W. Hawks]

CLAN CHISHOLM (3) 1944-1962

O.N. 169420 9,581g 5,083n

487.7 x 63.0 x 29.9 feet.

Two T.3-cyl. by John G. Kincaid and Co. Ltd., Greenock, with a low-pressure exhaust steam turbine, double-reduction geared to twin screws; 1,370 NHP.

23.6.1944: Launched by the Greenock Dockyard Co. Ltd., Greenock (Yard No. 457).

19.10.1944: Registered in the ownership of for The Clan Line Steamers Ltd. (Cayzer, Irvine and Co. Ltd., managers), London as CLAN CHISHOLM.

21.10.1944: Delivered.

3.1962: Transferred to King Line Ltd. (Cayzer, Irvine and Co. Ltd., managers), London.

7.5.1962: Fire in hold whilst on a voyage from Glasgow to Dar-es-Salaam with general cargo including explosives and ammunition.

10.5.1962: Fire extinguished after she arrived at Mombasa, but extent of damage made repairs were uneconomic.

14.5.1962: Sold for £76,000 to Shiu Wing Hong and Co., Hong Kong, for demolition.

21.8.1962: Handed over at Hong Kong.

18.9.1962: Breaking up began.

The interior views show the officers' dining room (right), their smoke room (middle) and the master's day room and bedroom (bottom). *[Glasgow University Archives GD319/18/2/9/6, 7, 9, 8, 10 and 11/Archie Munro collecton]*

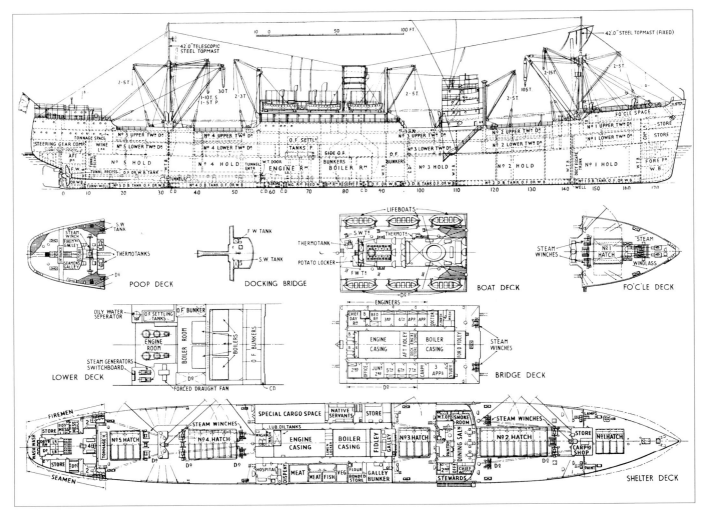

Above: General arrangement drawings of the *Clan Cumming* (3).
Below: *Clan Cumming* (3) on trials. *[Glasgow University Archives GD319/18/2/11/1 / Archie Munro collection]*

CLAN CUMMING (3) 1946-1962

O.N. 169480 7,812g 3,326n
486.5 x 63.0 x 29.9 feet.
Two T.3-cyl. by John G. Kincaid and Co.
Ltd., Greenock, with a low-pressure
exhaust steam turbine, double-reduction
geared to twin screws; 1,372 NHP.
3.5.1946: Launched by the Greenock
Dockyard Co. Ltd., Greenock (Yard No.
459).
8.8.1946: Registered in the ownership of
The Clan Line Steamers Ltd. (Cayzer,
Irvine and Co. Ltd., managers), London as
CLAN CUMMING.
15.8.1946: Completed.
5.10.1962: Delivered at Corunna to
Francisco Munoz Barrientos and Manuel
Grana Carrera, trading as Desguaces
Fontan S.A., for demolition, having been
sold for £80,000.
18.10.1962: Arrived at Vigo.
10.11.1962: Demolition commenced.

Clan Cumming (3) at Cape Town in 1959, note the deepening of the white paint on her bulwarks (top). A view of the bridge (middle) and (bottom) two deck views which clearly show some of the 15 steam winches with which she had been fitted and other pieces of deck equipment. *[Top: J. and M. Clarkson collection, middle and lower: Glasgow University Archives GD323/7/ 9/2/459/11, GD319/18/2/11/12 and GD319/18/2/11/10]*

CLAN BUCHANAN (4) 1946-1962
O.N. 169477 7,467g 3,511n
487.7 x 63.0 x 29.9 feet.
Two T.3-cyl. by John G. Kincaid and Co.
Ltd., Greenock, with a low-pressure exhaust
steam turbine, double-reduction geared to
twin screws; 1,370 NHP.
26.5.1941: Launched by William Denny and
Brothers Ltd., Dumbarton (Yard No. 1356)
for the Admiralty as a seaplane carrier.
She had been laid down for The Clan Line

Steamers Ltd. with the intended name
CLAN BUCHANAN, but taken over by the
Admiralty who initially proposed to convert
her to an armed boarding vessel under the
name EMPIRE MIGHT.
22.11.1941: Completed as the aircraft
transport HMS ENGADINE.
1.1945: Laid up in reserve.
3.1946: Began rebuilding as a cargo steamer
by Greenock Dockyard Co. Ltd.
26.6.1946: Registered in the ownership of

The Clan Line Steamers Ltd. (Cayzer, Irvine
and Co. Ltd., managers), London as CLAN
BUCHANAN.
22.10.1946: Delivered by the Greenock
Dockyard Co. Ltd., Greenock following
conversion for £120,000.
10.11.1962: Arrived at Cartagena for
demolition by Juan Antonio Tolon de Gali,
Alicante, and Gabriel Moncho Alacren of
Valencia, having been sold for £65,000.
1.1963: Work commenced.

The Clan Buchanan (4) was taken over by the Admiralty whilst building and, after several changes of mind by their lordships, was completed as the aircraft transport HMS *Engadine*, seen on the page opposite discharging aircraft at a Clyde anchorage in June or July 1944 preparatory to a refit on the Tyne.

Following the war she was substantially rebuilt to give the *Clan Buchanan* (4), as in the upper photograph on this page. She and *Clan Brodie* had the stump mast aft and the low superstructure of the pre-war *Clan Cameron* class, but a smaller funnel and a distinctly different bridge structure with walkways that extend around its front. The lower photograph shows her in final condition with a heightened funnel and deep white topside strakes.

Whilst waiting to lock into Antwerp docks from the River Scheldt on 25th November 1947, *Clan Buchanan* was blown ashore in a gale. Her master had repeatedly signalled for tugs, but none came to his assistance. Once aground, tug owners boarded the ship and requested the master to sign Lloyd's Open Form, and when this was done sent no fewer than ten tugs, an unnecessarily large number according the master, especially as on subsequent dry docking in Glasgow *Clan Buchanan* was found to be undamaged. The tug owners' claim was subsequently settled for £4,000. *[Opposite: National Maritime Museum N13165 and N13166; this page top: John MacRoberts/Archie Munro collection; bottom: B. and A. Feilden/J. and M. Clarkson collection]*

CLAN BRODIE 1947-1962

O.N. 169474 7,473g 3,508n
487.7 x 63.0 x 38.1 feet.
Two T.3-cyl. by John G. Kincaid and Co.
Ltd., Greenock, with a low-pressure
exhaust steam turbine, double-reduction
geared to twin screws; 1,370 NHP.
1939: Laid down for The Clan Line
Steamers Ltd. with the intended name
CLAN BRODIE but work suspended on
the outbreak of the Second World War.
Subsequently purchased by the
government.
1.10.1940: Launched by the Greenock
Dockyard Co. Ltd., Greenock (Yard No.
444) and towed to Dalmuir Basin for
fitting out and conversion by John Brown
and Co. Ltd.
10.1941: Completed for the Admiralty as
the aircraft transport HMS ATHENE.
1.1945: Laid up in reserve.
3.5.1946: Registered in the ownership of
The Clan Line Steamers Ltd. (Cayzer,
Irvine and Co. Ltd., managers), London as
CLAN BRODIE.
12.6.1946: Began rebuilding as a cargo
steamer by Greenock Dockyard Co. Ltd.
16.2.1947: Delivered following
conversion for £110,000.
22.10.1962: Transferred to King Line Ltd.
(Cayzer, Irvine and Co. Ltd., managers),
London.
19.7.1963: Arrived at Hong Kong.
22.7.1963: Handed over to Hong Kong
Salvage and Towage Co. Ltd., Hong Kong
for demolition, having been sold for
£88,050.
30.7.1963: Work began by Mollers Ltd.,
Hong Kong.

Clan Brodie as HMS *Athene* (top). After her war service, Clan planned to have her reconverted to a cargo ship at Rotterdam, but the price proved too high and the work went instead to Greenock Dockyard. She is seen as *Clan Brodie* at Cape Town (middle) and in the English Channel (bottom). *[Top: World Ship Photo Library, middle and bottom: J. and M. Clarkson collection]*

CLAN DAVIDSON (2) 1948-1961
O.N. 182100 8,067g 3,697n
487.7 x 63.0 x 29.9 feet.
Two T.3-cyl. by John G. Kincaid and Co. Ltd., Greenock, with a low-pressure exhaust steam turbine, double-reduction geared to twin screws; 1,370 NHP.
27.10.1942: Launched by the Greenock Dockyard Co. Ltd., Greenock (Yard No. 452).
She had been laid down for The Clan Line Steamers Ltd. (Cayzer, Irvine and Co. Ltd., managers), London but was taken over by the Admiralty 9.1942.
31.1.1943: Completed by Scott's Shipbuilding and Engineering Co. Ltd., Greenock as the midget submarine depot ship HMS BONAVENTURE (F.139).
23.3.1948: Acquired by The Clan Line Steamers Ltd. (Cayzer, Irvine and Co. Ltd., managers), London for £135,000, and sent for conversion into a general cargo ship by Greenock Dockyard Co. Ltd.
20.10.1948: Registered as CLAN DAVIDSON.
22.10.1948: Delivered after conversion.
2.10.1961: Transferred to King Line Ltd. (Cayzer, Irvine and Co. Ltd., managers), London.
28.12.1961: Arrived at Hong Kong and sold to Sigma Shipping Co. Ltd., Hong Kong for demolition.
13.2.1962: Demolition commenced.

Upper: HMS *Bonaventure* at the Tail of the Bank on 30th January 1943, the day before she was officially completed, and immediately prior to moving to Kames Bay to act as a depot and training ship for the first midget submarines. Launched by Greenock Dockyard, she had been fitted out at the neighbouring Scotts' yard, which was more experienced at naval work. Major alterations included encasing all of number 3 hatchway and lengthening number 2 hatch to allow two submarines to be stowed in the hold. All other hatches were plated over to provide stowage for the submarines: two on deck abreast of number 2 hatch under the 50-ton derrick and four under the 40-ton derrick at number 4 hatch. *[Imperial War Museum A2948]*
Lower: In Kames Bay near Rothesay on 17th December 1944, the 50-ton derrick of HMS *Bonaventure* handles one of the midget submarines stowed on her foredeck. Note the anti-submarine netting. In March 1943 HMS *Bonaventure* moved to the remote Loch Chàirn Bhàin in Sutherland from where in September 1943 her boats attacked the German battleship *Tirpitz* in Altenfjord, putting her out of action for seven months. In February 1945 HMS *Bonaventure* left Kames Bay for the Far East and in July launched her submarines from Brunei to successfully attack the Japanese cruiser *Takao* in Singapore harbour. *[Imperial War Museum A26927/Rick Cox collection]*

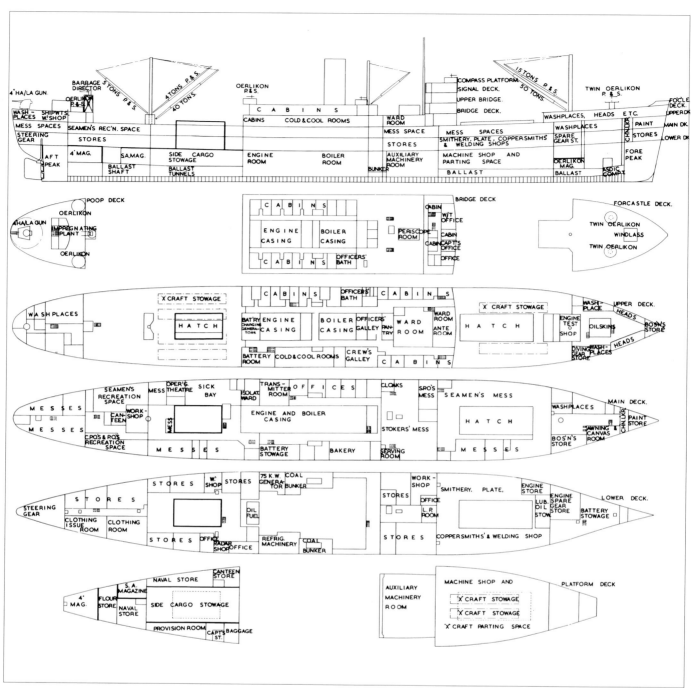

Above: General arrangement of HMS *Bonaventure*.
Right: HMS *Bonaventure* on the North Wall of the Royal Navy Dockyard at Hong Kong in 1945. The monument on the left hand peak behind the ship is the Japanese war memorial ordered by Lt.General Isogai and built by Allied prisoners of war in 1943 who were made to carry every stone from the harbour to the top of the 2,000 foot Mount Cameron. The memorial is believed to have been demolished in 1946.
[Norman G. Tacey collection]

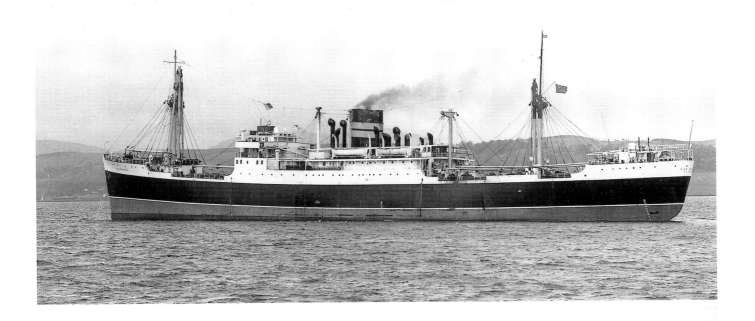

HMS *Bonaventure* paid off in April 1947, and in August of that year was reduced to reserve status. Greenock Dockyard staff inspected her in December, but it was not until February 1948 that the Admiralty decided to dispose of her. Following a further visit by Dockyard staff in early March, she was reacquired by Clan, and moved to a riverside berth at Greenock, moving into Greenock Dockyard to begin conversion to a conventional cargo ship on 22nd March.

Emerging in October as *Clan Davidson* (2), she initially had a narrow white ribbon between black hull and boot topping as seen at anchor during her trials (upper). Note that a clumsy attempt has been made to paint out the anchor chain on the negative. She has a distinctly different funnel to other members of the group, shorter and fatter but significantly raked, giving her a unique appearance. Although number 3 hatchway and hold was reinstated after war service, it remained trunked through the accommodation.

Clan Davidson reintroduced passenger carrying to the company by providing accommodation for 12 passengers when redelivered to Clan Line in October 1948. She was the last of the twin-screw class to enter service, 12 years after the first had been delivered. Mitchell and Sawyer's 'Empire Ships' lists her yard number, 452, as having been laid down as *Clan Campbell*, so perhaps when this hull was requisitioned by the Admiralty the name *Clan Campbell* was re-allocated to number 453. In the lower photograph the hull has been repainted without the white band above the boot topping. *[Upper: Glasgow University Archives; lower: Roy Fenton collection]*

SIX-HOLD REEFERS

The refrigerated Clan Macdonald *and her three successors represented a further advance in size with an extra hold to facilitate handling and storage of frozen cargoes.* Clan Macdonald *was diesel engined, and* Lanarkshire *was fitted with steam turbines and watertube boilers for comparative purposes.* Clan Urquhart *was intended to be a repeat of* Lanarkshire, *but unavailability of gearing meant reciprocating engines were substituted for the turbines, although the intended watertube boilers were fitted (and gave much trouble), and her wartime completion meant there were no wooden decks or other frills. She was slightly shorter, but extra beam gave her much the same capacity.* Clan Macdougall *was a repeat of* Clan Macdonald, *but again had steel rather than wooden decks.*

CLAN MACDONALD (4) 1939-1970

O.N. 165971 9,653g 5,719n
505.3 x 64.7 x 27.4 feet.
Two 10-cyl. 4SCSA Burmeister and Wain-type oil engines by John G. Kincaid and Co. Ltd., Greenock, geared to twin screws; 1,631 NHP, 16 knots.
15.8.1939: Launched by the Greenock Dockyard Co. Ltd., Greenock (Yard No. 436).
4.12.1939: Registered in the ownership of The Clan Line Steamers Ltd. (Cayzer, Irvine and Co. Ltd., managers), London as CLAN MACDONALD.
9.5.1940: Requisitioned by the British government.
7.10.1960: Transferred to Houston Line Ltd. (Cayzer, Irvine and Co. Ltd., managers), London.
6.8.1970: Arrived at Shanghai for demolition.
14.8.1970: Delivered to the China National Machinery Import and Export Corporation, Peking.

Workers watch as the *Clan Macdonald* (4) takes to the water on the 15th August 1939. *[Glasgow University Archives GD323/7/9/2/436/1]*

The refrigerator ship *Clan Macdonald* (4) (middle and bottom). The lower photograph shows the sixth hold worked into her structure. *[Middle: J. and M. Clarkson collection; bottom: Newall Dunn collection]*

LANARKSHIRE 1940-1959

O.N. 165973 9,816g 5,822n
505.4 x 64.7 x 29.9 feet
Six steam turbines single-reduction geared to twin screws by Parsons Marine Steam Turbine Co. Ltd., Wallsend-on-Tyne; 1,549 NHP, 16 knots.
30.11.1939: Launched by the Greenock Dockyard Co. Ltd., Greenock (Yard No. 437).

30.3.1940: Registered in the ownership of the Scottish Shire Line Ltd. (Turnbull, Martin and Co. Ltd., managers), London as LANARKSHIRE.
4.1940: Completed.
31.3.1959: Transferred to Bullard, King and Co. Ltd., London and renamed UMGAZI.
12.1959: Transferred to Springbok Line Ltd., London.

1.1960: Transferred to Springbok Shipping Co. Ltd., Cape Town, South Africa.
8.1960: Renamed GRYSBOK.
1.7.1961: Managers became South African Marine Corporation Ltd., Cape Town and subsequently renamed SOUTH AFRICAN FARMER.
20.1.1963: Arrived Aioi, Japan to be broken up by Ataka and Co. Ltd.
1.3.1963: Work began.

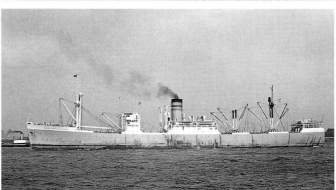

Clan wanted to name this Scottish Shire Line ship *Ayrshire*, but this was rejected by the Registrar of Shipping as a Hull trawler of the name had been completed in 1938. Because of the war *Lanarkshire* was launched without ceremony.
Top: *Lanarkshire* with buses on deck off Cape Town in July 1948. *[J. and M. Clarkson collection]*
Middle left: Arriving in the James Watt Dock, Greenock on 25th September 1956 to discharge tobacco. The new *Argyllshire* (2) is alongside fitting out. *[Archie Munro collection]*
Middle right: Sailing from Antwerp in 1956. *[National Maritime Museum N.35325]*
Bottom: Seen as *Umgazi* in April 1959 (left) and as *South African Farmer* (right). *[J. and M. Clarkson collection]*

CLAN URQUHART (3) 1944-1966

O.N. 169404 9,726g 5,607n
500.5 x 65.8 x 37.9 feet.
Two T.3-cyl. by John G. Kincaid and Co.
Ltd., Greenock each with a low-pressure
exhaust steam turbine, double-reduction
geared to twin screws; 1,283 NHP.
30.6.1943: Launched by the Greenock
Dockyard Co. Ltd., Greenock (Yard No.
454).
19.1.1944: Registered in the ownership of
The Clan Line Steamers Ltd. (Cayzer,
Irvine and Co. Ltd., managers), London as
CLAN URQUHART.
26.1.1944: Completed.
4.1.1944: Requisitioned by the British
government until 18.5.1946.
25.10.1960: Transferred to Houston Line
Ltd. (Cayzer, Irvine and Co. Ltd.,
managers), London.
8.4.1966: Arrived at Kaohsiung for
demolition.
13.4.1966: Delivered to the Chin Ho Fa
Steel and Iron Company, Taipei, having
been sold for £142,500.
6.1966: Work commenced.

Possibly because she was built under difficult wartime conditions, *Clan Urquhart* (3)
had very considerable teething troubles. She proceeded on trials on 17th December
1943, but returned to dock, and underwent further trials on Boxing Day 1943. She
sailed on her first voyage in ballast to Buenos Aires on 15th January 1944, but had
to put into Rio de Janeiro with boiler problems. Further boiler repairs were needed
at Buenos Aires, and she put into both Pernambuco and St. Vincent, Cape Verde on
her way home to Avonmouth. Completion of her first voyage without any involuntary
stoppages was worthy of a note in the Clan Line board minutes for November 1945.

She is shown first running trials on a sunny Clyde during December 1943,
then still in war rig and early post-war colours on 4th October 1947, next in an
experimental colour scheme with a narrow white hull ribbon, and as finally repainted.
*[Top; Glasgow University Archives GD319/18/2/6/2, middle; John MacRoberts/J.
and M. Clarkson, bottom left; S.G. Docker/Roy Fenton collection, bottom right; J.
and M. Clarkson collection]*

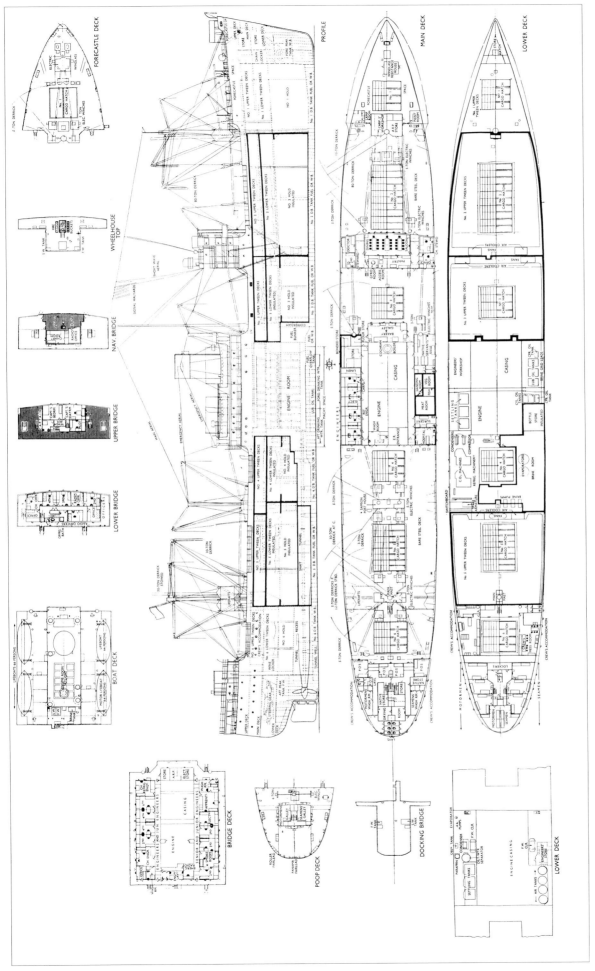

General arrangement drawing of *Clan Macdougall*.

CLAN MACDOUGALL (3) 1944-1971

O.N. 169411 9,710g 5,630n
505.5 x 64.7 x 35.6 feet.
Two 10-cyl. 4SCSA Burmeister &
Wain-type oil engines by John G.
Kincaid and Co. Ltd., Greenock,
geared to twin screws; 1,631 NHP.
10.11.1943: Launched by the
Greenock Dockyard Co. Ltd.,
Greenock (Yard No. 455).
1.5.1944: Registered in the ownership
of The Clan Line Steamers Ltd.
(Cayzer, Irvine and Co. Ltd.,
managers), London as CLAN
MACDOUGALL.
6.5.1944: Completed.
10.5.1944: Requisitioned by the
British government until 22.5.1946.
7.10.1960: Transferred to Houston
Line Ltd. (Cayzer, Irvine and Co. Ltd.,
managers), London.
30.11.1962: Transferred to Huntley,
Cook and Co. Ltd., London.
4.10.1971: Sold to Castle Shipping
Ltd., Famagusta, Cyprus (Mavroleon
Brothers Ltd., London) and renamed
VRYSI.
23.11.1971: Sailed from Singapore for
Kaohsiung, where she arrived previous
to 8.12.1971.
15.12.1971: Li Chon Steel and Iron
Works, Kaohsiung, commenced
demolition.

Clan Macdougall (3) was essentially a wartime utility version of *Clan Macdonald* (4) of 1939. By a whisker *Clan Macdougall*
was the last survivor of this group of reefers, delivered to Taiwan breakers some days after Blue Star's diesel-conversion
Caledonia Star.
Top: on trials in grey during March 1944. *[Glasgow University Archives GD 319/18/2/7/2]*
Middle: in early post-war colours on 16th March 1947. *[John MacRoberts/J. and M. Clarkson]*
Bottom: a splendid view of *Clan Macdougall* in superb condition in her final colour scheme. *[John G. Callis]*

FIVE-HOLD REEFERS

Two hulls were completed to government account, slightly shorter reflecting the revised internal layout with five holds. Externally the main difference from the Clan Line reefers was in the arrangement of cargo gear aft of the superstructure, so they resembled the non-refrigerated twin-screw ships. Empire Wisdom was given to Clan to manage, and Empire Might to Blue Star to help compensate for losses of their refrigerator ships. For some reason, there was an exchange at the end of the war, Empire Might coming into Clan ownership as Clan Macrae and Empire Wisdom becoming Blue Star's Royal Star.

EMPIRE WISDOM 1942-1944

O.N. 168989 9,205g 5,065n
487.6 x 63.0 x 38.1 feet.
Two T.3-cyl. by John G. Kincaid and Co. Ltd., Greenock, with a low-pressure exhaust steam turbine, double-reduction geared to twin screws; 1,370 NHP.
10.1961: Two 5-cyl. 2 SCSA M.A.N.-type oil engines by Bremer Vulkan, Vegesack; 9,000 BHP, 12.5 knots.
29.7.1942: Launched by the Greenock Dockyard Co. Ltd., Greenock (Yard No. 451).
26.10.1942: Registered in the ownership of the Ministry of War Transport (Cayzer, Irvine and Co. Ltd., managers), London as EMPIRE WISDOM.

14.11.1942: Completed.
20.9.1944: Blue Star Line Ltd. appointed managers.
19.9.1946: Sold to Union Cold Storage Co. Ltd. (Blue Star Line Ltd., managers), London, and renamed ROYAL STAR.
1950: Owners became Union International Co. Ltd. (Blue Star Line Ltd., managers), London.
1961: Transferred to Blue Star Line Ltd., London, re-engined and renamed CALEDONIA STAR.
9.12.1971: Delivered to Ta Yung Steel Co. Ltd., Kaohsiung for demolition.
1.1.1972: Work commenced.
25.2.1972: Demolition completed.

Empire Wisdom and *Empire Might* were essentially wartime refrigerated versions of the *Clan Menzies* of 1938. The Cayzer, Irvine-managed *Empire Wisdom* is seen in war-rig at anchor during trials on the Clyde (top). She was transferred to Blue Star management in 1944, and went on to have a 30-year career in this company's ownership, first as *Royal Star* (middle) and later as the motor ship *Caledonia Star* (bottom). [Top: Glasgow University Archives; GD 319/18/2/3/5; middle and bottom: J. and M. Clarkson collection]

197

CLAN MACRAE (3) 1946-1959

O.N. 168986 9,221g 4,873n 10,145d
487.6 x 63.0 x 38.1 feet.
Two T.3-cyl. by John G. Kincaid and Co.
Ltd., Greenock, with a low-pressure
exhaust steam turbine, double-reduction
geared to twin screws; 1,372 NHP.
17.4.1942: Launched by the Greenock
Dockyard Co. Ltd., Greenock (Yard No.
450).
2.7.1942: Registered in the ownership of
the Ministry of War Transport (Blue Star
Line Ltd., managers), London as EMPIRE
MIGHT.
29.7.1942: Completed.
17.4.46: Acquired by The Clan Line
Steamers Ltd. (Cayzer, Irvine and Co. Ltd.,
managers), London and renamed CLAN
MACRAE.
29.1.1959: Transferred to Bullard, King
and Co. Ltd., London.
7.5.1959: Renamed UMGENI.
12.1959: Transferred to the Springbok
Line Ltd., London.
1.1960: Transferred to Springbok
Shipping Co. Ltd., Cape Town, South
Africa.
8.1960: Renamed GEMSBOK.
1.7.1961: Managers became South African
Marine Corporation Ltd., Cape Town and
renamed SOUTH AFRICAN
FINANCIER.
20.1.1962: Arrived Antwerp and sold to
Rederij Wijsmuller, Baarn, Holland and
renamed SANTA MARIA DE ORDAZ for
delivery voyage to Spanish shipbreakers.
10.2.1962: Arrived at Valencia.
3.1962: Breaking up began by Juan
Antonio Tolon de Gali and Gabriel
Moncho Alacren.

Clan Macrae (3) (top) at sea, as *Umgeni* (middle) on the Mersey and *Gemsbok*
(bottom). Her appearance is rather like the *Clan Cameron* of 1936, but with a smaller
funnel and more open bridge, although the latter was altered at some point. *[J. and
M. Clarkson collection]*

MISCELLANEOUS MANAGED SHIPS

Clan Line were appointed managers of several ships that fell into government hands when their owners' countries were over-run or, in the case of some Vichy French ships, when captured and put into Allied service. Clan Line minutes reveal that not all of these management roles were free from problems, as described in the captions. A further French ship, Ville de Majunga *(6,174/1931), is listed by Duncan Haws as managed by the company but her registration documents show that she was managed by Union-Castle Mail Steam Ship Co. Ltd. throughout her UK service.*

ROBERT MÆRSK 1940-1943

O.N. 166210 2,290g 1,346n
341.7 x 46.2 x 17.9 feet.
Oil engine 6-cyl. 4SCSA by Burmeister &
Wain Maskin og Skibsbyggeri, Copenhagen;
355 NHP, 2,450 IHP, 13.5 knots.
19.12.1936: Launched by Odense
Staalskibsvaerft, Odense (Yard No. 64) for A.
P. Moller A/S, Denmark.
2.1937: Completed for A/S D/S Svendborg
(A.P. Moller A/S, managers), Copenhagen,
Denmark as ROBERT MÆRSK.
13.4.1940: Brought into Calcutta after being
intercepted by British warships.
7.11.1940: Registered in the ownership of the
Ministry of Shipping (Cayzer, Irvine and Co.
Ltd., managers), London.
9.4.1941: Owners became the Ministry of War
Transport, London.
3.2.1943: T. and J. Brocklebank Ltd.,
Liverpool appointed managers.
24.7.1946: UK register closed on return to
owners.
1955: Sold to D/S Jutlandia A/S (Ove Toft,
manager), Copenhagen and renamed
BIRGITTE TOFT.
1958: Sold to Cathay Shipping Co. Ltd.,
Singapore and renamed EVER GLORY.
1962: Sold to Chin Yeong Co. Ltd., Singapore.
1965: Sold to Teck Hwa Shipping Co. Ltd.,
Singapore.
1967: Renamed SINGAPORE PEARL.
1968: Sold to State Marine Enterprises S.A.,
Panama (Kuo International Ltd., Singapore)
and renamed TANDJUNG LAYANG.
3.4.1970: Arrived at Hong Kong to be broken
up by the Leung Yau Shipbreaking Company.

VILLE D'AMIENS 1941-1942

O.N. 166317 6,975g 4,216n
411.0 x 53.7 x 28.5 feet.
T.3-cyl. by J.G. Kincaid and Co. Ltd.,
Greenock with a low-pressure turbine; 3,500
IHP, 11.7 knots.
1931: Fitted with Bauer-Wach low-pressure
exhaust turbine.
11.1924: Completed by the North of Ireland
Shipbuilding Co. Ltd., Londonderry (Yard No.
98) for Compagnie Havraise Péninsulaire de
Navigation à Vapeur, Le Havre, France as
VILLE D'AMIENS.
1928: Sold to Société des Services
Contractuels des Messageries Maritime,
Marseilles, France.

After Germany invaded Denmark, Moller's motor ship *Robert Mærsk* was requisitioned by the British government and, under Clan Line's management, loaded at Calcutta. The Ministry of Shipping insisted that the crew comprised a mix of willing Danes and Britons, all on British articles, but Clan had misgivings which turned out to be well founded. She sailed from Calcutta to Durban, where some elements of the crew staged a strike. This seems to have been settled, but at Alexandria in February 1942, Clan Line's Captain A.V. Gordon came ashore suffering from a nervous breakdown, apparently due to continuing troubles with the crew. The naval authorities acquiesced in this, and she sailed under Chief Officer Neilson's command. When Captain Gordon recovered and went back on board, Neilson and the Danish crew members refused to sail with him. At Port Sudan Clan again attempted to impose their will, and Chief Officer Fox from *Clan Mactavish* was told to take command of *Robert Mærsk*. However, the Ministry of War Transport insisted that, as part of their agreement with the crew, she should have a Danish master, and confirmed Neilson in command. This was too much for Clan Line, who could not tolerate Neilson continuing as he had disobeyed their orders. They therefore relinquished management which was taken over by Brocklebanks.

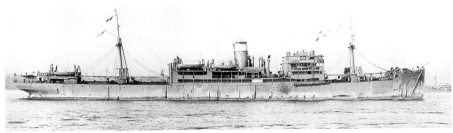

Ville d'Amiens in Australian waters on 26th September 1942 under Clan Line management.

In December 1940, when they realised *Ville d'Amiens* was loading in Australia for the United Kingdom, her French crew objected, feeling that their war was over with the fall of France and not wishing to sail into dangerous waters. They were replaced at Sydney, and some dropped off at Madagascar during the voyage to Durban.

In late 1942, Clan were deprived of the management of *Ville d'Amiens* for what they described as 'political reasons'. She was transferred to Moxey, Savon and Co. Ltd. who were London-based associates of owners Messageries Maritimes. Later, her UK registration was closed when transferred to Compagnie Maritime Française, a company operating under the auspices of the French Committee for National Liberation in London. *[Ian J. Farquhar collection]*

18.9.1940: Requisitioned by Free French
authorities at Papeete and transferred to UK
control.
5.4.1941: Registered in the ownership of the
Ministry of Shipping (Cayzer, Irvine and Co.
Ltd., managers), London.
9.4.1941: Owners became Ministry of War
Transport, London.
10.11.1942: Managers became Moxey, Savon
and Co. Ltd., London.

4.9.1943: Managers became Gonneville Ltd.,
Cardiff.
13.10.1944: UK register closed on transfer to
Compagnie Maritime Française, London
1945: Returned to owners.
1948: Owners became Compagnie des
Messageries Maritimes, Marseille.
27.2.53: Arrived at La Seyne to be broken up
by Serra Frères.
10.3.53: Work began.

LIEUTENANT ST. LOUBERT BIÉ
1941-1945

O.N. 168238 6,126g 3,460n
451.0 x 57.2 x 27.3 feet.
T.3-cyl. by J.C. Tecklenborg A.G.,
Wesermünde with a low-pressure turbine;
3,000 BHP, 3,750 IHP, 11 knots.
7.10.1911: Launched by J.C. Tecklenborg
A.G., Wesermünde (Yard No. 244).
6.11.1911: Completed for Deutsch-
Australische Dampfschiffahrts Gesellschaft,
Hamburg, Germany as MANNHEIM.
25.3.1919: Delivered to the French
Government, Paris as war reparations.
1922: Sold to Compagnie des Messageries
Maritimes, Marseille and renamed
LIEUTENANT ST. LOUBERT BIÉ.
1931: Fitted with Bauer-Wach low-pressure
exhaust turbine.
18.5.1941: Intercepted by HMS
NEWCASTLE about 250 miles south east
of Saint Helena in position 21.31 south by
05.56 west and brought into Durban.
20.11.1941: Registered in the ownership of
the Ministry of War Transport (Cayzer,
Irvine and Co. Ltd., managers), London.
17.9.1945: UK register closed on return to
owners.
26.5.1950: Damaged by a mine and
beached downriver from Saigon whilst
outbound.
6.6.1950: Refloated and taken to Saigon.
6.9.1950: Arrived at La Seyne to be broken
up by Société de Materiel Naval du Midi.

DÉSIRADE 1942-1944

O.N. 168811 9,645g 6,018n
483.4 x 58.9 x 34.6 feet.

The former Vichy French steamer *Lieutenant St. Loubert Bié* under a dramatic wartime sky. She was condemned as a prize and initially taken over by the South African government but then transferred to the Ministry of War Transport, London. Amongst the Clan Line crew put on board were the pitifully few survivors from the *Clan Buchanan*. *[National Maritime Museum P23221]*

Two T.3-cyl. by Ateliers and Chantiers de
France, Dunkirk driving twin screws; 679
NHP, 5,800 IHP, 11 knots.
6.1921: Completed by Ateliers et Chantiers de
France, Dunkirk (Yard No. 101) for
Compagnie Française de Navigation à Vapeur
Chargeurs Réunis, Le Havre, France as
DÉSIRADE.
1940: Transferred to Compagnie Maritime
des Chargeurs Réunis, Le Havre.
17.6.1941: Intercepted by the armed merchant
cruiser HMS PRETORIA CASTLE off Saint
Helena and ordered to Cape Town.
28.2.1942: Registered in the ownership of the
Ministry of War Transport (Cayzer, Irvine and
Co. Ltd., managers), London.
5.9.1944: Management transferred to the
French Committee of National Liberation,
London.

24.9.1945: UK register closed, returned to
owners.
9.5.1950: Left Bordeaux under tow for
Bruges to be broken up by Van Heyghen
Frères.

BANGKOK II 1942-1946

O.N. 168828 8,056g 5,077n
445.0 x 58.0 x 37.3 feet.
Two T.3-cyl. by the Uraga Dock Co. Ltd.,
Uraga driving twin screws; 719 NHP,
4,600 IHP, 10 knots.
12.1919: Completed by the Uraga Dock
Co. Ltd., Uraga (Yard No. 144) for Société
de Navigation à Vapeur France-Indo
Chine, Le Havre, France as BANGKOK.
1932: Transferred to Compagnie Française
de Navigation à Vapeur Chargeurs Réunis,
Le Havre.

Désirade was built with considerable passenger accommodation and refrigerated space for a service from France to South America. Captured off St. Helena in 1941, she was ordered to Cape Town, but not all her Vichy French crew were happy about this, and there was significant sabotage to her propelling and refrigerating machinery. Some of the French crew were happy to continue, and were supplemented by officers from *Clan Cumming* (2) who were returning home from the Mediterranean, plus South Africans. *[Ambrose Greenway collection]*

1940: Transferred to Compagnie Maritime des Chargeurs Réunis, Le Havre.
2.11.1941: Captured by British warships 200 miles south of Durban whilst on a voyage from Madagascar to Dakar in a French convoy.
4.6.1942: Renamed BANGKOK II.
1.7.1942: Registered in the ownership of the Ministry of War Transport (Cayzer, Irvine and Co. Ltd., managers), London.
17.8.1945: Register closed on return to owners and reverted to BANGKOK.
1949: Transferred to Compagnie Maritime des Chargeurs Réunis S.A., Paris.
1950: Sold to Z.P. Troiano, Camberley, Surrey and put under the Honduras flag, but remained laid up at Marseille.
30.8.1954: Arrived in tow at La Spezia to be broken up by Cantiere Navale del Golfo.
6.9.1954: Work began.

The captured *Bangkok*, managed by the company as *Bangkok II*, required protracted repairs at East London and Durban. *[National Maritime Museum P21538]*

COMMANDANT DORISE 1941-1946
O.N. 167854 5,529g 3,470n
400.4 x 54.5 x 27.4 feet.
T.3-cyl. by the Mitsubishi Dockyard and Engine Works, Kobe; 510 NHP, 10.5 knots.
16.5.1917: Launched by the Mitsubishi Dockyard and Engine Works, Kobe (Yard No. 66) as KUREHA MARU.
6.1917: Completed for Compagnie des Messageries Maritime, Marseille, France as COMMANDANT DORISE.
3.11.1941: Captured by a British warship 300 miles south of Durban.
1941: Taken over by the Ministry of War Transport (Cayzer, Irvine and Co. Ltd., managers), London.
10.6.1942: Registered.
5.1944: Returned to owners.
1951: Sold to Pierre Atychides, Piraeus, Greece and renamed MARO.
1954: Sold to Kenfig Steamship Co. Ltd. (S. Catsell and Co. Ltd., managers), London and renamed SAN NICOLAS.
1955: Sold to Compania de Navegacion San Antonio Ltda., Puerto Limon, Costa Rica (L. Minacoulis) and renamed SAN NICOLOS II.
1959: Sold to Mollers Ltd., Hong Kong.
23.3.1959: Arrived at Hong Kong to be broken up by her owners.

Commandant Dorise also needed to be repaired in South Africa before entering service. She is seen in Bedford Basin, Halifax, Nova Scotia, Canada in May 1943. *[National Maritime Museum P21910]*

HOOGKERK 1945-1946
O.N. 143311 5,125g 3,205n
410.0 x 54.7 x 26.7 feet.
Q.4-cyl. by Flensburger Schiffsbau Gesellschaft, Flensburg; 563 NHP, 12 knots.
12.8.1911: Launched by Flensburger Schiffsbau Gesellschaft, Flensburg (Yard No. 312).
21.9.1911: Completed for Roland Linie A.G., Hamburg, Germany as ATTO.
4.8.1914: Seized at Antwerp by Belgian authorities and remained there until after the end of the First World War.
24.4.1919: Delivered to the UK.
3.7.1919: Registered in the ownership of the Shipping Controller (Houlder, Middleton and Co. Ltd., managers), London as ATTO.
29.12.1920: Sold to the David Steamship Co. Ltd. (William S. Mitchell, manager), London.

14.2.1921: Renamed ST. AUGUSTINE ABBEY.
14.1.1922: Register closed on sale to Vereenigde Nederlandsche Scheepvaart Maatschappij, The Hague, Holland, and renamed HOOGKERK.
4.1.1945: Registered in the ownership of the Ministry of War Transport (Cayzer, Irvine and Co. Ltd., managers), London.
1946: Owners became the Ministry of Transport.
2.8.1946: UK register closed on return to owners.
1947: Sold to Royal Netherlands Government, The Hague as a stevedore training ship at Schiedam.
1949: Renamed VETERAAN.
4.1958: Demolished by N.V. Simon's Scheepsloperij, Rotterdam.

Hoogkerk is seen in Dutch ownership, with neutrality markings. *[Newall Dunn collection]*

The Liberty *Clan Macfarlane* (3) sails from the Mersey. *[J. and M. Clarkson]*

LIBERTIES MANAGED AND OWNED

In July 1943, Clan Line was asked to provide three crews for Liberties building in the USA and which were to be transferred to the British flag. A month later this was increased to ten crews, all of whom were sent to North America to man the ships. The delivery dates quoted below come from Clan Line records, and presumably indicate when the completed ships came under British control. Known registration dates are typically months later, as they were registered only when they reached a British port. For the voyage to the UK the ships were loaded on account of United States Lines.

Unlike other British cargo liner companies who took a good number of Liberties, Clan seemed to prefer the US-built Ocean type, and in post war years bought just two of the Liberties, Sambrian becoming Clan Macfarlane and Samderwent becoming Clan Macfadyen.

Lengths quoted here are the between perpendiculars figures found in contemporary Lloyd's Registers. The overall length of the Liberties was 441.8 feet.

SAMBRIAN/CLAN MACFARLANE (3) 1943-1961

O.N. 169716 7,258g 4,424n
441.7 x 57.0 x 34.8 feet.
T.3-cyl. by the Vulcan Ironworks, Wilkes-Barre, Pennsylvania, USA; 2,500 IHP.
21.8.1943: Launched by the North Carolina Shipbuilding Corporation, Wilmington, USA (Yard No. 186) for the United States War Shipping Administration, Washington, USA as JOHN BRANCH.
27.8.1943: Delivered to the Ministry of War Transport (Cayzer, Irvine and Co. Ltd., managers), London as SAMBRIAN.
1947: Acquired by The Clan Line Steamers Ltd. (Cayzer, Irvine and Co. Ltd., managers),

London and renamed CLAN MACFARLANE.
20.4.1961: Sold to Vesta Maritime Corporation, Monrovia, Liberia (Frinton Shipbrokers Ltd. (J.N., D.N., D.S. and F.H. Inglessis), London) for £106,500 and renamed NICHOLAS under the Lebanese flag.
10.10.1961: Driven aground during a typhoon at Hachinoe, Honshu, Japan and abandoned by all except two officers. She was on a ballast voyage from Kamaishi to Vancouver.
27.10.1961: Refloated.
5.11.1961: Arrived in tow at Kanagawa, Japan and declared a constructive total loss.
25.1.1962: Arrived at Yokosuka, Japan for demolition.

SAMPENN 1943-1946

O.N. 169633 7,219g 4,380n
422.8 (b.p.) x 57.0 x 34.8 feet.
T.3-cyl. by the General Machinery Corporation, Hamilton, Ohio, USA; 2,500 IHP, 11 knots.
30.8.1943: Launched by Bethlehem-Fairfield Shipyard Inc., Baltimore,

Maryland, USA (Yard No. 2224) for the United States War Shipping Administration, Washington, USA as JOHN H. HATTON
7.9.1943: Delivered as SAMORA.
5.11.1943: Registered in the ownership of the Ministry of War Transport (Cayzer, Irvine and Co. Ltd., managers), London as SAMPENN.
20.3.1946: Owner became the Ministry of Transport, London.
30.4.1946: Managers became Charles Strubin and Co. Ltd., London.
14.9.1948: Register closed on return to the United States Maritime Commission, Washington, and laid up at Newport News.
13.9.1968: Delivered from the Reserve Fleet at Beaumont, Texas to Southern Scrap Material Company, New Orleans to be broken up.

SAMAYE 1943-1947

O.N. 180496 7,219g 4,380n
441.6 x 57.0 x 34.8 feet.
T.3-cyl. by the Worthington Pump and Machinery Corporation, Harrison, New Jersey; 2,500 IHP.
31.8.1943: Launched by Bethlehem-

Sampenn photographed by the United States Coast Guard on 4th April 1944. *[Ships in Focus collection]*

Samaye at Cardiff about 1947. [National Museums and Galleries of Wales, Department of Industry 1145/1245]

Fairfield Shipyards Inc., Baltimore, Maryland (Yard No.2223) for the United States War Shipping Administration, Washington as JAMES T. EARLE.
8.9.1943: Delivered as SAMAYE.
2.10.1943: Registered in the ownership of the the Ministry of War Transport (Cayzer, Irvine and Co. Ltd., managers), London.
30.4.1946: Owners became the Ministry of Transport, London.
21.4.1947: Sold to the Queen Line Ltd. and the Cadogan Steamship Co. Ltd. (Thomas Dunlop and Sons, managers), Glasgow and renamed QUEEN VICTORIA.
14.1.1949: Sold to the Charente Steam Ship Co. Ltd. (T. and J. Harrison, managers), Liverpool for £165,000 and renamed HISTORIAN.
19.12.1962: Sold to the Jayanti Shipping Co. Ltd., Bombay, India and renamed PARVATI JAYANTI.
6.9.1967: Damaged by Israeli gunfire in Suez Harbour.
22.2.1968: Grounded at Azenmour, 50 miles south of Casablanca, whilst on a voyage from Alexandria to Bombay with a cargo of cotton.
23.2.1968: Refloated, towed into Casablanca and subsequently declared a constructive total loss.
14.4.1968: Arrived under tow at Aviles to be broken up by Desguaces y Salvamentos S.A.

ADOLPH S. OCHS 1943-1946
O.N. 169658 7,219g 4,380n
422.8 (b.p.) x 57.0 x 34.9 feet.
T.3-cyl. by the General Machinery Corporation, Hamilton, Ohio, USA; 2,500 IHP, 11 knots.

The name *Samwyo* was hastily changed back to *Adolph S. Ochs* when those who had sponsored her objected to losing the name. In British service she was referred to as 'Adolf's Socks' which was somewhat irreverent as the ship had a distinguished war record, sailing in no fewer than six hazardous North Russian convoys. *[George Scott collection]*

23.9.1943: Launched by Bethlehem-Fairfield Shipyard Inc., Baltimore, Maryland, USA (Yard No. 2239) for the United States War Shipping Administration, Washington, USA as ADOLPH S. OCHS.
2.10.1943: Delivered as SAMWYO.
3.12.1943: Registered in the ownership of the Ministry of War Transport (Cayzer, Irvine and Co. Ltd., managers), London as ADOLPH S. OCHS.

20.3.1946: Owner became the Ministry of Transport, London.
30.4.1946: Managers became George Nisbet and Co., Glasgow.
25.6.1948: Register closed on return to the United States Maritime Commission, Washington.
13.9.1968: Delivered from the Reserve Fleet at Wilmington, North Carolina to Union Minerals and Alloys Corporation, New York and broken up at Kearny, New Jersey.

SAMNEBRA 1943-1946
O.N. 169655 7,270g 4,451n
441.7 x 57.1 x 34.8 feet.
T.3-cyl. by General Machinery
Corporation, Hamilton, Ohio, USA; 276
NHP, 2,500 IHP, 10.5 knots.
12.9.1943: Keel laid.
10.10.1943: Launched by Bethlehem-
Fairfield Shipyard Inc., Baltimore,
Maryland, USA (Yard No. 2247) for the
United States War Shipping
Administration, Washington, USA as
LYON G. TYLER.
18.10.1943: Delivered as SAMNEBRA.
3.12.1943: Registered in the ownership of
the Ministry of War Transport (Cayzer,
Irvine and Co. Ltd., managers), London.
30.4.1946: Owners became the Ministry of
Transport (Frederick C. Perman, manager),
London.
22.8.1947: Register closed on return to the
United States War Shipping
Administration, Washington.
4.9.1947: Registered in the ownership of
the Chellew Navigation Co. Ltd. (Frank C.
Perman, manager), London as PENTIRE.
4.9.1948: Manager became Baden H.
Roberts.
23.7.1955: Register closed when sold to
Compania de Navegacion Gaviota S.A.,
Panama (Mario Zoboli, Genoa, Italy) and
renamed CUACO.
18.6.1963: Arrived at Hirao, Japan to be
broken up by Matsukura K.K.
5.12.1963: Work began.

SAMOKLA 1943-1946
O.N. 169698 7,219g 4,380n
422.8 (b.p.) x 57.0 x 34.8 feet.
T.3-cyl. by the General Machinery
Corporation, Hamilton, Ohio, USA; 276
NHP, 2,500 IHP.
23.10.1943: Launched by Bethlehem-
Fairfield Shipyard Inc., Baltimore,
Maryland, USA (Yard No. 2260) for the
United States War Shipping Administration,
Washington, USA as JOSE ARTIGAS.
3.11.1943: Delivered as SAMOKLA.
20.12.1943: Registered in the ownership of
the Ministry of War Transport (Cayzer,
Irvine and Co. Ltd., managers), London.

Samnebra. *[National Maritime Museum P.23954]*

20.3.1946: Owner became the Ministry of
Transport, London.
30.4.1946: Managers became Dene
Shipping Co. Ltd., London.
19.4.1948: Returned to the United States
Maritime Commission, Washington,
renamed JOSE ARTIGAS and laid up.
9.8.1961: Delivered from the Reserve
Fleet at Wilmington, North Carolina to T.
J. Stevenson and Co. Inc., New York.
Subsequently resold and broken up at
Newport News.

SAMFIELD 1943-1947
O.N. 169765 7,219g 4,380n
441.7 x 57.0 x 34.9 feet.
T.3-cyl. by the Worthington Pump and
Machinery Corporation, Harrison, New
Jersey, USA; 276 NHP, 2,500 IHP, 11
knots.
20.11.1943: Launched by Bethlehem-
Fairfield Shipyard Inc., Baltimore,
Maryland, USA (Yard No. 2276) for the
United States War Shipping
Administration, Washington, USA as
DANIEL APPLETON.
29.11.1943: Delivered as SAMFIELD.
21.2.1944: Registered in the ownership
of the Ministry of War Transport
(Cayzer, Irvine and Co. Ltd., managers),
London.
20.3.1946: Owner became the Ministry of
Transport, London.

15.5.1947: Register closed on return to the
United States Maritime Commission,
Washington.
15.5.1947: Registered in the ownership of
the Moor Line Ltd. (William Runciman and
Co. Ltd., managers), Newcastle-upon-Tyne
as SOUTHMOOR.
10.7.1950: Sold to Marine Enterprises Ltd.
(Maurice H. Polglase, manager), London.
13.7.1950: Renamed MARINE PRIDE
18.4.1951: Register closed on sale to Mar
del Sur Compania Naviera S.A., Panama
(Lyras Brothers Ltd., London) and renamed
ST. SPERO under the Costa Rican flag.
1953: Sold to Luciferus Compania Maritima
S.A., Panama (S.G. Embiricos Ltd., London)
and renamed ENDEAVOUR under the Costa
Rican flag.
1959: Sold to Ocean Span Corporation,
Monrovia, Liberia (Ocean Carriers
Corporation (Antony Culucundis and Elias J.
Kulukundis), New York) and renamed
VALIANT LIBERTY.
1960: Renamed SKYLLAS.
1960: Sold to Taiwan Ming Sung Industrial
Co. Ltd., Taipeh, Formosa and renamed
HWEI SUNG.
30.10.1961: Grounded at Naoyetsu, Honshu,
Japan whilst discharging at anchor.
7.11.1961: Refloated. Subsequently
declared a constructive total loss.
2.1962: Broken up at Osaka by Amakasu
Sangyo Kisen K.K.

Samokla on 2nd December 1943. *[Ships in Focus collection]*

SAMDON 1944-1946
O.N. 169781 7,219g 4,380n
422.8 (b.p.) x 57.0 x 34.8 feet.
T.3-cyl. by the Springfield Machine and
Foundry Company, Springfield,
Massachusetts, USA; 276 NHP, 2,500
IHP.
20.12.1943: Launched by the New
England Shipbuilding Corporation,
Portland, Maine, USA (Yard No. 2210)
for the United States War Shipping
Administration, Washington, USA.
3.3.1944: Registered in the ownership of
the the Ministry of War Transport
(Cayzer, Irvine and Co. Ltd., managers),
London as SAMDON.

12.2.1946: Register closed on return to the United States Maritime Commission, Washington and laid up.
20.3.1961: Delivered from the Reserve Fleet at the James River to the Northern Metal Co., Philadelphia and broken up at Philadelphia.

SAMPORT 1943-1948
O.N. 169786 7,219g 4,380n
422.8 (b.p.) x 57.0 x 34.8 feet.
T.3-cyl. by the General Machinery Corporation, Hamilton, Ohio, USA; 276 NHP, 2,500 IHP.
6.12.1943: Launched by Bethlehem-Fairfield Shipyard Inc., Baltimore, Maryland, USA (Yard No. 2287) for the United States War Shipping Administration, Washington, USA as ISRAEL WHEELAN.
14.12.1943: Delivered as SAMPORT.
3.3.1944: Registered in the ownership of the Ministry of War Transport (Cayzer, Irvine and Co. Ltd., managers), London.
20.3.1946: Owner became Ministry of Transport.
28.4.1948: Register closed on return to the United States Maritime Commission, Washington and renamed ISRAEL WHEELAN.
14.11.1962: Delivered from the Reserve Fleet at Mobile Bay, Alabama to Union Minerals and Alloys Corporation and demolished at Panama City, Florida.

SAMBALT 1943-1946
O.N. 169766 7,219g 4,380n
441.6 x 57.0 x 34.8 feet.
T.3-cyl. by the General Machinery Corporation, Hamilton, Ohio, USA. 2,500 IHP, 11.5 knots.
9.12.1943: Launched by Bethlehem-Fairfield Shipyard Inc., Baltimore, Maryland, USA (Yard No. 2290) for the United States War Shipping Administration, Washington, USA as ROBERT WICKLIFFE.
18.12.1943: Delivered to the Ministry of War Transport (Cayzer, Irvine and Co. Ltd., managers), London as SAMBALT.
30.4.1946: Owners became the Ministry of Transport, London (David Alexander and Sons, Glasgow, managers).
18.4.1947: Returned to United States War Shipping Administration, Washington.
4.1947: Sold to Mollers Ltd., Hong Kong and renamed LILIAN MOLLER.
15.4.1948: Sold to the Charente Steamship Co. Ltd. (T. and J. Harrison, managers), Liverpool and subsequently renamed SPEAKER.
1.3.1962: Sold to Epos Marine Enterprises S.A., Panama (J.C. Yemelos, Piraeus, Greece) and renamed BYZANTION under the Greek flag.
1965: Managers became J.C. Carras and Sons (Shipbrokers) Ltd., London.

Samchess. [Ships in Focus collection]

6.4.1967: Stranded near Ras Gombo Lighthouse, Assab.
9.4.1967: Refloated, but when dry docked at Livorno found to be severely damaged.
1969: Sold to Koshin Sangyo K.K., Japan to be broken up.
5.5.1969: Demolition began at Onomichi, Japan.

SAMCHESS 1944-1946
O.N. 169823 7,219g 4,380n
441.7 x 57.0 x 34.9 feet.
T.3-cyl. by the General Machinery Corporation, Hamilton, Ohio, USA; 276 NHP, 2,500 IHP, 11 knots.
20.1.1944: Launched by Bethlehem-Fairfield Shipyard Inc., Baltimore, USA (Yard No. 2312).
1.1944: Completed.
24.3.1944: Registered in the ownership of the Ministry of War Transport (Cayzer, Irvine and Co. Ltd., managers), London as SAMCHESS.
20.3.1946: Owners became Ministry of Transport, London.
25.7.1946: Manager became Robert S. Dalgleish, Newcastle-upon-Tyne.
28.5.1947: Register closed on return to United States Maritime Commission, Washington.
29.5.1947: Registered in the ownership of the Alpha South African Steamship Co. Ltd. (Moller Line S.A. (Proprietary) Ltd.), Durban, South Africa as ALPHA MOOI.
14.7.1948: Sold to the Somerset Shipping Co. Ltd. (Counties Ship Management Ltd., managers), London.
26.7.1948: Renamed PORLOCK HILL.
21.12.1951: Stranded during a gale two miles south east of Famagusta, Cyprus whilst on a voyage from Southampton to Port Said with army stores

22.12.1951: Broke in two. Subsequently salvaged.
29.4.1952: Both parts of ship arrived at Alexandria in tow for discharge.
14.5.1952: Arrived at Palermo for demolition.
14.7.1952: Register closed.

SAMDERWENT/CLAN MACFADYEN (3) 1944-1958
O.N. 169959 7,219g 4,427n
441.7 x 57.0 x 34.84 feet.
T.3-cyl. by the Springfield Machinery and Foundry Company, Springfield, Massachussetts, USA; 2,500 IHP.
7.3.1943: Launched by the New England Shipbuilding Corporation, Portland, Maine, USA (Yard No. 2224) for the United States War Shipping Administration, Washington, USA.
14.3.1944: Completed for lease to the Ministry of War Transport (Cayzer, Irvine and Co. Ltd., managers), London as SAMDERWENT.
1947: Acquired by The Clan Line Steamers Ltd. (Cayzer, Irvine and Co. Ltd., managers), London and renamed CLAN MACFADYEN.
22.5.1958: Sold to Compania Naviera Betacruz S.A., Panama (Adolphi Vergottis Ltd., London) for £125,000 and renamed BETAVISTA under the Liberian flag.
1968: Sold to Thakur Shipping Co. Ltd., Bombay, India, and renamed VARUNA DEVI.
31.3.1971: Arrived at Hong Kong and sold to Wallem and Company for breaking up.
21.4.1971: Arrived at Kaohsiung under tow for demolition by Nan Feng Steel Enterprise Company.
30.4.1971: Work began.
10.5.1971: Work completed.

Samderwent in a South Wales port (top). *[National Museums and Galleries of Wales, Department of Industry, Hansen 1192/ 1292]. Clan Macfadyen* (3) photographed on the Mersey on 3rd July 1947 in early peacetime colours and still with wartime rig (middle), and later with a white topside strake and with topmasts on the fore and mizzen masts (bottom). *[J. and M. Clarkson collection]*

Whilst *Clan Macfadyen* was discharging at Queen Elizabeth II Quay at Colombo in May 1957, one of guys attached to the starboard derrick at number 4 hatch carried away as a sling of cargo was going overside. The derrick ended up wrapped round the mast stay, like a bent elbow. *[Brian Smith]*

HEAVY-LIFT SHIPS MANAGED

EMPIRE ELAINE 1942-1947

O.N. 167744 7,513g 5,133n
433.4 x 66.7 x 31.0 feet.
3-cyl. 2SCSA oil engine by William
Doxford and Sons Ltd., Sunderland;
516 NHP, 12 knots.
30.7.1942: Launched by Vickers-
Armstrongs Ltd., Barrow-in-Furness
(Yard No. 856).
23.10.1942: Registered in the
ownership of the Ministry of War
Transport (Cayzer, Irvine and Co. Ltd.,
managers), London as EMPIRE
ELAINE.
6.11.1942: Completed.
1946: Owners became the Ministry of
Transport, London.
1947: Sold to Marine Enterprises Ltd.,
London and renamed JOHN LYRAS
1952: Managers became Lyras Brothers
Ltd.
1959: Transferred to Viking Shipping
Corporation, Piraeus, Greece (Lyras
Brothers Ltd., London).
1964: Transferred to the Liberian flag.
1970: Sold to New Frontier Shipping
Co. Inc., Panama (Grindrod, Gersigny
and Co., Durban, South Africa) and
renamed BOUNDARY
Prior to 9.9.1972: Arrived at Kaohsiung
for breaking up by the Yi Ho Steel
Corporation.
11.10.1972: Work began.

Empire Elaine (lower middle) was
the first of a group of nine heavy lift
ships ordered by the British
government to a design based on
ships built pre-war for Christen
Smith of Oslo, with derrick capacity
increased to 120 tons. Company
management resulted from Clan's
experience with heavy loads, but
the company disdained these ships
in post-war years, and did not
acquire either of those it managed,
although at least one, *Empire
Byng*, was chartered. In 1947
Empire Elaine was sold to London
Greeks and became *John Lyras*
(right). *[Lower middle: National
Maritime Museum; right: Ships in
Focus]*

Clan Macfadyen under the Indian flag as *Varuna Devi*. *[Roy Fenton collection]*

207

EMPIRE CANUTE 1946-1947

7,750g 4,475n
469.9 x 66.7 x 31.0 feet.
Steam turbine by the General Electric Company, Erith, driving a single screw through electric motors.
10.1954: 8-cyl. 2SCSA oil engine by Bremer-Vulkan, Vegesack, West Germany.
24.12.1945: Launched by the Greenock Dockyard Co. Ltd., Greenock (Yard No. 462) for the Ministry of War Transport, London as EMPIRE CANUTE.
1946: Managers became Cayzer, Irvine and Co. Ltd., London.
6.1947: Completed for Belships Co. Ltd. Skibs A/S (Christen Smith and Co., managers), Oslo, Norway as BELOCEAN
10.1954: Re-engined.
1964: Sold to Bacong Shipping Co. S.A., Panama (Southern Industrial Products Inc, Manila, Philippines) and renamed SOUTHERN SUN.
1968: Sold to Manila Interocean Lines Inc., Manila and renamed MARIE ANN.
29.7.1976: Arrived at Gadani Beach to be broken up.

The last Empire heavy lift ship built, *Empire Canute* was probably entrusted to the company's management by default, as at the end of the war she was left incomplete in the wholly-owned shipyard at Greenock. Fitting out began in November 1946 and she was completed in the following June for Christen Smith and Co.of Oslo as *Belocean* (above). As she never sailed under the British flag, management could not have been arduous for Cayzer, Irvine. *[Glasgow University Archives GD323/7/9/ 2/462/2]*

Again because of their heavy-load capability, two moderate-sized ships were managed by the company for the government. *Empire Malta* (middle) was photographed on trials, and close ups of her cargo gear (bottom) were taken whilst she was alongside. With several others of this small, West Hartlepool-built class, she was sold to work in the east. Renamed *Hangsang* (opposite top left) she was used mainly in the timber trade between North Borneo and Hong Kong. *[Middle and lower: Yeoman and Co./ Newall Dunn collection (3); opposite top left: Ambrose Greenway collection]*

EMPIRE MALTA 1944-1946
O.N. 180072 3,610g 2,265n
328.0 x 46.5 x 22.1 feet.
T.3-cyl. by the Central Marine Engine
Works, West Hartlepool.
24.3.1944: Launched by William Gray and
Co. Ltd., West Hartlepool (Yard No. 1167).
19.5.1944: Registered in the ownership of
the Ministry of War Transport (Cayzer,
Irvine and Co. Ltd., managers), London as
EMPIRE MALTA.

1946: Sold to S.T. Williamson, Hong Kong.
1946: Sold to Indo-China Steam
Navigation Co. Ltd., Hong Kong and
renamed HANGSANG.
11.1960: Sold to Continental Enterprises
and Navigation Ltd., Hong Kong (Far East
Corporation Ltd., Singapore) and renamed
SLIGHT WIND.
12.1964: Sold to Sunbeam Navigation Co.
S.A., Panama (Patt, Manfield and Co. Ltd.,
Hong Kong) and renamed SUNBEAM.

23.7.1969: Engine failed in position 13.56
north by 114.30 east whilst on a voyage
from Malaysia to Kaohsiung. She was
towed to Kaohsiung, discharged, and laid
up.
30.11.1970: Breaking up began by Keun
Hwa Iron and Steel Works and Enterprises
Ltd. at Kaohsiung.
10.12.1970: Work completed.

Empire Perlis under the Hong Kong flag as the *Hinsang* (top right) and under her original name (above) in the Mersey: for a comparatively small ship she has impressively heavy derricks which were replaced with lighter ones in peacetime. *[Top right: Ambrose Greenway collection, above: National Maritime Museum P.22420]*

EMPIRE PERLIS 1944-1946
O.N. 180074 3,610g 2,265n
328.0 x 46.5 x 22.1 feet.
T.3-cyl. by the Central Marine Engine
Works, West Hartlepool.
22.5.1944: Launched by William Gray and
Co. Ltd., West Hartlepool (Yard No. 1168).
28.7.1944: Registered in the ownership of
the Ministry of War Transport (Cayzer,

Irvine and Co. Ltd., managers), London as
EMPIRE PERLIS.
7.1946: Sold to Indo-China Steam
Navigation Co. Ltd., Hong Kong and
renamed HINSANG.
3.1965: Sold to Kinabatangan Shipping Co.
Ltd. (United China Shipping Co. Ltd.),
Hong Kong and renamed KOWLOON.
12.1968: Transferred to Concordia

Kinabantangan Shipping Co. S.A., Panama
(United China Shipping Co. Ltd., Hong
Kong) and renamed HORIS.
29.12.1969: Abandoned, capsized and sank
in the Celebes Sea, 200 miles off Tawau,
Sabah in position 03.53 north by 119.23
east after water entered her hold and engine
room during a voyage from Surabaja to
Hong Kong with general cargo.

SPLIT-SUPERSTRUCTURE EMPIRES ACQUIRED

Replacing Clan's war losses with purpose-built ships was going to be a protracted and expensive business, so the company invested heavily in the various standard ships built for the British government. This process got under way as early as the summer of 1943, following an agreement between the Ministry of War Transport and the General Council of British Shipping. Clan bought three existing freighters at cost price less depreciation on the understanding that they were to continue under Ministry control. The outward sign of the change was that they went under Cayzer, Irvine management,

formal transfer to Clan and renaming not occurring until late 1945 or early 1946.

In 1946 Clan took on bareboat charter for a period of five years a further three British war-built ships plus seven of the Ocean type. The Ministry refused to allow Clan to rename them, and they operated with their original names although in Clan colours. Late in 1947 the company exercised its option to purchase, and at the very end of that year they became Clan vessels.

All of the group in the following list were of the split superstructure type, but not all were identical. The majority were of the B type, the most numerous tramp types built in British yards during the war, and which

had a distinctly wide gap between funnel and bunker hatch kingposts, plus a full height forecastle. Clan Alpine was to a design of J.L. Thompson and Sons Ltd. of Sunderland which could be distinguished by the closeness of the funnel and the king posts to the bunker hatch and by its flush deck. Not surprisingly her profile was like that of the Ocean and the Fort and Park types which were themselves based on a Thompson design. The Stirlingshire from Harland and Wolff was built to the X type, an early standard design, and was relatively unusual in being diesel-driven. The distinctly different D-types are listed separately.

Seen at Cape Town in original (above) and later condition (below), *Clan Angus* was originally transferred to the company's management in July 1943 as *Empire Prince*. The three 'Clan A' ships spent time under the ownership of Bullard, King, presumably to suit conference arrangements. [Above: R.M. Scott/Newall Dunn Collection; below: Ships in Focus]

EMPIRE PRINCE/CLAN ANGUS 1943-1956/1959-1962

O.N. 166214 7,015g 4,225n
446.3 x 56.3 x 35.2 feet.
T.3-cyl. by the North Eastern Marine Engineering Co. (1938) Ltd., Newcastle-upon-Tyne.
31.3.1942: Launched by the Caledon Shipbuilding and Engineering Co. Ltd., Dundee (Yard No. 394).
13.5.1942: Registered in the ownership of the Ministry of War Transport, London (Gibbs and Co., Cardiff, managers) as EMPIRE PRINCE.
22.7.1943: Managers became Cayzer, Irvine and Co. Ltd., London.
3.1.1946: Acquired by The Clan Line Steamers Ltd. (Cayzer, Irvine and Co. Ltd., managers), London for £181,000 and renamed CLAN ANGUS.
1.6.1956: Transferred to Bullard, King and Co. Ltd., London, and renamed UMKUZI.

9.1959: Transferred to The Clan Line Steamers Ltd. (Cayzer, Irvine and Co. Ltd., managers), London and renamed CLAN ANGUS.
22.4.1962: Arrived in Hirao Roads, Japan.

2.7.1962: Handed over to Kinoshita K.K., Tokyo for demolition having been sold for £61,400.
20.10.1962: Work began at Hirao.

EMPIRE FOREST/CLAN ALLAN 1943-1958/1959-1961

O.N. 168653 7,043g 4,261n
446.4 x 56.2 x 35.2 feet.
T.3-cyl. by John Readhead and Sons Ltd., South Shields.

15.1.1942: Launched by John Readhead and Sons Ltd., South Shields (Yard No. 526).

14.3.1942: Registered in the ownership of the Ministry of War Transport, London (Smith, Hogg and Co., West Hartlepool, managers) as EMPIRE FOREST.

13.8.1943: Managers became Cayzer, Irvine and Co. Ltd., London.

2.12.1945: Acquired by The Clan Line Steamers Ltd. (Cayzer, Irvine and Co. Ltd., managers), London, for £180,000 and renamed CLAN ALLAN.

21.3.1958: Transferred to Bullard, King and Co. Ltd., London and renamed UMTALI.

9.1959: Transferred to The Clan Line Steamers Ltd. (Cayzer, Irvine and Co. Ltd., managers), London and renamed CLAN ALLAN.

1.6.1961: Transferred to King Line Ltd. (Cayzer, Irvine and Co. Ltd., managers), London.

6.8.1961: Sold to Mullion and Co. Ltd., Hong Kong for £97,500 and renamed ARDSIROD.

12.10.1966: Arrived at Kaohsiung to be broken up by the China National Machinery Import and Export Corporation.

27.10.1966: Work began.

Clan Angus as *Umkuzi* at Cape Town in April 1958. *[J. and M. Clarkson collection]*

A somewhat war-weary *Empire Forest* prepares to enter the Manchester Ship Canal at Eastham (above). As *Clan Allan* (below) she received a new funnel and topmasts, and looked altogether brighter in Clan's later livery. *[Above: National Maritime Museum P.22294; below: FotoFlite/J. and M. Clarkson collection]*

EMPIRE BARRIE/CLAN ALPINE (4) 1943-1957

O.N. 169016 7,103g 4,265n
441.5 x 57.2 x 34.9 feet.
T.3-cyl. by George Clark (1938) Ltd., Sunderland.

17.1.1942: Launched by J.L. Thompson and Sons Ltd., Sunderland (Yard No. 615).

7.4.1942: Registered in the ownership of the Ministry of War Transport, London (Allan, Black and Company, Sunderland, managers) as EMPIRE BARRIE.

26.8.1943: Managers became Cayzer, Irvine and Co. Ltd., London.

28.11.1945: Acquired by The Clan Line Steamers Ltd. (Cayzer, Irvine and Co. Ltd.), London for £173,000 and renamed CLAN ALPINE.

1957: Transferred to Bullard, King and Co. Ltd., London and renamed UMVOTI.

9.1959: Transferred to The Clan Line Steamers Ltd. (Cayzer, Irvine and Co. Ltd., managers), London and renamed CLAN ALPINE.

10.11.1960: Driven from her moorings at Chittagong by a cyclone and deposited in paddy fields at Shonai Chori, 11 miles north north west from the entrance to the Karanfuli River whilst on passage with general cargo from Glasgow to Chittagong, from where she was to continue Japan. Subsequently declared a constructive total loss.

31.1.1961: Sold to Koshin Sangyo K.K., Kobe for £65,000 for scrap.

14.2.1961: Sold for £46,000 to East Bengal Trading Corporation Ltd., Pakistan, who demolished vessel as she lay.

Empire Barrie (top) became *Clan Alpine* (middle and bottom) when acquired by Clan in November 1945. Compare the gap between the funnel and kingposts, and the bulwark plating alongside the accommodation with these features in the views of *Clan Allan* and *Clan Angus*. [Top: National Maritime Museum P.22218, middle: B. and A. Feilden/J. and M. Clarkson collection, bottom: FotoFlite]

Clan Alpine (4) was the subject of tests on her hull, which followed worrying accidents in which all-welded ships built in the United States broke in two. Clan Alpine was chosen as she was wholly riveted, and her behaviour under stress was compared with the wholly-welded Ocean Vulcan. In the summer of 1946 Clan Alpine was first sent to the Tyne to have instrumentation fitted and then proceeded to Falmouth where bending tests were carried out by flooding various combinations of holds and measuring the strain on the hull with an array of gauges. [Imperial War Museum: A31359, A31360, A31367 and A31364]

Clan Alpine's end was almost farcical. Sold to Japanese breakers, she made one final voyage east but before she could discharge her last cargo at Chittagong she was blown inland by a cyclone, ending up in a paddy field some distance from the sea. A water supply was arranged so that her steam machinery could run and work her winches, and cargo was discharged into trucks. There was no economical way to refloat the ship, which was already on the way to the scrap yard, and she was sold to local breakers who demolished her on the spot. *Clan Mackinnon* (3) also broke adrift in the same cyclone, but damage was minimal. *[Top: Newall Dunn collection, middle left: Andy Skarstein, others: John R. Woodley]*

EMPIRE CATO/CLAN MACKENZIE
(4) 1946-1960

O.N. 168949 7,025g 4,850n
446.3 x 56.2 x 35.2 feet.
T.3-cyl. by the Central Marine Engine
Works, West Hartlepool.
10.11.1942: Launched by William Gray and
Co. Ltd., West Hartlepool (Yard No. 1138).
21.12.1942: Registered in the ownership of
the Ministry of War Transport (Hain
Steamship Co. Ltd., managers), London as
EMPIRE CATO.
12.4.1946: Bareboat chartered by The Clan
Line Steamers Ltd. (Cayzer, Irvine and Co.
Ltd., managers), London.
31.12.1947: Acquired by The Clan Line
Steamers Ltd. (Cayzer, Irvine and Co. Ltd.,
managers), London for £107,833.
1948: Renamed CLAN MACKENZIE.
1960: Sold to Wheelock, Marden and Co.
Ltd., Hong Kong.
14.10.1960: Arrived at Hong Kong.
11.1960: Breaking up began.

Empire Cato sails from Cape Town in June 1946 (top), soon after being taken on charter by Clan, and is seen again as *Clan Mackenzie* (4) with Clan funnel (middle), and Scottish Shire colours in company with a steam collier (bottom). *[Top: R.M. Scott/Newall Dunn collection; middle: B. and A. Feilden/J. and M. Clarkson; bottom: J. and M. Clarkson collection]*

EMPIRE PICKWICK/CLAN MACKENDRICK 1946-1961

O.N. 169053 7,068g 4,851n
446.2 x 56.2 x 35.2 feet.
T.3-cyl. by John Readhead and Sons Ltd., South Shields.
31.8.1943: Launched by John Readhead and Sons Ltd., South Shields (Yard No. 536).
25.10.1943: Registered in the ownership of the Ministry of War Transport, London (Donaldson Brothers and Black Ltd., Glasgow, managers) as EMPIRE PICKWICK.
11.1943: Completed.
1946: Managers became Cayzer, Irvine and Co. Ltd.
25.5.1946: Bareboat chartered by The Clan Line Steamers Ltd. (Cayzer, Irvine and Co. Ltd., managers), London.
31.12.1947: Acquired by The Clan Line Steamers Ltd. (Cayzer, Irvine and Co. Ltd., managers), London for £115,426 and renamed CLAN MACKENDRICK.
28.3.1961: Sold to Mullion and Co. Ltd., Hong Kong for £77,500 and renamed ARDPATRICK.
1966: Sold to the National Shipping Corporation, Karachi, Pakistan and renamed HARINGHATA.
16.7.1968: Arrived at Karachi for repairs which were deferred.
7.5.1969: Breaking up began by Ghanchi Rerolling Mills, Karachi.

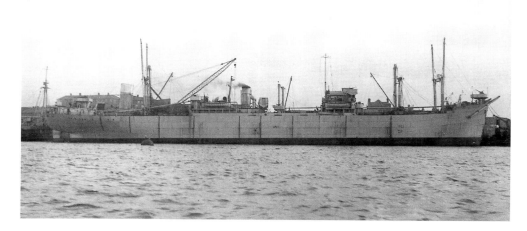

Empire Pickwick (top) was transferred to company ownership in 1946 after Clan committed to purchase her. As *Clan Mackendrick* (middle) she had the dubious distinction of being the last of the company's war-built acquisitions to burn coal, not being converted to oil firing until mid 1952. In 1966 she was sold to one of Clan's rivals, the National Shipping Corporation of Karachi and renamed *Haringhata* (bottom). *[Top: National Maritime Museum; middle: B. and A. Feilden/J. and M. Clarkson; bottom: Warwick Foote]*

EMPIRE LANKESTER/ CLAN MACKELLAR (2) 1946-1961

O.N. 180071 7,067g 4,844n
446.3 x 56.2 x 35.2 feet.
T.3-cyl. by the Central Marine Engine Works, West Hartlepool.

24.2.1944: Launched by William Gray and Co. Ltd., West Hartlepool (Yard No. 1161)

26.4.1944: Registered in the ownership of the Ministry of War Transport, London (Joseph Robinson and Sons, North Shields, managers) as EMPIRE LANKESTER.

27.8.1946: Bareboat chartered by The Clan Line Steamers Ltd. (Cayzer, Irvine and Co. Ltd., managers), London.

31.12.1947: Acquired by The Clan Line Steamers Ltd. (Cayzer, Irvine and Co. Ltd., managers), London for £121,236 and renamed CLAN MACKELLAR.

6.2.1961: Transferred to King Line Ltd. (Cayzer, Irvine and Co. Ltd., managers), London for £77,500.

10.5.1961: Sold to Mullion and Co. Ltd., Hong Kong and renamed ARDGROOM.

20.2.1967: Delivered to Lee Sing Company, Hong Kong for demolition.

20.3.1967: Work commenced.

HESIONE (2) 1946-1960

O.N. 169050 7,044g 4,869n
446.4 x 56.2 x 35.2 feet.
T.3-cyl. by John Readhead and Sons Ltd., South Shields; 558 NHP, 2,550 IHP; 11 knots.

20.1.1943: Launched by John Readhead and Sons Ltd., South Shields (Yard No. 532).

9.3.1943: Registered in the ownership of the Ministry of War Transport (Glen Line Ltd., managers), London as EMPIRE CAPULET.

5.1946: Acquired by the British and South American Steam Navigation Co. Ltd. (Houston Line (London) Ltd., managers), London for £140,000 and renamed HESIONE.

1957: Owners became Houston Line Ltd. (Cayzer, Irvine and Co. Ltd., managers), London.

5.10.1960: Arrived at Hong Kong for demolition by Shun Hing Ironworks Ltd.

28.10.1960: Demolition commenced.

Clan Mackellar (2) in the Mersey with a substantial deck cargo. *[B. and A. Feilden/J. and M. Clarkson]*

Empire Capulet (middle) was bought in 1946 and renamed *Hesione* as which she ran in Houston ownership until disposal 14 years later (bottom). *[Middle: Archie Munro collection; bottom: Fotoflite]*

STIRLINGSHIRE (2) 1946-1963

O.N. 168536 7,006g 4,080n
448.0 x 56.3 x 34.3 feet.
6-cyl. 4SCSA oil engine by Harland and
Wolff Ltd., Glasgow.
2.9.1944: Launched by Harland and Wolff
Ltd., Belfast (Yard No. 1276).
1.2.1945: Registered in the ownership of
the Ministry of War Transport (Blue Star
Line Ltd., managers), London as EMPIRE
FALKLAND.
21.2.1945: Completed.
15.5.1946: Acquired by the Scottish Shire
Line Ltd. (Turnbull, Martin and Co. Ltd.,

managers), London for £326,500 and
renamed STIRLINGSHIRE.
20.9.1960: Transferred to Houston Line
Ltd. (Cayzer, Irvine and Co. Ltd.,
managers), London.
1963: Transferred to Huntley, Cook and
Co. Ltd., London.
1965: Transferred to Houston Line Ltd.
(Cayzer, Irvine and Co. Ltd., managers),
London.
2.9.1966: Delivered at Ghent for
demolition by Van Heyghen Frères having
been sold for £60,000.

The X-type standard ship *Stirlingshire*
had a squat motor ship funnel. *[Top :
FotoFlite, left: J. and M. Clarkson
collection, above: Roy Fenton collection]*

EMPIRE D TYPE

*Clan had a propensity for the
prefabricated D type ship built as part of
the British wartime standard ship
programme, with their distinctive
composite superstructure and V-shaped
transom sterns. Three of these which had
been managed from new were bought in
1946, and two more of the class bought*

*for Houston on completion, to become
Hesperia and Hesperides. Just as in the
aftermath of the First World War, these
standard ships were the only newbuildings
Houston received during the company's
ownership by Clan.*

*Clan may also have contem-
plated buying another of the type, Empire
Ronaldsay (7,331/1947), building at the*

*Shipbuilding Corporation yard on the
Wear, and a price of £209,500 is mentioned
in the board minutes for March 1946.
However, the ship's completion was
delayed by lack of materials, which
probably caused the sale to Clan to fall
through, and she was completed in July
1947 as* Lagosian *for the United Africa Co.
Ltd., London*

EMPIRE FAWLEY/CLAN MACKINLAY (2) 1945-1962

O.N. 180221 7,382g 4,685n
449.0 x 56.3 x 35.6 feet.
T.3-cyl. by Vickers-Armstrongs Ltd.,
Barrow-in-Furness.
25.4.1945: Launched by John Readhead
and Sons Ltd., South Shields (Yard No.
545).
5.1945: Completed.
27.6.1945: Registered in the ownership of
the Ministry of War Transport (Cayzer,
Irvine and Co. Ltd., London, managers),
London as EMPIRE FAWLEY.
1946: Acquired by The Clan Line
Steamers Ltd. (Cayzer, Irvine and Co. Ltd.,
managers), London for £198,500 and
renamed CLAN MACKINLAY.
2.11.1962: Arrived at Hong Kong for
demolition, having been sold for £56,050.
6.11.1962: Delivered to Hong Kong
Salvage and Towage Company Ltd.
24.11.1962: Demolition commenced by
Peninsula Shipbreaking Company, Hong
Kong.

EMPIRE DUNNET/CLAN MACKINNON (3) 1945-1961

O.N. 180086 7,373g 4,611n
449.0 x 56.2 x 35.6 feet.
T.3-cyl. by the Central Marine Engine
Works, West Hartlepool.
10.7.1945: Launched by William Gray and
Co. Ltd., West Hartlepool (Yard No.
1177).
19.9.1945: Registered in the ownership of
the Ministry of War Transport (Cayzer,
Irvine and Co. Ltd., managers), London as
EMPIRE DUNNET.
13.9.1946: Acquired by The Clan Line
Steamers Ltd. (Cayzer, Irvine and Co. Ltd.,
managers), London for £203,500 and
renamed CLAN MACKINNON.
15.12.1954: Transferred to the British and
South American Steam Navigation Co.
Ltd. (Houston Line (London) Ltd.,
managers), London for £79,000.
1957: Transferred to Houston Line Ltd.
(Cayzer, Irvine and Co. Ltd., managers),
London.
22.7.1960: Transferred to The Clan Line
Steamers Ltd. (Cayzer, Irvine and Co. Ltd.,
managers), London.
16.2.1961: Transferred to King Line Ltd.
(Cayzer, Irvine and Co. Ltd., managers),
London for £85,000.
1961: Sold to Mullion and Co. Ltd., Hong
Kong and renamed ARDROSS.
1962: Sold to Kinabatangan Shipping Co.
Ltd. (United China Shipping Co. Ltd.),
Hong Kong and renamed LABUAN BAY.
1963: Transferred to Concordia
Kinabatangan Shipping Co. Ltd., Panama
(United China Shipping Co. Ltd., Hong
Kong).
27.10.1967: Arrived at Hong Kong and
subsequently sold for demolition at
Kaohsiung.
9.11.1967: Arrived at Kaohsiung.

Clan Mackinlay (2) escorted by a 'Cock' tug in the Mersey and at anchor, with only one topmast. *[Both: J. and M. Clarkson collection]*

Clan Mackinnon (3) on the Mersey in a colour scheme which was not generally adopted, with two white ribbons, one between hull colour and boot topping and one just below the upper white strake (middle). In the bottom view she is seen at anchor on the Thames. *[Upper: S.G. Docker/Roy Fenton collection; bottom: Ships in Focus]*

EMPIRE GUNFLEET/CLAN MACKAY (5) 1945-1962

O.N. 180223 7,389g 5,255n
449.0 x 56.3 x 35.6 feet.
T.3-cyl. by John Readhead and Sons Ltd., South Shields.
10.8.1945: Launched by John Readhead and Sons Ltd., South Shields (Yard No. 547).
5.11.1945: Registered in the ownership of the Ministry of War Transport (Cayzer, Irvine and Co. Ltd., managers), London as EMPIRE GUNFLEET.
9.8.1946: Acquired by The Clan Line Steamers Ltd. (Cayzer, Irvine and Co. Ltd., managers), London for £204,500 and renamed CLAN MACKAY.
6.6.1962: Sold to Compania de Navigation Victoria Neptuno S.A., Panama (Teh-Hu Steamship Company, Hong Kong, managers) for £63,395 and renamed BABYLON.
25.9.1966: Laid up at Hong Kong.
15.2.1966: Ming Hing Company, Hong Kong, commenced demolition.

HESPERIA (2)/CLAN MURDOCH (2) 1946-1962

O.N. 180865 7,375g 4,738n
449.0 x 56.0 x 35.6 feet.
T.3-cyl. by the North Eastern Marine Engineering Co. (1938) Ltd., Sunderland; 2,500 IHP.
16.1.1946: Launched by Bartram and Sons Ltd., Sunderland (Yard No. 306) for the Ministry of War Transport, London as EMPIRE SOUTHWOLD.
15.5.1946: Registered in the ownership of the British and South American Steam Navigation Co. Ltd. (Houston Line (London) Ltd., managers), London as HESPERIA having been acquired for £209,500.
1957: Owners became Houston Line Ltd. (Cayzer, Irvine and Co. Ltd., managers), London.

Clan Mackay (5) (top) and as *Babylon* (above) under the flag of Panama. *[Top: Roy Fenton collection, above: Ships in Focus collection]*

Hesperia (2) showing the distinctive transom of the D type, off Gravesend on 11th June 1960. *[F.W. Hawks/Roy Fenton collection]*

Clan Murdoch (left) and in September 1976 as the *Denizhanlar* in Turkish waters (right). *[Left: Archie Munro collection, right: Malcolm Cranfield/J. and M. Clarkson collection]*

22.7.1960: Transferred to The Clan Line Steamers Ltd. (Cayzer, Irvine and Co. Ltd., managers), London and renamed CLAN MURDOCH.

23.10.1961: Transferred to King Line Ltd. (Cayzer, Irvine and Co. Ltd., managers), London.

22.1.1962: Sold to Sadikzade Rusen Ogullari Denizcilik Limited Kollektif, Istanbul, Turkey and renamed MUSTAFA.

1974: Sold to Hakan Vapuru Donatma Istiraki (Ziya Sonmez, manager), Istanbul for £138,500.

1974: Transferred to Denizhanlar Vapuru Donatma Istraki (Ziya Sonmez, manager), Istanbul and renamed DENIZHANLAR.

3.1979: Zeki Verel began demolition at Aliaga, Turkey.

HESPERIDES (2)/CLAN MURRAY (4) 1946-1962

O.N. 180929 7,375g 4,738n
449.0 x 56.0 x 35.6 feet
T.3-cyl. by the North Eastern Marine Engineering Co. (1938) Ltd., Sunderland; 2,500 IHP.

2.5.1946: Launched by the Shipbuilding Corporation Ltd. (Wear Branch), Sunderland (Yard No. 9) for the Ministry of Transport, London as EMPIRE LONGSTONE.

Hesperides (above) and lit by evening light as *Clan Murray* (4) (below). *[Above: FotoFlite/J. and M. Clarkson collection, below: Ships in Focus]*

12.8.1946: Registered in the ownership of the British and South American Steam Navigation Co. Ltd. (Houston Line (London) Ltd., managers), London as HESPERIDES.

1957: Owners became Houston Line Ltd. (Cayzer, Irvine and Co. Ltd., managers), London.

26.8.1960: Transferred to The Clan Line Steamers Ltd. (Cayzer, Irvine and Co. Ltd., managers), London and renamed CLAN MURRAY.

25.11.1962: Arrived at Hirao.

28.11.1962: Delivered to Matsukura K.K.

15.12.1962: Breaking up began at Hirao.

OCEANS, CHARTERED AND BOUGHT

Along with the three Empires mentioned above, Clan first took on bareboat charter and then at the end of 1947 bought seven of the Ocean type, built by two shipyards in the United States for British Government account. An oddity of these ships was that official registration as a British ship was often long delayed, in several cases until over a year after completion. Ships bought abroad were allowed to trade on a temporary British registration issued by a consul for six months, or until they first visited a British port. No doubt this period was extended in wartime.

An interesting little quirk is that those built at Portland, Maine were given Clan names beginning Macb, whilst those from Richmond, California were given Clan names beginning with the letter K. Two more Oceans, one from each of these yards, broke this rule when transferred from a recently acquired subsidiary in 1950 and 1951, becoming Clan Macqueen *and* Clan Macquarrie. *The* Hellenes, *similarly transferred in 1952, brought the total to ten giving the largest fleet of Oceans under non-government ownership.*

Ocean Glory leaves no doubt she is a coal burner (upper). As *Clan Macbeth* (2) she was photographed on 1st May 1949 with the white line at boot topping level (lower). She was converted to burn oil fuel in July 1950. *[Upper: R.M. Scott/Ships in Focus; lower: John McRoberts/J. and M. Clarkson]*

OCEAN GLORY/CLAN MACBETH (2) 1946-1959

O.N. 169176 7,178g 4,352n
441.5 x 57.0 x 34.8 feet.
T.3-cyl. by John Inglis and Co. Ltd, Toronto, Ontario, Canada; 505 NHP, 2,500 IHP.
18.10.1942: Launched by the Todd-Bath Iron Shipbuilding Corporation, South Portland, Maine, USA (Yard No. 30).
11.1942: Completed.
13.12.1943: Registered in the ownership of the Ministry of War Transport (J. and C. Harrison, managers), London as OCEAN GLORY.
1946: Bareboat chartered by The Clan Line Steamers Ltd. (Cayzer, Irvine and Co. Ltd., managers), London.
31.12.1947: Acquired by The Clan Line Steamers Ltd. (Cayzer, Irvine and Co. Ltd., managers), London for £107,343 and renamed CLAN MACBETH.
7.1950: Converted to burn oil fuel.
4.4.1959: Sold to Panamanian Oriental Steamship Corporation, Panama (Wheelock, Marden and Co. Ltd., Hong Kong) for £70,000 and renamed MADONNA.
1961: Sold to Sincere Navigation Corporation (V.K. Eddie Hsu), Taipeh, Taiwan and renamed SINCERE TRADER.
15.10.1964: Left Osaka for Kaohsiung.
11.1964: Demolition began by the China National Machinery Import and Export Corporation, Kaohsiung.

OCEAN COURIER/CLAN MACBEAN (2) 1946-1960

O.N. 168840 7,129g 4,250n
441.5 x 57.0 x 34.8 feet.
T.3-cyl. by the Dominion Engineering Works Ltd., Montreal, Canada; 2,500 IHP.

7.9.1942: Launched by the Todd-Bath Iron Shipbuilding Corporation, South Portland, Maine, USA (Yard No. 24).

10.1942: Completed.

9.11.1942: Registered in the ownership of the Ministry of War Transport, London (Larrinaga Steamship Company, Liverpool, managers) as OCEAN COURIER.

30.7.1944: Damaged by German E boats in the English Channel.

11.5.1946: Bareboat chartered by The Clan Line Steamers Ltd. (Cayzer, Irvine and Co. Ltd., managers), London.

31.12.1947: Acquired by The Clan Line Steamers Ltd. (Cayzer, Irvine and Co. Ltd., managers), London for £106,466 and renamed CLAN MACBEAN.

9.1949: Converted to burn oil fuel.

5.8.1960: Arrived at Tokyo and sold for demolition to the Hong Kong Salvage and Towage Co. Ltd. for £95,000.

20.8.1960: Arrived at Hong Kong in tow.

21.9.1960: Breaking up began by the Chiap Hua Manufacturing Co. (1947) Ltd., Hong Kong.

Ocean Courier was photographed at Cape Town in February 1947 (top), and in October 1948 after she had been transferred to Clan ownership as *Clan Macbean* (2) (middle). The third photograph shows her in final condition. *[Top/middle: R.M. Scott/ Newall Dunn collection (2); bottom: Ships in Focus]*

OCEAN GYPSY/CLAN MACBRIDE (2)
1946-1958

O.N. 169067 7,128g 4,344n
441.5 x 57.0 x 34.8 feet.
T.3-cyl. by John Inglis and Co. Ltd.,
Toronto, Ontario, Canada; 2,500 IHP.
18.10.1942: Launched by the Todd-Bath
Iron Shipbuilding Corporation, South
Portland, Maine, USA (Yard No. 29).
11.1942: Completed.
1.11.1943: Registered in the ownership of
the Ministry of War Transport (J. and C.
Harrison Ltd., managers), London as
OCEAN GYPSY.
28.7.1946: Bareboat chartered by The Clan
Line Steamers Ltd. (Cayzer, Irvine and Co.
Ltd., managers), London.
31.12.1947: Acquired by The Clan Line
Steamers Ltd. (Cayzer, Irvine and Co. Ltd.,
managers), London for £108,185 and
renamed CLAN MACBRIDE.
2.1950: Converted to burn oil fuel.
22.5.1958: Sold to Panamanian Oriental
Steamship Corporation, Panama (Wheelock,
Marden and Co. Ltd., Hong Kong) for
£110,000 and renamed ALICE.
1961: Sold to Valles Steamship Co. Ltd.,
Panama (C.S. Koo, Hong Kong).
7.10.1966: Arrived at Hirao, Japan for
demolition.
13.10.1966: Matsukuru Kaiji K.K.
commenced work.

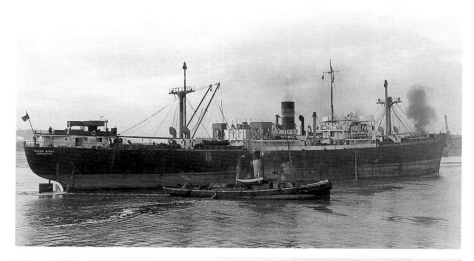

Three distinct colour schemes were
carried by some Oceans. Top at Cardiff
Ocean Gypsy is in war rig and with
wholly black topsides, middle at Cape
Town as *Clan Macbride* (2) she has two
white hull ribbons, and as finally painted
she passes a pilot cutter in home waters
(bottom). *[Top: Hansen collection,
National Museums of Wales, 1346/1445,
middle: David Whiteside collection,
bottom: FotoFlite/ J. and M. Clarkson
collection]*

OCEAN MESSENGER/CLAN MACBRAYNE (2) 1946-1961

O.N. 168638 7,129g 4,252n
441.5 x 57.0 x 34.8 feet.
T.3-cyl. by John Inglis and Co. Ltd., Toronto, Ontario, Canada; 2,500 IHP.
7.9.1942: Launched by the Todd-Bath Iron Shipbuilding Corporation, South Portland, Maine, USA (Yard No. 25).
10.1942: Completed.
17.11.1942: Registered in the ownership of the Ministry of War Transport, (Watts, Watts and Company, managers), London as OCEAN MESSENGER.
21.8.1946: Bareboat chartered by The Clan Line Steamers Ltd. (Cayzer, Irvine and Co. Ltd., managers), London.
31.12.1947: Acquired by The Clan Line Steamers Ltd. (Cayzer, Irvine and Co. Ltd., managers), London for £108,087 and renamed CLAN MACBRAYNE.
12.1949: Converted to burn oil fuel
23.12.1960: Transferred to King Line Ltd. (Cayzer, Irvine and Co. Ltd., managers), London.
15.3.1961: Arrived at Kobe, Japan and sold for demolition.
27.3.1961: Handed over to Nichimen K.K. at Mihara.

OCEAN VICEROY/CLAN KENNETH (2) 1946-1958

O.N. 168734 7,174g 4,272n
441.5 x 57.0 x 34.8 feet.
T.3-cyl. by the General Machinery Corporation, Hamilton, Ohio, USA; 2,500 IHP.
22.5.1942: Launched by the Permanente Metals Corporation, Shipyard No. 1, Richmond, California, USA (Yard No. 25).
7.1942: Completed.
24.9.1942: Registered in the ownership of the Ministry of War Transport, London (P. Henderson and Co., Glasgow, managers) as OCEAN VICEROY
21.6.1946: Bareboat chartered by The Clan Line Steamers Ltd. (Cayzer, Irvine and Co. Ltd., managers), London.
31.12.1947: Acquired by The Clan Line Steamers Ltd. (Cayzer, Irvine and Co. Ltd., managers), London for £104,809 and renamed CLAN KENNETH.
2.1951: Converted to burn oil fuel.
8.10.1958: Sold to Compania Concordia de Navegacion S.A., Panama (Elias Xenios, Piraeus, Greece, manager) for £105,000 and renamed OMONIA II under the Greek flag.
13.4.1966: Caught fire whilst discharging at Amsterdam after arriving from Colombo. The affected hold was flooded and the vessel towed to a safe area outside Amsterdam harbour and beached. During discharge of the remaining cargo further fires broke out but were extinguished.
15.7.1966: Arrived at Hamburg under tow to be broken up by Eisen und Metall A.G.
3.1967: Work began.

Clan Macbrayne (2) appears to have just been re-painted. *[B. & A. Feilden/J. & M. Clarkson]*

Ocean Viceroy is seen (top to bottom) leaving Cape Town in October 1946 with an all-black hull whilst on charter to Clan, deep laden after sale to Clan, repainting and renaming *Clan Kenneth* (2) and as *Omonia II* shortly after her sale to Greek buyers. *[Top to bottom: R.M. Scott/Newall Dunn Collection; J. and M. Clarkson collection (2)]*

Clan Keith (2) was Clan's last casualty involving serious loss of life, indeed, she was one of its worst peacetime losses with 63 fatalities. The enquiry into her loss found that Captain Pitts was at fault in not setting a correct course when he found the vessel was southward of her intended position. Instead of passing to the north of Galita Island, he altered course southward, and failed to check that he would clear rocks at Ecueils des Sorelles. Neither did he send out distress signals to summon assistance. The crew had not been adequately instructed in emergency procedures. The inability to launch one of the boats correctly cost three lives, and there were suggestions that at least some of the boats were in no fit state for launching. The captain's certificate was suspended for 18 months and he was dismissed from Clan Line's employment, although as a gesture the company paid his wife £30 per month during the duration of his suspension. Both the official enquiry and that conducted by Clan Line blamed the casualty on a stranding, but an officer who was on *Clan Keith* during a previous voyage has recently gone on record that her hull was in poor condition. *[J. and M. Clarkson collection]*

OCEAN VERITY/CLAN KEITH (2)
1946-1961
O.N. 167858 7,174g 4,272n
441.5 x 57.0 x 34.8 feet.
T.3-cyl. by General Machinery Corporation, Hamilton, Ontario; 2,500 IHP.
14.5.1942: Launched by Permanente Metals Corporation, Shipyard No.1, Richmond, California, USA (Yard No.24).
6.1942: Completed.

21.9.1942: Registered in the ownership of the Ministry of War Transport (Glen Line Ltd., managers), London as OCEAN VERITY
23.9.1946: Bareboat chartered by The Clan Line Steamers Ltd. (Cayzer, Irvine and Co. Ltd., managers), London.
31.12.1947: Acquired by The Clan Line Steamers Ltd. (Cayzer, Irvine and Co. Ltd., managers), London for £106,270 and renamed CLAN KEITH.
4.1950: Converted to burn oil fuel.

5.11.1961: Wrecked during a gale and poor visibility on Ecueils des Sorelles rocks, near Cape Bon, 11 miles south of Galita Island, Tunisia, whilst on a voyage from Middlesbrough and Malta to Colombo with general cargo. The after-part sank the same day and the forepart the next. Only five of her crew of 68 survived, these being picked up by the motor vessel DURHAM TRADER (6,214/1959).

Ocean Viscount. [National Maritime Musuem/Archie Munro collection]

Clan Kennedy (2) leaves Cape Town in September 1948 still with wartime rig, over three years after hostilities had ended (upper) and in peacetime colours (lower). *[Upper: R.M. Scott/Ships in Focus, lower: Malcolm Cranfield collection]*

OCEAN VISCOUNT/CLAN KENNEDY (2) 1947-1959
O.N. 165840 7,174g 4,272n
441.5 x 57.0 x 34.8 feet.
T.3-cyl. by the General Machinery Corporation, Hamilton, Ohio, USA; 2,500 IHP.
9.5.1942: Launched by the Permanente Metals Corporation, Shipyard No. 1, Richmond, California, USA (Yard No. 23).

6.1942: Completed
17.9.1942: Registered in the ownership of the Ministry of War Transport, London (Bibby Brothers Ltd., Liverpool, managers) as OCEAN VISCOUNT
9.1.1947: Bareboat chartered by The Clan Line Steamers Ltd. (Cayzer, Irvine and Co. Ltd., managers), London.
9.1948: Acquired by The Clan Line Steamers Ltd. (Cayzer, Irvine and Co. Ltd.,

managers), London for £107,949 and renamed CLAN KENNEDY.
6.1951: Converted to burn oil fuel.
7.8.1959: Sold to the Eddie Steamship Company, Keelung, Taiwan and renamed KELLY.
4.8.1959: Sold to Japanese breakers.
21.3.1960: Demolition began at Yokohama.

OCEAN VESPER/CLAN
MACQUEEN 1950-1958

O.N. 168630 7,131g 4,259n
441.5 x 57.0 x 34.8 feet.
T.3-cyl. by the General Machinery
Corporation, Hamilton, Ohio, USA; 505
NHP, 2,500 IHP.
30.11.1941: Launched by the
Permanente Metals Corporation,
Shipyard No. 1, Richmond (Yard No. 6).
1.1942: Completed.
15.4.1942: Registered in the ownership
of the Ministry of War Transport (Kaye,
Son and Co. Ltd., managers), London as
OCEAN VESPER.
1942: Managers became Connell and
Grace Ltd., Newcastle-upon-Tyne.
1946: Managers became Thompson
Steamshipping Co. Ltd., Cardiff.
1950: Sold to Thompson Steamshipping
Co. Ltd., Cardiff.
20.4.1951: Transferred to The Clan Line
Steamers Ltd. (Cayzer, Irvine and Co.
Ltd., managers), London for £184,500,
and renamed CLAN MACQUEEN.
3.12.1953: Transferred to the British and
South American Steam Navigation Co.
Ltd. (Houston Line (London) Ltd.,
managers), London and renamed
HERMINIUS.
3.1958: Sold to Pan Norse Steamship
Company S.A., Panama (P.S. Li, Hong
Kong) (Wallem and Co. Ltd., Hong
Kong, managers) and renamed EKBERG.
1963: Transferred to Marine
Development and Supply S.A., Panama
(P.S. Li, Hong Kong).
11.12.1964: Arrived at Onomichi, Japan
for demolition.
12.12.1964: Demolition began by Koshin
Sangyo K.K.
10.2.1965: Demolition complete.

Ocean Vesper departs Cape Town under a banner of smoke (top), whilst managed
by Thompson. She is seen again as *Clan Macqueen* (middle) and leaving Cape
Town as the *Herminius* (2) (bottom). *[Top: R.M. Scott/Ships in Focus; middle: David
Whiteside collection; bottom: Archie Munro collection]*

CLAN MACQUARRIE (2) 1951-1953

O.N. 168636 7,131g 4,259n
441.5 x 57.0 x 34.8 feet.
T.3-cyl. by Canadian Allis Chalmers Ltd., Montreal, Canada; 505 NHP, 2,500 BHP, 12 knots.
16.8.1942: Launched by the Todd-Bath Iron Shipbuilding Corporation, South Portland, Maine, USA (Yard No. 19).
9.1942: Completed.
13.10.1942: Registered in the ownership of the Ministry of War Transport (Thompson Steamshipping Co. Ltd., managers),

London as OCEAN WAYFARER.
20.3.1946: Owners became the Ministry of Transport, London.
27.1.1951: Sold to the Thompson Steamshipping Co. Ltd., London.
2.2.1951: Transferred to The Clan Line Steamers Ltd. (Cayzer, Irvine and Co. Ltd., managers), London for £189,500.
5.4.1951: Renamed CLAN MACQUARRIE.
31.1.1953: Grounded during a gale ten miles west of the Butt of Lewis whilst on a voyage from Dundee to Glasgow in ballast.

16.3.1953: Refloated and taken to Stornoway and on 22.3.1953 to the Clyde. Following inspection declared a constructive total loss.
2.4.1953: Towed to the Holy Loch and laid up.
7.1953: Sold by the Salvage Association to Sea Tankers Inc., Monrovia, Liberia for £50,000.
29.10.1953: Towed to Troon to be broken up by West of Scotland Shipbreaking Co. Ltd.
21.11.1953: Register closed.

Clan Macquarrie (2) was the shortest lived of Clan's Oceans. During a ballast voyage around the north of Scotland, she became unmanageable in a south westerly gale with winds gusting up to 112 mph, and despite putting out two anchors was blown ashore on the island of Lewis (bottom). The crew were taken ashore by breeches buoy by the local coast guard. Salvage attempts eventually succeeded and she was taken to Stornoway, but this was not regarded as a 'place of safety' as specified by the Lloyd's Open Form of salvage agreement, and so she was towed to Faslane on the Clyde. Dry docking at Elderslie revealed serious damage and tenders for repair were as high as £341,000, against her book value of £242,500. She was therefore declared a constructive total loss and abandoned to the underwriters. Intriguingly, she was sold to a Liberian company who sold her on to breakers in the West of Scotland. An internal inquiry by Clan decided that her master had made a serious error of judgement and he was asked to resign, although given a pension by the company. He went on to command with the India Steamship Co. Ltd. *[Upper: Ships in Focus; middle: Archie Munro collection; bottom: The Ness Historical Society]*

HELLENES (2) 1952-1958

O.N. 168815 7,174g 4,272n
441.5 x 57.0 x 34.8 feet.
T.3-cyl. by the General Machinery
Corporation, Hamilton, Ohio; 505 NHP,
2,500 IHP.
1941: Launched by the Permanente Metals
Corporation, Shipyard No. 1, Richmond,
California, USA (Yard No. 8).
1.1942: Completed,
13.4.1942: Registered in the ownership of
the Ministry of War Transport (Kaye, Son
and Co. Ltd., managers), London as
OCEAN VESTAL.
18.11.1946: Sold to Thompson
Steamshipping Co. Ltd., London and
renamed FARNINGHAM.
1952: Transferred to the British and South
American Steam Navigation Co. Ltd.
(Houston Line (London) Ltd., managers),
London and renamed HELLENES.
1957: Transferred to The Clan Line
Steamers Ltd. (Cayzer, Irvine and Co. Ltd.,
managers), London.
1958: Sold to Malabar Steamship Co. Ltd.,
Bombay, India and renamed JANMADA.
15.4.1962: Breaking up began by Abid
and Company at Bombay.

Hellenes (2) at Cape Town (top).
Before and after: The *Farningham* in
Australian waters (middle) and dis-
charging overside into lighters and
sailing barges in the Thames as the
Janmada in September 1958 (bottom).
[Top: Ships in Focus, middle: J. Y.
Freeman/Archie Munro collection;
bottom: J. and M. Clarkson]

FROM REBUILDING TO RETREAT: 1947-1981

Peace with problems

With the massive purchase and charter of war-built tonnage recorded at the end of the previous chapter, the Clan fleet was quickly getting back to strength, but the company along with other British lines was to encounter fresh competition which it was more-or-less powerless to oppose. Independence for India and Pakistan was very quickly followed by claims by local shipping companies for a share of trade. The first claim, as early as February 1947, was by the India Steamship Co. Ltd. of Calcutta, applying for admission to the Calcutta Conference. With its eight ships it was initially granted rights as an 'affiliate' without a vote in the conference. Fears that other companies would follow suit were fully justified: in 1948 the Bombay-based Scindia Steam Ship Co. Ltd. applied: a more serious rival, as this well-established company had a fleet of 20 ships. The *Jalabala* (4,557/1924) took the first Scindia sailing from Liverpool in May 1948. By 1950, both these Indian companies were demanding full conference rights which were conceded, although the established companies managed to restrict the sailings by the Indian ships. Pakistani companies had less resources: late in 1950 the Pakistan government pressed the claim of the Muhammadi Steamship

Co. Ltd. to conference rights, but the company did not have sufficient tonnage.

New competition to the established conference was not confined to lines on the Indian subcontinent. At the beginning of 1950 South African Lines Ltd. entered the South African Conference with one sailing per month, and soon afterwards Safmarine made a separate request to join. Clan Line board minutes in June 1950 record that the latter's *Vergelegen* (7,605/1945) loaded a full cargo in Liverpool, Newport and Glasgow, ports which had long been Clan's fiefdom. Partly as a response to these entrances, Springbok Shipping Co. Ltd. was established in South Africa with capital from Sir Vernon Thomson of Union-Castle. Despite these unwelcome incursions, trade was buoyant and Clan needed to charter ships to meet its requirements. In December 1948, three tramps were on charter plus the Greenock Dockyard-built heavy lift ship *Empire Byng* (7,832/1945) to carry carriages for South African Government Railways and Rhodesian Railways. Possibly Clan was now regretting the decision not to buy one of these ships when it was available.

The new lines sponsored or supported by governments of countries to which Clan had traded could not

Clan Urquhart (3), *Lanarkshire* and *Perthshire* at Hamilton Reach, Brisbane River, 18th July 1947 (top). *Clan Urquhart* and *Lanarkshire* were completing loading homewards for Hull and London respectively. *Perthshire* was at her last port of discharge from Cape ports. *[Archie Munro collection]*
Empire Byng in the Mersey on 14th May 1949 (bottom). *[John McRoberts/J. and M. Clarkson collection]*

be denied access to conferences, but a newcomer from eastern Europe was opposed, Gdynia America Line, whose service from Poland to India began making calls at ports in western Europe and the Mediterranean in 1950. Further competition came from the German lines which were rebuilding their shattered fleets and re-entering old trades. Hansa Line reopened its Bombay service late in 1950, and in 1951 Deutsche Ost-Africa Line began monthly sailings to East Africa.

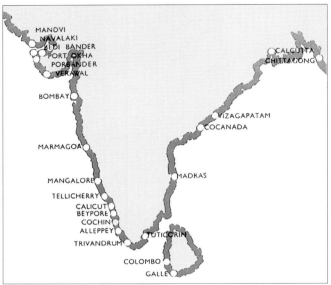

Pre-war ports of call on the Indian peninsula re-established by Clan after the war.

As well as nationalist feelings when it came to shipping lines, partition of India caused Clan other problems. Jute from what had become Pakistan was subject to duty when it crossed the border into India to be exported from Calcutta. Instead it was despatched from Chittagong, and Clan felt it advisable to reopen direct sailings from this port to the USA, although they were miffed that Brocklebanks were muscling in on the trade from Chittagong which Clan regarded as its own. Partition also led to Pakistan developing a new port at Chalna, and Houston's *Halesius* (2) was the second ship to load there in December 1950. Ill feeling between India and Pakistan led to dockers at certain ports refusing to handle ships that had called at ports in the other country. Clan began to operate separate services to India and Pakistan. When war broke out between the two countries in 1965 Clan ships avoided damage, but some rearrangement of crews was needed. The ships also had to be certain not to call at both an Indian and Pakistani port during the same voyage, as otherwise cargo for the one country could be treated as contraband by the other.

The mid-1950s saw problems in many of the ports served by Clan in both India and Pakistan, with a dockers' go-slow in Calcutta, congestion at Bombay and Beira, problems at Chittagong and even in the new port of Chalna, with situations at Madras and Vizagapatam described as 'chaotic'. Ships were taking an average of 51 days to complete discharge at Indian ports. There were also difficulties at home, with a shortage of dock labour at Liverpool, and a dock strike in London which led to some sailings being diverted to Bremerhaven. In 1955 at least one strike was reported at each monthly board meeting, and such were the delays that chartered ships were needed to supplement the fleet.

The nationalisation of the Suez Canal by Egypt in July 1956 gave Clan fewer problems than anticipated. There were minor delays whilst waiting for the Egyptian pilots, and as a precaution ships for Australia were routed via the Cape. However, the invasion of Egypt by Britain, France and Israel in October 1956 did cause major disruption, with the outward-bound *Clan Brodie* turning back in the Mediterranean and going round the Cape, whilst *Clan Mackinnon* (3) was called back to Aden and with other homeward-bound Clans was sent round the Cape. As a result Clan, always anxious to protect its revenue, imposed a 15% surcharge on rates to India and Pakistan. The British government did not allow British ships to use the Canal again until May 1957, and after this Clan reported few delays but noted that the standard of pilotage fluctuated considerably, with groundings being not uncommon.

The last of the post-colonial problems for Clan was the unilateral declaration of independence by Southern Rhodesia in 1965. The board initially seemed quite relaxed about this, even welcoming the increased loading of tobacco and asbestos at Beira, with Zambian copper still reaching the port on the railway through Rhodesia. However, sanctions against Rhodesia did eventually make themselves felt.

Grounded on the Shipwash Sands, off Harwich — see map — lies the 9,500-ton steamer Clan Chatton, her screws above water, rudder showing. Vain efforts were made yesterday to refloat her.
Aerial picture by " Daily Graphic " staff cameraman Stanley Devon.

Problems came in different shapes and sizes. In September 1950 the *Clan Chattan* (3) went aground on the Shipwash Sands as reported by the 'Daily Graphic'. She was safely refloated.

Acquisition, amalgamation, aviation

Like several British companies, Clan took tentative steps to become tanker owners in the 1950s, but the operation never seemed to gain the momentum achieved by Norwegian and other owners. It set up the Scottish Tanker Co. Ltd. in August 1950, and placed a contract with Swan, Hunter for two tankers which became *Scottish Lion* (1) (11,169/1952) and *Scottish Eagle* (1) (11,202/1952), each with a five-year charter to the Anglo-Iranian Oil Co. Ltd. A third near sister, *Scottish Hawk* (11,148/1955), was ordered from Greenock Dockyard, and the slightly larger *Scottish Ptarmigan* (12,685/1958) from John Brown. In May 1961 an offer was made for Hector Whaling Ltd., which was no longer interested in whaling but was

operating two tankers and had a bulk carrier building. The bulker, already named *Hector Halcyon* (15,500/1962), was sold whilst building, and after a few years the tankers *Hector Heron* (12,795/1959) and *Hector Hawk* (10,252/1959) were transferred to Scottish Tankers Ltd., although several former Clan cargo liners were registered in the name of Hector Whaling Ltd. The tanker operation survived its parent company, and two products tankers delivered by Cammell Laird remained in service, albeit for King Line, until 1985 and 1986 with the names *Scottish Lion* (2) (32,996/1979) and *Scottish Eagle* (2) (32,995/1979).

Clan were also on the look out for a tramp shipping company, and in 1950 bought the Thompson Steamshipping

Tankers were never registered in the ownership of The Clan Line Steamers Ltd., but were owned by associated companies. The upper photograph shows the *Scottish Ptarmigan* of the Scottish Tanker Co. Ltd. running trials on a wintry Clyde in January 1958. Her funnel appears to be in Clan Line colours, but the two red bands were separated by a narrow blue band. *Scottish Ptarmigan* was sold in 1968. *[Glasgow University Archives]*

The lower photograph shows the Spanish-built *Hector Heron*, part of the small fleet of Hector Whaling Ltd. She was transferred to the Scottish Tanker Co. Ltd. in 1966 and remained in its ownership until 1975. *[J. and M. Clarkson collection]*

Farringham was the only Thompson ship retained by Clan who put her under the Houston flag as *Hellenes* (3). *[Ships in Focus]*

Co. Ltd. with its one Ocean and two Empires, *Amersham* (5,536/1941) and *Cheltenham* (5,194/1942). Only the Ocean, *Farningham*, was retained, becoming *Hellenes* (3). Thompson was dormant for a few years, to be reactivated in 1956 as a British and Commonwealth subsidiary to purchase the tanker *Scottish Hawk* (11,148/1955).

The major change to affect Clan in post-war years was the amalgamation with Union-Castle which on 1st November 1955 created British and Commonwealth. The merger brought into the fold Union-Castle subsidiaries Bullard, King and Co. Ltd. and King Line Ltd. Whether this was merger or takeover must remain a moot point, however, although both employees and historians of Union-Castle believed it was the latter. Clan was the larger of the two organisations, valued at £3,360,000 compared with £2,192,000 for Union-Castle, giving Clan a 57.4% share. It was third time lucky for the Cayzers: they had offered to buy Union-Castle in 1935 following the Kylsant crash, and again in 1944, but both were resisted by Sir Vernon Thomson. The eventual success is put down to Thomson not preparing himself a successor as chairman, and indeed it was the prospect of Union-Castle as a major competitor falling into other and more aggressive hands on Thomson's death that precipitated the Cayzers' actions. But it was not achieved without some pain. A legal challenge was mounted by financiers and shipowners on the grounds that whilst Union-Castle's articles of association prohibited it being sold beyond British control, Clan Line's constitution had no such clause. This challenge was not upheld, but

In 1958 Sir Nicholas Cayzer became chairman of British and Commonwealth when he took over from Sir Herbert Cayzer. *[Newall Dunn collection]*

other demands of shareholders had to be met before the merger could formally proceed.

Accomplishing the amalgamation seems to have been the pinnacle of his career for Sir Herbert Cayzer, Lord Rotherwick. He was in ill health when he became chairman of British and Commonwealth, and survived only until March 1958, when Sir Nicholas Cayzer took over as chairman. At first, changes in the fleet as a result of the merger were few, but these accelerated as time went on and accountants had their way. The first significant change to affect Clan was the transfer in December 1959 of six King Line ships. They retained their names but all eventually painted up the Clan Line funnel. Early in 1961 it was reported that three ships described as 'cargo/tramp' types were to be ordered from Greenock, and these were duly named as *King Canute*, *King Edward* and *King Harold*. Within a few months, however, it was decided that these should be developments of the *Clan Fergusson* class for the Indian trade, but beamier, with remote machinery control, an enhanced speed of 16 knots, and modified hatch covers. They emerged as *Clan Macgillivray* (2), *Clan Macgregor* (3) and *Clan Macgowan*.

One of the first results of the merger was that crews could be appointed to almost any ship in the group, which now included passenger and mail ships running to the Cape, Clan Liners serving Calcutta or Chittagong with Asian crews, King Line ships which were tramping or on charter and crewed by white crews from the local shipping pool, tankers and, some time later, newsprint carriers managed on

King George (top), one of the six King Line vessels transferred to Clan ownership in December 1959. She is seen here loading timber in a British Columbian port.

Clan Macgowan (middle) was completed in 1963 having been laid down as the *King Harold* and was the last to be delivered of three ships originally intended for the King Line. With remote control of their machinery they were developments of the Clan Fs represented by the *Clan Finlay* (bottom) seen on her trials on 2nd October 1962.

[Top and middle: Newall Dunn collection; bottom: Tyne and Wear Archives, 2931/1933/1]

behalf of the Bowaters Steamship Co. Ltd. Fifty years later, there is still controversy amongst British and Commonwealth pensioners as to whether or not this was a good thing. Some men welcomed the opportunity for new experiences. Some complained that those from other parts of the group were treated preferentially in terms of seniority and were given preference when appointments were made. One officer has expressed his disgust at being appointed to 'the floating slums' of King Line, although this company had a fair reputation and ran good class tramp ships: the critic himself has been accused of missing the easy life on a Clan ship with its large Asian crew.

Although this account concerns itself almost exclusively with ships, and particularly Clan ships, aviation merits a mention. Reorganisation in 1951 brought a small Australian airline into Clan's ownership. Cayzer, Irvine had acquired Trans-Oceanic Airways Ltd., an operator of Short Solent flying boats on services including that to Lord Howe Island. A combination of the loss of one of its boats, the *City of London*, and poor management saw Trans-Oceanic become bankrupt, apparently before it could adopt the name Clanair Ltd., but undaunted Clan sought other aviation opportunities. Late in 1953 it entered a partnership with the Hunting Group, Britain's largest independent tanker operator, both organisations investing £500,000 in Hunting Clan Aviation Ltd. Vickers Viscounts and later Bristol Britannias were ordered, but the Clan Line board only really got excited when these aircraft, or orders for them, were sold on at a profit. In February 1957, for example, £225,000 profit was recorded from sales of Viscounts and spares. The amalgamation that spawned British and Commonwealth brought other aviation interests into the fold, and in 1960 these, plus Hunting Clan and other interests, were merged to produce British United Airways.

Shipbuilding and repairing

For many years Clan had workshop facilities at Glasgow to carry out repairs to ships which finished their voyages on the Clyde. In 1948 this was renamed Scottish Lion Ship Repairing and Engineering Co. Ltd., a title reflecting Clan's Scottish connections and their use of a lion on their house flag and bow crests. It might be wondered why this facility was kept separate from the company's own shipyard, and indeed the company was acquired by Greenock Dockyard Co. Ltd. in June 1954.

Uncertainty amongst Clan board members about the state of trade, and horror that new buildings such as *Clan Shaw* (3) were costing as much as £765,000, led to a disruption in the flow of orders to Greenock in 1949. Two hulls of turbine-driven ships, which were to have been *Clan Skene* and *Clan Stewart*, were sold to Pacific Steam, and this company then placed repeat orders. Together with a hull building for Scottish Tankers, this meant that no berths were free for further Clan Line vessels until March 1951.

Greenock Dockyard had received almost all orders for Clan Line vessels since 1934, and apart from government building during wartime had worked largely for Clan and Scottish Shire Lines. However, disillusionment with the yard seemed to be growing during the 1950s, and this relatively cosy arrangement was increasingly questioned. In 1954 the Clan Line board gave serious consideration to a proposal for investing in a new yard in South Wales, the Atlantic

Looking west: Queens Dock is in the foreground with the Clyde beyond. Scottish Lion's premises are at the east end of the dock. *[George O'Hara collection]*

Shipbuilding Co. Ltd. Clan would have invested about half a million pounds to have a share of at least 50% in the venture, and proposed transferring their building from Greenock Dockyard. However, on examining the scheme it was found not to offer any substantial savings, especially as main engines would have to be moved to South Wales from the builders who were on the Clyde, Tyne or Wear. Instead, it was felt preferable to extend facilities at Greenock, where a modernisation programme was begin in 1957.

In July 1959 the board declared that its orders would no longer automatically go to Greenock Dockyard, despite the recent modernisation, as there were suspicions that the yard was not giving best value for money. Occasional orders which could not be handled at Greenock had been placed with John Brown at Clydebank, but this yard was not a good comparator as it did much high-end passenger ship work, and was notoriously expensive for cargo ships, as British Shipbuilders was later to find out when it compared prices for a standard ship. The suspicions concerning Greenock Dockyard were soon confirmed when an order for the second batch of ships with engines three-quarters aft was put out to tender to two British and four continental yards. The winner was the recently-modernised Wallsend facility of Swan, Hunter and Wigham Richardson Ltd. which bid £1,100,000 each. However, the Clan board were horrified to note that Greenock Dockyard submitted the highest bid of the six. The yard was told to make itself more competitive, and to its credit it took the warning to heart, and secured further orders not just from Clan but from other members of the British and Commonwealth Group. Appendix 3 gives a brief history of the yard, and lists the yard numbers built during ownership by Clan and British and Commonwealth.

The high building cost of the *Clan Shaw* (3) (top) resulted in the ships intended to be *Clan Skene* and *Clan Stewart* being sold to the Pacific Steam Navigation Company. The *Clan Skene* and *Clan Stewart* were completed as *Kenuta* (middle) and *Flamenco* (right). Pacific Steam then went on to order a further two from the Greenock Dockyard which they named *Potosi* and *Pizarro*. Note that *Kenuta* does not yet have the distinctive top to her funnel.
[Top: Archie Munro collection; middle and bottom; Glasgow University Archives GD323/7/9/ 2/473/5 and GD323/7/9/2/474/5]

Clan gatherings: above and right are two views of the Clan Line berths in Vittoria Dock, Birkenhead and beyond. That above, looking towards the Mersey, can be dated to on or about 11th August 1965, thanks to the 'Ships in Port' sections of 'Lloyd's Lists'. In the innermost berth of Vittoria Dock is the turbine steamer *Clan Sutherland* (2), readily distinguished by her heavy-lift derrick and by then the only member of her class still in Clan Line colours. Next to her and stern-on is the war-built refrigerated steamer *Clan Urquhart* (3), which was just eight months away from the breakers. Beyond are two ships which allow a comparison between the turbine- and diesel-driven members of the first post-war class, the oil-engined *Clan Maclean* (3) nearer the camera in Vittoria Dock itself, and beyond, in the East Float, the turbine-driven *Clan Maclennan*, with a floating crane alongside.

In the distance is a former Clan Liner, the *South African Shipper*, formerly *Clan Robertson* (3). Also of interest, and helping to fix the date of the photograph, is the *Manchester Commerce* (8,724/1963), moored ahead of her. An unusual visitor to Birkenhead, the Manchester Liner is doubtless discharging grain from the Great Lakes. Note that the sheds alongside the south side of Vittoria Dock are being rebuilt, which accounts for the complete lack of Blue Funnels.

The view to the right was taken a year later, early in August 1966 by when the Blue Funnel berths were working again. Nearest the camera is *Clan Mactaggart* (2), loading salt or chemicals from a motorised Weaver packet. The next ship has been identified as *Clan Macnair* (2), and beyond her is an interloper, Union-Castle's *Rothesay Castle* (9,650/1960), also with a floating crane alongside. Note the bridge in the foreground which swung to let vessels in to and out of Vittoria Dock. Despite the apparently ample size of the transit sheds alongside Clan Line's berth, there is much cargo stacked in the open on the roadway beyond. *[Both aerial views: Newall Dunn collection]*

Opposite page: smart and not so smart, the four refrigerated R class ships completed in 1965 were impressive at sea as in the aerial view of *Clan Ross* (4), but she looks less so in dry dock, surrounded by the paraphernalia of repair and survey. *[Opposite top: Fotoflite/J. and M. Clarkson collection; opposite bottom: Ships in Focus]*

Clan Farquharson (above), seen in New Zealand waters, was sold to Iranian buyers after only six years service. *Clan Alpine* (5) on trials (below). Completed by Scotts' in April 1967 the *Clan Alpine* was named after the first Clan Line ship and was the last true cargo liner built for the company. *[Above: Ian J. Farquhar, below: GUA. GD323/7/9/2/708/20]*

The retreat begins

In September 1965 the fleet of Clan and its two close associates, Houston and Scottish Shire, stood at 45 ships, with several on charter. With the last war-built ships sold, all of these were steam turbine or motor ships built post-war for Clan or King Line. It was a large, relatively modern fleet, but it represented the company's zenith, for in 1965 a decision was taken which signalled the beginning of the run down of the fleet. Offers were received from the Scindia Steam Navigation Co. Ltd. for the *Clan Fraser* (4) and *Clan Fergusson*, which were barely three years old. The bid of £850,000 was higher than the ships' book values and, with export incentives making it even more attractive, the offer was accepted. The remaining three F class ships were also sold prematurely, this time to Iran. Board minutes note rather lamely that it was preferable to charter ships where necessary, but figures quoted for daily rates hardly bear this out: £440 a day for the ageing 11-knot *Inchdouglas* (7,275/1943), £660 for the 17-knot *Turkistan* (9,531/1963), but only £550 per day for a company ship which must have been the equal of the 17-knot vessel. This was shortly followed by the order for the last true Clan Line ship which was placed to sweeten the purchase of Greenock Dockyard by Scotts' Shipbuilding and Engineering Co. Ltd. She was to be named *Clan Alpine* (5) after Cayzer's first steamship, a somewhat ironic acknowledgement of history, as the company was turning its back on its nine decades of proudly running its own ships, through good times and bad, and establishing traditions and a reputation second to none.

There were several factors which persuaded the owners to run down the fleet. Containerisation was imminent, with British and Commonwealth making a 20% investment in the consortium Overseas Containers Ltd. National shipping companies seemed to be going from strength to strength, a process abetted by Clan selling its F class to two such fleets. Some of the cargo ships' trades were being taken by specialist vessels such as bulk carriers and reefers. To be fair, British and Commonwealth did invest in both these types of ships. Bulkers came into the King Line fleet and in late December 1981 the *King Alfred* became by a few days the very last, if quite untypical, ship owned by The Clan Line Steamers Ltd. Reefers were more Clan's style, but although built by Greenock Dockyard and named and painted as Clan ships, the *Clan Ramsay* and her three sisters were doing Union-Castle work, running largely in the seasonal fruit trade from South Africa and often laid up out of season. Nominal owner of these reefers was Union-Castle, and the apparently random ownership pattern amongst the fleet, although it no doubt pleased the accountants, was another outward sign that the company had lost its sense of tradition and continuity.

In 1978 the British and Commonwealth Group reported the first trading loss on its shipping business, and ship sales plus earnings from air transport were what, if the metaphor can be pardoned, kept the group afloat. A trickle of ship sales became a flood, and with the ending of new buildings the fleet rapidly declined. A number of ships did see out most of their economic life with Clan – the very last to be sold in 1981, *Clan Macgillivray* (2) and *Clan Macgregor* (3), were 19 years old – and few were to have lengthy further careers. The East African trade was largely containerised in April 1981, and with the Indian trade following, the new year of 1982 dawned with no ships owned by Clan or with Clan names for the first time in over one hundred years. The bulk carriers and the products tankers added in the late 1970s did briefly restore the fortunes of British and Commonwealth Group's shipping division, but this was short-

lived. The Group sold its last ship, the reefer *Speedster Universal* (9,073/1979), in October 1986.

Epilogue

For the British and Commonwealth Group, which was basically a Cayzer brainchild, life after Clan was nasty, brutish and rather short. In September 1987 the four remaining Cayzers on the board resigned en masse. The family sold most of its holdings for £427,000,000, much of which went into the Cayzer Trust and its investment vehicle, Caledonia Investments. In contrast to Caledonia, whose investments have largely prospered, British and Commonwealth Holdings, as it became, collapsed spectacularly less than three years after the Cayzers' exit.

The great wealth of the Cayzers is due in large part to Clan Line, and it was solid family management that steered Clan through its years of greatness. Mistakes were made, such as the Mexican misadventure, but overall Clan's story is one of the great successes of British shipping. Clan's routes and services were sufficiently diverse to ensure that, if one was doing poorly, spare tonnage could be transferred to another that was prospering. The company was not afraid to dirty its holds with bulk cargoes when these were the best prospect of earning a decent freight. Its building policy resulted in some of the finest cargo ships in the British fleet - and at the time that meant in the world - but it was not adverse to taking more basic vessels when the need arose. From the point of view of the enthusiast, there was never a Clan ship that did not look like a real ship. A quarter of a century since the last Clan liner was sold, they are still sadly missed.

The last to go: *King Alfred* was bought by the King Line in 1968, transferred to Houston in 1977, to Clan Line in 1980 and sold to China in 1983. *[Newall Dunn collection]*

THE FIRST POST-WAR CLASS

Ordered in November 1944, the first entirely new ships to emerge post war had single screws, composite superstructure and goalpost masts, and an extended fore deck to accommodate long loads. Although the goalposts were not repeated, the success of the Clan Maclaren *class was outstanding, and few ship owners of the period could have had such service from a group of ships: between 24 and 30 years.*

Two of this group were turbine-driven and four had diesels, the mix resulting from lack of engineering capacity in wartime, which may also explain the single-screw design. The two turbine steamers were marginally cheaper – Clan Maclennan cost £420,000 compared with £436,000 for the motor vessel Clan Macleod (4) – but had shorter lives because their higher running costs became critical when fuel prices began to rise in the 1970s.

CLAN MACLAREN (2) 1946-1976

O.N. 169488 6,021g 2,344n
466.0 x 60.9 x 26.1 feet.
Doxford-type 6-cyl. 2SCSA oil engine by Barclay, Curle and Co. Ltd., Whiteinch, Glasgow; 15 knots.
25.9.1946: Launched by the Greenock Dockyard Co. Ltd., Greenock (Yard No. 463).
17.12.1946: Registered in the ownership of The Clan Line Steamers Ltd. (Cayzer, Irvine and Co. Ltd., managers), London as CLAN MACLAREN.
20.12.1946: Completed.
22.12.1958: Transferred to Houston Line Ltd. (Cayzer, Irvine and Co. Ltd., managers), London.
12.11.1960: Transferred to The Clan Line Steamers Ltd. (Cayzer, Irvine and Co. Ltd., managers), London.
23.1.1963: Transferred to Hector Whaling Co. Ltd. (Cayzer, Irvine and Co. Ltd., managers), London.
12.1967: Transferred to Clan Line Steamers Ltd. (Cayzer, Irvine and Co. Ltd., managers), London.
1976: Sold to Seymour Shipping Ltd., London and renamed SEEMOOR.
17.5.1977: Arrived at Gadani Beach for demolition.

A shipyard worker checks the trigger mechanism before the launch of the *Clan Maclaren* (2). *[Glasgow University Archives GD323/7/9/2/463/1]*

The launching party: Lady and Lord Rotherwick along with the sponsor The Hon. F. B. Wyldebore-Smith, sister of Sir Herbert Cayzer. *[Glasgow University Archives GD323/7/9/2/463/12]*

Clan Maclaren (2) shortly after her launch with only one of her three goalposts standing. *[Glasgow University Archives GD323/7/9/2/463/5]*

Don't trust the French

Clan Maclaren (2) was unloading at Boulogne in June 1948 when a fire started in her cargo of jute, blamed on an electrical discharge from one of the port's cranes. However, the master did not trust the local fire services and, refusing to open the hatch to the affected hold, sailed to Dover where the 'very efficient' Kent Fire Brigade extinguished the blaze. *Clan Maclaren* then returned to Boulogne to continue discharging. Quite possibly this insult to municipal pride did not help when Clan attempted to pursue a claim against the port authorities and local stevedores.

The lead ship of this class, *Clan Maclaren* (2), was by a small margin the longest-lived. Sold in 1976, after almost 30 years in Clan Line service, she become *Seemoor* for a rather anonymous London-based company for one last voyage to the east. The top photograph, dated 24th August 1947, shows her as built in the early post-war colour scheme and in the middle photograph she has the two white bands. Below, *Clan Maclaren* as later and more attractively painted: note the black and white bands on the stays. In the *Clan Maclaren* and the two steamers of this class the bridge front overhung the master's accommodation. *[Top: John McRoberts/J. and M. Clarkson, middle: Newall Dunn collection, bottom: FotoFlite/J. and M. Clarkson collection]*

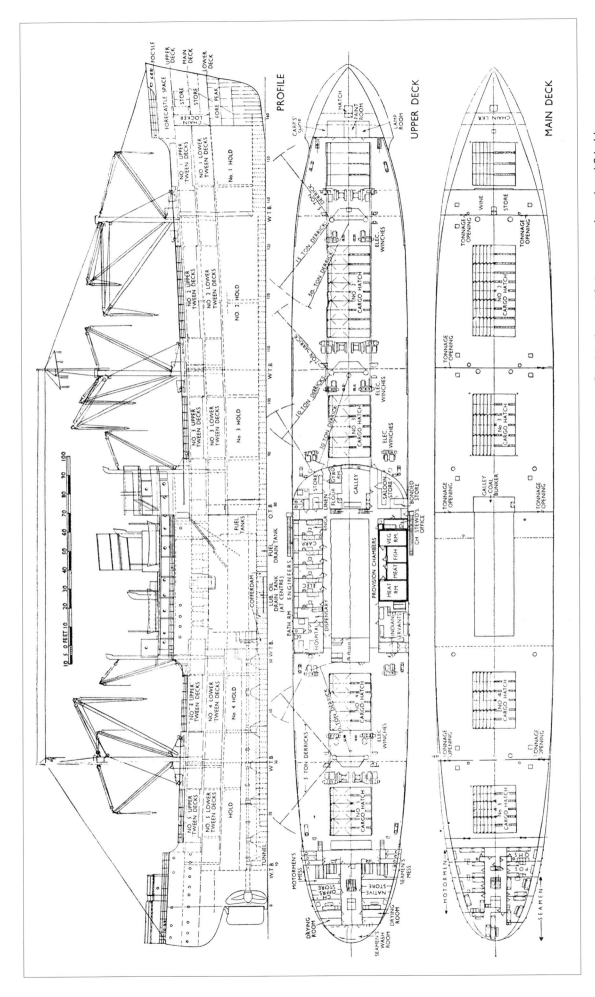

General arrangement drawing of the *Clan Maclaren* (2) as designed. As built the topmast was fitted to the mast between numbers 1 and 2 holds.

CLAN MACLACHLAN (2) 1947-1971
O.N. 169493 6,365g 3,178n
466.0 x 60.8 x 26.1 feet.
Three steam turbines single-reduction
geared to a single screw shaft by David
Rowan and Co. Ltd., Glasgow; 1,440
NHP; 15 knots.
23.12.1946: Launched by the Greenock
Dockyard Co. Ltd., Greenock (Yard No.
464).

28.5.1947: Registered in the ownership
of The Clan Line Steamers Ltd.
(Cayzer, Irvine and Co. Ltd.,
managers), London as CLAN
MACLACHLAN.
4.6.1947: Completed.
23.1.1963: Transferred to Hector
Whaling Co. Ltd. (Cayzer, Irvine and
Co. Ltd., managers), London.
12.1967: Transferred to The Clan Line

Steamers Ltd. (Cayzer, Irvine and Co. Ltd.,
managers), London.
1971: Transferred to King Line Ltd.
(Cayzer, Irvine and Co. Ltd., managers),
London.
19.10.1971: Arrived at Shanghai.
23.10.1971: Delivered to the China
National Machinery Import and Export
Corporation for demolition.

Shedding blades

Both *Clan Maclachlan* (2) and *Clan Maclaren* (2) had the unusual problem of their propellor blades falling off. At £750 per blade, this was not a matter to be taken lightly, as four plus two spares for each of the six ships made a total of 36 blades. In 1949 Lloyd's Register were called in to carry out a technical investigation as to whether the fault was due to excessive vibration. As the problem affected both a motor ship and a turbine vessel, it seemed more likely that faulty design or manufacture was to blame, and eventually the manufacturers agreed to replace 24 of the 36 blades needed for the class.

When delivered *Clan Maclachlan* (2) became Clan's commodore ship. She originally had a similar height funnel (top) to *Clan Maclaren* (2) but set further aft. In *Clan Maclachlan* and the other turbine-driven vessel of this class, *Clan Maclennan*, this was heightened to carry smoke clear of the boat deck (middle and bottom), and distinguished them from the four motor ships of the class. *[Top: Archie Munro collection, middle: J. and M. Clarkson, bottom: Malcolm Cranfield collection]*

CLAN MACLEAN (3) 1947-1976

O.N. 169500 6,017g 3,328n
466.0 x 60.9 x 26.1 feet.
Doxford-type 6-cyl. 2SCSA oil engine by
Barclay, Curle and Co. Ltd., Whiteinch,
Glasgow; 15 knots.
2.6.1947: Launched by the Greenock
Dockyard Co. Ltd., Greenock (Yard No.
465).
10.10.1947: Completed.
11.10.1947: Registered in the ownership
of The Clan Line Steamers Ltd. (Cayzer,
Irvine and Co. Ltd., managers), London as
CLAN MACLEAN.
1976: Sold to Singapore Islands Line
(Pte.) Ltd. (Singapore Shipping Agencies
(Pte.) Ltd.), Singapore and renamed
SENTOSA ISLAND.
8.5.1979: Arrived at Kaohsiung to be
broken up by Long Long Industry Co. Ltd.

Clan Maclean (3) seen at her
launch (upper), in superb lighting
on the Mersey (middle) and sailing
from Fowey in 1959 assisted by the
local tugs after loading a part cargo
of china clay (right). She was the
only member of the class to remain
nominally owned by The Clan Line
Steamers Ltd. throughout her
company career, an impressive 29
years. Converted to burn heavy oil
in 1952, at the same time her heavy
lift capacity was upgraded to 80
tons. *[Top: Newall Dunn collection;
middle: B. and A. Feilden/J. and M.
Clarkson; bottom: Ambrose
Greenway]*

CLAN MACLENNAN 1947-1971
O.N. 182080 6,366g 3,168n
466.0 x 60.8 x 26.1 feet.
Three steam turbines single-reduction geared to a single screw shaft by David Rowan and Co. Ltd., Greenock; 1,441 NHP; 15 knots.
16.9.1947: Launched by the Greenock Dockyard Co. Ltd., Greenock (Yard No. 466).
12.12.1947: Registered in the ownership of The Clan Line Steamers Ltd. (Cayzer, Irvine and Co. Ltd., managers), London as CLAN MACLENNAN.
18.12.1947: Completed.
23.1.1963: Transferred to Hector Whaling Co. Ltd. (Cayzer, Irvine and Co. Ltd., managers), London.
12.1967: Transferred to The Clan Line Steamers Ltd. (Cayzer, Irvine and Co. Ltd., managers), London.

1971: Transferred to King Line Ltd. (Cayzer, Irvine and Co. Ltd., managers), London.
27.8.1971: Left Mombasa for China.
16.9.1971: Arrived at Shanghai for demolition.
21.9.1971: Handed over to China National Machinery Import and Export Corporation.

Clan Maclennan was somewhat accident prone, with a definite propensity for running into BP tankers. On 2nd December 1961 she hit *British Defender* (6,138/1950) off Beira, and on 24th November 1966 it was the turn of *British Crusader* (11,346/ 1954) in fog in the Thames Estuary. Note the large funnel carried by the two turbine-driven ships of this class. *[Upper: B. and A. Feilden/J. and M. Clarkson, lower: Malcolm Cranfield collection]*

CLAN MACLEOD (4) 1948-1976
O.N. 182090 6,073g 3,367n
466.0 x 60.9 x 26.1 feet.
Doxford-type 6-cyl. 2SCSA oil engine by
Barclay, Curle and Co. Ltd., Whiteinch,
Glasgow; 15 knots.
13.2.1948: Launched by the Greenock
Dockyard Co. Ltd., Greenock (Yard No. 467).
29.6.1948: Registered in the ownership of
The Clan Line Steamers Ltd. (Cayzer,
Irvine and Co. Ltd., managers), London as
CLAN MACLEOD.

3.7.1948: Completed.
22.12.1958: Transferred to Houston Line
Ltd. (Cayzer, Irvine and Co. Ltd.,
managers), London.
20.9.1960: Transferred to The Clan Line
Steamers Ltd. (Cayzer, Irvine and Co. Ltd.,
managers), London.
23.1.1963: Transferred to Hector Whaling
Co. Ltd. (Cayzer, Irvine and Co. Ltd.,
managers), London.

12.1967: Transferred to The Clan Line
Steamers Ltd. (Cayzer, Irvine and Co. Ltd.,
managers), London.
1976: Sold to Alligator Shipping Co. Ltd.,
Limassol, Cyprus (Mitchurst Ltd. (M.M.
and M.Y. Shaikh), London, managers) and
renamed PAPAJI.
6.11.1977: Arrived at Karachi following
sale for demolition.
2.1978: Breaking up began at Gadani
Beach.

New, on the Clyde and a fine aerial view of *Clan Macleod* (4) in the English Channel. In the upper view note the white line
above the boot topping, done away with later, and the white bulwarks. *[Top: Newall Dunn collection; bottom: FotoFlite/J. and
M. Clarkson collection]*

CLAN MACLAY 1949-1976

O.N. 182109 6,075g 3,367n
466.0 x 60.9 x 26.1 feet.
Doxford-type 6-cyl. 2SCSA oil engine by
Barclay, Curle and Co. Ltd., Whiteinch,
Glasgow; 15 knots.
7.5.1948: Launched by the Greenock
Dockyard Co. Ltd., Greenock (Yard No.
468).
23.2.1949: Registered in the ownership of
The Clan Line Steamers Ltd. (Cayser,
Irvine and Co. Ltd., managers), London as
CLAN MACLAY.
2.3.1949: Completed.
23.1.1963: Transferred to Hector Whaling
Co. Ltd. (Cayzer, Irvine and Co. Ltd.,
managers), London.
12.1967: Transferred to The Clan Line
Steamers Ltd. (Cayzer, Irvine and Co. Ltd.,
managers), London.
1976: Transferred to King Line Ltd.
(Cayzer, Irvine and Co. Ltd., managers),
London.
1976: Sold to Climax Shipping
Corporation, Monrovia, Liberia (Maldives
Shipping Ltd., Male) and renamed
CLIMAX AMETHYST under the Panama
flag.
25.4.1979: Arrived at Singapore and
offered for sale.
12.5.1979: Arrived at Kaohsiung under the
name ANGELOS.
28.5.1979: Demolition began by Keun
Hwa Iron and Steel Works.

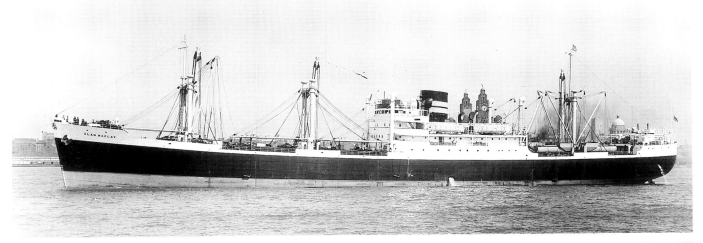

The only ship of this name, *Clan Maclay* is launched with kingposts erected but none of her goalpost masts (top). She is also seen on trials (upper middle), on the Mersey at 2.30 pm according to the clock on the Liver Buildings (lower middle) and after sale to Maldives Shipping Ltd. as *Climax Amethyst*. [Top pair: Glasgow University Archives GD323/7/9/2/468/ 12 and 1; bottom pair: J. and M. Clarkson (2)]

THE LAST TWIN-SCREW SHIPS

The two ships of this class ordered in November 1946 were the last twin-screw and the last three-island design in the Clan fleet, their successors having just a forecastle and poop with the superstructure amidships built on the main deck. They were also the most expensive ships yet at £678,000 each. The heavy-lift derricks of this pair of ships helped the company move many railway locomotives and other items of railway rolling stock to Africa and India. The locomotives often originated from the works of the North British Locomotive Co. Ltd. at Springburn, although others were shipped from builders in Lancashire. In Glasgow they were loaded either by floating crane in the King George V Dock or at the 175-ton capacity Stobcross Crane. The ship's own gear was often necessary to unload them at their destination.

Clan Mactaggart (2) is seen in the Channel with her main topmast slightly raked (top). She is also pictured in the Mersey after the addition of an ungainly radar aerial to her funnel (middle). She and her sister dispensed with the goalpost pasts of the previous class, had a longer forecastle and 125-ton derricks, amongst the largest Clan had yet installed. This derrick is used to tranship a piece of heavy equipment from the *Southern Coast* (869/1943) (bottom). *[Top: Fotoflite; middle: J. and M. Clarkson; bottom: Ballast Trust]*

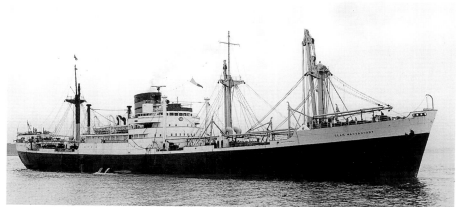

CLAN MACTAGGART (2) 1949-1971

O.N. 182111 8,035g 3,924n
505.5 x 65.6 x 28.4 feet.
Six steam turbines double-reduction geared to twin screw shafts by Parsons Marine Steam Turbine Co. Ltd., Newcastle-upon-Tyne.
8.10.1948: Launched by the Greenock Dockyard Co. Ltd., Greenock (Yard No. 469)
14.3.1949: Registered in the ownership of The Clan Line Steamers Ltd. (Cayzer, Irvine and Co. Ltd., managers), London as CLAN MACTAGGART.
17.3.1949: Completed.
1971: Transferred to King Line Ltd. (Cayzer, Irvine and Co. Ltd., managers), London.
12.11.1971: Arrived at Bilbao for breaking up.
16.11.1971: Handed over to E. Vaxela.
1.1972: Demolition completed.

CLAN MACTAVISH (3) 1949-1971

O.N. 182124 8,035g 3,926n
505.5 x 65.6 x 28.4 feet.
Six steam turbines double-reduction geared to twin screw shafts by Parsons Marine Steam Turbine Co. Ltd., Newcastle-upon-Tyne.
2.3.1949: Launched by the Greenock Dockyard Co. Ltd., Greenock (Yard No. 470).
21.6.1949: Completed.
22.6.1949: Registered in the ownership of The Clan Line Steamers Ltd. (Cayzer, Irvine and Co. Ltd., managers), London as CLAN MACTAVISH.
1971: Transferred to King Line Ltd. (Cayzer, Irvine and Co. Ltd., managers), London.
22.10.1971: Arrived at Whampoa for demolition.
27.10.1971: Handed over to the China National Machinery Import and Export Corporation.

Top: A deck view of *Clan Mactavish* (3) immediately after launching. The launch ways can be seen above the extreme port side edge of the forecastle. The tugs will take her into James Watt Dock for fitting out. The 150-ton crane in this dock is on the left hand edge of the photograph.
Middle: *Clan Mactavish* (3) could be distinguished from her sister by the lattice mast on the bridge which carries the radar aerial, a feature continued in the next class.
Bottom: Underway off Tarifa Point, west of Gibraltar. *[Top: Glasgow University Archives GD323/7/9/2/470/1; middle: B. and A. Feilden/J. and M. Clarkson; bottom: Ambrose Greenway]*

TURBINE-DRIVEN *CLAN SHAWS*

One of the authors has to declare a prejudice at this point: he has felt since a schoolboy that the group of ships beginning with Clan Shaw *(3)* and ending with Ayrshire *(2)* represented the apotheosis of British cargo liner design. With a well balanced layout, an imposing funnel with its tall cowl (reportedly known as 'the helmet' to those in Greenock), turbines for smoothness, accommodation for 12 passengers following successful experience with Clan Davidson *(2)*, and the Clan Line colour scheme, the class rivalled even the Blue Funnel 'A' class, with which they could be compared in Birkenhead's Vittoria Dock. However, their careers were somewhat less than impressive,

marked by a significant stall in the building programme, early transfers and sales, and by two of the class coming to violent ends.

In May 1949, whilst this class was building at Greenock Dockyard, the Clan Line board started panicking about a downturn in trade they thought they could detect and, also worried by escalating ship prices, sold the ships which were to be Clan Skene *(yard number 473)* and Clan Stewart *(yard number 474)* to Pacific Steam Navigation Company, who renamed them Kenuta *(8,494/1950)* and Flamenco *(8,491/1950)*. Obviously impressed, Pacific Steam ordered two more from Greenock (Potosi, *8,564/1955* and Pizarro, *8,564/1955)* and a fifth from William Denny and Co. (Cotopaxi, *8,559/1954)*.

Three of the four completed for Clan were transferred to other companies within the British and Commonwealth Group, and as a result only Clan Sutherland *(2)* saw out all her allotted span of years with Clan Line, and then only because her particularly heavy lift gear made her very useful. It was reported that the freight for a single heavy lift item sent out to Australia on Clan Sutherland could pay for her entire voyage.

Two different figures are quoted for the shaft horsepower of these vessels: 9,400 and 10,340, with respective speeds of 16.5 and 17 knots. It has been assumed the former figures apply to the first two ships.

CLAN SHAW (3) 1950-1959

O.N. 182140 8,101g 4,630n 10,955d
512.6 x 66.3 x 28.0 feet.
Three steam turbines double reduction geared to
single screw shaft by Parsons Marine Turbine Co.
Ltd., Wallsend-on-Tyne; 9,400 SHP, 16.5 knots.
23.8.1949: Launched by Greenock Dockyard Co.
Ltd., Greenock (Yard No. 471).
3.1.1950: Completed and registered in the ownership
of The Clan Line Steamers Ltd. (Cayzer, Irvine and
Co. Ltd., managers), London as CLAN SHAW at a
cost of £765,200.
30.11.1959: Transferred to Bullard, King and Co.
Ltd., London for £410,000.
12.1959: Transferred to Springbok Line Ltd.,
London.
1.1960: Transferred to Springbok Shipping Co. Ltd.,
Cape Town, South Africa.
8.1960: Renamed STEENBOK.
1.7.1961: Managers became South African Marine
Corporation Ltd., Cape Town and subsequently
renamed SOUTH AFRICAN SEAFARER.
1966: Renamed S.A. SEAFARER.
1.7.66: Stranded in a heavy swell at Green Point in
the entrance to Table Bay whilst on a voyage from
Glasgow to Beira with general cargo and broke her
back, becoming a constructive total loss. The
passengers and crew were taken off by helicopter.

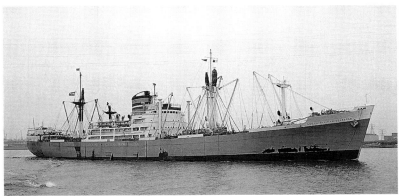

A classic view of *Clan Shaw* (3) on the Mersey
(opposite page upper). Notice the lattice mast
which carried her radar scanner. As she steams
past lightly-laden her 'helmet' top to her funnel
seems to be doing its job of clearing smoke
(right). Her early career had a moment of
splendour when she was chosen to represent
the company at the Coronation Review at
Spithead in 1953, and had one of her 'tween
decks fitted out as a lounge. In 1959 she left
Clan ownership, becoming *Steenbok* some
months later (top). In 1961 she was renamed
South African Seafarer (upper middle) and in
1966 this was abbreviated to *S.A. Seafarer*
(lower middle). Later that year she met a violent
end, driving ashore in a gale and breaking up in
full view of Cape Town (bottom). *[Opposite
upper: B. and A Feilden/J. and M. Clarkson;
opposite lower: David Whiteside collection; this
page top: Ships in Focus; upper middle: J. and
M. Clarkson; lower middle J. and M. Clarkson;
bottom: The Cape Argus]*

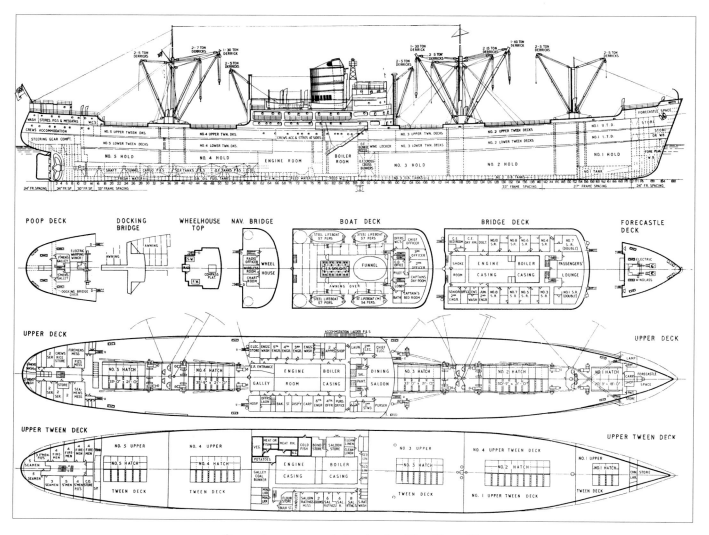

General arrangement drawing for *Clan Shaw* (3).

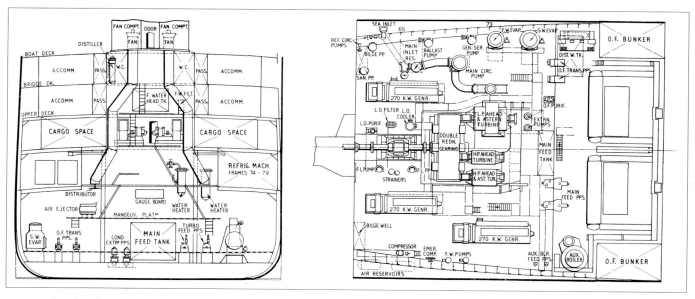

Section through engine room at frame 78 looking forward and engine room plan at floor level for *Clan Shaw* (3).

Clan Sinclair (3) entering Durban on 8th June 1950 during her maiden voyage (opposite top); as Springbok Line's *Bosbok* (opposite middle), and in Safmarine colours at Cape Town as *South African Statesman* (opposite bottom). [Top: Archie Munro; middle: Ships in Focus; bottom: Roy Fenton collection]

CLAN SINCLAIR (3) 1950-1959

O.N. 182148 8,405g 4,430n 11,000d
512.6 x 66.3 x 27.9 feet.
Three steam turbines double-reduction geared to single screw shaft by Parsons Marine Turbine Co. Ltd., Wallsend-on-Tyne; 9,400 SHP, 16.5 knots.

17.1.50: Launched by the Greenock Dockyard Co. Ltd., Greenock (Yard No. 472).
20.4.1950: Completed.
21.4.1950: Registered in the ownership of The Clan Line Steamers Ltd. (Cayzer, Irvine and Co. Ltd., managers), London as CLAN SINCLAIR.
9.1959: Transferred to Bullard, King and Co. Ltd., London.
12.1959: Transferred to Springbok Line Ltd., London.
1.1960: Transferred to Springbok Shipping Co. Ltd., Cape Town, South Africa.
8.1960: Renamed BOSBOK.
1.7.1961: Managers became South African Marine Corporation Ltd., Cape Town and subsequently renamed SOUTH AFRICAN STATESMAN.
1966: Renamed S.A. STATESMAN.
3.11.72: Arrived at Kaohsiung, Taiwan.
7.11.1972: Delivered to Li Chong Steel Corporation.
9.11.1972: Breaking up began.
31.1.1973: Demolition completed.

CLAN SUTHERLAND (2) 1951-1971
O.N. 182167 8,436g 4,434n
512.6 x 66.3 x 27.9 feet.
Three steam turbines double-reduction
geared to single screw shaft by Parsons
Marine Steam Turbines Co. Ltd.,
Wallsend-on-Tyne; 10,340 SHP, 17 knots.

28.12.1950: Launched by the Greenock
Dockyard Co. Ltd., Greenock (Yard No.
475).
27.3.1951: Registered in the ownership of
The Clan Line Steamers Ltd. (Cayzer,
Irvine and Co. Ltd., managers), London as
CLAN SUTHERLAND.
30.3.1951: Completed.

8.1971: Transferred to King Line Ltd. (Cayzer,
Irvine and Co. Ltd., managers), London.
10.11.1971: Arrived at Kaohsiung for
demolition by the China National Machinery
Import and Export Corporation.
However, resold to the People's Republic of
China and renamed ZHE HAT 3.
1979: Still in service. Her fate is unknown.

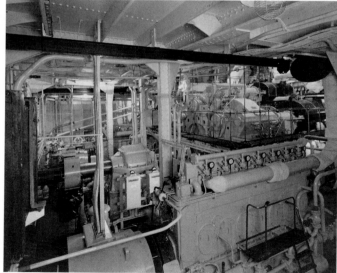

A bad day at Beira

Whilst entering Beira on 20th June 1953, *Clan Sutherland* (2) struck the Lloyd Triestino motor vessel *Risano* (3,191/1934),
fracturing her own stem plate, and causing damage to the *Risano* which cost Clan Line (and their underwriters) some £8,000.
But worse was to follow. After the Clan Liner berthed at Beira, petrol leaking from the Norwegian tanker *Fenheim* (10,370/
1943) caught fire and was carried by the ebbing tide past *Clan Sutherland* and *Clan Macaulay* (2). Both Clans were engulfed
in the flames, and those on board attempted to fight the fire, which consumed lifeboats and deck fittings on the latter and
blistered paint on both ships. A number of the fire fighters were burned, including the *Clan Sutherland's* surgeon, Dr. Forrest,
who sadly died of his injuries, Captain Starkey, the third officer, the second electrical engineer and two firemen from *Clan
Macaulay*. Although Clan Line pursued claims against the *Fenheim*, it proved impossible to determine who was responsible
for the tragedy.

Clan Sutherland (2) as built with a 65-ton derrick on her foremast (opposite upper), and two views of her engine room when new (opposite lower).

Between August and December 1960 the original derrick was replaced at Greenock Dockyard with one of 165 tons safe working load, the largest carried by a Clan Liner and indeed the largest supplied by a British manufacturer, in this case Stewarts and Lloyds Ltd. The work involved the removal of the vessel's existing foremast and heavy derrick. Structural alterations included special stiffening through the upper and lower 'tween deck spaces and the lower hold to the tank top. All decks in the vicinity were removed for strengthening and a new series of 'tween deck bulkheads erected to house the new heavy lift winches and other equipment. Guy tripods were built and arrangements were made to take the solid steel stays and shrouds from the foremast. At the same time, Greenock Dockyard modified *Clan Sutherland's* passenger accommodation to provide for 12 cadets, and altered the crew accommodation to take a white rather than a Lascar crew.

The top two photographs on this page show a weight of 181.5 tons being used to test the derrick on 21st December 1960: bags can be seen on top of the load to make up its weight. This very useful accessory spared her transfer to other British and Commonwealth Group companies, and she traded world wide for Clan (this page middle).

The final photograph is some-thing of a mystery. Taken in the Huangpu River, it shows the Chinese *Zhe Hai 3*, the former *Clan Sutherland*, but is dated July 1979, eight years after she is reported to have been scrapped. She has lost her heavy lift derrick, had her top masts replaced and received a

new radar mast, but the solid steel stays for the 165-ton derrick are still visible, proving she was indeed *Clan Sutherland*. [Opposite upper: J. and M. Clarkson; opposite lower pair: Glasgow University Archives GD323/7/9/2/475/ 23 and 24; top left: GD323/7/9/2/475/ 67; top right: Newall Dunn collection; middle: Malcolm Donnelly; bottom: Roy Fenton collection]

CLAN STEWART 1954-1961/ KINPURNIE CASTLE 1962-1968

O.N. 185001 8,163g 4,587n 11,070d
512.6 x 66.3 x 28.0 feet.
Three steam turbines double-reduction
geared to single screw shaft by Parsons
Marine Steam Turbines Co. Ltd.,
Wallsend-on-Tyne; 10,340 SHP, 17
knots.

22.10.1953: Launched by the
Greenock Dockyard Co. Ltd.,
Greenock (Yard No. 481).
20.1.1954: Registered in the
ownership of The Clan Line Steamers
Ltd. (Cayzer, Irvine and Co. Ltd.,
managers), London as CLAN
STEWART.
24.2.1954: Completed.
6.1961: Transferred to Springbok
Shipping Co. Ltd., London. It was
intended to rename her SPRINGBOK.
5.8.1961: Transferred to the South
African Marine Corporation, Cape
Town, South Africa for £650,000 and
renamed SOUTH AFRICAN
SCULPTOR.
18.4.1962: Transferred to The Clan
Line Steamers Ltd. (Cayzer, Irvine and
Co. Ltd., managers), London and
renamed KINPURNIE CASTLE.
1967: Transferred to King Line Ltd.
(Cayzer, Irvine and Co. Ltd.,
managers), London.
1968: Sold to Astro Firme Compania
Naviera S.A., Panama (D. Th.
Petropoulos, London) and renamed
HELLENIC MED under the Greek
flag.
15.3.1978: Arrived at Gadani Beach
for demolition.
5.1978: Demolition complete.

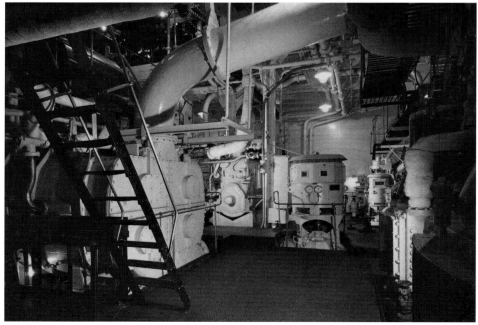

Clan Stewart was the first of this name, although Clan Stuart had been used several times before. During testing of Clan Stewart's 105-ton capacity derrick on 23rd January 1954, it failed at a weight of 115.5 tons, which was not judged a sufficient safety margin, and delivery of the ship was declined, although she had already been registered. Clan Stewart became one of the company's cadet ships, carrying 12 cadets instead of passengers.

She is seen on the Clyde in what is certainly a trials shot, although she is carrying several items of deck cargo (opposite page top). Her bridge and part of her turbines were also photographed (opposite page middle and bottom).

The photographs on this page show her in each of her later guises, as South African Sculptor in the Thames on 10th September 1961 (top), after returning to Clan as Kinpurnie Castle in 1962 when she was painted in Union-Castle colours and carried a Zulu crew (middle) and under the Greek flag as Hellenic Med (bottom).
[Opposite top: W. Ralston Ltd.; interiors: Glasgow University Archives GD323/7/9/2/481/32 and 13; this page top and middle: Roy Fenton collection; bottom: J. and M. Clarkson collection]

MODIFIED *CLAN SHAWS*

Clan Robertson *(3)* and Clan Ross *(3)* had their superstructures extended aft and trunked around the fourth hatch. This partly reflected the rearrangement of the passenger accommodation, with the lounge and dining room being on the same deck as the two double- and eight single-berth cabins. It was the lowly members of the crew who were berthed alongside the fourth hatch and had their sleep disturbed by cargo working. An 80-ton derrick was fitted to the mast serving number 3 hatch. A third member of the class was ordered as Greenock Dockyard number 486, but this was altered to become a reefer and emerged as Argyllshire *(2)*. Number 486 is repeatedly referred to as Clan Rose *in the board minutes. This is unlikely to have been a* clerical error for Clan Ross *as this name appears in the same list alongside her correct yard number 487.*

CLAN ROBERTSON (3) 1954-1959

O.N. 185012 7,898g 4,111n 10,118d
502.8 x 65.7 x 27.3 feet
Three steam turbines double-reduction geared to single screw shaft by Parsons Marine Turbine Co. Ltd., Wallsend-on-Tyne; 10,340 SHP, 17 knots.
17.3.1954: Launched by the Greenock Dockyard Co. Ltd., Greenock (Yard No. 482).
25.6.1954: Completed and registered in the ownership of The Clan Line Steamers Ltd. (Cayzer, Irvine and Co. Ltd., managers), London as CLAN ROBERTSON.
29.1.1959: Transferred to Bullard, King and Co. Ltd., London and renamed UMZINTO.

12.1959: Transferred to Springbok Line Ltd., London.
1.1960: Transferred to Springbok Shipping Co. Ltd., Cape Town, South Africa.
8.1960: Renamed ROOIBOK.
1.7.1961: Managers became South African Marine Corporation Ltd., Cape Town and subsequently renamed SOUTH AFRICAN SHIPPER.
1966: Renamed S.A. SHIPPER.
26.11.1975: Arrived at Kaohsiung, Taiwan to be broken up.
4.12.1975: Handed over to Ling Cheng Yung Iron and Steel Co. Ltd.
27.12.1975: Demolition began.

Opposite is a sequence of photographs of *Clan Robertson* (3) just launched by Mrs Anthony Cayzer, piped into James Watt Dock by Henry Laird, fitting out, dry docked in the Garvel Dry Dock for underwater painting, and on trials in the Clyde. The launch photograph was taken from the top of an 180-foot dockyard crane by the wife of the proprietor of James Hall (Photographers) Ltd.

On this page *Clan Robertson* is seen in subsequent ownership, as *Umzinto* at Cape Town in June 1959 (top), as *Rooibok* (middle) and as *S.A. Shipper*, again at Cape Town (bottom). [Opposite: Newall Dunn collection (5); this page: J. and M. Clarkson (3)]

A sequence showing the accommodation of *Clan Robertson* (3), from the top the master's day room, the master's cabin, the officer's smoking room, the passenger lounge, a double state room and two views of the galley – a part of the accommodation not often photographed. *[Glasgow University Archives GD323/7/9/2/482/35, /37, /33, /28, / 23, /42 and /41]*

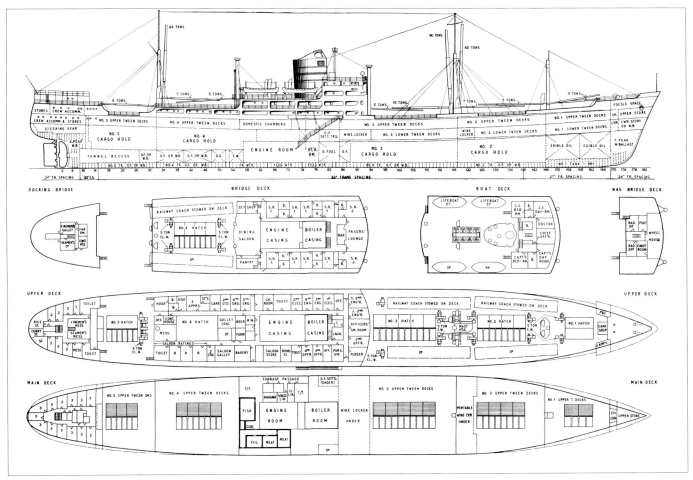

General arrangement drawing of *Clan Robertson* (3).

CLAN ROSS (3) 1956-1961/
KINNAIRD CASTLE 1962-1975
O.N. 185040 7,698g 4,263n 10,075d
502.8 x 65.7 x 27.3 feet
Three steam turbines double-reduction
geared to single screw shaft by Parsons
Marine Steam Turbine Co. Ltd., Wallsend-
on-Tyne; 10,340 SHP, 17 knots.
17.1.1956: Launched by the Greenock
Dockyard Co. Ltd., Greenock (Yard No.
487).

12.4.1956: Completed and registered in
the ownership of The Clan Line Steamers
Ltd. (Cayzer, Irvine and Co. Ltd.,
managers), London as CLAN ROSS.
7.1961: Transferred to the South African
Marine Corporation, Cape Town, South
Africa for £883,000 and renamed SOUTH
AFRICAN SCIENTIST.
9.4.1962: Transferred to The Clan Line
Steamers Ltd. (Cayzer, Irvine and Co. Ltd.,

managers), London and renamed
KINNAIRD CASTLE.
1966: Transferred to King Line Ltd.
(Cayzer, Irvine and Co. Ltd., managers),
London.
1975: Sold to Dasonab Compania Naviera
S.A., Panama (Monnoo Overseas Ltd.,
Dubai) and renamed NAZEER.
26.4.1978: Arrived at Gadani Beach for
demolition.
5.1978: Demolition began.

Launch of the *Clan Ross* (3) and the ship's sponsor Miss Nichola Cayzer, daughter of
Sir Nicholas Cayzer. *[Glasgow University Archives GD323/7/9/2/487/12 and 487/13]*

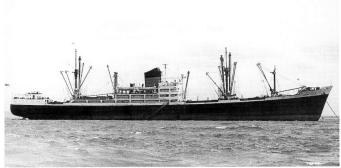

Clan Ross (3) (top) also became a cadet ship, this time with a mix of six deck and six engineering cadets. After transfer to Safmarine and being renamed *South African Scientist* (upper middle), she returned to Clan ownership, but not colours, as *Kinnaird Castle* seen in Safmarine colours on 10th June 1962 (lower middle left) and in Union-Castle colours (lower middle right). The last photograph shows her under the Panama flag as *Nazeer* (bottom). *[Top: Roy Fenton collection; upper middle: Ships in Focus; lower middle left: C.L. Reynolds; lower middle right: Roy Fenton collection; bottom: W.A. Schell]*

Life before the merger

There is little doubt that seagoing life in the Clan Line changed after the merger with Union-Castle and its associated companies in 1956, even if only imperceptibly to begin with; but how could it ever have been otherwise in a fleet of 60 ships which suddenly overnight was combined into one of a hundred, including the tramps of King Line Ltd. Perhaps if the merger had been made with a company or group with closer interests and trades, such as Ellermans which even shared most of the Clan routes with comparable ships and the same Indian crews, the new conglomerate would have been the more palatable, but of course that was hardly the purpose of the financial gain intended from economies of scale.

From a fleet which numbered 55 ships in 1939, the company found itself at the end of hostilities (including wartime replacements) with a post-war fleet of just 27 ships and therefore with a colossal undertaking to regain its position on established trade routes. The end of the Liner Requisition Scheme in 1946 allowed this task to begin and with various standard ship acquisitions and new buildings the fleet had increased to 42 units by November 1947, and two years later to 52 ships and therefore almost at the pre-war level, although 14 were due for disposal as being between 15 and 34 years old. By the date of the merger in 1956 the fleet had stabilised at the pre-war figure of 55 ships although 40 per cent were of the standard 10-knot wartime types i.e. Empires, Liberties and Oceans.

In the decade from the end of the Second World War until the merger in 1956 the deck department of the Clan Line, in common with that of many other companies, was staffed by officers from diverse backgrounds who might have joined as juniors from other liner companies, a few from tramp companies and even a unique entry from a tanker company under the flag of Panama. Those who began their service in Clan Line as cadets (they did not have indentured apprentices) for the most part did so after pre-sea training in such establishments as Pangbourne, Conway or Worcester, which then allowed them one year's remission of sea service before sitting the examination for second mate. Others served ten months on an approved cadet course such as provided by the School of Navigation in Glasgow which allowed six months remission of sea service. There was also a small but diminishing number who joined direct from school and had to serve the full four years. In the long run the company must have benefited from this progressive policy of engaging such a wide range of junior officers, although the habitual wastage of cadets, common to most companies, was sufficient for the Clan Line's principal marine superintendent to publish a lengthy paper entitled 'Why young men leave the sea'.

Unlike their brothers in the deck department, Clan Line engineering officers served their time ashore in the workshops of marine engine builders, such as Kincaids in Greenock which built the boilers, triple-expansion steam engines and Burmeister & Wain diesels for so many of the company's ships. Others trained in Barclay, Curle or John Brown's works which built Doxford diesels, or other licensed builders including those on the Tyne and Wear, some at Weirs of Cathcart which built pumps, J. and E.

Hall which manufactured refrigerating machinery and many other marine and electrical engineering companies throughout the United Kingdom. There were others, like those in the deck department, who joined with previous seagoing experience gained in other shipping companies. The percentage of Scots amongst all the company's officers both deck and engineering is unknown; however, the uniform braid worn by the company's officers did not embrace the standard diamond pattern of the Merchant Navy but that of the ring worn by the Royal Navy, from which the Clan Line was known colloquially as the 'Scots Navy'.

The number of Europeans carried on any one ship varied according to type; the basic wartime standard ships carrying a master and three mates, two cadets, five engineers, a radio-officer, chief steward and carpenter, which totalled 14. On the *MacL* class this number increased to 19 by the addition of two more engineers, two electricians and a second steward. On the S class ships extra catering and cabin crew were required to attend the 12 passengers thereby increasing the total to an extent that a surgeon and fourth mate were also carried. The greatest number of Europeans was carried by *Clan Macdonald* (4) and *Clan Macdougall* (3), a total of 26 which included ten engineers, two carpenters and three refrigerating engineers.

From the earliest times Clan Line, in common with others in the Indian trades, employed deck and engine room ratings from that very country who, unlike their European counterparts, hardly ever went ashore during the course of a voyage, preferring to save all their money to support themselves and their families at home. Because they often lacked the physique of a European, more were required to perform equivalent tasks, but they were infinitely reliable in port for essential work when other races were often tempted ashore. Few could read or write but most were able to recognise important marks and symbols. The Clan Line engaged their crews from the Chittagong district of East Bengal, part of India until partition in 1947, East Pakistan thence to 1971 when it became the independent republic of Bangladesh. The deck serang (i.e. bosun) was the all-abiding master of his crew and widely believed to have selected each man from friends and relatives in his immediate neighbourhood. They were of the Muslim faith long before the advent of extremists, while the catering crew usually from the Portuguese colony of Goa, on India's west coast, comprised a large proportion of Christians. A typical Clan Line Indian crew of that period numbered 55 all told.

During the 1950s the Indian government became aware that British companies in the Indian trade were employing Pakistanis rather than those widely accepted to be 'Indian' crews. From this point onwards some of those crews were replaced by Indian (Hindu) crews, highly trained and educated seamen going about their work in a wholly European manner, on occasion taking photographs and sending them with captions to the company's magazine for publication. This was unheard of with a Muslim crew.

In the autumn of 1948 the management launched a quarterly house magazine appropriately entitled *The*

Clansman of 20 odd pages in glossy quarto format. The contents were introduced by a message from the Chairman, Lord Rotherwick, and comprised articles and contributions from both ship and office staff alike, newsletters from all three of the company's British offices, from its stevedoring company in Glasgow, its agents abroad and a list of appointments. This publication proved highly successful and was soon expanded to allow more illustrations, including pen and ink sketches and group photographs, from every possible source. Soon it was listing those on the seagoing staff who gained certificates of competency in addition to promotions, and from 1955 listed each ship which had begun its voyage since the previous issue, complete with every European appointment on board. Undoubtedly the magazine instilled all personnel with a keen sense of belonging while the seagoing staff was presented with a means of compiling a rough and ready guide to their probable steps on the all important ladder for promotion.

Growing up in the company in those years and being part of that great Clan family was something of which one had to be intensely proud. New ships of steadily improving design were constantly under construction in the company's own Greenock Dockyard, and with the eldest of the twin-screw type now 20 years old, it seemed obvious that their replacement and that of the slow wartime standard ships was well in hand and that the fleet would soon eclipse that of its rivals. The company was pre-eminent on the outward Durban express service (which had no rival) and on the homeward Calcutta service with almost weekly sailings to London during the tea season. It also appeared that Clan lifted by far the bulk of the homeward cargoes from East Pakistan, together with those from the Madras and Malabar coasts of India. As many as eight ships were on the Australian service at any one time, and from Beira in Portuguese East Africa some homeward ships were being filled to capacity with copper wire bars and casks of tobacco originating from the Rhodesias. Everyone and everything felt secure.

It was therefore hardly possible in that period of time to escape the general feeling of wellbeing that pervaded the entire fleet. The principal marine superintendent and his assistant were established in the company's head office at 2 St Mary Axe within the City of London. There was a further marine superintendent at Royal Liver Buildings in Liverpool and yet another at the company's registered office, at 109 Hope Street, Glasgow, who with his retinue made daily inspections to each one of the company's ships then berthed in that port whether loading, discharging, repairing or in dry dock. There were in addition dock superintendents based at Tilbury, where ships from India discharged, at the Vittoria Dock loading berths in Birkenhead and at King George V Dock in Glasgow. Machinery overhauls in Glasgow were looked after by Clan Line's own Scottish Lion Ship Repairing and Engineering Co. Ltd.

Nor was one able to lose one's sense of identity when abroad; all ships visiting South Africa called at Durban where the company's affairs were looked after by the Clan Line South Africa (Pty.) Ltd., with a resident marine superintendent responsible for ships on both the south and east African coasts of that continent. In India,

the Glasgow firm of James Finlay and Co. Ltd., with whom Clan Line had been closely linked since 1878, acted as agents in Bombay, Karachi, Colombo, Chittagong and Calcutta where another marine superintendent was stationed to look after matters on that continent. At all these ports the Clan Line house flag was prominently displayed whether on windows, doorways, paperwork, envelopes or on flagpoles; even at outlying anchorages attended by other agencies, and especially by Pierce Leslie at Cochin, whose pristine Glasgow-built Kelvin launches prominently flew the Clan house flag when attending any of the company's ships. The African Mercantile Company represented Clan Line in East African ports while in Australia, McArthur Shipping and Agency acted in both Brisbane and Sydney, and William Haughton in Melbourne.

One hardly noticeable but invaluable aspect of seagoing life in the Clan Line was variety. By means of a judicious written request a cadet could, in his three or more years' training, gain varied experience on a slow coal-burner, on a fast motorship or steam turbine dry cargo or refrigerated ship trading on two routes to South Africa, one to the Red Sea and East Africa, three routes to India, another to Australia and occasional cross voyages between India and the United States and from there to South Africa. It was a vast network which from 1952 had the additional advantage of service on tankers trading on BP charters on a worldwide basis.

Unlike other companies such as Glen Line, which had eight identical fast ships devoted to one strictly scheduled service between London and the Far East, Clan Line had no such guaranteed repetitive programme to offer any of its ships; the policy appearing to be simply that which put the best and most suitable ships on a particular loading berth. By this means when on the homeward leg of any voyage it was practically impossible to guess what the next voyage might be. When outward bound to Australia or India one could be certain of loading homewards from that continent, but not the ports, which were only made known while discharging. When on any outward service to South or East Africa, the homeward possibilities ranged from returning from any of these same ports, or proceeding to any of several ports in India or Australia, even on occasions completing discharge at Beira then anchoring outside that port, with charts and courses prepared for either of those continents while awaiting orders to proceed.

In respect of life at sea in the Clan Line, the deck and engine room work and general watch keeping was no different from the pattern in any other cargo liner company. The ships were maintained to a very high standard. Cargo gear was overhauled outbound and the ship painted overall homeward. Contact was usually made with other Clan ships when berthed together in ports abroad. When at sea the radio officer kept in touch by wireless telegraphy with other company ships within range, each exchanging noon positions and where bound, to and from with present course and speed. Occasionally two ships on opposite courses passed each other close to, hoisting ensigns and house flags and blowing the whistle to mark the occasion. Cargo work on the South African or Australian coasts generally adhered to daytime hours or at least finished each day in the early evening; in

India the major ports worked day and night but the anchorage ports mostly daylight hours only.

It was widely acknowledged that Clan Line specialised in heavy lifts to the extent that all ships other than the wartime standard freezer, *Stirlingshire* (2), were equipped with at least one derrick of 50 to 80 tons capacity serving the major (number 2) hold, while most ships also had a secondary heavy derrick, but of lesser capacity, fitted at the mainmast. Clan Line maintained their heavy derricks in a state of short readiness with the purchase and topping lifts fully rigged. However, activating these derricks for service remained a labour-intensive operation for the deck crew when retrieving and rigging the guy pennants and tackles, whose tails were then led to the most accessible winches, of which two had to be at adjacent hatches. In the twin-screw classes the 'remote winches' were at number 3 hatch and on the warping drum of the windlass. Depending on the weight of the actual lift, preventer stays had also to be set up on the mast. Finally it was simply a matter of breaking out the derrick from its housing to have it ready for use, from which point onwards all six winches were invariably driven by stevedores' own labour.

In the early fifties exports from the United Kingdom were booming and outward sailings were generally loaded to capacity so it was unusual to be without heavy lifts of one kind or another to any of the three continents served by Clan Line. It might be Centurion tanks of 42 tons to Australia, Vulcan or North British locomotives to India or the lengthy Beyer-Garrett locomotives each in five parts totalling 126 tons to Beira for Rhodesian Railways: all these were frequent items of freight during this period. There was often congestion at Beira causing delays of 50 days or more (but not as bad as Chittagong in 1949 when six Clan ships were delayed there for periods from 91 to 124 days). To assist the rolling stock movement to Beira and obviate delays to their own ships, Clan Line chartered the heavy lift ship *Empire Byng* during 1950-51 for a number of voyages between Birkenhead and Beira.

A good example of the flexibility provided by Clan for heavy lifts was shown during the maiden voyage of *Clan Shaw* (3) in January 1950. Two complete Beyer-Garrett locomotives were shipped out to Beira on this ship, each comprising a boiler unit, front and rear units, together with front and rear tanks; the heaviest units being 40 tons. In Lourenço Marques were loaded two further identical sets which had been landed previously from *Clan Macdonald* (4) to prevent delaying this ship which was required to load in East Africa for Australia. All four complete Beyer-Garrett locomotives were landed at Beira direct to the rails on the wharf by *Clan Shaw*'s own heavy derrick.

The much-talked about merger between Clan Line and Union-Castle with associated companies became effective at the end of January 1956, under the chairmanship of the familiar Lord Rotherwick, who had served on the board of the Clan Line for 40 years. He died in 1958 and was succeeded by his nephew, Sir W. Nicholas Cayzer. From the time of the merger much focus was put on to the mail ships of Union-Castle but whose end was a mere two decades ahead, and that of Clan Line itself only a handful of years beyond that again.

THE LAST SCOTTISH SHIRES

Designed to replace the ageing pre-war and wartime-built refrigerated ships, the Ayrshire *(2) and her sister ship* Argyllshire *(2) were the last to be built for the company's trade between the United Kingdom and Australia. They adopted the names of the last two ships owned by Turnbull Martin's Scottish Shire Line when taken over by the Clan Line 38 years earlier. Yard number 488,* Ayrshire, *was actually the first ordered, but it was then decided to alter the order for yard number 486, ordered as a member of the* Clan Robertson *class, into a reefer. Number 486 emerged as* Argyllshire, *some time before the* Ayrshire.

The ships were enlarged versions of the Clan Robertsons, *with number 1 hold trunked down through an extended forecastle and added an extra number 6 hold immediately forward of the poop giving, if anything, an even better and more balanced profile. The ships were the last to have the distinctive funnel top introduced on the* Clan Shaw *(3) of 1949. Of the six holds, numbers 2, 3, 4 and 5 were insulated in eight separate compartments (63 per cent of the total cargo space) for the carriage of refrigerated meat, fruit and dairy produce from the two continents of Australasia and Africa. There were two 'tween decks in numbers 1 to 4 holds and one each in numbers 5 and 6, the heights being particularly designed for the maximum stowage of baled wool.*

Accommodation was provided to a high standard for 28 European officers, 73 Indian, Pakistani and Goanese crew and 12 passengers, a total complement of 113 which, astonishingly, was almost as many as that carried on the twin-screw, coal-burning freezer trio built twenty years earlier. However, the general layout was very different as the company had adopted a policy of mixing the European accommodation, rather than the customary 'engineers around the easing' and 'mates below the bridge' system which had evolved in a bygone era. The radio officer and pilot were berthed on the port side of the navigating bridge deck abaft the wheelhouse, with the chartroom and radio room to starboard. On the boat deck immediately below the bridge was a block of accommodation which, five years earlier, would have been the sole preserve of the master, but now also housed the chief engineer, the chief officer and the doctor with the senior pair occupying suites on the outboard corners, the master being to starboard. On the bridge deck below were ten passenger cabins, with a double on each forward corner and four singles down each side. Across the fore end was a passenger lounge-bar with seating for 22 while the aft end, looking out to number 4 hatch, was the combined passenger and officers' saloon accommodating 34 at one sitting.

Until the spring of 1965 these two ships were continually employed on either the South African or Australian trades, making, altogether, 13 round voyages out and home to South Africa, the same number out and home to Australia, a further ten outward to South Africa and homeward from Australia, five out to South Africa and home from East Africa and one out to East Africa and home from Australia: a total of 42 voyages of which 24 loaded home from Australia. During those years, however, the Australian homeward trade for cargo liners began to decline as that country sought to align itself with closer markets amongst its nearer Asian neighbours. In 1950 the Clan and Scottish Shire Lines provided 15 refrigerated homeward sailings from Australia, but in 1953 just 11 and in 1957 a mere 8. The rundown continued so that only six sailings were made in 1960 and following the withdrawal of the Clan Macdougall *(3) to the South African route in 1961 this dropped to five.* Argyllshire *continued in service until 1975, mostly on the Cape or East African route, but made another six voyages to Australia before the container ships displaced all the conventional cargo liners on this route in 1969.*

ARGYLLSHIRE (2) 1956-1975
O.N. 185047 9,299g 5,267n
534.9 x 69.3 x 28.4 feet.
Three steam turbines double-reduction geared to a single screw shaft by Parsons Marine Steam Turbine Co. Ltd., Wallsend-on-Tyne.
23.5.1956: Launched by the Greenock Dockyard Co. Ltd., Greenock (Yard No. 486).
18.10.1956: Registered in the ownership of The Clan Line Steamers Ltd. (Cayzer, Irvine and Co. Ltd., managers), London as ARGYLLSHIRE.
24.10.1956: Completed.
22.9.1960: Transferred to the Scottish Shire Line Ltd. (Cayzer, Irvine and Co. Ltd., managers), London.
1975: Sold to Gulf East Marine Inc., Monrovia, Liberia (Monnoo Overseas Ltd., Dubai) and renamed SCHIVAGO.
3.8.1977: Arrived at Gadani Beach for demolition.

Argyllshire (2) fitting out in the James Watt Dock, Greenock. This was a protracted business on refrigerated tonnage with so many compartments to be insulated and the work lasted five months, including dry docking in Glasgow for final painting before returning to Greenock for the first three weeks of October. She is also seen on trials in the Clyde (middle) and from the air in the English Channel with Harrison Line's *Adventurer* (8,971/1959) in the background (bottom). *[Top three: Newall Dunn collection (3); bottom: FotoFlite/J. and M. Clarkson collection]*

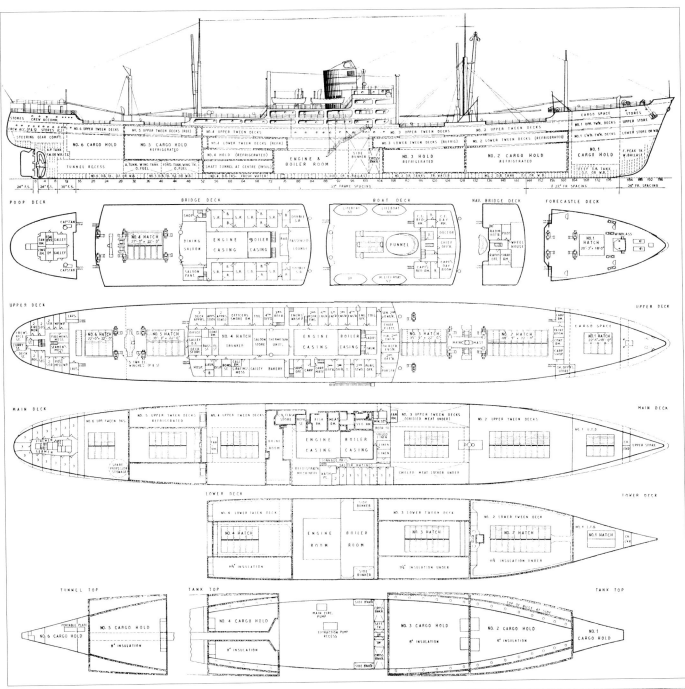

General arrangement drawing of the *Argyllshire* and the dining saloon. This room was designed to seat 32 persons. The walls were pastel green with an eggshell finish and there was access to the deck aft on both sides through the decorative forged iron grill doors.

AYRSHIRE (2) 1957-1965

O.N. 300171 9,360g 5,302n
534.9 x 69.3 x 28.4 feet.
Three steam turbines double-reduction geared to a single screw shaft by Parsons Marine Steam Turbine Co. Ltd., Wallsend-on-Tyne; 17 knots.
19.10.1956: Launched by the Greenock Dockyard Co. Ltd., Greenock (Yard No. 488).
2.5.1957: Completed for The Clan Line Steamers Ltd. (Cayzer, Irvine and Co. Ltd., managers), London as AYRSHIRE.
25.10.1960: Transferred to the Scottish Shire Line Ltd. (Cayzer, Irvine and Co. Ltd., managers), London.
23.3.1965: Struck uncharted submerged rock at Abd-al-Kuri near Socotra, 430 miles east south east of Aden, in position in position 12.08 north by 52.16 east, whilst on a voyage from Liverpool to Brisbane with general cargo.
26.4.1965: Refloated but grounded again.
27.4.1965: Salvage attempts abandoned.

Photographed on trials and in South Africa, *Ayrshire* (2) was arguably the finest in the fleet. Below is the engine room, looking aft and the forward end of the boiler room. *[Top: Newall Dunn collection; middle: R. Pabst; bottom: Glasgow University Archives GD323/7/9/2/488/46 and 45]*

Loss of the *Ayrshire*

In 1956 Clan and Scottish Shire Line's proud flagship *Ayrshire* (2) was abandoned to the elements on the south side of Abd-al-Kuri, a remote, little-known island lying 50 miles north east of the Horn of Africa (or Cape Guardafui as it was known to passing mariners), but now named Raas Caseyr.

In February 1963, *Ayrshire* was advertised on the Dowie and Marwood berth in Liverpool for Australia, accepting cargo in the Gladstone Dock for Brisbane, Gladstone and Sydney. The commodore ship left Liverpool on 1st March with a total complement of 94 consisting of 24 European officers, 62 Asian crew, seven passengers, and the chief officer's wife. Delayed for seven days at Gibraltar with boiler defects, she sailed from the bunkering port of Aden at 14.00 hours on 22nd March.

At that time of year fine weather generally prevails over the Gulf of Aden and northern Indian Ocean from the gentle breezes of the north east monsoon. It is the cruising man's dream with clear blue skies and no more than a few puffs of fine cumulus clouds, extreme visibility, temperatures in the high 70s and a relative humidity similar to a UK summer.

Ayrshire was due to call at Cochin on the Malabar coast of western India to change the Indian crews, a long-standing feature of the company's Australian trade, although Colombo in Sri Lanka was occasionally used as an alternative to Cochin. In the fair weather season a direct straight line course can be steered all the way from Aden to Cochin over a distance of 1,850 miles. Unlike most of the traffic between the Gulf of Aden and Bay of Bengal or Malacca Straits or beyond, which passes fairly close to Cape Guardafui and then

directly to the Eight Degree Channel through the Maldives, the direct course to Cochin passes 25 miles north of Cape Guardafui and then close south of Abd-al-Kuri, an obscure island lying midway between Socotra and the Horn of Africa. Abd-al-Kuri has very few inhabitants and lies on an east-west axis, is 20 miles in length and one to three miles in width. The western half is hilly and the eastern half mountainous with peaks of almost 2,500 feet allowing them to be seen for 50 miles in good clear weather. At about the mid-length, which is low lying and the narrowest part of the island, lies the wide south facing shore of Bandar Saleh backed by sandhills and soon to become a prominent feature of this story. The remainder of the south coast consists of cliffs. The entire island, which is uncultivated, presents a barren, desolate aspect to the passing mariner. It is surrounded by a shoal bank which showed on the chart as 17 fathoms close to the southern coast and 100 fathoms five miles offshore.

After a pleasant overnight passage from Aden, the *Ayrshire* was in sight of the bold Capo Elephante on the distant northern Somali coast next forenoon, 23rd March, while noon sights confirmed the ship to be on course and making good a speed 16.88 knots. By 13.30 hours Cape Guardafui was abeam 25 miles distant and within the next hour the pinkish peaks of Abd-al-Kuri came into view fine on the port bow. During the afternoon the wind increased from very light to a moderate easterly breeze, which veered to the south east as the island was approached and by the change of the watch at 16.00 hours was south south east force 4, by which time the ship was almost abeam the western tip of the island and four miles south of it.

Seen here at Aden the *Ayrshire* was an extremely powerful-looking ship, especially when belching clouds of black smoke.
[Ambrose Greenway]

As the course line approached the projecting south easterly end of the island the distance off gradually reduced but nevertheless placed the ship in a minimum 17 fathoms of water on a draft of 27 feet. The master was on the bridge with the chief officer and one of the passengers who was recording the scene on cine film.

Ayrshire strikes

While passing the steep southern cliffs abreast the highest part of the island, just before 17.00 hours, in an area where the chart indicated a depth of almost 20 fathoms, the *Ayrshire* struck an uncharted submerged object. The helm was immediately put hard-a-starboard, the engines stopped and the carpenter sent around to sound the bilges, which soon revealed a serious ingress of water to numbers 2, 3 and 4 holds. With the echo sounder still showing 20 fathoms, the engines were put half ahead and the ship turned around to a westerly course to place the wind and sea on the port quarter. Meanwhile, as a precautionary measure while the situation was being assessed, the crew were set to clearing away the boats. At 17.40 the engines were again stopped and the two after boats manned and lowered into the water, followed soon after by the port forward boat, into which were distributed a total of 73 personnel including the passengers and the chief officer's wife. This left the master and 20 other officers and crew aboard for the essential tasks of maintaining pumping and manoeuvring the ship.

With darkness approaching the boats were set on long painters astern of the ship, which at 18.07 again proceeded at half speed, steering a west-north-west course back towards the centre of the island, but 15 minutes later with the ingress of water increasing and the vessel listing to starboard, it was decided to beach the ship in Bandar Saleh and the boats were cut adrift.

At 18.48 hours both anchors were dropped, the vessel touched bottom and full speed ordered for five minutes to drive the ship securely on to the sandy beach; by 19.03 the engines were rung off and shut down. The chief officer then set off in the motor lifeboat to locate the other boats, all of which were recovered and hoisted back on board by 23.00 hours. For the time being the ship was safe, but with numbers 2, 3 and 4 holds flooded to sea level, in addition to four of the double bottom tanks, diesel tank and duct keel, her position was indeed precarious and in urgent need of a major salvage effort.

Some 20 minutes after striking the underwater object, *Ayrshire* had transmitted a distress message by wireless telegraphy on 500 kc/s, asking 'Vessels in the vicinity to stand by'. Twelve minutes later a further message indicated the *Ayrshire* was 'making water and might require assistance'.

By that same evening of 23rd March the owners in London were made aware of the vessel's plight and next morning fully advised of the extent of damage and flooding.

Fortunately the engine room, although holed in the double bottom, remained dry thus keeping the main engines, generators and pumps serviceable but even so were unable to cope with the ingress of water to numbers 2, 3 and 4 holds, which had led to the decision to beach.

Lloyd's Open Form signed

During the next day, 24th March, the owners contracted with L. Smit and Co. of Rotterdam on Lloyd's Open Form, with their first tug *Oceaan* (497/1951) expected in four to five days, and *Poolzee* (328/1942) due at Aden in six days where she was to ship the necessary salvage equipment. Smit's Salvage Inspector and the Clan Line Marine Superintendent flew out to Aden next day. Further investigation on 24th March revealed damage to the starboard diesel and fresh water tanks and contamination with seawater, although there was sufficient in the port tanks for all immediate needs.

The owners meanwhile instructed their nearest ship, *Clan Mactaggart* (2), to divert to the casualty on her outward voyage to East Africa. Having come out from London on the Union-Castle berth via Genoa and Naples, the *Clan Mactaggart* left Aden in the late evening of 23rd March and reached the *Ayrshire* at 02.40 on the 25th, where she remained standing by until relieved by the homeward *Clan Malcolm* (2) at 20.30 that day and then resumed her voyage. On passage from Cochin to London the former 12-passenger ship was then carrying 12 cadets in lieu, and these were asked to volunteer their assistance for the forthcoming salvage operations. On the morning of 26th March the passengers and chief officer's wife, four saloon ratings and accompanying baggage were transferred from the *Ayrshire* to *Clan Malcolm* in exchange for six cadets. The latter ship then continued her voyage, leaving the *Ayrshire* to await the arrival of Smit's tugs and pumping equipment. It was found during this day that flooding had spread to another two double bottom tanks and yet another by the following evening.

At 10.15 on Sunday 26th March, HMS *Anzio*, on passage from Aden to Mombasa, berthed alongside the *Ayrshire* and pumped aboard 110 tons of fresh water. Whilst alongside, her naval divers carried out a preliminary examination of the bottom which revealed the *Ayrshire* was unevenly supported along her entire length. The divers reported that number 1 double bottom had apparently been pierced by a rock when beaching; there were eight holes in the plating of number 2 and 3 double bottoms, a rivetted seam in way of number 4 and 5 double bottom was open for 30 feet over a four inch wide gap, and there were additional suspected damages towards the centreline, which were not investigated. HMS *Anzio* departed at 14.04 the same day for Mombasa and, with the impending arrival of the first tug, the ship's crew were set to opening the hatches to provide ready access for pumping equipment. Little else could be done until the salvors arrived, but clearly the

Ayrshire was in a perilous condition and, being on the south side of the island, would be fully exposed to the effects of the south west monsoon expected in less than two months time. It would be a race against time if the vessel was to be saved.

The first tug to reach the stricken vessel was the *Oceaan*, of 1,300 SHP, which had been relieved by the *Thames*

Oceaan was the first tug to arrive on the scene. [J. and M. Clarkson]

(664/1961) when towing two barges to the Persian Gulf. Smits directed the *Thames* to meet the *Oceaan*, transfer salvage pumps and take over the tow. The *Oceaan* subsequently arrived alongside the *Ayrshire* at 14.10 local time on 29th March. The pumps were quickly transferred and began operating from number 2 hold within two hours, but were stopped for the night at 22.30 having had little effect.

By next day the *Ayrshire* had been a week on the beach and had started to move slightly in the light swell which had set in. Conditions in the engine room began to deteriorate, with an increasing leak on the forward bulkhead and the starboard boiler connections breaking adrift. Despite having plenty of reserve on the engine room pumps, the master asked that arrival of tug *Poolzee* and salvage equipment be expedited. The derricks were rigged and the officers and crew began jettisoning cargo to help lighten the ship, initially from a shipment of 96 tons of bagged salt stowed in number 5 'tween deck. As a first salvage attempt, the anchors were weighed and, while pumping continued, the *Oceaan* made an effort to tow the vessel afloat, but was unsuccessful.

Further pumping and cargo jettisoning continued throughout the last day of March, by dumping drums of chemicals from number 1 hold, and with the vessel now bumping on the bottom, the *Oceaan* made another high water attempt to refloat her but was again unsuccessful and the tow rope parted. Meanwhile *Poolzee* had that day reached Aden, where she shipped one eight-inch and one three-inch pump, plus diving gear, together with the owner's superintendent, Smit's inspector and a surveyor from the Salvage Association, who had all arrived at Aden by air. The *Poolzee* had been recalled from a Mediterranean location and left Aden at 19.00 en route to Abd-al-Kuri.

On 1st April conditions in the engine room of the *Ayrshire* continued to deteriorate from buckling and fracturing of tank top girders, and from leaking and shearing rivets. Whilst the pumps were holding the water in numbers 2 and 3 at a very low level, there was insufficient capacity to reduce the level in

number 4 hold. *Oceaan* laid out a kedge anchor to assist another refloating attempt but was again unsuccessful when the anchor dragged. About 100 tons of cargo was jettisoned from number 1 hold while 250 tons of oil fuel was pumped overboard from the side bunkers to ease the weight in the engine room. The remaining fuel in the cross and side bunkers was also pumped overboard.

Next morning the tug *Noordzee* (333/1949) arrived at the ship and placed two more pumps aboard which were set to reduce the level of water in number 4 hold, which then had the highest ingress at 18 feet. The ship was now experiencing a moderate westerly wind on the port beam with a slight to moderate swell. That evening the *Poolzee* arrived alongside the starboard side of *Ayrshire* with the salvage party and two additional pumps. Another arrival at this time was the Aden coaster *Seiyun* (514/1945), into which cargo was to be transferred by the ship's crew.

During the next three days, cargo was worked from numbers 2 and 3 shelter decks into the *Seiyun*, while Smit's divers examined the bottom and found the vessel to be resting on rock and sand from forward to the aft end of number 3 hold. The wind worked round to a moderate south east with a slight sea and swell, while the salvors made an encasement for the 30-foot bottom crack on the hull, and began plugging over 100 holes in the 45-foot cracking tower stowed on deck, in preparation for floating and towing it to Aden. Cargo continued to be jettisoned from numbers 1, 2 and 6 holds, and after taking fresh water from the *Seiyun*, this coaster left for Aden at 13.00 on 5th April.

On the morning of 6th April, after almost two weeks on the beach, it was found that three of the double bottom fuel tanks were contaminated with seawater and, with a view to conserving fresh water, rationing was implemented by drawing on a hand pump from the peak tanks. A consignment of bricks, paper sacks of chemicals, and water-stained bales were jettisoned over the next five days whilst the wind fell light and variable.

Clan Maclean (3). [Malcolm Cranfield]

With a view to further reducing the number of unnecessary crew, the owners diverted their outbound *Clan Maclean* (3) which arrived at the scene during the afternoon of Saturday, 10th April. The *Poolzee* was used to transfer provisions to the casualty and seven Indian ratings with their baggage to the *Clan Maclean*, which then resumed her voyage to Madras and Chittagong.

Bank in Holland the salvors were making strenuous efforts to provide additional pumping equipment. A Luxemburg cargo aircraft was chartered, into which were loaded hoses, pipes, tools and no less than ten more pumps. This aircraft flew to Aden, where its cargo was then loaded into the chartered Panamanian steamer *Ais Nicolas* (4,125/1930), which subsequently berthed alongside the *Ayrshire* at 08.00 on Sunday 11th April. After transferring the vital salvage equipment, the *Ais Nicolas* began receiving heavy lifts by the *Ayrshire's* jumbo derrick from number 2 hold and 'tween deck, and thereafter miscellaneous cargo from numbers 3 and 5 'tween decks. The bottom situation continued to deteriorate when it was found that numbers 1 and 4 port double bottoms were contaminated and slowly filling with sea water.

Refloating attempted

The first major attempt at refloating was made on 16th April after the *Ayrshire* had been ashore for 25 days, by which time 900 tons of cargo had been transferred and 623 tons jettisoned, a total of 1,523 tons. The *Ais Nicolas* was moved off to an anchorage and with all pumps working to capacity, the *Oceaan* and *Poolzee* were made fast aft and began towing but the attempt was unsuccessful and abandoned at nightfall with the ship listing 7.5 degrees to starboard. The wind had now returned to a moderate south east and the pumps were rearranged to increase the flow from number 4 hold. With the failure of the refloating attempt, Smits ordered another tug to proceed to the casualty at maximum speed, the *Mississippi* (674/1960) of 2,500 BHP, which was en route light from Ras Gharib in the Gulf of Suez to Dubai.

At 07.00 next day the *Ayrshire's* second officer, with the senior cadet and 34 Indian crew with their baggage were transferred to the *Ais Nicolas*, which then sailed for Aden. A further refloating attempt was abandoned as unsuccessful at 16.00 hours, and prompted the Salvage Association surveyor to declare that the effective pumping capacity was insufficient, and unless it was quickly increased the vessel would become a constructive total loss. Meanwhile preparations were continued to offload the vacuum tower while another coaster was sought to discharge more of the readily accessible cargo. Although the weather continued favourable, the utmost urgency was now required if the vessel was to be refloated before the approach of the south west monsoon.

On 19th April the *Ayrshire's* 105-ton derrick discharged overside the 45-ton cracking tower, which had been ballasted with 1.5 tons of naphthalene to prevent it rolling when waterborne. It was then towed away by the *Poolzee* to Aden while the *Oceaan* carried the accompanying chocks and slings. The cracking tower was subsequently carried from Aden to Brisbane by another ship. As soon as these tugs had left, the *Mississippi* arrived alongside and transferred another three salvage pumps to the *Ayrshire* while the crew resumed the dumping of cargo from number 1 hold.

The *Clan Matheson* (5), homeward bound from Australia, arrived at the scene on the morning of 20th April to transfer stores and take *Ayrshire's* mail for onward posting at Aden. By that evening a total of 2,329 tons of cargo had been discharged and jettisoned from the *Ayrshire*. Next day the wind increased to fresh from the south south east, although the swell remained slight.

Yet more salvage pumps were being despatched to the casualty; six were flown out to Aden to be shipped onward by the *Oceaan*. On 23rd April the salvors stated their intention of making another refloating attempt when these additional

The scene on deck as the cracking tower is lifted from the deck and lowered overside into the sea to be towed to Aden. *[Archie Munro collection]*

pumps were set to work. It was planned to move the ship half a length only, whilst an examination was made on the ability to cope with the ingress of water, and, if satisfactory, the *Ayrshire* would be moved to a sheltered location at Guardafui. The south west monsoon was now believed to be imminent, the wind continued fresh from the south south east with a moderate swell. The Aden coaster *Shibaun* arrived alongside and began receiving cargo while the destroyer HMS *Cambrian* reported herself keeping station on the other side of the island for the next four days.

The tug *Oceaan* returned from Aden with the six additional pumps at 21.00 on 24th April. A further refloating attempt was again unsuccessful. Some of the pumps were now becoming choked with debris from the lower holds but, even more ominous, it was found that when maximum pumping lightened the ship sufficiently to be nearly afloat, she began rolling and bumping on the bottom. The *Poolzee* returned from Aden with the second officer on the morning of 25th April. Another unsuccessful refloating attempt was made that afternoon by which time it was found the vessel was only aground just aft of amidships. The pumps had to be frequently cleared from blockages and were rearranged for a major refloating attempt next day, but overnight the vessel moved six feet inshore. However, the weather was again fine with a smooth sea and the prospects for a successful refloating were never brighter.

After being 35 days aground, having jettisoned and transferred over 3,000 tons of cargo, fuel and water, and with 34 of Smit's salvage pumps going flat out to lower the level of water in the holds, the tugs finally and successfully refloated the *Ayrshire* at 16.20 local time on Monday, 26th April. The ship was towed approximately one ship length astern when, with the starboard anchor down, one tug aft, another alongside and one at anchor, the vessel swung ashore and again became fast aground and began bumping heavily parallel to the shore and heading east.

Having been afloat for only eight minutes, the *Ayrshire* was again aground and pinned broadside on to the reef by a two-knot current. The tugs *Oceaan* and *Mississippi* were made fast aft but failed to move the ship and, with most of the water ingress having been pumped out, there was little else that could be done to lighten the ship. After twelve hours continuous towing overnight, the tugs' efforts proved unavailing. The engine room, which had until now remained remarkably dry, now began to show increasing signs of leakage. The weather continued fine but it was obvious no more could be done to salvage the ship before the onset of the monsoon. Whilst the two tugs continued towing from the starboard quarter, Smit's salvage crew began disconnecting the pumps and preparing them for removal. The salvage attempt was officially abandoned that day and next morning, 28th April, the *Poolzee* and *Mississippi* left for Aden with part of the salvage party and the *Ayrshire* personnel. Finally, at 15.00 local time, the *Oceaan* left the *Ayrshire* taking with her the master and all remaining personnel. The chief officer's last work instruction had been to paint out the two red bands on the funnel. Effectively the *Ayrshire* was no longer part of the Clan Line fleet and had been abandoned.

No cure, no pay

There can be no doubt that Smits made a major effort to salve the ship with every means at their disposal, but with the bottom open for two thirds of her length and the ship fully exposed to the impending monsoon, the situation became hopeless and forced them to abandon the attempt. A total of 1,400 tons of cargo, which included 12 dogs and a great number of cars, together with the 45-ton cracking tower and numerous other heavy lifts, was safely recovered out of a total of 4,100 tons. All this had been accomplished by the officers and crew, working mostly under very trying conditions, learning the stevedore's job virtually from day to day by making up or adapting slings and strops to suit the wide range of cargo on hand, and had to include the peculiar art of slipping jettisoned loads overside.

On 30th April the three tugs arrived at Aden from where the salvage equipment was returned to Holland and from where the master and officers of the *Ayrshire* were flown to London. It was a tragic and sad end to a fine ship, but not quite the end of the story.

The Salvage Association now enquired if other salvors might be interested, which resulted in the Danish *Svitzer* (666/1921) arriving at the casualty one week later. This tug spent over five hours at the *Ayrshire* and reported a moderate south west wind but the swell six to eight feet high, which made it imprudent to get alongside. The *Ayrshire* was found to be six feet deeper in the water and the *Svitzer's* divers found the port side to be resting on stone and sand and embedded to bilge keel level from the stem to number 6 hold. All the holds except number 5 were flooded to sea level, in addition to the engine and boiler rooms, tunnel and steering gear flat. The surface of the water in three of the holds was covered in fuel oil. The ship was found to be constantly moving and in the high swell bumping heavily on the ground. The shaking had pushed up the rudder post and was felt through the steering engine and the whole ship. The port boiler was moving by an inch, while some of the forward rails and bulwark were partly cracked and opening up. The accommodation had been invaded, ransacked, looted and severely damaged by the natives who had also salvaged all manner of goods, including carpets, which were strewn on the beach. The ship was fully exposed to the south west monsoon which would soon prevent the movement of any personnel or materials to the ship. On 12th May the Salvage Association confirmed the chances of salving any more cargo to be non-existent in view of the ever increasing swell and the approaching monsoon, now reported to be active 200 miles south of Guardafui. The *Ayrshire* and her remaining cargo were now officially abandoned.

British Admiralty charts had long provided worldwide coverage to an international community of mariners. Their reliability was widely accepted and no one then could have anticipated the hidden dangers encountered by the *Ayrshire*. Nowadays, an area extending almost two miles offshore from the southernmost tip of Abd-al-Kuri is shown to embrace underwater rocks rated dangerous to navigation.

The authors are indebted to Captain A.T Campbell, formerly chief officer of Ayrshire*, and to Eliane de Man of Smit Tak BV, for information. A version of this text appeared in 'Ships Monthly' for October 1998.*

Clan Macintosh (3). *[Paul Boot]*

CLAN MACINTOSH CLASS

The Clan Macintosh *trio were essentially updated versions of the diesel-engined* Clan MacIs, *but with accommodation for 12 passengers. They were five feet longer, had the same beam and used the same six-cylinder Doxford machinery. All had satisfactorily long careers with Clan Line.*

CLAN MACINTOSH (3) 1951-1978

O.N. 184959 6,558g 3,605n
471.0 x 60.7 x 26.1 feet.
Doxford-type 6-cyl. 2SCSA oil engine by John Brown and Co. Ltd., Clydebank; 6,000 BHP.
19.7.1951: Launched by John Brown and Co. Ltd., Clydebank (Yard No. 665).
19.11.1951: Registered in the ownership of The Clan Line Steamers Ltd. (Cayzer, Irvine and Co. Ltd., managers), London as CLAN MACINTOSH.
23.11.1951: Completed.
1978: Sold to Sanil Shipping Co. Ltd., Hong Kong (Ali Khalifa and Mirchandani Shipping Co. Ltd. (Nirmal Mirchandani), Kuwait) and renamed SANIL.
28.8.1980: Arrived at Bombay.
30.8.1980: Handed over to the Haryana Steel Company for demolition.

CLAN MACINTYRE (3) 1952-1976

O.N. 184963 6,560g 3,602n
471.0 x 60.7 x 26.1 feet.
Doxford-type 6-cyl. 2SCSA oil engine by John Brown and Co. Ltd., Clydebank; 6,000 BHP.
31.10.1951: Launched by John Brown and Co. Ltd., Clydebank (Yard No. 666).
21.2.1952: Registered in the ownership of The Clan Line Steamers Ltd. (Cayzer, Irvine and Co. Ltd., managers), London as CLAN MACINTYRE.
28.2.1952: Completed.
1976: Transferred to King Line Ltd. (Cayzer, Irvine and Co. Ltd., managers), London.

A spotless *Clan Macintyre* (3) in the Mersey on 8th May 1954 (middle). During a major repair on Tyneside this unusual photograph was taken of the engine room with the crankshaft exposed. *[Middle: B. and A. Feilden/J. and M. Clarkson; bottom: Tyne and Wear Archives DT/TU/55652J]*

1976: Sold to Renown Bay Shipping Co. Ltd., Panama (Gulf Shipping Lines Ltd. (Abbas K. and Murtaza M. Gokal), London) (Gulfeast Ship Management Ltd., Hong Kong, managers) and renamed EASTERN EXPRESS.

22.12.1979: Stranded in a gale half a mile south of Marina di Carrara, Italy whilst on a voyage from La Spezia to Sardinia. Subsequently declared a constructive total loss.

Eastern Express, the former *Clan Macintyre* (3). [Ships in Focus]

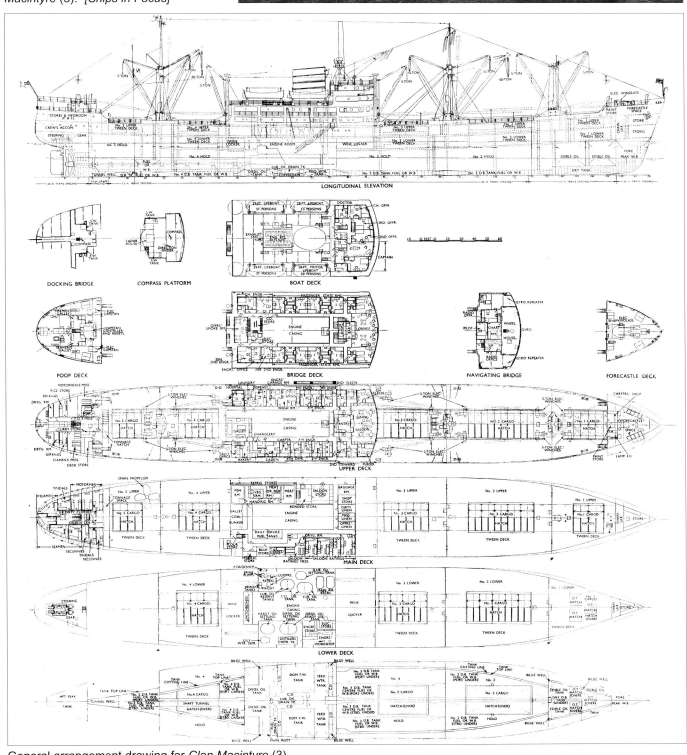

General arrangement drawing for *Clan Macintyre* (3).

CLAN MACINNES (3) 1952-1977
O.N. 184974 6,588g 3,621n
471.0 x 60.7 x 26.1 feet.
Doxford-type 6-cyl. 2 SCSA oil engine by
John Brown and Co. Ltd., Clydebank;
6,000 BHP.
9.4.1952: Launched by The Greenock

Dockyard Co. Ltd., Greenock (Yard No.
478).
30.6.1952: Registered in the ownership of
The Clan Line Steamers Ltd. (Cayzer,
Irvine and Co. Ltd., managers), London as
CLAN MACINNES.
2.7.1952: Completed.

1977: Sold to Ali Khalifa and Mirchandani
Shipping Co. Ltd. (Nirmal Mirchandani),
Kuwait and renamed ATHOUB.
15.10.1979: Arrived at Kaohsiung for
demolition by Lung Ching Steel Enterprise
Co. Ltd.
16.10.1979: Work began.

Clan Macinnes (3). *[J. K. Byass/J. and M. Clarkson collection]*

A round voyage in *Clan Macinnes*
Brian Scott

I commenced my cadetship with the Clan Line in October 1952 after leaving school the previous July. My first ship was the steamer *Clan Mackinnon* (3). I made two voyages in her from the UK/Europe to India/Pakistan, with short deviations carrying British military cargo to various trouble spots. After one year I was transferred to the *Clan Brodie* for a voyage from the UK to South Africa, Mauritius and India.

My next ship was the *Clan Macinnes* (3), a two-year-old motor vessel. My first voyage in her was from the UK to South Africa, then from the UK to India followed by a third voyage from the UK to Australia. Having enjoyed my visits to South Africa and Australia, the thought of another voyage to India did not motivate me at all, so when I received my recall to the *Clan Macinnes*, loading in Glasgow, at the end of my leave in early May 1955, my first reaction was to check the 'Journal of Commerce' to learn which ports we were loading for. Much to my delight it was South Africa and Portuguese West and East Africa. So off I went to Glasgow to rejoin my ship.

Loading cargo in Glasgow was typical of the mid-1950s with plenty of whisky, frozen kippers, and numbers 2, 3, 4 and 5 lower holds floored off with rails for the Rhodesian railways, plus many heavy lifts for new power stations and sugar factories. As a result we had a good bottom weight.

At number 2 hatch we had a 60-ton heavy-lift derrick, and at number 4 hatch aft there was a 30-ton derrick. Our other derricks had safe working loads of 15, 10 and 5 tons, so we

could rig them in all the various permutations of union purchase: doubled-up in union purchase; 'Frisco rig; and as swinging derricks with steam guys. This meant that the ship was self-sustaining for handling heavy lifts in the ports of developing countries.

We sailed from Glasgow to Birkenhead with the Clan Line's appropriated Liverpool pilot on board, so were soon on our final loading berth. The *Clan Macinnes* soon filled up with general cargo in the upper and lower 'tween decks, with more heavy lifts stowed in the lower holds over the railway lines loaded in Glasgow. These included 49-ton Centurion tanks for the South African Army. On the foredeck we loaded two railway locomotives and two small towboats. On the after deck we loaded one railway passenger carriage and one rail tank wagon. There were reconditioned Second World War army vehicles stowed on the hatches which were securely lashed and covered with tarpaulins. Number 1 hatch had an upper 'tween deck and a lower 'tween deck, but instead of a lower hold had three deep tanks fitted with heating coils and could be used for the carriage of vegetable oil cargoes or water ballast. With the heating coils removed, this space could be used for dry cargo. On this particular outward voyage the tanks were full of a partially refined soap-making product being shipped by Lever Brothers of Port Sunlight to their factory at Maydon Wharf in Durban. It would be necessary to monitor the liquid's temperature twice daily until it was pumped ashore.

Outward bound

We sailed on a Saturday afternoon and after disembarking the company pilot at Point Lynas we were on our way down the Irish Sea bound for Dakar for oil bunkers and fresh water. Like those of most UK liner companies, Clan Line masters doubled-up bridge watches until past Ushant. As the *Clan Macinnes* carried four mates and two cadets, the cadets were spared four-on and four-off watches.

Once south of the latitude of Ushant normal shipboard routine fell into place. The first mate could do little on deck because of the clutter. The normal outward bound routine on board Clan Line vessels was to strip down all running gear on the derricks for survey and overhaul. On this voyage we had to make do with a visual inspection, and the greasing and oiling of topping lifts, runners, guys and cargo blocks.

The cadets got on with their usual jobs; first the life-saving apparatus and fire-fighting equipment was checked, and then a start was made on the lifeboats. The *Clan Macinnes* was used to trial new types of paints and this voyage we had to start stripping out the lifeboats one at a time, clean them thoroughly inside and out, and then apply different paints to the metal hulls. This was a pleasant enough task as it was flying fish weather and not too hard physically.

We carried 12 passengers in quite luxurious accommodation and they spent their days on the boat deck. The Indian stewards always passed us the leftover tab nabs after morning coffee and afternoon teas. One of the lady passengers asked the captain why he mixed up white sailors with the lascars. This was probably prompted by the fact that chippie and the cadets usually looked dirtier and sweatier than the kelassies!

The cadets' routine at sea was quite pleasant. Our Indian steward woke us at 06.30 with a mug of tea and hot buttered toast. At 07.00 the Scottish carpenter took his soundings while one cadet took the temperatures in the holds and the liquid cargo tanks. The other cadet went on the wheel so the seacunny (quartermaster) could help his mate clean the wheelhouse windows and brasswork. We then had breakfast at the second sitting and we always enjoyed a good hearty meal along with the fourth mate, carpenter, assistant purser, junior engineers and electricians. During the day we worked on our allotted tasks until 17.00, when we took the afternoon temperature readings. We did not work on Wednesday afternoons as we had study for our correspondence courses. On Sunday mornings the cadets went to the bridge to practise taking morning and noon sun sights, and in the evenings we joined the first and fourth mates to take star sights.

Around Africa

After a brief stop at Dakar for bunkers and fresh water we continued southwards towards the port of Lobito in Angola, Portuguese South West Africa to discharge vehicles for the Portuguese army. We then sailed for Cape Town, keeping well off the coast to avoid the treacherous currents off the Skeleton Coast of Namibia, between the Swakop and Kunene rivers.

It was good to arrive in Cape Town again and berth in the Duncan Dock. Cargo work in South African ports was from 08.00 until 20.00 so, with four mates and two cadets on the *Clan Macinnes*, we got some shore leave. The Seamen's Mission had a couple of large taxi-type cars, so we put money into their petrol fund and enjoyed some very good guided tours of the city and countryside.

We discharged our railway locomotives and rolling stock at Cape Town, which made cargo work much easier. We did this by using our heavy lift derricks and winding ship. Our coastal voyages from Cape Town to Port Elizabeth (420 miles), then Port Elizabeth to East London, (130 miles) and from East London to Durban (260 miles) were uneventful. At Durban we spent some time at Maydon Wharf alongside Lever Brothers' soap factory.

Durban is a large sub-tropical city with a long surf beach. It is a major port but also a well-known holiday resort. The weather is warm all the year round and due to the Agulhas Current the seawater remains warm. During the summer the weather gets hot and humid with spectacular thunderstorms.

By this time we began to wonder what our homeward loading programme would be. Would we retrace our outward route or proceed up the coast of East Africa to Dar-es-Salaam

Clan Macinnes (3) secured for sea in the English Channel. *[FotoFlite/J. and M. Clarkson collection]*

and Mombasa? But no, we loaded bagged rice in our empty 'tween decks for Mauritius, and then proceeded north to Lourenço Marques (now Maputo) to continue discharging our outward cargo. Lourenço Marques was a beautiful city comparable to Cape Town or Rio de Janeiro. We then steamed the 475 miles north to Beira which was the principal port for the Rhodesias, where we discharged our rails for the Rhodesian Railways, and cleaned out our deep tanks and removed the heating coils. There was serious port congestion at this time both at Lourenço Marques and Beira, but our much-needed cargo secured us priority berthing, and we were soon on our way south of Madagascar, bound for Mauritius.

On the voyage to Mauritius the crew cleaned out the holds whilst chippie and his mate, the winchwallah, and the two cadets cleaned out the bilges and repaired the limber boards and spar ceiling: not a pleasant task as we were light ship and there was a strong swell running. I took a spare bucket down the holds and it was needed by all four of us.

On arrival at Port Louis, Mauritius, we discharged our part cargo of rice. Once again we asked, what was our homeward cargo to be? Would it be a full load of sugar for the UK or might we proceed light ship to the Malabar Coast in India to load ironsand, tea and gunnies? Both guesses were wrong. We received orders to proceed to Fremantle, Western Australia, to lift a homeward cargo for Scottish Shire Line.

On the Australian coast
We soon departed from Port Louis and set course for Fremantle. It was all go on deck, as all cargo gear was overhauled, hatch boards repaired and 'tween deck lifelines rigged in preparation for the Australian Government surveyor's inspection.

A few days before arriving at Fremantle we received a radio message to break out the two heavy-lift derricks, as we had been granted a permit to carry Australian coastal cargo, namely a civil engineering contractor's fleet of heavy earth-moving vehicles from Fremantle to our first loading port, Port Pirie. We duly arrived at Fremantle, bunkered, took on fresh water and loaded the oversize vehicles in numbers 2 and 4 lower holds and on deck. We then sailed for the Spencer Gulf through a rough Australian Bight. On arrival at Port Pirie we discharged our heavy-lift cargo and rehoused the jumbo derricks and our passengers disembarked.

It was now the first week in September 1955. Port Pirie was the best provincial port in southern Australia and had a great maritime history. It had the largest lead smelting and refining plant in the world. There was also a bulk grain silo for export cargoes. Rail transport was important and three different rail gauges served the town and port, the tracks running down the main street.

We loaded lead ingots in the 'tween decks and lower holds and a few days later sailed for Brisbane to load canned fruit, mainly pineapples. Loading was quite quick and the cadets had a break from work to go and caddie for the captain and ship's doctor on the famous golf course. In the mid 1950s Brisbane was fairly quiet and so we organised a social evening for our shoreside friends to repay the generous hospitality they had offered us during the week.

We sailed from Brisbane to Newcastle where we loaded wool and then proceeded to Sydney where our berth was at the Woolloomooloo Wharf just below the Royal Botanical Gardens. There we loaded more wool which came down to the wharf on lorries and was then put through the wool dumping presses before being loaded on board.

By this time our Indian crew had been away from home for a year and were agitating for a crew change. At the same time we were waiting for cargo to go into our number 1 deep tanks and expected to load wet hides as on a previous voyage. However, we received a shipment of large crates from the Royal Australian Navy labelled 'Indian Navy, Port of Cochin, Malabar Coast, India'. This cheered up the crew and they became their usual happy selves again. And so we filled number 1 hold deep tanks and 'tween decks with the naval cargo and we knew that we would be going the long way home.

We had been fortunate with the weather in our loading ports and had not had too much of the expected rain. We sailed from Sydney to Melbourne where we berthed at Station Pier and loaded wool. We completed filling the holds and then stowed more wool on the hatches between the derricks and covered it with tarpaulins which were well lashed down. After a busy social life in Melbourne we were glad to depart for Fremantle to take on bunkers and fresh water. We had a new group of 12 passengers on board which pleased our old doctor as he had some bridge partners. Our doctor was about 70 years of age, ex Indian Army and Colonial Service, and as well as medal ribbons for both World Wars he had other exotic ones such as North West Frontier, and he could rival Kipling when he told us about his army career.

Heading home via India
After a brief stop at Fremantle we were on our way to India. The crew washed down and painted the masts, derricks and the midships accommodation block. The cadets scraped and repainted number 2 lifeboat with the second batch of trial paints, this time a rubbery type, so we were glad of the warmer weather.

On our arrival at Cochin we tied up at the buoys offshore from Willingdon Island, named after a former Viceroy of India. It was a mainly man-made island and apart from a pleasant civilian hotel and swimming pool, was used as a civil/military airfield and naval base. As we had not loaded wool on number 1 hatch we soon discharged our naval cargo into lighters alongside. Then chippie and the two cadets fitted the steam heating coils in the three number 1 deep tanks, followed by shore cleaning gangs to hand clean the tanks prior to inspection by a cargo surveyor. We then loaded 450 tons of cashew nut oil from road tankers carried on barges alongside. This oil is a thick, black, smelly liquid which we were told was used to make the black insulation on heavy duty electric power cables. It was for discharge at Barry, South Wales. We carried out a crew change and then loaded coconut mats and matting in the number 1 'tween decks. All this took two days.

Once clear of Cochin we settled into sea routine with the crew cleaning and painting the steel decks. The cadets went into signwriting and varnishing mode until arrival at Aden for a brief stop for bunkers and fresh water. Our job on passage up the Red Sea was to make a set of new wire preventer guys for the derricks.

The *Clan Macinnes* arrived at the anchorage at Suez Roads in the early morning, fully expecting to wait for a northbound convoy later in the day. A water barge came out to us and we quickly took on fresh water. A canal pilot then boarded. He was a bi-lingual Mauritian and an ex-Clan Line officer, so he was pleased at the prospect of a curry and rice lunch later. One of our quartermasters injured his wrist whilst housing the accommodation ladder, so I was nominated to replace him on the wheel for the canal transit. As we had no cargo for Port Said we were allocated a convoy position at the end of 12 oil tankers which were just passing through and so we had a relatively fast passage. The ship steered well as always and when darkness fell the chippie and the second electrician operated the searchlight in the bow.

Once clear of Port Said we felt that we were really heading home. During the passage through the Mediterranean the cadets landed the job of painting both the mate's and the tally clerks' offices, and then carried out a stocktaking of all the remaining deck stores. By this time we had passed Gibraltar and we carried out a final check of the fire-fighting equipment and then completed our correspondence course assignments. By the time we were off Santander in Spain and entering the Bay of Biscay with rough seas and poor visibility we were put on bridge watches with the mates, and I got the 8 to 12.

We called in at Dunkirk for the duration of one tide and quickly discharged our deck cargo of wool with the shore cranes lifting 16 bales at a time. Our kindly mentor, the first mate, signed off as he had to return to Glasgow having obtained a position as a River Clyde pilot.

From Dunkirk we sailed close in to the shore with a French pilot on board until we embarked a River Scheldt pilot to take us into Antwerp. This entailed the usual long stand-by up the river. We locked into the Antwerp docks for one tide only and more wool was quickly discharged at the rate of 16 bales per lift using shore cranes.

The passage down the English Channel and up the Bristol Channel was tiring with rough seas, poor visibility and the usual heavy shipping traffic. We had radar and Decca navigator operating so we coped well and did not lose any time.

We arrived at Barry where our passengers disembarked and we discharged the coconut matting from number 1 'tween decks, and then pumped the 450 tons of cashew nut oil ashore into road tankers. We then filled the three number 1 deep tanks with dock water, poured a drum of detergent into each and kept the steam heating coils hot, in the hope that on passage to Manchester the tanks would partially self clean.

One of the Clan Line 'choice' Liverpool pilots boarded in Barry in order to avoid an open sea transfer off Point Lynas. We had a fast passage from Barry to the River Mersey where we entered the Manchester Ship Canal at Eastham. As it was late afternoon and getting dark we moored up at the crane berth just inside the canal. That evening the shore crane assisted our crew to lower the topmasts and the radar mast. As I lived close by, I went home for a few hours to visit my family. We had an early breakfast and commenced our inward canal transit at 08.00 with the company pilot and his helmsman on the bridge.

As usual with a large vessel in the Manchester Ship Canal we had some long stand-bys awaiting outward-bound vessels to pass us, and when we were in the various locks. By late afternoon it was getting dark and so we moored overnight at a lay-by berth. Next morning we resumed our passage up the Canal to Manchester, arriving at lunchtime. Cargo work commenced immediately and the bales of wool went off to the mills of Bradford, while the lead ingots were loaded on to rail wagons for the Midlands. The local tank cleaning vessel arrived alongside to clean out our deep tanks which took until 23.30, and so it was another long day.

The following day the coastal relief team of officers arrived on board with the Shipping Master, and we signed off articles with instructions to be ready to rejoin the ship at Cardiff on or about 28th December 1955 for a direct voyage to Australia.

This account by the late Captain Brian Scott of Whangarei, New Zealand of his voyage as a Clan Line cadet in the 1950s appeared in the 'Bulletin' of the Liverpool Nautical Research Society in March 2005 and is reproduced here, slightly abbreviated, by kind permission of the editor, John Shepherd.

Clan Macinnes (3) in the Bristol Channel in May 1963. *[W. D. Harris/J. and M. Clarkson collection]*

CLAN MALCOLM CLASS

These three motor ships were simply a diesel-engined version of the Clan Robertson *(3) and* Clan Ross *(3), the motor ship at last triumphing over the steam turbine, although the latter ships were a knot or so faster in service. It was originally intended that they should have twin screws, but this was estimated to cost an extra £150,000 compared with a single-screw turbine ship. A rethink saw them redesigned first with turbines, and then with a two-stroke Doxford diesel driving a single screw. It is extraordinary that the order for these ships was placed in the spring of 1951, yet they were not delivered until six years later. They were the last Clans to have passenger accommodation.*

CLAN MALCOLM (2) 1957-1979

O.N. 300181 7,686g 4,181n
502.9 x 65.8 x 27.3 feet.
Doxford-type 6-cyl. 2SCSA oil engine by the Wallsend Slipway and Engineering Co. Ltd., Wallsend-on-Tyne; 8,000 BHP.
29.4.1957: Launched by the Greenock Dockyard Co. Ltd., Greenock (Yard No. 490).
13.8.1957: Completed for The Clan Line Steamers Ltd. (Cayzer, Irvine and Co. Ltd., managers). London as CLAN MALCOLM.
1979: Sold to Bective Shipping Corporation, Panama (Javelin Co. Ltd., Hong Kong) and renamed TRINITY FAIR.
9.7.1979: Arrived at Shanghai for demolition.

CLAN MATHESON (5) 1957-1978

O.N. 300186 7,685g 4,180n
502.8 x 65.8 x 27.3 feet.
Doxford-type 6-cyl. 2SCSA oil engine by the Wallsend Slipway and Engineering Co. Ltd., Wallsend-on-Tyne; 8,000 BHP.
26.8.1957: Launched by the Greenock Dockyard Co. Ltd., Greenock (Yard No. 489).
18.12.1957: Completed for The Clan Line Steamers Ltd. (Cayzer, Irvine and Co. Ltd., managers). London as CLAN MATHESON.
12.12.1978: Handed over to Keun Hwa Iron and Steel Works and Enterprise Ltd., Kaohsiung for demolition.
21.12.1978: Work commenced.

Above: Clan Malcolm (2) at Brisbane in 1957. She served as a cadet ship for a number of years. [J. and M. Clarkson]
Below: Clan Matheson (5) on trials. [Newall Dunn collection]

CLAN MENZIES (3) 1958-1979

O.N. 300200 7,685g 4,180n
502.8 x 65.8 x 27.3 feet.
Doxford-type 6-cyl. 2SCSA oil engine by the Wallsend
Slipway and Engineering Co. Ltd., Wallsend-on-Tyne;
8,000 BHP.
22.1.1958: Launched by the Greenock Dockyard Co.
Ltd., Greenock (Yard No. 491).
21.5.1958: Completed for The Clan Line Steamers Ltd.
(Cayzer, Irvine and Co. Ltd., managers), London as
CLAN MENZIES.
1979: Sold to Bective Shipping Corporation, Panama
(Javelin Co. Ltd., Hong Kong) and renamed TRINITY
SPLENDOUR.
1980: Sold to the China Ocean Shipping Company,
Peking, China and renamed XING KONG.
1984: Transferred to the Hebei Province Subcorporation
China Ocean Shipping Company, (COSCO/HEBEI).
1989: Broken up in China.

Clan Menzies (3) just prior to launch on 22nd June 1958 (top right), on trials (bottom) and looking into her engine room. The name originally intended for her was *Clan Morrison. [Launch and trials: Newall Dunn collection (2); engine room: Glasgow University Archives GD323/7/9/2/491/29]*

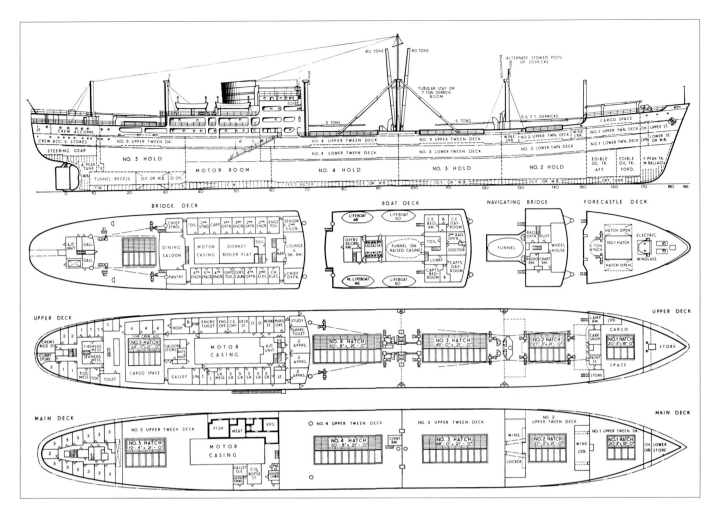

ENGINES THREE QUARTERS AFT

Clan Maciver (3) was the first of the company's ships to have the bridge and accommodation moved aft to between holds four and five. Cargo gear in Clan Maciver featured two bipods, one conventional but unstayed mast, and three pairs of kingposts, but this was altered to three bipods for the two subsequent ships. The bipod between holds three and four carried two 80-ton derricks. The technical press remarked that she was unusual for a ship carrying an Asian crew in having fully air-conditioned accommodation, but she was rather anachronistic in having an almost fully riveted hull construction.

With this class passenger accommodation was discontinued, and on visiting the completed Clan Maciver a board member was irate because he felt the lounge and bar area too generous for the crew alone. It was resolved that it would be smaller in subsequent ships.

CLAN MACIVER (3) 1958-1979

O.N. 300214 7,350g 3,686n
494.0 x 61.8 x 26.4 feet.
Doxford-type 5-cyl. 2SCSA oil engine by Barclay, Curle and Co. Ltd., Glasgow; 5,400 BHP.
23.6.1958: Launched by the Greenock Dockyard Co. Ltd., Greenock (Yard No. 492).
11.1958: Completed for The Clan Line Steamers Ltd. (Cayzer, Irvine and Co. Ltd., managers), London at a cost of £1,260,000 as CLAN MACIVER.
1979: Sold to Quin Ace Maritime S.A., Panama (Javelin Co. Ltd., Hong Kong) for $640,000 and renamed TRINITY PRIDE.
31.1.1980: Arrived at Shanghai for demolition.
9.2.1980: Work began.

On 25th September 1958 the *Clan Maciver* almost capsized in the James Watt Dock during the final stages of fitting-out. During ballast trials a hole which had been cut in the port side to facilitate pumping the bilges allowed water into the port side of the engine room, causing a rapidly increasing list. The ship's mooring wires became taut and carried away one after another. Capsize was only averted when the sluice of the dock gate was opened to lower the water level and allowing the port bilge of the ship to rest on the bottom, by then at an angle of 35°. Salvage teams worked throughout the next night to locate and plug the hole and this allowed the list to be gradually corrected. Delivery of the ship was only delayed by two weeks. *[Archie Munro]*

General arrangement drawing of *Clan Maciver* (3) (opposite top), photographed leaving Brisbane on 4th August 1960 (opposite bottom) and as *Trinity Pride* (bottom right). She could be distinguished from her two later sisters by the combination of bipod, conventional mast and bipod on the long fore deck, *Clan Macindoe* (2) and *Clan Macilwraith* (2) having three bipods. The bipods may not have been a success: they did not appear on subsequent ships.

The detail photographs show the business end of the heavy lift derrick (above), the top platform in the engine room showing the upper piston rod guides and in the distance the six-ton overhaul crane (middle), and the starting platform (middle right).
[Opposite: J. and M. Clarkson; this page: Glasgow University Archives GD323/7/9/2/492/27-28 (2); bottom: Trevor Jones/D. Salisbury collection]

Clan Macindoe (2) differed from her immediate predecessor in having three bipod mast rather than two, presumably experience with the former benefiting her design. She was owned by British and Commonwealth subsidiary Neptune Shipping Co. Ltd. of Hamilton, Bermuda, and bareboat chartered to Clan Line. She disgraced herself when a thrust block seized during trials on 11th November 1959, delaying delivery by nine days. *Clan Macindoe* was photographed on the New Waterway. *[J. and M. Clarkson]*

CLAN MACINDOE (2) 1959-1979

O.N. 301401 7,359g 3,754n
492.5 x 61.8 x 26.4 feet.
Doxford-type 5-cyl. 2SCSA oil engine by John Brown and Co. (Clydebank) Ltd., Clydebank; 5,400 BHP.
20.8.1959: Launched by John Brown and Co. (Clydebank) Ltd., Clydebank (Yard No. 712).
20.11.1959: Completed for Neptune Shipping Co. Ltd., Hamilton, Bermuda (Cayzer, Irvine and Co. Ltd., managers), London at a cost of £1,320,000 and bareboat chartered to The Clan Line Ltd., London as CLAN MACINDOE.
7.1979: Sold to Gulf Shipping Lines Ltd. (Abbas K., Murtaza M. and Mustafa Gokal) (Gulfeast Ship Management Ltd., managers), London and renamed GULF HERON.
11.9.1980: Arrived at Basrah, from Recife. Later that month damaged by shell fire during the Iran-Iraq war and grounded in the Shatt Al Arab. Subsequently declared a compromised total loss.

CLAN MACILWRAITH (2) 1960-1979

O.N. 301428 7,354g 3,690n
494.0 x 61.7 x 26.4 feet.
Doxford-type 5-cyl. 2SCSA oil engine by the Wallsend Slipway and Engineering Co. Ltd., Wallsend-on-Tyne; 5,400 BHP.
27.5.1960: Launched by the Greenock Dockyard Co. Ltd., Greenock (Yard No. 496).
14.12.1960: Completed for The Clan Line Steamers Ltd. (Cayzer, Irvine

and Co. Ltd., managers), London at a cost of £1,360,000 as CLAN MACILWRAITH.

1979: Sold to Guan Guan Shipping (Private) Ltd., Singapore for $725,000 and renamed GOLDEN CITY.

17.7.1986: Fire broke out in number 1 hold in the Malacca Straits in position 05.02 north by 97.58 east whilst on a voyage from Colombo to Singapore.

24.7.1986: Arrived at Singapore. Subsequently declared a constructive total loss.

21.10.1986: National Shipbreakers (Private) Ltd. began demolition at Jurong.

Clan Macilwraith (2) being launched (opposite middle), from the stern (opposite bottom), and in run down condition as *Golden City* (above). [Opposite middle: Newall Dunn collection; opposite bottom: J. K. Byass; above: W.A. Schell]

SIX KINGS

Six King Line motor ships were transferred to Clan Line late in 1959. Although not renamed and continuing with British crews, they painted up Clan's funnel colours. It is said that this was to tidy up the King Line fleet, which henceforth was to consist only of bulk carriers, but if so untidiness was to reign further, with several Clan Liners transferred to King Line for their last days, the latter company being better able to use the investment allowance. There was some reluctance amongst Clan officers to serve on what they regarded as mere tramp ships.

KING ARTHUR 1959-1972

O.N. 185856 8,255g 5,157n
466.5 x 59.2 x 25.8 feet.
Burmeister & Wain-type 6-cyl. 4SCSA oil engine by Harland and Wolff Ltd., Belfast; 3,300 BHP.

19.11.1952: Launched by Harland and Wolff Ltd., Belfast (Yard No. 1462).

16.5.1953: Registered in the ownership of King Line Ltd., London as KING ARTHUR.

3.1953: Completed.

6.10.1959: Transferred to The Clan Line Steamers Ltd. (Cayzer, Irvine and Co. Ltd., managers), London.

1.1.1963: Transferred to King Line Ltd. (Cayzer, Irvine and Co. Ltd., managers), London.

5.1972: Sold to Kition Compania Naviera S.A., Panama (Alassia Steamship Co. Ltd. (Vassos

Haji Ioannou), London) and renamed TOULLA under the Cyprus flag.

1980: Renamed DESPO under the Panama flag.

1980: Sold to Basco Enterprises (Private) Ltd. (Lucky Dragon Enterprises Private Ltd. (Joseph Muttiah), Singapore) and renamed PEARL RAINBOW under the Panama flag.

1981: Sold to Greenleaf Navigation S.A., Panama (Smipt Shipping and Trading Private Ltd. (Joseph Muttiah), Singapore) and renamed GREENLEAF.

14.7.1982: Arrived at Trincomalee in tow after taking on water during a voyage from Port Kelang to Aden.

Prior to 30.6.1983: Arrived at Chittagong.

30.7.1983: Breaking up began by Emzed Enterprises, Dakar.

King Arthur. [J. and M. Clarkson collection]

King Henry (above) was the newest of the King Line motor ships transferred to Clan, and the only one with a composite superstructure.

'Big' ships were uncommon visitors to Preston (right) and *King Henry* caused a stir when she arrived on 2nd February 1961 from Vancouver, via Garston, with 743 standards of timber, sailing on 13th February for Cardiff in ballast.

Her arrival was unusual for two reasons; firstly she was one of the beamiest ships to visit the port - she had little spare room in the locks - and secondly timber cargoes from British Columbia generally came in old Greek ships. In this photograph her hull is in an unusually poor state for a Clan liner. [Both: J. and M. Clarkson collection]

KING HENRY 1959-1972
O.N. 300806 8,331g 4,953n
466.5 x 59.2 x 25.8 feet.
Burmeister & Wain-type 6-cyl. 4SCSA oil engine by Harland and Wolff Ltd., Belfast; 3,300 BHP.
15.8.1958: Launched by Harland and Wolff Ltd., Belfast (Yard No. 1587).
12.1958: Completed for King Line Ltd., London as KING HENRY.
29.10.1959: Transferred to The Clan Line Steamers Ltd. (Cayzer, Irvine and Co. Ltd., managers), London.
1.1971: Transferred to Houston Line Ltd. (Cayzer, Irvine and Co. Ltd., managers), London.
12.1972: Sold to Grandmar Compania Naviera S.A., Panama (Athanasios Marco-poulos, Piraeus, Greece) and renamed AFRICAN LION under the Greek flag.

1981: Sold to Grifos Maritime Co. S.A., Panama (Seahorse Shipping Co. S.A., Panama) (N. Evangelatos, Piraeus, Greece) and renamed KLADITIS EMMANUEL under the Greek flag.
1983: Sold to Verbier Shipping Ltd., Valletta, Malta and renamed VERBIER.
14.4.1983: Arrived at Gadani Beach.
24.5.1983: Demolition began by Amin Steel Company.

KING CHARLES 1959-1973
O.N. 187593 8,160g 4,926n
466.5 x 59.2 x 25.8 feet.
Burmeister & Wain-type 6-cyl. 4SCSA oil engine by Harland and Wolff Ltd., Belfast; 3,300 BHP.
15.3.1957: Launched by Harland and Wolff Ltd., Belfast (Yard No. 1556).

21. 6.1957: Registered in the ownership of King Line Ltd., London as KING CHARLES.
27.11.1959: Transferred to The Clan Line Steamers Ltd. (Cayzer, Irvine and Co. Ltd., managers), London.
1.1970: Transferred to Houston Line Ltd. (Cayzer, Irvine and Co. Ltd., managers), London.
2.1973: Sold to Cephissos Shipping Co. Ltd., Famagusta, Cyprus (Aegis Shipping Co. Ltd., Athens, Greece), and renamed AEGIS MIGHT.
1976: Transferred to Marmaris Shipping Corporation Ltd. (Aegis Shipping Co. Ltd., Athens, Greece).
27.7.1979: Arrived at Kaohsiung for demolition.
6.8.1979: Kao Yung Steel Enterprise Co. began work.

King Charles in the Mersey 1st July 1972, heading for Eastham, in the full Clan livery and with her top masts already dropped for her passage up the Manchester Ship Canal. *[J. and M. Clarkson]*

KING GEORGE 1959-1972
O.N. 187694 8,160g 4,926n
466.5 x 59.2 x 25.8 feet.
Burmeister & Wain-type 6-cyl. 4SCSA oil engine by Harland and Wolff Ltd., Belfast; 3,300 BHP.
27.8.1957: Launched by Harland and Wolff Ltd., Belfast (Yard No. 1557).
13.12.1957: Registered in the ownership of King Line Ltd., London as KING GEORGE.

7.12.1959: Transferred to The Clan Line Steamers Ltd. (Cayzer, Irvine and Co. Ltd., managers), London.
1.1970: Transferred to Houston Line Ltd. (Cayzer, Irvine and Co. Ltd., managers), London.
11.1972: Sold to Lemythou Compania Naviera S.A., Panama (Alassia Steamship Co. Ltd. (Vassos Haji Ioannou), London) and renamed ELENI under the Cyprus flag.

2.1980: Sold to Hong Kong Maritime Inc., Panama (Jaguar Shipping Corporation Ltd., Hong Kong) and renamed TAICHUNG 2.
9.10.1982: Arrived at Kaohsiung for demolition.
7.12.1982: Sie Horng Steel Enterprises began work.
14.12.1982: Demolition completed.

King George looking smart in full Clan colours. At the end of her life, ten years after her sale, she was broken up in the extraordinary short time of seven days, according to Lloyd's Register's records. *[J. and M. Clarkson collection]*

King Malcolm. [Newall Dunn collection]

KING MALCOLM 1959-1972
O.N. 184575 8,197g 4,979n
466.5 x 59.2 x 25.8 feet.
Burmeister & Wain-type 6-cyl. 4SCSA oil
engine by Harland and Wolff Ltd., Belfast;
3,300 BHP.
29.11.1951: Launched by Harland and
Wolff Ltd., Belfast (Yard No. 1450).
26.2.1952: Registered in the ownership of
King Line Ltd., London as KING
MALCOLM.
29.12.1959: Transferred to The Clan Line
Steamers Ltd. (Cayzer, Irvine and Co.
Ltd., managers), London.
1.1.1963: Transferred to Hector Whaling

Co. Ltd. Cayzer, Irvine and Co. Ltd.,
managers), London.
6.1972: Sold to Soloi Compania Naviera
S.A., Panama (Alassia Steamship Co. Ltd.
(Vassos Haji Ioannou), London),
managers), and renamed KANARIS under
the Cyprus flag.
1980: Sold to Dimitra Shipping Company
(Demitris P. Kavadas), Piraeus, Greece,
and renamed DIMITRA K.
24.10.1981: Arrived at Chittagong and
arrested.
7.1983: Arash Shipbreakers began
demolition at Faujderhat Beach,
Chittagong.

KING ALEXANDER 1959-1972
O.N. 184628 8,194g 4,992n
466.5 x 59.2 x 25.8 feet.
Burmeister & Wain-type 6-cyl. 4SCSA oil
engine by Harland and Wolff Ltd., Belfast;
3,300 BHP.
14.2.1952: Launched by Harland and
Wolff Ltd., Belfast (Yard No. 1451).
2.5.1952: Registered in the ownership of
King Line Ltd., London as KING
ALEXANDER.
29.12.1959: Transferred to The Clan Line
Steamers Ltd. (Cayzer, Irvine and Co.
Ltd., managers), London.
1.1.1963: Transferred to Hector Whaling

King Alexander at Durban with Clan Line funnel colours but without Clan's distinctive white hull strake (above) and on the
River Tees on 8th May 1971 (opposite top). *[J. and M. Clarkson collection]*

Co. Ltd. (Cayzer, Irvine and Co. Ltd., managers), London.
9.1972: Sold to Ilyssia Compania Naviera S.A., Panama (Alassia Steamship Co. Ltd. (Vassos Haji Ioannou), London) and renamed ELLI 2 under the Cyprus flag.
1980: Sold to Bangkok Maritime Inc., Panama (Jaguar Shipping Corporation (I. Wang), Hong Kong) and renamed BANGKOK 2.
19.8.1982: Arrived at Gadani Beach.
12.9.1982: Ahmad Mercantile Ltd. began demolition.

CLAN Fs AND Gs

These seven ships represented the largest class Clan Line had built for fifty years. As with all the company's ships, rather than being a radical departure the design evolved subtly, in this case from that of Clan Maciver (3). Larger and faster, they had conventional unstayed masts rather than bipods, and the sixth hold aft managed with one set of kingposts rather than two. Sulzer-type engines were fitted, virtually ending Clan's loyalty to Doxford diesels.

The Clan Fs represented the only time Clan was significantly unfaithful to Greenock Dockyard. Swan Hunter considerably undercut the Scottish yard which, of the seven orders, only received two, distinguished by being given Clan G names. However, one wonders if the ships from the Tyne were quite as well built as those from the Clyde, as all the Fs were sold within seven years, whilst the Clan Graham (5) and Clan Grant (4) had careers with Clan of almost 20 years.

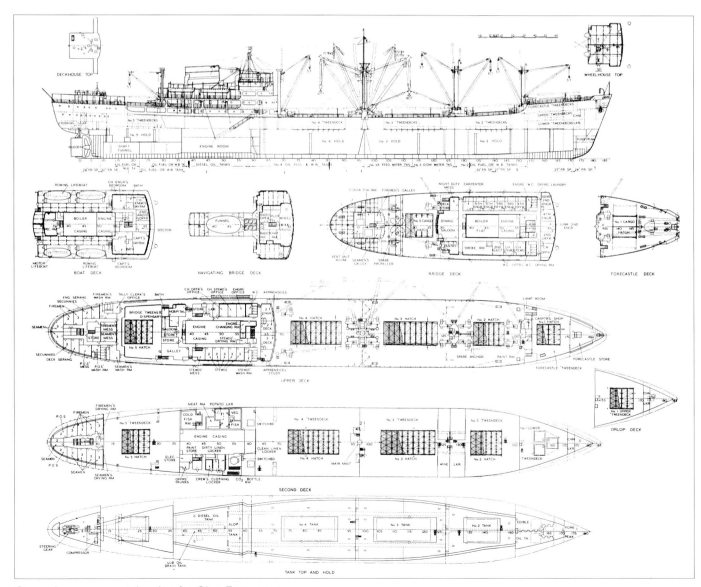

General arrangement drawing for *Clan Fergusson.*

CLAN FERGUSSON 1961-1965

O.N. 301439 9,242g 4,993n
496.6 x 62.4 x 28.2 feet.
Sulzer-type 6-cyl. 2SCSA oil engine by the
Wallsend Slipway and Engineering Co.
Ltd., Wallsend-on-Tyne; 7,700 BHP, 15.25
knots.
3.11.1960: Launched by Swan, Hunter and
Wigham Richardson Ltd., Wallsend-on-
Tyne (Yard No. 1917).
31.3.1961: Completed for The Clan Line
Steamers Ltd. (Cayzer, Irvine and Co.
Ltd., managers), London at a cost of
£1,151,000 as CLAN FERGUSSON.
1962: Transferred to King Line Ltd.
(Cayzer, Irvine and Co. Ltd., managers),
London.
17.3.1965: Sold to Scindia Steam
Navigation Co. Ltd., Bombay, India for
£850,000 and renamed JALAPANKHI.
5.2.1983: Arrived at Bombay for
demolition.
6.1983: Work began by Rai Metal Private
Ltd.

Clan Fergusson on trials (top). The previous two ships named after this Clan had managed with only one letter S. The interior views on this page show the dining saloon (above), the chief engineer's cabin and his dayroom (bottom). *[Top: Newall Dunn collection; interiors: Tyne and Wear Archives 2931/1917/10; 2931/ 1917/15; 2931/1917/16]*

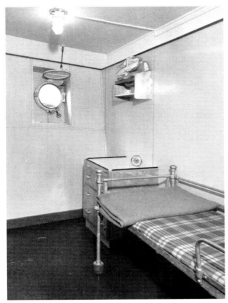

On this page are a typical crew cabin (far left), the electrical switchboard (left), the wheelhouse (upper middle left), the engine room control platform (upper middle right), and views of the lower part of the engine room (lower middle). The final shot shows her after sale to a major rival to become *Jalapankhi* (bottom). *[Tyne and Wear Archives 2931/1917/17; 2931/1917/18; 2931/1917/9; 2931/1917/4; 2931/1917/7; 2931/1917/6; below: Roy Fenton collection]*

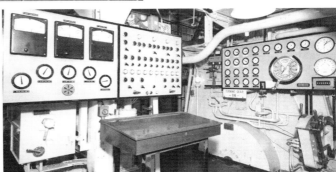

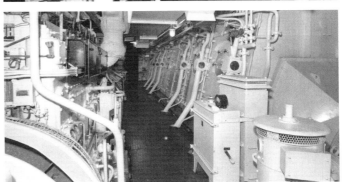

CLAN FORBES (4) 1961-1968

O.N. 301454 9,292g 4,992n
496.7 x 62.4 x 28.2 feet.
Sulzer-type 6-cyl. 2SCSA oil engine by the
Wallsend Slipway and Engineering Co.
Ltd., Wallsend-on-Tyne; 7,700 BHP, 15.25
knots.

2.3.1961: Launched by Swan, Hunter and
Wigham Richardson Ltd., Wallsend (Yard
No. 1919) for King Line Ltd., London as
CLAN FORBES.

23.6.1961: Completed for The Clan Line
Steamers Ltd. (Cayzer, Irvine and Co.
Ltd., managers), London at a cost of
£1,120,000.

7.5.1968: Transferred to King Line Ltd.
(Cayzer, Irvine and Co. Ltd., managers),
London.

11.9.1968: Sold to Arya National Shipping
Lines S.A., Tehran, Iran and renamed
ARYA MAN.

1980: Owners became Islamic Republic of
Iran Shipping Lines, Tehran and renamed
IRAN HEMMAT.

3.7.1985: Arrived at Alang, India for
demolition.

5.7.1985: Trilokchand Family Trust began
work.

Clan Forbes (4) running trials (top and
middle) and after her sale to Arya
National Shipping Lines (bottom) to
become *Arya Man*. [Top: Newall Dunn
collection, middle: Tyne and Wear
Archives, 2931/1919/2, bottom: J. and
M. Clarkson collection]

CLAN FRASER (4) 1961-1965

O.N. 301461 9,292g 4,992n
496.7 x 62.4 x 28.2 feet.
Sulzer-type 6-cyl. 2SCSA oil engine by the
Wallsend Slipway and Engineering Co.
Ltd., Wallsend-on-Tyne; 7,700 BHP, 15.25
knots.
27.7.1961: Launched by Swan, Hunter and
Wigham Richardson Ltd., Wallsend-on-
Tyne (Yard No. 1921) for King Line Ltd.
(Cayzer, Irvine and Co. Ltd., managers),
London as CLAN FRASER.
27.9.1961: Completed for The Clan Line
Steamers Ltd. (Cayzer, Irvine and Co.
Ltd., managers), London at a cost of
£1,120,000.
1.3.1965: Sold to Scindia Steam
Navigation Co. Ltd., Bombay, India for
£850,000 and renamed JALAPALAKA.
20.11.1979: Burnt out at Bombay.
17.11.1980: Breaking up began at Bombay
by Jalyan Udyog, Calcutta.

CLAN GRAHAM (4) 1962-1979

O.N. 301465 9,308g 5,105n
496.6 x 62.8 x 28.2 feet.
Sulzer-type 6-cyl. 2SCSA oil engine by
Barclay, Curle and Co. Ltd., Whiteinch,
Glasgow; 7,700 BHP, 15.5 knots.
25.8.1961: Launched by the Greenock
Dockyard Co. Ltd., Greenock (Yard No.
498).
16.1.1962: Completed for The Clan Line
Steamers Ltd. (Cayzer, Irvine and Co.
Ltd., managers), London at a cost of
£1,220,000 as CLAN GRAHAM.
5.1969: Transferred to King Line Ltd.
(Cayzer, Irvine and Co. Ltd., managers),
London.
1977: Transferred to the Clan Line
Steamers Ltd. (Cayzer, Irvine and Co.
Ltd., managers), London.
1979: Managers became Cayzer, Irvine
Shipping Ltd.

Clan Fraser (4) on trials off the North East coast (top). She was another early sale, becoming *Jalapalaka* in 1965 (middle). *[Top: Newall Dunn collection; middle: Ships in Focus]*

Clan Graham (4) launched at Greenock on 25th August 1961. *[Newall Dunn collection]*

Clan Graham (4) in service. [FotoFlite/J. and M. Clarkson collection]

4.1981: Sold to Kinsdale International S.A., Panama (Navegante Shipping Agency Ltd., Hong Kong, managers) for $2,100,000 and renamed MARIANNE.
1983: Renamed CANDELARIA.
26.3.1984: Arrived at Kaohsiung for demolition.
3.4.1984: Kvo Dar Steel and Iron Enterprise Co. Ltd. began work.

CLAN FARQUHARSON 1962-1968
O.N. 301475 9,240g 4,993n
496.6 x 62.4 x 28.2 feet.
Sulzer-type 6-cyl. 2SCSA oil engine by the Wallsend Slipway and Engineering Co.

Ltd., Wallsend-on-Tyne; 8,500 BHP; 15.5 knots.
19.1.1962: Launched by Swan, Hunter and Wigham Richardson Ltd., Wallsend-on-Tyne (Yard No. 1931).
13.4.1962: Completed for King Line Ltd. (Cayzer, Irvine and Co. Ltd., managers), London as CLAN FARQUHARSON.
19.9.1962: Transferred to The Clan Line Steamers Ltd. (Cayzer, Irvine and Co. Ltd., managers), London.
20.4.1968: Transferred to King Line Ltd. (Cayzer, Irvine and Co. Ltd., managers), London.

1968: Sold to Arya National Shipping Lines S.A., Tehran, Iran and renamed ARYA SEP.
1980: Owners became Islamic Republic of Iran Shipping Lines, Tehran and renamed IRAN OKHUVAT.
1982: Transferred to Irano-Hind Shipping Co. Ltd., Tehran, Iran and renamed OKHUVAT.
1985: Sold to Indian shipbreakers.
24.9.1985: Anchored off Mangalore awaiting demolition.
28.9.1985: Nathani Industrial Services began work at Mangalore.

Clan Faquharson on trials. [Tyne and Wear Archives, 2931/1931/1]

Arya Sep, the former *Clan Farquharson*, photographed by Peter Foxley in the Malacca Straits (top).
      Clan Grant (4) on trials (middle) and as *Enriqueta* (bottom), still in good condition but note how changing the paint scheme alters the appearance of the ship. *[Top: J. and M. Clarkson collection; middle: Newall Dunn collection; bottom: J. and M. Clarkson collection]*

CLAN GRANT (4) 1962-1980
O.N. 301480 9,022g 4,804n
496.6 x 62.7 x 28.2 feet.
Sulzer-type 6-cyl. 2SCSA oil engine by Barclay, Curle and Co. Ltd., Whiteinch, Glasgow; 8,500 BHP, 15.5 knots.
22.12.1961: Launched by the Greenock Dockyard Co. Ltd., Greenock (Yard No. 499).
2.5.1962: Completed for The Clan Line

Steamers Ltd. (Cayzer, Irvine and Co. Ltd., managers), London at a cost of £1,220,000. as CLAN GRANT.
5.1969: Transferred to King Line Ltd. (Cayzer, Irvine and Co. Ltd., managers), London.
1976: Transferred to The Clan Line Steamers Ltd. (Cayzer, Irvine and Co. Ltd., managers), London.

1979: Managers became Cayzer, Irvine Shipping Ltd.
12.1980: Sold to Venables Steamship S.A., Panama (Navegante Shipping Agency Ltd., Hong Kong, managers) for $1,900,000 and renamed ENRIQUETA.
15.1.1985: Arrived in China for demolition having been sold to China National Metals and Minerals.

CLAN FINLAY 1962-1968
O.N. 304143 9,124g 4,875n
496.6 x 62.4 x 28.2 feet.
Sulzer-type 6-cyl. 2SCSA oil
engine by the Wallsend Slipway
and Engineering Co. Ltd.,
Wallsend-on-Tyne; 8,500 BHP.
29.6.1962: Launched by Swan,
Hunter and Wigham Richardson
Ltd., Wallsend-on-Tyne (Yard
No. 1933).
5.10.1962: Completed for King
Line Ltd. (Cayzer, Irvine and
Co. Ltd., managers), London as
CLAN FINLAY.
27.11.1962: Transferred to The
Clan Line Steamers Ltd.
(Cayzer, Irvine and Co. Ltd.,
managers), London.
28.4.1968: Transferred to King
Line Ltd. (Cayzer, Irvine and
Co. Ltd., managers), London.
1968: Sold to Arya National
Shipping Company S.A.,
Tehran, Iran and renamed ARYA
FAR.
1971: Sold to Tat On Shipping
and Enterprises Co. Ltd. (Yick
Fung Shipping and Enterprises
Co. Ltd., managers), Hong
Kong and renamed ATLANTIC
OCEAN under the Somali flag.
1975: Transferred to China
Ocean Shipping Co., Peking,
China and renamed LU CHUN.
1983: Transferred to Guanzhou
Ocean Shipping Company,
(COSCO/ GUANZHOU),
China.
20.2.1991: Deleted from Lloyd's
Register as continued existence
in doubt.

Clan Finlay of 1962 was the only ship to use the name (top). She was sold after only six years to mainland China, who initially hid its ownership under the Hong Kong flag as Yick Fung's *Atlantic Ocean* (middle) seen sailing from Birkenhead on 23rd October 1971. Only in 1975 did she appear under true Chinese colours as *Lu Chun* (bottom), photographed at Singapore in March 1981. *[Top: Newall Dunn collection; middle: J. and M. Clarkson; bottom: Roy Fenton collection]*

CLAN F EXTENDED

Contemporary with the previous class, Clan built two slightly longer ships, one at Greenock and one at Clydebank. The only distinguishing feature from the Clan Fs was the flat front to the superstructure. We shall probably never know why the facility to walk round in front of the superstructure was denied to those on Clan Macnab *(4) and* Clan Macnair *(2).*

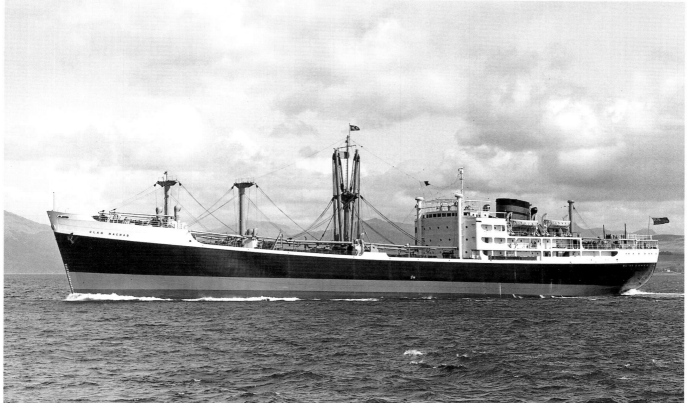

CLAN MACNAB (4) 1961-1980

O.N. 301448 9,428g 4,995n
506.9 x 61.7 x 26.6 feet.
Sulzer-type 6-cyl. 2SCSA oil engine by the Wallsend Slipway and Engineering Co. Ltd., Wallsend-on-Tyne; 7,700 BHP.

31.1.1961: Launched by the Greenock Dockyard Co. Ltd., Greenock (Yard No. 497).

5.5.1961: Completed for The Clan Line Steamers Ltd. (Cayzer, Irvine and Co. Ltd., managers), London at a cost of £1,380,000 as CLAN MACNAB.

1979: Managers became Cayzer, Irvine Shipping Ltd.

23.4.1980: Sold to New Eagle Navigation S.A., Panama (Sin Chiao Shipping (Private) Ltd., Singapore) for $1,425,000 and renamed NEW EAGLE.

1.11.1984: Arrived at Shanghai for demolition having been sold to Shanghai Foreign Trade. The name originally allocated was CLAN MACINDOE.

Clan Macnab (4) leaving dry dock (top), in the Clyde for trials (middle) and in the river at Kilindini (bottom).   *[Top and middle: Newall Dunn collection; bottom: Ambrose Greenway collecton]*

CLAN MACNAIR (2) 1962-1980

O.N. 301468 9,137g 4,928n

506.2 x 61.8 x 26.7 feet.

Doxford-type 6-cyl. 2SCSA oil engine by John Brown and Co. (Clydebank) Ltd., Clydebank; 6,400 BHP.

26.10.1961: Launched by John Brown and Co. (Clydebank) Ltd., Clydebank (Yard No. 713).

9.2.1962: Completed for Neptune Shipping Co. Ltd., Bermuda (Cayzer, Irvine and Co. Ltd., London, managers) at a cost of £1,400,000 and bareboat chartered to The Clan Line Steamers Ltd., London as CLAN MACNAIR.

1979: Managers became Cayzer, Irvine Shipping Ltd.

1980: Sold to Uni-Ocean Lines (Private) Ltd., Singapore for $1,622,500 and renamed LICHIANG.

7.4.1987: Arrived at Kaohsiung for demolition.

15.4.1987: Chi Hsiang steel Enterprises began work.

21.4.1987: Demolition completed.

Clan Macnair (2) was built by John Brown at Clydebank, presumably because Greenock Dockyard had no berths available, and she had the last Doxford engine fitted in a Clan Line vessel. In the first photograph she waits on the slip to be launched: she had been named on 24th October 1961, but due to bad weather was launched two days later. She is also seen sailing from the Manchester Ship Canal (middle), at Gibraltar (bottom left) and in the Malacca Straits after sale to Singapore owners who renamed her *Lichiang* (bottom right). *[Top: Newall Dunn collection; middle: J. and M. Clarkson collection; bottom left: Ambrose Greenway; bottom right: J. and M. Clarkson collection]*

INTENDED TO BE KINGS

Three ships were ordered in 1961 as 'cargo/tramp' types, to be given King Line names. However, before building was far advanced a change of mind saw them becoming modifications of the Clan Fergusson design. Main distinguishing features were a tapered funnel, the accommodation not being carried right to the stern, and a single mast replacing the after set of king posts. A fourth vessel, Clan Alpine (5), followed four years after Clan Macgowan, but with only minor differences.

Clan Macgillivray (2) was the first British cargo liner with remote machinery control. A control room at the forward end of the engine room contained conventional levers mechanically connected to the main engine. The room also had panels carrying distance-reading thermometers, pressure gauges and counters. The diesel generators and pumps could also be started by remote control. The watch-keeping engineer was normally stationed in the control room, and a saving in manpower of 20% was anticipated. It was a step on the way to the complete bridge control of engines which electronic systems were soon to make possible.

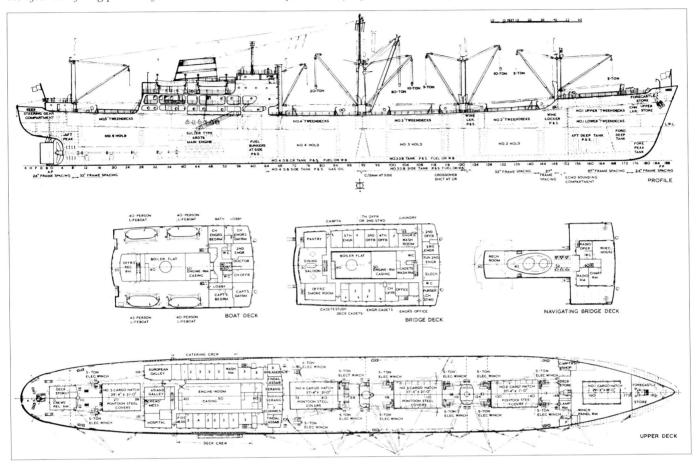

General arrangement drawing of Clan Macgillivray (above). Shown on trials (right), Clan Macgillivray (2) was reputedly the last Clan Line ship sold, although not the last in service as she was laid up at the time in Chittagong. She kept her Clan connection after her sale, being renamed Clan Macboyd, and had the last clan name listed in register books. [Newall Dunn collection]

Interior views of *Clan Macgillivray* (2) show the wheelhouse (right), the main switchboard (middle left), the control room (middle right and lower left) and the cylinder tops of the main engine (lower right). *[Glasgow University Archives GD323/7/9/2/ 500/12; GD323/7/9/2/500/32; GD323/7/9/2/500/30; GD323/7/9/2/500/31; GD323/7/9/2/500/29]*

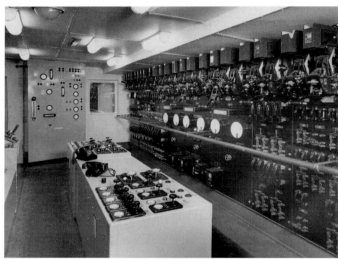

O.N. 304140 8,811g 4,813n
507.8 x 63.3 x 28.5 feet
Sulzer-type 6-cyl. 2SCSA oil engine by Barclay, Curle and Co. Ltd., Whiteinch, Glasgow; 8,500 BHP, 16.5 knots.
1962: Keel laid by the Greenock Dockyard Co. Ltd., Greenock (Yard No. 500) as KING CANUTE.
9.5.1962: Named CLAN MACGILLIVRAY, but not launched owing to a tug strike.
22.5.1962: Launched.

31.8.1962: Completed for King Line Ltd. (Cayzer, Irvine and Co. Ltd., managers), London.
16.11.1962: Transferred to The Clan Line Steamers Ltd. (Cayzer, Irvine and Co. Ltd., managers), London.
5.1969: Transferred to King Line Ltd. (Cayzer, Irvine and Co. Ltd., managers), London
1977: Transferred to The Clan Line Steamers Ltd. (Cayzer, Irvine and Co. Ltd., managers), London.

1979: Managers became Cayzer, Irvine Shipping Ltd.
1981: Sold to Gateway Shipping Ltd. (Anglo-Eastern Shipping Co. Ltd.), Hong Kong for $1,875,000 and renamed CLAN MACBOYD.
17.9.1984: Sailed from Singapore.
Prior to 1.10.1984: Arrived at Shanghai for demolition.

CLAN MACGREGOR (3) 1962-1981
O.N. 304151 8,811g 4,909n
507.8 x 63.3 x 28.5 feet.
Sulzer-type 6-cyl. 2SCSA oil engine by
Barclay, Curle and Co. Ltd., Whiteinch,
Glasgow; 8,500 BHP, 16.5 knots.
1962: Keel laid by the Greenock Dockyard
Co. Ltd., Greenock (Yard No. 501) as
KING EDWARD.
26.9.1962: Launched.
21.12.1962: Completed for King Line Ltd.
(Cayzer, Irvine and Co. Ltd., managers),
London as CLAN MACGREGOR.
1963: Transferred to The Clan Line
Steamers Ltd. (Cayzer, Irvine and Co.
Ltd., managers), London.
5.1969: Transferred to King Line Ltd.
(Cayzer, Irvine and Co. Ltd., managers),
London.
1977: Transferred to The Clan Line
Steamers Ltd. (Cayzer, Irvine and Co.
Ltd., managers), London.
1979: Managers became Cayzer, Irvine
Shipping Ltd.
7.1981: Transferred to Scottish Shire Line
Ltd. (Cayzer, Irvine and Co. Ltd.,
managers), London.
11.1981: Sold to Raft Shipping Company
(Dedalos Compania Naviera S.A.
managers), Athens, Greece and renamed
ANGELIKA R.
9.11.1982: Caught fire sixty miles south
east of Cyprus in position 33.45 north by
33.15 east whilst on a voyage from Mersin
to Bombay.
10.11.1982: Towed into Larnaca Roads,
Cyprus and laid up.
Subsequently towed to Piraeus for
disposal.
8.3.1983: Arrived at Larium in tow.
9.1983: Breaking up began by G.
Perdikaris and Company.

Photographed on trials (top), *Clan Macgregor* (3) is believed to have been the last
Clan Liner in service, sold after discharging in Manchester in November 1981.
She was to work for her new owner for barely a year. The second photograph
shows a very rare repainting of the Clan funnel whilst on charter to Harrison Line.
[Top: Newall Dunn collection; above: Captain M. D. R. Jones]

CLAN MACGOWAN 1963-1970
O.N. 304153 8,811g 4,909n
507.8 x 63.3 x 28.5 feet.
Sulzer-type 6-cyl. 2SCSA oil engine by the
Wallsend Slipway and Engineering Co.
Ltd., Wallsend-on-Tyne; 8,500 BHP, 16.5
knots.
1962: Keel laid by the Greenock Dockyard
Co. Ltd., Greenock (Yard No. 502) as
KING HAROLD.

14.12.1962: Launched.
3.4.1963: Completed for King Line Ltd.
(Cayzer, Irvine and Co. Ltd., managers),
London as CLAN MACGOWAN.
1963: Transferred to The Clan Line
Steamers Ltd. (Cayzer, Irvine and Co.
Ltd., managers), London.
5.1969: Transferred to King Line Ltd.
(Cayzer, Irvine and Co. Ltd., managers),
London.

1970: Sold to the India Steamship Co. Ltd., Calcutta, India and renamed INDIAN TRIBUNE.

16.4.1984: Damaged in collision with the Swedish motor vessel BANDAR ABBAS EXPRESS (9,000/1978) at Bombay.

24.5.1984: Laid up at Calcutta.

3.10.1985: Demolition began at Calcutta by Chaudhary Shipbreaking Co.

CLAN ALPINE (5) 1967-1981

O.N. 307670 8,713g 4,798n

507.9 x 63.2 x 28.6 feet

Burmeister & Wain-type 7-cyl. 2SCSA oil engine by J.G. Kincaid and Co. Ltd., Glasgow; 8,500 BHP, 16.5 knots.

1.12.1966: Launched by Scotts' Shipbuilding and Engineering Co. Ltd., Greenock (Cartsdyke Yard No. 708).

4.1967: Completed for The Clan Line Steamers Ltd. (Cayzer, Irvine and Co. Ltd., managers), London as CLAN ALPINE at a cost of £1,520,000.

1979: Managers became Cayzer, Irvine Shipping Ltd.

1.1981: Sold to Delibra Shipping Co. Inc., Monrovia, Liberia (China Marine Corporation, Taipeh, Taiwan) (Golden Peak Maritime Agencies Ltd., Hong Kong, operators) for $3,300,000 and renamed AFRICAN DIAMOND.

1982: Renamed PACIFIC AMBER.

1983: Operators became Island Navigation Corporation (Ship Management) Ltd., Hong Kong.

2.5.1984: Arrived at Kaohsiung for demolition by Gwo Feng Steel Enterprise Co.

15.5.1984: Work completed.

Clan Macgowan, seen at Brisbane on 4th July 1965 (top), had a relatively short life with Clan, the company selling her to one of their rivals, the Calcutta-based India Steamship Co. Ltd. who renamed her *Indian Tribune* (middle). Even at this late stage, Clan could come up with a name not previously used. *[Top: Warwick Foote; middle: J. and M. Clarkson]*

Opposite bottom, above and right: The last ship for Clan was ordered as part of the agreement to sell the Cartsdyke yard of Greenock Dockyard to the owners of the neighbouring yard, Scotts. She was basically a repeat of the *Clan Macgillivray* (2), with minor details including an enlarged winch platform between holds 3 and 4, minor external differences to the superstructure, just two lifeboats, and modified bulwarks aft. Another difference was that, by the time of the order, Burmeister & Wain-type engines were favoured over Sulzers. Fittingly, *Clan Alpine* (5) commemorated the name of Charles Cayzer's first steamer. *[Opposite: Glasgow University Archives GD323/7/9/2/708/17; above: George O'Hara collection; right:J. and M. Clarkson]*

THE LAST REEFERS

These four refrigerator ships could be forgiven for being schizophrenic: nominally owned by Union-Castle and serving largely on their traditional South African fruit trades, they were bareboat chartered to Houston Line, yet named and painted as Clans.

Their five holds were largely refrigerated, giving over half-a-million cubic feet of insulated space. Space in numbers 4 and 5 'tween decks could be further cooled for the carriage of meat. Reflecting their intended use, derricks were relatively light, of no more than five tons capacity. Their specialised role as fruit ships meant that they were laid up, usually at Southampton, for part of the year. Given 'Castle' names in 1977, they remained in the British and Commonwealth Group until the early 1980s

Clan Ramsay, the first of the reefers, on her trials. *[Newall Dunn collection]*

CLAN RAMSAY 1965-1977
O.N. 304194 7,955g 4,272n
529.4 x 68.9 x 28.5 feet.
Burmeister & Wain-type 7-cyl. 2SCSA oil
engine by J.G. Kincaid and Co. Ltd.,
Glasgow; 10,350 BHP, 17.5 knots.
26.8.1964: Launched by the Greenock
Dockyard Co. Ltd., Greenock (Yard No.
506).

3.1965: Completed for the Union-Castle
Mail Steamship Co. Ltd. (Cayzer, Irvine
and Co. Ltd., managers), London at a cost
of £1,950,000 as CLAN RAMSAY.
1977: Renamed WINCHESTER
CASTLE.
1979: Managers became Cayzer, Irvine
Shipping Ltd. and renamed
WINCHESTER UNIVERSAL.

10.1980: Sold to Braganza Bay Shipping
Corporation, Monrovia, Liberia (Kappa
Maritime (G. Kollakis), London) and
renamed LADY MADONNA under the
Greek flag.
29.4.1984: Laid up at Falmouth.
25.4.1985: Arrived at Gadani Beach for
demolition by Seikh Miran Bux Ltd. who
started work the same day.

Clan Ramsay: the only occasion the name was used. She is seen on trials (opposite top), as the *Winchester Castle* (opposite bottom) and as the *Lady Madonna* (right). [Opposite top: Archie Munro collection; opposite bottom: J. and M. Clarkson collection; right: Newall Dunn collection]

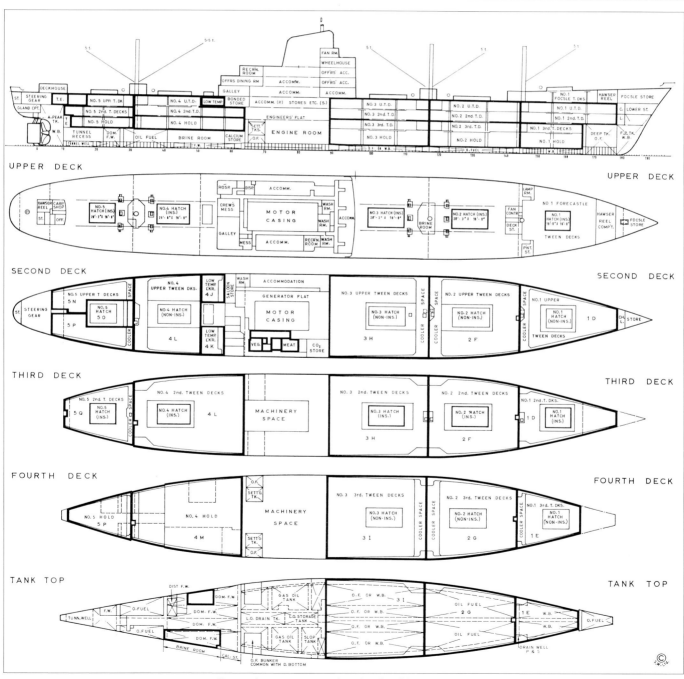

General arrangement drawing for *Clan Ramsay*.

Interior views of *Clan Ramsay* showing (from left to right and top to bottom) one of her holds (she had a total of 19 insulated spaces for fruit which could be refrigerated for carrying meat), the wheelhouse, radar console, her wheel and auto-pilot, chart table (with echo sounder, Decca navigator, direction finder and course recorder mounted above), the galley (this was fitted with a food lift to the dining saloon pantry), the officers' lounge and the dining saloon. *[Glasgow University Archives]*

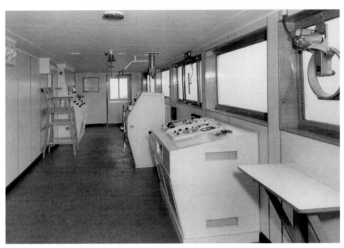

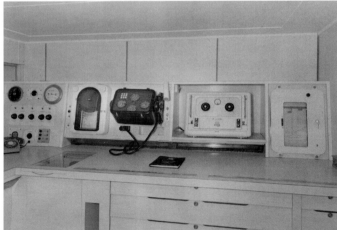

CLAN RANALD (4) 1965-1977
O.N. 307627 7,955g 4,272n 11,730d
529.4 x 68.9 x 28.5 feet.
Burmeister & Wain-type 7-cyl. 2SCSA oil
engine by J.G. Kincaid and Co. Ltd., Glasgow;
10,350 BHP, 17.5 knots.
21.12.1964: Launched by the Greenock
Dockyard Co. Ltd., Greenock (Yard No. 507).
16.6.1965: Completed for the Union-Castle
Mail Steamship Co. Ltd. (Cayzer, Irvine and
Co. Ltd., managers), London at a cost of
£1,950,000 as CLAN RAMSEY.
1.1977: Renamed DOVER CASTLE.
1979: Managers became Cayzer, Irvine
Shipping Ltd. and renamed DOVER
UNIVERSAL.
6.1981: Sold to Invergordon Shipping
Corporation, Monrovia, Liberia (Kappa
Maritime (G. Kollakis), London) and renamed
GOLDEN SEA under the Greek flag.
16.5.1984: Laid up at Falmouth.
11.5.1985: Demolition began by Abdul Noor
Mohammad and Co. at Gadani Beach.

Clan Ranald (4) (top and middle) and as *Dover Castle* in full Union-Castle colours (bottom). Although striking and retaining a midships superstructure, the appearance of these ships, and especially their funnels and lack of sheer, meant that the design has not worn as well as the Clans of the fifties and even the three-quarters aft ships of the sixties. *[Top: Newall Dunn collection; middle: Fotoflite/J. and M. Clarkson collection; bottom: Newall Dunn collection]*

CLAN ROBERTSON (4) 1965-1976

O.N. 307638 7,955g 4,272n 11,730d 529.4
x 68.9 x 28.3 feet.
Burmeister & Wain-type 7-cyl. 2SCSA oil
engine by J.G. Kincaid and Co. Ltd.,
Glasgow; 10,350 BHP, 17.5 knots.
3.5.1965: Launched by the Greenock
Dockyard Co. Ltd., Greenock, (Yard No.
508).
1.11.1965: Completed for the Union-Castle
Mail Steamship Co. Ltd. (Cayzer, Irvine
and Co. Ltd., managers), London at a cost
of £1,950,000 as CLAN ROBERTSON.
11.1976: Renamed BALMORAL CASTLE.
1979: Managers became Cayzer, Irvine
Shipping Ltd. and renamed BALMORAL
UNIVERSAL.
12.1982: Sold to National History
Compania Naviera S.A., Panama
(Comninos Brothers Shipping Company
S.A., Piraeus, Greece managers) and
renamed PSARA REEFER under the Greek
flag.
19.6.1984: Arrived at Chittagong Roads to
be broken up by Saleh Steel Industries Ltd.
30.6.1984: Work began.

Clan Robertson (4) at anchor off
Cowes (top) and laid up at
Southampton between *Clan Ramsay*
and *Rothesay Castle* (middle upper).
When renamed *Balmoral Castle* she
painted up Union-Castle colours (lower
middle). Her final appaearance in
British and Commonwealth ownership
was as *Balmoral Universal* (bottom).
*[Top: Ambrose Greenway collection;
upper middle: J. and M. Clarkson
collection; lower middle: Newall Dunn
collection; bottom: Roy Fenton
collection]*

CLAN ROSS (4) 1966-1976

O.N. 307645 7,955g 4,272n
11,918d
529.4 x 68.8 x 28.2 feet.
Burmeister & Wain-type 7-cyl.
2SCSA oil engine by J.G. Kincaid
and Co. Ltd., Glasgow; 10,350
BHP, 17.5 knots.
24.9.1965: Launched by the
Greenock Dockyard Co. Ltd.,
Greenock (Yard No. 509).
11.3.1966: Completed for
Houston Line Ltd. (Cayzer, Irvine
and Co. Ltd., managers), London
at a cost of £1,950,000 as CLAN
ROSS.
12.1976: Transferred to Union-
Castle Mail Steamship Co. Ltd.
(Cayzer, Irvine and Co. Ltd.,
managers), London and renamed
KINPURNIE CASTLE.
1979: Managers became Cayzer,
Irvine Shipping Ltd. and
renamed KINPURNIE
UNIVERSAL.
12.1982: Sold to National
Heritage Compania Naviera
S.A., Panama (Comninos
Brothers Shipping Company
S.A., Piraeus, Greece, managers)
and renamed SYROS REEFER
under the Greek flag.
5.2.1984: Grounded during a
gale at Grave Point, in Berkeley
Sound, 14 miles north west of
Port Stanley in the Falkland
Islands. Later refloated and
taken to Port Stanley.
31.7.1984: Arrived at Chittagong
to be broken up by National
Shipbreakers who began work
the same day.

Clan Ross (4) on trials (top) and dropping her pilot (middle), not long before Clan Line did the same. As *Kinpurnie Castle* she sails from Hull in 1977 (bottom). *[Top: Newall Dunn collection; middle: Roy Fenton collection; bottom: J. and M. Clarkson collection]*

SOLITARY BULKER

KING ALFRED 1977-1981

O.N. 335920 29,419g 22,033n
713.8 x 97.2 x 39.5 feet.
Burmeister & Wain 8-74VT2BF-160 type
8-cyl. 2SCSA oil engine by Eriksbergs
Mekaniska Verksted A/B, Gothenburg,
Sweden; 12,000 BHP.
2.4.1968: Launched by Eriksbergs
Mekaniska Verkstads A/B, Gothenburg,
Sweden (Yard No. 616) for I/S Angelus (H.
Angel Olsen, manager), Sandefjord,
Norway as ANGELUS.
11.5.1968: Sold to Olsen and Ugelstad A/S,
Oslo, Norway and renamed HEMSEFJELL.
23.7.1968: Sold to King Line Ltd. (Cayzer,
Irvine and Co. Ltd., managers), London and
renamed KING ALFRED.
9.1968: Completed.
1977: Transferred to Houston Line Ltd.,
(Cayzer, Irvine and Co. Ltd., managers),
London
2.1.1980: Transferred to Clan Line
Steamers Ltd. (Cayzer, Irvine and Co. Ltd.,
managers), London.
29.12.1981: Transferred to Cayzer, Irvine
and Co. Ltd. (Cayzer, Irvine Shipping Ltd.,
managers), London.
1983: Sold to Guangzhou Ocean Shipping
Company (COSCO/GUANGZHOU),
Guangzhou, China and renamed LUO FU
SHAN.
1997: Transferred to China Shipping
International Co. Ltd., Shanghai, China.
2.2007: Still in existence.

Rather ironically, the last ship owned by Clan Line by a matter of weeks was the bulk carrier *King Alfred*, which spoils the authors' ambitions that every ship shown in this book should be an attractive one. In the aerial view she appears to have a plain black funnel (above), but when photographed on the Thames (below) she seems to have the old King Line funnel, yellow with a black top. *[Newall Dunn collection (2)]*

CLANS
IN COLOUR

Right: *Clan Mackinnon* (2) painted flying a full set of flags: stem jack, her signal hoist, Clan Line house flag and ensign. *[G. Young/The British Mercantile Marine Memorial Collection]*

Middle: Pier head painter H. Crane's depiction of the Turret *Clan Buchanan* (2) again with all flags flying. *[H. Crane/The British Mercantile Marine Memorial Collection]*

Bottom: *Banffshire*, the former *Clan Macrae* (2), with Scottish Shire Line funnel and house flag. *[H. Crane/The British Mercantile Marine Memorial Collection]*

Top: The long-lived refrigerator ship *Clan Macdonald* (4) photographed on the New Waterway. *[Roy Kittle]*

Middle: War-built near-sister *Clan Macdougall* (3) at anchor off Southend. *[Roy Kittle]*

Bottom: Shepherded by a tug and a health launch on the Thames on 2nd October 1959 is *Clan Cumming* (3), last built of the big class of twin-screw general cargo ship. *[F.W. Hawks]*

Right: The Liberty-type *Clan Macfarlane* (3) passes Runcorn on the Manchester Ship Canal with her top masts struck, but with her funnel still in place. *[Eddie Jackson]*

Left: The Ocean-type *Clan Kenneth* (2) on the Thames, 1st June 1957. *[R. Snook/F.W. Hawks]*

Right: Another Ocean image from the camera of veteran Thames photographer Rupert Snook, the *Clan Macbean* (2) on 19th September 1959. *[R. Snook/F.W. Hawks]*

Below: *Clan Macleod* (4). sailing from Eastham on 2nd July 1975. *[Paul Boot]*

315

Top: The motor ship *Clan Maclaren* (2), first of a new post-war class, picks up speed as she sails from Eastham after leaving the Manchester Ship Canal on a sunny 4th December 1974. *[Paul Boot]*
Middle: Sister motor ship *Clan Maclean* (3) approaches Eastham on 28th July 1975 with her topmasts and large derricks lowered to transit the Manchester Ship Canal. *[Paul Boot]*
Bottom left: *Sentosa Island*, the former *Clan Maclean* (3). *[Michael Green]*
Bottom right: *Climax Amethyst*, ex-*Clan Maclay*. *[Paul Boot collection]*

Top: With Cock tugs ahead and one of Johnston Warren's steam tugs alongside, *Clan Sinclair* (3) passes Hartley's Victoria Tower on the Liverpool waterfront.
[F.W. Hawks collection]

Middle: *Clan Sutherland* (2) soon after fitting her 165-ton heavy lift derrick.
[Malcolm Donnelly]

Bottom: A beautifully lit *Clan Stewart* on the Tyne, 2nd August 1961. *[Malcolm Donnelly]*

Top: *Clan Macintosh* (3) leaves Eastham on 18th January 1975. *[Paul Boot]*
Middle: Sister *Clan Macintyre* (3), distinguished by her taller radar mast, in the Mersey on 13th April 1974. *[Paul Boot]*
Bottom left: *Clan Macinnes* (3) arriving at Durban. *[Michael Green collection]*
Bottom right: *Sanil*, the former *Clan Macintosh* (3), in 1979. *[Bob Allen]*

Above: With her unlucky sister *Ayrshire* (2), the *Argyllshire* (2) was arguably the finest ship Clan produced, turbine-driven, partly-refrigerated and with accommodation for 12 passengers. She was photographed leaving Cardiff in 1971. *[John and Andrew Wiltshire]*

Below: The design of *Argyllshire* was developed from that of the *Clan Ross* (3), seen here as *Kinnaird Castle* off Gravesend in September 1974. *[Paul Boot collection]*

Top: With the *Clan Malcolm* (2) and her two sisters, the motor ship was finally established in the Clan fleet. She is seen off Avonmouth on 28th April 1973. *[John Wiltshire/Nigel Jones collection]*

Middle: *Clan Matheson* (5). *[John Wiltshire/Nigel Jones collection]*

Bottom: *Clan Menzies* (3) in the Mersey on 9th March 1972. *[Paul Boot]*

Top: *King George,* with Clan Line funnel but still not in full Clan hull colours, passes Runcorn outward bound. *[Eddie Jackson]*

Middle: Composite-superstructure *King Henry*, in full Clan livery, in Birkenhead Docks on 2nd July 1970. *[Paul Boot]*

Bottom: The former *King Arthur*, now renamed *Greenleaf*, anchored off Singapore on 12th February 1983. *[Nigel Jones]*

Top: *Clan Maciver* (3) approaches Eastham, ready for a Manchester Ship Canal transit, on 26th May 1978. *[Paul Boot]*
Middle: Sailing from Eastham on 3rd December 1974, *Clan Macindoe* (2) illustrates the difference in cargo gear from *Clan Maciver*. *[Paul Boot]*
Bottom left: *Clan Macindoe* (2) has now become *Gulf Heron*. *[Ian Shifffman/David Sailsbury collection]*
Bottom right: The third member of the first engines-three-quarters-aft trio, *Clan Macilwraith* (2) was photographed as Guan Guan's *Golden City*. *[Don Brown/David Salisbury collection]*

Top: *Clan Fraser* (4), a name which commemorated her predecessor, lost on a Malta convoy. She was photographed off South Shields, not far from her birthplace, on 4th June 1962. *[Malcolm Donnelly]*
Middle: The Tyne-built Clan Fs had short Clan careers: *Clan Fraser* became Scindia's *Jalapalaka* as which she is seen on 30th April 1976. *[Nigel Jones]*
Bottom left: *Arya Sep*, the former *Clan Farquharson*. *[David Salisbury]*
Bottom right: *Arya Man*, ex *Clan Forbes* (4). *[Michael Green]*

Top: Clan Line often chartered ships, and one which would have been familiar in Birkenhead Docks was Bibby's *Herefordshire* (8,320/1944), photographed in the Mersey during the early 1960s. *[Eddie Jackson]*

Middle: *Clan Macnab* (4) on 31st December 1979. By this late stage, containers were becoming common deck cargoes. *[Paul Boot]*

Bottom: Of Clan's last engines-three-quarters-aft design, *Clan Macgregor* (3) makes an interesting contrast with the *Clan Macnab* above. She was photographed on 31st February 1973. *[Paul Boot collection]*

Top: A deep-laden *Clan Macgillivray* (2) on 23rd March 1972. *[John Wiltshire/Nigel Jones collection]*

Right: Last ship to carry a Clan name, albeit no longer in the company's ownership, was *Clan Boyd*, the former *Clan Macgillivray*, looking somewhat more restrained colour-wise than during her Clan Line days on 23rd March 1972. *[Michael Green collection]*

Bottom: Approaching Eastham on 14th April 1979 ready for a voyage to Manchester, *Clan Grant* (4) has reverted to a colour scheme with no white topside strake. Her hull is also in poor condition for a Clan Line ship in home waters. *[Paul Boot]*

Top: As *Indian Tribune*, the former *Clan Macgowan* still looks very well cared for as she docks at Tilbury. *[David Salisbury]*

Right: *Clan Macnair* (2) on the Manchester Ship Canal. *[Michael Green]*

Below: *Clan Macnair* is seen again, now as *Lichiang*, anchored off Singapore on 10th February 1983. *[Nigel Jones]*

Top: *Clan Ramsay* approaches Cardiff on 19th September 1976. *[Nigel Jones]*

Middle: A tug nestles up to *Clan Robertson* (4) on the Mersey, 20th October 1974. *[Paul Boot]*

Bottom: *Clan Ross* (4) as *Kinpurnie Castle* at Southampton. *[Michael Green]*

Top: The last true Clan, *Clan Alpine* (5). *[Fotoflite incorporating Skyfotos]*

Middle: *Clan Alpine* (5) seen again just after entering the Manchester Ship Canal on 11th June 1972. *[Paul Boot]*

Bottom: *Clan Macgregor* in Gladstone Docks, Liverpool wearing Harrison Line colours on 13th February 1974. *[Paul Boot]*

Appendix 1:

CHRONOLOGICAL LIST

In contrast to the main listing of ships by class, this list is strictly chronological by date of registration in the company's ownership. It includes all ships listed in this book: of Clan, of Houston and Scottish Shire Lines from 1919, vessels in their naming schemes, and managed ships but not proposed names or those not carried in service.

Clan Alpine (1)	1878-1899
Clan Fraser (1)	1878-1898
Clan Ranald (1)	1879-1899
Clan Gordon (1)	1879-1897
Clan Stuart (1)	1879-1890
Clan Lamont (1)	1879-1890
Clan Macduff	1881
Clan Maclean (1)	1881-1903
Clan Macleod (1)	1881-1883
Clan Murray (1)	1881-1897
Clan Monroe (1)	1881-1899
Clan Mackay (1)	1882-1891
Clan Macdonald (1)	1882-1897
Clan Cameron (1)	1882-1900
Clan Buchanan (1)	1882-1905
Clan Graham (1)	1882-1905
Clan Mackenzie (1)	1882-1905
Clan Cambell (1)	1882
Clan Drummond (1)	1882-1898
Clan Forbes (1)	1882-1902
Clan Macgregor (1)	1882-1899
Clan Sinclair (1)	1882-1905
Clan Ogilvie	1882-1888
Clan Grant (1)	1883-1900
Clan Macarthur (1)	1883-1905
Clan Macintosh (1)	1883-1905
Clan Macpherson (1)	1883-1905
Clan Matheson (1)	1883-1905
Clan Macneil (1)	1891-1902
Clan Macleod (2)	1891-1902
Clan Mackinnon (1)	1891-1902
Clan Macintyre (1)	1891-1902
Clan Macnab (1)	1891-1902
Clan Macalister (1)	1891-1902
Clan Ross (1)	1894-1913
Clan Campbell (2)	1894-1913
Clan Mackay (2)	1894-1913
Amara	1895
Gorji	1895
Tigris	1895
Clan Macrae (1)	1895-1899
Clan Menzies (1)	1896-1925
Clan Lindsay (1)	1896-1898
Imperialist/Clan Shaw (1)	1896-1898
Clan Chisholm (1)	1896-1924
Bullionist	1896-1898
Clan Ogilvy (1)	1896-1913
Clan Sutherland (1)	1896-1921
Clan Macdonald (2)	1897-1922
Clan Murray (2)	1897-1917
Clan Monroe (2)	1897-1905
Clan Robertson (1)	1897-1922
Clan Macfarlane (1)	1898-1915
Clan Ferguson (1)	1898-1917
Clan Cumming (1)	1899-1925
Clan Macaulay (1)	1899-1929
Clan Colquhoun (1)	1899-1925
Clan Maclaren (1)	1899-1924
Clan Farquhar (1)	1899-1917
Clan Macfadyen (1)	1899-1921
Clan Urquhart (1)	1899-1929
Clan Alpine (2)	1899-1917
Clan Maclachlan (1)	1900-1917
Clan Fraser (2)	1900-1917
Clan Gordon (2)	1900-1919
Clan Lamont (2)	1900-1928
Clan Ranald (2)	1900-1909
Clan Stuart (2)	1900-1914
Clan Cameron (2)	1900-1917
Clan Macmillan (1)	1901-1917

The Turret steamer *Clan Lamont* (2) of 1900 seen at Algoa Bay, South Africa in 1926. *[Archie Munro collection]*

Clan Macleod (3) of 1903 at Buffalo Harbour, East London, about 1910. *[J. and M. Clarkson collection]*

Clan Macgregor (2)	1902	*Clan Macewen/Buteshire*	1912-1947
Clan Grant (2)	1902-1914	*Clan Macbride* (1)	1912-1937
Clan Shaw (2)	1902-1917	*Clan Macarthur* (2)/*Berwickshire*	1912-1944
Clan Leslie	1902-1916	*Clan Mactavish* (1)	1913-1916
Clan Lindsay (2)	1902-1931	*Clan Mackellar* (1)	1913-1937
Clan Chattan (1)	1902-1930	*Clan Macbeth* (1)	1913-1937
Clan Mackinnon (2)	1903-1927	*Clan Maccorquodale*	1913-1917
Clan Macalister (2)	1903-1915	*Clan Macquarrie* (1)	1913-1943
Clan Forbes (2)	1903-1918	*Clan Campbell* (3)	1914-1916
Clan Macneil (2)	1903-1918	*Clan Ross* (2)	1914-1942
Clan Macintyre (2)	1903-1928	*Clan Ogilvy* (2)	1914-1941
Clan Macleod (3)	1903-1915	*Clan Macbrayne* (1)	1916-1947
Clan Macdougall (1)	1904-1918	*Clan Stuart* (3)	1916-1940
Clan Macnab (2)	1905-1918	*Clan Mackay* (3)	1916-1918
Clan Maclean (2)	1905-1919	*Clan Ranald* (3)	1917-1944
Clan Macpherson (2)	1905-1918	*Clan Malcolm* (1)	1917-1935
Clan Macintosh (2)	1906-1932	*Clan Mackenzie* (3)	1917-1937
Clan Matheson (2)	1906-1914	*Clan Matheson* (3)	1917-1918
Clan Graham (2)	1907-1920	*Clan Macmaster*	1917-1923
Clan Sinclair (2)	1907-1933	*Ayrshire* (1)	1918-1926
Clan Buchanan (2)	1907-1933	*Argyllshire* (1)	1918-1929
Clan Macinnes (1)	1907-1914	*Clan Kenneth* (1)	1918-1934
Clan Maciver (1)	1907-1913	*Clan Macbeolan/Halesius* (1)	1918-1936
Clan Macphee	1911-1940	*Clan Kennedy* (1)	1918-1924
Clan Mackenzie (2)	1911-1912	*Clan Macbean* (1)	1918-1946
Clan Macgillivray (1)	1911-1948	*Clan Keith* (1)/*Hilarius* (2)	1918-1937
Clan Macnaughton (1)	1911-1915	*Clan Monroe* (3)	1918-1940
Clan Macrae (2)/*Banffshire*	1911-1943	*Clan Morrison*	1918-1940
Clan Davidson (1)	1912-1917	*Clan Macvicar*	1918-1936

Clan Campbell (3) of 1914. Built by Napier and Miller she was the first Clan Line steamer with a cruiser stern. Employed as a transport she was torpedoed and sunk in April 1916. *[Archie Munro collection]*

Berwickshire of 1912, formerly the *Clan Macarthur* (2), in the Mersey in Clan Line colours. *[J. and M. Clarkson collection]*

Clan Alpine (3)	1918-1943	*Hesperides* (1)	1921-1937
Clan Macmillan (2)	1918-1924	*Hesione* (1)	1921-1937
Clan Macvey	1918-1918	*Clan Macnair* (1)	1921-1954
Herminius (1)	1918-1922	*Oaxaca*	1921
Horatius	1918-1919	*Sinaloa* (1)	1921-1922
Hyanthes	1918-1923	*Guerrero*	1921
Honorius	1918-1925	*Clan Maciver* (2)	1921-1951
Hortensius	1918-1925	*Clan Mactavish* (2)	1921-1942
Hostilius	1918-1926	*Clan Macnaughton* (2)	1921-1942
Hellenes (1)	1918-1925	*Clan Macfarlane* (2)	1922-1940
Hilarius (1)	1918	*Clan Macneil* (3)	1922-1952
Harmodius (1)	1918-1919	*Clan Macfadyen* (2)	1923-1942
Harmonides (1)	1918-1919	*Sinaloa* (2)	1923-1933
Hydaspes	1918-1930	*Clan Macilwraith* (1)	1924-1950
Hypatia	1918-1929	*Clan Macdonald* (3)/*Stirlingshire* (1)	1928-1940
Hyacinthus	1918-1930	*Clan Macdougall* (2)	1929-1941
Hyperia	1918	*Clan Grant* (3)	1929-1938
Homerus	1918-1920	*Clan Graham* (3)	1929-1938
Halizones (1)/*Willcasino*/*Clan Macwhirter*		*Clan Macpherson* (3)	1929-1943
	1918-1920/1923-1942	*Clan Macalister* (3)	1930-1940
Clan Mackinlay (1)	1918-1940	*Heraclides*	1930-1939
Clan Macwilliam	1918-1927	*Clan Urquhart* (2)	1932-1937
Clan Murray (3)/*Halizones* (3)	1919-1948	*Clan Colquhoun* (2)	1933-1947
Clan Skene/*Halocrates*/*Clan Skene*	1919-1942	*Clan Farquhar* (2)	1933-1948
Clan Matheson (4)/*Harmodius* (3)	1919-1951	*Clan Robertson* (2)	1934-1938
Haliartus	1919-1932	*Clan Macarthur* (3)	1936-1943
Clan Murdoch (1)/*Halesius* (2)	1919-1948	*Perthshire*	1936-1964
Harmodius (2)	1919-1941	*Clan Macaulay* (2)	1936-1963
Clan Mackay (4)	1920-1934	*Clan Cameron* (3)	1937-1959
Harmonides (2)	1920-1942	*Clan Campbell* (4)	1937-1942
Clan Macinnes (2)	1920-1947	*Clan Chattan* (2)	1937-1942
Clan Macindoe (1)	1920-1943	*Clan Chisholm* (2)	1937-1939
Halizones (2)	1920-1943	*Clan Buchanan* (3)	1938-1941
Hellopes	1920-1927	*Clan Cumming* (2)	1938-1941
Clan Mactaggart (1)	1920-1942	*Clan Ferguson* (2)	1938-1942
Clan Macnab (3)	1920-1941	*Clan Forbes* (3)	1938-1959
Chihuahua	1921	*Clan Menzies* (2)	1938-1940
Colima	1921	*Clan Fraser* (3)	1939-1941
Chiapas	1921	*Clan Lamont* (3)	1939-1961
Hesperia (1)	1921-1938	*Clan Macdonald* (4)	1939-1970

Clan Allan, ex *Empire Forest*, heads an impressive line-up on Stobcross Quay, Glasgow. *[Archie Munro collection]*

Empire Song	1940-1941	*Clan Urquhart* (3)	1944-1966
Robert Maersk	1940-1943	*Samfield*	1944-1946
Ville d'Amiens	1941-1947	*Samdon*	1944-1946
Lieutenant St. Loubert Bié	1941-1945	*Samport*	1944-1948
Désirade	1942-1944	*Sambalt*	1944-1947
Commandant Dorise	1942-1944	*Samchess*	1944-1946
Bangkok 1	1942-1945	*Samderwent/Clan Macfadyen* (3)	1944-1958
Empire Elaine	1942-1947	*Clan Macdougall* (3)	1944-1971
Empire Wisdom	1942-1944	*Empire Malta*	1944-1946
Clan Campbell (5)	1943-1961	*Clan Chattan* (3)	1944-1962
Empire Prince/Clan Angus	1943-1956	*Empire Perlis*	1944-1946
Empire Forest/Clan Allan	1943-1958/1959-1961	*Clan Chisholm* (3)	1944-1962
Empire Barrie/Clan Alpine (4)	1943-1957/1959-1961	*Hoogkerk*	1945-1946
Sambrian/Clan Macfarlane (3)	1943-1961	*Empire Fawley/Clan Mackinlay* (2)	1945-1962
Samaye	1943-1946	*Empire Dunnet/Clan Mackinnon* (3)	1945-1961
Sampenn	1943-1946	*Empire Gunfleet/Clan Mackay* (5)	1945-1962
Adolph S. Ochs	1943-1946	*Empire Canute*	1946-1947
Samnebra	1943-1946	*Empire Cato/Clan Mackenzie* (4)	1946-1960
Samokla	1943-1946	*Clan Macrae* (3)	1946-1959

Empire Might was completed in 1942 and managed by the Blue Star Line Ltd. In 1946 she was acquired by The Clan Line and renamed *Clan Macrae* (3). *[Archie Munro collection]*

A fine picture of a fine ship: *Clan Mactaggart* (2) on trials. *[Newall Dunn collection]*

Empire Pickwick/Clan Mackendrick	1946-1961	*Clan Stewart/Kinpurnie Castle*	1954-1961/1962-1968
Hesione (2)	1946-1960	*Clan Ross* (3)/*Kinnaird Castle*	1956-1961/1962-1975
Clan Brodie	1946-1963	*Argyllshire* (2)	1956-1975
Hesperia (2)/*Clan Murdoch* (2)	1946-1962	*Ayrshire* (2)	1957-1965
Stirlingshire (2)	1946-1963	*Clan Malcolm* (2)	1957-1979
Clan Buchanan (4)	1946-1962	*Clan Matheson* (5)	1957-1978
Ocean Glory/Clan Macbeth (2)	1946-1959	*Clan Menzies* (3)	1958-1979
Ocean Courier/Clan Macbean (2)	1946-1960	*Clan Maciver* (3)	1958-1979
Ocean Viceroy/Clan Kenneth (2)	1946-1958	*King Arthur*	1959-1973
Ocean Gypsy/Clan Macbride (2)	1946-1958	*King Henry*	1959-1972
Hesperides (2)/*Clan Murray* (4)	1946-1962	*Clan Macindoe* (2)	1959-1979
Clan Cumming (3)	1946-1962	*King Charles*	1959-1970
Ocean Messenger/Clan Macbrayne (2)	1946-1961	*King George*	1959
Empire Lankester/Clan Mackellar (2)	1946-1961	*King Malcolm*	1959-1972
Ocean Verity/Clan Keith (2)	1946-1961	*King Alexander*	1959-1972
Clan Maclaren (2)	1946-1976	*Clan Macilwraith* (2)	1960-1979
Ocean Viscount/Clan Kennedy (2)	1947-1959	*Clan Fergusson*	1961-1965
Clan Maclachlan (2)	1947-1971	*Clan Macnab* (4)	1961-1980
Clan Maclean (3)	1947-1976	*Clan Forbes* (4)	1961-1969
Clan Maclennan	1947-1971	*Clan Fraser* (4)	1961-1965
Clan Davidson (2)	1948-1961	*Clan Graham* (4)	1962-1979
Clan Macleod (4)	1948-1976	*Clan Macnair* (2)	1962
Clan Maclay	1949-1976	*Clan Farquharson*	1962-1968
Clan Mactaggart (2)	1949-1971	*Clan Grant* (4)	1962-1980
Clan Mactavish (3)	1949-1971	*Clan Macgillivray* (2)	1962-1981
Clan Shaw (3)	1950-1960	*Clan Finlay*	1962-1968
Clan Sinclair (3)	1950-1959	*Clan Macgregor* (3)	1962
Clan Macquarrie (2)	1951-1953	*Clan Macgowan*	1963-1970
Clan Sutherland (2)	1951-1971	*Clan Ramsay*	1965-1977
Ocean Vesper/Clan Macqueen/Herminius (2)	1951-1958	*Clan Ranald* (4)	1965-1977
Clan Macintosh (3)	1951-1978	*Clan Robertson* (4)	1965-1976
Hellenes (2)	1952-1958	*Clan Ross* (4)	1966-1976
Clan Macintyre (3)	1952-1976	*Clan Alpine* (5)	1967-1981
Clan Macinnes (3)	1952-1977	*King Alfred*	1980-1981
Clan Robertson (3)	1954-1959		

Appendix 2:

CHRONOLOGICAL LIST OF TOTAL LOSSES

Losses listed are those through marine causes, including collisions in convoys and casualties which resulted in the ship being broken up. Those from direct enemy action are listed in tables 5 and 9. More details will be found in the fleet lists. It is noteworthy that human error in the form of faulty navigation or defective charts led to almost all the casualties: only four Clans were lost through foundering, and in two cases this may have been due to faulty stowage of the grain cargo.

Year	Date	Ship	Cause and location
1881	21st October	*Clan Macduff*	Foundered during gale in Irish Sea
1882	22nd September	*Clan Campbell* (1)	Wrecked at Mauritius
1888	8th January	*Clan Ogilvie*	Wrecked in Straits of Bonifacio
1891	9th March	*Clan Mackay* (1)	Wrecked near Galle, Ceylon
1891	30th May	*Clan Lamont* (1)	Wrecked on Vindiloas Point, Ceylon
1897	16th October	*Clan Gordon* (1)	Wrecked in the River Umlalazi, Zululand
1898	19th March	*Clan Lindsay* (1)	Wrecked in Mareppa Bay, East London
1898	28th November	*Clan Drummond*	Foundered off northern Spain
1899	4th September	*Clan Macgregor* (1)	Collision off St. Vincent
1902	1st June	*Clan Macgregor* (2)	Wrecked at Martha's Point, Cape Colony
1903	13th August	*Clan Maclean* (1)	Wrecked near Cape St. Vincent, Spain
1905	1st July	*Clan Monroe* (2)	Wrecked at Cape Peninsula, South Africa

The inclinometer of the *Clan Monroe* (2) was salvaged from her wreck. [*Newall Dunn collection*]

1909	1st January	*Clan Ranald* (2)	Foundered off Edithburg, South Australia
1912	30th December	*Clan Mackenzie* (2)	Wrecked near Cadiz
1914	21st November	*Clan Stuart* (2)	Wrecked at Simon's Bay, South Africa
1917	19th July	*Clan Maclachlan* (1)	Collision off Gibraltar
1918	11th May	*Clan Mackay* (3)	Collision in North Atlantic
1918	23rd May	*Clan Matheson* (3)	Collision in North Atlantic
1919	30th July	*Clan Gordon* (2)	Foundered off North Carolina
1919	23rd November	*Clan Maclean* (2)	Wrecked on Mafamede Island
1920	11th November	*Clan Graham* (2)	Collision in the Scheldt
1922	18th June	*Herminius* (1)	Wrecked in fog off Vigo, Spain
1923	30th September	*Clan Macmaster*	Wrecked on Isle of Man
1924	16th January	*Clan Kennedy* (1)	Wrecked on Sizewell Bank, Suffolk
1924	21st June	*Clan Macmillan* (2)	Wrecked on Preparis Island, Bay of Bengal
1926	28th November	*Ayrshire (1)*	Abandoned on fire in the Indian Ocean.
1929	29th October	*Hypatia*	Wrecked on Robben Island, South Africa
1927	24th December	*Clan Macwilliam*	Fire at Vavau, Friendly Isles
1929	20th October	*Hypatia*	Wrecked on Whale Rock, Robben Island, Cape of Good Hope
1932	4th May	*Haliartus*	Wrecked near Mossel Bay, South Africa
1934	19th October	*Clan Mackay* (4)	Wrecked at Sierra Leone
1935	26th September	*Clan Malcolm* (1)	Wrecked at The Lizard, Cornwall
1937	23rd October	*Clan Mackenzie* (3)	Collision in Liverpool Bay
1940	11th March	*Clan Stuart* (3)	Collision off Start Point, English Channel
1940	17th July	*Clan Macfarlane* (2)	Collision off Socotra
1941	17th March	*Clan Macnab* (3)	Collision near Cape Verde Islands
1943	26th April	*Clan Macindoe* (1)	Fire at Alexandria
1953	31st January	*Clan Macquarrie* (2)	Stranded near the Butt of Lewis, Hebrides
1960	10th November	*Clan Alpine* (4)	Stranded near Chittagong in typhoon
1961	5th November	*Clan Keith* (2)	Wrecked near Cape Bon, Tunisia
1965	23rd March	*Ayrshire* (2)	Stranded near Socotra

Appendix 3:

GREENOCK DOCKYARD CO. LTD.

The title Greenock Dockyard Co. Ltd. dates from 1919, when a new company was set up to own the yard which had been acquired by Cayzer, Irvine and Co. Ltd. in 1918. However, its shipbuilding history is much older, involving a number of owners and one change of site. The original yard was the first on the lower Clyde to build an iron ship, the paddle steamer *Glasgow*, in 1844. It later came under the control of Russell and Co. and in 1899 became the Clyde yard of the Grangemouth Dockyard Co. Ltd., subsequently becoming the Grangemouth and Greenock Dockyard Co. Ltd. As such it specialised in cargo ships and tankers.

Its takeover by Cayzer, Irvine did not see an immediate rush of orders for Clan Line, for which it built just five hulls in the 1920s. The yard continued to build a number of tankers, of which *Voreda* was left on the stocks for a long period during the recession of the interwar years. The yard was sandwiched between two others owned by Scotts' Shipbuilding and Engineering Co. Ltd., and in 1928 an exchange of yards was arranged so that Greenock Dockyard now occupied the eastern yard at Greenock. Cayzer, Irvine seem to have woken up the value of its asset only in the 1930s, when Greenock Dockyard began the rebuilding programme which led to a long sequence of fine twin-screw cargo and refrigerated ships for Clan. From then, and with important exceptions such as during Second World War, Greenock Dockyard built mainly for Clan and from 1956 its partners in the British and Commonwealth Group. However, it also had very extensive repair facilities, and an enormous amount of work was carried out with a total of 830 vessels repaired or converted in the peak year, 1943. Repair work for a variety of owners continued after the war.

The Greenock Dockyard Co. Ltd. was transferred to the ownership of The Clan Line Steamers Ltd. in 1944, something of a paper transaction as the control of both Clan and Cayzer, Irvine was in the hands of the Cayzers. The yard did build for other owners in the 1950s and, given its pre-war

experience in this field, built several tankers. In 1957 a modernisation programme saw £1,750,000 spent on improving fabrication methods, installing travelling cranes and reducing the number of berths from three to two. At this time the Cartsdyke yard had about one thousand employees. Concerns about the yard's productivity were voiced in the 1960s, when Clan went to Swan, Hunter for five ships, but the yard managed to recover its share of work for the British and Commonwealth Group.

Once the *Clan Ramsay* class reefers were completed in 1966, it was apparent that the yard would have no further orders, and its future seemed bleak as part of a shipping group which was looking towards vessels bigger than Cartsdyke could accommodate. Fortuitously, the Geddes Report on the shipbuilding industry, published in 1966, recommended that existing British shipbuilders be merged, and the Cartsdyke yard fitted logically and geographically into a group consisting of Scotts' Shipbuilding and Engineering Co. Ltd. and Lithgows Ltd. As a preliminary to this larger merger, in April 1966 control of Greenock Dockyard Co. Ltd. passed to Scotts' Shipbuilding and Engineering Co. Ltd., who owned the adjacent yard. As part of the agreement for Scotts' to take over the yard, for which they paid £264,000, British and Commonwealth agreed to place a further order worth £1,520,000 with the Cartsdyke yard. The *Clan Alpine* as it became was laid down by Greenock Dockyard but launched and completed by Scotts' as yard number 708. The Cartsdyke yard ceased building in 1979, whilst Scott Lithgow Ltd., as its owners became, continued until 1986.

The list includes all ships known to have been built by Greenock Dockyard Co. Ltd. following its acquisition by Cayzer, Irvine in 1919. Names of ships ordered or built for Clan Line ownership or Cayzer, Irvine management are in bold. Launch or proposed names are given first, with the initial in-service name on a subsequent line.

No.	Name	O.N.	Launch	Completed	gt	Engine	Type	Original owner
396	*War Canna*							The Shipping Controller
	> *Grangepark*	143746	12.9.1919	11.1919	5,131	ss	C	J. and J. Denholm Ltd., Greenock
397	*War Coleus*							The Shipping Controller
	> *Elmpark*	143753	6.2.1920	5.1920	5,132	ss	C	J. and J Denholm Ltd., Greenock
398	*War Broom*							The Shipping Controller
399	> *Oakpark*							J. and J. Denholm Ltd
	> *Orowaiti*	145213	27.1.1921	4.1921	6,684	ss	Tk	Union S.S. Co. of New Zealand Ltd., London
399	*Mont Agel*	———	29. 4.1920	6.1920	4,493	ss	C	Soc. Gen. de Trans. Maritime á Vapeur, Marseille
400	*Staur*	———	30.8.1920	10.1920	5,653	ss	PC	N.V. Hollandsche Zuid Afrikansche, Rotterdam
401	*Nordkyn II*	146322	30.9.1921	11.1921	4,584	ss	C	Albert Harloff, Bergen
402	*Cedarpark*	145606	22.06.1922	8.1922	5,087	ss	Tk	Denholm Shipping Co. Ltd., Greenock
403	***Clan Macilwraith*** (1)	147931	14.8.1924	11.1924	4,958	ss	C	The Clan Line Steamers Ltd.
404	*Mirasol*	———	9.5.1924	6.1924	788	-	ltr	Cia. Argentina de Lanchas, Buenos Aires
405	*Garza Azul*	———	30.5.1924	6.1924	788	-	ltr	Cia. Argentina de Lanchas, Buenos Aires
406	*Valetta*	148853	12.3.1925	5.1925	4,903	ss	Tk	Gow, Harrison and Co., Glasgow
407	*Mobiloil*	148653	8.6.1925	8.1925	5,090	ss	Tk	Vacuum Oil Co Ltd., London
408	*Barrdale*	148882	30.9.1925	11.1925	5,072	ss	C	Barr, Crombie and Co Ltd., Glasgow
409	*Hirondelle*	148710	27.10.1925	12.1925	893	ss	C	General Steam Nav. Co. Ltd., London

Built for other owners: *Orowaiti* (top) had been laid down as the *Oakpark* for British owners. Completed in 1921 for the Union Steamship Co. of New Zealand Ltd. she had only a short life, being wrecked on the Californian coast in August 1924. *Barrdale* (middle) was completed in 1925 for the Barr Shipping Co. Ltd. (Barr, Crombie and Co. Ltd.), Glasgow. Sold to Reardon Smith in 1941 she was torpedoed and sunk in May of the following year whilst on passage from New York to Table Bay, Basra and Abadan with general cargo. The tanker *Virgilia* (bottom) was one of a series built for Gow, Harrison and Co., Glasgow. As with many ships from this period she too had only a short life being torpedoed and sunk in November 1941 on a voyage from New York to London with oil products. *[Top: Ian J. Farquhar collection; middle and bottom: World Ship Society Ltd.]*

410	*Woodcock*	149831	5.4.1927	5.1927	1,827	ss	C	General Steam Nav. Co. Ltd., London
411	*Virgilia*	160179	30.8.1927	10.1927	5,728	ss	Tk	Gow, Harrison and Co., Glasgow
412	*Vancouver*	160207	18.5.1928	6.1928	57,29	ss	Tk	Gow, Harrison and Co., Glasgow
413	*British Reliance*	160357	8.12.1927	2.1928	7,000	mv	Tk	British Tanker Co Ltd., London
414	**Clan Macdonald** (3)	160210	21.2.1928	6.1928	6,051	mv	C	The Clan Line Steamers Ltd.
415	**Clan Macdougall** (2)	160234	28.9.1928	1.1929	6,843	mv	C	The Clan Line Steamers Ltd.
416	**Clan Macpherson** (3)	160249	9.3.1929	5.1929	6,940	ss	C	The Clan Line Steamers Ltd.
417	*Barrwhin*	161890	5.9.1929	10.1929	4,998	ss	C	Barr, Crombie and Co. Ltd., Glasgow
418	**Clan Macalister** (3)	161909	29.1.1930	4.1930	6,795	ss	C	The Clan Line Steamers Ltd.
419	*Melmay*	161931	9.6.1930	9.1930	5,413	ss	C	T.L. Duff and Co., Glasgow
420	*Voreda*	164049	22.1.1935	4.1935	7,216	ss	Tk	Gow Harrison and Co., Glasgow
421	*British Resource*	162547	23.12.1930	3.1931	7,209	mv	Tk	British Tanker Co. Ltd., London
422	*British Energy*	162588	2.4.1931	5.1931	7,209	mv	Tk	British Tanker Co. Ltd., London

Built at Cartsdyke East Yard

423	**Clan Macarthur** (3)	164066	14.10.1935	1.1936	10,528	2ss	CR	The Clan Line Steamers Ltd.
424	**Perthshire**	164087	26.3.1936	7.1936	10,496	2ss	CR	Scottish Shire Line Ltd.
425	**Clan Macaulay** (2)	164100	7.8.1936	11.1936	10,492	2ss	CR	The Clan Line Steamers Ltd.
426	**Clan Cameron** (3)	164108	15.10.1936	2.1937	7,243	2ss	C	The Clan Line Steamers Ltd.
427	**Clan Campbell** (4)	164112	14.1.1937	4.1937	7,255	2ss	C	The Clan Line Steamers Ltd.
428	**Clan Chattan** (2)	165907	12.4.1937	7.1937	7,262	2ss	C	The Clan Line Steamers Ltd.
429	**Clan Chisholm** (2)	165915	21.7.1937	10.1937	7,256	2ss	C	The Clan Line Steamers Ltd.
430	**Clan Cumming** (2)	165924	18.10.1937	1.1938	7,264	2ss	C	The Clan Line Steamers Ltd.
431	**Clan Buchanan** (3)	165929	21.12.1937	2.1938	7,266	2ss	C	The Clan Line Steamers Ltd.
432	**Clan Ferguson** (2)	165937	22.3.1938	6.1938	7,347	2ss	C	The Clan Line Steamers Ltd.
433	**Clan Menzies** (2)	165947	15.6.1938	9.1938	7,336	2ss	C	The Clan Line Steamers Ltd.
434	**Clan Forbes** (3)	165951	8.9.1938	11.1938	7,529	2ss	C	The Clan Line Steamers Ltd.
435	**Clan Fraser** (3)	165960	20.12.1938	2.1939	7,529	2ss	C	The Clan Line Steamers Ltd.
436	**Clan Macdonald** (4)	165971	15.8.1939	12.1939	9,653	2mv	CR	The Clan Line Steamers Ltd.
437	**Lanarkshire**	165973	30.11.1939	4.1940	9,816	2st	CR	Scottish Shire Line Ltd.
438	**Clan Lamont** (3)	165965	22.3.1939	6.1939	7,673	2ss	C	The Clan Line Steamers Ltd.
439	not used							
440	not used							
441	not used							
442	not used							
443	**Empire Song**	166991	18.6.1940	10.1940	9,228	2ss	C	Ministry of War Transport, London (Cayzer, Irvine and Co. Ltd., managers).
444	**Clan Brodie**							The Clan Line Steamers Ltd.
	requisitioned on stocks							
	> **HMS Athene,**		1.10.1940	10.1941	7,473	2ss	N	Royal Navy, seaplane depot ship
	handed back and refitted							
	> **Clan Brodie**	169474				2ss	C	The Clan Line Steamers Ltd.
445	*Empire Rainbow*	166999	27.12.1940	5.1941	6,942	mv	X	Ministry of War Transport, London
446	*Empire Ray*	167003	25.3.1941	6.1941	6,919	mv	X	Ministry of War Transport, London
447	*Empire Stanley*	168967	15.7.1941	9.1941	6,921	mv	X	Ministry of War Transport, London
448	*Empire Kingsley*	168972	19.9.1941	11.1941	6,996	ss	Y	Ministry of War Transport, London
449	*Empire Homer*	168976	19.11.1941	1.1942	6,993	ss	Y	Ministry of War Transport, London
450	*Empire Might*	168986	17.4.1942	7.1942	9,221	2ss	CR	Ministry of War Transport, London
	> **Clan Macrae** (3)							The Clan Line Steamers Ltd.
451	**Empire Wisdom**	168989	29.7.1942	11.1942	9,205	2ss	CR	Ministry of War Transport, London (Cayzer, Irvine and Co. Ltd., managers)
452	**Clan Campbell**							The Clan Line Steamers Ltd., Glasgow
	requisitioned on the stocks							
	> HMS *Bonaventure*		27.10.1942	1.1943	8,067	2ss	N	Royal Navy, midget submarine depot ship
	handed back and refitted							
	> **Clan Davidson** (2)	182100				2ss	C	The Clan Line Steamers Ltd.
453	**Clan Campbell** (5)	168761	23.2.1943	5.1943	9,545	2ss	C	The Clan Line Steamers Ltd.
454	**Clan Urquhart** (3)	169404	30.6.1943	1.1944	9,726	2ss	CR	The Clan Line Steamers Ltd.
455	**Clan Macdougall** (3)	169411	10.11.1943	5.1944	9,710	2mv	CR	The Clan Line Steamers Ltd.
456	**Clan Chattan** (3)	169413	9.3.1944	6.1944	9,585	2ss	C	The Clan Line Steamers Ltd.
457	**Clan Chisholm** (3)	169420	23.6.1944	10.1944	9,581	2ss	C	The Clan Line Steamers Ltd.
458	*Empire Byng*	169521	16.11.1944	4.1945	7,832	te	HLS	Ministry of War Transport, London
459	**Clan Cumming** (3)	169480	3.5.1946	8.1946	7,812	2ss	C	The Clan Line Steamers Ltd.
460	*Empire Marshal*	169525	14.5.1945	8.1945	7,836	te	HLS	Ministry of War Transport, London
461	*Empire Wallace*	169527	4.9.1945	12.1945	7,800	te	HLS	Ministry of War Transport, London
462	**Empire Canute**		24.12.1945					Ministry of War Transport, London (Cayzer, Irvine and Co. Ltd., managers)
	> *Belocean*	———	6.1947		7,750	te	HLS	Skibs A/S Belships Co Ltd., Oslo
463	**Clan Maclaren** (2)	169488	25.9.1946	12.1946	6,021	mv	C	The Clan Line Steamers Ltd.

464	*Clan Maclachlan* (2)	*169493*	*23.12.1946*	*6.1947*	*6,365*	*st*	C	*The Clan Line Steamers Ltd.*
465	**Clan Maclean** (3)	169500	2.6.1947	10.1947	6,017	mv	C	The Clan Line Steamers Ltd.
466	**Clan Maclennan**	182080	16.9.1947	12.1947	6,366	st	C	The Clan Line Steamers Ltd.
467	**Clan Macleod** (4)	182090	13.2.1948	7.1948	6,073	mv	C	The Clan Line Steamers Ltd.
468	**Clan Maclay**	182109	7.5.1948	3.1949	6,075	mv	C	The Clan Line Steamers Ltd.
469	**Clan Mactaggart** (2)	182111	8.10.1948	3.1949	8,035	2st	C	The Clan Line Steamers Ltd.
470	**Clan Mactavish** (3)	182124	2.3.1949	6.1949	8,035	2st	C	The Clan Line Steamers Ltd.
471	**Clan Shaw** (3)	182140	23.8.1949	12.1949	8,101	2st	C	The Clan Line Steamers Ltd.
472	**Clan Sinclair** (3)	182148	17.1.1950	4.1950	8,386	2st	C	The Clan Line Steamers Ltd.
473	**Clan Skene**							The Clan Line Steamers Ltd.
	Sold on stocks							
	> *Kenuta*	183788	22.5.1950	8.1950	8,494	st	C	Pacific Steam Navigation Co., Liverpool
474	**Clan Stewart**							The Clan Line Steamers Ltd.
	Sold on stocks							
	> *Flamenco*	183799	28.8.1950	12.1950	8,491	st	C	Pacific Steam Navigation Co., Liverpool
475	**Clan Sutherland** (2)	182167	28.12.1950	3.1951	8,436	st	C	The Clan Line Steamers Ltd.
476	*Thorskog*	————	20.7.1951	11.1951	11,325	mv	Tk	A/S Thor Dahl, Sandefjord
477	*Corato*	184590	14.12.1951	3.1952	11,387	mv	Tk	Hadley Shipping Co Ltd., London
478	**Clan Macinnes** (3)	184974	9.4.1952	7.1952	6,517	mv	C	The Clan Line Steamers Ltd.
479	*Imperial Transport*	184753	24.10.1952	1.1953	11,365	mv	Tk	Houlder Bros. and Co. Ltd., London
480	*Alva Cape*	185954	15.5.1953	9.1953	11,252	mv	Tk	Alva S.S. Co. Ltd., London
481	**Clan Stewart**	185001	22.10.1953	2.1954	8,163	st	C	The Clan Line Steamers Ltd.
482	**Clan Robertson** (3)	185012	17.3.1954	6.1954	7,878	st	C	The Clan Line Steamers Ltd.
483	**Scottish Hawk**	185020	11.11.1954	3.1955	11,148	mv	Tk	Scottish Tanker Co Ltd.
484	*Potosi*	185520	23.2.1955	5.1955	8,564	st	C	Pacific Steam Navigation Co., Liverpool
485	*Pizarro*	187115	20.5.1955	9.1955	8,564	st	C	Pacific Steam Navigation Co., Liverpool
486	**Clan Rose**							
	Launched as							
	> **Argyllshire** (2)	185047	23.5.1956	10.1956	9,299	st	CR	The Clan Line Steamers Ltd.
487	**Clan Ross** (3)	185040	17.1.1956	4.1956	7,698	st	C	The Clan Line Steamers Ltd.
488	**Ayrshire** (2)	300171	19.10.1956	5.1957	9,360	st	CR	The Clan Line Steamers Ltd.
489	————						Tk	Scottish Tanker Co. Ltd.
	Cancelled, built as							
	> **Clan Matheson** (5)	300186	26.8.1957	12.1957	7,685	mv	C	The Clan Line Steamers Ltd.
490	**Clan Malcolm** (2)	300181	29.4.1957	8.1957	7,686	mv	C	The Clan Line Steamers Ltd.
491	**Clan Morrison**							
	> **Clan Menzies** (3)	300200	22.1.1958	5.1958	7,685	mv	C	The Clan Line Steamers Ltd.
492	**Clan Matheson**							
	> **Clan Maciver** (3)	300214	23.6.1958	11.1958	7,350	mv	C	The Clan Line Steamers Ltd.
493	*Swan River*	183369	2.11.1958	3.1959	9,637	mv	C	Houlder Bros.and Co. Ltd., London
494	*Rotherwick Castle*	301038	19.8.1959	12.1959	9,650	mv	CR	Union-Castle Mail S.S. Co. Ltd., London
495	*Rothesay Castle*	301158	30.12.1959	6.1960	9,650	mv	CR	Union-Castle Mail S.S. Co. Ltd., London
496	**Clan Macilwraith** (2)	301428	27.5.1960	12.1960	7,354	mv	C	The Clan Line Steamers Ltd.
497	**Clan Macindoe**							
	Completed as							
	> **Clan Macnab** (4)	301448	31.1.1961	5.1961	9,428	mv	C	The Clan Line Steamers Ltd.
498	**Clan Graham** (4)	301465	25.8.1961	1.1962	9,308	mv	C	The Clan Line Steamers Ltd.
499	**Clan Grant** (4)	301480	22.12.1961	5.1962	9,022	mv	C	The Clan Line Steamers Ltd.
500	**Clan Macgillivray** (2)	304140	22.5.1962	9.1962	8,811	mv	C	The Clan Line Steamers Ltd.
501	**Clan Macgregor** (3)	304151	26.9.1962	12.1962	8,811	mv	C	The Clan Line Steamers Ltd.
502	**Clan Macgowan**	304153	14.12.1962	4.1963	8,811	mv	C	The Clan Line Steamers Ltd.
503	*S.A. Letaba*							Safmarine
	Completed as							
	> *Letaba*	350339	20.8.1963	12.1963	6,897	mv	C	Huntley Cook S.A. (Pty.) Ltd., Cape Town
504	*S.A. Drakenstein*							Safmarine
	Completed as							
	> *Drakenstein*	350353	18.12.1963	4.1964	6,837	mv	C	Huntley Cook S.A. (Pty.) Ltd., Cape Town
505	*S.A. Tzaneen*							Safmarine
	Completed as							
	> *Tzaneen*	350361	15.4.1964	8.1964	6,837	mv	C	Huntley Cook S.A. (Pty.) Ltd., Cape Town
506	**Clan Ramsay**	304194	26.8.1964	2.1965	7,955	mv	CR	Union-Castle Mail S.S. Co. Ltd., London
507	**Clan Ranald** (4)	307627	21.12.1964	6.1965	7,955	mv	CR	Union-Castle Mail S.S. Co. Ltd., London
508	**Clan Robertson** (4)	307638	3.5.1965	11.1965	7,955	mv	CR	Union-Castle Mail S.S. Co. Ltd., London
509	**Clan Ross** (4)	307645	24.9.1965	3.1966	7,955	mv	CR	Union-Castle Mail S.S. Co. Ltd., London
510	*Geestcape*	306444	25.3.1966	9.1966	7,678	mv	CR	Geest Industries Ltd., Boston

31.3.1966 merged with the adjoining yard and now known as Scotts' Shipbuilding and Engineering Co Ltd., Cartsdyke Shipyard

511	*Geesthaven*	306445	21.7.1966	12.1966	8,042	mv	CR	Geest Industries Ltd., Boston

Key to types:

C	Cargo ship	CR	Refrigerated cargo ship
HLS	Heavy lift cargo ship	Ltr	Lighter
N	Naval craft	Tk	Tanker
X	X-type war standard cargo ship	Y	Y-type war standard cargo ship

This list has been based on information kindly provided by the Yard List Team of the World Ship Society.

Consecutive yard numbers 482 and 483 were both for Cayzers. The completed *Clan Robertson* (3), yard number 482, seen above coming into the James Watt Dock on 2nd June 1954, was completed in that month whereas the motor tanker *Scottish Hawk*, yard number 483, and seen below on trials, was finished nine months later. *[Glasgow University Archives GD323/7/9/2/ 482/14 and 483/6]*

The shipyards at Greenock were active in the summer of 1961 with naval and mercantile work. HM Submarine *Otter* is fitting out in Scotts' dry dock, and to the left is Elder Dempster's cadet ship *Fourah Bay* (7,704/1962) with near-sister *Falaba* (7,703/1962) alongside and HM Submarine *Otus* on the next slipway. Greenock Dockyard can be seen in the top right-hand corner, with *Clan Graham* (4) soon to be launched. Almost hidden, *Clan Grant* (4) is next to her. *[George O'Hara collection]*

In the Cartsdyke Yard of Greenock Dockyard is yard number 500, *Clan Macgillivray* (2), almost ready for her launch on 22nd May 1962. The dias for the launching party is virtually complete. Next to her, at an early stage of construction, is yard number 501, *Clan Macgregor* (3), which would be launched in September 1962. *[George O'Hara collection]*

INDEX OF SHIPS
All ships mentioned are indexed

343

The Turret steamer *Clan Chattan* (1) of 1902 as photographed in the Clyde by the well-known photographer Dan McDonald. The view illustrates the unusual appearance of the type when seen from directly ahead. *[The Ballast Trust]*